Proceedings

C000203940

Fifth IEEE International Workshop
on Policies for Distributed Systems
and Networks

POLICY 2004

Proceedings

Fifth IEEE International Workshop on Policies for Distributed Systems and Networks

POLICY 2004

7-9 June 2004 • Yorktown Heights, New York

Sponsored by

IEEE
COMPUTER
SOCIETY

◆IEEE

Los Alamitos, California

Washington   •   Brussels   •   Tokyo

IEEE Computer Society Order Number P2141
ISBN 0-7695-2141-X
Library of Congress Number 2004103508

Additional copies may be ordered from:

IEEE Computer Society	IEEE Service Center	IEEE Computer Society
Customer Service Center	445 Hoes Lane	Asia/Pacific Office
10662 Los Vaqueros Circle	P.O. Box 1331	Watanabe Bldg., 1-4-2
P.O. Box 3014	Piscataway, NJ 08855-1331	Minami-Aoyama
Los Alamitos, CA 90720-1314	Tel: + 1 732 981 0060	Minato-ku, Tokyo 107-0062
Tel: + 1 800 272 6657	Fax: + 1 732 981 9667	JAPAN
Fax: + 1 714 821 4641	http://shop.ieee.org/store/	Tel: + 81 3 3408 3118
http://computer.org/cspress	customer-service@ieee.org	Fax: + 81 3 3408 3553
csbooks@computer.org		tokyo.ofc@computer.org

Individual paper REPRINTS may be ordered at: reprints@computer.org

Editorial production by Stephanie Kawada
Cover art production by Joe Daigle/Studio Productions
Printed in the United States of America by The Printing House

Proceedings

Fifth IEEE International Workshop on Policies for Distributed Systems and Networks

POLICY 2004

Table of Contents

Session 1: Policies for Self-Management

Session 2: Routing and Mobile Networks

Session 3: QoS and Storage

Session 4 (Short Papers): Automation and Control

Session 5: Security Policy in Large Scale Systems

Session 6: Trust and Filtering

Session 7 (Short Papers): Security

Session 8 (Short Papers): Quality of Service

Session 9: Analysis and Refinement

Preface

These proceedings collect the papers presented at the 5th IEEE International Workshop on Policies for Distributed Systems and Networks (POLICY 2004), held at the IBM T.J. Watson Research Laboratories, New York, in June 2004.

This forum, also known as the *Policy Workshop,* brings together researchers and practitioners working on policy-based systems across a wide range of application areas including networking, security management, storage area networking, and enterprise systems. POLICY 2004 is the 5th in a series of successful workshops which since 1999 have provided a forum for discussion and collaboration between researchers, developers, and users of policy-based systems. The *policy* community has grown substantially in the last year as witnessed by the increase in the number of submissions and in the overall interest for the conference. Two particular trends have become apparent and deserve particular mention:

- Knowledge within the community is consolidating with substantial interest in formal specifications for policy, policy analysis, policy transformation and combination of techniques toward realizing self-adaptive systems.
- The application domains of policies have diversified into many new areas, including new security models and trust management, mobile systems, large-scale computing, and pervasive systems. Policies are seen as the main paradigm for providing adaptation in response to changes in distributed systems and networks.

These trends are well reflected in the set of papers presented below. These papers, comprising 18 full papers and 15 short papers, were selected from 87 submissions after a rigorous review process.

A forum like this can not be organized without the help of many volunteers. We would like to express our gratitude to the members of the Steering Committee, Organizing Committee, and Program Committee who were key to the success of this workshop. This year, more than in any previous one, the interest in the conference has seen a tremendous increase, which in turn has required increased efforts from all those involved in its organization. We would like to thank Prof. Morris Sloman, Dr. Seraphin Calo, Dr. Naranker Dulay, Ms. Paridhi Verma, and Mr. Arosha Bandara who have helped tremendously in many ways throughout the last year. We would also like to thank Stephanie Kawada for compiling and editing these proceedings. Finally, we are indebted to the IEEE for their continuous support for the conference and to IBM Research for their financial support and for hosting this event.

Dinesh Verma and **Murthy Devarakonda,** *General Chairs*
Emil Lupu and **Madhur Kohli,** *Program Chairs*

London and New York, June 2004

Organizing Committee

General Chairs
Dinesh Verma, *IBM Research*
Murthy Devarakonda, *IBM Research*

Technical Program Chairs
Emil Lupu, *Imperial College, London*
Madhur Kohli, *Relativistic Systems*

Finance Chair
Seraphin Calo, *IBM Research*

Publicity Chair
Rebecca Montanari, *University of Bolgna*

Web Chair
Paridhi Verma, *IBM Research*

Publications Chair
Ritu Chadha, *Telcordia*

Program Committee

Jean Bacon, *University of Cambridge, UK*
Arosha Bandara, *Imperial College London, UK*
Elisa Bertino, *University of Milano, Italy*
Marcus Brunner, *NEC, Germany*
Mark Burgess, *University College, Oslo, Norway*
Seraphin Calo, *IBM T.J. Watson, USA*
Ritu Chadha, *Telcordia, USA*
Jan Chomicki, *University at Buffalo, USA*
Asit Dan, *IBM T.J. Watson, USA*
Murthy Devarakonda, *IBM T.J. Watson, USA*
Naranker Dulay, *Imperial College, London, UK*
Paulo Ferreira, *INESC, Portugal*
Francisco Garcia, *Agilent, UK*
Virgil Gligor, *University of Maryland at College Park, USA*
Terence Halpin, *Conceptual Modeling, USA*
Heinz-Gerd Hegering, *Leibniz-Rechenzentrum, Germany*
Stan Hendryx, *Northface University, USA*
Boyd Hays, *SUN Microsystems Inc., USA*
Christian Jensen, *Technical University of Denmark, Denmark*
Peter Linington, *University of Kent, UK*
Jorge Lobo, *USA*
Hanan Lutfiyya, *University of Western Ontario, Canada*
Ian Marshall, *University of Kent, UK*
Bret Michael, *Naval Postgraduate School, USA*
Zoran Milosevic, *DSTC, Australia*

Naftaly Minsky, *Rutgers University, USA*
Jonathan Moffett, *University of York, UK*
Rebecca Montanari, *University of Bologna, Italy*
Ken Moody, *Cambridge University, UK*
Clifford Neuman, *ISI, USA*
Gerard Parr, *University of Ulster, UK*
George Pavlou, *University of Surrey, UK*
Louiqa Raschid, *University of Maryland, USA*
Babak Sadighi Firozabadi, *SICS, Sweden*
Akhil Sahai, *HP Labs, USA*
Pierangela Samarati, *University of Milan, UK*
Ravi Sandhu, *George Mason University, USA*
Kent Seamons, *Brigham Young University, USA*
Morris Sloman, *Imperial College, London, UK*
John Strassner, *IntelliDEN, USA*
Joe Sventek, *University of Glasgow, UK*
Toshio Tonouchi, *NEC, Japan*
Vijay Varadharajan, *Macquarie University, Australia*
Dinesh Verma, *IBM T.J. Watson, USA*
Vincent Wade, *Trinity College, Dublin, Ireland*
Andrea Westerinen, *Cisco Systems, USA*
Duminda Wijesekera, *George Mason University, USA*
William Winsborough, *George Mason University, USA*
Marianne Winslett, *University of Illinois at Urbana-Champaign, USA*

Reviewers

Ehab Al-Shaer
Xuhui Ao
Arosha Bandara
Jean Bacon
Moritz Becker
Elisa Bertino
Konstantin Beznosov
Rakesh Bobba
Marcus Brunner
Mark Burgess
Seraphin Calo
Ritu Chadha
Cho-Yu Jason Chiang
Jan Chomicki
Asit Dan
Murthy Devarakonda
Naranker Dulay
Paulo Ferreira
Olivier Festor
Tim Finin
Joe Finney
Francisco Garcia
Virgil Gligor
Tyrone Grandison
Frédéric Grasset
Elizabeth Gray
Boyd Hays
Heinz-Gerd Hegering
Mihail Ionescu
Christian Jensen
Jesper Kampfeldt
Yasusi Kanada
Guenter Karjoth
Alexander Keller
Sye Loong Keoh
Radostina Koleva
George Lapiotis
Peter Linington
Jorge Lobo
Hanan Lutfiyya
Leonidas Lymberopoulos
Jeff Magee
Ian Marshall

Jean Philippe Martin-Flatin
Julie McCann
Bret Michael
Zoran Milosevic
Naftaly Minsky
Jonathan Moffett
Rebecca Montanari
Ken Moody
Takahiro Murata
Clifford Neuman
Olle Olsson
Gerard Parr
George Pavlou
Louiqa Raschid
Erik Rissanen
Alessandra Russo
Babak Sadighi Firozabadi
Akhil Sahai
Pierangela Samarati
Ravi Sandhu
Junaid Saiyed
Kent Seamons
Jean-Marc Seigneur
Constantin Serban
Marek Sergot
Peter Sewell
Morris Sloman
Rolf Stadler
John Strassner
Niranjan Suri
Joe Sventek
Toshio Tonouchi
Son Cao Tran
Vijay Varadharajan
Dinesh Verma
Vincent Wade
Eero Wallenius
Andrea Westerinen
Duminda Wijesekera
William Winsborough
Marianne Winslett
S. Felix Wu

Session 1:
Policies for Self-Management

An Artificial Intelligence Perspective on Autonomic Computing Policies

Jeffrey O. Kephart and William E. Walsh
IBM Thomas J. Watson Research Center
Yorktown Heights, New York 10598

Abstract— We introduce a unified framework that interrelates three different types of policies that will be used in autonomic computing systems: *Action*, *Goal*, and *Utility Function* policies. Our policy framework is based on concepts from artificial intelligence such as states, actions, and rational agents. We show how the framework can be used to support the use of all three types of policies within a single autonomic component or system, and use the framework to discuss the relative merits of each type.

I. INTRODUCTION

In order to cope with the ever increasing complexity of managing distributed, heterogeneous computing systems, it has been proposed that the systems themselves should manage their own behavior in accordance with *high-level objectives from human administrators* [1]. This vision of self-managing systems is sometimes referred to as *autonomic computing*[2]. Given these high-level objectives, autonomic computing systems will autonomously perform many of the tasks that are now beginning to overwhelm human administrators, including configuration, optimization, healing, and protection.

Numerous and varied definitions of policy (e.g., [3], [4], [5], [6], to cite just a few) have been put forward in recent years. Common to most of them is the notion that policies are a form of guidance used to determine decisions and actions. Given the numerous disciplines that are brought together under the umbrella of autonomic computing, any single formal definition of policy is likely to be too restrictive to cover all of the many forms of behavioral guidance that will be required. Instead, we prefer to adopt a very broad, loose definition of *policy* for autonomic computing: a *policy* is any type of formal behavioral guide. Clearly, then, policies as we define them have a fundamentally important role to play in autonomic computing.

In this paper, we approach autonomic computing policies from the perspective of the artificial intelligence (AI) field.[1] AI is an appropriate core discipline from which to borrow concepts and techniques for autonomic computing, as automated decision making is its central focus. More specifically, one popular view of the field of AI—outlined by Russell and Norvig in their standard text on AI [7]—is that it is fundamentally concerned with the design of *rational agents*. A rational agent is any entity that perceives and acts upon its environment, selecting actions that, on the basis of information from sensors and built-in knowledge, are expected to maximize the agent's objective. Since this is precisely the behavior we demand of autonomic components, it is essential that they be designed as rational agents.

Russell and Norvig outline a series of progressively more sophisticated and flexible approaches to rational agent design. We review three here. A *reflex agent* uses if-then *action rules* that specify exactly what to do under the current condition. In this case, rational behavior is essentially compiled in by the designer, or somehow pre-computed. A *goal-based agent* exhibits rationality to the degree to which it can effectively determine which actions to take to achieve specified goals, allowing it greater flexibility than a reflex agent. A *utility-based agent* is rational to the extent that it chooses the actions to maximize its utility function, which allows a finer distinction between the desirability of different states than do goals.

As we demonstrate in this paper, these three notions of agenthood can fruitfully be codified into three policy types for autonomic computing. The **Action policies** that form the basis of reflex agents will be essential for early autonomic systems, and will likely continue to prove useful in more advanced systems. However, higher-level **Goal policies** and **Utility Function policies** are necessary to realize the vision of truly self-managing systems.

For expository simplicity, Russell and Norvig describe these three types of policies (although they do not refer to them as such) as being embodied in different types of agents. However, a sophisticated agent in a complex environment such as an autonomic computing system may potentially use a mixture of these different policy types for various types of decisions. Moreover, in an autonomic computing system, there will be a multiplicity of autonomous agents serving a variety of purposes, each potentially relying on different types of policies. In order to support multiple policy types within a single autonomic component or system, we propose a unified framework that interrelates Action, Goal, and Utility Function policies. The framework also helps to clarify the relative advantages and disadvantages of different types of policy, such as their susceptibility to mutual conflicts, and the situations in which each is most appropriate.

It is beyond the scope of this paper to explore the full range of technical issues involved in creating and deploying policies in a real system. Rather, we outline the relationship between policies in the unified framework and, using an autonomic

---

[1]In AI, there is a more specific definition of policy, described later. Except where noted, we use our specified definition of policy.

data center scenario, we highlight some of the complexities of applying the different policy types at multiple levels in the data center system. In Section II, we define these three types of policies and outline a unified framework into which they all fit, including the relationships among the three types. In Section III, we discuss a prototype system in which we have implemented these types of policies and describe how they are used in practice, focusing in particular on policies for system performance management and resource allocation. We conclude in Section IV.

II. UNIFIED FRAMEWORK

The unified framework we outline for autonomic computing policies is based upon the notions of states and actions that are quite familiar in the computer science literature, particularly in the realm of AI. In general, one can characterize a system, or a system component, as being in a state S at a given moment in time. Typically, the state S can be described as a vector of attributes, each of which is either measured directly by a sensor, or perhaps inferred or synthesized from lower-level sensor measurements. A policy will directly or indirectly cause an action a to be taken, the result of which is that the system or component will make a deterministic or probabilistic transition to a new state σ.[2] This sequence of events is depicted in Figure 1.

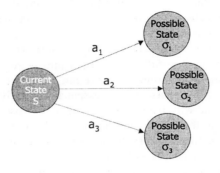

Fig. 1. States and actions: the basis for a unified framework for autonomic computing policy.

At least three types of policy will be useful for autonomic computing. We present them in order from the lowest to the highest level of behavioral specification.

- **Action Policies**. An Action policy dictates the action that should be taken whenever the system is in a given *current* state. Typically this takes the form of IF(*Condition*) THEN(*Action*), where *Condition* specifies either a specific state or a set of possible states that all satisfy the given *Condition*. Note that the state that will be reached by taking the given action is not specified explicitly. Presumably, the author knows which state will be reached upon taking the recommended action[3], and deems this

state more desirable than states that would be reached via alternative actions. This is generally necessary to ensure that the system is exhibiting rational behavior. Related work on using Action policies for network and systems optimization includes [8], [9], [10], [11].

- **Goal Policies**. Rather than specifying exactly what to do in the *current* state S, Goal policies specify either a single *desired* state σ, or one or more criteria that characterize an entire set of desired states. Implicitly, any member of this set is equally acceptable—Goal policies cannot express fine distinctions in preference. The system is responsible for computing an action a (or possibly a sequence of actions or a workflow) that will cause the system to make a transition from the current state S to some desired state σ. Rather than relying on a human to explicitly encode rational behavior, as in Action policies, the system generates rational behavior itself from the Goal policy. This permits greater flexibility, and frees human policy-makers from the necessity of knowing low-level details of system function, at the cost of requiring reasonably sophisticated planning or modeling algorithms. Related work on using Goal policies for network and system optimization includes [12], [13], [14].

- **Utility Function Policies**. A Utility Function policy is an objective function that expresses the value of each possible state. Utility Function policies generalize Goal policies. Instead of performing a binary classification into desirable vs. undesirable states, they ascribe a real-valued scalar desirability to each state. Because the most desired state is not specified in advance, it is computed on a recurrent basis by selecting from the present collection of feasible states the one that has the highest utility. Utility Function policies provide more fine-grained and flexible specification of behavior than Goal and Action policies. In situations in which multiple Goal policies would *conflict* (i.e. they could not be simultaneously achieved), Utility Function Policies allow for unambiguous, rational decision making by specifying the appropriate tradeoff. On the other hand, Utility Functions policies can require policy authors to specify a multi-dimensional set of preferences, which may be difficult to elicit, and furthermore they require the use of modeling, optimization, and possibly other algorithms. Related work on using Utility Function policies for network and systems optimization includes [15], [16], [17], [18], [19], [20], [21].

It is instructive to compare our broad definition of policy to the standard definition used in AI, namely that a policy specifies a mapping from any state to the action that should be taken in that state [7]. In our terms, this notion of policy is a *set* of Action policies, in which the Conditions fully cover the state space, and in which each state is mapped to a unique action. Implicit in their definition, there are no policy conflicts, and the policy is a single coherent, consistent mapping from state to action. In order for an autonomic system or component to exhibit rational behavior, an Action *policy set* must cover

---

[2]For the sake of simplicity, we implicitly assume *deterministic* transitions in most of this paper.

[3]Or the probability distribution of states that could be reached, in the case of probabilistic state transitions.

every state in the relevant state space and provide a single unique action for each. Unfortunately, when even moderately large sets of Action policies are created manually by people, it is quite difficult to ensure that the resulting policy set satisfies this criterion. Recognizing then the fallibility of humans in specifying Action policies, we need additional mechanisms to help reduce the potential for conflicts, and to handle them when they do arise. We discuss this further in the next section.

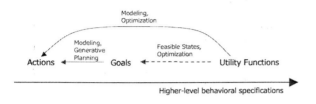

Fig. 2. Relationships between different types of policy.

Alternatively, coherent action can be automatically derived from the higher level forms of policy. Figure 2 illustrates the relationships between the three types of policy in a unified framework. Goal policies are translated into actions during system operation by any of a variety of methods including generative planning [7, chapter 11] for example. To generate a sequence of actions that achieves the desired goal, generative planning necessarily takes into account the results of performing an action. This in turn requires that the system have a model of itself that indicates how actions change the state of the system. In simple cases, translation of Goal policies into actions can be achieved purely via modeling without any planning, as will be illustrated in the next section.

Implementing Utility Function policies requires optimization algorithms. Because Utility Functions are a function of states, it might appear easy and natural to use optimization to directly identify the most desirable state as a Goal from which actions can then be derived via planning and/or modeling. However, one needs to identify the most valuable *feasible* state, and in general that identification requires system modeling. A likely byproduct of such modeling is knowledge of the low-level actions that result in a given state. Thus, once the most optimal state is identified, it is likely that the actions required to achieve that state are already known, so the intermediate step of establishing a goal state can be bypassed. Furthermore, deriving actions directly from the Utility Function policy allows the optimizer to take into account the potential costs of actions. Costs could include explicit monetary costs (such as the cost of power for running a server or the cost of obtaining computation from a data center), or opportunity costs (the cost, not explicitly modeled in the utility function, of not doing something else of value).

In many dynamic autonomic computing scenarios Utility Function policies would be optimized online to compute the best actions for the current state. There can also be situations in which it is feasible to use the utility function to compute an entire Action policy set offline, which is then interpreted by the running system. This approach is taken in the decision-theoretic planning literature by using Markov Decision Processes [22] to compute the actions that should be taken *every* state such that the optimal expected sum of (discounted) utility is obtained over the sequence of all states visited. A hybrid approach can also be taken, whereby the policy set is periodically recomputed online when conditions change sufficiently to make the old policy set suboptimal.

It is worth noting that Utility Function policies can be properly viewed as generalizations of Goal policies. Indeed, conceptually, a utility function can be defined by specifying a complete set of disjoint goals and assigning values to them. (This is not generally feasible when there is a large state space, and is impossible if the state space is continuous. In these cases, more compact functional expressions of utility functions are more practical.) On the other hand, although Action policies are computed by optimizing Utility Function policies, there is no meaningful sense in which Utility Function policies can be derived from Action policies because Action policies are defined over the *current* state space and Utility Function policies are defined over the *desired* state space.

Although not shown, there may also be self-loops in Fig. 2. For example, Utility Functions may be translated into other forms of Utility Functions for use in multiple levels of decision making. In this case, different Utility Functions correspond to the same value system translated into different state spaces. For instance, a Utility Function at one level could specify the relative value of different service levels—to be used for optimizing the performance of a stream of transactions in one part of the system—while a Utility Function at another level could specify the value for obtaining different amounts of computational resources—to be used for optimally allocating resources throughout the system. Generally, to derive some Utility Function B from Utility Function A, a procedure must compute, for each state in the space of B, the optimal value that could be obtained in the space of B. This requires optimization algorithms and a model of how available actions can transform the state space of B to the state space of A. The next section will demonstrate via a simple example how a service-level utility function by one autonomic component can be transformed into a resource-level function to be used by another autonomic component. One can easily imagine other examples in which Goal policies at one level can be transformed into Goal policies at another level.

III. DATA CENTER SCENARIO

The previous section introduced and discussed (somewhat abstractly) three types of policies and a framework that encompassed them. In this section, we shall illustrate and compare the three types of policy more concretely via a data center scenario that is based on a prototype that we and our colleagues at IBM Research have implemented [23], [21].

As shown in Figure 3, the model data center is comprised of a number of *Application Environments* that provide application services to customers. Application Environments are logically separated from each other, each providing a distinct application

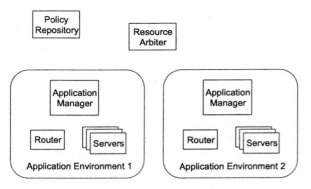

Fig. 3. A data center model.

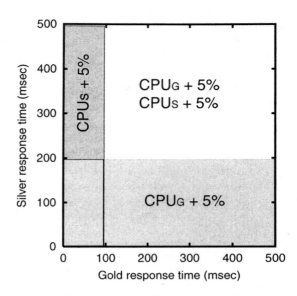

Fig. 4. Action policies for Gold and Silver transaction classes as a function of *current* measured response times for each class.

service using a dedicated (but dynamically allocated) pool of resources. For simplicity of exposition, we assume that resources are identical servers. Each Application Environment is managed by an *Application Manager* (AM), which is responsible for implementing the policies obtained from a *Policy Repository*.

Each AM continually adjusts resource usage in accordance with its policies. When demand changes significantly, some AMs may not be able to adequately implement their policies with available resources. When this occurs, they can appeal to the *Resource Arbiter* for additional resources. The *Resource Arbiter* will consider such resource requests, and may under some circumstances even remove resources from one AM to give them to another if it deems this desirable.

Next, we illustrate in greater detail how policies of each type might drive the resource allocation behavior of the AMs and the Resource Arbiter, using this as a basis for comparing the relative merits of each type of policy.

A. Action policies

In this subsection, we consider three Action policy sets that might be used in our data center model: one to govern an AM's apportionment of its current resources among different transaction classes, a second to govern an AM's resource requests to the Resource Arbiter, and a third to govern the Resource Arbiter's allocation of resources across different AMs.

First, consider the following policy set, which specifies how an AM should apportion resources to Gold and Silver transaction classes:

G. IF ($RT_G > 100$ msec) THEN (Increase CPU_G by 5%)
S. IF ($RT_S > 200$ msec) THEN (Increase CPU_S by 5%)
$$(1)$$

where RT_G and RT_S represent measured average response times for Gold and Silver transaction classes, respectively, and CPU_G and CPU_S represent the fraction of the CPU on each machine that is devoted to serving Gold and Silver class transactions, respectively. The policy pair is represented graphically in Figure 4.

The policy pair of Eq. (1) is quite plausible: the fraction of CPU devoted to each transaction class should be increased

whenever the response time for that class exceeds a given threshold. Another part of each policy (not shown in Eq. (1)) would indicate the conditions under which it was to be applied; for instance there could be a periodic trigger that causes re-evaluation once every 30 seconds. Thus, if a class is still failing to make its objective after a first application of the pertinent policy, subsequent applications of the policy will result in further increases in the fraction of CPU devoted to that class, until finally the response time goal is met.

In terms of our framework, the space of possible current input states can be represented as a two-dimensional space (RT_G, RT_S). The condition of each Action policy defines an entire subspace of input states that do and do not meet the condition. The condition of the Gold policy pertains to all states lying to the right of the vertical line at $RT_G = 100$msec in Figure 4, while that of the Silver policy pertains to all states lying above the horizontal line at $RT_S = 200$msec. These two intersecting lines create four regions. In the upper left region, only the Silver condition applies. In the lower right region, only the Gold condition applies. In both of these cases, the action to be taken is absolutely unambiguous. In the lower left region, neither condition applies. In this region, the policies do not explicitly state what action is to be taken, but a reasonable default policy is to take no action in this case. The system is satisfying both response time objectives, so no actions are warranted. Finally, in the upper right region, *both* conditions apply. If it is possible to increase both the Gold and the Silver CPU shares by 5%, then there are no conflicts, and both of these actions should be taken.

However, if the current state is in the upper right region and Gold and Silver are already sharing the entire CPU between them, then it is impossible to honor the Gold and Silver policies simultaneously. With the Gold and Silver policies in

6

conflict, the policy set as a whole is providing ambiguous, ill-defined guidance to the system. There are several ways to remove the ambiguity in the disputed upper right region of Fig. 4. One approach is to add meta-policies to disable some of the conflicting policies or triggering conditions [24], [25]. For instance, one could add the following rule to resolve the potential conflict:

$$\begin{aligned}
\text{IF } ((\text{ACTION}_1 &: \text{Increase CPU}_G \text{ by } 5\%) \\
\text{AND } (\text{ACTION}_2 &: \text{Increase CPU}_S \text{ by } 5\%) \\
\text{AND } (\text{CPU}_G &+ \text{CPU}_S > 90\%)) \\
\text{THEN}(\text{Ignore ACTION}_2)&
\end{aligned} \quad (2)$$

Here, we use "$\text{ACTION}_i: X$" to indicate that X is specified as an action by an active rule. We label the action by i.

Another method entails modifying the individual policies to eliminate overlapping conditions [26]. Suppose for example that one wishes the Gold class to receive extra CPU in the disputed region. One could add an additional clause to the condition of the silver policy that restricts its application to the upper left region whenever resources are sufficiently scarce, e.g.,

$$\begin{aligned}
\text{IF } ((\text{RT}_S &> 200\text{msec}) \\
\text{AND } ((\text{RT}_G &< 200\text{msec}) \text{ OR } (\text{CPU}_G + \text{CPU}_S < 90\%))) \\
\text{THEN } (\text{Increase CPU}_S & \text{ by } 5\%)
\end{aligned}$$
$$(3)$$

A third method is to leave the individual policies alone, but to permit policies to override one another in the case of conflict. One approach is to associate priorities with each policy with the understanding that, among those policies whose conditions are satisfied simultaneously, only the one with the highest priority will be executed [27]. Using priorities, one could achieve the same effect as in Eq. (3) merely by assigning to the Gold policy and Silver policies priorities of 10 and 5, respectively (with higher numbers indicating higher priorities). A more elegant and flexible approach is to express policies in logic that handles conflicts, and define additional policies that explicitly describe conditions under which overriding occurs [24], [28], [29], e.g., "Gold policy always has priority over Silver policy".

Since it is inherently difficult for humans to compose policy sets that map each and every condition into a single unique action, it is essential for systems that employ Action policies to provide methods for detecting and resolving conflicts among policies. In some cases, static analysis of a set of policies may be adequate to detect conflicts [26], [27]. For example, if is known *a priori* that the Gold and Silver classes together share the entire CPU, then one can determine statically that the Silver and Gold policies of Eq. (1) are in conflict whenever both of their conditions are satisfied, and the system can prompt the policy author to either modify or prioritize the rules to remove the ambiguity. In a more complex system in which CPU may be consumed by several other processes not explicitly mentioned in the policies, static analysis can only suggest the possibility of a conflict, and it is only during the

running operation of the system that a definite conflict can be detected [30]. In this case, a possible solution is to establish which policy should take precedence in the event of a conflict. However, this is not a fully general solution for at least two reasons. First, one might want to base the choice on the nature of the conflict itself. For example, in terms of Fig. 4, the choice between the Gold and Silver policies might depend on the exact location within the upper right hand rectangle, with preference given to the class that is furthest from its response time target. Second, and more importantly, one might want to compromise between the proposed actions, rather than selecting one over the other. For example, suppose that Gold and Silver are both failing, and are together consuming 94% of the available CPU. One might wish to allocate just 4% more CPU to Gold, and the remaining 2% CPU to Silver.

Now, consider a second policy set that guides the AM's resource requests to the Resource Arbiter, for example:

$$\begin{aligned}
\text{IF } (\text{RT}_G &> 100\text{msec OR RT}_S > 200\text{msec}) \\
\text{AND } (\text{CPU}_G &+ \text{CPU}_S > 98\%) \\
\text{THEN } (\text{Request } & 1 \text{ server})
\end{aligned} \quad (4)$$

This policy could be invoked repeatedly until the system achieves its response time goals, or is rebuffed once too often by the Resource Arbiter. Note that the terms regarding the CPU threshold in policy 4 need to be commensurate with the CPU thresholds in policies 2 and 3. In general, the policy writer is forced to think very carefully about how each newly added rule may interact with the ones that are already present in the rule set.

Finally, consider a third policy set used by the Arbiter to adjudicate among resource allocation requests from three different Application Managers, e.g.,

$$\begin{aligned}
\textbf{Arb1. } & \text{IF } (\text{AM}_A \text{ requests } n \text{ servers}) \text{ THEN Grant} \\
& : \text{Priority} = 10 \\
\textbf{Arb2. } & \text{IF } (\text{AM}_B \text{ requests } n \text{ servers}) \text{ THEN Grant} \\
& : \text{Priority} = 8 \\
\textbf{Arb3. } & \text{IF } (\text{AM}_C \text{ requests } n \text{ servers}) \text{ THEN Grant} \\
& : \text{Priority} = 5
\end{aligned} \quad (5)$$

Note that the priority-based scheme does not permit compromises among the various requests, which might well be desirable in this situation. One way to achieve partial granting of requests is to write enumerate a set of rules—one for each possible triple of requests. However, this solution would be quite unwieldy, and would not generalize if more Application Managers joined the system.

B. Goal policies

Here we illustrate how the data center's behavior might be guided by Goal policies. First, the policy set used by an AM to govern apportionment of resources between the Silver and Gold transaction classes would take the form of performance targets, e.g.,

$$\begin{aligned}
\textbf{G. } & \text{RT}_G \leq 100\text{msec} \\
\textbf{S. } & \text{RT}_S \leq 200\text{msec}
\end{aligned} \quad (6)$$

(Strictly speaking, only the goals themselves appear in (6); the full policy would be for the system to *act so as to achieve these goals*. In what follows, we shall not make fine distinctions between Goal policies and the goals on which they are based.) The policy set of (6) is illustrated graphically in Fig. 5.

Fig. 5. Goal policies for Gold and Silver transaction classes as a function of *desired* measured response times for each class. Response-time states to the left of the vertical line at 100 msec satisfy the Gold criterion; those below the horizontal line at 200 msec satisfy the Silver criterion. Labels within each of the four regions formed by the intersection of these two thresholds indicate which policies are satisfied within that region. Hyperbolic curves represent boundary of feasible regions for a fixed workload and for various assumptions about total resource; the feasible region lies above and to the right of these boundaries.

Note that, in contrast to the policy set of Eq. (1), the state space in question is defined by the *desired* response times for Gold and Silver transactions, as opposed to the *current* response times. The two policies in Eq. (1) each define a set of goal states that are acceptable; the set of acceptable goal states for the policy set is given by the intersection—the shaded lower left hand rectangle of Fig. (5).

The policies contain no hints about *how* the goals are to be attained; instead, the system must employ other mechanisms in order to translate these goals into actions. Many such mechanisms are conceivable, but one can reason about them in general terms as follows. Denote the response time vector (T_G, T_S) of the two transaction classes by $\vec{T}$. In general, there will be some functional dependency $\vec{T}(\vec{\lambda}, \vec{C})$ of the response times upon the request rates $\vec{\lambda} = (\lambda_G, \lambda_S)$ and the apportionment of resource among the various classes $\vec{C} = (\text{CPU}_G, \text{CPU}_S)$.

Treating the quantity of CPU resource in absolute (rather than fractional terms, as in the previous subsection), suppose that the total amount of CPU resource available for the Gold and Silver classes is a constant CPU capacity C_0. Then the set of feasible states are those defined by $\vec{T}(\vec{\lambda}, \vec{C})$, for all

$\vec{C}$ satisfying the constraint $C_G + C_S \leq C_0$, evaluated at the current value of the demand vector $\vec{\lambda}$. In general, this will define a region of state space with a nonlinear boundary. For example, suppose that the system can be modeled as a simple M/M/1 queue, and that the response time for each class is proportional to the amount of CPU devoted to it. Then

$$T_i = \frac{1}{\alpha C_i - \lambda_i}, \qquad (7)$$

where α is some constant of proportionality that relates service time to CPU resource. The resulting feasible regions are bounded by hyperbolas, as shown in Fig. 5 for three different choices of C_0.

There are several cases to consider. First, suppose there is enough resource to satisfy both the Gold and the Silver Goal policies. Then the regions of desired and feasible states overlap. In Fig. 5, this occurs when $C_0 = 50$ servers—note the roughly triangular region of overlap between the desired states in the lower left rectangle and the feasible states bounded by the hyperbola. *Any* state in this triangle of intersection is equally acceptable. Then the appropriate action is to set $\vec{C}$ to any value such that $\vec{T}$ lies within the desired region.

However, if there is insufficient resource to satisfy both goals, but enough to satisfy either the Gold or the Silver goal alone, then there is a policy conflict. In Fig. 5, this occurs when $C_0 = 10$ servers—the hyperbolically bounded feasible region overlaps with the upper left rectangle (representing states that satisfy only the Gold policy) and with the lower right rectangle (representing states that satisfy only the Silver policy), but not with the lower left rectangle (representing states satisfying both the Silver and Gold policies).

A common approach to meeting quality of service goals in network environments is to restrict requests whose required goal cannot be met [12], [13]. However, data centers are typically obliged to service all requests (at least up to a certain request rate threshold). An alternative approach to resolving the policy conflict is to assign priorities to the policies, as with action policies. However, this conflict resolution strategy is not quite as clear-cut as one might expect. A naive approach is to successively give up on lower priority goals until one finally achieves intersection between the feasible and the desirable states. However, for some values of $\vec{\lambda}$ and C_0, it may be the case that the Silver goal can be achieved, but the Gold goal cannot. In Figure 6, this occurs when there are fewer than five servers. Should the AM then meet the Silver goal, but choose a state such that the deviation from the Gold response time threshold is minimized? Or should most of the resource be given to Gold to get it as close as possible to the desired response time goal, even if this means driving the Silver response time to a very unacceptable level? The possibilities get even more complex when one considers more than two transaction classes. Finally, if neither goal can be satisfied individually, then the policy set offers no guidance for how the system should behave. There is no way to distinguish any of the feasible states from one another. All are equally undesirable, because all represent failure, and goal policies express only a binary success or failure, not degrees of failure.

As we discussed in the case of Action policies, if the current resource is insufficient to satisfy the goals, the AM can appeal to the Resource Arbiter for more resource. In the previous subsection, this function required a separate policy set. For Goal policies, this is not strictly necessary. A capacity planning engine armed with a good system model might be able to achieve this purely from the Goal policies of Eq. (6). From knowledge of the current value of λ and the function $\vec{T}(\lambda, \vec{C})$, it could compute a value of $\vec{C}^*$ required to achieve overlap between the feasible and desired state and request from the Resource Arbiter enough additional servers to bring the total resource to $C_G^* + C_S^*$. In practice, there might be additional policies that establish further conditions that govern when the AM would request additional resources.

In response to a request for resource from the AM, the Arbiter would also ask the other AMs how many servers they need to meet their Goal policies before determining the global reallocation of servers. The Arbiter might employ the Action policies of Policy Set (5). As noted in the previous subsection, this particular policy set has some protection against resource allocation conflicts that occur when the total number of available servers is inadequate to satisfy the total expressed resource needs of the AMs. However, the situation may be more subtle. Suppose for example that there are several AMs. If the highest priority AM requests all of the resources, the other AMs would get nothing. This may not always reflect what is really desired. An alternative is for the Arbiter to itself use a Goal policy, e.g.,

$$\text{Ensure that at least } 3/4 \text{ of the AMs are satisfied.} \quad (8)$$

Since this policy set contains just a single goal, there is no danger of conflict in this case. Such a Goal policy could be reasonable if the data center is configured with sufficient servers to ensure it can be met. However, if Goal policy 8 cannot be satisfied, there is no guidance as to what the Arbiter should do.

One can envisage much more complex Arbiter policies that take into account other information, such as the state or the importance of each Application Environment; the mechanisms required to execute them may need to be rather sophisticated.

C. Utility Function policies

Now we illustrate how the data center's behavior might be guided by Utility Function policies. With a Utility Function policy, the system acts so as to optimize a given utility function, for example by setting control parameters or allocating resources appropriately. In the remainder of this section, we focus on the utility functions themselves, and do not make fine distinctions between Utility Function policies and the utility functions on which they are based.

First, we consider how utility functions can be used to apportion resource between the Gold and Silver transaction classes. Figure 6 shows two utility functions (measured in a monetary unit such as dollars): one for average response time of Gold transactions, and the other for the average response time of Silver transactions. The utility functions can be thought of as softened versions of the individual goals of Eq. (6). For Gold utility, the utility peaks at response times of just less than 100 msec, dropping significantly as the response time rises above 100 msec. The Silver utility curve has a similar shape, with a threshold at 200 msec, but a more gradual transition from maximum to minimum utility. These two utility functions can be mathematically combined into a single utility function in any number of ways. The two-dimensional utility function of Fig. 7 is obtained simply by summing the individual Gold and Silver utility functions U_G and U_S, e.g.

$$U(\text{RT}_G, \text{RT}_S) = U_G(\text{RT}_G) + U_S(\text{RT}_S). \quad (9)$$

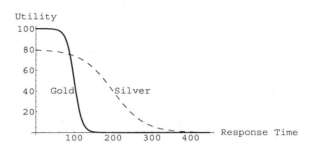

Fig. 6. Utility functions providing the utility in monetary units as a function of response time. The solid curve shows the utility for response time of Gold transactions and the dashed curve shows the utility for response time of Silver transactions.

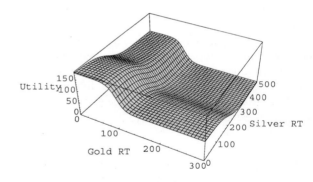

Fig. 7. A single utility function, providing the utility in monetary units as a function of joint average response time for Gold and Silver transactions.

The Goal policies of the previous section established a binary classification of all states into either "desirable" or "undesirable". The objective was then to place the system into any state that was both desirable and feasible—something that is not possible if these sets do not intersect. With Utility Function policies, each state has a real value rather than just a Boolean one, and the objective is to place the system into the feasible state with the highest utility. Thus there is never a failure. Also, note that a single utility function maps all states of interest into a single unique value, and as such only one is needed. Therefore there cannot be any conflicts.

It may however be the case that the highest attainable utility is deemed unacceptably low. This may be indicated by adding an additional Goal policy of the form

$$\text{The utility should be at least 50} \qquad (10)$$

If the utility falls below 50, the AM could redress the problem by appealing to the Resource Arbiter for more resources. Rather than specifying a fixed number of servers, the AM could compute a *resource-level* utility function indicating the value as a function of the number of additional servers and send this function to the Resource Arbiter. To determine the resource-level utility function, each AM must compute, for each number r of servers, the maximal utility it could obtain if it had r servers and optimized its service-level utility function. Using the notation from Section III-B, the utility function for CPU capacity C_r obtained from r servers is

$$U(C_r) = \max_{\vec{C} \mid C_G + C_S \le C_r} U(\vec{T}(\vec{\lambda}, \vec{C})) \qquad (11)$$

To compute the optimal service-level utility that can be obtained from a particular resource level, each AM must possess a performance model that maps resource level and client demand into performance.

The Arbiter would query other AMs for their resource-level utility functions, and apply its policy to compute a best allocation. A typical policy for the Arbiter might be:

$$\text{Maximize sum of utilities of all AMs} \qquad (12)$$

Although this optimization could be expensive (and may need to be approximated), it is conceptually simple. There are no conflicts that need be resolved. Instead, the complexity is placed inside the AMs.

Although Utility Function policies have the benefit of being naturally conflict free, they impose an added burden of precisely specifying numeric values over the entire state space. It is well established that humans have difficulty specifying utility functions, and much work has been done to understand and ameliorate the difficulty [31], [32], [33]. In our data center domain, there are at least three challenges associated with specifying a utility function. One is to determine the appropriate shape of the function. Another challenge is to put multiple metrics on a common value scale. For the sake of exposition, this paper has explored a single simple performance metric only. In a real system, one would employ utility functions expressing preferences for a variety of performance metrics, as well as metrics describing availability, security, and any other service attributes of interest. Combining utility functions for individual metrics into a common multi-dimensional utility function requires (say via summation) that the individual utility function share a common value scale; some monetary unit would be a reasonable choice. A third challenge is to evaluate the relative value of multiple Application Environments.

At first blush, it would seem that Action and Goal policies are easier and more natural for humans to think about and specify. We acknowledge this to be true in relatively simple cases, but as we have shown, policy conflicts can complicate this process significantly. Indeed, the problem of evaluating the relative importance of different metrics and of different Application Environments becomes manifest in even moderately complex systems. While Utility Function policies place the burden on humans to be more precise about these relative tradeoffs, they have the advantage of forcing humans to consider these issues. In contrast, Action and Goal policies allow these issues to be swept under the rug, which can result in conflicts. Determining the appropriate shape for Utility Functions can be challenging, but often one can simplify this problem by starting out with what are effectively smoothed out goals, as with the Utility Function policies of Figure 6.

D. Mixing Policy Types

Observe that different components can use different types of policies. In Section III-B we showed an example in which an Application Manager used Goal policies and the Arbiter used an Action policy. As another example, the Arbiter can use a Utility Function policy even if the AMs are using other types of policies. For instance, if the AMs are using either Action or Goal policies for requesting more servers (as in sections III-A or III-B), the AM might use the following Utility Function policy:

$$\text{Maximize num(AMs) whose resource requests are granted} \qquad (13)$$

However, policy types cannot be mixed arbitrarily. For example, the Arbiter's policy has to be consistent with the form of the resource requests, which depend on the type of policy used by the AM issuing the request. Policies (8) and (13) would not be meaningful if the AMs expressed the resource requests in terms of resource utility functions, as in Eq. (11). Likewise, the Arbiter could not use a Utility Function policy such as (12) if the AMs issued requests for a specific quantity of resource, as in section III-B. These examples hint at the careful relationship that must be maintained between policies used by various elements in an autonomic computing system and the protocols for interaction between the elements.

Handling multiple policy types within the same component is also possible, but much more complicated. Here we highlight some of the salient issues. Overall, Utility Function and Goal policies tend to be more naturally compatible with one another than either is with Action policies. The reason is simple: both are expressed in terms of the space of desired states rather than the current state. We anticipate that one common pattern for combining Utility Function and Goal policies within a single component will involve using a Goal policy as a constraint on the optimization problem defined by the Utility Function policy.

For example, consider an Application Manager with a Policy Set consisting of two policies: the Utility Function shown in Figure 7, plus the Goal policy $RT_G \le 200\text{msec}$. Expressed as a constraint to the optimization procedure, the Goal policy would simply exclude the region of state space lying above $RT_G = 200\text{msec}$. As another example, consider the communication between this AM and the Resource Arbiter. The hard constraint on RT_G might translate into a hard constraint on the minimum number of servers that the AM must obtain in order to satisfy its Policy Set. In other words, the AM could submit the constraint "Obtain at least 1 server" along with its utility function. If the Resource Arbiter uses a Utility Function policy like (12), and it is willing to accept this constraint by dynamically (and temporarily) adding it to its own Policy Set, then the Resource Arbiter's Policy Set is likewise a mixture of Utility Function and Goal policies.

Of course, since Goal policies introduce constraints, and thus eliminate regions of state space, Policy Sets that mix Utility Function and Goal policies possess the same problems as pure Goal Policy Sets. Chief among these problems are the possibility of failure to satisfy the Policy Set (which necessitates other policies that govern behavior in the event of failure), and the possibility of conflict if there are multiple constraints that are not mutually satisfiable (which is really just a special case of Policy Set failure).

Combining Action policies with Utility Function policies or Goal policies is more problematic. If the optimizer that operates upon the utility function tries to control variables that appear in the Action clause of an Action policy, conflicts are bound to occur. Unfortunately, the control variables available to the optimizer (e.g. the CPU devoted to each class, in our simple example) are typically not mentioned explicitly in the utility function. Therefore, pure syntactic checking of the Policy Set alone cannot reveal potential conflicts. If it is somehow determined that there is a potential conflict (through detailed knowledge of the control variables available to the optimizer, for example), then the various options for conflict resolution discussed in Section III-A may be explored, such as assigning priorities to the policies or writing more general metapolicies.

A possible way to minimize the risk of conflicts between Action and Utility Function policies employed within the same component is to ensure that they are applied to very different classes of service attributes, such as performance and availability or security. However, this is not a surefire solution because the control variables that underlie performance, availability and security are not necessarily mutually exclusive. For example, consider a utility function for performance. The optimizer that takes the utility function as its objective may have as one of its control variables the number of servers allocated to each transaction class. An Action policy may govern the availability characteristics for the Gold class by controlling (among other things) the number of servers that are allocated to it. Once again, conflict is possible.

Another way to avoid conflict is to ensure that the optimizer cannot control any variable mentioned in the Action clause of an Action policy. This may work, although it is still possible that indirect interactions among variables will cause trouble. For example, certain actions (such as installation of new software) may temporarily make a resource (along with any associated control variables) temporarily unavailable. If the optimizer is not aware of this outage, and it relies on some of these control variables, it may produce inappropriate results.

IV. CONCLUSION

We have presented a unified view of different types of autonomic computing policy from an AI perspective. States and actions are the key concepts that relate Action, Goal, and Utility Function policies. In accordance with the AI principle of rational agents, the purpose of a policy is to provide guidance for an autonomic system to choose actions that move it into desirable states. Still, only if the policies are complete and coherent can rationality be realized in the system and correct behavior be achieved.

To this end, policies must cover the entire state space and provide unambiguous guidance to the system. Because this cannot generally be achieved by considering individual policies in isolation, Policy *Sets* are the right way to think about policy. Unfortunately, people typically think of policies individually, rather than as Policy Sets, because they have difficulty comprehending and reasoning about Policy Sets in systems of realistic complexity. As seen in section III-A, even small Policy Sets can exhibit subtle complexities. This points to a need for mechanisms to enforce the use of Policy Sets, and to support their creation and management.

Possessing a unified view of policy gives us the power to mix the different types of policy within a system, so long as we ensure that unambiguous action is guaranteed across the entire state space. Our data center scenario illustrated some inherent advantages and disadvantages of each of the different types of policy.

A nice feature of Action policies is that they do not require an operational model of the system in order to be used. In real systems, performance models will be considerably more complex than the simple M/M/1 queuing model given in Eq. 7. It will be hard to obtain accurate models of real, complex systems, and by and large they do not exist today. For this reason, we expect Action policies to predominate in early autonomic computing systems. One might argue that Action policies are also appealing in their simplicity, but this is debatable. Action policies require the user to know about the space of control variables as well as the state space, which typically requires a large amount of domain expertise. Furthermore, even in the simple examples of this paper, we found it necessary to reconceive our two simple initial Action rules—which seem quite reasonable on first inspection—to ensure that the AM would avoid conflict. Although our example is idealized, the revised rule (3) is somewhat complex, and requires a bit of thought for a human to verify its correctness. Priority schemes are another approach, but in either case it seems clear that even moderately larger policy sets would become quite unwieldy.

As system models and planners become better and more widely available, Goal based policies will become more feasible and more prevalent. Goal policies have an advantage over Action policies because they give an autonomic system the flexibility to choose the best actions under the current conditions. Furthermore, Goal policies reduce the burden on the user because they are expressed only in terms of the state space, leaving to an automated mechanism like an optimizer or planner the task of dealing with the space of control variables (such as CPU allocation in our simple example). Thus the user need only deal with a smaller and easier set of variables. However, Goal policies are dependent upon system models and planning algorithms, and moreover they are still susceptible to conflict. When not all goals can be realized, the Goal policies alone provide no guidance. Additional policies and mechanisms may be needed to resolve the impasse, all of which can complicate the resulting Policy Set.

Utility Function policies are quite appealing for advanced autonomic computing systems because they inherently avoid conflicts. Optimizing a utility function is conceptually more straightforward than having to patch a Policy Set with additional policies, priorities, and various conflict resolution mechanisms, as is necessary for Action and Goal policies. However, as with Goal policies, Utility Function policies rely on the existence of potentially complex system models and optimization algorithms. Furthermore, since it is difficult for humans to specify them, Utility Function policies will not be very usable until we have good interfaces and algorithms for eliciting them. It may take a some years of solid research effort to address all of these issues, but ultimately the inherent advantages of Utility Function policies may make them the predominant form of policy.

ACKNOWLEDGMENTS

The authors thank Rajarshi Das and Gerald Tesauro for sharing their insights on utility functions, policy, and artificial intelligence, and for numerous helpful comments on this paper.

REFERENCES

[1] J. O. Kephart and D. M. Chess, "The vision of autonomic computing," *Computer*, vol. 36, no. 1, pp. 41–52, 2003.

[2] "Autonomic computing: IBM's perspective on the state of information technology," http://www.research.ibm.com/autonomic/manifesto/autonomic_computing.pdf%.

[3] M. Bearden, S. Garg, and W. jyh Lee, "Integrating goal specification in policy-based management," in *2nd International Workshop on Policies for Distributed Systems and Networks*, 2001.

[4] N. Damianou, N. Dulay, E. Lupu, and M. Sloman, "The Ponder policy specification language," in *2nd International Workshop on Policies for Distributed Systems and Networks*, 2001.

[5] J. Strassner, "How policy empowers business-driven device management," in *3rd International Workshop on Policies for Distributed Systems and Networks*, 2002.

[6] A. Westerinen, J. Schnizlein, J. Strassner, M. Scherling, B. Quinn, S. Herzog, A. Huynh, M. Carlson, J. Perry, and S. Waldbusser, "Terminology for policy-based management," University of Wolverhamptons School of Computing and Information Technology, http://www.scit.wlv.ac.uk/rfc/, Tech. Rep. RFC 3198, 2001.

[7] S. Russell and P. Norvig, *Artificial Intelligence: A Modern Approach*, 2nd ed. Prentice Hall, 2003.

[8] C. Efstratiou, A. Friday, N. Davies, and K. Cheverst, "Utilising the event calculus for policy driven adaptation on mobile systems," in *3rd International Workshop on Policies for Distributed Systems and Networks*, 2002, pp. 13–24.

[9] H. Lutfiyya, G. Molenkamp, M. Katchabaw, and M. Bauer, "Issues in managing soft QoS requirements in distributed systems using a policy-based framework," in *2nd International Workshop on Policies for Distributed Systems and Networks*, 2001.

[10] L. Lymberopoulos, E. Lupu, and M. Sloman, "An adaptive policy based management framework for differentiated services networks," in *3rd International Workshop on Policies for Distributed Systems and Networks*, 2002, pp. 147–158.

[11] A. Ponnappan, L. Yang, and R. Pillai.R, "A policy based QoS management system for the IntServ/DiffServ based internet," in *3rd International Workshop on Policies for Distributed Systems and Networks*, 2002, pp. 159–168.

[12] S. Wang, D. Xuan, R. Bettati, and W. Zhao, "Providing absolute differentiated services for real-time applications in static-priority scheduling networks," in *IEEE Infocom*, 2001.

[13] J. Yoon and R. Bettati, "A three-pass establishment protocol for real-time multiparty communication," Texas A&M University, Tech. Rep. 97-006, 1997.

[14] A. Chandra, W. Gong, and P. Shenoy, "Dynamic resource allocation for shared data centers using online measurements," in *International Workshop on Quality of Service*, 2003, pp. 381–400.

[15] J. S. Chase, D. C. Anderson, P. N. Thakar, and A. M. Vahdat, "Managing energy and server resources in hosting centers," in *18th Symposium on Operating Systems Principles*, 2001.

[16] T. Kelly, "Utility-directed allocation," in *First Workshop on Algorithms and Architectures for Self-Managing Systems*, 2003.

[17] R. Rajkumar, C. Lee, J. P. Lehoczky, and D. P. Siewiorek, "Practical solutions for QoS-based resource allocation problems," in *IEEE Real-Time Systems Symposium*, 1998, pp. 296–306.

[18] S. Lalis, C. Nikolaou, D. Papadakis, and M. Marazakis, "Market-driven service allocation in a QoS-capbable environment," in *First International Conference on Information and Computation Economies*, 1998.

[19] P. Thomas, D. Teneketzis, and J. K. MacKie-Mason, "A market-based approach to optimal resource allocation in integrated-services connection-oriented networks," *Operations Research*, vol. 50, no. 4, 2002.

[20] H. Yamaki, M. P. Wellman, and T. Ishida, "A market-based approach to allocating QoS for multimedia applications," in *Second International Conference on Multi-Agent Systems*, 1996, pp. 385–392.

[21] W. E. Walsh, G. Tesauro, J. O. Kephart, and R. Das, "Utility functions in autonomic systems," in *International Conference on Autonomic Computing*, 2004.

[22] C. Boutilier, T. Dean, and S. Hanks, "Decision-theoretic planning: Structural assumptions and computational leverage," *Journal of Artificial Intelligence Research*, vol. 11, pp. 1–94, 1999.

[23] D. Chess, A. Segal, I. Whalley, and S. White, "Unity: Experiences with a prototype autonomic computing system," in *International Conference on Autonomic Computing*, 2004.

[24] H. V. Jagadish, A. O. Mendelzon, and I. S. Mumick, "Managing conflicts between rules," in *Fifteenth ACM SIGACT-SIGMOD-SIGART Symposium on Principles of Database Systems*, 1996, pp. 192–201.

[25] J. Chomicki, J. Lobo, and S. Naqvi, "A logic programming approach to conflict eesolution in policy management," in *Seventh International Conference on Principles of Knowledge Representation and Reasoning*, 2002, pp. 121–132.

[26] M. Koch, L. V. Mancini, and F. Parisi-Presicce, "Conflict detection and resolution in access control policy specifications," in *5th International Conference on Foundations of Software Sicence and Computation Structures*, ser. LNCS. Springer, 2002, no. 2303.

[27] E. C. Lupu and M. Sloman, "Conflicts in policy-based distributed systems management," *IEEE Transactions on Software Engineering*, vol. 25, no. 6, 1999.

[28] B. N. Grosof, Y. Labrou, and H. Y. Chan, "A declarative approach to business rules in contracts: courteous logic programs in XML," in *ACM Conference on Electronic Commerce*, 1999, pp. 68–77.

[29] R. Agrawal, R. Cohrane, and B. Lindsay, "On maintaining priorities in a production rule system," in *17th International Conference on Very Large Data Bases*, 1991, pp. 479–487.

[30] N. Dunlop, J. Indulska, and K. Raymond, "Dynamic conflict detection in policy-based management systems," in *Sixth International Enterprixe Distributed Computing Conference*, 2002, pp. 15–26.

[31] C. Boutilier, "A POMPDP formulation of preference elicitation problems," in *Eighteenth National Conference on Artificial Intelligence*, 2002, pp. 239–246.

[32] V. Iyengar, J. Lee, and M. Campbell, "Evaluating multiple attribute items using queries," in *3rd ACM Conference on Electronic Commerce*, 2001, pp. 144–153.

[33] R. L. Keeney and H. Raiffa, *Decisions with Multiple Objectives: Preferences and Value Tradeoffs*. Cambridge University Press, 1993.

Policy Transformation Techniques in Policy-based Systems Management

Mandis S. Beigi　　　　Seraphin Calo　　　　Dinesh Verma

IBM T.J. Watson Research Center

mandis@us.ibm.com　　　scalo@us.ibm.com　　　dverma@us.ibm.com

Abstract

Policy based systems management provides a means for administrators, end-users and application developers to manage and dynamically change the behavior of computing systems. One advantage of policy-based management is that it simplifies and automates the administration of IT environments. A significant part of the simplification is obtained by allowing the system administrator to specify only the objectives or goals that are to be met, rather than having to specify detailed configuration parameters for each of the different devices in the system. It may not be obvious to the administrator how the goals can be achieved without having to know the internals of the system. This knowledge thus needs to be captured in the policy driven actions. The existing algorithms for mapping policy objectives to specific configuration details tend to be specific to each policy discipline. This makes the policy-based approach harder to deploy for new disciplines. In this paper, we address different types of policy transformations and propose methods, which are not discipline specific for mapping objectives to system configurations.

1. Introduction

Most distributed computing environments today are very complex and time consuming for a human administrator to manage. The policy based management approach [1][16][18][19] provides a mechanism that can simplify the management of distributed computing systems, and can be applied in large computer networks [2][3], or in the context of Grid Computing [4]. This simplification of management functions is obtained primarily because of two aspects of the policy-based architecture employed, namely centralization and business level abstractions. Centralization refers to the process of defining all the device provisioning and configuration policies at a single point rather than separately provisioning and configuring each individual device in the distributed system. Business level abstractions make the job of the policy administrator simpler by allowing the policies to be defined in terms of a language that is closer to the business needs of an organization rather than in terms of the specific technology needed to implement them. Therefore, the administrator need not know all the details of the technology and 'how' these business needs can be met.

The mechanisms necessary for transforming service objectives into configuration parameters currently available in the literature are specific to the domains in which policy-based management is being applied [5][6][15]. The ad-hoc domain specific transformation mechanisms only increase the amount of work that is required to apply policy-based techniques to a new domain. Clearly, generic transformation mechanisms, which can be applied to many different disciplines, are needed. In this paper, we introduce the different types of policy transformations needed in a system managed by the use of policies, propose methods for performing such generic transformation mechanism, and study their effectiveness.

The paper is organized as follows: Section 2 describes a general policy based systems management architecture as employed in many environments; in Section 3 we show how this can be extended to incorporate policy transformation; in Section 4 we describe a number of different methods for determining the right set of system configuration parameters to meet a business objective or goal; Section 5 presents three solution scenarios for policy transformation; Section 6 describes experimental results for a policy transformation solution using case based reasoning; in Section 7 online or real time transformation is discussed; and, finally, conclusions and future work are presented in Section 8.

13

2. Policy based systems management architecture

A policy based systems management architecture based on the IETF framework consists of four main components: a policy management tool, a policy repository, a policy decision point, and a policy enforcement point. Figure 1 shows a general architecture for such a policy based management system [18]. Most current systems employing policies follow such an architecture.

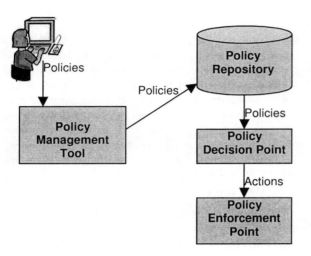

Figure 1. A general policy based systems management architecture

The system administrator enters the policies into the policy management tool. These policies are then sent to and are stored in the policy repository. The policies stored in the repository must be in a form that corresponds to the information model specified by the Policy Framework Working Group [1]. This ensures interoperability across products from different vendors. The decision points (PDPs) retrieve their policies from the repository. The PDP is responsible for interpreting the policies stored in the repository and communicating them to the policy enforcement points (PEPs).

The PEP is the system component that actually applies and executes the policies. The PEP and the PDP may both be located on a single device or they can be on different physical devices. Different protocols can be used for various parts of the architecture; e.g., the COPS protocol [7] or the SNMP protocol [8] can be used for communication between the PDP and the PEP. A repository could be a network directory server accessed using the LDAP protocol [9].

3. The policy transformation module

In general, high-level business-oriented policies will need to be transformed into lower level technology-oriented policies in order for them to be used by the various components of the system. Such a policy transformation can be done by a module within the policy management tool that takes the policies entered by the system administrator and converts them from one form to another before they are deployed and interpreted by the enforcement points. This transformation module should be bi-directional in that it should be able to transform technology-oriented policies (i.e. configuration parameters) into high-level policies or business goals. The reverse transformation feature is useful for an advisor tool where an administrator is told what level of service (i.e. set of goals) he or she can achieve given the specified set of configuration values.

Transformation may be done in one of two places: either before the policies are sent to the repository, or at the decision point before the policies are sent to the enforcement point. Policy transformation can be done either offline or online. The former will be referred to as static transformation, and the latter will be referred to as real time transformation.

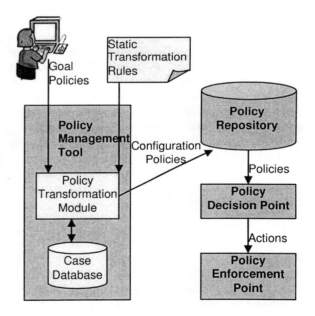

Figure 2. A policy based systems management architecture enabled with static policy transformation

Static (or offline) policy transformation uses static data and predetermined transformation rules to convert high level goals to sets of specific policies that can be applied to the components of the system. Figure 2 shows a policy-based systems management architecture incorporating static policy transformation within the policy management tool.

In real time policy transformation, the system uses an online component that dynamically monitors the behavior of prescribed elements within the system in order to ensure that the specified objectives are being met. In such a system, observations of system behavior are used by the transformation module to dynamically modify the configuration of the system to achieve the user's goals.

In the following sections of the paper, we describe different approaches for performing policy transformation and propose a generic algorithm that is discipline independent.

4. Existing Solution approaches

The problem of determining the right set of configuration parameters to meet a business objective or a goal can be solved by various approaches. We go over some of these approaches in the following subsections.

4.1. Analytic Models

If an analytic model exists that can be used to determine the business objective as a function of the configuration parameters, one could solve for the model parameters that satisfy the required business objective. As an example, if an analytical expression existed to relate a website's outbound bandwidth to its inbound traffic rate, one could invert the expression to obtain the requisite traffic rate for any desired limit on outbound bandwidth.

The problem with analytical expressions is that they do not exist in most real-life environments. In order to obtain a tractable analytical expression, one generally needs to make simplifying assumptions, which are rarely satisfied in practice. For example, in the case where one needs to model the relationship between the network bandwidth required and the connection rate supported, it is generally necessary to make assumptions such as: that the distribution of the arrival traffic is Poisson, or that the traffic characteristics are constant over time. Neither of these assumptions may actually hold, making it difficult to obtain tractable analytical expressions.

4.2. Online Adaptive Control

One could use concepts from control theory [10] to determine online schemes for controlling and fine-tuning the parameters needed to obtain a business objective. Another approach would be to develop a neural network model [11] as a mechanism for determining the impact of specific configuration parameters on the requisite business objective. The neural network or the adaptive control scheme could then be used to modify the business parameters dynamically online [12]. While these approaches seem attractive from the point of view of flexibility, there are two principal drawbacks. The first is that the control algorithm or the neural network needs to be trained on a characteristic workload for it to operate effectively, and it is often impossible to generate a synthetic workload that will have the same characteristics as the real workload in the system. The second drawback is that the development of the training model for a discipline is a laborious discipline-specific process, and it is hard to develop generic software that could be used readily across multiple disciplines.

4.3 Simulation Approach

An alternative to developing an analytic or a control model is to use a simulation system to model the behavior of a system, and use simulation based schemes to build a scheme for transforming higher level business objectives into lower level system configuration parameters. The simulation approach can offer a more flexible approach than an analytic model, and can encompass more realistic assumptions than the analytic model. Simulation based approaches do not suffer from the limitations of a training set in order to learn how to transform the system.

The significant limitation of the simulation approach is its lack of generality. Developing a good simulator for meaningful policy transformation requires a significant amount of effort, and depends upon many nuances of the domain and environment in which policies are being used. A simulation based approach can be used to build a customized policy transformation engine, but is hard to use in a generic manner.

5. Our Proposed Approach

We categorize the usage of policy transformation into three different scenarios. We go over these scenarios in the following subsections and propose a generic solution.

5.1. Scenario 1: Transformation using static rules

Transformation using static rules is the simplest type of transformation but can be very useful in simplifying the policy language as seen by the system administrator. In this scenario, we assume that there is set of static transformation rules for converting policies in terms of high-level goals into policies in terms of low-level configuration parameters understandable by the system. The rules follow a policy language that is more detailed and complicated than the one used by the goal policies as seen by the system administrator. These rules are defined by an expert user, who knows the details of the system and the definitions of the various objectives, such as what it means to provide gold level service in terms of performance, security, etc. The transformation module simply transforms the objectives to low-level configuration parameters using the definitions specified by the transformation rules. This kind of transformation is well suited for a policy management system in which there are groupings of administrators, and different administrators have different authorities and access rights for retrieving and editing policies.

As an example, the transformation module would receive a policy of the form: If the *user* is from *Schwab*, then provide *Gold* level service. This policy would be transformed into the following more specific policy: If the *user* is from the subnet *9.10.3.0/24*, then reserve a *bandwidth* of *20 Mbps* and provide an *encryption of 128 bits*. In this case, the transformation rule specifies that a Schwab user is on the 9.10.3.0/24 subnet. It also specifies that a Gold service be defined to provide a bandwidth of 20 Mbps and an encryption of 128 bits. Since policy transformation is bi-directional, a user is also able to query the module to find out the level of goals that can be achieved given a set of low-level configuration parameters.

5.2. Scenario 2: Transformation by policy table lookup

In this scenario, we assume the transformation module holds a table of policies appropriate for the system. The system administrator queries the module with a set of configuration parameters in order to obtain a set of goals that can be achieved given the input.

In order to perform transformation, each policy in the table needs to be first mapped into an N-dimensional hyperspace object, where N or the dimension of the space is the number of configuration parameters in the policy. Each policy is considered to be a region in the hyperspace, which may be connected or disconnected. Each hyper-cube points to a set of goals or actions. The system needs to match the hyper-cube corresponding to the policy being queried against all the hyper-cubes representing all the policies in the table. It finds the hyper-cube from the table that fully contains the specified hyper-cube.

Note that the specified hyper-cube might not be fully contained in any single hyper-cube from the table. In other words, it might overlap several hyper-cubes, in which case the incoming hyper-cube needs to be split into smaller hyper-cubes where each new hyper-cube now corresponds to a different set of goals. In order to make sure we find a match for all segments of the incoming hyper-cube, we need to perform a coverage check on the policy table.

The coverage checker is based on the ability to subtract two regions (i.e. perform group difference): A - B = {x | x in A but not in B} where A and B are two regions and A-B denotes the difference between A and B. Coverage checking is performed by subtracting from the region of interest all the regions defined by the group of policies. Once the region of interest becomes empty, then coverage is deemed *complete*. If, after iterating through all the policies the region of interest is not empty, then the coverage is deemed *incomplete*.

Figure 3 shows a simple 2-dimensional hyperspace with 4 policies shown as A, B, C, and D. The policy being queried is shown with a dashed pattern and is shown to overlap policies B, C and D.

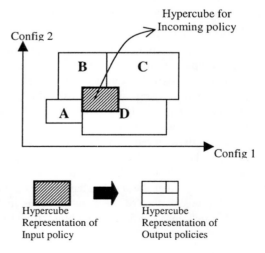

16

Figure 3. Hypercube representation of policies for a 2-dimensional space

5.3. Scenario 3: Transformation using case based reasoning

One can use a case database or history of system behavior to provide an experiential basis for the transformation of high-level policies or goals into low-level configuration parameters and vice versa. In this approach, the transformation module uses the knowledge learned from the behavior of the system in the past to predict its present and future behavior.

Case based reasoning is widely used in many applications such as diagnostics, planning, prediction, object classification, and in electronic commerce for such functions as product selection [13].

In the case based reasoning approach, the system learns experientially from the operational behavior it has seen in the past. The system maintains a database of past cases, where each case is a combination of the system configuration parameters and the business objectives that are achieved by the specific combination of the system configuration parameters. When the configuration parameters needed for a new business objective are required, the case database is consulted to find the closest matching case, or an interpolation is performed between the configuration parameters of a set of cases to determine the appropriate configuration parameters that will result in the desired business objective. The adaptation to each discipline requires that the discipline identify the configuration parameters and the business objectives that constitute a case and identify the strategies for interpolation among cases, but the same case manipulation software and algorithms can be used across all the different disciplines.

However, the effectiveness of the case based reasoning approach depends on having a rich enough set of cases that can be consulted in order to map the business objectives into the desired set of configuration parameters. In a system that has been running for an extended period of time, it is possible to build cases from prior experiences. However, at bootstrap time, the system has no case history to use. Thus, one has to solve the bootstrap problem by using some heuristic (an analytical expression or rules of thumb), or by pre-populating the system with a set of cases observed in pre-operational tests. The bootstrapping case suffers from the same limitations as the previously mentioned approaches described in section 4. Later on in this section, we will describe methods that can help

increase the accuracy of the cased based approach when there is only a small amount of data available. Despite this bootstrapping issue, it is felt that the case based reasoning approach offers the best solution for a generic mapping of business objectives to the configuration parameters.

The format of the case database – The case database contains measurements of various parameters of a system over a long period of time. Each case contains an N-dimensional set of configuration parameters and an M-dimensional set of corresponding goal values. Each case corresponds to measurements taken at one point in time. The cases may or may not be ordered chronologically and may or may not be associated to timestamps. Table 1 shows an example of a case table in a 2-tiered web server measuring the user response times as a function of the number of disks and nodes in tiers 0 and 1. In this example N=4 and M=1.

N: # of configuration parameters
M: # of measured goal values

It is assumed that the table may contain more information than necessary, such as configuration parameters that have no correlation with any of the corresponding goal values, or goal values that have no correlation with any of the configuration parameters. If this is the case, there is a need for an automated management system that with little or no human interaction can deal with such ambiguities in the data. Ideally, the user of the system would not need to know which measurements are necessary and relevant.

We also assume that the database may contain inconsistent cases. Two cases are considered inconsistent when the same values of configurations result in different goal values. This may be the result of bad measurements or it may be caused by other unknown variables affecting the system behavior, which are not present in the case database. Conversely, in cases when different values of configuration parameters map to the same set of goals and objectives, one may combine these cases together to form a hyper-cube as described in section 5.2 in order to increase the performance of the table lookup.

It may also occur that some measurements might be missing in the table due to measurement problems. We will present later in this section a way of handling such difficulties by including data pre-processing steps that remove noise and redundant data.

Tier0 # of Disks	Tier1 # of Disks	Tier0 # of Nodes	Tier1 # of Nodes	User Response Time
1	4	1	2	0.039 sec
3	2	2	4	0.029 sec
2	3	2	4	0.082 sec
4	1	1	2	0.015 sec
2	1	3	3	0.042 sec
2	4	1	2	0.053 sec
1	2	2	4	0.032 sec
3	2	3	4	0.098 sec

Table 1. Sample of a case database of the performance of a 2-tiered web site

Due to the high sensitivity of the case based reasoning approach to noise in the data, we consider grouping the data values into clusters. Clustering also improves the performance of the system by decreasing the data lookup time.

K-nearest neighbor clustering – We use the k-nearest neighbor clustering technique to cluster the data points into a fixed number (k) of clusters. The clusters are initially created by taking k data points randomly from the database and assigning each point to a cluster. The rest of the data points are then subsequently all assigned to these clusters. There are two different assignment techniques. The first and easier method is to find the closest cluster to the new point (i.e., the one for which the distance between the new point and the mean of the cluster is smallest). The second method is more accurate, especially when the data has lots of large overlaps (i.e., variances are large). It assumes that each cluster has a Gaussian distribution, and so we find the most probable cluster for the new point using the Gaussian density function. Every time a point is assigned to a cluster, the mean of the cluster is recalculated. The points may be reassigned from one cluster to a closer cluster. The reassigning of the points continues until the means of the clusters remain the same or vary by a very small amount.

The clustering technique is more computationally intensive than the regular CBR technique but is more robust to noise in the data. It also can be used to effectively limit the search space to distinctly different cases, and thereby improve performance. In most systems, cases that are very close should be coalesced, since they do not capture any significantly different behavior. Figure 4 shows simple clustering in a 2-dimensional space.

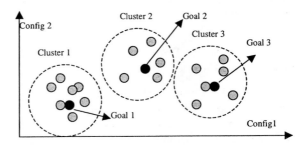

Figure 4. Clustering in a simple 2-dimensional space

Data pre-processing – In order to improve the usefulness of the case database, it is desirable to perform various pre-processing techniques on the data. This is needed to remove noise in the data as well as to remove irrelevant or redundant [20] data. The techniques that we are considering are discussed in the following.

Dimensionality reduction: A managed system may have hundreds of configuration knobs or *features*. Also, based on our assumption that the database may contain all the features, related or unrelated to any of the goal values, the dimensionality of the data may become too large thus increasing the computational overhead of the subsequent processing stages. A method for reducing the dimensionality will be of great use in our case based approach. In order to get accurate and meaningful results, we need many cases. The minimum number of cases needed depends on the number of dimensions [1]. Therefore, another way of getting accurate results, without having lots of data (i.e. many cases or instances) is to reduce the number of dimensions.

One form of dimensionality reduction technique is called feature selection. In this technique, all features are evaluated and weighted using some criteria and the features with the highest scores are selected. In our experiments, we have used accuracy as the evaluation criteria. First, we start with all the features in place and evaluate the accuracy of the clustering technique by comparing our predicted goal values with the actual values the simulator calculates for the same set of configuration values. We then take one feature out at a time and reevaluate the accuracy. This is called a backward feature generation. There are other generation schemes such as forward and bi-directional, which will not be discussed here. The search strategy we have used is a complete search, which means we

---

[1] The rule of thumb is to have 10 data points per dimension

cover all combinations of all the features. However, a complete search is time consuming and one can instead use heuristic or non-deterministic search strategies to improve the performance of the system.

Another method we have considered for reducing the dimensions is performing principal component analysis (PCA) [17] on the data. PCA is a powerful and well-established technique for finding the most informative or explanatory features in a collection of data[2]. The basic idea in PCA is to find those components, which explain the maximum amount of variance in a set of linearly transformed components. In particular, PCA substantially reduces the complexity of the data in which a large number of variables (e.g. thousands) are interrelated. PCA accomplishes this by computing a new, much smaller set of uncorrelated variables that best represent the original data.

Calculating the cross correlation matrix of the entire data allows us to select and be able to inform the user of the correlated parameters. A correlation matrix contains the strength as well as the direction of the relationship between all the variables. The correlation values are all in the range [-1, 1]. A positive number indicates a direct relationship between the variables, where as one variable goes up the other goes up as well. On the other hand, a negative number indicates an inverse relationship between the two variables. A number at or near zero indicates there is virtually no relationship at all between the variables. The cross correlation matrix is of size (M+N) x (M+N) where M is the number of configuration parameters and N is the number of goals.

Normalizing: Some configuration parameters may have values that are several orders of magnitude larger than others. For example a user response time is usually on the order of milliseconds while a bandwidth or throughput value is usually tens of Mega bits per second. Therefore we need to normalize the data for all the dimensions before we perform clustering in order to get accurate results.

Data unit consistencies: In order for the data to be meaningful, it needs to have consistent units of measures.

6. Experiments and Results

We have used the IBM High Volume Web Sites simulator [14] to produce a database containing a rich set of observations or cases. The simulator estimates the performance of complex configurations of a multi-tiered web site. Figure 5 shows a 3-tiered web site configuration. The simulator can accommodate different workload patterns such as online shopping, trading, reservations, auctions etc. It also allows changing of other aspects of the simulation such as varying the user session characteristics, as well as the software and hardware characteristics in each tier. In the experiments performed, we have modified 21 configuration parameters and observed 16 different output values or goals. Therefore, in this case, N=21 and M=16.

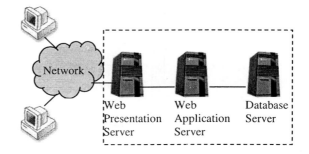

Figure 5. A 3-tier web sites architecture

Figure 6 shows the components of the transformation module. To generate each instance of data or a case, we generate a set of 21 uniformly distributed random variables. The configuration parameters of the simulator are set to these values and the resultant values or goals are measured. We have generated as many as 100,000 cases in this fashion and placed them in a repository (i.e., a case database). The case database is then passed to the pre-processing components, then to the feature reduction component, and finally into the clustering component of the transformation module.

---

[2] PCA is only effective for dimensions that have linear dependencies with each other

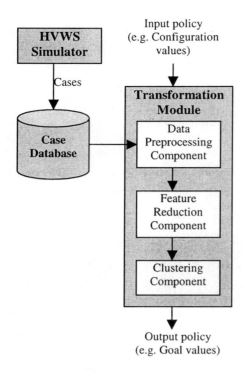

Figure 6. Components of the policy transformation module

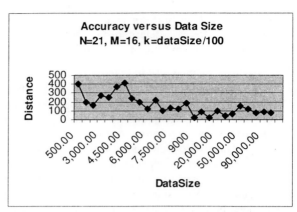

Figure 7. Accuracy of the system versus the size of the data used for learning (e.g. history of the system)

Figure 7 shows a plot of the accuracy of the system using the clustering technique as a function of the data size or the number of instances learned by the system. The y-axis is the Euclidean distance of the predicted goal vector from the actual goal vector. As expected, the distance tends to decrease as the system collects more data or instances. As mentioned earlier, the input vector or the configuration vector has a dimension of 21 (e.g. N=21) and the goal vector has a dimension of 16 (e.g. M=16). The configuration values are normalized to be real values between 0 and 100. The number of clusters, k is set to be dataSize/100. We have used three different distance metrics: Euclidean distance, weighted Euclidean distance, and Mahalanobis distance [17]. All the three mentioned distance metrics resulted in the same accuracy levels.

The feature reduction component using the PCA technique has been able to reduce M (e.g. the dimension of the measured goal values) from 16 to 6. This is quite substantial, and leads to a corresponding reduction in the complexity of the data analysis. This method can be used to reduce N as well since in a real environment the configuration parameters or knobs are correlated to each other as well. But in our simulations, since we use a uniform distribution to generate our random values for the configuration knobs, we are not able to show that.

We have calculated the cross correlation matrix for 10,000 instances of data. The correlation matrix shows a strong direct correlation value (e.g. +0.949) between the configuration knob 'ThinkTime' and the goal value 'SessionTime'. It also shows a direct high correlation value (e.g. +0.805) between the configuration knob 'BackgroundUtilization' and the goal value 'CPUUtilization'.

Table 2 shows the correlation values between various configuration and goal parameters. As it shows, the average response time of the web site has a higher dependency on the number of nodes in tier 1 than it does on the number in tiers 0 and 2. This shows that one can improve the web site's performance by adding more nodes to the application server tier rather than the database and the Web presentation server tiers.

	Tier0 #ofNodes	Tier1 #ofNodes	Tier2 #ofNodes
AvgRespTime	0.08	0.18	0.13

Table 2. Correlation values between various configuration (i.e. Tier0-Tier2 # of nodes) and a goal value (i.e. AvgRespTime)

In order to reduce the dimensionality one can throw away all goal parameters that show very little or no dependency on any of the configuration parameters.

7.   Online   or   real   time   policy transformation

In Real time policy transformation an online monitoring component is used which dynamically monitors the behavior of its agents to ensure the objectives are being met. In such a system, the transformation module dynamically modifies the configuration of the system based on its observations in order to achieve the user's goals.

Figure 8 shows an adaptive policy-based systems management architecture, which enables transformation of business level objectives into system configuration parameters. The policy management tool allows the system administrator to specify business level objectives or goal level policies. These policies are transformed into system configuration parameters by the policy transformation module and then sent to the repository.

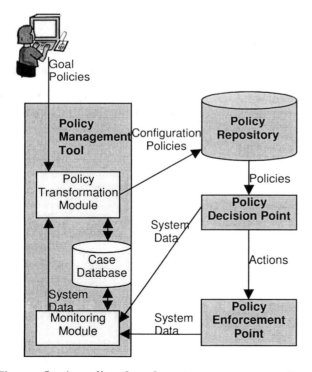

Figure 8. A policy based systems management

architecture enabled with static policy transformation

The transformation module interacts with a monitoring module, which is responsible for monitoring the current behavior of the system and determining whether the specified business objectives are being met. The transformation module obtains the current system configuration from the repository, and changes it if needed to a new system configuration, which is better suited for meeting the performance goals. The transformation module can also send the new modified system configuration to the policy repository.

This type of transformation is useful for handling those disciplines where the mapping from business level objectives to system configuration is dependent on the current state of the system. As an example, mapping the response time objectives to configuration parameters like network bandwidth limits is dependent on the current traffic load on the system, and an initial configuration tool can only provide estimates. Therefore, an adaptive architecture is much more appropriate for such a task. Depending on the nature of the discipline, an adaptation component may communicate changed configuration parameters directly to the PEPs, or may be incorporated as part of the management tool running as a system daemon process.

The monitoring module is responsible for monitoring the system and obtaining its current measure of the business objective that is supported, as well as reporting the current set of configuration parameters that are effective within the system. The information captured by the monitoring module is averaged over several measurement intervals to produce a new case history based on the averages observed during that period. The cases thus observed are stored in the case database.

8. Conclusions and future work

In this paper, we have addressed different types of policy transformations and proposed discipline independent methods for mapping objectives to system configurations and vice versa. We have described different scenarios for using a transformation module in a policy-based management system. A transformation module may use static data or it may be used real time in an adaptive system that uses a monitoring component for capturing real time data. We have used a high volume web site simulator to produce a database containing a rich set of observations for testing the case based reasoning approach. The proposed case-based reasoning approach seems to be practical for performing offline as well as real time transformation.

Our future work in this area is to explore a system modeling approach that predicts the impact of the system configurations on the goal values. One way to do this would be to come up with a state transition model for the system.

9. References

[1] The IETF Policy Framework Working Group: Charter available at the URL: http://www.ietf.org/html.charters/policy-charter.html.

[2] L. Lymberopoulos, E. Lupu and M. Sloman, "An adaptive Policy based Management Framework for Differentiated Services Network", IEEE International Policy Workshop 2002, Monterey, CA, June 2002.

[3] A. Ponnappan, L. Yang, R. Pillai, and P. Braun, "A Policy Based QoS Management System for the IntServ/DiffServ Based Internet", Policy Workshop 2002, Monterey, CA, June 2002.

[4] D. Verma, S. Sahu, S. calo, M. Beigi, and I. chang, "A Policy Service for GRID Computing", Grid Workshop 2002, Baltimore, MD, Oct. 2002.

[5] M. Bearden, S. Garg, and W. Lee, "Integrating Goal Specification in Policy-Based Management", IEEE International Workshop on Policies for Distributed Systems and Networks, Bristol, U.K., January 2001, pp.153-170.

[6] D. Verma, "Simplifying Network Administration using Policy based Management", IEEE Network Magazine, March 2002.

[7] The IETF Resource Allocation Protocol Working Group. Charter available at the URL http://www.ietf.org/html.charters/rap-charter.html.

[8] W. Stallings, "*SNMP, SNMPv2, SNMPv3, and RMON 1 and 2*", Addison Wesley, ISBN 0201485346, 1999.

[9] T. Howes, M. Smith, and G. Good, "Understanding and Deploying LDAP Directory Services", MTP, ISBN 1578700701, 1999.

[10] W. Brogran, "Modern Control Theory", Prentice Hall, October 1990.

[11] S. Haykin, "Neural networks: A Comprehensive Foundation", Prentice Hall, July 1998.

[12] Y. Diao, N. Gandhi, J. Hellerstein, S. Parekh and D. Tilbury, "Using MIMO Feedback Control to enforce Policies for interrelated metrics with application to the Apache Web Server", Proceedings of NOMS, April 2002.

[13] http://www.cbr-web.org/

[14] http://www.ibm.com/websphere/developer/zones/hvws

[15] D. Verma, M. Beigi, and R. Jennings, "Policy Based SLA Management in Enterprise Networks", IEEE International Workshop on Policies for Distributed Systems and Networks, Bristol, U.K., January 2001, pp.137-152.

[16] http://www-dse.doc.ic.ac.uk/research/policies

[17] R. Duda, P. Hart, and G. Stork, "Pattern Classification", John Wiley & Sons, Second edition, 2001.

[18] RFC 3060: Policy Core Information Model -- Version 1 Specification

[19] RFC 3198: Terminology for Policy-Based Management

[20] H. Liu and H. Motoda, "Feature selection for knowledge discovery and data mining", Kluwer Academic Publishers c1998, ISBN: 079238198X.

Policy Based Management for Internet Communities

Kevin Chekov Feeney, Dave Lewis, Vincent P. Wade

Knowledge and Data Engineering Group, Trinity College Dublin, Ireland

kefeeney@cs.tcd.ie, Dave.Lewis@cs.tcd.ie, Vincent.Wade@cs.tcd.ie

Abstract

Policy Based Management (PBM) is a research topic that has been driven by the tremendous complexity inherent in the administration and management of present-day networking and telecommunications systems and services. The increasingly diverse organisational forms of modern industry represent a significant component of this complexity. Internet communities offer extreme examples of organisational diversity, since they often lack any central authority and many subsections operate with almost complete autonomy. This paper argues that PBM systems offer great potential in this domain due to the complexity of management arrangements. However, since these communities lack any single trusted administrative hierarchy, a centralised solution to policy engineering and management is not possible. This paper proposes an approach to modelling communities for PBM systems. This approach focuses on the concept of communities within a hierarchy of authority as the fundamental unit of organisational analysis. As such, the model reflects the distribution of authority in the real-world community, the resulting policies reflect the community's operational needs and contracts between the various groups and individuals that make up the community. Policy conflicts are used to identify organisational conflicts that must be resolved. In order to illustrate and validate these concepts, the paper presents a conceptual architecture and case study based on the secure management of an open publishing network.

1. Introduction

Policy Based Management (PBM) is currently attracting considerable research focus as an enabling technology for managing large scale, heterogeneous information systems and communications infrastructure [1]. It has the potential to achieve a unified method of managing enterprise information resources, including such areas as access control, network management (in particular quality of service management) and configuration management. This unified method aims to enable administrators to manage entire networks through the authoring of policy rules (or other elements of a policy language), preferably in a single, simple language. The ultimate aim of a policy-based system is to derive these policies from business goals, so that information systems can respond dynamically to changes in those goals. The motivation being that the resultant management system behaviour is more focused on achieving the business goals of the organisation [2].

PBM rests on the assumption that a common set of rules can be applied to sets of entities in the system, rather than merely to individual entities. Thus, policy languages include constructs to group entities together. This facilitates management by allowing the definition of rules that apply to sets of entities rather than to individuals. Policy rules are divided into *authorisation policies* for access control management and *obligation policies* for resource management [2]. PBM systems which include support for both types of policy promise to provide a complete solution to the problem of managing complex electronic networks.

Internet communities often manage large and complex networks of information resources and much of the research into policy specification languages and management architectures is equally applicable in this domain. However, Internet communities have several characteristics which lead to problems in accurately modelling their organisational structures and managing the administration of PBM systems. Most importantly, they tend towards a decentralised, non-hierarchical model of decision making, with resource ownership distributed across the community, rather than being centralised, as is generally the case with hierarchical organisations. Access control models that are commonly associated with PBM systems, such as Role Based Access Control (RBAC) [3], lack this notion of distributed ownership. They also require the construction of a detailed model of the human organisation. However, the fluidity and heterogeneity of the groupings that make up large Internet communities render centralised approaches to this modelling impossible.

This paper examines the possibilities of applying PBM approaches to the problem of managing the information resources of large voluntary Internet communities. It describes a community policy framework for applying PBM solutions to these communities, a framework which facilitates the distributed, decentralised modelling of the community structure and the building of an organisational structure to reflect the distribution of ownership of the resources managed by the community. It aims to enable the secure management of resources shared between different subsections of the community.

Although this paper particularly focuses on Internet communities, many of the issues addressed are increasingly relevant to traditional hierarchical organisations, where new organisational paradigms, including team-working, virtual organisations and cost-centres share many of these characteristics.

2. Internet Communities and Policy

Voluntary Internet communities are a new form of organisation, enabled by mass networked computing. It is difficult to generalise about this type of organisation, due to the diversity of forms that they take. However, we can at least note a few characteristics that they tend to exhibit - especially when contrasted with traditional bureaucratic organisations. They depend upon volunteer labour; their membership and goals can be fluid; they are widely distributed and often all community interaction is electronic; they tend towards flat hierarchies and often have wide membership involvement in decision making; their structures evolve over time; they can be composed of multiple autonomous sub-communities with independent decision making mechanisms and different internal organisations.

There are several well-known examples of such communities such as the open-source software-development community responsible for the Linux operating system. The success of the model has been proved by the widespread adoption of Linux by the IT industry and has prompted a closer examination of this form of working within traditional hierarchical organisations [4].

Although this type of community has flourished in the past decade, there remain several widespread problems to their development. The majority of projects have remained very small and have had problems in expanding, lacking any means of regulating access to project resources and management responsibilities in a controlled way [5]. They have often remained centred on a single individual maintainer, responsible for all decision making, who becomes a bottleneck to management, thus restricting the expansion of the project. Larger projects, which have succeeded in attracting greater numbers of members, have had problems in integrating the various sub-systems, which work in practice as autonomous projects, require a large amount of manual negotiation and ultimately often depend on a single maintainer to carry out management functions. For these reasons, a PBM approach, with its potential for extensive automation of management tasks, should be particularly attractive to Internet communities.

2.1. Case Study: Indymedia Network

This paper will focus on one example of such a community - the Indymedia Network [6], a global open-publishing community - and examine the problems of applying a PBM solution to the management of this community's resources. This community has been selected as its size, complexity and decentralisation provide a good example of the difficulty of applying policy solutions to distributed non-hierarchical organisations. One of the authors has been closely connected to the community for several years and has been involved in developing the *Oscailt* open publishing system, a software package developed to facilitate management of nodes in the network.

Indymedia is a global open-publishing network that consists of 123 local independent media centres (IMCs) in 52 countries. Each IMC operates as a producer and distributor of locally-produced open-source media content. Although each IMC is autonomously managed, the community is held together by a shared technical infrastructure and a common set of policies, or contracts between each IMC and the rest of the network. The technical infrastructure is developed and managed by a network of working groups and project groups, some of which are sub-communities of a particular IMC and manage local resources, while others - those that are responsible for the development and management of the infrastructure on a regional and global level - draw their membership from across the global network [7].

This complex structure owes little to central planning. It has evolved through a process of *specialisation* and *incorporation*, typical of Internet communities [8]. Specialisation takes place as a community divides itself into sub-groupings and delegates specific areas of responsibility to them. For example, IMCs generally start as a single working group. Over time many have sub-divided into a combination of editorial, video, audio and other groups, each responsible for managing different resources. Incorporation occurs when previously independent groups join the community, bringing resources with them. Thus, many local IMC's were independent projects with a similar aim before being incorporated into the Indymedia community.

The task of co-ordinating management responsibilities and enforcing the various contracts between the working groups requires a significant amount of administrative work and largely depends upon the good faith of the individual administrators of community resources. However, the rapid expansion of the community - from a single IMC with a few dozen members in 1999, to a huge global network involving tens of thousands of people by 2003 and in several thousand working groups - has caused the community to seek automated solutions for enforcing policies. A PBM approach would prove particularly attractive to this community as it offers the promise of automating much of the administration, while also providing an enforcement mechanism for the contracts that bind the groups together.

2.2. Policy Engineering for Communities

Modern policy languages and PBM frameworks are technically capable of providing solutions for many of the administrative problems experienced by Internet communities such as Indymedia, as these are largely the same problems encountered when dealing with any large organisation. Working groups could be modelled as roles, domains, groups or some other policy language construct and access control policies could be applied to these, thereby making access control administration significantly more efficient.

Access control models like RBAC, security policy frameworks like Oasis [9], and PBM frameworks like Ponder [10] are based on the assumption that the organisation can be modelled in its entirety, in a centralised requirements engineering phase before deployment. Even when dealing with centralised bureaucratic organisations, this is a difficult task and "the policy development process alone can take months to refine and implement" [11]. However, regardless of the sophistication of the modelling process, there are a number of characteristics of Internet communities which render this entire approach problematic:

- The fluidity of the community's structures mean that by the time the requirements have been captured and modelled as policies, the community structure will inevitably have changed considerably.
- Two work groups with the same overall set of duties and rights with respect to the system may differ greatly in their internal organisation. Thus, there is no guarantee that useful, reusable grouping abstractions like roles will exist across working groups.
- The internal organisation of the working groups may be private. Although they may participate in a broader community contract and share in the management of community resources, they may not be willing to expose the division of rights and duties within the group

- In hierarchical organisations we can assume that the ultimate authority over the organisation's resources lies at the top of the organisational hierarchy. In Internet communities we can make no such assumption. Many of the shared resources are ultimately owned by autonomous independent groups within the community. Although the administration of these resources may be shared across the community, the groups that own the resources must be able to retain ultimate control over them.

3. Community Policy Framework

In this section, we provide the basic outlines of a PBM framework for communities, where the organisational structure of a community is modelled as a set of interrelated communities. Authority over particular resources is distributed throughout the organisation using delegation between communities. This model is intended to reflect the way that these communities work in practice. Rather than creating the structure through a centralised modelling process, the framework enables a policy based approach to be applied to the management of the processes of sub-division, delegation of authority and incorporation through which these communities dynamically define their own structures and operational rules.

Delegation between groups is used to create a hierarchical map of authority over each resource. This authority map also forms the basis for a single integrated model of the community, incorporating users, administrators, managed resources, automatic policy conflict resolution and negotiation, community decision making and controlled management of policy refinement.

For the purpose of this discussion we use the Ponder notation for specifying policy rules. In Ponder authorisation and obligation policies, both positive and negative, are specified as having a *subject*, *action* and *target* which describe who performs the action, what action they carry out and which resource they are acting upon. Obligation policies also include an *event*, which triggers the evaluation of the policy rule, while all policies are also subject to *constraints*, which limit the set of conditions under which the policy rule is valid. The content of Ponder policies can also be constrained by *meta-policies*, which limit the types of policies or their policy elements.

3.1. Community Specification

Our conception of the community has many similarities to the Enterprise viewpoint RM-ODP definition of a community [12]. However, rather than providing a full model of an enterprise and its associations with external organisations, it aims to provide an authority context to policy rules that apply to resources. Therefore, its specification is less complex than that of an RM-ODP community and, for example, does not include any concept of roles. In our framework the community is specified as:

• A set of *membership rules*. The membership rules are similar to the role activation constraints of constrained RBAC [13] or OASIS [14], in that they allow us to specify the conditions that must be met before an individual is admitted into the community.

• A set of *sub-communities*. Sub-groups within the overall community are themselves modelled as communities, their membership being a subset of the parent community.

• The set of policies that apply to the community. This is all of the policy rules in the system which have the community as their subject.

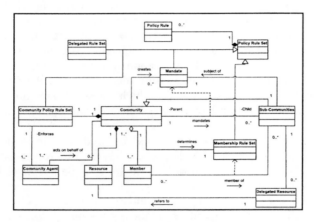

Figure 1. Community Entity Relationships

• The set of resources that the community has authority over and the set of policies that the community has applied to these resources. A resource can be composed of other resources and is not tied to any particular implementation. Having authority over a resource implies that the community can author policies whose target is that resource. There are two types of resources that a community may have authority over, namely owned resources and delegated resources. Owned resources are resources which a community can apply policies to without any restrictions. Delegated resources are references to resources that are owned by a different community that has delegated a portion of their authority over this resource to this community.

3.2. Sub-Communities

At its simplest, an Internet community is modelled as a single undifferentiated top-level community. The modelling of specific groups within the community is

achieved through the creation of *mandated sub-communities* or *child-communities*, each made up of a subset of the top-level community. Sub-communities can themselves create their own sub-communities. The creating community becomes the parent community of the sub-community. Each sub-community has exactly one parent to ensure a simple hierarchical relationship, or partial order, between communities. Any community can create a sub-community by defining membership rules for it. The sub-community is described as *mandated* because the parent community may create policy rules whose subject is the sub-community. That is to say that the parent community may define what the sub-community is authorised to do (by defining authorisation policies whose subject is the sub-community) and what it is obliged to do (similarly, by defining obligation policies). The set of policies that have been defined by the parent community and whose subject is the sub-community is the mandate of the sub-community.

3.3. Delegation of authority and rights

Delegation of authority and rights is fundamental to the community policy framework. Any community can delegate authority over any subset of its resources and policies to its sub-communities. If a community has *authority over* a resource, this means that it can author policies whose target is that resource. When this authority is delegated to a sub-community the sub-community can author policies whose target is that resource. A community can also delegate a subset of its rights to its sub-communities. Delegation of *rights* means that a community that is the subject of an authorisation policy can pass this authorisation policy on to its sub-communities, effectively making the sub-community the subject of the authorisation policy. The creation of sub-communities and the delegation of authority and rights allows the dynamic creation of an organisational structure for the overall community.

This concept of delegation differs from the concept of delegation in Ponder. Ponder's delegation model allows individuals to nominate others who are trusted to act on their behalf to perform certain tasks, independent of the delegated individual's position in the organisational structure. We describe this type of delegation as *delegation of identity*, as the delegated individual acts as if she was the delegating individual, by effectively assuming their identity for the enactment of particular tasks. Delegation of identity is an important feature for any PBM system, as it is a common practice in all organisations. However, it is a different concept to the delegation of authority and rights between communities and the two concepts are entirely compatible within a PBM system.

Practically, delegation of authority amounts to entering a reference to that resource in the set of

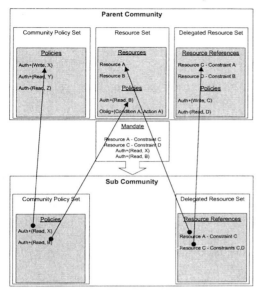

Figure 2. Delegation to sub-community

delegated resources of the sub-community, as shown in figure 2. Similarly a policy that applies to a community can be delegated to its sub-community by inserting the policy rule into the sub-community's set of policies. Negative policies are not explicitly delegated since if a negative policy applies to a community, then it implicitly applies to its sub-communities. A community can't permit its sub-community to do something that it is not itself permitted to do. Similarly, constraints that apply to policies, whether they be meta-policies limiting the form of the policy rule or constraints on the conditions under which a policy is valid, are implicitly propagated from a community to its sub-communities.

3.4. Policy Refinement and Resource Semantics

This propagation of authority and rights through the community structure would be of limited use if a community could only delegate precisely those rights that it possesses. However, our model allows for sub-division of rights in delegation. If we consider a community authorisation policy to have the form *auth{action, target, constraints}* (the community is implicitly the subject of the rule), then we can delegate a policy *auth{action', target', constraints'}* to a sub-community as long as *auth{action, target, constraints}* logically implies *auth{action', target', constraints'}*. For example, if a community has a policy which authorises the writing of files to diskA without any constraints, written as *Auth{write, diskA}*, then it can delegate the policy *Auth{read, fileA}* to a sub-community if the semantics of

the target resource specify that write authority implies read authority and fileA is a subset of diskA (these semantics are typically dependant on the operating system). Similarly, if the community possesses authority to author policies with targets *{A,B,C}*, constrained by meta-policies *{X,Y,Z}*, then the community can delegate authority to its sub-community with meta-policies *{X',Y',Z'}* as long as the delegated resources are a subset of *{A,B,C}*. The constraints that apply to policies authored by the sub-community are the union of the existing meta-policies and the new meta-policies applied by its parent, that is *{X,Y,Z,X',Y',Z'}*. In effect, this propagation of rights and authorities through the community structure means that policies are organically refined as they are distributed through the community structure. As we get further down the community hierarchy, we can expect that policy rules will become more precise and limited in scope as large areas of responsibility are broken down into specific tasks and delegated to various sub-communities.

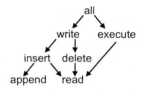

Figure 3. Example of a *implies* hierarchy

This process of policy refinement through delegation of rights depends upon the availability of semantic information about the target resource. This semantic information is stored with the resource in the form of a hierarchical tree of actions, relating to the resource. This hierarchical tree provides a partial order on actions, according to the *implies* relationship, described in [15].

Target resources are also organised in a hierarchical directory structure. This enables the community management system to ensure that all delegations are valid. If a community possesses a right *Auth{ActionA, TargetA}* then a delegated right *Auth{ActionB, TargetB}* is validated by ensuring that the right to take *ActionA* implies the right to take *ActionB* with respect to *TargetA* and that *TargetA* is higher or equal to *TargetB* in the directory structure.

3.5. Decision making and community agents

What do we mean when we say that the community can define policies and that the community is the subject of policy rules? The community is not a single entity and can be made up of many individuals with independent motivations, who can not be trusted to always carry out the community's will. Thus, we introduce the concepts of community decision-making mechanisms and community agents into our model. Community agents, whether human or automated, carry out actions on behalf of the community. A community member becomes a community agent when a decision has been made by the community to carry out a specific action. Decision making mechanisms define the process through which a community reaches a decision. This is particularly important when modelling Internet communities as they often operate on a democratic basis. Each community can attach specific decision making rules to particular policy rules. Thus, a community may decide that some actions can be taken on behalf of the community by any member of the community, while other actions may require agreement by several members, or even a majority vote, before they can be taken on behalf of the community. Once a decision has been made the community issues a certificate to the community agent which permits the agent to perform the action on behalf of the community.

3.6. Internal Privacy and Hierarchies

Authority over resources may be delegated repeatedly from communities to their sub-communities and each may apply policy rules to the resource. However, each community delegates only to its immediate sub-communities and allows them to subdivide the authority between their own sub-communities. Thus communities are only aware of their parent community and their immediate children. This allows communities to keep their internal organisation private from the rest of the broader community. When a community delegates a policy to a sub-community, only an agent of that sub-community can act upon the policy.

Although Internet communities contain many democratic elements, they also contain hierarchies. For example, many users of community provided services may be considered to be part of the community, yet only those who put time into community development may have an input into community decisions. This can be accommodated in our model by specifying a particular sub-community as a *control community*. A control community acts on behalf of its parent community, that is to say that an agent of the control community is always an agent of its parent community.

3.7. Interpreting Policy Hierarchically

Through the process of communities sub-dividing and delegating authority to their sub-communities, a hierarchical tree of communities is built up within the overall community and this amounts to a model of the distribution of authority over each resource managed by the community. This model is used in the delegation process, to ensure that any authority delegated is a subset of the authority possessed. However, it also provides us with a means of enforcing policies in a hierarchical way to automatically resolve policy conflicts.

Even when a parent community delegates authority over a particular resource to a sub-community, the parent may still author policies whose target is the resource. This creates potential policy conflicts on particular resources due to conflicting policies being defined by communities and their sub-communities (which may occur several steps of delegation away). To get around this problem, policy is hierarchically enforced. Thus, policies authored by the community that owns the resource have precedence over policies authored further down the hierarchy. As the hierarchy is based upon authority with respect to the resource, this policy precedence is correct by definition. This is an important feature since it allows us to define community-wide policies at the most general levels, policies that will continue to be enforced irrespective of any policies that are applied in sub-communities. For example, we can impose community-wide security guarantees on all resources in the top-level community while leaving the sub-communities free to define extra policies in their specific areas of responsibility, without the risk that these policies may inadvertently violate the security guarantees.

When a new policy is authored anywhere in the community structure (step 1 in figure 4), it passes up through its parent communities (step 2) until it reaches the owning community of the target resource. At each stage the parent automatically checks to ensure that the new policy rule does not conflict with its existing policies for the target resource (step 3) before issuing a community agent certificate and passing it on to its parent community (step 4). When the rule reaches the owning community, it is deployed to the target resource (step 6). If a policy conflict is detected before deployment, the new policy rule is either rejected or, if possible, automatically rewritten to limit the target domain in order to avoid the conflict. A rejected policy is returned to the authoring community with an indication of the level on which the conflict was detected. The authoring community can then choose to manually rewrite the policy rule to avoid the conflict, or can attempt to

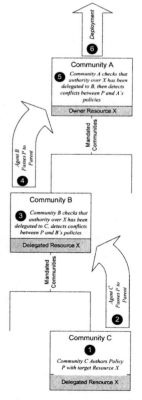

Figure 4. Hierarchical Policy Model

negotiate a change in the policy rule at the level where the conflict was detected (which it is by definition a subset of). As policy conflicts can be the result of genuine conflicts between communities, caused by conflicting demands and resource competition, there is no way to avoid all cases of manual re-negotiation of policy rules. In these cases, we need to know at what level of the organisation the conflict must be resolved and the community policy achieves this by identifying the nearest common ancestor of the conflicting communities.

This hierarchical enforcement of policy depends upon a conflict detection mechanism. The discussion of conflict detection is beyond the scope of this paper, for a comparison of various approaches see [16, 17]).

4. Implementation and Case Study

Although it is not directly implementable in any existing PBM system, since they lack community constructs with the required semantics, the community policy framework is not tied to any specific policy language and uses broadly the same policy concepts as other existing PBM systems. Therefore, the approach of mapping the community based model to an existing PBM framework was thought prudent rather than devising yet another Policy language and architecture. The Ponder framework and its suite of tools, along with the source code, are freely available to download on the Internet. Ponder uses a declarative object-oriented language which is specifically designed for simple policy specification - particularly suitable for this domain where policy rules are not authored by experts. Furthermore, Ponder provides a range of grouping constructs and the fact that Ponder policies are themselves managed resources allows a great degree of flexibility in designing an administrative model. Therefore, Ponder was used in our experiments as an underlying policy framework.

As a case study and proof of concept, we modelled a simplified version of one branch of the Indymedia Internet community. At the highest level, Indymedia is specified as a single community, incorporating all users of the system. This community owns all of the resources that are shared across the community. The global decision making community is the control community of the top-level community, since it makes decisions on behalf of the whole community and has authority over all global resources.

There are other sub-communities of the top-level community, which have delegated authority over subsets of the global resources, such as projects and technical infrastructure. These communities can author policies whose targets are these delegated resources, subject to any constraints that the global decision-making community may impose upon the content of these

policies. There is also a European regional community, which is delegated authority from the global community to author policies whose target is the global newswire. For example, they may wish to author a policy forbidding certain types of content from the global newswire. The European community also introduces new resources into the community, namely the European newswire. This is autonomously managed from the global community and the global community cannot author policy whose target is this resource.

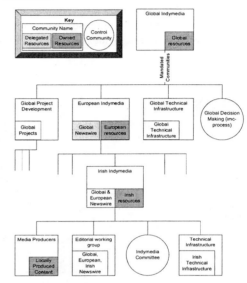

Figure 5. Community Model of Indymedia

The Irish Indymedia community is one sub-community of the European Indymedia community. Again it has delegated authority over certain resources that are owned at higher levels and authority over its own resources that it controls autonomously. This authority is further delegated to working groups covering the various areas of the local IMC's operations.

When new policies are authored they pass through a similar hierarchical enforcement process. For example if the Irish editorial group wishes to create a policy banning users from posting images to the European newswire, it would create a policy of the form *Auth-{Post-image, European Newswire}*. Once this new policy has been ratified by the community's decision making mechanism, it is passed to the Irish Indymedia community where it is checked to ensure that authority over the European Newswire has been delegated to the Editorial Group. Then it is checked to ensure that the policy obeys all the meta-policies that have been imposed by the parent community. Then it is checked to ensure that the policy does not conflict with any of the parent community's policies. If all of these tests are passed, the parent community attaches its agent certificate to the policy and passes it onto its parent where the checks are repeated in turn before deployment.

The community structure is defined in XML and interpreted with a custom software application, written in the Java language using the JAXML, JNDI and Ponder libraries. It validates each delegation of authority to ensure that the delegated authority is possessed by the parent community. This is currently achieved by using a simplified hierarchy of actions and target resources that are organised in a hierarchical directory structure. Any constraints placed upon policies by parent communities are also checked. Currently, the software only detects those conflicts that Lupu describes as modal [17], such as

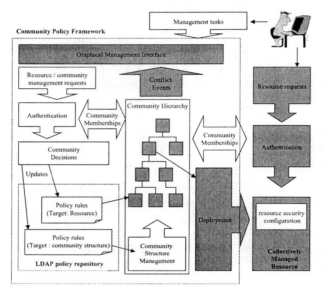

Figure 6. Policy Framework Architecture

the existence of positive and negative authorisation policies with the same subjects and targets. Once all of these checks are passed, a set of domains, policies and roles to implement the rules of the community structure is created in an LDAP directory, corresponding to Ponder language constructs. The membership rules are evaluated and Ponder user objects are created and assigned domains. Communities are mapped to Ponder domains and a set of policies that dictates the rights and obligations of the members of the domain. The hierarchy of the communities is reflected in the resulting Ponder domain hierarchy. In the current version each member of a community acts as an agent of the community, without decision-making mechanisms, as this concept is not supported by the software framework. Furthermore, the concept of hierarchical enforcement of policy does not fit easily into Ponder's deployment framework, and this has not been implemented in the current version. Nevertheless, the Ponder mapping of the community

structure is capable of implementing many of the features of the community model. In particular, the delegation of authority through the community is validated by the software and mapped into a simple set of domains, roles, policies and meta-policies in Ponder.

5. Related Work

The Rei policy language [18] incorporates attribute-based subject credentials, from which one could easily build community membership, but it does not support community-based semantics. The language includes detailed delegation semantics, including the ability to restrict the ability for delegates to further delegate authority, which is excluded by our model, where communities have autonomy over delegation of rights and authority to sub-communities. Although the language supports two different types of delegation, *while delegation* and *when delegation*, neither of these corresponds closely with the notion of delegation of authority between communities and delegation is seen as an ancillary issue of individual trust rather than as the basis for the organisational model.

Kaos [19], like Rei, incorporates semantic web languages. Although it doesn't include any support for community based semantics, the policy framework could be extended by adding the community concept to the ontology. It would be conceivable to implement our community policy framework based on either Kaos or Rei, instead of Ponder, as they are all sufficiently expressive and general. However, none provide native support for community semantics and hierarchical policy deployment and enforcement.

In [20], Wasson and Humphrey describe some of the important issues in implementing policies for Virtual Organisations. However, they assume that policies for shared resources will be specified by centralised administrators and do not consider the possibility that the authoring of policies for resource management could be decentralised and distributed among the bodies who provide the resources.

The Organisation Based Access Control model (Or-BAC) [21] provides means for specifying different security policies for organisations that are structured into several sub-organisations with distinct security policies. However, it does not address the problems of distributed resource ownership or the problem of modelling decentralised communities.

6. Conclusion

This paper has presented a community-based model for the management of policies in the context of a large Internet community. This model builds upon previous work in the field of Policy Based Management, but simplifies the specification of the organisation by using a single grouping construct, the community, to model the organisation. It introduces a concept of delegation whereby authority and rights are delegated to dynamically build a model of the organisation. Communities retain all of the advantages of specifying policies for roles or domains: policy decisions are made on the basis of the communities that a person belongs to, rather than their identity and policy can be composed through conjunction of the communities that an individual belongs to.

However, communities also extend the standard role-model in several ways. In particular, communities provide a means of incorporating group context and decision making; they integrate administration into the model and allow policy rules to be interpreted with respect to the overall structure of authority in the organisation. They facilitate the self-modelling of groupings within the community, autonomous control of shared resources and allow for privacy of different parts of the structure. A hierarchy of communities provides a means for modelling the organisation in a much more succinct and intuitive way than by using roles with a variety of different relationships between them.

A primary strength of this framework is that it does not require a detailed process of requirements engineering to create a model of the organisation. We can create the most basic structure and allow the detailed divisions of responsibility and the organisational groupings to evolve in an organic manner. Thus, we can introduce a PBM system by merely modelling the entire organisation as a single community, with authority over the full set of resources managed by the system. As the needs arise, we can create sub-communities and delegate to them responsibility for specific resources. The analysis of policy conflicts can be used to signal structural problems in our model and in the underlying real-world community, thus providing constant feedback to refine the model.

Organisations such as the military with structures that are centrally-planned, static and hierarchical, with clearly defined and delineated roles, would have limited use for these features. However, most organisations are dynamic to a certain extent and the ability to alter the organisational structure without a costly phase of requirements engineering has the potential to make PBM systems significantly more economic to deploy.

By implementing a community policy framework, based on the Ponder framework, we have demonstrated the feasibility of implementing a community structure in a general policy language. However, there are particular features of the community model, notably the hierarchical enforcement of policies, which are not supported by available PBM systems. Therefore, these concepts have yet to be tested in practice.

Although this paper has specifically looked at the problem of managing policies in large Internet communities, the model is not restricted to this domain. The Internet paradigm, of autonomous groups co-operating as part of larger organisations, is increasingly being employed by traditional organisations. SME value chains, collaborative projects between corporations, virtual organisations and the practice of corporate divisions being run as independent businesses all conform to this paradigm to a certain extent. All of these organisations encounter the same problems as Internet communities in relation to the management of their shared resources. They need a way to distribute authority without sacrificing ultimate control. The community-based model could prove to be a promising model for introducing a PBM approach in these cases.

7. Further work

We are currently introducing the community policy framework to manage certain areas of the Indymedia Internet community mentioned in the paper. The system will be introduced to first mirror and then directly manage a CVS repository, which contains the development code of one of the community's content management systems. The community will create sub-communities and delegate various authorities to them. For example, there will most likely be a 'developer' working group which will have the authority to add files to the repository, while the 'tester' workgroup will only be permitted to add files to certain branches. The experience of using this PBM approach in a real-world community will provide us with further proof of the concept as well as empirical evidence relating to the usefulness of this management solution. Metrics such as administrative work hours, volume of administrative communication and administrator response times will be measured through user-surveys and monitoring and analysis of communication channels such as mailing lists, to evaluate the usefulness of the approach.

Although this paper has presented an approach to resolving application specific policy conflict by alignment with the natural decision making processes of an organisation, it does not address the more general problem of mapping high-level user objectives to system level objectives. Policy languages in general fail to address this problem because of the shallowness of the semantic model of the managed resource that is incorporated into these frameworks.

Our approach also introduces a variation of this problem, when we wish to get automated assistance in ensuring the community-generated policies are correctly mapped from the community mandate within the constraints of the relevant resource semantics. A likely solution to this problem is to employ ontologies as explicit mechanisms for describing resource semantics. The growing popularity of this approach in the Semantic Web may ensure that increasing numbers of resources will be available with accompanying semantic mark-up.

We will examine the use of ontology languages for defining our communities, resources and community policies. We aim to benefit not only from better policy mapping due to more accurate resource models, but also from the availability of a wide range of ontology-compatible inference and rule engines to provide policy enforcement, mapping and conflict detection support.

8. Acknowledgements

This research was conducted with funding from the Irish Higher Education Authority under the M-Zones Programme. Kevin Feeney holds an Ussher fellowship at Trinity College Dublin, which co-funds his research.

9. References

[1] Wright, S., Lapiotis, P., Chadha, R. "Policy-Based Networking", *IEEE Network*, Vol. 16, no. 2, 2002, p 8-9.

[2] Sloman, M., Lupu, E. "Security and Management Policy Specification", *IEEE Network*, Vol. 16, no. 2, 2002, p 10-19.

[3] Sandhu, R.S. et al., "Role Based Access Control Models", *IEEE Computer*, vol. 29, no.2, 1996, p 38-47

[4]. Thompson P. and McHugh, D., *Work Organisations*, Palgrave, New York, 2002.

[5] Krishnamurthy, S. "Cave or Community?: An Empirical Examination of 100 Mature Open Source Projects" *First Monday*, vol. 7, no. 6, June 2002, Available from: http://firstmonday.org/issues/issue7_6/krishnamurthy/

[6] Hyde, G., "Independent Media Centers: Cyber-Subversion and the Alternative Press", *First Monday*, vol. 7, no. 4, April 2002. http://www.firstmonday.dk/issues/issue7_4/hyde/

[7] See Indymedia Documentation Project, Global Section. http://docs.indymedia.org/view/Global/ImcProcess. Accessed November 2003.

[8] Iannacci, F. "The Linux managing model", *First Monday*, vol. 8, no. 12, December 2003, Available from: http://www.firstmonday.org/issues/issue8_12/iannacci/

[9] Bacon J., Moody K. and Yao W. "A model of OASIS role-based access control and its support for active security", *ACM Transactions on Information and System Security (TISSEC)*, Vol.5, No. 4 (November), pp 492-540, ACM Press, New York, NY, 2002.

[10] Damianou, N., "A Policy Framework for Management of Distributed Systems", PhD Thesis, Imperial College, University of London, 2001.

[11] Jude, M., "Policy-based Management: Beyond the Hype" *Business Communications Review*, March 2001. pp 52-56.

[12] ISO/IEC 15414:2002 JTC1/SC7 *Information technology - Open Distributed Processing - Reference Model - Enterprise Viewpoint*, ISO/IEC 2002

[13] Sandhu, R. et al. "The ARBAC97 model for role-based administration of roles: Preliminary description and outline", *Proceedings of 2nd ACM Workshop on Role-Based Access Control*, Fairfax, VA, November 6-7 1997.

[14] Hine, J., Yao, W., Bacon, J. and Moody, K.. "An Architecture for Distributed OASIS Services", *Proceedings of Middleware 2000*, New York, USA, *Lecture Notes in Computer Science*, Springer-Verlag, 4-8 April 2000. pp 107-123.

[15] Shen, H., Dewan, P. "Access Control for Collaborative Environments", *Proceedings of the ACM Computer-Supported Cooperative Work Conference*, Toronto, Canada 1992, pp 51-58

[16] Tonti, G., Bradshaw, J.M., Jeffers, R., Montanari, R., Suri1, N., Uszok, A., "Semantic Web Languages for Policy Representation and Reasoning: A Comparison of KAoS, Rei, and Ponder" *Proceedings of 2nd International Semantic Web Conference (ISWC2003)*, October 20-23, 2003, Sanibel Island, Florida, USA

[17] Lupu, E.C, Sloman, M. "Conflicts in Policy-Based Distributed Systems Management", *IEEE Transactions on software engineering*, vol. 25, no. 6, November 1999.

[18] Kagal, L., Finin, T., Joshi, A., "A Policy Language for a Pervasive Computing Environment" *Proceedings of IEEE 4th International Workshop on Policies for distributed Systems and Networks*, June 2003 Lake Como, Italy p 63-77

[19] Uszok, A., et al. "KAoS Policy and Domain Services: Toward a Description-Logic Approach to Policy Representation, Deconfliction, and Enforcement" *Proceedings of IEEE 4th International Workshop on Policies for distributed Systems and Networks*, June 2003 Lake Como, Italy pp 93-99

[20] Wasson, G., Humphrey, G., "Towards Explicit Policy Management in Virtual Organizations" *Proceedings of IEEE 4th International Workshop on Policies for distributed Systems and Networks*, June 2003 Lake Como, Italy. pp 173-182.

[21] El Kalam, A.A, Benferhat, S., Miège, A., El Baida, R., Cuppens, F., Saurel, C., Balbiani, P., Deswarte, Y., Trouessin, Y., "Organization based access control" *Proceedings of IEEE 4th International Workshop on Policies for distributed Systems and Networks*, June 2003 Lake Como, Italy.

Session 2:
Routing and Mobile Networks

Policy-Based Mobile Ad Hoc Network Management*

Ritu Chadha, Hong Cheng, Yuu-Heng Cheng, Jason Chiang, A. Ghetie, Gary Levin, Harshad Tanna
{chadha,hong,yhcheng,chiang,aag,gary,tannah}@research.telcordia.com
Telcordia Technologies, 445 South Street, Morristown NJ 07960.

Abstract

Ad hoc networking is the basis of the future military network-centric warfare architecture. Such networks are highly dynamic in nature, as mobile ad hoc networks are formed over wireless links that are susceptible to failure. Strict requirements on security and reliability combined with the dynamic nature of the network provide a strong motivation for self-forming, self-configuring, and self-healing capabilities in the network. This paper describes a policy-based mobile ad hoc network management system that addresses these needs. The system provides the capability to express networking requirements in the form of policies at a high level and have them automatically realized in the network by intelligent agents. Our system provides the following capabilities: flexible monitoring and reporting that enables collection of management information from network elements at configurable intervals; automated configuration and re-configuration of network elements based on reported network status; user-definable aggregation and filtering of monitored management information at the source of the data so as to reduce management station processing and network transmission overhead.

1. Introduction

Today's military networks are mobile ad hoc wireless networks, where every node acts as a router and can route traffic to other nodes. Such networks pose stringent requirements for security and reliability. They are highly dynamic in nature, as mobile ad hoc networks are formed over wireless links. Links are susceptible to failures because of mobility of nodes, or loss of connectivity due to volatility of wireless links. Strict requirements on security and reliability combined with the dynamic nature of the network provide a strong motivation for self-forming, self-configuring, and self-healing capabilities in the network. In order to address these needs, we have developed a policy-based network management system that provides the capability to express networking requirements at a high level and have them automatically realized in the network by configuration agents, without requiring further manual updates. This approach provides the network administrator with the capability to specify high-level policies that:

- Specify *long-term, network-wide* configuration objectives, e.g.
  o All control traffic must get the highest level of QoS priority;
  o All private communications must be encrypted.

- Provide an *automated feedback loop* so that information reported by monitoring agents can be used to automatically trigger correction of network problems based on policies, e.g.
  o "If server response time > 5 seconds, determine whether to relocate the server".

Once policies such as those described above are defined, they are automatically enforced by the management system. These capabilities can provide military personnel as well as commercial network operators with very powerful tools to configure and control their network, and to re-configure their network in response to network conditions, with the highest possible level of automation. Some examples of added functionality that would be enabled by policy-based management include:

- Dynamically changing the role of a node to act as a server (e.g. DNS server), based on relevant capabilities such as computing power, battery power, signal strength, hardware, etc. Capabilities that are important in a certain environment may not be relevant in others (e.g. battery power may be important at night but not during the daytime for

---

* The research reported in this document/presentation was performed in connection with contract number DAAD19-01-C-0062 with the U.S. Army Research Laboratory. The views and conclusions contained in this document are those of the authors and should not be interpreted as presenting the official policies or position, either expressed or implied, of the U.S. Army Research Laboratory, or the U.S. Government unless so designated by other authorized documents. Citation of manufacturer's or trade names does not constitute an official endorsement or approval of the use thereof. The U.S. Government is authorized to reproduce and distribute reprints for Government purposes notwithstanding any copyright notation hereon.

solar-powered nodes); such constraints are captured as policies.

- Switching between proactive (e.g. Optimized Link State Routing [10]) and reactive (e.g. Ad hoc On-demand Distance Vector [7]) routing protocols to optimize performance depending on the known density of nodes in the network.

- Adjusting auto-configured address pool sizes based on density of nodes in the network to conserve address space.

- Setting network-wide values for auto-configuration parameters; etc.

This paper describes a policy-based mobile ad hoc network management system, developed under the U.S. Army CERDEC DRAMA (Dynamic Re-Addressing and Management for the Army) program [3], that addresses the special needs posed by mobile ad hoc networks. The system provides the capability to express networking requirements at a high level and have them automatically realized in the network by agents, without requiring further manual updates. Network management functionality is realized by policy agents that are organized in a hierarchy to provide both scalability and autonomy. Survivability is achieved by enabling any component to take over the management role of another component in the case of failure.

1.1. Related work

The characteristics of mobile ad hoc networks (commonly called *MANETs*) are sufficiently different from commercial wireline networks to have generated a great deal of work in alternate management paradigms. The task of managing MANETs involves frequent reconfiguration, due to node mobility and consequently dynamically changing network topology. Network nodes often have limited battery power and storage capacity, and wireless radio link capacity and quality varies dynamically based on environmental conditions (weather, terrain, foliage, etc.). These differences have resulted in an emergence of paradigms particularly suited for managing MANETs. As an example, although SNMP is the management protocol of choice for monitoring the vast majority of network elements available on the market today in wireline networks, alternative protocols have sprung up that are specifically designed for mobile ad hoc networks. ANMP (Ad hoc Network Management Protocol) [32] is a management protocol that is compatible with SNMPv3 [35], and uses hierarchical clustering of nodes to reduce the number of messages exchanged between the manager and the agents. In the management system described in this paper, we make use

of YAP (Yelp Announcement Protocol) [8] for efficiently reporting management information. YAP relies on periodic information reporting from agent to manager instead of having a manager that regularly polls network elements for status (as is done with SNMP). Another function of a network management protocol is to present the topology of the network to the network manager. In a wireline network, this causes minimal network overhead as network topology changes very infrequently; however, in a MANET, the extremely dynamic network topology results in a high volume of network management traffic. When this is coupled with the habitually scarce bandwidth and computing resources in MANETs, the result is significant network burden for reporting network topology to the manager. We use a hierarchical management system organization as well as dynamically adjustable reporting intervals to minimize the impact of reporting management information such as topology details across the network.

Another significant difference from wireline networks is that the dynamic nature of MANETs can cause frequent network partitions. This may be due to limited node battery power, high node mobility, etc. The resultant fragmented networks need to be able to autonomously reconfigure themselves to function independently. Conversely, when two network partitions merge, they need to be able to negotiate a suitable reconfiguration for the merged network. The U.S. Army CERDEC MOSAIC (Multi-functional On-the-move Secure Adaptive Integrated Communications) Ad hoc Mobility Protocol Suite (AMPS) [31] provides mechanisms for dynamically merging and splitting networks, which we have adopted in our testbed. The work in this paper describes a management system for managing networks running AMPS protocols.

Policy-based networking [4],[5] is a powerful approach to automating network management, as evidenced by the numerous industry efforts in this area dealing with diverse networking domains, e.g., configuration management [14], quality of service control [1], [15], [9], traffic engineering [6], security [29], etc. A policy implies a pre-determined action pattern that is repeated by an entity whenever certain system conditions appear [24]. The first "policy-based" applications in the area of computing were in the expert systems area, where "if-then" rules were programmed to determine the decisions of computer software in a specific knowledge domain. More recently, in the area of distributed systems management, work in [18] outlined an approach to providing automated support for analysis of policy hierarchies for the management of very large distributed systems. The reason for using policy hierarchies was to enable specification of high-level policies and automatic generation of lower-level policies. In 1997, the idea of modeling and using policies for network management resulted in the creation of the Directory-Enabled Networks (DEN) initiative, which was later incorporated into the Common Information Modeling (CIM) effort in the DMTF (Distributed Management Task Force) [28], [11]. More recently, the use of policy-based management for QoS management in wireless ad hoc networks has been studied; [33] proposes a solution suite including k-hop clustering, Dynamic Service Redundancy (DynaSeR), inter-domain policy negotiation, and automated service discovery.

The IETF Policy Framework work group [13] was created to leverage and extend standardization of policy information modeling from the CIM/DEN [11] working groups in the DMTF. The architectural components of the Policy Framework developed by this work group include a policy management tool, used for defining policy rules; a Policy Decision Point (PDP) and Policy Enforcement Points (PEP); and a policy repository. The policy management tool allows entry of policy rules which are stored in the policy repository. These rules are used by the PDP, which interprets and translates the policy data to a device-dependent format and configures the relevant PEPs. The output of this working group includes several information models for representing policies. The Policy Core Information Model (PCIM) [19], [21] defines object classes that represent generic constructs such as policy rules, conditions, actions, policy groups, and policy repositories. The most common policy repository access protocol is the Lightweight Directory Access Protocol (LDAPv3) [30], and a mapping of PCIM to an LDAP schema has been defined in [27]. Other information models defined by this workgroup are specific to QoS policies [26], [20].

1.2. System Overview

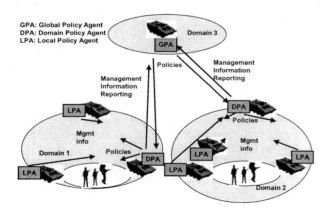

Figure 1. High-level architecture

The high-level architecture of our system is shown in Figure 1. As shown here, a collection of Policy Agents

manage all the nodes in the mobile ad hoc network. At the highest level, the Global Policy Agent, or GPA, manages multiple Domain Policy Agents, or DPAs. A DPA can manage multiple DPAs or Local Policy Agents (LPAs). An LPA manages a node. LPAs perform local policy-controlled configuration, monitoring, filtering, aggregation, and reporting, thus reducing management bandwidth overhead. Policies are disseminated from the GPA to DPAs to LPAs, or from DPAs to LPAs. Policy Agents react to network status changes on various levels (globally, locally, domain-wide) by automatically reconfiguring the network as needed to deal with fault and performance problems. In this architecture, any node can dynamically take over the functionality of another node to ensure survivability. A flexible agent infrastructure allows dynamic insertion of new management functionality.

This paper is organized as follows. Section 2 gives an overview of our system design and describes all the components of the management system. The kinds of policies that are used in the system are described in Section 3. Our implementation experience and a sample use case are described in Section 4, and we conclude with a summary in Section 5.

2. Intelligent Agent-Based Network Management System Design

As shown in Figure 2, the management system is organized into a number of policy domains. A policy domain is a collection of entities subject to the same set of policies and managed by a policy agent, known as the Domain Policy Agent. A policy domain may contain one or more policy domains, organized in a hierarchical structure.

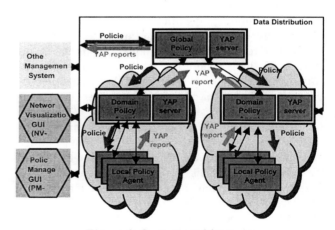

Figure 2. System architecture

A Policy Agent is an entity responsible for managing and enforcing the policies of a policy domain. The Policy

Agent of an atomic policy domain (i.e. one that does not contain any other policy domain) is referred to as a Local Policy Agent (LPA). The Policy Agent of the top-level policy domain is referred to as the Global Policy Agent (GPA). Intermediate Policy Agents are referred to as Domain Policy Agents (DPA).

The Data Distribution Service (DDS) provides the mechanism for distributing policies and for reporting information. Policies created at the GPA are distributed to the DPAs which, in turn, distribute them to the LPAs. Policies are distributed using a combination of DRCP/DCDP [36] and unicast messaging. The *scope* of a policy determines whether the policy is applicable to a particular policy domain. The LPAs collect local management information and report the information to higher-level policy agents using an enhanced version of the YAP protocol [8]. The policy agents implement a standard interface for use by external systems, such as GUIs. This interface is also used for inter-policy-agent communication. This section provides an overview of the components of our policy-based ad hoc network management system, depicted in Figure 3.

Policy Agent Platform: A GPA, DPA, or LPA have the same basic structure and consist of the same code base. They have similar functionality but different scope. Different agents can be installed within a GPA, DPAs, and LPAs to enable different functionality.

Policy Enforcer: The Policy Enforcer is the entity responsible for enforcing policies. Policies consist of event, condition, action, and scope, and are described in more detail in Section 3. The Policy Enforcer monitors events and evaluates conditions to decide which agent should be instructed to perform its management actions.

When a policy is activated, the Policy Enforcer listens for the event associated with that policy, if the policy definition includes an event. When this event is received, the Policy Enforcer identifies all the policies that are triggered by that event. For each of these policies, the Policy Enforcer evaluates the policy condition, if one exists. If the condition evaluates to true, the corresponding action is performed by instructing the appropriate agent to perform the action. The Policy Enforcer can receive events published by other system components via an Event Bus. For a policy that does not contain any event or condition, the Policy Enforcer immediately launches the appropriate agent to perform the policy action. This design provides an easy and flexible way of adding new management functionality. Each agent implements a standard interface that enables the Policy Enforcer to communicate with the agents. The Policy Enforcer is then able to launch agents, set/modify their parameters, and terminate them. Management policies can therefore be defined in terms of the actions that could be performed by these agents. The standard

interface also enables other systems to query the agents to determine their functionality and associated parameters.

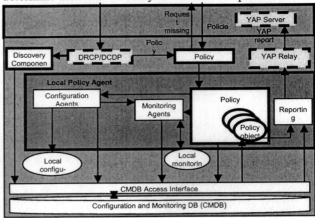

Figure 3. System components

Management Agents: Management Agents are instantiated when policies are activated and triggered as described in the previous section. These management agents perform different types of actions. Currently, the following types of management agents have been defined:

- **Configuration Agents:** These agents perform configuration on a local managed element, or node. Configuration Agents may invoke local system commands to perform the configuration. They may also perform the configuration by writing to the Configuration and Monitoring Database, or CMDB (described later in this section). An example of this is to configure a node to act as a SIP server by changing certain attribute values in the CMDB. If configuration is successful, Configuration Agents write the configuration data to the CMDB.

- **Monitoring Agents:** These agents collect information at configurable intervals from the local node and store it in the CMDB. A monitoring agent may collect information about the local platform using various mechanisms, including SNMP, operating system calls, log files, or via an Element Management System.

- **Reporting Agents:** Reporting agents report two types of information: monitoring and configuration information. The information is reported at configurable intervals via YAP. Information monitored by Monitoring Agents or produced by Aggregation Agents may be reported on demand by Reporting Agents. Configuration information, however, is reported regularly to verify that nodes are configured correctly. If the configuration has changed, the new configuration is reported. However, if configuration remains the same since the last reporting, a "hash value" of the configuration is computed and reported in order to conserve bandwidth.

- *Aggregation Agents:* These agents perform aggregation of locally collected data before the information is reported. For example, an Aggregation Agent may compute the average value of an attribute over a given period of time using the last five monitored values of the attribute. The enables pre-processing of information at the node where this information is being monitored, and reduces the amount of information that needs to be reported. It also provides flexibility in the type of information that could be reported.

- *Filtering Agents:* Filtering Agents report information via YAP only when certain conditions are met. For example, a policy can be created that specifies that battery power should only be reported when it drops below a certain threshold. These agents perform intelligent filtering of monitored data, thus reducing processing effort of management stations and the communication overhead due to transmission of monitoring information.

- *General-Purpose Agents:* General-Purpose Agents are designed to perform special management functions. For example, a General-Purpose Agent may implement an algorithm that determines which node to move a server to, when the current node hosting the server is experiencing performance degradation.

Policy Distributor: The function of the Policy Distributor is to receive policy updates from a remote node and to send these updates to the Local Policy Agent on its node. Policies are disseminated to all the nodes that need to implement the policies in accordance with the defined policy scope. Policies will typically be created via a Policy Manager GUI, or by other related management systems. The Policy Agent Interface at the GPA assigns a sequence number to this policy update, and propagates the sequence number to all nodes using DCDP/DRCP, based on the scope of the policy. Sequence numbers are assigned sequentially, and are strictly increasing. Once a policy sequence number arrives at a remote node, the Policy Distributor component on the node receives this sequence number from the local DRCP process and determines whether it is missing any policies by comparing the transmitted sequence number with its last received sequence number. If the new sequence number is larger than the last received sequence number, the Policy Distributor requests the missing policies from the GPA. The GPA responds with all the missing policies to the requesting node.

YAP Server and Relay: YAP (Yelp Announcement Protocol) [8] is a lightweight management protocol designed for the MANET environment and used for reporting management information to a higher-level manager. Rather than using an SNMP-like polling paradigm for gathering management information, YAP enables a managed element to periodically or asynchronously report management information. YAP is designed to efficiently and robustly relay (via *YAP relays*) network management information about a node to a designated node running a *YAP server* that collects and stores this information in a database. Other applications can then query this information as needed. We have enhanced YAP with five new message types to enable it to report arbitrary information content, and to enable other management entities to subscribe to receive information updates about specific data that they are interested in. We use policies to control what data is reported by YAP and how frequently it is reported.

DRCP/DCDP: The Dynamic Configuration Distribution Protocol (DCDP) [36] is a robust, scalable, low-overhead, lightweight protocol designed to distribute configuration information about address pools and other IP configuration information (e.g., DNS Server's IP address, security keys, routing protocol, etc.). Designed for a dynamic wireless environment, it operates without central coordination or periodic messages. Moreover, DCDP does not rely on a routing protocol to distribute information. DCDP relies on the Dynamic and Rapid Configuration Protocol (DRCP) [36] to actually configure the interfaces. DRCP borrows heavily from DHCP, but adds features critical to roaming users. DRCP can automatically detect the need to reconfigure (e.g., due to node mobility) through periodic advertisements. In addition, DRCP allows: a) efficient use of scarce wireless bandwidth, b) dynamic addition or deletion of address pools to support server fail over, c) message exchange without broadcast, and d) clients to be routers. We have enhanced DCDP/DRCP to distribute policy sequence numbers from the GPA to DPAs and from DPAs to LPAs.

CMDB: The Configuration and Monitoring Database (CMDB) is used to store configuration and monitoring data on a node. This information is stored locally on every node in a repository implemented as a MySQL database server [22]. Configuration data is written to the CMDB by Configuration Agents, and monitoring data is written to the CMDB by Monitoring Agents. A configurable amount of history is stored in a History Database for both monitoring and configuration data. In order to provide a convenient interface for components to access data in the CMDB, object identifiers, or OIDs, are used to uniquely name every data element in the CMDB. The CMDB provides a wrapper, the CMDB Access Interface that translates these OIDs into the appropriate

SQL queries to retrieve or store the referenced data elements in the database.

The CMDB database schema is the same on an LPA, DPA, or GPA. The difference is that on a node that is not acting as a DPA or GPA, the CMDB will only contain information about the local node; whereas on a node that is acting as a DPA or GPA, the CMDB will contain information about the local node as well as about all the nodes within its management jurisdiction. On a DPA/GPA, data about nodes other than the local node is obtained from remote nodes via YAP reporting and is stored in the CMDB by the YAP server.

Discovery Component: The Discovery Component is an entity responsible for initializing the Local Policy Agent (LPA) configuration and monitoring database (CMDB), for updating the LPA CMDB when values are changed by external software components, and for accessing the CMDB on behalf of these components.

3. Policies

Policies provide a means of specifying the desired behavior of a network at a high level. They are implemented and enforced by Policy Agents, and stored in a Policy Repository implemented as a MySQL database server. Policy enforcement involves translating the specification of desired network behavior into appropriate monitoring, evaluation, filtering, aggregation, configuration and reporting actions that establish and maintain the desired network behavior. Policies can have four components:

Event: An event is a named event in the local policy domain that triggers execution of a policy. Whenever the event occurs, the policy condition (if present) is evaluated. If it evaluates to true, the action is executed.

Condition: A condition is a binary expression that is evaluated by a Policy Agent to determine if the corresponding action needs to be executed for a given scope of the policy. If the condition is absent from a policy, it is considered trivially "true". If it is specified, it consists of two components: operator and operands. Operators supported include less than ($<$), greater than ($>$), equal to ($==$), not equal to ($<>$), etc. The first operand is an object identifier of a data element in the CMDB, and the second operand is a literal value (e.g. number or string).

Action: An action describes a task to be executed. Actions may need additional parameters to define actual operations that will be carried out by the action. Thus an action can be sub-divided into two components: action name (sometimes referred to as action *agent*) and Action parameters.

Scope: The scope of a policy indicates its targets, i.e. at which nodes it should be enforced. Currently, two scopes are supported: *GPA* and *All_LPAs*. A scope of

GPA indicates that the policy is to be enforced only at the GPA; whereas a scope of *All_LPAs* indicates that the policy is to be enforced at all LPAs.

Event, Condition and Scope are optional. If neither Event nor Condition are present in a policy, the policy action is immediately executed. If Event is not present but Condition is, an implicit event is assumed which triggers condition evaluation every time the variable operand of the condition changes. If a Condition expression is not provided, it defaults to *true* so that the Action is executed immediately after policy execution is triggered. In the absence of a Scope, the policy scope defaults to "*All_LPAs*", i.e. universal scope.

From the functional classification viewpoint, six different types of policies may be defined for Policy Agents: general-purpose, monitoring, configuration, reporting, filtering, and aggregation policies. These are described in more detail below.

A **General-Purpose Policy** consists of four components: event (optional), condition (optional), action and scope. When an event is specified, it triggers evaluation of the condition. When an event is not specified, the evaluation of the condition is triggered implicitly as described above. If the specified condition is true, the action specified in the action component is performed. This action is performed by a general-purpose agent.

A **Monitoring Policy** specifies information that needs to be monitored, and the interval at which the information needs to be monitored. A Monitoring Policy consists of two components: monitoring action (performed by a monitoring agent) and parameters, and scope. Thus a Monitoring Policy has no event or condition. The parameters for Monitoring Policy are further classified into parameter names and their associated monitoring granularity. The parameter name component specifies the information that needs to be monitored. The granularity component specifies the time interval at which the specified information needs to be monitored. In order to support monitoring, information needs to be collected from the network and stored in the CMDB.

A **Configuration Policy** is a special case of the General-Purpose policy, where the action to be taken involves setting the values of one or more configuration parameters. Thus a Configuration Policy consists of four components: event, condition, configuration action (performed by a configuration agent), and scope. When an event is specified, it triggers evaluation of the condition. If the specified condition is true, the configuration action specified in the action component is performed. The configuration action is specified by a list of attribute-value pairs, where the semantics are that each attribute must be set to the specified value.

A **Reporting Policy** specifies information that needs to be reported, and the interval at which reporting needs to be performed. A Reporting Policy consists of two components: a reporting action (performed by a reporting agent) with parameters, and scope. The parameters of the action specify the information that needs to be reported and the time interval at which the specified information needs to be reported.

A **Filtering Policy** is also a special case of the General-Purpose policy, where the action to be taken involves reporting specified parameter values if the specified condition is true. A Filtering Policy consists of four components: event (optional), condition, filtering action, and scope. When an event is specified, it triggers evaluation of the condition. When an event is not specified, the evaluation of the condition is triggered upon update of the condition operand. If the specified condition is true, the filtering action specified in the action component is performed by a filtering agent.

An **Aggregation Policy** specifies information that needs to be computed, and the interval at which computation needs to be performed or the number of previous values of a data element to be aggregated. An Aggregation Policy consists of two components: action (performed by an aggregation agent) and its parameters, and scope. The action component specifies what type of aggregation needs to be performed (e.g. averaging a data element over time; returning the maximum of several data elements; etc.). Its parameters specify the operands for the computation task and the time interval at which the specified information needs to be computed. The information generated from computation is stored and is indexed by the policy name.

4. Implementation

The management system described in this paper has been implemented under the U.S. Army CERDEC DRAMA program and demonstrated at Technology Readiness Level 5 (TRL-5) [34]. The software was implemented on Red Hat Linux release 8.0. Our testbed is shown in Figure 4 and consisted of two wireless 802.11b ad hoc routing domains (Oscar and Emmy in the figure below) connected by a wired backbone network. In theory, the wired backbone network is a stand-in for a satellite or wireless backbone network that provides connectivity through a satellite, aircraft, or other advantaged node. We installed the MOSAIC AMPS (Ad hoc Mobility Protocol Suite) protocols [31] in our MANET testbed. Infrastructure servers such as a SIP server (for mobility management as described in [31]) and a Bandwidth Broker (for QoS management as described in [31]) were placed on machines in the wired backbone. Two desktop machines (Oscar and Emmy) were used as border routers for the two ad hoc routing domains, and the other two desktop machines (DRAMA-gw and Grammy) were used to host the infrastructure servers

described above. Two laptop computers were used in each ad hoc routing domain as the mobile nodes. Each laptop had an 802.11b wireless interface card, as did the two border routers Oscar and Emmy. The GPA was running on the DRAMA-gw machine, and LPAs were running on all other machines in the network. A Policy Manager GUI was used on DRAMA-gw to create and modify policies.

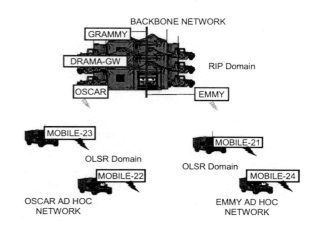

Figure 4. Mobile ad hoc network testbed

Below is a description of some of the scenarios that were demonstrated during our TRL-5 demonstration:

- Network monitoring: The following monitoring policy was created via the Policy Manager GUI and distributed to all nodes: *Monitor CPU utilization every 30 seconds.* Upon receipt of this policy, monitoring agents on all nodes began to monitor the local CPU utilization and store it in the local CMDB every 10 seconds.

- Reporting of management information: The following reporting policy was created via the Policy Manager GUI and distributed to all nodes: *Report CPU utilization every 10 seconds.* Upon receipt of this policy, reporting agents on all nodes began to report the local CPU utilization via YAP every 10 seconds to the GPA. The YAP server on the GPA stored this reported information in the local CMDB (i.e. on the DRAMA-gw node).

- Survivability: In order to demonstrate survivability, one of the mobile nodes (mobile-23) was manually disconnected from the network. In practice, this could happen if the node moved away and could not hear the radio signal from the other nodes in the network, or if the node temporarily lost power, etc. Following this disconnection, the following policy updates were made via the Policy Manager GUI and distributed to all nodes (note that due to its being disconnected, mobile-23 could not receive these policy updates):

o Deactivate the previous reporting policy
o Create a new filtering policy: Report CPU utilization via YAP if it exceeds 70%.

Following this, mobile-23 was reconnected to the network and automatically received the above policy updates that it had missed while it was disconnected, using the sequence number mechanism described earlier to identify and request missing policies. The result of replacing the reporting policy with the filtering policy was that all nodes ceased to report their CPU utilization to the YAP server on the GPA node. This was due to the fact that the CPU utilization on all the nodes was below the threshold of 70%. This demonstrated the ability to save network bandwidth by suppressing unnecessary information reporting.

- Filtering management information reports: The next step was to manually increase the CPU utilization on mobile-23 so that it exceeded 70%. When this was done, mobile-23 began to report its CPU utilization to the YAP server on the GPA node. The other nodes continued to suppress their YAP reporting.

- Reporting aggregated management information: Following the above scenarios dealing with CPU utilization monitoring, reporting, and filtering, a number of new policies were created to monitor, aggregate, and send filtered reports about SIP server response time. A SIP server is used in this network to allow lookups of a node's new IP address when the latter changes due to mobility (see [31] for a detailed explanation of this process). Thus the following policies were created via the Policy Manager GUI:

o Monitoring policy: Monitor SIP server response time on all nodes every 30 seconds.
o Aggregation policy: Average SIP server response times over the last 3 sampled values.
o Filtering policy: Report aggregated SIP server response time to the GPA via YAP if it exceeds 5 seconds.

Following the distribution of these policies to all nodes, all nodes began to monitor and aggregate the observed SIP server response time at their local nodes. No reports were sent to the GPA as the SIP server response time was well below the specified threshold of 5 seconds. The idea behind aggregating and filtering reported information was to reduce the management bandwidth overhead in the network by performing aggregation and filtering at the source.

- Server relocation upon soft failure: The next scenario was used to demonstrate the capability to automatically reconfigure the network based upon reported network status. First, the following general-purpose policy was created via the Policy Manager GUI: *Switch SIP server if the average SIP server response time for the network exceeds 8 seconds*. In order to make the decision to change the location of a SIP server, we built a ServerSwitchover agent responsible for such decision-making running at the GPA. This agent makes decisions about whether to relocate the SIP server or not, and if so, where it should be relocated. The agent runs an algorithm that determines whether to relocate servers or not based on data reported by network nodes via YAP. This policy was restricted to the GPA (i.e. its scope was "GPA", so that it would be implemented only on the GPA).

Next, we introduced a high level of packet loss on the link connecting desktop machine Grammy, which hosted the SIP server for this network, to the rest of the network. This was done using NIST Net tools [2] to drop a percentage of the traffic on this link. The idea was to simulate a node that is experiencing intermittent connectivity, which could be due to a variety of causes including interference due to weather or terrain, etc. The net result of this was that all nodes in the network began to experience degraded SIP server response times. When the threshold of 5 seconds was crossed, nodes began to report the high observed response times to the GPA. The agent implementing the action for the above general-purpose policy obtained these response times, and when the threshold of 8 seconds was exceeded, it relocated the SIP server to desktop machine Oscar. The result of this relocation was an immediately improved SIP server response time at all nodes.

The process of relocation was handled by replicating the contents of the SIP server database on Grammy to Oscar; halting the SIP server on Grammy and starting the SIP server on Oscar; and sending DCDP/DRCP messages throughout the network to inform all nodes about the new location of the SIP server. All of this was done automatically in reaction to the high SIP server response times.

Note that this scenario demonstrated the ability to handle *soft* failures in the network, as opposed to a hard failure where the SIP server failed. The ability to recover from hard failures is often handled automatically by implementing a failover mechanism to a secondary server; however, we have found that soft failures such as degraded performance are often not handled automatically and are typically resolved manually by having a human being troubleshoot the problem.

- Automated QoS policy reconfiguration: The final scenario was to demonstrate automated reconfiguration of the QoS policies in the network in response to a mission change or other external input into the system. The motivation here is that a change in mission often means that the kinds of communication and their priorities will be different from those in the previous mission, thus necessitating a change in QoS policies. The initial set of QoS policies configured in the network are shown below. The table shows the amount of bandwidth reserved for the different Diffserv [12] traffic classes supported, which included AF1-AF4 (Assured Forwarding) [16], EF (Expedited Forwarding) [17], CTRL for control traffic, and BE (Best Effort).

Table 1. Origin bandwidth allocation

Diffserv Class	Bandwidth
AF1	2Mbps
AF2	2Mbps
AF3	2Mbps
AF4	2Mbps
EF	1Mbps
CTRL	1Mbps
BE	5Mbps

The following general-purpose policy was created via the Policy Manager GUI: *Upon receipt of mission change event, reconfigure QoS policies everywhere as shown*:

Table 2. Reconfigured bandwidth allocation

Diffserv Class	Bandwidth
AF1	4Mbps
AF2	1Mbps
AF3	1Mbps
AF4	2Mbps
EF	1Mbps
CTRL	1Mbps
BE	5Mbps

Two video flows were then started (flow1 and flow2) from mobile-24, acting as a video server, to mobile-22 (acting as a video client). This video was being sent as best effort. Contention traffic was introduced using iperf [23] and the video quality was observed

to degrade considerably due to congestion in the network. In order to obtain better quality of service for the video flows, admission requests were sent to the Bandwidth Broker [25] to admit flow1 and flow2 into the AF1 traffic class, which was used for video traffic. The request for flow1 was granted, but the request for flow2 was denied due to insufficient bandwidth available in the AF1 traffic class. Thus the quality of flow1 was observed to improve, whereas the quality of flow2 remained poor.

The next step was to manually send a mission change event to the Policy Management system. This event triggered the above QoS reconfiguration policy, and resulted in the reconfiguration of the QoS policies on all nodes as shown in the second table above. Note that the bandwidth for AF1 was thereby doubled (from 2Mbps in the first table to 4Mbps in the second). The admission request for flow2 into traffic class AF1 was then repeated, and this time it was admitted and the quality of flow2 improved too. This effectively demonstrated the result of changing the QoS policies in effect in the network.

5. Summary

The management system described in this paper was prototyped and demonstrated in a realistic environment. Our implementation results showed that a substantial reduction in management traffic overhead is achievable by controlling the content and frequency of management information reporting, and by aggregating and filtering management information at the source before sending it across the network. We also demonstrated the ability to automatically trigger reconfiguration actions in the network in response to network status, thus achieving a high degree of management automation, and improving the performance of the network. Future work will address integration of this management system with fault diagnosis technology being developed under the DRAMA program. This work is also being transitioned to the U.S. Army under the SDD (System Design and Development) phase of the Future Combat Systems program.

The views and conclusions contained in this document are those of the authors and should not be interpreted as representing the official policies, either expressed or implied, of the Army Research Laboratory or the U. S. Government.

6. References

[1] R. Bhatia et al., "Policy Evaluation for Network Management", *INFOCOM* 2000.

[2] National Institute of Standards and Technology, NIST Net tools, http://snad.ncsl.nist.gov/itg/nistnet/.

[3]   R. Chadha et al., "System Design Report", *CERDEC Intelligent Agent-based Management for the Army Environment Project Deliverable*, Contract DAAD19-01-C-0062, CDRL A003, Sept. 2003.

[4]   R. Chadha et al., "PECAN: Policy-Enabled Configuration Across Networks", *IEEE 4th International Workshop on Policies for Distributed Systems and Networks*, Como, Italy, June 2003.

[5]   R. Chadha, G. Lapiotis, S. Wright, "Policy-Based Networking", *IEEE Network special issue*, March/April 2002, Vol. 16 No. 2, guest editors.

[6]   R. Chadha et al., "Policy Framework MPLS Information Model for QoS and TE", http://search.ietf.org/internet-drafts/draft-chadha-policy-mpls-te-01.txt, December 2000.

[7]   C. Perkins et al., "Ad hoc On-Demand Distance Vector (AODV) Routing", RFC 3561, July 2003; www.rfc-editor.org/rfc/rfc3561.txt.

[8]   C. Chiang et al., "Generic Protocol for Network Management Data Collection and Dissemination", MILCOM 2003, Boston MA, October 2003.

[9]   A. Chiu, S. Civanlar, R. Rajan, "A Policy based approach for QoS on demand over the Internet", *8th Intl. Workshop on QoS (IWQoS)*, Pittsburgh, 2000.

[10] T. Clausen, P. Jacquet, "Optimized Link State Routing Protocol", Int. Draft, http://www.ietf.org/internet-drafts/draft-ietf-manet- olsr-11.txt, 2003.

[11] DMTF CIM Standards, http://www.dmtf.org/spec/cims.html.

[12] S. Blake et al., "An Architecture for Differentiated Services", RFC 2475, December 1998.

[13] IETF Policy Framework Working Group, http://www.ietf.org/html.charters/policy-charter.html.

[14] IETF SNMPCONF Working Group, "Configuration Management with SNMP", http://www.ietf.org/html.charters/snmpconf-charter.html.

[15] K. Kim et al., "A Bandwidth Broker Architecture for VoIP QoS", ITCOM 2001.

[16] J. Heinanen et al., "Assured Forwarding PHB Group", RFC 2597, June 1999.

[17] B. Davie et al., "An Expedited Forwarding PHB (Per-Hop Behavior)", RFC 3412, March 2002.

[18] J. Moffett, M. Sloman, "Policy Hierarchies for Distributed Systems Management", *IEEE JSAC*, Vol 11, No. 9, Dec. 1993.

[19] B. Moore et al., "Policy Core Information Model Extensions", Internet Draft, May 2002, http://www.ietf.org/internet-drafts/draft-ietf-policy-pcim-ext-08.txt.

[20] B. Moore et al., "Information Model for Describing Network Device QoS Datapath Mechanisms", http://www.ietf.org/internet-drafts/draft-ietf-policy-qos-device-info-model-08.txt, May 2002.

[21] B. Moore et al., "Policy Core Information Model - Version 1 Specification", RFC 3060, February 2001, http://www.ietf.org/rfc/rfc3060.txt.

[22] MySQL Database Server information, http://www.mysql.com.

[23] Iperf, http://dast.nlanr.net/Projects/Iperf/.

[24] J. Saperia, "IETF Wrangles over Policy Definitions", *Network Computing*, Jan. 2002, p. 36.

[25] I. Sebuktekin et al., "Initial DS/BB Protocol Design Document, Version 1.0", CECOM MOSAIC Project, Contract DAAB07-01-C-L534, MOSAIC ATD, CDRL C001, January 2002.

[26] Y. Snir et al., "Policy QoS Information Model", http://www.ietf.org/internet-drafts/draft-ietf-policy-qos-info-model-04.txt, November 2001.

[27] J. Strassner et al., "Policy Core LDAP Schema", http://www.ietf.org/internet-drafts/draft-ietf-policy-core-schema-16.txt, October 2002.

[28] J. Strassner, "Directory Enabled Networks", *Technology Series*, New Riders Publishing, 1999.

[29] D. Trcek, "Security Policy Management for Networked Information Systems", NOMS 2000.

[30] M. Wahl et al., "Lightweight Directory Access Protocol (v3)", RFC 2251, December 1997.

[31] K. Young et al., "Ad Hoc Mobility Protocol Suite for the MOSAIC ATD", MILCOM, Boston, MA.

[32] W. Chen, N. Jain and S. Singh, "ANMP: Ad hoc Network Management protocol", *IEEE Journal on Selected Areas in Communications* 17(8) (August 1999) 1506-1531.

[33] K. S. Phanse, "Policy-Based Quality of Service Management in Wireless Ad Hoc Networks", Ph.D. thesis, 2003, http://scholar.lib.vt.edu/theses/available/etd-09082003-110529/.

[34] J. C. Mankins, "Technology Readiness Levels", *NASA White Paper*, http://ipao.larc.nasa.gov/Toolkit/TRL.pdf, April 1995.

[35] D. Harrington, R. Presuhn, B. Wijnen, "An Architecture for Describing Simple Network Management Protocol (SNMP) Management Frameworks", RFC 3411, December 2002.

[36] K. Manousakis et al., "Routing domain autoconfiguration for more efficient and rapidly deployable mobile networks", 23rd Army Science Conference, Dec. 2002, Orlando FL, http://www.asc2002.com/manuscripts/O/OO-04.PDF.

Routing with Confidence:
Supporting Discretionary Routing Requirements in Policy Based Networks

Apu Kapadia,* Prasad Naldurg, Roy H. Campbell

Dept. of Computer Science
University of Illinois at Urbana-Champaign
Urbana, IL, USA
{akapadia, naldurg, rhc}@uiuc.edu

Abstract

We propose a novel policy-based secure routing framework that extends the mandatory nature of network access-control policies and allows users to exercise discretionary control on what routes they choose in a given network. In contrast to existing research that focuses mainly on restricting network access based on user credentials, we present a model that allows users to specify discretionary constraints on path characteristics and discover routes based on situational trust attributes of routers in a network. In this context, we present three levels of trust-attribute certification based on inherent, consensus based, and inferred characteristics of routers. We also define a "confidence" measure that captures the "quality of protection" of a route with regard to various dynamic trust relationships that arise from this interaction between user preferences and network policy. Based on this measure, we show how to generate paths of highest confidence efficiently by using shortest path algorithms. We show how our model generalizes the notion of Quality of Protection (QoP) for secure routing and discuss how it can be applied to anonymous and privacy-aware routing, intrusion tolerant communication, and secure resource discovery for ubiquitous computing, high performance, and peer-to-peer environments.

1 Introduction

With the advent of Policy Based Networking (PBN), network administrators now have the ability to spec-

---

*Apu Kapadia is funded by the U.S. Dept. of Energy's High-Performance Computer Science Fellowship through Los Alamos National Laboratory, Lawrence Livermore National Laboratory, and Sandia National Laboratory.

ify, administer, and enforce an organization's network-access and utilization policies more effectively. PBN has traditionally focused on *which* users have access to *what* resources in a network [9]. A PBN framework uses bandwidth management, traffic-flow management, firewalling, caching, and other routing protocol and network security solutions such as IPSec, VPNs, etc., to provide differentiated services to groups of users in a dedicated network.

For most part, the policies in a PBN refer to *mandatory* access control (MAC) and utilization policies that the network, as a system, applies to its users. The PBN architecture [10] organizes different network objects such as resources and services into different *object roles*, and defines a policy as a relationship between these object roles and different *user groups*. For example, traffic from certain groups of users can be treated preferentially, or access to certain network resources can be restricted to users belonging to a specific group. In addition, policies can be defined based on the attributes of the traffic itself—e.g., music file transfers or other application specific packets can be bandwidth-limited. PBN Policies are stored in a (possibly distributed) policy repository and enforced at Policy Enforcement Points (PEPs) on firewalls, routers and switches, etc., using a wide variety of mechanisms such as access control, filtering, and queue management.

The PBN framework has greatly simplified the management and administration of organizational network security policies. In this paper, we propose a novel extension to this framework that incorporates a user's expectations and preferences, with the existing mandatory network policies, to influence the path chosen by a user's traffic within this setting. Our motivation stems from the observation that the *discretionary* demands of users have been largely ignored in any formulation of PBN policies.

In addition to a user's identity and group membership

information, our extended framework explicitly models static and dynamic trust attributes of both users and network objects and effectively captures the changing trust relationships between them as the system evolves over time. To illustrate this, consider a user who may want to avoid certain routers based on the knowledge that the routers may be compromised because they are running outdated software with known security holes. The system administrator may not have installed the latest patch, or the patch may not be available. Note that the user's demands in this situation do not violate the mandatory system policy in any way. While a user would be dependent on the administrator in a traditional PBN, in our proposed model, a user can encode this requirement and discover a path dynamically, consisting of routers that do not have this vulnerability, and use only these routers until the vulnerability is patched.

Other examples of a user's discretionary policies in this setting include the ability to exclude routers that belong to an administrative domain that the user does not trust, or exclude routers that are dropping an unacceptable fraction of packets, and so on. A point to note here is that the trust attributes of both the user and the network object are *dynamic*, in the sense that they may change over time. We list different types of attributes of both user groups and network objects and classify them according to whether they are inherent, consensus based, or need to be inferred by the user in some way. This extends the traditional notion of "Quality of Service" to what we refer to broadly as the "Quality of Protection" (QoP) [3, 14] of a network route. We explore the issue of trust management and describe what entities are needed to enable certification and validation of dynamic trust attributes.

In order to capture the effect of dynamically changing trust values and relationships on the quality of routes our model can discover, we introduce a quantitative measure called *confidence*. Using this metric, we describe different functions to combine meaningfully the confidence values of individual links along a route, presenting what we believe is a novel quantitative model of *trust* relationships. This metric reflects the perceived threat quantitatively, and users change the confidence levels in response to exposed threats and vulnerabilities. We show how we can efficiently compute routes that maximize the confidence a user can expect given the current threat model and trust relationships. We explore these issues in the context of three representative environments—a military network, a ubiquitous computing scenario, and a peer-to-peer network.

Yi et al. [13] propose the notion of *secure routing* for ad-hoc military environments. To the best of our knowledge, this is the only work besides ours that attempts to accommodate users' demands on secure routing. While

their work was limited to ad-hoc wireless routing environments and to certain credentials of the users, we present a generalized protocol based on different types of attributes of users and routers, as well as trust and threat assumptions between these entities.

In addition to security, a user may also be interested in setting up routes that preserve their privacy, in terms of location anonymity or identity anonymity. Our model enables users to set up routes through routers in a way that does not compromise their privacy, leveraging on our experience with Mist [1]. Users can specify trust and threat attributes to avoid certain nodes and prefer some routes over others, rather than relying on the system to make anonymous routing decisions.

We envision a network in which users operate under the overall network MAC policy, but have the flexibility to apply dynamic trust attributes and relationships for improved confidentiality, privacy, and availability guarantees of their communication. In the future we propose to study different computational models of confidence and extend our model with probabilistic analysis to capture stochastic behavior, and sensitivity analysis to study how changing trust relationships and threat models can impact the overall security of routes in a given network.

Overview—In Section 2 we present an overview of our system's architecture. Section 3 discusses how users can specify path requirements based on desired path properties. Section 4 describes our trust model and how we quantify "good quality" routes. We present some applications of our approach in Section 5. After a discussion in Section 6, we present our conclusions in Section 7.

2 Architecture

In this section, we present a high-level architectural view of our proposed model consisting of different network elements. Similar to traditional PBNs, our network includes a policy database, PEPs, and PDPs. We focus our attention on corporate or private networks that are effectively isolated from the Internet at large and provide the adequate support to enforce cohesive administrative and management policies across this network. Within our network we also have the ability to certify different static and dynamic attributes of users and network objects, through a centralized or distributed trust authority.

As shown in Figure 1, users connect to our routing infrastructure through *access points*. Services can be connected to access points, or certain services may be available at the routing nodes itself (e.g., discovery services that are part of the routing infrastructure). Based on the certified attributes that the user chooses to disclose to the authenticating system (for privacy reasons the users may disclose only a subset of their current attributes),

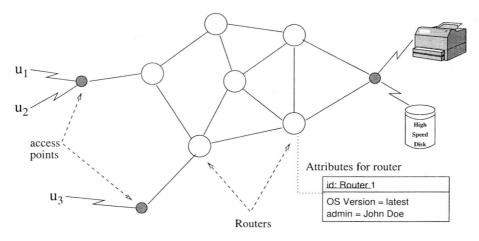

Figure 1. Architecture Overview

the user is presented with a snapshot of the system consisting of different network elements, including routers, links and servers. Note that this snapshot is a restricted view of the network, reflecting what resources a user is authorized to use based on the user's disclosed credentials [1], according to the *mandatory* access policies of the organization.

The user hence possesses a logical view of the routers, their attributes, and their connectivity. When a user wishes to communicate with another entity on the network, he or she looks up the access point of the destination and computes a route to that access point. Within this view of the network, our framework allows users to restrict their preferences for routers, services and routes even further, in accordance with their discretionary demands. In the next few subsections we describe how each part of this process works, along with the trust negotiation and bootstrapping that occurs in the system. We begin with how attributes can be certified in our proposed system.

2.1 Attributes

We define three types of attributes to capture both the static and dynamic nature of evolving trust relationships in our system—*inherent attributes, consensus-based attributes* and *inferred attributes*. As we show later, these attributes help us quantify the trust relationships in the system.

Inherent attributes: These attributes are relatively static characteristics of an entity, which can be certified by a Certificate Authority (CA). Examples of inherent user attributes include identity, role, age, and gender. In-

herent router attributes include physical location, administrative authority, physical security, clearance level, and firewall security. A CA can create these certificates for inherent attributes and distribute them a priori to users and routers. For example, users can use these attributes to set up routes through routers that are physically secure and that belong to a certain trusted administrative entity.

Consensus-based attributes: These attributes relate to the behavior of an entity with respect to other entities in the system. For example, routers in the network can vouch for the integrity of neighboring routers if they appear to be routing packets correctly. A compromised router may stop forwarding packets, and neighboring routers would degrade their trust in that router with respect to packet delivery. Users can therefore use these dynamic attributes to set up routes through routers that have been routing packets reliably on a need-to-use basis. Routers may decide that a certain user is not honoring routing policies and exclude that user from future negotiations. For example, the user may be running a transfer protocol that does not have any congestion control mechanism (e.g., non TCP-friendly multimedia flows, or a denial of service attack). Hence routers may or may not vouch for a user's behavior, which would hurt the user's ability to set up future routes. This encourages good behavior of both users and routers within the network. Since these certificates are issued for the current behavior of a router or a user, it is impractical to have the CA issue such certificates.

Therefore, we need a robust and efficient protocol where routers and users can generate, agree, and distribute these relatively dynamic attributes. Since users and routers, especially compromised ones, can lie about these attributes, we plan to explore different intrusion

---

[1] We use *credentials* and *attributes* interchangeably since attributes are certified and are presented as credentials

47

tolerant consensus protocols in the future, with different assumptions (including Byzantine failure) for this part of the framework. One option is to use COCA [16], an online certification authority that uses threshold cryptography to issue these certificates. The basic idea is that at least k out of n routers would need to agree on an attribute to issue a certificate for that attribute. COCA comes with built-in intrusion tolerance for Byzantine failures, and is reasonably efficient.

Inferred attributes: While entities in the network may have inherent or consensus-based attributes, users may have reasons not to trust certain routers, and likewise, certain routers may not trust certain users. For example a user might use probes to infer that certain routers are running outdated versions of software with a known vulnerability. This is an indicator that the router may be compromised and is not trustworthy. Hence a user may want to avoid such routers. Since these are attributes that the user assigns to routers (or vice versa), these attributes are local to the entity making the inference. No certification is required for such attributes. Other examples include latest patches, daemon processes, past behavior observed by the user, etc.

In the next subsection, we briefly explore how to accommodate a user's privacy preferences.

2.2 Trust negotiation

We desire a system that honors the privacy of users. A user would like to reveal only those attribute certificates that are absolutely necessary to accomplish the user's goals. For example, a user may want to use the network as a *Student*, without revealing the actual identity. Since the logical view of the network depends on the credentials of the user, this view is restricted based on the attributes the user reveals to the network. Moreover, when a user demands consensus-based attributes of routers, the router may first demand that user present credentials appropriate to that demand. For example the router may disclose routing statistics only to users with a high level of security clearance (high-priority users). This suggests the use of trust negotiation protocols such as those proposed by Yu et al. [15]. Such protocols can be effectively used to bootstrap trust between users and routers based on inherent and consensus based attributes.

2.3 Routing model

In this subsection, we formalize our routing model and describe how users can specify their discretionary policies based on attributes of routers in the organization. As explained before, users can obtain a map of the network that they are authorized to view according to the organizational mandatory policy at startup. This map lists all the routers, and links, and labels each router with the set of static attributes that are valid on that router. Users are allowed to update this map with dynamic attributes at any point in time.

We model our network as a Kripke structure in order to take advantage of what is called model checking [4] and its accompanying formalism. Formally, a Kripke structure is the tuple $M = \langle S, S_0, R, L \rangle$, where S is a set of states, S_0 is the set of initial or start states, $R \subseteq S \times S$ is a total transition relation between states, and $L : S \rightarrow \mathcal{P}(AP)$ is a labeling function where $\mathcal{P}(AP)$ is the power set of atomic propositions AP. Given a state $s \in S$, $L(s)$ is the set of atomic propositions that are true in s.

Note how this formalism corresponds almost exactly with the attribute-based routing framework we propose. The set of routers corresponds to the set of states S in the model. If two routers s_1, s_2 are connected then $(s_1, s_2), (s_2, s_1) \in R$ since we assume symmetric links. Note relation R is total since our links are bidirectional. Each relation in R corresponds to the connectivity between routers. The set of attributes at each router can be viewed as atomic propositions (or truth valued statements) about attributes in that that state. Therefore the set AP is the set of all possible attribute-value pairs in our system. Note, this set is finite in our model. The set of start states S_0 are specified by the user.

Since the network is logically mapped to a Kripke structure, users can define their discretionary policies as path characteristics using temporal logic formulas that can be interpreted over what is called a computation tree of a Kripke structure. Formally, an infinite computation tree is obtained by unwinding the state-transition graph by starting with a fixed start state and applying all transitions from that state to other states in the model, and so on. Different types of temporal logic have been studied extensively in the past [4] to describe properties of these infinite computation trees. We believe that the most useful logic for our case is Linear Temporal Logic (LTL) which is used to specify characteristics of paths in this tree. We do not define the syntax and semantics of LTL as it is well known, but explain how we can use it to specify properties in the next section.

Our biggest motivation for using this formalism is the availability of automatic tools that can compute efficiently whether there exists a path in our model that satisfies the constraints imposed by the LTL formula. This process is called model checking. A model checker always provides a counter-example (if one exists) to a property specified by the user. Specifying the negation of a desired property, yields a path (counter-example) with the desired property. Model checkers can be modified to return more than one counter-example to yield all paths that satisfy a specific type of LTL formula [8].

We show how we can adapt this technique in the next section, and present a discussion on the suitability of model checking, its time complexity, and highlight specific characteristics of our model that make it particularly scalable with respect to the "state space explosion" problem.

3 Path specification

LTL formulas are a powerful way for users to express path requirements. As explained in the previous section, model checkers can be used to generate multiple paths, when they exist, that satisfy these constraints between a source access point and a destination access point in our model. Model checking algorithms for LTL formulas in general have time complexity $O(|M|2^{O(|f|)})$, where $|f|$ is the size of the LTL formula. However, note that the algorithm is tractable in general for LTL formulas of small size, and we expect that user specified LTL formulas will be reasonable in size. As we discuss below, there is more of a concern with the state space explosion problem (the size $|M|$), which is not a concern for us since $|M|$ is the size of the network, and there is no state space explosion in our model.

In this paper, we describe how we can optimize this algorithm for a subset of LTL formulas that reduces to the shortest path problem, which is polynomial in time (e.g., Dijkstra's shortest path algorithm). For future work, we plan on exploring the utility of more complex LTL formulas. It is useful to note here that model checking is associated with what is called the "state space explosion problem," which usually makes it unusable for a large system with dynamic behavior. Typically, a state transition occurs in a Kripke model when the truth values of the atomic propositions in that state change. As a result, computation trees that represent all possible behaviors of the system by enumerating states and transitions for all combinations of changes of these values, can become very large. In our case, the attribute certificates are fixed for a particular view of the network. We do not model the changing values of these attributes as different states for each router. The transitions can only occur between routers that have links between them in the real network we are modeling. Therefore, we can limit the size of our model by number of routers, links, and attributes in our network. In terms of model checking overhead, we do not suffer from the state-space explosion problem, and we are only limited by the complexity of algorithms for verifying LTL formulas. In general, if the length of the formula $|f|$ is small in comparison to size of the network (Kripke structure), then for all practical purposes the model checking takes place in asymptotic linear time with respect to the size of the network. Hence we believe that the use of model checking

for computing paths according to LTL specifications can be a powerful and efficient tool.

Manna and Pnueli [6] in their discussion on the expressive power of temporal logic discuss three useful classes of path properties—Invariance, Response, and Precedence. Invariance properties are true in every state in a path. These properties are useful to model user constraints such as "Only route through nodes that support IPSec." Response properties are useful to model quantitative properties of bidirectional paths, e.g., in terms of round trip latency or available bandwidth. Precedence properties capture the causal relationships between properties along a path. We explore these properties in turn and show they can be specified in LTL.

3.1 Global or invariance properties

Consider LTL formulas of the form $\mathbf{G}\,p$. $\mathbf{G}$ is the "globally" operator which means that in all states along the path, proposition p must evaluate to true. We restrict p to propositions on the attributes. The user requires that p must hold at all routers. The algorithm for computing paths that satisfy $\mathbf{G}\,p$ first eliminates all nodes from the graph (Kripke structure) where p does not hold. This solely depends on attributes at each router, and attributes at one router do not affect the satisfiability of p at another router. The graph that we are left with represents the routers that the user is willing to route through.

3.2 Response properties

These properties are of the form $\mathbf{G}\,(p \rightarrow \mathbf{F}\,q)$ where $\mathbf{F}$ is the "finally" operator. The formula asserts that it is always true on our path that if proposition p is satisfied at any node, eventually proposition q will be satisfied. This property is useful to specify bounded-response and causal relationships between attributes. Quantitative versions of these properties (obtained by augmenting both the model and the temporal logic carefully with time variables as in [2]) can be used to specify path latencies and bandwidth constraints.

3.3 Precedence properties

We look at the case when certain attributes along the path must occur in a specific order. For example, the user may want to set up a path that goes through routers in a non-decreasing order of classification levels. Once a packet enters a router with high level of security, it must not pass through a node with lower security. Consider the case when routers append sensitive information to packets. If the packet is at a certain router, it can never contain previous data from a higher clearance router, and hence there is no information leakage. The user can specify an attribute ordering $p_1, \ldots, p_n$, where exactly one of these is true at every router. If p_i and p_j occur along a path, it must be the case that p_i occurred before p_j. This can be specified with the LTL formula: $\neg \bigvee_{i>j} \mathbf{F} (p_i \rightarrow \mathbf{F} p_j)$. Given this specification, we can remove all edges from the graph that violate the attribute ordering. Consider an edge (s_1, s_2). If $i > j$, and $p_i \in L(s_1), p_j \in L(s_2)$, then we remove the edge (s_1, s_2) from the graph. Hence no path in the resulting graph can violate the precedence specified by the user. Moreover, any valid path that satisfies the precedence property in the original graph, also exists in the resulting graph, and these paths are exactly those in the original graph that satisfy the precedence property.

Note that the user can specify global and precedence properties independently. These transformations on the graph described above are commutative. Given global, response, and/or precedence requirements specified by the user, we combine the resulting graph with the trust model described next to find paths of highest "confidence."

4   Trust model

Once a user transforms the graph (as described above) of the network satisfying the attribute requirements (e.g., via the user supplied $\mathbf{G} p$ LTL formula or precedence formula), the user would like to set up a route to a destination. A naïve solution would be to obtain the shortest path (in terms of hops) to the destination. However, if the network is under attack, some paths are more trustworthy than others. For example, it may be known that there are intruders in the system with physical access to machines. One would like to degrade trust in routers that have lower physical security. It may be known that certain machines have been compromised without knowing the specific machines. In such a case, users may degrade trust for machines run by certain administrators, or for those machines that are running out of date software.

Such a scenario suggests that we integrate this notion of threats in the graph-based formalism we proposed so far. We propose a quantitative measure of this interplay between threat and trust as the *confidence* a user has in the validity of the attribute under question. Users can assign confidence levels to routers as a function of one or more of their attributes of interest.

Definition 1. *Given a router $s \in S$ with attributes $L(s)$, a user's* **confidence function** $C : S \times \mathcal{P}(AP) \rightarrow [0, 1]$ *returns the* **confidence level** *for a router. We abbreviate the confidence level $C(s, L(s))$ of router s as c_s.*

The exact nature of this confidence function will depend on the types of attributes and how these values

can be composed to compute the confidence value of a path. The confidence function we choose will depend on this composition operator as we explain in the next section. We believe that assigning these confidence levels to routers is an important area of study and propose to work on it in the future. In the next subsection, we discuss how we can compute paths of high overall confidence based on confidence levels of routers along the path.

4.1   Trusted paths

We refer to any path from router a to router b as an a, b-path. We assume that the user/sender is connected through access point a, and that $c_a = 1$ since the user has to use that as their first hop, and that the destination is either b or a user whose access point is b. In either case we treat a and b as the endpoints of communication.

Definition 2. *The* **path confidence** $\mathcal{C}_\pi$ *of an a, b-path π is obtained by applying a* **combiner function** $K(c_1, \ldots, c_n)$ *that takes all the confidence levels c_i of the n routers s_i along the path π from a to b ($s_1 = a, s_n = b$), and returns a confidence value for the path in $[0, 1]$.*

We explore different combiner functions in this context. To illustrate, consider the concept of "weakest link." There may be routers that are highly vulnerable, and it is extremely likely that they will be chosen for attack. The path confidence in this case can be defined as the *minimum* of all confidence values of routers along the path. Here $K(c_1, \ldots, c_n) = \min\{c_1, \ldots, c_n\}$. So when a user needs to pick a path based on its combined confidence value, he or she can avoid paths with the lowest path confidence levels.

Also consider the following example. A user may conclude that the DoS vulnerability of a router is proportional to the number of incoming links. Hence the user would like a path that minimizes the average sum of incoming links over all routers along a path, and does not include any nodes with very high connectivity. In this case, the user can use a second order statistic such as variance to decide which path has the best "Quality of Protection" for the given scenario.

One combiner function we focus on in the next subsection is the multiplication function. A multiplicative measure of path confidence can be used to model various properties of interest to a user: probability of success of delivery, probability of no information leakage, probability that routers along a path will not collude, etc. In the next subsection, we explore this in some detail and describe efficient algorithms to compute path confidence values using a multiplicative combiner function.

We note that there may be policies that combine several such models and seeks optimal paths based on several constraints (additive, multiplicative, weakest-link, etc.). We are currently classifying such policies and their corresponding algorithms.

4.2 Multiplicative combiners

We consider the case when $K(c_1, \ldots, c_n) = c_1 \ldots c_n$, the product of confidence levels of routers along a path. This multiplicative model of path confidence that we focus on, applies to confidence levels that were computed independently along a path. In this model, a user assigns confidence levels based on the probability of "good things happening" at each node. Assuming independence, the probability of the desired property being true along the entire path is simply the product of all the confidence levels. We now present an efficient method for computing paths of high path confidence under the multiplicative model.

The main idea behind computing paths of high confidence is that by applying the correct weights to edges in a network connectivity graph, we can use shortest path algorithms (that use additive weights) to find paths with highest overall confidence (based on multiplicative weights).

Consider the directed graph G that represents the connectivity of routers specified by the Kripke structure M. For each $s \in S$, we now assign $-\ln(c_s)$ to be the *weight* of all incoming edges to s. Note that all weights are non-negative since confidence levels are in the range $[0, 1]$. We now have a weighted directed graph G. Consider a source node a and a destination node b.

Lemma 1. *Let s be the sum of weights on the a, b-path π in G. The path confidence $\mathcal{C}_\pi$ of π is equal to e^{-s}.*

Proof. Let $c_1, \ldots, c_n$ be the confidence levels of all the routers in π except a. $\mathcal{C}_\pi = c_1 c_2 \ldots c_n$ since $c_a = 1$. Now $s = \sum_{i=1}^{n} -\ln(c_i) = -\sum_{i=1}^{n} \ln(c_i) = -\ln(c_1 c_2 \ldots c_n)$. Hence $e^{-s} = e^{\ln(c_1 c_2 \ldots c_n)} = c_1 c_2 \ldots c_n = \mathcal{C}_\pi$.

Note that if there exists a $c_i = 0$, then the path confidence is 0. Here, $s = \infty$ since $-\ln(0) = \infty$ and $e^{-s} = 0$, and there is no discrepancy for confidence levels of 0. Essentially, any path which includes a router of 0 confidence will not be chosen by the user. □

Lemma 2. *For any two a, b-paths π_1, π_2 with total weights w_1, w_2, we have $w_1 \leq w_2$ if and only if $\mathcal{C}_{\pi_1} \geq \mathcal{C}_{\pi_2}$.*

Proof. From Lemma 1 we have that $w_1 \leq w_2 \Leftrightarrow -w_1 \geq -w_2 \Leftrightarrow e^{-w_1} \geq e^{-w_2} \Leftrightarrow \mathcal{C}_{\pi_1} \geq \mathcal{C}_{\pi_2}$. □

Theorem 1. *The k shortest a, b-paths in G correspond to the k a, b-paths of highest path confidence in G.*

Proof. This follows from Lemma 2 since if we order all the a, b-paths in G in increasing order of weight, they are ordered in decreasing order of path confidence.

□

Since all edge weights are non-negative, Theorem 1 allows us to apply k shortest simple (loopless) path algorithms to find cycle-free paths of highest confidence. For example, Dijkstra's algorithm is the special case when $k = 1$ and will yield a path with maximum path confidence. Several algorithms have been proposed for obtaining the k shortest simple paths in a directed graph. The best known worst case time complexity of these algorithms is $O(kn(m + n\log n))$ [11, 12]. Hershberger et al. [5] propose an algorithm that provides a $\Theta(n)$ improvement in most cases. For small k (for example, the user may want the 3 highest confidence paths) these algorithms are efficient for all practical purposes. Hershberger et al. [5] provide results of their algorithm for large graphs (e.g., 5000 nodes, 12000 edges) based on real GIS (Geographic Information Services) data for road networks in the United States.

In addition to the models we present in this section, we argue that the ability to specify both threat and trust relationships using a combined metric is extremely powerful. We plan to study how these values can vary over time, using sensitivity analysis, stochastic analysis and other techniques.

5 Applications

We present three concrete examples that showcase the benefits of our new framework. We present the first example in more detail, and suggest two other uses.

5.1 High performance and military environments

Consider an MLS (Multilevel Security system) user u_1 with sensitivity level *Confidential* in compartment $\{Navy\}$, connected at the access point s_1. User u_2 has security clearance $\{Confidential, \{Army\}\}$ and is connected at access point s_{19}. Based on u_1's clearance (u_1 chooses to only reveal this, not its identity), the system presents the user with a logical view of the network as shown in Figure 2(a). All routers in this system are cleared for $\{Confidential, \{Army, Navy\}\}$. For simplicity we look at only two inherent attributes: *physical security*, which can be *high* (unshaded nodes) or *low* (shaded nodes), and *domain*, which can be D_1, D_2, D_3 or D_4 (we only show D_1 and D_2 in Figure 2(a) since we

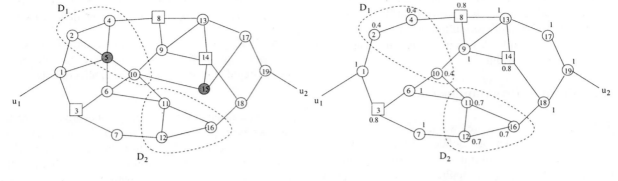

(a) Logical view for u_1

(b) Resultant view based on user's policy, including confidence levels

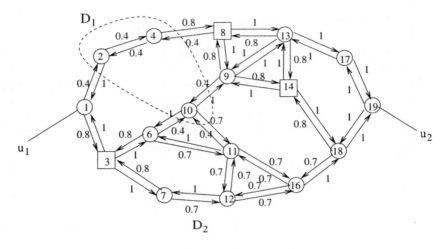

(c) Resultant digraph for use with k shortest path algorithms

Figure 2. Military network example

use them as one of the constraints later). D_1 can correspond to a confidential network owned by the Army for example.

User u_1 desires to communicate with u_2 and determines that u_2's access point is s_{19}. We assume a network component analogous to dynamic DNS which can respond with a user's current access point (u_2 has chosen to register its access point with the service). Now u_1 has been informed by trusted sources that there is an intruder physically located on the premises, and that low physical security routers should be excluded. u_1 specifies the following LTL formula **G** *physical security = high*. This eliminates s_5, s_{15} from the logical view and results in the graph shown in Figure 2(b).

By means of network probes, u_1 determines the inferred attribute *OS version*, which can be *outdated* (square nodes) or *latest* (round nodes). u_1 assigns a confidence level of 1 to all routers. Routers with outdated

operating system versions (*OS version = outdated*) have their confidence levels multiplied by 0.8 since they may be compromised. Lastly, u_1 would like to avoid machines in domain D_1 because of a suspected insider attack in that domain. User u_1 multiplies the confidence levels of routers in this domain by 0.4. User u_1 has experienced large delays when routing through D_2, and degrades confidence in those routers by multiplying their confidence levels by 0.7. Figure 2(b) shows these confidence levels for each node. Figure 2(c) shows the resulting digraph with multiplicative weights. As described in Section 4.1 we replace these weights by their negative natural logarithm, and then apply k shortest path algorithms [5] to obtain the three paths of highest confidence. In this example it is easy to see that the following are paths with the three highest path confidences: $\langle 1, 3, 7, 12, 16, 18, 19 \rangle$, $\langle 1, 3, 6, 11, 16, 18, 19 \rangle$, and $\langle 1, 3, 6, 10, 9, 13, 17, 19 \rangle$. The first two paths have a path confidence of 0.392 (with respect to the logarithmic weights, the total weight is 0.9365), and the third has a path confidence of 0.32 (weight 1.139).

Once these three paths are obtained, the user needs to set up a path through the routers. This is done using a scheme that encrypts the packet multiple times, based on the routers in the path, similar to *onion* routing [7], since public keys of routers are assumed to be well known to u_1. The user encrypts the path in reverse order using the keys of the routers in the reverse path. Each subsequent router decrypts the received route setup packet to obtain the next hop and an encrypted route setup packet for the next router. This technique hides the path from the routers, which only know the previous and next hops in the path. By means of this route setup, u_1 can establish the chosen path to u_2. Packets from u_2 to u_1 are simply forwarded on the reverse path.

5.2   Ubiquitous computing

The previous example provided a detailed overview on how our system works in a military environment. In this section we briefly discuss applications to ubiquitous computing. Users in ubiquitous computing environments seamlessly interact with numerous devices and services. In such an environment *discovery* of services is one of the main applications. However, with such an environment it is very easy for the ubiquitous system to track a user's movements or record user patterns. Using our system as a basic infrastructure or service, users can maintain their privacy. Users only need to reveal as much information as necessary to get a logical view of the ubiquitous environment. Again, this is achieved by trust negotiation as described in [15]. In a university setting, a user may want to avoid using routers or services that belong to other research groups, and eliminate these by using global property specifications. While connecting to certain services, a user may choose to maintain location anonymity (for example, using Mist [1]) by creating a route that is hard to trace back. The user can assign lower confidence levels to the domains that the user does not trust since routers within a domain can presumably collaborate to expose the location of the user. This will give paths of higher confidence that the user trusts for higher location privacy.

5.3   Peer-to-peer overlay networks

We consider peer-to-peer networks where it is feasible for users to obtain topological information of the overlay. We assume the user can form a logical view of the overlay network based on information available to the user. The user desires to perform searches for content available at each peer. Applications include distributed file systems, file sharing, etc. Based on attributes of peers in the overlay, the user can choose to only search for content at routers that satisfy global property specifications. That is, the user can avoid performing searches at untrusted nodes for privacy reasons. Additionally, the user may assign lower confidence levels to nodes on which it expects the search to fail. This can be based on past performance (inferred attribute). If certain nodes seldom have content of interest to the user, the user can assign lower confidence levels. On the other hand, if a biology student is searching for research papers related to cell division, confidence levels for peers in the computer science department can be degraded since there is a very low chance of finding useful content. Hence the user can set up a search path with the highest confidence, so that the probability of the directed search succeeding is high.

6   Discussion and future work

In this paper we focus on particular LTL specifications and provide efficient algorithms for finding paths that meet those specifications. Pnueli et al. [6] argue that global, response and precedence properties are of most interest as path properties, and this provides some justification to this focus. We are currently exploring more complex user specifications in LTL and possible algorithms for computing such paths. We are also interested in using model checkers as a blackbox. The user can provide complex LTL formulas and the model checker would return paths according to the specification. Sheyner et al. [8] use a similar technique for generating attack graphs in a network, although they are susceptible to the state space explosion problem because of the way they model attack paths. Despite its benefits, LTL may be somewhat limiting since all requirements do not have an equivalent LTL specification. For example, a user may want a path that passes through a certain threshold number of domains, which cannot be represented without quantification on the domain attributes, which is not allowed in LTL. In anonymous routing, this would ensure that multiple domains would have to cooperate to expose a users location. This suggests the use of a higher level language (possibly graphical) coupled with efficient algorithms.

We also want to explore how a user can assign confidence levels to routers through a confidence function. We believe that this is a powerful model for intrusion-tolerant routing in networks under attack conditions. Users can assume a certain threat model and update confidence levels of routers that are suspected of being compromised. Our algorithm will compute paths of highest confidence, which can then be used for intrusion tolerant routing by routing along multiple high-confidence paths. From a usability perspective, it is unreasonable to expect users to be experts in policy definition languages. Users would need a more intuitive interface for making discretionary demands, which would then be translated to LTL formulas. We defer higher-level policy languages for future consideration.

We assume global knowledge of router connectivity within a network. While this assumption is reasonable for private networks, a scalable solution for larger networks may require aggregation of routers, where attributes are applied to aggregates. Applying our model to ad-hoc networks would require further consideration based on the degree of mobility of nodes. Users may have to work with partial information on global connectivity, and would need to reestablish routes more often.

7   Conclusion

We extend the mandatory access control nature of PBN systems by empowering users to make discretionary routing choices within a network. We propose a formal model based on Kripke structures and define a metric we call *confidence level* that captures both trust and threat attributes quantitatively. We present techniques for computing routes with high *path confidence* based on a user's preferences, within the constraints of a mandatory organizational policy, for two cases—global and precedence specifications. Based on confidence levels provided by the user, we provide a transformation of the graph using negative logarithmic weights that allows us to use k shortest path algorithms to efficiently obtain paths of highest confidence.

8   Acknowledgments

We thank John Fischer, Erin Wolf and Mahesh Viswanathan for their helpful comments.

References

[1] J. Al-Muhtadi, R. Campbell, A. Kapadia, D. Mickunas, and S. Yi. Routing Through the Mist: Privacy Preserving Communication in Ubiquitous Computing Environments. In *Proceedings of The 22nd IEEE International Conference on Distributed Computing Systems (ICDCS)*, 2002.

[2] R. Alur and T. A. Henzinger. Logics and models of real time: A survey. In *Real Time: Theory in Practice, Lecture Notes in Computer Science 600, Springer-Verlag, pp. 74-106.*, 1992.

[3] R. H. Campbell, Z. Liu, M. D. Mickunas, P. Naldurg, and S. Yi. Seraphim: Dynamic Interoperable Security Architecture for Active Networks. In *OPENARCH 2000*, Tel-Aviv, Israel, March 26–27, 2000.

[4] E. Clarke, O. Grumberg, and D. Peled. *Model Checking*. MIT Press, 2000.

[5] J. E. Hershberger, M. Maxel, and S. Suri. Finding the k shortest simple paths: a new algorithm and its implementation. In *Proceedings, 5th Workshop Algorithm Engineering & Experiments (ALENEX)*. SIAM, Jan 2003.

[6] Z. Manna and A. Pnueli. The temporal logic of reactive and concurrent systems. *Springer-Verlag*, 1992.

[7] M. G. Reed, P. F. Syverson, and D. M. Goldschlag. Anonymous Connections and Onion Routing. *IEEE Journal on Selected Areas in Communication: Special Issue on Copyright and Privacy Protection*, 1998.

[8] O. Sheyner, S. Jha, and J. M. Wing. Automated Generation and Analysis of Attack Graphs. In *Proceedings of the IEEE Symposium on Security and Privacy, Oakland, CA*, May 2002.

[9] M. Sloman and E. Lupu. Security and Management Policy Specification. *Special Issue on Policy-Based Networking*, 16(2), March 2002.

[10] A. Westerinen, J. Schnizlein, J. Strassner, M. Scherling, B. Quinn, S. Herzog, A. Huynh, M. Carlson, J. Perry, and S. Waldbusser. Terminogy for Policy-Based Management. RFC 3198, November 2001.

[11] J. Y. Yen. Finding the K shortest loopless paths in a network. In *Management Science*, volume 17, pages 712–716, 1971.

[12] J. Y. Yen. Another algorithm for finding the K shortest loopless network paths. In *Proceedings of 41st Mtg. Operations Research Society of America*, volume 20, 1972.

[13] S. Yi, P. Naldurg, and R. Kravets. Security-Aware Ad Hoc Routing for Wireless Networks. Poster presentation, ACM Symposium on Mobile Ad Hoc Networking & Computing (Mobihoc), 2001.

[14] S. Yi, P. Naldurg, and R. Kravets. Integrating Quality of Protection into Ad Hoc Routing Protocols. In *The 6th World Multi-Conference on Systemics, Cybernetics and Informatics (SCI), Orlando, Florida*, August 2002.

[15] T. Yu, M. Winslett, and K. E. Seamons. Supporting Structured Credentials and Sensitive Policies through Interoperable Strategies in Automated Trust Negotiation. *ACM Transaction on Information and System Security*, February 2003.

[16] L. Zhou, F. B. Schneider, and R. van Renesse. COCA: A Secure Distributed On-line Certification Authority. *ACM Transactions on Computer Systems*, 20(4):329–368, November 2002.

Transaction Policies for Mobile Networks*

Nuno Santos, Luís Veiga, Paulo Ferreira
INESC-ID/IST
Distributed Systems Group
Rua Alves Redol N 9, 1000-029 Lisboa
[nuno.santos, luis.veiga, paulo.ferreira]@inesc-id.pt

Abstract

Advances in wireless technology and affordable info-appliances are making mobile computing a reality. Such appliances can both communicate with a fixed station or with other info-appliances in an ad-hoc manner. In both scenarios the transaction paradigm is vital to provide applications with consistent access to durable data.

However, current mobile transactional systems fail to provide the so much needed adaptability to the large set of usage scenarios and applications semantics (e.g. disconnected work, relaxed ACID properties, etc.).

We present a transactional object-based mobile system, called MobileTrans, that supports the definition and enforcement of transaction policies. Such policies are separated from the application code and specify transactions behavior: (1) how data is fetched, (2) how updates are performed, (3) the degrees of consistency and atomicity required. Transaction policies can be either declarative (e.g. XML) or programmatic (e.g. Java, C#).

1. Introduction

Mobile and portable devices, such as PDAs and laptops, are growing in number, features and diversity, making mobile computing a reality. These devices are equipped with wireless interfaces that allow them to communicate within mobile networks with fixed stations or with other info-appliances in an ad-hoc manner. Mobile networks are characterized by the mobility and/or disconnection of one or more hosts. In ad-hoc networks, dynamics is higher since nodes interact in an arbitrary way, they are connected for limited amounts of time and their connections may fail when nodes enter and leave the network. Furthermore, due to its size, portable devices resources are still scarce (memory, processing, power, etc.).

*This work was partially funded by FCT/FEDER.

In such scenarios, data sharing both between portable devices and between them and fixed stations, is clearly needed. However, the data required by the applications is not often accessible. Thus, due to the instability of the network topology, the transaction paradigm is necessary to ensure that shared data is accessed in a consistent way in the presence of disconnections. In addition, transactions provide a high level interface that relieve the developers of having to deal with the complexities of the environment. Therefore, a transaction system is an important tool for developing applications for such networks.

Current mobile transactional systems [17, 15, 13] already provide some mechanisms for dealing specifically with mobile networks. One is the ability to handle disconnections of the mobile host. Care must be taken so that frequent disconnections are not handled as failures causing the abortion of transactions. The other mechanism adapted to mobile scenarios is the relaxation of one or more properties of the ACID model [10]. In fact, the classical ACID transactions are clearly too restrictive for such mobile scenarios.

However, current mobile transactional solutions still have some important drawbacks leading either to unnecessary aborts or to unnecessary reduced data availability:

- Typically, if a transaction is not able to commit, it is forced to abort. In most proposals, alternatives instead of aborting the transaction are not provided or the existing alternatives are neither flexible nor simple enough to program by application developers.

- The requirements of applications in terms of the transaction properties can be very different. Some applications may require strict atomicity, while others may admit to discard some changes and still commit the transaction successfully. Other applications may desire to abort the transaction immediately if some node is not reachable while others may desire to postpone the commitment of the transaction.

- Different degrees of control (e.g. in terms of consis-

55

tency) may be required by developers for each application. Some developers may not desire to configure every detail of the transaction behavior, while others may even want to react to the changes of the environment in realtime.

- Finally, it is complex to specify the transactions behavior because it is necessary to think about all the situations and problems that can occur. In addition, if we need to adjust the transaction properties, it is necessary to change the code of the transaction.

In short, there is a lack of available options to prevent a transaction from aborting and there is a lack of flexibility and adaptability in current mobile transactional systems. Thus, current mobile transactional systems fail to provide the so much needed adaptability to the large set of usage scenarios and applications. This adaptability is strongly dependent on the semantics of applications.

To solve the above mentioned problems we designed and implemented MobileTrans, a transactional object-based peer-to-peer mobile system that supports the definition and enforcement of mobile transaction policies. By means of a policy specification and a carefully designed platform, MobileTrans supports the flexibility and adaptability needed for mobile networks of info-appliances with a minimum programming effort.

Each node running MobileTrans is able to access objects provided by any other node. When serving objects to others, a node works as a server; when getting objects from a remote node, it works as a client. Objects may contain references to other objects on others nodes, forming distributed graphs of objects. Objects are only allowed to be accessed in the context of a transaction. Transactions are executed under a distributed optimistic concurrency control protocol ensuring serializable histories.

The transactions' behavior can be adapted in run-time to deal with the specific scenarios and applications needs. In particular, MobileTrans transaction policies focus on dealing with disconnection and on specifying the minimum consistency and atomicity properties of a transaction:

- *Consistency*: It is possible to specify consistency rules that allow the usage of outdated versions of objects if the corresponding remote node is not available. This can be done per object or per set of objects.

- *Fetching*: The policy describes if (and how many) objects must be pre-fetched before executing the transaction or if objects should be fetched on demand while the transaction executes.

- *Delegation*: When a transaction is about to be committed, it is possible to delegate the transaction, i.e. to transfer the commit responsibility to other node.

- *Atomicity*: The policy can specify if the transaction can commit even if it not all nodes involved in the transaction are reachable, i.e. if some changes can be dropped.

- *Caching*: When executing transactions, it is possible to store both the fetched objects and the committed objects by local transactions, in a node's cache. This feature is essential for providing access to data during disconnection.

- *Failure Handling*: The policy is also responsible for determining how to react when the specified conditions of consistency, fetching and atomicity do not hold (due to contingencies of the network). For instance, the policy may specify that the transaction should be suspended until some event occurs. The policy is also allowed to change the transaction configuration in runtime in order to handle failures accordingly.

To implement a transaction, in addition to its code (i.e. objects methods), the application developer must specify and provide a transaction policy. The specification of a policy consists simply on assigning a set of attributes that will determine the behavior of a transaction. It declares the conditions that a transaction must hold and the procedure to be executed in case those conditions can not be enforced. The same policy can be applied to several transactions.

MobileTrans provides a high degree of flexibility in two ways. First, for the application developer: the policy can be either declarative (e.g. XML) or programmatic (e.g. Java, C#); in the later case, the developer has a high degree of control and can react and change, in runtime, the specifications enforced by the policy. Second, for the platform developer: MobileTrans is designed to be extensible in order to allow the inclusion of other attributes to support features not yet predicted.

Thus, the main contribution of MobileTrans is its support for transactional awareness in the sense that a transaction behaves according to a policy previously specified so that it can adapt to applications and mobile scenarios.

This paper is organized as follows. In the next section we present an overview of MobileTrans focusing both on its architecture and on the transaction model. Section 3 exposes the transaction policy mechanism of MobileTrans. In Sections 4 and 5 we present the details of the current implementation and its evaluation, respectively. Section 6 compares our work with others and in Section 7 we draw some conclusions and present future directions.

2. System Overview

We consider both a network which can be simply made of mobile nodes with no other infrastructure, i.e. an ad-hoc

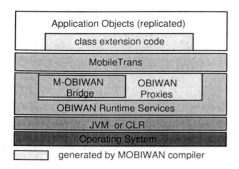

Application Objects (replicated)	
class extension code	
MobileTrans	
M-OBIWAN Bridge	OBIWAN Proxies
OBIWAN Runtime Services	
JVM or CLR	
Operating System	

☐ generated by MOBIWAN compiler

Figure 1. System architecture overview.

network, and also a scenario in which mobile nodes connect to the fixed network. Thus, mobile nodes may connect both to others mobile nodes or to other fixed nodes, typically for limited amounts of time, and their connections may fail due to its inherent mobility. In addition, due to its size, such portable devices are resource constrained (memory, processing, power, etc.).

While working as a server, a node provides information in the form of objects. Objects contain references to other objects building *graphs* of objects. A node where an object was created is called the object's *home node*.

Any object, which is part of a graph of objects, may be given a human readable name. Such objects can be seen as *roots* of a (sub)graph. An object graph may contain several named objects, i.e. roots. Applications obtain references to such objects, from a name service, given their name.

Nodes access objects (i.e. a single object, a full graph or subgraphs), provided by others, by replicating them locally; we call this operation, object *fetching*. Such access is done within a transaction and replication is performed automatically and transparently.

2.1. Architecture

MobileTrans is a middleware platform (see Figure 1) that provides support for the development and execution of applications. Applications are able to access objects according to a distributed transaction semantics. MobileTrans has two main components; its kernel, called MOBIWAN, and MobileTrans itself. We describe both in the next sections.

2.1.1 MOBIWAN

MOBIWAN is an evolution of OBIWAN [19, 8], a middleware platform that provides transparent, yet adaptive, incremental replication of object graphs. OBIWAN has been extended in order to both accommodate the transactional needs of MobileTrans and also to improve its performance on resource constrained devices (e.g. PDAs).

MOBIWAN supports the incremental replication of large object graphs into mobile nodes, allows the creation of dynamic clusters of data, and provides hooks for the application programmer to implement a set of application specific properties such as relaxed transactional support or updates dissemination (which MobileTrans uses).

MOBIWAN is a set of runtime services on top of either the Java or .Net virtual machines. It is comprised of five parts: runtime services, a mobile-device bridge (for communication purposes between nodes), an open-compiler (that generates code automatically), proxies and class extension code (automatically generated). The base runtime services include, mainly, object registration, name service, object repository discovery and connection, and custom event-handling.

For the purpose of this paper, the most relevant MOBIWAN data structures are the proxy-out/proxy-in pairs [18]. A proxy-out (an out-going proxy) stands in for an object that is not yet locally replicated. For each proxy-out there is a corresponding proxy-in (an in-coming proxy).

When a not yet locally replicated object is invoked for the first time, the corresponding proxy-out interacts with its counterpart proxy-in (residing at the remote node) to perform the replication of the corresponding object. This enables the incremental replication of object graphs. Once objects are locally replicated, invocations are direct, i.e. with no indirection at all. This is achieved by careful combination of proxies and referring objects. Proxies also mediate object updating, i.e. when local replicas are sent back to remote nodes. This happens when a transaction commits.

Replication of more than a single object is also permitted, obviously. In particular, the programmer may specify at run-time the amount of objects that should be replicated. So, a whole cluster (i.e. a subgraph of objects) can be replicated in a single step instead of replicating a single object individually. This mechanism is extremely useful as it allows to replicate, as a whole, a set of objects that are to be accessed within a transaction.

Communication among nodes is performed using a bridge based on a set of web-services. These services are set-up on each node, and are invoked by proxies-out and runtime services. The web-services encapsulate all communication and delegate requests on to other nodes.

An open-compiler, called *obicomp*, automatically generates code for proxy classes and augment application classes. This augmentation process does not interfere with application-logic methods. It simply implements, automatically, special-purpose code so that classes are able to create replicas of their instance objects. Proxy and class-extension code do not include communication related code in order to increase flexibility in object replication and updating.

To simplify design, increase modularity and allow different, more sophisticated replication techniques, every step of object replication (into a mobile node) and update (back to remote nodes) is performed by handling specially defined events. Specific events (e.g., *before-replica*, *after-replica*, *before-update*, etc.) are triggered by MOBI-WAN. Default handlers for these events are implemented in the base runtime services performing basic semantics expected. Nonetheless, the application, either explicitly or in its declarative setup/configuration can define different handlers with added versatility, flexibility, different Qos and fault-tolerance, either replicating objects or performing their update. These primitives are used by MobileTrans as they are the basis upon transactional concurrency control and transactional policy mechanisms are built.

2.1.2 MobileTrans

MobileTrans runs on top of MOBIWAN and makes extensive use of the provided hooks. In other words, it implements the event handlers related to object replication (i.e. fetching of objects being accessed within a transaction) and to object update back into the remote nodes (i.e. when the transaction commits). These event handlers implement specific transaction mechanisms concerning concurrency control, atomicity, etc.; in particular, they behave according to a *transaction* policy previously defined.

2.2. Transaction Model

Within a transaction, object graphs provided by other nodes (the *coordinator* and the *cohort* nodes in transactional terminology) are replicated (i.e. fetched) into a mobile node where they are then read and written. The set of fetched objects that are read/written is called the *readset/writeset*; the union of the read and the write sets is the *dataset*. A transaction that performs reads and writes is called a *read-write* transaction; a transaction that only performs reads is a *read only* transaction.

Concurrency control is based on a distributed multiversion parallel validation algorithm (MVPV) [2]. MVPV is an optimistic concurrency control protocol that ensures serializable histories. It consists on three phases: the *read*, the *validation* and the *write* phases. MVPV is also a multiversion scheme, where new object versions are created once updates are made. Each running transaction, when in the read phase, is provided with a consistent view, which is the result of a serial execution of transactions that has already committed when the transaction started. The distribution of this algorithm is based on the 2PC protocol.

MVPV has important benefits for a mobile environment. Since a transaction does not see the results of concurrent read-write transactions, transactions behave predictably and read-only transactions need not be validated. It is only necessary to validate against read-write transactions to enforce

```
void AddAppointment(Appointment ap, String[] hosts,
    TransactionPolicy policy) {
    Transaction t = new Transaction(policy);
    t.Begin();
    for (int i = 0; i < hosts.length; i++) {
        bool unscheduled = true;
        Appointment a = t.Get("Schedule",hosts[i]);
        for(Appointment i=a; a!=null; a=a.next()) {
            if (a.Collide(ap)) {
                unscheduled = false; break;
            }
        }
        if (unscheduled && a != null) { a.Append(ap); }
    }
    t.Commit();
}
```

Figure 2. Example of a transaction.

serializable histories. Furthermore, cascading rollbacks can not occur; the cohorts do not store any state for remote transactions; and there is no need to contact the cohorts if the transaction is aborted. However, since a new version is created once an object is updated, the amount of storage space need is significant. However, this is not a drawback because such versions are only kept if there is enough space (subject to policy specification).

MobileTrans uses a modified version of the MVPV algorithm, in two ways. First, it is adapted for handling objects instead of database relations. Second, based on policy specification, it provides configuration facilities adapting the transaction behavior and increasing its flexibility.

Application developers must use a set of primitives to implement a transaction: Begin, Get, Set, Commit and Abort. A transaction's lifespan can be divided in two phases: the *fetch phase* and the *commit phase*. The fetch phase consists on the read phase of the MVPV. It starts with a Begin primitive and admits arbitrary invocations of the Get and Set primitives for fetching and updating objects, respectively. The commit phase begins when Commit is performed, and the transaction is aborted with Abort. Commit phase performs both the validation and the write phases of MVPV.

3. Transaction Policies

Consider a scenario where each network node exports a schedule which contains a list of appointments. It is a linked list of objects, each representing an appointment. The schedule head list is assigned a well know name Schedule. The code of Figure 2 presents a trivial yet motivating example of a transaction in such scenario.

This transaction consults the lists of a set of nodes and attempts to schedule a new appointment. For example, if this method was called with hosts={"a.pt","b.pt","c.pt"}, the transaction would fetch the schedules of the listed hosts. For each schedule, the transaction checks if the new appointment conflicts with an already scheduled appointment. If

Attributes				
Name		**Value**		**Arguments**
consistency	.object	required		–
		replica		–
		dispensable		–
	.degree	high		–
		medium		–
		low		–
fetching	.object	random		depth
		node		depth, node
		randset		depth,{node}
	.mode	ondemand		–
		prefetch		{obj}
delegation	.coordinator	random		–
		node		node
		randset		{node}
	.responsibility	local		–
		foreign		–
atomicity	.object	mandatory		–
		tentative		–
	.degree	high		–
		low		–
caching	.read	yes		–
		no		–
	.write	yes		–
		no		–
failure	.consistency .fetching .delegation .atomicity .user.*	abort		–
		retry		attribute
		suspend	.timeout	time, attribute
			.reshape	attribute
			.user	attribute

Table 1. Attributes of transactions.

it does, the appointment is not added to the schedule. The transaction does not demand every schedule to have a free slot. This example is used for the remainder of the paper to help understand how MobileTrans can support different behaviors for the same transaction, without changing its code.

3.1. Configuration Facilities

In MobileTrans, it is possible to specify the exact behavior of a transaction according to a set of predefined parameters called *attributes*. The full list of MobileTrans transaction attributes is presented in Table 1.

An attribute is identified by a unique *name*. This name is hierarchical (a sequence of identifiers separated by dots) to provide a better organization of the attribute namespace. This structure is purely syntactic. For example, consistency.object and consistency.degree are names of attributes.

An attribute can be assigned a *value*. Some values, such as *suspend.timeout*, can also be parameterized with arguments. The set of values that can be assigned to an attribute is called the *domain*. Each attribute has its own domain. The domain of attribute consistency.object is the set {*required*, *replica*, *dispensable*}. The value namespace is also organized hierarchically (e.g. *suspend.timeout* and *suspend.reshape*).

It is said that an attribute is *instantiated* when a value is assigned. The *instance* is the pair $i_{attr} = < name, value >$, which represents that assignment. Instances are valid in the context of a transaction and are only valid during the transaction life span. Instances of one transaction do not interfere with other transactions.

Some attributes are relevant for the whole transaction, while others refer to a specific object of the transaction's dataset. The former ones are called *transaction attributes*, the later ones are called *object attributes*.

A transaction is said to be *configured* when all its attributes are instanciated. This means that MobileTrans is now fully instructed about the desired behavior for that transaction and the transaction can be executed. Thus, configuring the behavior of a transaction consists on choosing the values of the transaction's attributes.

In the remainder of this section, we present the major configuration facilities of MobileTrans and describe the attributes relevant for each facility.

3.1.1 Consistency

MobileTrans provides facilities to control the quality of the fetched data, by specifying the relevance of each object's consistency to a transaction. There are two relevant attributes. One is the object attribute consistency.object. It is evaluated by MobileTrans whenever the object is fetched. The other is the transaction attribute consistency.degree. It defines degrees of consistency for the transaction according to the consistency requirements of objects. This attribute is read before the read stage begins and is used every time an object is fetched.

The semantics is as follows. If the value of consistency.degree is *high*, it is required that all objects be fetched from its home nodes. If some object is required for reading, the transaction can not proceed until it is possible to get a replica of the object from the home node. This ensures that the transaction gets a consistent view of data.

If the consistency.degree value is *medium*, only the home nodes of the objects marked as *required* must be directly reachable. If the home nodes of objects marked as *replica* or *dispensable* are not reachable, MobileTrans must provide a copy of the objects from the local cache or from caches of online nodes. Is not guaranteed that objects fetched from caches are consistent.

Finally, if the degree is *low*, the home nodes of the data marked as *required* must be reachable, and, at least, some version of the objects marked with *replica* must also be reachable. If the data marked as *dispensable* is not reachable, the transaction may still proceed and are returned null references to the transaction.

In the example, suppose the schedule of a is marked as *required*, b as *replica* and c as *dispensable*, respectively. This makes sense, if hosts a and b are more relevant than c. If all nodes are online, it makes sense that the degree be *high*, and the transaction can be executed among all the nodes. However, if c is not online, it may still be important to execute the transaction. Hence the degree would be set to *low*. The intermediate attributes can also be useful if it is preferable to fetch inconsistent object versions than none at all.

3.1.2 Fetching

In MobileTrans it is possible to fetch an object according to two semantics: on a *prefetch* basis, which means that objects (sub)graphs are fetched into the transaction's context before the transaction starts executing; or *on-demand*, in which case, objects (sub)graphs are only fetched upon the first access, on transaction execution.

For this purpose, the object attribute fetching.object must be provided. It informs MobileTrans about the host from which to fetch the object and the depth[1] of its graph. There are three possibilities: (1) to fetch the object randomly from one of the nodes currently online (*random*); (2) to fetch randomly from a list of possible nodes (*randset*), where it is necessary to provide the name of the possible hosts; or (3) to fetch the object from a specific node (*node*). This attribute is evaluated before each object is fetched.

The fetching.mode attribute tells MobileTrans if it is necessary to prefetch the objects or not. In the first case, the value is *prefetch*, and it is necessary to provide the identifier of the root object whose graph is to be prefetched. Objects not listed are fetched on demand. If the value is *ondemand*, every object is fetched on demand, i.e. when read by the first time.

In the schedule example, suppose that host c is about to leave the network or to become powerless. In this case, it is interesting to prefetch the whole object graph to prevent the inaccessibility of data. Since the other nodes will continue online, objects can be fetched on-demand. But, if b leaves the network during the transaction, by specifying the *fetching.object* attribute, MobileTrans, can be instructed to fetch a version of that object from other node.

3.1.3 Delegation

The coordinator is responsible for the initiation and coordination of a transaction. In MobileTrans it is possible to delegate the responsibility of commitment to another node, i.e. the role of "coordinator" will be performed by other node. This role consists on the execution of the 2PC protocol.

This feature is configured by assigning the transaction attribute delegation.responsibility with values *local* or *foreign*. The former means that the coordinator remains the same. The later activates delegation.

---
[1]Depth of a root object, is the number of object references that need to be transversed from the root to any other object, reachable from the root.

If delegation is specified, it is necessary to assign the transaction attribute delegation.coordinator which identifies the node of the new coordinator. Similarly to fetching, there are three possibilities of identifying the nodes: *random*, *ranset* or *node*.

3.1.4 Atomicity

MobileTrans can be instructed to drop some changes made by the transaction. It is possible to specify the identification of the objects that must be updated during commit and the objects that do not cause the transaction to abort in case it is not possible to commit them successfully (e.g. the home node is not online).

For this purpose it uses two attributes: the object attribute atomicity.object, which is evaluated by MobileTrans whenever the commit protocol is executing; and the atomicity.degree attribute that defines the desired atomicity degree for the transaction. The latter attribute is necessary before the commit protocol starts.

The procedure is as follows. If atomicity.degree is *high*, the home nodes of all the modified objects (writeset) must be reachable and the local commit of all the participants must be valid. All the changes must be stored, thus providing the higher level of atomicity.

The alternative is to set atomicity degree as *low*. In this case, only the home nodes of the objects marked as *mandatory* have to commit successfully. If the home nodes of objects marked as *tentative* are not reachable or if they cannot commit locally, these changes can be discarded and the transaction can still commit.

In the example, suppose that the schedules of a.pt and b.pt were marked as *mandatory* and c.pt as *tentative*. If the degree was *high*, the transaction would only commit if all changes where submitted. But if the degree was dropped to *low*, if host c.pt becomes unreachable during commit, for example, the transaction would still commit. Obviously this assignment is dependent on the application semantics.

3.1.5 Caching

MobileTrans can be configured to store copies of objects that belong to the transaction's dataset in the local cache. Two attributes are relevant. The caching.read attribute, informs MobileTrans if the fetched replica of object must be locally cached or not. The caching.write attribute, if the object is modified and is successfully committed, tells MobileTrans that its new version must be stored (or not) in the local cache. By specifying such attributes, it is possible to make data available even if it is not possible to fetch objects from its home nodes. Thus, this facility can be quite useful to keep on working even while disconnected.

3.1.6 Failures

If the conditions specified by the current attribute instances can not hold, MobileTrans provides a facility for describing how such failures should be handled. The relevant failure conditions are associated with the attributes failure.consistency, failure.delegation, failure.atomicity and failure.fetching. The first two are evaluated when the degrees of consistency or atomicity, respectively, can not be ensured. The others are evaluated when fetching can not be executed.

The value assigned to each of these attributes informs MobileTrans of the action that must be taken to overcome the respective failure. However, given the set of available actions, application developers may need to execute a recovery procedure that involves a sequence of actions. Therefore, MobileTrans provides a way for describing such sequence. It consists on allowing developers to add new attributes to the failure.user.* namespace which represent a step in the recovery procedure. These attributes can be used as arguments of the value associated with the failure attributes. Thus, MobileTrans can be informed of the next attribute to be read and, hence, to describe the next action to be taken.

All the failure.* attributes have the same domain. When the *abort* value is assigned, it means that the transaction should be immediately aborted. The other values are designed to make possible to recover the transaction by reevaluating the condition that gave rise to the failure. The *retry* value, performs this reevaluation and it must be given, as argument, the user attribute that must be read in case the associated condition can not still be performed. Since this action performs a new attempt immediately, MobileTrans also provides the *suspend.** values which means that the transaction should be suspended until some specific event happens. Currently, there are three predicted events, which define three attributes: *suspend.timeout*, suspending the transaction for a specified period of time; *suspend.reshape*, which suspends the transaction until the system detects a change of the network topology (some node enters or leaves the network); and *suspend.user*, where the transaction is suspended until it is sent an event by the application (dependent on the application semantics) using the MobileTrans API. All the *suspend.** values expect, as argument, a user attribute. When the suspend event is triggered, MobileTrans consults the user attribute which contains the next action to be performed.

For example, suppose that when some object could not be fetched, we would like to retry the fetching after the network topology has changed, to check if the searched node is in range. If the node does not appear, the transaction must abort. In this case it would be necessary to define the following instances:

$i_1 = <$failure.fetching,*suspend.reshape(*failure.user.attr1*)>*,

$i_2 = <$failure.user.attr1,*retry(*failure.user.attr2*)>*,

$i_3 = <$failure.user.attr2,*abort>* .

```
POLICY( AName  n ,  CtxData  c ,  EnvData  e )  →  AValue {
    AppData  a ;
    switch(n) {
        case  attribute₁.name:
            // value₁ₓ ∈ attribute₁.domain
            if  rule₁₁(c,e,a)  → <value₁₁,arg₁₁(c,e,a)>;
            ...
            if  rule₁ₙ(c,e,a)  → <value₁ₙ,arg₁ₙ(c,e,a)>;
            if  TRUE  → <value₁₋default>;
        ...
        case  attributeₘ.name:
            // valueₘy ∈ attributeₘ.domain
            if  ruleₘ₁(c,e,a)  → <valueₘ₁,arg₁₁(c,e,a)>;
            ...
            if  ruleₘₙ(c,e,a)  → <valueₘₙ,arg₁₁(c,e,a)>;
            if  TRUE  → <valueₘ₋default>;
    }
}
```

Figure 3. Model of the transaction policy.

Policies make possible that during these recovery procedures, any attribute of the transaction can be reassigned. Thus, it is possible to describe complex recovery procedures according to the application semantics.

3.2. Policy Rationale

The specification of the attribute instances for a transaction in MobileTrans is a *transaction policy*. Until now, we have assumed that the transaction is fully configured before the transaction begins. However, using a transaction policy, the attribute instances can be provided at runtime. When necessary, MobileTrans asks the transaction policy for the value of each attribute. The policy returns a value from the attribute domain along with its arguments.

The model of the transaction policy is depicted in Figure 3. A transaction policy can be viewed as a sequence of *rules*. A rule is a function which associates an attribute to a value of the attribute's domain, according to some test condition. These conditions can take into account data items from several sources:

- *Context data*: This information is provided by Mobile-Trans in the CtxData data structure. This data structure contains information related to the transaction (e.g. the read set, the write set, the transaction identifier). In case the requested attribute is an object attribute, this parameter also contains information about the object, such as: the object's name and the object's home node name.

- *Environment data*: It is also provided by MobileTrans to the policy in the EnvData data structure. It is a resource to get information about the environment. Namely, it describes: the current online nodes, the available bandwidth and the current power availability.

```
<!-- Excerpt of conf.xml -->
<transaction>
    <attribute name="consistency.object">
        <rule cond="o[host]=='a.pt'" value="required"/>
        <rule cond="o[host]=='b.pt'" value="replica"/>
        <rule cond="o[host]=='c.pt'" value="dispensable"/>
        <rule cond="true" value="required"/>
    </attribute>
    <attribute name="consistency.degree">
        <rule cond="true" value="high">
    </attribute>
    ...
</transaction>

// Application code
TransactionPolicy p = new TransactionPolicy("conf.xml");
...
```

Figure 4. Declarative specification.

```
class A {
    AValue RuleCO(AName n, CtxData c, EnvData e) {
        if (c["object.host"] == "a.pt") {
            return new AValue("required");
        }
        if (c["object.host"] == "b.pt") {
            return new AValue("replica");
        }
        if (c["object.host"] == "c.pt") {
            return new AValue("dispensable");
        }
        return new AValue("required");
    }
    AValue RuleCD(AName n, CtxData c, EnvData e) {
        return new AValue("high");
    }
}
// Application code
TransactionPolicy p = new TransactionPolicy();
A a = new A();
p["consistency.object"].AddRule(a.RuleCO);
p["consistency.degree"].AddRule(a.RuleCD);
```

Figure 5. Programmatic specification.

- *Application data*: The policy can also contain internal semantic information related to the application. Thus, the application can also be determinant in the way values are assigned to attributes. This data is represented as the type AppData.

Several rules can be associated for each attribute. When the policy is queried, the rules of the corresponding attribute are evaluated in cascade. MobileTrans requires that each attribute provides a default rule.

3.3. Policy Specification

A policy is implemented as a class which implements the policy rules. The application developer is responsible for creating and initializing the policy that will be used for configuring the transaction. There are two approaches for such initialization: *declarative* and *programmatic*.

A declarative specification consists on describing the policy rules on a XML file. The initialization of the transaction policy consists on loading the policy with rules stored in the file. An example can be seen in Figure 4.

The programmatic approach (see Figure 5) consists on providing the transaction policy all the required rules. The rule is a method that receives, as arguments, the attribute name, the context data and the environment data, and must return a value. Its implementation fully depends on the application. These methods are called by MobileTrans when it is necessary to get the values of attributes.

4. Implementation

The prototype implementation was developed both on .Net and .Net Compact Frameworks, using C# as primary language. The OBIWAN runtime services and MobileTrans were developed using Remoting services. The MOBIWAN Bridge was developed as a web-service, and runs on top of Internet Information Server. The obicomp compiler automatically generates proxies coded in C#. Parsing of class code only accepts C# source code and extends classes with replication-specific code. Due to this last feature, applications must still be developed only in C#. This is not a major drawback. Nonetheless, we intend to address this issue by also parsing VB.Net code. The platform library and proxy code need not be changed since the .Net VM is able to mix execution of assemblies written in different languages. In application code, the programmer simply needs to insert instructions to discover and fetch repositories. From that on, only application-logic code is required and communication is transparently handled by proxies. Once objects are replicated, their local proxies are discarded by the local garbage collector. The programmer never needs to invoke object replication explicitly.

5. Evaluation

To demonstrate how transaction policies can be used to improve the adaptability of transactions, consider the scenario referred in Section 3. Suppose that nodes a, b, c and x are in a room. Then, x decides to execute the transaction AddApointment, with the other nodes names as argument.

Before the transaction begins, suppose that x already knows that a is going to leave the room temporarily but will come back again. So, it prefetches a's schedule while it is online. The transaction executes normally on x. If the schedule was not changed, the transaction is read-only. Therefore, the transaction can commit even if a does not come back online. Otherwise, if it is a read-write transaction, the transaction only commits if a comes back online.

Suppose that it is a read-write transaction, but a had to go out definitely. In this case the user may not desire to

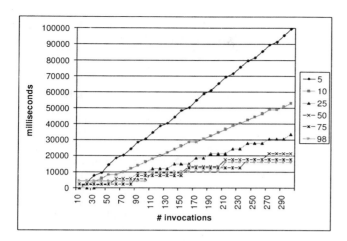

Figure 6. Performance with various replication depths.

wait indefinitely. He may prefer to discard the updates on a, but still commit the transaction with the other online nodes b and c. Thus, the atomicity degree of the policy can be dropped to allow the commitment of the transaction.

Consider instead that a must get the updates and the transaction must commit, but node x has to leave the room. Nodes b and c still remain in the room. In that case, the commitment of the transaction can be delegated to one of the nodes. Thus, when a returns, all the transaction cohorts are present and the transaction will be able to commit.

In these situations, just by specifying the transaction policy, without changing the transaction code, the transaction is able to adapt according to the application needs.

5.1. Quantitative Evaluation

Besides the qualitative evaluation, we analyzed the prototype performance with a micro-benchmark: series of iterations were executed on a hypothetical list of appointments with 1000 elements with a payload of 64 bytes each.

The performance tests were executed with the following infrastructure: a Pentium 4, 2.8 Ghz, 512 MB PC, an IPAQ 3360 Pocket PC and a Bluetooth USB adapter.

Cold connection setup time was about 8500 ms in each experiment. The replication mechanism was configured, by means of different policies, to replicate objects on-demand with a depth of 5, 10, 25, 50, 75 and 98 objects at a time. This way, every time a proxy is replaced and the corresponding object is replicated, a number of others, referenced by it, are also pre-fetched.

The limit depth, 98, is imposed by stack restriction on .Net CF. The graph shows that replication performance is latency-bound, i.e., it is most efficient when several (more than 25) objects are replicated each time.

These are rather encouraging result for various reasons: i) naturally, on-demand object replication of objects masks communication latency and minimizes memory usage by applications, ii) the number of objects pre-fetched for near optimal results needs not be too large (25 or 50). Best results are achieved with higher replication depths (75 or 98) but these could waste more memory if only a few of the objects pre-fetched are actually accessed.

6. Related Work

Most research on mobile transaction systems considers networks where mobile hosts (MHs) connect wirelessly to fixed base stations. In other words, they do not consider ad-hoc networks of MHs. Thus, their solutions are typically client-server based.

In such systems, one important issue is the disconnection of MHs. Concerning disconnection, the most common approaches (e.g. Pro-Motion [17], Clustering [16] and Gold Rush[4]) were inspired by the Coda file system [12]. When the MH is connected to the fixed network through a base station, data is cached in the MH. While the MH is disconnected, data locally cached can be accessed inside transactions and logged in the MH. Upon reconnection, transactions are reconciled in the database server (accessed through the base stations). The Prewrite model [15] handles disconnection differently, dividing the transaction in two phases: one that must be executed online, and other that can be executed while disconnected.

Some mobile transaction systems use semantic information to adapt the behavior of transactions. In Pro-Motion data is encapsulated in *compacts* which allow the definition of consistency rules to be applied to such data set as a whole. In Clustering it is possible to specify consistency degrees among replicated data. Moflex [13] also provides a mechanism for describing the associated behavior while crossing wireless cells. With Toggle [7], it is possible to specify different atomicity and isolation degrees, by dividing a transaction in vital and non-vital subtransactions.

It's worthy to note that most of the above mentioned proposals use semantic atomicity as its correctness criteria. This has two drawbacks. First, it is not possible to ensure serializability, thus it is not general enough for developing transactions that require serialization. Second, the developer, for each transaction, must implement a compensating transaction, which can be complex and time consuming.

Research has been done also to extend transaction models (ETM) [3], in order to make them more suitable for the requirements of mobile applications. Some frameworks where developed with focus on the design of such ETMs using application's semantic information. The ACTA framework [5] constructs a theoretical model that helps reasoning about and compare different ETMs. Inspired by ACTA,

Asset [1] allows users to define custom transaction semantics for specific applications. It provides primitives that can be composed together to define a variety of ETMs. Aster [9]presents a formal method for the systematic synthesis of transactional middleware, based on the formal specification of transaction properties and stub code generation.

Solutions have also been proposed that provide facilities for configuring the concurrency control protocol according to application's semantic information. CORD [11] introduced the Concurrency Control Language (CCL); CCL allows the application developer to specify a concurrency control policy tailored to the behavior of the transaction manager. PJama [14] is a proposal that is inline to what is pursued by MobileTrans. Using PJama, application developers can define the desired transaction behavior while maintaining transaction independence.

In short, in all these proposals, the support provided for transactional policy specification is not appropriate for the usage scenarios considered by MobileTrans.

7. Conclusions and Future Work

In this paper we introduced the design and implementation of MobileTrans, a transactional object based system for mobile networks, that supports the definition and enforcement of transaction policies. MobileTrans uses a distributed optimistic concurrency control protocol.

Application developers, when using MobileTrans, along with the transaction code, must specify a transaction policy. This specification can be declarative by means of a configuration file or programmatic which allow a higher degree of control, even in runtime. Using transaction policies, developers are able to configure several aspects of the transaction behavior, such as the specification of consistency and atomicity requirements, how the objects are fetched, if data is to be locally cached, if delegation is required and how failures are handled. Thus, transaction policies provide a powerful and flexible mechanism for configuring the behavior of transactions according to application semantics.

MobileTrans is a platform under development, hence, several features are now under study (e.g. refining the concurrency control protocol, adding agent based technology, automatic determination of the optimal depth on fetching). Thus, it will be necessary to add new attributes in order to increase the application awareness.

We also intend to increase the expressiveness of how policies are declaratively specified. For that purpose, we are considering an approach similar to the one presented in [6], for developing a transaction policy specification language.

References

[1] A. Biliris et al. ASSET: A system for supporting extended transactions. In R. T. Snodgrass and M. Winslett, editors, *Proc. of the 1994 ACM Intl. Conf. on Management of Data*, pages 44–54, 1994.

[2] D. Agrawal, A. Bernstein, P. Gupta, and S. Sengupta. Distributed multi-version optimistic concurrency control with reduced rollback. *Distributed Computing*, 2(1), 1987.

[3] N. S. Barghouti and G. E. Kaiser. Concurrency control in advanced database applications. *ACM Computing Surveys*, 23(3):269–317, 1991.

[4] M. Butrico, H. Chang, A. Cocchi, N. Cohen, D. Shea, and S. Smith. Gold Rush: Mobile transaction middleware with java-object replication. In *Proc. of the Third USENIX Conference on Object-Oriented Technologies*, pages 91–101, 1997.

[5] P. K. Chrysanthis and K. Ramamritham. Synthesis of extended transaction models using ACTA. *ACM Transactions on Database Systems*, 19(3):450–491, 1994.

[6] N. Damianou, N. Dulay, E. Lupu, and M. Sloman. The ponder policy specification language. *Lecture Notes in Computer Science*, 1995:18–39, 2001.

[7] R. A. Dirckze and L. Gruenwald. A toggle transaction management technique for mobile multidatabases. In *Proc. of the CIKM 98*, pages 371–377, 1998.

[8] P. Ferreira, L. Veiga, and C. Ribeiro. Obiwan - design and implementation of a middleware platform. *IEEE Trans. on Parallel and Distributed Systems*, 14(11):1086–1099, Nov 2003.

[9] G. S. Blair et al. The role of software architecture in constraining adaptation in component-based middleware platforms. In *IFIP/ACM Intl. Conf. on Dist. Systems Platforms*, pages 164–184. Springer-Verlag New York, Inc., 2000.

[10] J. N. Gray and A. Reuter. *Transaction Processing: Concepts*. Morgan Kaufmann, 1993.

[11] G. Heineman and G. Kaiser. The CORD approach to extensible concurrency control. In *13th IEEE Intl. Conf. on Data Engineering*, pages 562–571, April 1997.

[12] J. J. Kistler and M. Satyanarayanan. Disconnected operation in the coda file system. *ACM Transactions on Computer Systems*, 10(1):3–25, 1992.

[13] K. Ku and Y. Kim. Moflex transaction model for mobile heterogeneous multidatabase systems. In *Proc. of the 10th Intl. Workshop on Research Issues in Data Engineering*, 2000.

[14] L. Daynes et al. Customizable concurrency control for persistent java. In S. Jajodia & L. Kerschberg, editor, *Advanced Transaction Models and Architectures*. Kluwer, 1997.

[15] S. K. Madria and B. Bhargava. A transaction model for improving data, availability in mobile computing. *Distributed and Parallel Databases: An International Journal*, 10(2):127–160, 2001.

[16] E. Pitoura and B. Bhargava. Maintaining consistency of data in mobile distributed environments. In *Proc. of 15th Intl. Conf. on Distributed Computing Systems*, 1995.

[17] K. Ramamritham and P. K. Chrysanthis. A taxonomy of correctness criterion in database applications. *Journal of Very Large Databases*, 4(1), 1996.

[18] M. Shapiro. Structure and encapsulation in distributed systems: the proxy principle. In *Proc. of the 6th Intl. Conf. on Dist. Systems*, pages 198–204, Boston, May 1986.

[19] L. Veiga and P. Ferreira. Incremental replication for mobility support in OBIWAN. In *The 22nd Intl. Conf. on Distributed Computing Systems*, pages 249–256, July 2002.

Session 3:
QoS and Storage

DecisionQoS: an adaptive, self-evolving QoS arbitration module for storage systems

Sandeep Uttamchandani   Guillermo A. Alvarez   Gul Agha*

{sandeepu,alvarezg}@us.ibm.com

IBM Almaden Research Center, 650 Harry Rd., San José, California 95120, USA

Abstract

As a consequence of the current trend towards consolidating computing, storage and networking infrastructures into large centralized data centers, applications compete for shared resources. Open enterprise systems are not designed to provide performance guarantees in the presence of sharing; unregulated competition is very likely to result in a free-for-all where some applications monopolize resources while others starve. Rule-based solutions to the resource arbitration problem suffer from excessive complexity, brittleness, and limitations in their expressive power. We present DECISIONQOS, a novel approach for arbitrating resources among multiple competing clients while enforcing QoS guarantees. DECISIONQOS requires system administrators to provide a minimal, declarative amount of information about the system and the workloads running on it. That initial input is continuously refined and augmented at run time, by monitoring the system's performance and its reaction to resource allocation decisions. When faced with incomplete information, or with changes in the workload requirements or system capabilities, DECISION-QOS adapts to them by applying machine learning techniques; the resulting scheme is highly resilient to unforeseen events. Moreover, it overcomes significant shortcomings of pre-existing, rule-based policy management systems.

1   Introduction

Data centers are becoming increasingly popular in enterprise environments, as resources are consolidated to reap the benefits of statistical sharing and lower management costs. Consolidated resources are mainly computing power in the form of CPU cycles, network bandwidth, and storage sub-systems. Within a data center, hundreds or thousands of hosts typically access a terabyte or more of data each, stored in large, shared storage servers interconnected by a storage area network (SAN) such as Fibre Channel. A variety of applications such as web servers, online transaction processing and decision support systems runs on enterprise data centers. Many of those applications depend on predictable performance from the storage system in order to accomplish their goals, e.g., acceptable interactive transactions may require average I/O latencies to be under 5 ms. In general, a Service Level Agreement (*SLA*) prescribes the minimum quality of service (*QoS*) that a client application will experience, provided that its demands on the system do not exceed given bounds. We concentrate on the performance that the storage system must guarantee to its clients; other QoS dimensions include reliability, performability, and manageability.

Guaranteeing SLAs is a difficult problem, as the overwhelming majority of off-the-shelf devices, operating systems, and protocols allocate resources on a best-effort basis. The problem becomes still more difficult in consolidated systems [8, 21]. Storage consolidation introduces additional coupling, when previously unrelated workloads compete for resources such as disk drive actuators, network links and endpoints, switch backplanes, controller processors, data caches, system buses, and SCSI interconnects. Due to largely unpredictable and platform-dependent scheduling policies, unregulated competition will result in some applications starving while others use more than their fair share of the system's resources. Solutions based on static provisioning typically result in low levels of system utilization, and the only way of guaranteeing a fair allocation of resources is to resort to physical or logical separation. Static approaches also cope poorly with unforeseen events such as workload variations, failures, and additions of capacity to the system.

For additional flexibility, resource consumers can declare their needs in advance to an arbitrator (a model closer to that of admission control plus support for resource compartmentalization), or specialized QoS Arbitration Modules (*QAMs*) can modify resource allocations on the fly

---

*Department of Computer Science, University of Illinois at Urbana-Champaign. E-mail: agha@cs.uiuc.edu

whenever they are found to be inadequate. A QAM is responsible for ensuring that, as long as enough aggregate resources are present in the system, all SLAs will be satisfied[1].

The existing approach for building a QAM is using the rule-based paradigm [23]. Rules are used to define how the resources are partitioned among client applications. In AI terminology, the rule-based approach for specifications are referred to as *pattern directed procedure invocation* [15, 16]. While the advantage of procedural rule-based schemes is that they allow the specification of direct interaction between facts and eliminate the need for wasteful run-time searching [14], the disadvantage is that writing procedures (i.e., rules) are like programs that are difficult to write, modify and error-prone [10]. In contrast, this paper introduces DECISIONQOS which is a declarative, i.e., non-procedural paradigm [13] for building QAMs, based on Polus [25]. In DECISIONQOS, the administrator is not required to specify how the resources should be partitioned in different system states. Instead, the administrator simply specifies facts and constraints as logical formulas which are easy to write and modify. These logical formulas are combined at run-time with prepackaged formalisms (referred to as *reasoning*), to decide resource partitioning among the client applications. Logic-based specifications were originally considered deficient in capturing heuristic knowledge, which led to MIT's "procedure-is-best" debate [29]. The debate ended in favor of logic-based approaches, after Kowalski's procedural interpretation of the behavior of a Horn-clause linear resolution proof finder [19].

In summary, DECISIONQOS's specifications are declarative; it does not require system administrators to encode policies as complex, brittle rule sequences. DECISIONQOS does not require accurate, detailed inputs [1] to make good decisions; it can take a potentially minimal amount of system and workload information, and then refine it at run time. The net effect is that of relieving users from the burden of making sensitive, error-prone decisions (e.g., setting decision thresholds), and achieving nimble responses to changes in the operating conditions. DECISIONQOS hides a significant amount of complexity that is not relevant to users; in so doing, it does not depend on human experts to tweak and maintain the rule sets.

We define our version of the QoS arbitration problem, and discuss the shortcomings of rule-based QAMs in Section 2. Section 3 introduces our main assumptions; Sections 4 and 5 present DECISIONQOS's architecture and internal operation, respectively. We put our work in context in Section 6 and draw some conclusions in Section 7.

---

[1]More stringent definitions are possible: QAMs could attempt to guarantee that resources will be fairly shared, or that they will be optimally utilized (e.g., load balancing). Such extensions are beyond the scope of this paper.

2 The resource arbitration problem

In our version of the problem, a QAM manages the assignment of available storage resources to host workloads. This mapping must ensure that no workload fails to meet its SLA (a *QoS violation*). The QAM is invoked each time a QoS violation is detected. Upon invocation, the QAM attempts to bring the system to a state where no SLAs are violated, by identifying workloads whose resource consumption should be *throttled*.

Choosing which workloads to throttle is a fairly complex task for many reasons. First, workload access patterns change constantly (e.g., as a result of burstiness). The amount of resources freed up by throttling a given workload to a given degree is a dynamic function. Second, a workload's behavior may be related, at the application level, to that of other workloads or even human users. For instance, throttling accesses to a database log will affect the transaction workloads. The QAM needs to consider these dependencies when they exist. Third, each workload uses a fixed set of physical components referred to as its *invocation path*. The QAM should make sure that the workloads being throttled share either invocation path elements or application-level dependencies with the workloads that are experiencing QoS violations—otherwise their performance would be independent of one another, so throttling them would not help remedy the problem. Fourth, failures occur at unpredictable times. Even if data remains accessible due to built-in redundancy (e.g., RAID) performance will typically suffer because of the decrease in the overall amount of available resources. QAMs need to adapt to these events within a fairly short time interval, reapportioning resources so that the system continues to satisfy the SLAs. Fifth, the QAM should be potentially able to throttle any subset of the workloads in the system (although doing so optimally is NP-hard); this results in an exponential number of possible decisions.

Our SLAs are *conditional*: they specify maximum average I/O latencies over short sampling periods, as long as workloads request up to a maximum number of bytes and I/Os (throughput) during said periods. If workloads inject load into the system at more than the rate prescribed in their SLAs, the system is under no obligation of guaranteeing any bound on latency. Obviously, such rogue workloads are prime choices for resource restriction; but in some extreme cases, well-behaved workloads may also need to be restricted in order for the QoS violations to disappear. When faced with several choices for a given set of QoS violations, the QAM should minimize the side effects of its actions, i.e., have as little impact as possible on the workloads that are neither experiencing inadequate performance nor being throttled directly.

Many existing implementations of storage QAMs are

based on flavors of policy-based management [17, 23] where system behavior is described as a set of rules that are invoked when certain system conditions are met. Most rules are variations on the theme of Event-Condition-Action (*ECA*), with the semantics that the action will be executed if both a given type of event occurs (e.g., a violation of a given QoS metric) and a condition is satisfied. Let us consider writing a few example rules to define the behavior of a hypothetical QAM[2]. The set of rules can be divided into two categories:

Rules for selecting candidate workloads: Workloads are throttled in increments of *step_size*.

Condition: If workload exceeds $(1.6 \text{ SLA}) \wedge inv\_path(w) \triangle inv\_path(w_{under\_provisioned})$
Action: Mark workload w as candidate and *step_size* = 15%

Condition: If workload is between $(1.25\text{–}1.6 \text{ SLA}) \wedge inv\_path(w) \triangle inv\_path(w_{under\_provisioned})$
Action: Mark workload w as candidate and *step_size* = 10%

Condition: If workload exceeds $(1.15 \text{ SLA}) \wedge inv\_path(w) \triangle inv\_path(w_{under\_provisioned})$
Action: Mark workload w as candidate and *step_size* = 3%

Rules for deciding which candidate workloads should be throttled: Relationships between workloads are represented as a set of *correlation probabilities* cp_w, that throttling workload w will indirectly throttle any other workload in the system. Let avg_cp, var_cp denote the average and variance of the correlation probability over all candidates.

Condition: If $num\_candidates > 1 \wedge avg\_cp < 0.4 \wedge var\_cp < 0.1$
Action: Throttle all w with $cp_w \leq 0.8$ by *step_size*

Condition: If $num\_candidates > 1 \wedge avg\_cp < 0.4 \wedge var\_cp > 0.3$
Action: For workloads with $cp < 0.2$, throttle 85% of excess demand; for workloads with cp between 0.2-0.6, throttle 45% of excess demand

Condition: If $num\_candidates > 1 \wedge avg\_cp > 0.6 \wedge var\_cp > 0.3$
Action: Select w_min such that cp_{w_min} is minimum, throttle by *step_size*.

The example highlights the main limitations of rule-based approaches for building QAMs:

- *Complexity*: writing rules to express the QAM logic is non-trivial and requires a fair amount of expertise. Rules have built-in threshold values that are quite difficult to determine in a practical system—but the effectiveness of the rules depends on their accuracy to

---

[2]Predicate $A \triangle B$ is true iff sets A and B have a nonempty intersection.

a significant extent. More importantly, while writing the rules, the system-builder has to (manually) account for all the possible states that the system can be in, and for all the possible steps that can be taken from those states. System administrators cannot cope with this level of complexity, resulting in error-prone policy setting. Since rules implicitly capture the reasoning details, it is difficult to understand and maintain the precise reasoning behind the creation of a set of rules.

- *Limitations on expressive power*: the rule-based paradigm is based on imperative specifications that trade off a relatively lightweight processing at run time by extensive reasoning required at rule creation time—when detailed information about system and workload may be hard to obtain. In addition, this largely static approach makes it difficult to express semantics such as throttling multiple workloads by varying amounts, or to reason about the best possible option in terms of minimizing domino effects due to correlations.

- *Brittleness*: this problem dates from the early days of expert systems, as a consequence of policies getting (unnaturally) encoded into sets of rules with little or no internal structure. In a QAM, making any changes to the workload selection policies is non-trivial. For example, assume that the host workloads now have an additional parameter for relative priorities. Rule specifications will have to be extensively changed to accommodate this change. A preferable solution would allow changes to simply add to the reasoning engine in an incremental way, which is one of the strengths of DECISIONQoS.

- *Order-dependence*: rules with overlapping conditions are common, and the typical way of ensuring that they right one will fire is to make sure they are evaluated in a known order. This fall-through mechanism is error-prone and not intuitive.

- *Lack of adaptivity*: specifications should be *self-evolving*, i.e., the QAM should be able to augment the information encoded in them by observing the behavior of the running system. This is especially required since the workload implications are continuously changing and statically defined rules may not always be effective. Frameworks based on ECA rules do not have this property. It is possible to define *ad hoc* variables within the rules for learning, but the rule-based model does not inherently support learning.

3 System model

Figure 1 depicts our system model. Multiple hosts $H_1, H_2....H_n$ connect to the storage devices in the *back end*

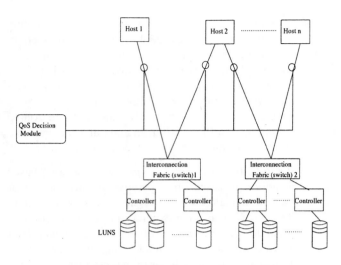

Figure 1. The system model

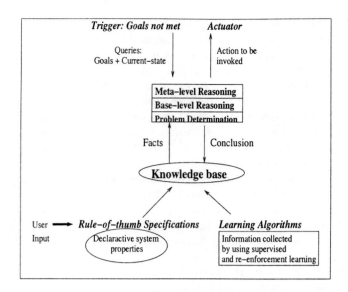

Figure 2. Bird's-eye view of DECISIONQOS

in such a way that the QAM can monitor every single I/O processed by the system. (One way of achieving this property [8] is by instrumenting the code running on a block-level virtualization appliance that is already present in the system to fulfill some other role.) The QAM can gather accurate information on the workload injected by each host, and on the latencies currently experienced by hosts. I/O requests originating from each host are grouped together into one or more workloads, e.g., $workloads(H_1) = \{W_1, W_8, ...W_\alpha\}$, according to which client applications issue them. All requests from a single client hosts could be grouped into a single workload without changing the semantics of the proposed framework, at the cost of making it more difficult to observe patterns at run-time—which are generally less identifiable in an aggregation of streams. Each workload has an SLA associated with it. At the physical level, the storage infrastructure is represented as a collection of elements (e.g., switches) that comprise the interconnection fabric IF; the system also contains the storage controllers SC and the logical disks (or $LUNs$) L. There is a one-to-many relationship between the IF and SC, e.g., $controllers(IF_1) = \{SC_3, SC_7, ...SC_\gamma\}$. Similarly, there is also a one-to-many relationship between SC and L such that a controller can have one or more LUNs that it manages, e.g., $luns(SC_1) = \{L_1, L_3, ...L_\beta\}$.

In this context, the invocation path I of a workload represents the storage components CO used to service the I/O requests of the workload, e.g., $inv\_path(w_1) = \{IF_2, SC_4, L_8\}$. Workloads differ in their access characteristics such as read/write ratio, block-size, sequential/random ratio. The exact amount of resources used by a given workload along its invocation path depend on the workload's access characteristics. In summary, workloads differ from each other in terms of the SLAs associated with

them, the access characteristics, the invocation paths, the resources being used to execute the workload.

4 Bird's-eye view of DECISIONQOS

DECISIONQOS is a logic-based approach. Contrary to existing imperative approaches in which the rule-specifications encode the workloads to be invoked for different system states, DECISIONQOS uses a combination of a declarative knowledge-base and logic-based reasoning to derive the workloads at run-time. The declarative knowledge-base defines details of a workload(referred to as *workload-object*, and capabilities of components present within the system. The logic used in the reasoning engine encodes the thinking process that is implicit while writing the rules in imperative approaches. Making the logic explicit allows for more efficient throttling decisions as it is possible to consider choices that are difficult to specify statically e.g. considering combinations of workloads and optimizing the throttling decision based on a particular goal-function such as minimizing side-effects. Additionally, DECISIONQOS proposes an innovative approach for creating the knowledge base, i.e., it uses a combination of specifications and learning algorithms to evolve the workload-objects within the knowledge. Specifications serve to prune to learning-space, allowing for faster convergence.

Within the knowledge base, the workload-objects are represented as "first-class" entities with attributes defining details such as the resource implication of throttling the workload, the invocation path(s) associated with the workload, the SLA goals of the workload. The details of the workload-object are derived using a combination of *declar-*

ative specifications and *learning*. The declarative specifications fundamentally enumerate the *feature-set*, which is used by the learning engine for interpolation.

Reasoning is a three step process. The *problem determination* step derives a list of components whose behavior needs to change. The *base-level reasoning* is expressed in first-order logic and is responsible for searching the workload-objects. It derives the candidate set of workloads that can be possibly used to satisfy the requirements generated by problem determination step. The *meta-level* decides between the candidate workloads using optimization functions. We have developed a working prototype, based on the ABLE toolkit [6], of the learning algorithms and policy-manipulation functions of DECISIONQOS; we plan to implement the remaining parts during the next few months.

5 Design details

The design details of DECISIONQOS are divided into:

- Representation of the workload objects

- Incremental creation of the workload objects using declarative specifications and learning

- Using of two-level reasoning to decide the workloads to be throttled

To make the discussion more concrete, we consider the following example (the example is kept simple for ease of explanation) : There are 3 workloads W_{e1}, W_{e2}, W_{e3} operating on the storage infrastructure. The infrastructure consists of a fibre-channel switch IF_α, a storage controller SC_β and two LUNS $L_{\gamma1}, L_{\gamma2}$. The workloads access a subset of the LUNs.

5.1 Representation of the workload objects

In DECISIONQOS, the workload objects are first-class entities with the following attributes:

- **Invocation path**: It represents the physical storage components being used by the workload. Additionally, for each component being used, the workload object has information about the percentage of the component's requests that are generated by this workload. Per-component usage values are dynamic; they are constantly updated by monitoring the system. The invocation path is represented as:
$I_{e1} = \{(IF_\alpha, V_1), (SC_\beta, V_2), (L_{\gamma2}, V_3)\}$
where V_1, V_2, V_3, represents the load as the percentage of the total number of requests handled by the component.

- **Implications**: This represents the resource impact of throttling the workload, i.e., the per-component resources that will be made available as a function of throttling the workload. The impact is dynamic as it depends on the access characteristics of the workload, which are constantly changing.
$\zeta(W_\alpha, \%throttling) = \{CO_n, \%usage\ change \mid \forall\ CO_n \in I_\alpha\}$
For example, the implication of W_{e1} is represented as:
$\zeta(W_{e1}, t) = \{(IF_\alpha, f(t)), (SC_\beta, g(t)), (L_{\gamma2}, m(t))\}$
where $f(t), g(t), m(t)$ are functions of the throttling percentage t.

- **Preconditions**: Based on the SLA for each workload (we use both terms interchangeably). The preconditions are generally of the form:
$\{(x, T_1)\ , (y, T_2)\ \mid \forall x, y\ ((y < T_2) \Rightarrow (x < T_1)) \land ((y > T_2) \Rightarrow (Best\_effort))\}$

For a precondition with performance goals, the preconditions are defined in terms of throughput and latency, where $x\ \epsilon\ latency$ and $y\ \epsilon\ throughput$.

5.2 Incremental creation of the workload objects using specifications and learning

In DECISIONQOS, the workload objects are generated using an innovative combination of declarative specifications and learning. An alternative would be to observe the system behavior (by monitoring the input and output values) and interpolate the attributes of the workload object using existing machine learning algorithms. For real-world systems, this pure black-box approach is not feasible because the number of observables present in the learning space is huge, making interpolation difficult.

5.2.1 Declarative Specifications

Specifications in DECISIONQOS are non-prescriptive, i.e., they simply enumerate properties of the workload. The entities used in the specifications are referred to as the *feature-set*. The feature-set is used by the learning algorithms for monitoring and interpolation. Specifications are *incomplete* in that they do not fully quantify the values associated with the feature-set. For example, the possible specification is *throttling workload x affects component y*. In this example, y is added to the feature-set of workload x. Further, the specification is not fully quantified in that it did not specify the percentage by which x affects y. The current version of DECISIONQOS takes as input a complete formulation of the invocation paths; this can be obtained from automatic configuration discovery tools.

Specifications in DECISIONQOS define the following:

- *The precondition associated with the workload* changes quite infrequently.

- *The components in invocation path of the workload.* This information is added to the Invocation path attribute of the workload object. It defines details such as the LUNs being used by the workload, the controllers used to access these LUNs, the port numbers on the switches that connect to these controllers. The interconnection details such as port numbers, etc are based on the physical interconnection and are relatively static. The invocation path specifications are used in conjunction with monitoring to derive information such as the per-component resource usage associated with the workload.

For example, specifications for workload W_{e1} are defined as:
Precondition: {(Latency, 5 ms), (Throughput, 1000 iops)}
Invocation: $\{IF_\alpha, SC_\beta, L_{\gamma 2}\}$
This information is added to the Preconditions and Invocation path attribute for the workload object W_{e1}.

5.2.2 Learning

Learning is used to derive information associated with the workloads and the components. In DECISIONQOS, learning is a combination of on- and off-line processing. After DECISIONQOS is initially deployed, it simply records the system activity without making any decisions (*training phase*). After initial training, DECISIONQOS then starts making decisions and uses reinforcement learning to refine the literals in the interpolation function. The information derived using learning is as follows:

- *Implication attribute of the workload object, i.e.,* ζ Each time a workload is throttled, its percentage change in the usage of each component in its invocation path is measured. A learning function such as a neural net (based on reinforcement learning [12, 18, 24]) is used to interpolate the ζ function. As mentioned earlier, ζ is a dynamic function whose value changes with the access characteristics of the workload namely read/write ratio, block-size, sequential/random ratio.

- *Correlation between the workloads* Workload W_a is correlated with W_b if throttling W_a also throttles W_b. Correlation arises due to the application-level dependencies of the workloads. For example, W_a may represent the log associated with the database application while W_b represents the query processing. Workload correlation is represented as a dependency graph with weights associated to the edges of the directed graph (Figure 3). The weights represent the probability, as shown in the figure, that throttling W_1 will affect W_3 is 20%.

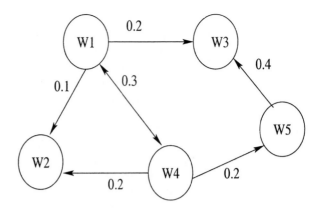

Figure 3. Correlation between the workloads

- *Behavior model of the storage components* The aim is to model the relationship between throughput and latency for each physical component such as switches, storage controllers, disks. The traditional, "hockey-stick" relationship between throughput and latency is represented by a curve where latency decreases for increasing throughput up to a point (the "knee" of the curve) beyond which increasing throughput drives latency up. The learning function interpolates the value of throughput, given the value for latency.

5.3 Reasoning

Reasoning is invoked when the SLA for any workload is violated. Reasoning is a three-step process:

- *The Problem determination* Determines the list of components whose behavior needs to change.

- *The Base reasoning* Based on the list of components whose behavior needs to be modified, this step analyzes the workload objects and derives a list of candidate workloads that can be throttled.

- *The Meta reasoning* Using the list of candidate workloads, this step determines the workloads to be actually throttled by optimizing based on the correlation between the workloads.

5.3.1 Problem determination

This step analyzes the components in the invocation path of the workload whose SLA is violated. The analysis uses the throughput-latency model of the component in conjunction with its current usage values. The algorithm for problem determination is as follows:
Input: Workloads $W_1, ..., W_\theta, ...$ whose SLA is violated
Output: A set η where each element is of the form: *(CO, Maximum change in throughput, Maximum change in*

latency)

Approach: For each workload W_θ whose SLA is violated:

- Determine the list of components in the invocation path $I_\theta = \{IF_\theta, SC_\theta, L_\theta\}$ of W_θ. Let the required change in latency for W_θ be χ.

- We want to determine the required change in the throughput of each component such that the overall latency of I_θ is reduced by χ.

- For each component, use the throughput-latency model. If the current operating point of the component is above the "knee point" (i.e., high throughput implies high latency), then continue. Else select the next component in the path.

- The maximum throughput change for a component is defined as moving the current operating point to the knee of the curve (i.e., beyond the knee, a change in throughput does not change latency). The corresponding change in latency is referred to as the maximum change in latency.

For example, assume W_{e3} is not meeting its preconditions (Goal latency = 6 ms, Current value = 10 ms, iops within specified threshold). The problem determination module analyzes the invocation path of W_{e3} which consists of $IF_\alpha, SC_\beta, L_{\gamma2}$. The average latency of $IF_\alpha = 0.5ms$, $SC_\beta = 2ms$, $L_{\gamma2} = 7.5ms$. Looking at throughput-latency for each of these components, the problem determination module determines that the number of requests serviced by SC_β can reduced by a maximum of 18% to reach the knee point, while that for $L_{\gamma2}$ by 43%. Component IF_α is operating at the knee point and does not need any changes.

5.3.2 Base reasoning

This step searches the workload objects. The semantics for searching the specifications are expressed in first-order logic.

Input: A set η of components whose behavior needs to change.

Output: A set where the elements are of the form: (Workload, *%Maximum possible throttling*)

Approach: Base reasoning is similar to constraint-solving. The input from the problem determination module can be represented as a constraint Ω: *"Find all workloads that actively use the components in η"*. The constraint is solved by analyzing the attributes of the workload object that are internally represented as *sentences* in propositional logic.

In simple words, the semantics for constraint solving are expressed in first-order logic as: *" A workload that is exceeding its SLA limits $\wedge$ Has the specified component in its*

invocation path $\wedge$ Has a non-zero implication function ζ for the specified component." Inference is carried out using first-order logic operations. In what follows, let w stand for a workload, c for a component, *curr_state* for the state of the system, and α for a requirement set such as η.

$$\forall\, w, \alpha \quad Satisfy(\alpha) \quad \Rightarrow \quad S_{Precondition}(w) \quad \wedge$$
$$S_{Invocation}(w, \alpha) \wedge S_{Implication}(w, \alpha)$$

$$\forall w \;\; S_{Precondition}(w) \Rightarrow \forall y \; Precondition(w, y) \wedge$$
$$Greater(Throughput(y), Throughput(curr\_state))$$

$$\forall\, w, \alpha \;\; S_{Invocation}(w, \alpha) \Rightarrow \exists c \; Invocation(w, c) \wedge$$
$$Equals(Component(\alpha), c)$$

$$\forall \quad w, \alpha \qquad S_{Implication}(w, \alpha) \qquad \Rightarrow$$
$$\exists! c \quad Component(\alpha) \quad \wedge \quad Implication(w, c) \quad \wedge$$
$$Greater(Interpolate(w, Access\_Patt(curr\_state), c), 0)$$

$$Equals = \{(x, y) \mid \forall\, x,\, y \; string(x) = string(y)\}$$

The function $Interpolate(x, y, z)$ approximates the impact of throttling workload x on component z, for its current access pattern y.

The base reasoning in addition to deciding the candidate workloads also prescribes the maximum allowable throttling, defined as follows:

$$\forall \quad w, t \;\; MaxThrottling(w, t) \quad \Rightarrow \quad Greater(t) \wedge$$
$$\neg\, S_{Precondition}(w)$$

In the example above, α is a workload that affects $(IF_\alpha \;\vee\; SC_\beta)$. Workload W_{e1} is selected as a candidate workload since the predicate $S_{Precondition}(W_{e1}) \wedge S_{Invocation}(W_{e1}, \alpha) \wedge S_{Implication}(W_{e1}, \alpha)$ is true.

5.3.3 Meta reasoning

This step selects the workloads to be throttled from the set of candidate workloads. This selection is based on an optimization goal such as minimizing the side-effects of throttling the workload, or minimize variance in resource utilization, etc. We describe details of meta reasoning with the goal function for minimizing the side-effects of throttling workloads.

Input: A set of candidate workloads W_C which is of the form (Workload, *%Max. possible throttling*, impact function for each component); plus a set of the form (Component, Max possible change in throughput); plus a set of constraints of the form (Set of components, Total required change in latency)

Output: The throttling decisions which is a set of the form: (Workload, *%Throttling*)

Approach: As mentioned earlier, the correlation between the workloads is represented as a directed graph (as in Figure 3). The weight on the edges is expressed as a probability $P(A \Rightarrow B)$.

- Let the set of all the workloads be represented by W.

- Calculate the weight associated with each workload in the set of candidate workloads W_C
  $$Weight_\Phi = \Sigma_{\Omega \in (W \cap W_C)}, P(\Phi \Rightarrow \Omega)$$

- The elements in W_C are sorted in ascending-order based on their weight. The smaller the weight, the more preferable is the workload.

- Throttle first element in W_C. If (SLA met) then terminate. Else remove the first element, and repeat this step.

6 Related work

The related research is divided into two domains:

- Resource arbitration frameworks

- Policy-based management and AI-based frameworks

6.1 Resource arbitration frameworks

Resource arbitration frameworks such as Façade [21] provide a per-workload storage performance monitoring and QoS enforcement capabilities. Façade is built using a central scheduler that regulates the rates of I/O workloads accessing a common storage container such as a RAID logical disk. Façade does not account for competing workloads sharing resources in various degrees, e.g., two logical units in the same vs. in different disk arrays; and it throttles all workloads to similar degrees when QoS violations occur. Sleds [8] can selectively throttle only the workloads supposedly responsible for the QoS violations, and has a decentralized architecture that scales better than Façade's. However, the policies for deciding which workload to throttle are hard-wired and will not adapt to changing conditions.

The problem of resource arbitration has also been addressed in domains other than storage systems. Many networking solutions [3] are based on selectively dropping packets [7]. They do not extend to widespread storage access protocols [2] for multiple reasons [28], including the severe consequences of packet loss. Proposals like Diff-Serv [7] are not rich enough to distinguish all service classes that may need to be treated differently.

6.2 Policy-based management and AI-based approaches

Policy based infrastructures have been used to automate the task of management [22, 26]. In these applications, the underlying policy specification model is based on ECA. There are multiple approaches (i.e., syntax) for specifying policies: Specified in terms of a special language that is processed and interpreted as a piece of software [4] or in terms of a formal specification language [9] or the simplest approach is to interpret policies as a sequence of rules. The IETF has chosen rule-based policy representation in its specifications [17, 23]. The problems of brittleness and complexity are one of the primary reasons limiting the wide-spread usages of policy-based management (which is precisely the problem a logic-based approach such as DECISIONQOS aims to solve).

A variation of policy-based management has been proposed in [27]. They use a Case-Based Reasoning approach, in which a system starts off with no specifications and uses the previously learnt cases to decide how a goal should be transformed, has been employed in the webserver configuration domain. The bootstrapping behavior of that approach is not attractive in real-world scenarios where the reasonable number of cases that need to be learned a priori are 0 (resource states, workload characteristics, goals, action set). Bearden *et al.* [5] propose an approach to separate the goal from the base rule specification. They create a mapping between each rule and user requirements, making it easy to validate a rule set. The DECISIONQOS approach is more sophisticated, in that it encodes the goal implications and uses them to automate the reasoning process.

An approach that uses genetic algorithms for self-tuning has also been proposed [11]. In this approach each system parameter is tuned by an individual algorithm and the genetic algorithm decides the best combination of algorithms. Unlike DECISIONQOS, this approach does not allow refinement of the decision-making based on learning. Zinky *et al.*, [30] present a general framework, called QuO, to implement QoS-enabled distributed object systems. The QoS adaptation is achieved by having multiple implementations. Each implementation is mapped to an environment and a QoS region. This approach is static, as it does not implement semantics for reasoning about the various possible configurations.

DECISIONQOS leverages concepts in AI and uses them as building blocks in its solution. Techniques for specification in expert systems are broadly classified as imperative (e.g., rule-based), declarative (e.g., logic programming) or mixed. Brittleness has been identified as the biggest drawback of imperative rule-based systems [10], whereas logic based systems overcome this problem by using a reasoning engine to combine facts/beliefs in the knowledge base to draw conclusions. The DECISIONQOS specification of action attributes is similar to the declarative approach. Further, reasoning in DECISIONQOS is a combination of specification search algorithms and higher-order operations. DECISIONQOS uses forward chaining to search the specifications, but it is possible to use other approaches such as backward chaining or heuristic-based searching. Other popular approaches for reasoning are: Model-based, Constraint-based, and Case-based reasoning [20]. Finally, learning in DECISIONQOS systematically refines the specifications. It leverages research in the domain of machine learning algorithms such as neural networks and reinforcement learning [12, 18, 24].

7 Conclusions

Most applications running on an enterprise data center depend on getting minimum performance levels from the storage system; if that cannot be provided, they fail. The typical scenario where many applications compete for relatively few high-end resources such as network switches and disk arrays is not well suited for predictable sharing. Because of their workload characteristics and of scheduling idiosyncrasies, resources will not be distributed according to each application's needs in the absence of a regulating entity.

We present DECISIONQOS, a novel paradigm for building resource arbitration modules, and discuss its application to storage systems. DECISIONQOS relies on declarative specifications and on machine learning techniques to keep an up-to-date body of knowledge about the storage system and the workloads running on it. This body of knowledge captures the concepts of physical and logical resource sharing, dependencies and correlations among different workloads, and fluctuations in the performance experienced by clients as a result of workload or system changes. DECISIONQOS does not require detailed descriptions as its initial input; system administrators can just supply whatever information is available to them, and DECISIONQOS will supplement and/or amend it by dynamically observing the system's behavior.

DECISIONQOS relieves users from the burdens (common in rule-based systems) of coding policies into unstructured sets of event-condition-action rules. Such rule sets are hard to tune, modify, and maintain, for they require users to foresee at rule-creation time all the relevant families of system states, the threshold values that determine when actions should be taken, and the particular actions prescribed for each state. In contrast, DECISIONQOS hides from users the complexity of individual decisions, letting users concentrate on the declarative, high-level aspects of system behavior. The important point about this work however is not that a declarative specification is preferable but rather that the

only rational course of action in QoS management is to relate policy to observation. This is because provisioning for QoS has intrinsic uncertainties that can only be solved by observing the system. The end result is that DECISIONQOS does not depend on human experts, and is significantly more resilient to the inevitable changes that will arise in practical systems.

References

[1] G.A. Alvarez, E. Borowsky, S. Go, T. Romer, R. Becker-Szendy, R. Golding, A. Merchant, M. Spasojevic, A. Veitch, and J. Wilkes. Minerva: An automated resource provisioning tool for large-scale storage systems. *ACM Transactions on Computer Systems*, 19(4):483–518, November 2001.

[2] ANSI. SCSI architecture model - 2 (SAM-2), September 2002. Draft Standard, Project 1157-D, Revision 24.

[3] C. Aurrecoechea, A. Campbell, and L. Hauw. A survey of QoS architectures. *Multimedia Systems*, 6(3):138–151, 1998.

[4] J. F. Barnes and R. Pandey. CacheL: Language support for customizable caching policies. In *Proceedings of the 4th International Web Caching Workshop*, 1999.

[5] M. Bearden, S. Garg, and W.J. Lee. Integrating goal specification in policy-based management. In *Proc. Int'l Workshop on Policies for Distributed Systems and Networks*, January 2001.

[6] J.P. Bigus, D.A. Schlosnagle, J.R. Pilgrim, W.N. Mills III, and Y. Diao. ABLE: A Toolkit for Building Multiagent Autonomic Systems. *IBM Sys. J.*, 41(3), September 2002.

[7] S. Blake, D. Black, M. Carlson, E. Davies, Z. Wang, and W. Weiss. An architecture for differentiated services. *IETF RFC 2475*, 1998.

[8] D. Chambliss, G. A. Alvarez, P. Pandey, D. Jadav, J. Xu, R. Menon, and T. Lee. Performance virtualization for large-scale storage systems. In *Proceedings of the 22nd Symposium on Reliable Distributed Systems*, October 2003.

[9] R. Darimont, E. Delor, P. Massonet, and A. van Lamsweerde. GRAIL/KAOS: An environment for goal-driven requirements engineering. In *Proc. ICSE'98 - 20th Intl. Conference on Software Engineering*, 1998.

[10] V. Dhar and H.E. Pople. Rule-based versus structure-based models for explaining and generating expert behavior. *Comm. ACM*, 30(6), June 1987.

[11] D. Feitelson and M. Naaman. Self-tuning systems. *IEEE Software*, 16(2):52–60, 1999.

[12] J. Ghosh and A. Nag. *An Overview of Radial Basis Function Networks*. Radial Basis Function Neural Network Theory and Applications, Physica-Verlag, 2000.

[13] C. Green. Application of theorem proving to problem solving. In B. L. Webber and N. J. Nilsson, editors, *Readings in Artificial Intelligence*, pages 202–222. Kaufmann, Los Altos, CA, 1981.

[14] F. Hayes-Roth. Rule-based Systems. *Comm. ACM*, 28(9), September 1985.

[15] C. Hewitt. Planner: A language for proving theorems in robots. In *Proc. of the 1st IJCAI*, pages 295–301, Washington, DC, 1969.

[16] C. Hewitt. Procedural embedding of knowledge in planner. In *Proc. of the 2nd IJCAI*, pages 167–182, London, UK, 1971.

[17] IETF Policy Framework Working Group. IETF Policy Charter. http://www.ietf.org/html.charters/policy-charter.html.

[18] T. Kohonen. *Self-Organizing and Associative Memory 3rd ed.* Springer-Verlag, 1988.

[19] R. Kowalski. Predicate logic as programming language. In Jack L. Rosenfeld, editor, *Proceedings of the Sixth IFIP Congress (Information Processing 74)*, pages 569–574, Stockholm, Sweden, August 1974.

[20] D.B. Leake. *Case-Based Reasoning: Experiences, Lessons and Future Directions*. AAAI Press, 1996.

[21] C. Lumb, A. Merchant, and G.A. Alvarez. Façade: Virtual storage devices with performance guarantees. In *Proc. 2nd Conf. on File and Storage Technologies (FAST)*, pages 131–144, April 2003.

[22] E. Lupu M. Sloman. Security and management policy specification. *IEEE Network*, March 2002.

[23] B. Moore. Network Working Group – RFC3060. Policy Core Information Model – Version 1 Specification. http://www.ietf.org/rfc/rfc3060.txt, 2001.

[24] D.E. Rumelhart, G.E. Hinton, and R.J. Williams. Learning Internal Representations Through Error Propagation. In D.E. Rumelhart and J.L. McClelland, editors, *Parallel Distributed Processing: Experiments in the Microstructure of Cognition, Vol. 1*. MIT Press, 1986.

[25] S. Uttamchandani, K. Voruganti, S. Srinivasan, J. Palmer, and D. Pease. Polus: Growing storage QoS management beyond a 4-year old kid. In *Proc. 3rd Conf. on File and Storage Technologies*, March 2004.

[26] D. Verma. Simplifying network administration using policy based management. (2), March 2002.

[27] D. Verma and S. Calo. Goal Oriented Policy Determination. In *Proc. 1st Workshop on Algorithms and Architectures for Self-Managing Sys.*, pages 1–6. ACM, June 2003.

[28] J. Wilkes. Travelling to Rome: QoS specifications for automated storage system management. In D. Hutchinson L. Wolf and R. Steinmetz, editors, *Proceedings of 9th International Workshop on Quality Of Service (IWQoS)*, pages 75–91. Springer Verlag, June 1991.

[29] T. Winograd. Frame representations and the declarative/procedural controversy. In R. J. Brachman and H. J. Levesque, editors, *Readings in Knowledge Representation*, pages 357–370. Kaufmann, Los Altos, CA, 1985.

[30] J. A. Zinky, D. E. Bakken, and R. D. Schantz. Architectural support for Quality-of-Service for CORBA objects. *Theory and Practice of Object Systems*, 3(1), 1997.

Policy-Based Validation of SAN Configuration

Dakshi Agrawal*   James Giles*   Kang-Won Lee*   Kaladhar Voruganti[†]   Khalid Filali-Adib[‡]
* *IBM T. J. Watson Research Center*   † *IBM Almaden Research*   ‡ *IBM Austin Research*
{*agrawal,gilesjam,kangwon,kaladhar,filali*}*@us.ibm.com*

Abstract

Historically, storage has been directly connected to servers for fast local access and easy configuration. In recent years, storage area networks (SANs) have defined an alternative storage paradigm that allows storage to be shared among servers using fast interconnects. One of the key challenges of SAN management is the large number of configuration problems that are encountered in a typical SAN deployment. These configuration problems can be addressed by SAN management software. However, hard-coding the SAN configuration rules into the management software is not a viable option since it is not possible to easily modify or replace old configuration rules and specify new policies and guidelines. In this paper, we propose a novel policy-based SAN configuration validation system that can be used to specify, store, and evaluate configuration policies for SANs. We also introduce five new operators for collection policies that are useful for evaluating a wide variety of practical SAN configuration policies found in practice. The policy-based SAN configuration checking approach proposed in this paper is discussed within the context of device interoperability constraints. However, this approach is extensible as it can also be used to enforce performance, reliability, and security-related configuration constraints.

1 Introduction

Historically, storage has been connected to servers in a direct attached storage paradigm. However, there is a limit to the amount of storage that can be added to a particular server, implying that increasing storage sometimes requires adding servers even if extra computing power is not needed. Another limitation of direct attached storage is that it is difficult to share storage among multiple servers because each server has to route its data requests for remote storage through the remote server associated with that particular storage. Storage area networks (SANs) define an alternative storage paradigm that allows storage to be shared among servers such that storage purchasing and server purchasing are decoupled. The dominant SAN protocol, Fiber Channel (FC), does not suffer from the distance and device connectivity limitations of the parallel SCSI transport protocol used for direct attached storage, and it is much more mature than competing network attached storage protocols such as the iSCSI transport protocol.

However, one of the key challenges of FC SAN management is the large number of configuration problems that are encountered when (a) adding/removing devices in an existing SAN, (b) provisioning new storage, (c) upgrading firmware or device drivers, and (d) trying to ensure a certain level of reliability and security in the SAN. System administrators spend many hours troubleshooting SAN configuration problems.

SAN configuration problems are typically caused by one or more of the following reasons:

- Absence of proper device drivers with the correct level of functionality.

- Connection of incompatible devices.

- Incorrect zoning of devices.

- Configuration of the SAN that does not satisfy the reliability, performance, and security requirements.

The above SAN configuration problems can be avoided by using SAN management software. SAN management software queries the SAN devices (both hardware and software components) to determine their status, configuration, and properties. Constraints can be encoded into the SAN management software that will allow it to detect configuration problems.

Hard-coding the SAN configuration constraints into the management software, however, is not desirable due to the following reasons:

- Newer versions of SAN software and hardware components have different interoperability track records. Thus, management software must be able to handle changes in existing SAN configuration rules.

- Changing business guidelines may require activation of new rules or deactivation of existing rules.

- Different actions may need to be taken when a particular rule is violated.

- In systems with thousands of rules, it is difficult for a human to determine conflicts between rules, assign priorities, and specify the sequence of execution of the rules.

Thus, it is necessary to enhance existing SAN management programs with policy management functionality to address these shortcomings of manual or hard-coded SAN configuration checking. Furthermore, it is also necessary for SAN management software to download the latest SAN configuration policies from a centralized repository (similar to anti-virus scan downloads that are located at a remote site). The policies defined in the centralized repository can be informed by input from field technicians, interoperability lab reports, and manufacturer product specifications.

In this paper, we propose a framework for policy-enabled SAN management software to address the SAN configuration checking problems. In the proposed framework, the configuration of a SAN is scanned periodically, or whenever a hardware or software component change occurs, or when the system administrator explicitly invokes a checking process. Alternatively, a detailed plan of a to-be-deployed SAN can be used as input so that the architect of a SAN may discover configuration errors during the design phase before actually deploying the plan. This configuration is dumped into a SAN Database in a canonical data format for consumption by the Policy Event Generator. Based on the changes in the SAN configuration, the Policy Event Generator creates new SAN policy events to trigger the Policy Evaluation process. If, during the evaluation process, a configuration violation has been detected, the corresponding actions to correct the error will be invoked.

This paper presents a design of the proposed SAN management architecture detailing the role of each component and the interactions between the modules. We also show that the composite nature of the SAN structure and the corresponding policy scopes can be exploited to build an efficient evaluator. Furthermore, we introduce five new operators for collection policies that are useful for evaluating a wide variety of practical SAN configuration policies defined by field experts. While in this paper we only address the issue of checking device interoperability constraints, our approach can easily be extended to enforce performance, reliability, and security related configuration constraints.

The remainder of this paper is organized as follows: Section 2 provides a brief introduction to SANs and presents a few example policies. Section 3 describes the overall architecture of the proposed SAN management system. Section 4 presents the policy model and collection policy operators. Section 5 presents details for components of the architecture. Section 6 presents work related to our paper. Section 7 discusses our conclusions and future work. Finally the appendix presents the 64 SAN configuration policies that we collected from SAN administrators and used in our design and prototype implementation.

2 Background

This section provides a simple introduction to storage area networks and illustrates some example policies used for configuration validation of SANs. Storage area networks provide interconnection between servers and consolidated storage devices. Current storage area networks are predominantly based on the Fiber Channel (FC) protocol, which provides reliable transport of storage I/O at gigabit speeds.[1]

Figure 1 shows a typical SAN configuration consisting of hosts (servers) and various types of storage devices. Hosts access the fabric via host bus adapters (HBAs), which play a role similar to network adapters and allow hosts to connect to the storage network. Similarly, storage devices are connected to the fabric via storage controllers. The fabric can include one or more of the following components: point-to-point link, arbitrated loop, and fabric switch. Point-to-point link provides a dedicated connection between two end-points (hosts, storage devices, or switches). Arbitrated loop is a shared media where multiple end-points connect in a logical ring topology. The operation of the loop is similar to that of the token ring; an end-point must first acquire a token before it sends data. The fabric switch provides data transport at the switched bandwidth of 100MBps per port. Additionally the fabric switch provides configuration capabilities including various types of zoning. By setting up zones, a SAN administrator can define an exclusive group of ports so that only permitted hosts can access certain storage devices.

Below we present some sample SAN configuration policies, which represent best practices for interoperability, performance, and security. In the appendix, we provide a comprehensive list of SAN configuration policies that have been defined by field experts.

- The same HBA cannot be used to access both tape and disk devices.

- No arbitrated loops are allowed in the FC fabric.

- The fabric cannot contain HBAs having a version below a certain level.

---

[1]Depending on types, the raw data rate of FC is either 1 or 2 Gbps. After the 8b/10b data encoding the actual data bandwidth of a 1 Gbps FC is about 100MBps.

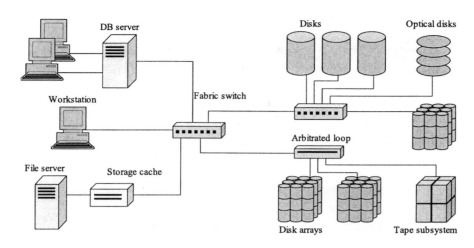

Figure 1. A typical storage area network configuration

- A host needs to have at least two disjoint paths to each storage device for reliability.

- The number of hops between the host and the storage device should be no more than N.

- All HBAs in a host logical partition must be of the same type.

- There cannot be more than 3 servers in an arbitrated loop.

As one can see, these configuration rules are easy to understand and describe in plain English. However, SANs are complex systems, consisting of multiple servers each with multiple HBAs, servers and HBAs with many software and firmware components, storage devices of multiple varieties with many different configuration parameters, and a SAN fabric consisting of various types of fabric switches, point-to-point links, and arbitrated loops. Because of this inherent complexity, manually validating these rules is a nightmare to the SAN administrator for even a modest-scale storage network. Furthermore, manually fixing the configuration problem is an error-prone process during which new errors may be introduced. The objective of this paper is to provide a policy framework that can automate the process of validating and enforcing the policies of the above type so that the SAN management can be greatly simplified.

3 Architecture Overview

In this section we provide an overview of the proposed SAN configuration management architecture as illustrated in Figure 2.

The SAN configuration management system is used to check the configuration of a SAN, which can either be a physically deployed SAN or planned SAN. For a physically deployed SAN, management agents query the SAN fabric and store the configuration information in a SAN Database using a format consistent with the Storage Management Initiative Standard (SMI-S) representation. For a planned SAN, the SAN planning software exports the designed configuration to a SAN Database.

The SAN configuration management system has a Policy Specification Tool that is used by a system administrator to author system configuration policies. The graphical user interface allows the author to build policies by combining system attributes with functions provided by the policy language. The policies in the SAN manager are specified in terms of a four-tuple: scope, condition, action, and priority, and are similar to those used by the PCIM specification [13]. Scope is used to group policies into sets that are applicable to particular system components, such as ports or HBAs, and identifies the set of attributes that may be included in the policy condition. Condition is a logical expression written on the attributes which determines if a policy is applicable for particular values of the attributes. Action describes the steps that should be taken by the system if the policy is applicable. Priority describes the relative importance of a policy (higher priority policies are chosen over lower priority policies when both the policies are applicable). The Policy Specification Tool stores authored policies in a policy repository.

The two types of policy repositories used by the SAN Manager are the Remote Centralized Policy Database and the Local Policy Database. The Remote Centralized Policy Database is a central repository that stores the configuration policies for many SAN managers. A distribution mechanism pushes policy updates from the Remote Centralized Policy Database to each SAN manager's Local Pol-

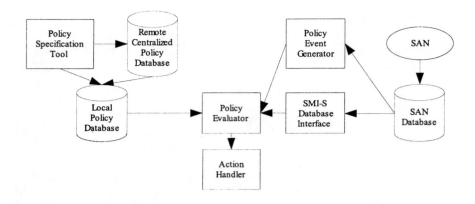

Figure 2. SAN management system architecture

icy Database. The Local Policy Database is co-located with an instance of a SAN manager and stores the configuration policies for that SAN manager. It can receive policies from a Remote Centralized Policy Database, or policies can be defined directly for the Local Policy Database by a system administrator using a Policy Specification Tool.

The Policy Event Generator component monitors changes to the SAN configuration by listening for changes in the SAN Database. When there is a change to an element in the SAN, the Policy Event Generator triggers an event and identifies the policy scopes that are applicable for the event. For example, a change to Fiber Channel port could trigger an event that would be relevant to port and host policies. The Policy Event Generator passes the applicable scopes to the Policy Evaluator for further processing. The Policy Event Generator can also be used by a system administrator to trigger configuration checking for subsets of the SAN, or the Policy Event Generator can be used by additional components to trigger configuration checking.

The Policy Evaluator component takes a list of scopes from the Policy Event Generator and selects the policies that are applicable to the scopes. To evaluate the selected policies, the Policy Evaluator identifies the SAN attributes referenced by the policies and requests those attributes from the SMI-S Database Interface. The gathered attributes are used to compute the condition of each of the selected policies. Among policies for which the condition evaluates to true, if any, the highest priority policy is selected. The action for the selected policy is passed to the Action Handler.

The Action Handler component takes actions passed from the Policy Evaluator, and invokes the specified actions. For example, the action can specify that an e-mail message be sent to a system administrator if the SAN configuration violates certain constraints. An action may also specify a function that can rectify a system configuration problem, such as performing a rezoning action when there is a zone configuration problem.

The SMI-S Database Interface collects system configuration attributes from the SAN Database or directly from the physically deployed system. It provides an abstraction for accessing system data so that the Policy Evaluator does not need to know the specifics of the SAN Database or how to query the SAN fabric.

4 Data and Policy Model

The typical size of SAN configuration data can easily run into several megabytes. Furthermore, there could be hundreds of configuration policies in the policy repository. A good organization of SAN configuration data and policies is critical for the good performance of the validation system.

4.1 Policy Scope Taxonomy

The first step toward data and policy modeling is to collect typical configuration policies and analyze them for the attributes that they validate. Using such policies, we modeled data for SAN components and major concepts such as host, switch, storage device, host bus adapter (HBA), port-controller, port, link, fabric, and zone. Our data models were inspired by the SMI-S standards, and they represent a subset necessary for the policy evaluation. For each given component type, we divide corresponding data into two parts: data describing *intrinsic properties* and data describing *associated components*. For example, for an HBA, its serial number, state, id, model name, vendor name, installed software, and hardware characteristics are defined to be its intrinsic properties. On the other hand, the ports contained in it, and the host in which the HBA is contained are defined to be the components associated with an HBA. This distinction of data for a component type turns out to be quite useful, since a close inspection of configuration policies reveals that there are three types of policies:

- **Intra-component Policies:** policies that validate constraints on the intrinsic properties of a single SAN component. An example policy is "An HBA from vendor X should have firmware level greater than Y". This policy may have been created because firmware levels less than or equal to Y for HBAs of vendor X are known to have a bug leading to sporadic data losses.

- **Inter-component Policies:** policies that validate intrinsic properties of one SAN component with respect to the intrinsic properties of another SAN component. An example of policy is "A host with operating system AIX version X should not have an HBA from vendor Y with firmware level greater than Z. This policy may be in force if the OS has only been certified up to a certain HBA firmware level.

- **Collection Policies:** policies that validate properties of a group of SAN components. An example policy is "All HBAs in a host should be from the same manufacturer". This policy may be enforced for reliability and interoperability reasons.

Based on our analysis of SAN components and policies we developed a policy scope taxonomy. In this classification, policies are first divided on the basis of the type of component they validate. Thus, a policy validating intra-HBA constraints would fall under the scope "HBAPolicies". A policy prescribing interoperability constraints between host OS and HBA firmware level would carry two scopes "HBAPolicies" and "HostPolicies". A policy mandating uniformity among HBAs of the same host would fall under "HBAPolicies". For each component type, the policies are further subdivided based on the three type of policies described above. Thus, all "HBAPolicies" may be divided into the following scopes, for instance:

- **IntraHBAPolicies.** Policies that validate constraints on the intrinsic properties of a single HBA.

- **InterHostHBAPolicies.** Policies that validate constraints between a host and a resident HBA.

- **InterHBAPortPolicies.** Policies that validate constraints between an HBA and a resident port.

- **HostHBACollectionPolicies.** Policies that validate constraints among all HBAs of a host.

- **ZoneHBACollectionPolicies.** Policies that validate constraints among all HBAs of a zone.

- **GeneralHBACollectionPolicies.** Policies that validate constraints among all HBAs in a SAN.

The advantage of making these policy subgroups will become clear in the next section when we describe architecture components in more detail. Essentially, this scope taxonomy allows us to build efficient policy evaluation for a given SAN event.

4.2 Collection Policies

In general, policies can be classified on the basis of the condition part of their four-tuple. At the first look, it may seem the conditions in the SAN configuration policies presented in the appendix do not present a structure for parsing and evaluation. However, more insight can be gained by expanding the Boolean expression representing the condition of a policy as an expression tree. We found that the expression tree of policy conditions mostly contains basic operators such as logical composite operators (AND, OR, NOT) and comparison operators ($>$, $<$, $\geq$, $\leq$, $==$) with the five notable exceptions. All five exceptions are operations on a collection of elements. In the following, we describe these new operations.

Assume that a collection C has elements $O_1, O_2, \ldots, O_n$. Further assume that each element in C has m attributes $p_1, \ldots, p_m$. Now consider the following five operations on the collection C.

- **Cartesian Property:** Given sets of values $A_1, \ldots, A_m$ for attributes $p_1, \ldots, p_m$ respectively, return all elements O_i in C that satisfy the condition $(O_i.p_1 \in A_1) \wedge \ldots \wedge (O_i.p_m \in A_m)$.
  - *Example Policy:* All HBAs of type Emulex 9002 must have firmware level of either 3.81a, 3.81b, 3.82, or 3.84.

- **Graph:** Given a directed graph $G = (E, C)$ (graph with elements in C as its vertices, and directed edges in E between them), and two elements O_i and O_j, return all directed paths between O_i and O_j.
  - *Example Policy:* All hosts must have more than k paths to target.

- **Exclusion:** Given sets of values $A_{1,1}, \ldots, A_{1,m}$ and sets of values $A_{2,1}, \ldots, A_{2,m}$, for attributes $p_1, \ldots, p_m$ respectively, return all elements O_i in C that satisfy the condition $(O_i.p_1 \in A_{1,1}) \wedge \ldots \wedge (O_i.p_m \in A_{1,m})$ while another element O_j, $j \neq i$, simultaneously satisfies $(O_j.p_1 \in A_{2,1}) \wedge \ldots \wedge (O_j.p_m \in A_{2,m})$.
  - *Example Policy:* Tape drives should not exist in a zone if it contains disk drives.

Cartesian	(1) (2) (4) (5) (6) (7) (11) (12) (15) (18) (19) (20) (21) (22) (23) (24) (25) (26) (27) (30) (31) (32) (33) (34) (35) (36) (37) (38) (40) (41) (42) (43) (47) (48) (49) (51) (52) (53) (54) (56) (57) (58) (60) (61) (62) (63)
Graph	(3) (15) (16) (17) (22) (23) (26) (34) (35) (51) (54) (57) (60) (61) (62)
Exclusion	(8) (28) (29) (50)
Many-to-One	(9) (10) (14) (39) (44) (45) (46) (59) (64)
One-to-One	(55)

Figure 3. Mapping of the SAN configuration policies to collection operators

- **Many-to-One:** The value of an attribute p_i, $1 \leqslant i \leqslant m$ should be the same for all elements in C. If this is not the case, then return subsets of C constructed by partitioning C according to the values of p_i.
  - *Example Policy:* Only one host type should exist in a zone.

- **One-to-One:** The value of an attribute p_i should be different for all elements in C. If this is not the case, then return subsets of C constructed by partitioning C according to the values of p_i.
  - *Example Policy:* No two devices in the system can have the same WWN (World-Wide Name).

In the appendix, we list 64 types of actual SAN configuration policies collected from field experts. Figure 3 shows how each policy can be modeled and expressed using the above five collection operators. The figure shows that the Cartesian Property operator is most popularly used and therefore the policy evaluator must implement it in an efficient manner.

5 Architecture Details

This section now describes the details of each component of the architecture.

5.1 Local Policy Repository

The design of the local policy repository has been driven by two critical requirements: First, the repository should be able to quickly retrieve all policies relevant to a Policy Request and pass it to the Policy Evaluator. Second, the repository should provide standard version control features: the ability to maintain multiple versions of policy documents, the ability to roll-back to an older version of a policy document, and the ability to maintain a coherent set of policies to the Policy Evaluator in the presence of concurrent modifications to the policy documents.

These requirements are met by implementing the policy repository in two parts: a persistent part that stores multiple versions of policy documents and resides in a concurrent version system, and a policy cache that stores the currently enforced policy document in a compiled format and resides in the random-access memory of the SAN management system. The persistent part maintains a history of policy documents and a coherent set of policies in the presence of multiple authors trying to modify the policy document. The cache stores policies in a hash table, hashed by their policy scope. If the policy scopes are chosen carefully, then each Policy Event only triggers policies corresponding to a small number of scopes, and the policy evaluator can query the cache and efficiently retrieve all policies in a compiled format.

Upon receiving a new policy document, the persistent part of the policy repository validates the syntax of the new policy document. If the document passes validation checks, then it notifies the policy cache. The policy cache retrieves the most recent policy document, compiles it to an expression tree suitable for policy evaluation and stores policies contained in the document in a temporary hash table. Once the compilation is finished, it switches to the newly compiled policies.

5.2 Policy Evaluator

The Policy Evaluator operates on the boolean expressions that represent the policy conditions. Boolean expressions are compiled into the form of an expression tree, with the nodes being the operators and the children nodes being the operands. The operators include logical operators and comparison operators, as well as the five collection operators discussed in the previous sections. The evaluator computes the value of the expression in a depth-first traversal order. The Policy Evaluator is optimized for performance by caching sub-expressions that appear more than once in the expression trees. Such sub-expressions representing the policy conditions are evaluated only once, with the results being cached to avoid repeated evaluations.

The policy evaluator obtains the data needed to evaluate the expression tree from the SMI-S Data Layer which is described in subsection 5.4. When a request for policy evaluation of a given scope is triggered, the attribute values for the corresponding objects are obtained by the SMI-S Data Layer and are cached so that they do not have to be fetched during evaluation of the tree for policies corresponding to the scope and its sub-scopes.

5.3 Policy Request Generator

The Policy Request Generator is responsible for sending properly formatted requests for configuration checks to the Policy Evaluator. The Request Generator sends a request based on input from two sources: the user interface where a user can ask the request generator to run a specific configuration check, or the SAN configuration database, where a stored procedure can send a notification every time a configuration change takes places. Typically, a user asks to run a specific configuration check for routine maintenance or for trouble-shooting a configuration problem. Alternatively, some typical actions that would trigger a notification by the SAN configuration database to the Policy Request Generator are as follows:

- Addition/removal/failure of SAN components.
- Firmware upgrade/downgrade of SAN component.
- Zoning operations.
- Software configuration changes.

Once the Policy Request Generator receives a triggering event, it examines the event to see if a new request for configuration checking should be generated. For example, the configuration of a SAN may change during business hours to provide more resources to business customers. The Policy Request Generator in our architecture filters out such triggering events. The filtering of events in the request generator is governed by meta-policies that are input by the system administrator. These meta-policies are stored in a local policy repository under a scope.

If the trigger event qualifies, the Policy Request Generator generates a corresponding request for configuration checking. The request for configuration checking includes a policy scope to indicate all the policies that need to be checked, and the identification of affected system component. For example, if the triggering event is an upgrade of the firmware of an HBA, then the attached scope would include HBAPolicies (policies checking configuration of a single HBA) and the request for checking configuration policies would carry the globally unique (GUID) of the affected HBA.

5.4 SMI-S Data Layer

Depending upon the scope of the involved policies, the policy evaluator obtains the necessary policy data from the storage management initiative standard (SMI-S) data layer. SMI-S is a SNIA standard that uses DMTF CIM modeling technology to model both physical storage devices such as switches, storage arrays and hosts, and also logical storage components such as volumes, extents, LUNs etc. Since the

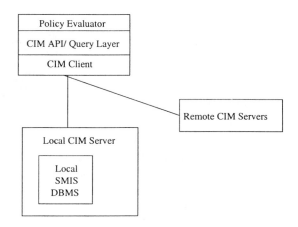

Figure 4. SMI-S Data Layer

SMI-S standard is being supported by most storage vendors, use of SMI-S entities and attributes in the policy framework to represent storage resources allows the policy framework described in this paper to be used in a vendor-neutral manner. As shown in Figure 4, the policy evaluator layer invokes the CIM-SMI-S APIs that could potentially be accessing data from a database management system (DBMS) under the covers, or could be directly contacting the storage devices. In either case, the SMI-S data layer maintains a cache of objects at the policy manager location to ensure that the same data is not retrieved multiple times if it is needed by multiple policies.

When the SMI-S data layer is utilizing a DBMS, it relies on the DBMS cache manager to provide the caching functionality and the CIM API/Query language layers leverage the SQL querying capability of the underlying DBMS to query the SMI-S database. The policy evaluator layer can potentially directly access (instead of CIM APIs or query language) the data from the DBMS but then the code will not be portable for cases where the data is being retrieved from remote storage devices and not from a local DBMS. As described above, use of the CIM API layer insulates the policy management software from the location details of where the information is stored (i.e. data could be located at remote devices).

Figure 5 shows the entities of the SMI-S schema that map to some of the key storage devices. ComputerSystem, PhysicalPackage, SoftwareElement, and FCPort are some of the SMI-S classes that are used in the SAN configuration checker. The ComputerSystem class represents a switch, a storage array, or a host. The PhysicalPackage class represents the hardware characteristics (manufacturer, model number) of a ComputerSystem, while the SoftwareElement class corresponds to software characteristics (firmware level, OS level, device driver level) of a ComputerSystem. It is important to note that the ComputerSystem

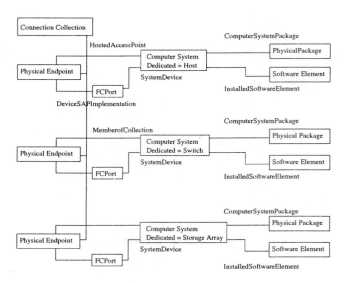

Figure 5. SMI-S Classes

class does not contain hardware and software information as its attributes, but instead it points to separate classes that contain this information. Finally, FCPort corresponds to Fiber Channel ports present in each of the storage devices.

Hence, the policy evaluator layer can use a combination of CIM-SMI-S query language or CIM hierarchy traversal APIs to access the device data. The following examples briefly illustrate how different types of data can be accessed from the SMI-S data layer:

- If the policy evaluator layer wants to get a list of all the hosts in the system then it can issue a SQL-like SMI-S query to the ComputerSystem class where it specifies the value of "HOSTS" for the dedicated field. The value "HOSTS" implies that it is searching for Hosts.

- If the policy evaluator layer wants to find the software installed on a particular host, then it can use the CIM Associator API to traverse the InstalledSoftwareElement link to arrive at the corresponding SoftwareElement class instance. Similarly, if it wants to find information about the manufacturer of a host then it can find this information by traversing the ComputerSystemPackage associator link.

5.5 Action Handler

The *Action Handler* is responsible for taking the actions specified by the Policy Evaluator component. The Action Handler is an extensible SMI-S compliant component that is capable of manipulating components in the SAN as well as generating workflows of predefined or customized actions. There are three broad types of actions that the action handler might issue. The first type of action is invoked by

calling well-defined procedures through the SAN management API (can be either SMI-S or non-SMI-S based) interfaces. For example, regrouping devices in a zone, creating a logical volume on a disk, or making a data copy from one storage device to another can be done by invoking SMI-S StorageConfigurationService and ZoneService methods. Thus, SMI-S is trying to standardize SAN management actions by defining various types of service classes. Another type of action is triggered by a workflow manager. For example, if a configuration violation is identified by a policy that specifies the action that the corresponding SAN components should be shut down, the Action Handler starts a workflow that manipulates the SAN components using the SMI-S specifications. Similarly, if the firmware version of a device does not conform to the version requirement indicated in the policy, then it may specify the Action Handler to start a workflow to replace the firmware of the device with a higher version. Finally, the third type of action is designed to help and bring attention to human operators. These predefined actions include the ability to send messages to a console or send e-mail to a system administrator. By extending the Action Handler, additional customized actions can easily be added.

6 Related Work

Policy-based management and auditing has been proposed for a wide variety of systems [14, 1]. For example, [12] proposed a policy management system for managing and validating Internet Security Protocol Suite (IPSec) policies to ensure end-to-end secure service. The IPSec management system allows users to define high-level security requirements, and then uses those requirements to detect and resolve conflicts in the specific IPSec policies.

There are many examples of policy management for network configurations to meet given quality of service requirements. The policy-based SLA management system [15] was proposed to control the Differentiated Services Architecture [4] for offering multiple classes of services in an IP network. PECAN [6] is a system that manages the configuration of Multi-Protocol Label Switching (MPLS) networks based on the quality of service guarantees that are required.

Recently, policy-based storage management has become an active research area in storage management [9, 8]. In this approach, system administrators specify high level policies (goals) that describe the required QoS with respect to performance, reliability, and security for the storage system. The storage management software maps the high level policies to low level storage actions. The mapping rules are usually written in the form of condition-and-action statements [9]. Thus, system administrators do not have to worry about the low level details of many different devices.

Systems like SAN Architect [11] from EMC and Bright-Stor SAN Designer [7] from Computer Associates also provide support for SAN configuration checking. However, to our knowledge these products do not utilize a policy-management framework similar to the one presented in this paper. Most of the current storage management software products contain only very primitive support for policy-based storage management because it is difficult for them to keep up with changing workloads and system configurations. Thus, new techniques are required to make it easier to express transformation from high level goals into low level system actions. Similarly, sophisticated policy conflict resolution methods need to be developed to detect both static and dynamic policy conflicts. Currently, there is support only for very rudimentary policy conflict detection mechanisms.

The SAN configuration checking framework presented in this paper can use any one of the existing policy specification mechanisms. That is, this approach is compatible with DMTF CIM Policy [10], IETF PCIM [13], and Web Services policy specification [5] approaches. Similarly, this framework can utilize any one of the many different policy execution engines such as the ABLE [3] or the Hypercube [2] policy evaluation engines. Finally, the configuration checking framework presented in this paper uses the SNIA SMI-S model by default, but it can also be extended to work with other proprietary data models.

7   Conclusion

In recent years, policy-based management and configuration validation has been proposed for various complex systems. In this paper, we have presented an architecture for a policy-based SAN configuration manager that can be used to specify, store, and evaluate interoperability policies for SANs. By explicitly using policies to drive the system rather than hard-coded configuration rules, the system can more easily adapt to changes in SAN software and hardware components and actions can be customized or extended as the needs of the SAN manager change. Furthermore, the SAN management system can profit from policy-specific functions such as efficient evaluation, validation, and conflict resolution. The generic policy components of the proposed architecture including the Policy Evaluator, Policy Specification Tool, Policy Database, and Action Handler can be used in many different scenarios and application domains. We are in the process of building policy-based design and planning tools, auditing tools, and configuration tools based on these generic policy components for a wide variety of application domains such as databases, networks, and messaging systems.

References

[1] M. Bearden, S. Garg, and W. J. Lee. Integrating Goal Specification in Policy Based Management. In *Proc. of IEEE Policy 2001*, January 2001.

[2] P. Bhattacharya, S. Kamat, R. Rajan, and S. Sarkar. Search tree for policy based packet classification in communication networks. U.S. Patent 6,587,466, July 2003.

[3] J. P. Bigus, D. A. Scholsnagle, J. R. Pilgrim, W. N. Mills III, and Y. Diao. ABLE: A toolkit for building multiagent autonomic systems. *IBM Systems Journal*, 41(3), April 2002.

[4] S. Blake, D. Black, M. Carlson, E. Davies, Z. Wang, and W. Weiss. An architecture for differentiated services. IETF RFC 2475, December 1998.

[5] D. Box, F. Curbera, M. Hondo, C. Kaler, D. Langworthy, A. Nadalin, N. Nagaratnam, M. Nottingham, C. von Riegen, and J. Shewchuk. Web Services Policy Framework (WS-Policy) version 1.1. http:// ifr.sap.com/ ws-policy/ ws-policy.pdf, May 2003.

[6] R. Chadha, Y.-H. Cheng, T. Cheng, S. Gadgil, A. Hafid, K. Kim, G. Levin, N. Natarajan, K. Parmeswaran, A. Poylisher, and J. Unger. PECAN: Policy-enabled configuration across networks. In *Proc. of IEEE Policy 2003*, June 2003.

[7] Computer Associates Corporation. Brightstor SAN designer. http:// www3.ca.com/ Solutions/ Product.asp?ID=4590.

[8] M. Devarakonda, J. Gelb, A. Saha, and J. Strickland. A policy-based storage management framework. In *Proc. of IEEE Policy 2002*, June 2002.

[9] M. Devarakonda, A. Segal, and D. Chess. Toolkit-based approach to supporting storage policy templates. In *Proc. of IEEE Policy 2003*, June 2003.

[10] DMTF. CIM Policy Model White Paper CIM Version 2.7. http:// www.dmtf.org/ standards/ documents/ CIM/ DSP0108.pdf, June 2003.

[11] EMC Corporation. SAN architect. http:// www.emc.com/ products/ software/ san_architect.jsp.

[12] Z. Fu, S. F. Wu, H. Huang, K. Loh, F. Gong, I. Baldine, and C. Xu. A policy-based storage management framework. In *Proc. of IEEE Policy 2001*, pages 39–56, January 2001.

[13] B. Moore, E. Ellesson, J. Strassner, and A. Westerinen. Policy core information model (PCIM) – version 1 specification. IETF RFC 3060, February 2001.

[14] A. Sahai, S. Singhal, R. Joshi, and V. Machiraju. Automated Policy-Based Resource Management in Utility Computing. In *Proc. of IEEE/IFIP*, 2004.

[15] D. Verma, M. Beigi, and R. Jennings. Policy Based SLA Management in Enterprise Networks. In *Proc. of IEEE Policy 2001*, pages 137–152, January 2001.

Appendix

In this appendix, we provide a list of 64 general SAN configuration policies that we used for designing the extensions of the policy evaluation primitives.

1. HBA Model and Firmware Level: Every HBA that has a vendor name X and that has a model Y must have a firmware level either n_1, n_2, or n_3.

2. Hardware Constraints: All host systems must be from vendor X.

3. Firmware Level: Firmware level of X must be upgraded to a version of at least n or higher.

4. Number of Ports per Zone: There must be no less than M ports and no more than N ports in a zone.

5. Number of Zones per Fabric: There must be no less than M zones and no more than N zones in a fabric.

6. Hard Zoning: All zones must be defined using domain or WWN.

7. Soft Zoning: All devices connected to an interconnect device must support name service to do soft zoning.

8. Device Selection in a Zone: Devices of type X and devices of type Y are not allowed in a same zone.

9. Host Selection per Zone: No two different host types should exist in a same zone.

10. HBA Selection per Zone: No two host HBAs should exist in a same zone.

11. Number of Zones per Port: No port should be a member of more than N zones.

12. Port Status in Active Zone: If a port has a good status, it must be in at least M zones and at most N zones.

13. Number of Ports in Fabric: The number of ports of type X in the fabric is less than N.

14. Domain IDs: All domain IDs throughout all monitored FC switches must be unique.

15. Equal Link Speed: FC link speed must be equal for all HBAs in system X connected to device type Y.

16. Logical Multiple Paths: A host can logically see multiple paths to target.

17. Physical Multiple Paths: A host physically has multiple paths to target.

18. System Type: All systems connected to SAN X must be of type Y or Z.

19. Port Type/System Type: All devices of type X must be connected to switch port of mode Y.

20. Tape and Port Loop Mode: All tape connections are loop.

21. G-Port Policy: No G-Port/In-Sync connections are allowed in the fabric.

22. Device Hop Constraints: There are no more than N hops between devices X and Y.

23. Switch Hop Constraints: There are no more than N hops between switches.

24. Environmental thresholding: Certain environmental parameters have to be within a specified range. For example, the room temperature must be between M and N degrees.

25. Host Hardware Profile: All fabric host hardware matches a user-defined profile.

26. Redundant Paths: There should be at least M and at most N paths to a device.

27. Active Zones: There should be no active zones having only a single port.

28. Tape/Disk and Zone: No tapes and disk should exist in a same zone.

29. HBA with Tape/Disk Devices: A host bus adapter cannot be used to access both tape and disk devices.

30. Tape Recovery Protocol: The tape recovery protocol should be enabled/disabled on HBA X in location Y.

31. Class of Service: All devices must run in class of service N, where $N = 2, 3$.

32. Loop Disk: No loop disk is allowed in the fabric.

33. Optic Mode: If optic link is in single mode, the BB_Credit[2] must be between M and N.

34. Connection to a Director Class Switch: No end-point devices can connect directly to a director class switch except for device X.

35. Connection to a Director Class Switch: No edge switches can connect to a director class switch unless the switch vendors are the same.

36. Link Speed: A link capable of X speed has been set to Y speed.

37. Port Mode: The device connection method is set to loop instead of FC port.

38. BB_Credits: A device running in mode E should have BB_credits between values M and N.

39. HBAs and LPAR: All HBA cards must be of the same type within an LPAR (logical partitioning).

40. Number of LUNs: A storage Port should have minimum/maximum number of LUNs.

41. Port Capacity: A storage Port should have a minimum/maximum capacity of k GB.

42. Device Type and Vendor: Device type X of Vendor type Y is not allowed.

43. Open System: An ESS array is not available to open systems if an iSeries system is configured to array.

44. HBA and Vendor: All the HBAs in a system should be from the same vendor.

45. Storage Type: The system should not have mixed storage types such as SSA, FC, and SCSI parallel.

46. Firmware Level: All firmware levels must be equal for device type X.

47. OS and Device types: Devices of type T should not be attached to an OS of type X.

48. OS Levels and Patches: A desired OS level and a list of the patches must have been install.

49. File System Types: Only a certain type of file systems can be on the system.

50. Interconnects: Copper and optical interconnects are not allowed on same device or system.

51. Active LUNs: All HBA devices must have at least one active LUN associated with it.

52. HBA and LUN: Each HBA on a host system has active LUNs associated with them.

53. Optics and Vendor: Optics must be of type X and at version Y in a device type Z if the vendor is Q.

54. LUN Masking: Proper LUN masking should have been enabled for a storage device that is accessed by multiple systems.

55. WWN Uniqueness: No two devices in the system can have the same WWN (World-Wide Name).

56. Serial Number Range: A certain serial number range for component X is not allowed.

57. Logical Paths: No less than two and no greater than four logical paths are allowed from endpoint A to endpoint B.

58. Switch Interoperability: Only the switches that are inter-operable can work together in the system.

59. Active Zone: Every fabric must have at least one active zone.

60. Core-Edge Policy: All edge switches must be connected to one or more core switches.

61. Redundant Paths: There must exist redundant SAN paths between host H and endpoint D.

62. Tape Device: Tape devices of type X may have at most one connection to any host.

63. No Sharing: Each zone should only contain the ports from a single host.

64. Alias: All hosts in the system must have at most X aliases.

---

[2]Buffer-to-buffer credit is used for flow control by FC classes 2 and 3.

RSVP Policy Control using XACML

Emir Toktar, Edgard Jamhour, Carlos Maziero

Pontifical Catholic University of Paraná, PUCPR, PPGIA

{toktar,jamhor,maziero}@ppgia.pucpr.br

Abstract

This work proposes a XML-based framework for distributing and enforcing RSVP access control policies, for RSVP-aware application servers. Policies are represented by extending XACML, the general purpose access control language proposed by OASIS. Because RSVP is a specific application domain, it is not directly supported by the XACML standard. Hence, this work defines the XACML extensions required for representing and transporting the RSVP access control policy information. The XACML-based framework is proposed as an alternative to the IETF PCIM-based approach. Both approaches are compared in this paper.

1. Introduction

Policy based network management (PBNM) is an important trend for IP-based networks. Recent works developed by IETF have defined a standard model for representing policies on different areas of network management. The groundwork of this model is the PCIM (Policy Core Information Model), defined by RFC 3060 [5]. PCIM is a platform independent object-oriented information model. The model defines a generic strategy for representing network policies as aggregations of rules expressed in terms of conditions and actions. PCIM is an abstract model, and it does not define sufficient elements for describing policies for particular areas of network management. To address particular areas, PCIM needs to be extended. IETF itself has already introduced PCIM extensions for representing IPsec and QoS [10] policies. Outside IETF, other works explored extensions of PCIM for the area of access control [6].

Besides IETF, others organizations are proposing standard policy models for PBNM. The OASIS (Organization for the Advancement of Structured Information Standards) proposed a language for representing access control policies, on general purpose, denominated XACML (eXtensible Access Control Markup Language). There are several differences between the PCIM and the XACML approach. While PCIM is a core model for representing policies on any area of network management, XACML is dedicated to

access control. Because PCIM is an abstract model, the implementation of policies models based on PCIM is a rather complex task. The XACML, by the other hand, is simpler of being implemented and deployed. However, XACML can lack the flexibility for addressing specific application domains.

Based on this argumentation, this work proposes the use of the XACML for modeling and distributing RSVP access control policies for RSVP-aware application servers. Because RSVP is a specific application domain, it is not directly supported by the XACML standard. Hence, this work defines the XACML extensions required for representing and transporting the RSVP access control policy information. The paper compares the proposed XACML-based approach with the standard PCIM-based approach with respect to implementation and deployment. By establishing the parallels with PCIM-based approach, this work defines the futures extensions required for extending this proposal to other network elements, such as routers.

This paper is structured as follows: section 2 presents a short review of the main aspects related to RSVP policy access control. Section 3 presents an analysis of the models that can be employed for describing RSVP access control policies, and the strategies for distributing and enforcing those policies. The section 4 presents a short review of the XACML model. The section 5 describes how the XACML can be used for describing RSVP policies, and presents the required extensions for adapting XACML to the RSVP issue. The section 6 describes how to implement the framework for distributing and enforcing the RSVP policies described in XACML. Finally, the conclusion reviews the principal aspects of this study and indicates the future works.

2. RSVP Policy Control

This section introduces a brief review of the RSVP protocol, defining the concept of RSVP policy control and presenting the important terms that will be utilized in the next sections. The RSVP signalization is composed by a set of standard messages. The most important messages are PATH and RESV. The emitter always initiates the QoS negotiation by sending the message PATH to the receiver. The PATH message has double function. It defines the QoS parameters the receiver should request for the network in order to satisfy the requisites of the application. It defines, as well, the path the other RSVP messages and the flow of data will follow between the emitter and the receiver. A flow of data on RSVP is a sequence of messages with the same origin, with same expected QoS, and one or more destinations. The receiver, on accepting the PATH message, initiates the process of flow reservation sending the RESV message to the emitter, along the reverse way defined by the PATH message. The RESV message consists of a flow descriptor, formed by the *flowspec* and *filterspec* objects. The *filterspec*, along with the specification of the session, defines which packets of data (RSVP flow) must benefit from the QoS reservation. The QoS specification is defined by *flowspec* using two data structures: *Rspec* (Reserve Spec), that indicates the service class expected and *Tspec* (Traffic Spec) that specifies what will be transmitted. During the resource reservation setup, two local decision modules evaluate a RSVP request: the "policy control module" and the "admission control module".

The admission control module determines whether the node (host or router) has sufficient resources available for satisfying the QoS request. The policy control module determines whether the user has administrative permission for obtaining the reservation [2]. The parameters for policy and admission control are not defined and controlled by the RSVP. The protocol merely transports the parameters to the appropriate module for interpretation. According to the RFC2205, the sender application must specify the type of service most appropriate for its requisites of transmission by passing the related information to the RSVP daemon in the host machine [2]. The RSVP daemon after being called, query the local decision modules, verifying resources and authorization and, being allowed, initiates the exchange of RSVP messages with the nearest network element in the path to the receiver.

As explained in the next sections, the purpose of the work described in this paper consists in defining and implementing a mechanism for configuring the RSVP access control policies ("policy control") for RSVP-aware application servers by using XACML, i.e., the policy control is implemented only by the application server. However, this proposal also supply the information for defining the *Tspec* and *Rspec* parameters transported in the PATH and RESV messages. Therefore, the XACML policy also provides the information used for "*admission control*" by the network elements along the path between the transmitter and the receiver.

3. RSVP Policy Control Strategies

In this paper, the strategy for representing, distributing and enforcing RSVP access control policies follows Policy Based Network Management (PBNM) approach. The concept of PBNM is already widely adopted by organizations that propose Internet standards, such as IETF [14] and the OASIS [7]. Although the definitions for PBNM could diverge according to the organization, the main concepts are relatively universal. The basic idea for PBNM is to offer a strategy for configuring policy on different network elements (nodes) using a common management framework, composed by a policy server, denominated PDP (Policy Decision Point) and various policy clients, denominated PEPs (Policy Enforcement Points) [12]. The PDP is the entity responsible for storing and distributing the policies to the diverse nodes in the network. A PEP is, usually, a network node component responsible for interpreting and applying the policies received from the PDP. The PBNM approach can be applied in various aspects of network management. This section will explore how this approach can be applied for managing access control policies in RSVP server (sender) applications.

The IETF explores the concept of PBNM according to two strategies, denominated outsourcing and provisioning. In the outsourcing strategy, the PEP sends a request to the PDP when it needs to make a decision. For example, considering the access problem on RSVP, the PEP would represent the server application (or more precisely, the policy component embedded in the server application). On receiving a request from a client, the PEP would send a request to the PDP in order to determine if the client has the permission for asking the reservation. The PDP then would interpret the policies and would send a final decision to the PEP, informing if the solicitation is permitted or denied. In the provisioning approach, the PEP, as being initialized, would receive from the PDP the set of policies needed for its decision. The policy information received from the PDP is locally stored by the PEP according to a locally defined scheme called PIB (Policy Information Base). On receiving a reservation request, the PEP would consult its locally stored policies and would make the decision by itself. In this approach, the communication between the PEP and the PDP is required only when there is necessity of updating the policies in the PEPs (e.g., the network administrator modifies a policy in the PDP concerning the PEP).

IETF define as well a standard protocol for supporting the communication between the PEP and the PDP. This protocol is denominated COPS (Common Open Policy Service). The basic structure of the COPS protocol is described in the RFC 2748 [1]. The COPS protocol supports both models of policy control, i.e., "outsourcing" and "provisioning". In the case of the provisioning approach, additional specifications were required and, the protocol was renamed to COPS-PR. The basic structure of the COPS-PR protocol is described in the RFC 3084 [3]. The IETF already published various works concerning the use of PBNM approach for RSVP policy control. The works cover the definition of a framework for admission control [14] and the utilization of COPS in outsourcing (COPS-RSVP) [4] and provisioning (COPS-PR) models. The provisioning approach is still under development, being necessary additional definitions for its complete specification.

The XACML proposal from OASIS also describes that its implementation could follow the approach PDP/PEP. However, OASIS does not make a distinction between the outsourcing and provisioning models, neither defines a standard protocol for supporting the communication between the PEP and the PDP. An analysis of the XACML indicates, however, that it was primarily conceived for supporting the outsourcing approach (see section 4). An important difference between the approaches adopted by OASIS and IETF relates to how policies are represented and stored. OASIS proposes XACML as a particular model for access control, represented and stored as XML documents. On the other side, IETF defines PCIM as a generic model, independent from the way the policies will be represented and stored. The PCIM model is abstract, and needs to be extended in order to support particular areas of management, such as QoS [10]. IETF indicates strategies for mapping the information models to LDAP (Lightweight Directory Access Protocol) schemas, but this form of storage requires a supplementary effort by developers.

A work describing the implementation and performance evaluation of a PBNM framework, using COPS in outsourcing model with RSVP (COPS-RSVP) was presented by Ponnappan [8]. The QoS policies were represented using QPIM (QoS Policy Information model), an IETF PCIM extension described by Snir [10]. The policies were represented and stored using LDAP .This work uses CORBA (Common Object Request Broker Architecture) for supporting the interaction between the application components.

4. XACML Review

The XACML (eXtensible Access Control Markup Language) is an OASIS proposal for modeling, storing and distributing descriptive access control policies [7]. XACML-based frameworks are supposed to be implemented using the PDP/PEP architecture in the outsourcing model. The XACML language is defined by two XML schemes: "*xacml context*" and "*xacml policy*". The "*xacml context*" defines how to represent policy request and policy response messages exchanged between the PEP and the PDP. The "*xacml policy*" defines how to represent the access control policies. Fig. 1 shows the UML diagram of the "*xacml policy*" scheme. The figure represents the classes and associations between XACML elements, but omits its attributes. According to the XACML strategy, a policy is described in terms of a set of access permissions (or access denials) by structures denominated Targets. A Target is expressed through the syntax: "users (Subject class) can (or cannot) apply actions (Action class) upon resources (Resource class)".

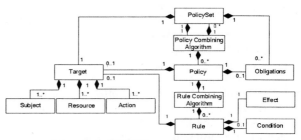

Figure 1. XACML policy scheme

Targets can be associated to a policy, to a policy set or to a rule. Targets associated to a policy or a policy set work as policy selectors, i.e., when a PEP request a decision concerning a Target, only the policies and policies sets that contain the Target elements need to be evaluated. Targets associated to rules permit to express conditional permissions (or denials). A rule is expressed by the syntax: "if the condition (Condition class) is satisfied then applies the effect (Effect class) upon the Target". The possible values for effect are: permit or deny. The effect defines the real sense of a Target as a permission or denial.

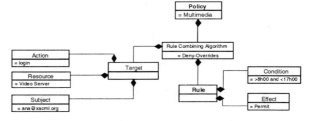

Figure 2. XACML policy example

Fig. 2 shows a simple policy example to illustrate the use of the XACML classes. The policy represented in the figure can be described textually as follows: "the user ana@xacml.org can **login** on a **Multimedia Server** in the period between **08:00AM** and **17:00PM**".

When a PEP sends a request to the PDP, it supplies the attributes permitting to identify the elements of a Target (Subject, Resource, Action). The PDP evaluates the policy rules and determines if exists a Target with those attributes, and then returns to the PEP the corresponding effect: *Permit* or *Deny*. If it fails to find a Target in its policies that satisfy the attributes supplied by the PEP, it will return "*NotApplicable*". The Obligations class, when defined, is returned to the PEP in conjunction with the decision. The Obligations class is supposed to inform a set of actions that must be performed by the PEP, concerning the decision. The XACML version (1.0) used in our study [7] does not specify the type of actions described in Obligations. The specification only defines the PEP must be capable of interpreting any information passed through the Obligations class. As will be explained further, our proposal uses the Obligations class to pass QoS parameters to a RSVP node.

Though the Obligations class offers an alternative for implementing some sort of policy "provisioning", we observe that XACML is primarily supposed to be implemented using the outsourcing approach, because the PDP basically returns decisions of type "*Permit*" or "*Deny*" to the PEPs. As it will be explained in the next section, the Obligations approach, as defined in XACML version 1.0, is rather limited, but the "concept" is flexible enough for providing "configuration information" to network nodes in several domains. Other limitations of the present XACML specifications concern the lack of definitions regarding the communication protocol for supporting the exchange of messages between the PDP and the PEPs, as well as definitions about the strategy for storing the XACML documents that represent the network policies.

```
<Policy PolicyId=" " RuleCombiningAlgId=" ">
  <Target>
    <Subjects>...</Subjects>
    <Resources>...</Resources>
    <Actions>...</Actions>
  </Target>
  <Rule RuleId=" " Effect=" ">
    <Target>...</Target>
    <Condition FunctionId=" ">...</Condition>
  </Rule>
  <Obligations>
    <Obligation ObligationId=" " FulfillOn=" "></Obligation>
  </Obligations>
</Policy>

<!— In Obligations, the attribute FulfillOn indicates if the obligation
must be executed when the resulting effect is Permit or Deny -->
```

Figure 3. A XACML Policy document

Fig. 3 illustrates how the UML model shown in Fig. 2 is represented in a XML document. The XML document "format" is formally described by the "*xacml policy*" scheme.

5. Proposal

This paper proposes a XACML-based framework for distributing and enforcing access control policies to RSVP-aware application servers. Fig. 4 illustrates a typical scenario for this framework. The PEP element represents a component of the server application, responsible for requesting policy decisions to the PDP and interacting with the RSVP daemon in the host computer. The code of the PEP must be integrated with the application server, as explained in section 6. In our proposal, the PEP is responsible for all interaction with the RSVP daemon, releasing the application from the task of any QoS negotiation. This interaction includes retrieving the traffic information for building PATH messages and granting or not the reservation request on receiving the RESV message. This approach can be implemented in any system that supports the RSVP APIs described in the RFC 2205.

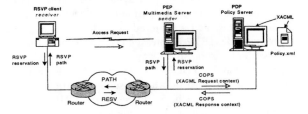

Figure 4. Policy control of RSVP with XACML

The sequence of events and messages exchanged by the elements in Fig. 4 during the establishment of a RSVP reservation, using the proposed framework, is described as follows:

1. A RSVP client requests a connection to a multimedia server for obtaining services with QoS.

2. In the multimedia server, the application calls the PEP for evaluating the request. Then, the PEP sends to the PDP a XACML request context message informing a "Target" containing its IP address (Resource), the IP address of the client (Subject) and the requested operation (Action).

3. The PDP evaluates the policy defined in XACML for the supplied target, and returns to the PEP a XACML response context message having, besides the result (permit or deny), the information of traffic specification (*Tspec*, supplied through the Obligations structure).

4. In case of positive decision, the PEP calls its RSVP daemon, informing the *Tspec* parameters. The RSVP daemon, then, sends a RSVP PATH message to the receiver (i.e., the RSVP client). The *Tspec* parameters are stored in the PEP for further analysis (see step 6).

5. The RSVP client, on receiving a RSVP PATH message, calls its RSVP daemon, which obtains the traffic parameters from the PATH message and formats a RESV RSVP message, returning it to the sender (i.e., the PEP).

6. On receiving the RESV message from the client, the RSVP daemon of the server triggers an event to the PEP forwarding the *Tspec* information. The PEP compares the *Tspec* information received from the client with the *Tspec* information saved in step 4. If the *Tspec* parameters are identical or smaller than those saved in step 4, the PEP confirms the reservation to the RSVP daemon. In this step, the RSVP daemon also verifies if it has enough resources to satisfy the request (admission control).

The steps 1 to 6 refer to a well-succeeded scenario of reservation, and exception treatment was omitted. A RSVP access solicitation differs from a conventional access solicitation (e.g., access to a file or directory) because the PDP needs to return the information necessary for the PEP building the PATH message. For this reason, extensions to the XACML framework features were required in order to describe and transport the QoS information.

The strategy adopted in this work for describing a RSVP policy in terms of XACML is illustrated in Figure 5.

```
<PolicySet PolicySetId="RSVP_Aware_Server_Application">
  <Target> <!—Defines the services (resources) to which the policy applies →
  </Target>
  <Policy PolicyId="Service Level 1"> <!—e.g. GOLD →
    <Rule>
      <Target> <!—Subjects to which the policy applies → </Target>
      <Condition> <!-- Time and client's IP addresses restrictions -->
      </Condition>
    </Rule>
    <Obligations> <!—TSpec specification for service level 1 →
    </Obligations>
  </Policy>
  <Policy PolicyId="Service Level 2"> ... </Policy> <!—e.g. SILVER →
  <Policy PolicyId="Service Level N"> ... </Policy> <!—e.g. BRONZE →
  <Policy PolicyId="Default Policy"> <!—usually denies all → </Policy>
</PolicySet>
```

Figure 5. RSVP XACML Policy Structure

In the proposed strategy each "RSVP-aware" server application (or group of applications) is mapped to a XACML <PolicySet>. Server applications can be described by the same policy set only if they offer the same "QoS Service Levels" for the same set of users, under the same restrictions. For example, distinct video streaming servers in a university campus that offer a

"GOLD" service for registered students and "SILVER" service for visitors (with the same Tspec definitions) can be represented by a single policy set. The policies are mapped to services through the <Target> element in the <PolicySet> structure (see the example in section 6). The <Policy> elements in the <PolicySet> are used for defining distinct QoS service levels offered by the same application. For example, "GOLD", "SILVER", etc. The <Rule> defines the users (subjects) that have authorization to receive the service level and the <Obligations> element describes the *Tspec* parameters.

The reason for defining a RSVP policy in terms of a <PolicySet> and not in terms of a single <Policy> element is related to the XACML definition. One observes in Figure 1 that the <Obligations> element is mapped to <Policy> or <PolicySet>, but it can't be mapped to Rules, i.e., all <Rules> in a policy defines the same <Obligations>. Therefore, distinct service levels can't be represented in a single policy.

Another important point is to define where the users and services information is located. If we consider the PCIM approach, defined by IETF, a logical approach would consist in representing users and services through CIM[1] objects. Because CIM is supposed to be supported by an important set of hardware and software vendors, it is an interesting choice for sharing the same information among heterogeneous systems. Both CIM and PCIM information can be stored in LDAP servers.

The XACML definition permits to define all the information concerning the policy (subjects, resources and actions) in the same XML document, as defined by the "*xacml policy scheme*". However, OASIS points that it will be possible to write XACML policies that refers to information elements stored in a LDAP repository. The 1.0 specification does not define how it can be done. However, because *xacml* is based on standard xml definitions, a possible solution would be create references in a policy to external documents using the *XML Pointer Language (XPointer)* strategy [15]. There are some references about the use of *XPointer* in the 1.0 OASIS specification, however, its use is limited to request documents (i.e., context scheme) and its use in policy documents is not supported. However, using *XPointer* for creating policies with reusable subjects and services information is a logical extension for future XACML versions.

Hence, this work adopts the use of XPointer for defining policies with reusable subjects (users) and

---

[1] CIM (Common Information Model), proposed by the DMTF (Distributed Management Task Force) is a information model compatible with PCIM that defines classes and associations for representing users, network elements and servies.

services information. In the future, this approach can be replaced by the LDAP approach without modifying the policy strategy.

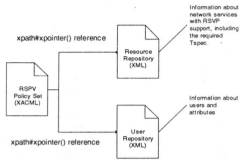

Figure 6. Policy, Resources and Users documents.

Figure 6 illustrates the relationship between the XML documents used for describing a policy. An example of how these documents can be defined are presented in case study in the next section (see Figures 8 and 9). The structure of the resource and user documents described in this work was chosen intentionally simple for didactical purposes. The QoS information is described in the resource document. A resource is defined as a network service that supports RSVP negotiations. Hence, the resource document accommodates the description of RSVP parameters required for building the PATH message, i.e., *Tspec* {r,b,p,m,M}, type of service (GS – guaranteed service or controlled load – CL) and reservation style as described in the RFC 2210 [13] and RFC 2215 [9].

Fig. 7 illustrates the XML scheme corresponding to the RSVP parameters. Our proposal assumes that a single service can offer different service levels. For example, a multimedia server can define various QoS modes for streaming video in order to support different resolutions. In this case, each QoS mode must receive a distinct class specification (attribute *RsvpClass*). The class enumerated in the scheme are define by ITU-T, and are included in the scheme for illustration purposes only. Observe in Fig. 7, that the RSVP resource scheme does not include the *Rspec* parameters. In this work, we suggest the PEP could reject the proposal received on the RESV message if the *Rspec* parameters are much larger than those specified by *Tspec*, not being necessary to consult the PDP again for validating the RESV message.

```
<xs:schema>
  <xs:element name="ResourceRsvp" type="xacml:ResourceRsvpType"/>
  <xs:complexType name="ResourceRsvpType">
    <xs:sequence>
      <xs:element ref="xacml:TspecBucketRate_r"/>
      <xs:element ref="xacml:TspecBucketSize_b"/>
      <xs:element ref="xacml:TspecPeakRate_p"/>
      <xs:element ref="xacml:TspecMinPoliceUnit_m"/>
      <xs:element ref="xacml:TspecMaxPacketSize_M"/>
      <xs:choice minOccurs="0" maxOccurs="1">
        <xs:element ref="xacml:RsvpStyle"/>
      </xs:choice>
      <xs:choice minOccurs="0" maxOccurs="1">
        <xs:element ref="xacml:RsvpService"/>
      </xs:choice>
    </xs:sequence>
    <xs:attribute name="AttributeId" type="xs:anyURI" use="required"/>
    <xs:attribute name="RsvpClass" type="xacml:RsvpClassType"
use="required"/>
  </xs:complexType>
  <xs:simpleType name="RsvpClassType">
    <xs:restriction base="xs:string">
      <xs:enumeration value="G711"/>
      <xs:enumeration value="G729"/>
      <xs:enumeration value="H263CIF"/>
      <xs:enumeration value="H261QCIF"/>
    </xs:restriction>
  </xs:simpleType>
  <xs:element name="RsvpService">
    <xs:simpleType>
      <xs:restriction base="xs:string">
        <xs:enumeration value="Null"/>
        <xs:enumeration value="Guaranteed"/>
        <xs:enumeration value="Controlled-load"/>
      </xs:restriction>
    </xs:simpleType>
  </xs:element>
  <xs:element name="RsvpStyle">
    <xs:simpleType>
      <xs:restriction base="xs:string">
        <xs:enumeration value="SE"/>
        <xs:enumeration value="WF"/>
        <xs:enumeration value="FF"/>
      </xs:restriction>
    </xs:simpleType>
  </xs:element>
  <xs:element name="TspecBucketRate_r">
    <xs:simpleType>
      <xs:restriction base="xs:double">
        <xs:minInclusive value="1"/>
        <xs:maxInclusive value="40000000000000"/>
      </xs:restriction>
    </xs:simpleType>
  </xs:element>
  <!--definitions for other elements: TspecBucketSize_b , etc-->
</xs:schema>
```

Figure 7. Tspec Scheme Definition

6. Case Study and Implementation

6.1. Case Study

In order to illustrated the use of the XACML approach for describing RSVP policies, the following scenario was considered: A set of "video streaming" servers in a university campus offers "tutorials" to registered and unregistered students (visitors). The policy adopted for having access to the video streaming is defined as follows:

a) Registered students have permission to access any server in the campus offering a *"TutorialVideoStreaming"* service without time restrictions. If a student connects to a server using a client host from inside the campus, he will receive a "GOLD" or "SILVER" service level. Otherwise, it will receive a "BRONZE" service level.

b)Unregistered students can have access to the *"TutorialVideoStreaming"* service only from the internal network and not in business-time. They can receive only the "BRONZE" service level.

```
<service serviceId="TutorialVideoStreaming">
  <description> tutorial videos in the campus university
  </description>
  <sap>
    <inetaddress> 192.168.200.10 </inetaddress>
    <inetaddress >192.168.5.3 </ inetaddress >
    <protocol>tcp</protocol>
    <port>8976</port>
  </sap>
  <serviceLevel serviceId="Gold">
    <ResourceRsvp AttributeId="qosG711" RsvpClass="G711">
      <TspecBucketRate_r>9250</TspecBucketRate_r>
      <TspecBucketSize_b>680</TspecBucketSize_b>
      <TspecPeakRate_p>13875</TspecPeakRate_p>
      <TspecMinPoliceUnit_m>340</TspecMinPoliceUnit_m>
      <TspecMaxPacketSize_M>340</TspecMaxPacketSize_M>
      <RsvpService>Guaranteed</RsvpService>
      <RsvpStyle>FF</RsvpStyle>
    </ResourceRsvp>
  </serviceLevel>
  <serviceLevel serviceId="Silver">
    <ResourceRsvp AttributeId="qosH261Q"
RsvpClass="H261QCIF">
      <TspecBucketRate_r>12000</TspecBucketRate_r>
      <TspecBucketSize_b>6000</TspecBucketSize_b>
      <TspecPeakRate_p>12000</TspecPeakRate_p>
      <TspecMinPoliceUnit_m>80</TspecMinPoliceUnit_m>
      <TspecMaxPacketSize_M>2500</TspecMaxPacketSize_M>
      <RsvpService>Controlled-load</RsvpService>
      <RsvpStyle>SE</RsvpStyle>
    </ResourceRsvp>
  </serviceLevel>
  <serviceLevel serviceId="Bronze">
    <ResourceRsvp AttributeId="qosH263C"
RsvpClass="H263CIF">
      <TspecBucketRate_r>16000</TspecBucketRate_r>
      <TspecBucketSize_b>8192</TspecBucketSize_b>
      <TspecPeakRate_p>16000</TspecPeakRate_p>
      <TspecMinPoliceUnit_m>80</TspecMinPoliceUnit_m>
      <TspecMaxPacketSize_M>8192</TspecMaxPacketSize_M>
      <RsvpService>Controlled-load</RsvpService>
      <RsvpStyle>WF</RsvpStyle>
    </ResourceRsvp>
  </serviceLevel>
</service>
```

Figure 8. Service Information

The service information is represented in the document illustrated in Figure 8. Note that the <SAP> structure defines the services in the campus that are subjected to the policy. The *Tspec* information concerning the <GOLD>, <SILVER> and <BRONZE> service levels are also defined in the file.

A XACML request from the video server (i.e., a PEP) will usually identify the user by its login (uid). However, the policy in the PDP will be described in terms of the student status (registered or unregistered). The mapping between the user id and the corresponding student status is represented by the XML document illustrated in Figure 9.

```
<subjects>
  <user>
    <cn>Emir Toktar</cn>
    <uid>etoktar</uid>
    <mail>toktar@ppgia.pucpr.br</mail>
    <businessCategory>RegisteredStudent</businessCategory>
  </user>
  <user>
    <cn>Luis Cezar</cn>
    <uid>lcezar</uid>
    <mail>ortega@ppgia.pucpr.br</mail>
    <businessCategory>RegisteredStudent</businessCategory>
  </user>
  <user>
    <cn>guest</cn>
    <uid>guest</uid>
    <businessCategory>UnregisteredStudent</businessCategory>
  </user>
</subjects>
```

Figure 9. User Information

The RSVP policy is defined in terms of a XACML <PolicySet>, as described in section 5. The <PolicySet> structure for the case study defines four policies, as shown in Figure 10. The Target structure in the <PolicySet> defines the resources to which the policy applies. Note <ResouceMatch> elements in the <Target> structure defined conditions that compares the information supplied by the PEP in the Request message (resource-id, and ip-address:sender) with the information described in the XML Service Information File (see Figure 8) .

Figure 11 illustrates the structure of "Policy 1" in the <PoliceSet>. This policy defines the conditions applied to the access of registered students from inside the campus. The <Subject> element in the <Rule> defines that the policy applies only to registered students. The <Condition> of the rule determines that the policy applies only to requests where the client host is located inside the university campus.

A typical policy request from a PEP to the PDP is illustrated in Figure 12. The <Subject> element will supply the information about the receiver, i.e., user id and IP address of its host. The <Resource> element supplies the information about the server (i.e., the sender), including its name (resource id) and IP address. The type of action requested is defined as "getResorceQoS", in this case, the only action supported by the policy.

```
<PolicySet PolicySetId="TutorialVideo"
PolicyCombiningAlgId=":policy-combining-algorithm:first-
applicable">
   <Target>
   <Resources>
     <Resource>
       <ResourceMatch MatchId=":function:string-equal">
         <AttributeValue DataType="#string">
         TutorialVideo</AttributeValue>
           <ResourceAttributeDesignator DataType="#string"
           AttributeId=":resource:resource-id"/>
       </ResourceMatch>
         <ResourceMatch MatchId=":function:xpath-node-match">
           <AttributeValue DataType="#string">
http://pdp/resources.xml#xpointer(//service[@serviceId="TutorialVide
oStreaming"]/sap/inetaddress/text())
           </AttributeValue>
           <ResourceAttributeDesignator DataType="#string"
AttributeId=":resource:authn-locality:ip-address:sender"/>
         </ResourceMatch>
       </Resource>
     </Resources>
   </Target>
   <!-- Policy 1: Registered Students from inside the campus -->
   <Policy PolicyId=":policy:TutorialRegStudentsInternal"
RuleCombiningAlgId=":rule-combining-algorithm:first-applicable">
   </Policy>
   <!-- Policy 02: Registered Studens from outside the campus -->
   <Policy PolicyId=":policy:TutorialRegStudentsExternal"
RuleCombiningAlgId=":rule-combining-algorithm:first-applicable">
   </Policy>
   <!-- Policy 03: Unregiestered Students -->
   <Policy PolicyId=":policy:TutorialRegStudentsGuest"
RuleCombiningAlgId=":rule-combining-algorithm:first-applicable">
   <!-- Policy 04 - Deny for All -->
   <Policy PolicyId=":policy:TutorialDenyForOthers"
RuleCombiningAlgId=":rule-combining-algorithm:first-applicable">
     <Rule RuleId=":Tutorial_Deny_Rule_For_Others"
Effect="Deny"/>
   </Policy>
</PolicySet>
```

Figure 10. Policy Set Structure

Finally, Figure 13 illustrates the response from the PDP to the PEP. The "Permit" information informs to the PDP that there are services to be offered to the client. The services are described in the <Obligations> structure. In this example, two *Tspec* specifications are returned to the PEP. These specification correspond to the service level "GOLD" and "SILVER" offered by the VideoStreaming server. An alternate approach could be return only the highest service level. The structure presented in the <Obligations> section is defined by the XACML context-schema.

```
<Policy PolicyId=":policy:TutorialRegStudentsInternal"
RuleCombiningAlgId=":rule-combining-algorithm:first-applicable">
<Rule RuleId="Reg_Students_Internal_Get_Gold_Silver" Effect="Permit">
  <Target>
    <Subjects> <Subject>
      <SubjectMatch MatchId=":function:xpath-node-match">
      <!-- return of a Bag attributes of elements 'uid' that are 'RegisteredStudent' -->
        <AttributeValue DataType="#string">
        http://pdp/resources.xml#xpointer(//subjects/user
        [businessCategory='RegisteredStudent']/uid/text())
        </AttributeValue>
        <SubjectAttributeDesignator AttributeId=":subject:subject-id"
        DataType="#string"/>
      </SubjectMatch>
    </Subject></Subjects>
    <Actions> <Action>
      <ActionMatch MatchId=":function:string-equal">
        <AttributeValue DataType="#string">getResourceQoS</AttributeValue>
        <ActionAttributeDesignator DataType="#string"
        AttributeId=":action:action-id:ServerAction"/>
      </ActionMatch>
    </Action></Actions>
  </Target>
  <Condition FunctionId=":function:or">
  <Apply FunctionId=":function:any-of">
    <Function FunctionId=":function:regexp-string-match"/>
    <AttributeValue DataType="#string">192.168.0.*</AttributeValue>
    <SubjectAttributeDesignator
      AttributeId=":subject:authn-locality:ip-address:receiver"
      DataType="#string"/>
  </Apply>
  </Condition>
</Rule>
<Obligations>
<Obligation ObligationId="GoldSilverStudentsInternal" FulfillOn="Permit">
  <AttributeAssignment AttributeId="qosG711" DataType="#string">
    http://pdp/resources.xml#xpointer(//service/serviceLevel
    [@serviceId='Gold']/ResourceRsvp/*)
  </AttributeAssignment>
  <AttributeAssignment AttributeId="qoSH261Q" DataType="#string">
    hdp://pdp/resources.xml#xpointer(//service/serviceLevel
    [@serviceId='Silver']/ResourceRsvp/*)
</AttributeAssignment>
  </Obligation>
</Obligations>
```

Figure 11. Policy Structure for Registered Students in Internal Network

```
<Request>
  <Subject>
    <Attribute AttributeId=":subject:subject-id" DataType="#string">
      <AttributeValue>etoktar</AttributeValue>
    </Attribute>
    <Attribute AttributeId=":subject:authn-locality:ip-address:receiver"
DataType="#string">
      <AttributeValue>192.168.0.1</AttributeValue>
    </Attribute>
  </Subject>
  <Resource>
    <Attribute AttributeId=":resource:resource-id" DataType="#string">
      <AttributeValue>TutorialVideoStreaming</AttributeValue>
    </Attribute>
    <Attribute AttributeId=":resource:authn-locality:ip-address:sender"
DataType="#string">
      <AttributeValue>192.168.200.10</AttributeValue>
    </Attribute>
  </Resource>
  <Action>
    <Attribute AttributeId=":action:action-id:ServerAction" DataType="#string">
      <AttributeValue>getResourceQoS</AttributeValue>
    </Attribute>
  </Action>
</Request>
```

Figure 12. Example of Policy Request

```
<Response>
  <Result>
    <Decision>Permit</Decision>
    <Status>
      <StatusCode Value=":status:ok"/>
    </Status>
    <Obligations>
      <Obligation ObligationId=":GoldSilverStudentsInternal"
FulfillOn="Permit">
        <AttributeAssignment AttributeId="RsvpClass#1"
          DataType="#string"> G711</AttributeAssignment>
        <AttributeAssignment AttributeId="TokenBucketRate_r#1"
          DataType="#double"> 9250.0</AttributeAssignment>
        <AttributeAssignment AttributeId="TokenBucketSize_b#1"
          DataType="#double"> 680.0</AttributeAssignment>
        <AttributeAssignment AttributeId="PeakRate_p#1"
          DataType="#double">13875.0</AttributeAssignment>
        <AttributeAssignment AttributeId="MinimumPoliceUnit_m#1"
          DataType="#integer">13875</AttributeAssignment>
        <AttributeAssignment AttributeId="MaximumPacketSize_M#1"
          DataType="#integer">13875</AttributeAssignment>
        <AttributeAssignment AttributeId="RsvpService#1"
          DataType="#string">Guaranteed</AttributeAssignment>
        <AttributeAssignment AttributeId="ServiceQoS#1"
          DataType="#string">FF</AttributeAssignment>

        <AttributeAssignment AttributeId="RsvpClass#2"
          DataType="#string">H261QCIF</AttributeAssignment>
        <AttributeAssignment AttributeId="TokenBucketRate_r#2"
          DataType="#double">12000.0</AttributeAssignment>
        <AttributeAssignment AttributeId="TokenBucketSize_b#2"
          DataType="#double">6000.0</AttributeAssignment>
        <AttributeAssignment AttributeId="PeakRate_p#2"
          DataType="#double">12000.0</AttributeAssignment>
        <AttributeAssignment AttributeId="MinimumPoliceUnit_m#2"
          DataType="#integer">80</AttributeAssignment>
        <AttributeAssignment AttributeId="MaximumPacketSize_M#2"
          DataType="#integer"> 2500</AttributeAssignment>
        <AttributeAssignment AttributeId="RsvpService#2"
          DataType="#string">Controlled-load</AttributeAssignment>
        <AttributeAssignment AttributeId="ServiceQoS#2"
          DataType="#string"> SE</AttributeAssignment>
      </Obligation>
    </Obligations>
  </Result>
```

Figure 13. Example of Policy Response

6.2. Implementation

On important advantage of the XACML approach with respect to PCIM refers to its implementation. Because it is defined in terms of XML, a XACML implementation benefits from the existing tools for developing XML applications. There are free packages for supporting XACML in Java language (Sun XACML project) and on C++ (by Jiffy Software).

The framework described in this paper was implemented using the Java™ 2 SDK, Standard Edition 1.4.2, and the Sun XACML package. The Sun XACML package includes the modules: *"com.sun.xacml. PolicySchema"* and *"com.sun.xacml.ContextSchema"*. The first module supports the interpretation of XACML policies (required for implemented a PDP) and the second, the exchange of messages between the PDP and the PEP.

The implementation permitted to evaluate if the proposed XACML extensions are compatible with existing implementation packages. The strategy adopted consisted in adding new functionalities to the XACML framework without modifying the scheme. We observed that it was not necessary to modify the package code, except in the case of treatment of the *<Obligations>* structure and the use of *XPointer* references to external files. The packet significantly simplifies the process of developing a PDP and embedding PEPs in existent applications.

Next, one presents some examples of utilization of the Sun XACML package for developing a PDP. The following code fragment illustrates the sequence of steps for creating a PDP instance, initialized with a policies file defined by "PolicyQoS.xml". The "policyModule.addPolicy" method permits to validate the policy with respect to the XACML policy schema. This method was used for validating the syntax of the schema extensions proposed in this work.

```
FilePolicyModule policyModule = new FilePolicyModule();
policyModule.addPolicy("Path/PolicyQoS.xml");
```

The XACML package offers classes that, through the Hash tables, simplify the process of searching policies (*PolicyFinder*) and attributes (*AttributeFinder*). The fragment of typical code for the creation of an instance of PDP is illustrated following.

```
PolicyFinder polFinder = new PolicyFinder();
Seth policyModules = new HashSet();
policyModules.add(policyModule);
policyFinder.setModules(policyModules);
AttributeFinder attrFinder = new AttributeFinder();
List attrModules = new ArrayList();
attrFinder.setModules(attrModules);
PDP pdp = new PDP(new PDPConfig(attrFinder, polFinder, null));
```

The next fragment of code illustrates the creation of a PEP. The RequestCtx class implements a PEP requests to a PDP. The attributes passed in the class constructor refers to the Target elements <Subject>, <Resource> and <Action>. The Environment attributed is used for passing other relevant information, concerning time, for example.

```
RequestCtx request = new RequestCtx(AttribSubjects,
AttribResource, AttribAction, AttribEnvironment);
```

The *ResponseCtx* class is used for receiving the PDP response. A *ResponseCtx* object encapsulates the decision, status code and the *<Obligations>* structure. The code fragment is presented next:

```
ResponseCtx response = pdp.evaluate(request);
```

7. Conclusion

In this work, XACML use was extended beyond the access control functionalities, because the decisions generated by the PDP include the *Tspec* parameters necessary for building the PATH messages. The capacity of returning configuration parameters through PDP decisions is an important feature for many PBNM scenarios. This feature, easily supported in IETF PCIM-based models, is quite difficult to implement in XACML. To support the RSVP scenario, modifications in the <Obligations> structure were required, including some features not supported by the XACML Sun package. The 1.0 XACML specification and the corresponding packet implementation are deficient in returning results that are not simple deny or permit decisions. In the proposed work, some features have been added to the XACML framework without modifying its scheme: <Obligations> are dynamically processed and XPointer references to external documents are used for creating policies with reusable resources and subjects.

Some modifications on XACML scheme, however, would be useful. First, we suggest a more flexible way of mapping conditional <Obligations> to policies. Mapping <Obligations> to <Rules> would permit to define different service levels in a single policy. This modification would certainly be useful for other application domains. Another suggested modification is to formalize the use of XPointer references in the XACML scheme.

9. References

[1] Boyle, J.; Cohen, R.; Durham, D.; Herzog, S.; Rajan, R.; Sastry, A. The COPS (Common Open Policy Service) Protocol, RFC2748, Jan. 2000.

[2] Braden, R.; Zhang, L.; Berson, S.; Herzog, S.; Jamin, S. Resource Reservation Protocol (RSVP) Version 1 Functional Specification, RFC2205, Sep. 1997.

[3] Chan K.; Seligson, J.; Durham, D.; Gai, S.; McCloghrie, K.; Herzog, S.; Reichmeyer, F.; Yavatkar, R.; Smith, A. COPS Usage for Policy Provisioning (COPS-PR), RFC3084, Mar. 2001.

[4] Herzog, S.; Rajan, R.; Sastry, A. COPS usage for RSVP, RFC2749, Jan. 2000.

[5] Moore, B.; Ellesson, E.; Strassner, J.; Westerinen, A. Policy Core Information Model - Version 1 Specification, RFC3060, Feb. 2001.

[6] Nabhen, R., Jamhour, E., Maziero C. "Policy-Based Framework for RBAC", Proceedings for the fourteenth IFIP/IEEE International Workshop on Distributed Systems: Operations & Management, October, Germany, Feb. 2003.

[7] OASIS, eXtensible Access Control Markup Language (XACML) Version 1.0. OASIS, Feb. 2003.

[8] Ponnappan, A.; Yang, L.; Pillai, R.; Braun, P. "A Policy Based QoS Management System for the IntServ/DiffServ Based Internet". Proceedings of the Third International Workshop on Policies for Distributed Systems and Networks (POLICY.02). IEEE, 2002 .

[9] Shenker, S.; Wroclawski, J. General Characteri-zation Parameters for Integrated Service Network Elements, RFC 2215, Sep. 1997.

[10] Snir, Y.; Ramberg, Y.; Strassner, J.; Cohen, R. "Policy QoS Information Model, work in progress, draft-ietf-policy-qos-info-model-05.txt". IETF, May. 2003.

[11] Toktar, E. Controle de Admissão de RSVP utilizando XACML. Dissertação de Mestrado, PPGIA, PUCPR. Aug. 2003.

[12] Westerinen, A. et. al. Terminology for Policy Based Management. RFC3198, Nov. 2001.

[13] Wroclawski, J. RSVP with INTSERV, RFC 2210, Sep. 1997.

[14] Yavatkar, R., Pendarakis, D.; Guerin, R. A Framework for Policy-Based Admission Control, RFC2753, Jan. 2000.

[15] W3C, XPointer Framework, W3C Recommendation, 25 March 2003.

Session 4 (Short Papers): Automation and Control

Policy-Based Autonomic Control Service

N. Badr
School of Computing and Mathematical Science, Liverpool John Moores University, Byrom Street, Liverpool L3 3AF, UK
cmsnbadr@livjm.ac.uk

A. Taleb-Bendiab
School of Computing and Mathematical Science, Liverpool John Moores University, Byrom Street, Liverpool L3 3AF, UK
a.talebbendiab@livjm.ac.uk

D. Reilly
School of Computing and Mathematical Science, Liverpool John Moores University, Byrom Street, Liverpool L3 3AF, UK
d.reilly@livjm.ac.uk

Abstract

Recently, there has been a considerable interest in policy-based, goal-oriented service management and autonomic computing. Much work is still required to investigate designs and policy models and associate meta-reasoning systems for policy-based autonomic systems. In this paper we outline a proposed autonomic middleware control service used to orchestrate self-healing of distributed applications. Policies are used to adjust the systems autonomy and define self-healing strategies to stabilize/correct a given system in the event of failures.

1. Introduction

Recently, there has been a considerable interest in both policy-based management, goal-based service management and autonomic distributed systems management [1-9]. Policies are often encoded as rules to specify for instance systems security, management properties, allowable states and/or obligations. Based on an ongoing study into requirements for self-adaptive software engineering and management, this paper outlines the interplay of self-managing and self-healing policies and deliberative reasoning models to orchestrate, enable and/or adjust application autonomy. The paper describes a prototype policy-based autonomic system, which is deployed as a middleware service. The system is based on: *service manager, system controller* and *JavaSpaces*, and self-healing policy repository.

The remainder of the paper is structured as follows: section 2 provides background material relating to our approach and in particular describes current trends in autonomic-based management and policy-based management approaches. Section 3, provides an overview of the policy-based autonomic control service. Section 4,

describes the development of the control service based on Jini middleware technology. Section 5, presents a case study and section 6, draws overall conclusions and mentions future work.

2. Background

Recent research has focused on the development of methods and techniques to support runtime management and self-governance of distributed applications, which is reviewed briefly below.

2.1 Policy-Based Management

Much research has addressed the use of policies for dynamic management of large distributed systems [1-3]. Moffett *et al.* [3] stated the necessity of representing and manipulating policy management of distributed systems. In policy management, action policies are represented as a policy hierarchy, where each policy in the hierarchy represents a plan that meets a specific objective. Sloman and Lupu [10] studied authorization and obligation policies' specification for programmable networks. Such policies are interpreted to facilitate runtime activation, de-activation and/or their modification without having to shutdown the network node. Other approaches to policy-based management have used condition-action rules to support a static policy configuration-based solution, in which human intervention is required for system reconfiguration and policy deployment. Moffett *et al.* [11] have proposed a framework for supporting automated policy deployment and flexible event triggers to permit dynamic policy configuration, focusing on solutions for dynamic adaptation of policies in response to changes within the managed environment. Other research efforts have focused on policy specification and enforcement for dynamic service management. For instance, the IETF

Policy Working Group is developing a QoS network management framework using the X.500 directory service, where policies are encoded as If-Then rules and stored in directories [12].

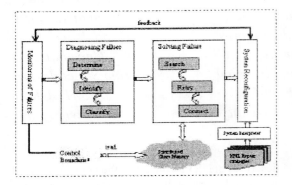

Figure 1: Autonomic management process model.

2.2 Autonomic-Based Management

Within the distributed system community work is underway to understand and design autonomic computing systems endowed with self-management and abilities to adjust to unpredictable changes [13]. The two main elements of autonomic management are the *functional unit* and the *management unit*. The functional unit performs the main operation and is provided by elements such as web services or databases. The management unit is responsible for system resources and operational performance and hence the reconfiguration of resources according to adaptive changes [5]. Autonomic systems have been defined by IBM [6] as system that have "*... The ability to manage themselves and dynamically adapt to change in accordance with policies and objectives...*". In other words, they have the ability to monitor, diagnose and heal themselves. This entails that systems have the ability to dynamically insert and remove code at runtime. *Hot swapping* [8, 9] is proposed as a means to enable autonomic software systems to *interpose and/or replace* components (code) in response of either failure or software maintenance.

3. Policy-Based Autonomic Control Service

Autonomic systems must discharge the intended self-management functionality in a safe, controllable and predictable manner avoiding any emerging, accidental errors or undesirable features [9-12]. This therefore requires that autonomic systems extend and integrate autonomic control models with policy-based service [9]. This formed the motivation for our work, which provides a self-governance mechanism based on a developed

Extensible Believe, Desire and Intension (EBDI) model for deliberative systems. The EBDI model is used to guide and manage an autonomic application's self-healing processes.

Figure 1 illustrates the autonomic management and interaction model used to monitor an application. The overall process starts with the monitoring process to detect conflicts using the control service internal and external polices. This followed by the diagnosis process and then the repair strategies, which are based on the proposed EBDI model (Sec. 4). The strategies are embedded in an external format such as XML, which may be parsed and translated into executable format by the system interpreter. In addition the distributed shared space is used to facilitate the remote integration and coordination of the distributed control services.

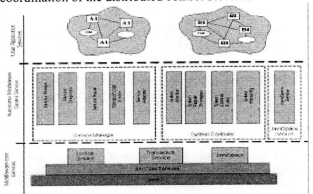

Figure 2:The control service architectural layers.

4. Design of the Proposed Control Service

As shown in Figure 2, the design of the policy-based autonomic control service combines three main services:

- *Service Manager:* is used to adapt the structural components and the dynamic behaviour of the services they provide. Structural components can evaluate their behaviour and environment against their specified goals with capabilities to revise their structure and behaviour accordingly [20]. This separation into distinct service managers eases their management by decentralizing the control of each individual application-level service. Service managers look after their application-level service and monitor its behaviour using an external and internal policies.

- *JavaSpace Service:* is a persistent distributed shared memory used by the self-healing process for awareness and coordination. It stores the required information and reports service states for use by the system controller service to repair and reconfigure the system in the event of any service failures. The JavaSpace service uses *external policies* to notify the system controller directly with remote events. The remote events may either notify of changes in application-level service states (as reported by the service manager) or notify the system controller if the lease of a service manager should expire.

- *System Controller:* is responsible for the dynamic reconfiguration of a given application by coordinating the activities of individual service managers. Each manager is used as a meta-service to monitor, repair and adapt its associated application-level services in the event of conflicts/failures. Service managers may then report their associated application-level service states using the JavaSpace service. Associated external policies can either trigger a notification event to the system controller or request a system controller service's activation to monitor a given application service states. For example, the action shown below may be used if the average latency of the control process exceeds the maximum allowed latency. If such a case occurs the control rule detects and triggers an execution failure notification leading to a self-healing process.

```
If (control_avLatency is larger than
        control_maxLatency)
start
    conflict_monitor(true);
    start_control_process();
end;
```

The development of system repair strategies and self-healing control is based on our proposed Extensible Beliefs, Desires and Intension (EBDI) model [11-13]. The model is concerned with situated intentional software that continuously monitors and/or observes its environment and acts to changes in accordance with its sets of policies.

This architecture is based on a control service model that follows a cycle of monitoring the target application, detecting undesirable behaviours (events), identifying conflicts/errors, prescribing remedial action plans and enacting change plans through reconfiguration[1].

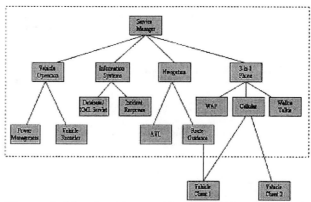

Figure 3: The Architectural view of the EmergeITS application.

5. Case Study

The policy-based autonomic control service has been developed and demonstrated through an industrial case-study, namely EmergeITS [12]. The latter was developed using Jini middleware as a proof-of-concept for self-healing software for intelligent networked appliances (vehicles). The case-study was developed in collaboration with the Merseyside Emergency Fire Service (Fig. 4). One of the EmergeITS services evaluated was the 3-in-1 phone, which allows a mobile phone or PDA device to be used in one of three different modes: a cellular phone, a WAP phone or a walkie-talkie. The 3-in-1 phone may be used for either voice communication or to receive multimedia content, subject to the requirements of the user and availability of a communication service provider. An autonomic middleware control service prototype was incorporated into the case study to provide the meta-control software to support EmergeITS over the network.

The 3-in-1phone service is hosted by an in-vehicle computer, which also acts as a gateway. If the local service deployment should fail, then a service manager is started to provide self-monitoring, self-diagnosis, self-repair and self-adaptation. In the event of failure, the service manager will select an appropriate repair strategy, thereby providing a degree of conflict resolution and fault tolerance. The service manager stores the 3-in-1 phone service state in a JavaSpace service and the system controller may check these states against external policies.

---

[1] A full description of the design and implementation of the autonomic middleware control service is out of the scope of this paper and can be found in a longer version of this paper [12].

```
<?xml version="1.0" ?>
<!-- Simple Description of 2in1 phone Strategies
 -->
<!DOCTYPE strategy [View Source for full doctype.]>
<Strategies>
<Strategy id="1" type="desire">
<Action id="1" type="plan" name="Connection">
<Properties>
<property id="1" name="host">cmsnbadr</property>
<property id="2" name="Location">GPS_loc</property>
<property id="3" name="Max_connected">maxNo</property>
<property id="4" name="Method">connect</property>
</Properties>
</Action>
</Strategy>
<Strategy id="2" type="intension">
<Action id="1" type="plan" name="Retry">
<Properties>
<property id="1" name="No_trial">twe</property>
<property id="2" name="ServiceStatus">not null</property>
<property id="3" name="Method">connect</property>
</Properties>
</Action>
<Action id="2" type="plan" name="Alternative">
<Properties>
<property id="1" name="host">cmsnbadr</property>
<property id="2" name="New Manager Interface">ManagerProxy</property>
<property id="3" name="Get Manager">getServiceManager</property>
<property id="4" name="Client Interface">ClientProxy</property>
<property id="5" name="Get Client">getClient</property>
<property id="6" name="Notify Client">notifyClient</property>
<property id="8" name="Max_connected">maxNo</property>
<property id="9" name="Method">connect</property>
</Properties>
</Action>
</Strategy>
</Strategies>
```

Figure 6: The XML description of a self-repair str
ategy.

7. Conclusions and Future Work

In this paper we have described the development of a policy-based autonomic control service, which has been implemented using Jini middleware technology. The control service incorporates the policies (either internal or external) within the architecture of the autonomic control service to achieve policy-based autonomic control of distributed applications at run time.

We have briefly described the proposed Extensible BDI (EBDI), which is a policy (normative)-based model that is used to examine the system external policies and for generating the appropriate repair strategy at runtime.

We have described the main services of our policy-based autonomic control service (service manager, JavaSpace service and system controller service) and demonstrated their use to control a 3-in-1-phone application service. In addition we have evaluated the performance of the autonomic control service using the elapsed time and the average latency as metrics of the system at runtime.

In our future work, we intend to improve/enhance the autonomic control service on two main fronts: self-protection and machine learning. There is a need to provide self-protection to provide security in untrustworthy environments. There is also a need to equip the current model with the machine learning capabilities so that the policy-based autonomic control service can access history and knowledge relating to the previous failure cases.

8. References

1. E. Lupu, et al. *A Policy Based Role Framework for Access Control*. in *First ACM/NIST Workshop on Role-Based Access Control*. 1995. Maryland USA: ACM.

2. J. Moffett and M.Sloman, *Policy Hierarchies for Distributed Systems Management*. IEEE Journal on Selected Areas in Communications, 1993. **11**: p. 1404–1414.

3. K. Yoshihara, M.Isomura, and H.Horiuchi. *Distributed Policy-based Management Enabling Policy Adaptation on Monitoring using Active Network Technology*. in *12th IFIP/IEEE International Workshop on Distributed Systems: Operations and Management*. 2001. Nancy France.

4. D. Chess, C.Palmer, and S.White, *Security an autonomic computing environment*. IBM SYSTEMS JOURNAL, 2003. **42**.

5. J. Appavoo, et al., *Enabling autonomic behavior in systems software with hot swapping,*. IBM SYSTEMS JOURNAL, 2003. **42**.

6. M. Sloman and E. Lupu. *Policy Specification for Programmable Networks*. in *First International Working Conference on Active Networks (IWAN'99)*. 1999. Berlin.

7. K. Barber, et al. *Conflict Representation and Classification in a Domain Independent Conflict Management Framework*. in *the Third International Conference on Autonomous Agents*. 1999. Seattle WA.

8. P. Horn, *Autonomic Computing: IBM's Perspective on the State of Information Technology*. IBM Corporation, 2001.

9. D. Reilly, et al. *An Instrumentation and Control-Based Approach for Distributed Application Management and Adaptation*. in *Workshop on Self-Healing Systems (WOSS'02)*. 2002. Charleston SC USA.

10. N. Badr, D. Reilly, and A. Taleb-Bendiab. *A Conflict Resolution Control Architecture for Self-Adaptive Software,* in *the International Workshop on Architecting Dependable Systems: WADS 2002 (ICSE 2002)*. 2002. Florida USA.

11. N. Badr, *An Investigation into Autonomic Middleware Control Service to Support Distributed Self-Adaptive Software*, PhD thesis, *School of Computing and Mathematical Sciences,* Liverpool JMU, 2003, www.cms.livjm.ac.uk/cmsnbadr.

12. N. Badr, D. Reilly and A. Taleb-Bendiab, *"Policy-Based Autonomic Control Service"*, Technical Report, School of Computing and Mathematical Sciences, Liverpool JMU, 2004, www.cms.livjm.ac.uk/cmsnbadr.

13. M. Bratman, *Intentions, Plans, and Practical Reason*. Harvard University Press, 1987.

An Hierarchical Policy-Based Architecture for Integrated Management of Grids and Networks

Ricardo Neisse, Evandro Della Vecchia Pereira, Lisandro Zambenedetti Granville,
Maria Janilce Bosquiroli Almeida, Liane Margarida Rockenbach Tarouco
Institute of Informatics - Federal University of Rio Grande do Sul
Av. Bento Gonçalves, 9500 - Porto Alegre, RS - Brazil
{neisse, edvpereira, granville, janilce, liane}@inf.ufrgs.br

Abstract

The management of the underlying network infrastructure, which supports the grid communications, is not proceeded through the same management systems used for the grid management. In this scenario, an integrated management of grids and networks could turn the maintenance processes easier. This paper proposes an hierarchical policy-based architecture, whose goal is to allow such desired integration, where grid policies are translated to network policies following mapping rules defined by network administrators. It also describes a prototype implemented based on the architecture.

1 Introduction

Due to the network requirements and the grid resource distribution, the implementation and management of a grid infrastructure is not a trivial task. Considering that, software libraries, called toolkits, were developed to provide the basic management services required to a proper grid maintenance [2] [1]. These toolkits provide basic services and try to reduce the initial work needed to install and manage a grid. Also, for the grid operation, the management of the network infrastructure is required because grid users access shared resources through the network. Therefore, it would be interesting to have an interaction between the grid toolkit and the network management in order to allow, for instance, a network bandwidth reservation issued from the toolkit but executed by the network management.

In addition to the grid management solutions found in the toolkits, policy-based grid solutions are being proposed to turn such management easier [9] [6]. These proposals do not allow the definition of network QoS parameters in order to allocate resources in the underlying communication

network. Moreover, the policy-based grid management architectures are not integrated with any toolkit mentioned before, although some proposals cite future integration efforts (e.g. Globus toolkit). That leads to a situation where the grid and network administrators are forced to manually interact with each other in order to proceed with the required configuration of the communication support.

Trying to solve this integration problem, this paper proposes an hierarchical policy-based architecture where network management policies, required in each network administrative domain for the grid operation, are derived from grid policies. The architecture translates grid to network policies through a mapping mechanism that uses mapping rules. These rules are defined by the network administrators (of each administrative domain that composes the grid) in order to control how the grid policies have to be mapped to the network policies. The remainder of this paper is organized as follows. Section 2 presents the proposed hierarchical policy-based management architecture, and Section 3 shows the prototype developed based on such architecture. Finally, Section 4 presents conclusions and future work.

2 Hierarchical Mapping Architecture

In the architecture proposed in this paper, grid policies are defined through higher abstraction structures that are mapped to network policies defined through lower abstraction structures. The policy mapping is carried out by a mapping mechanism based on mapping rules. Although the network administrator is not supposed to define network policies for grid operation, he or she is now supposed to define the mapping rules of the mapping mechanism. The network policies generated by the mapping mechanism are then translated to network configuration actions executed by PDPs (Policy Decision Points) [10] of a policy-based network management system (PBNMS).

2.1 Grid and Network Policies

Although we do not aim to define a new language to create grid management policies, we describe a set of elements required for such policies through an hypothetical language, which is based on some of the work previously presented [9] [8]. The support for such required grid policies elements can be accomplished by actual established policy languages like Ponder and PDL. New elements in defining grid policies are required because current grid policy languages does not allow the definition of network QoS requirements together with proxies. We suppose here, for simplicity, that a grid policy language supports both proxies and network QoS following the condition-action model from the IETF.

In the following example (Listing 1), two rules are used to define that the user `neisse` will access, at November 25th 2003, a grid cluster (`LabTec Cluster`) and, from such cluster, he will also access a storage server (`UFRGS Data Server`). In this last access, the `LabTec` cluster will also act as a user proxy. Besides, the user receives a network QoS that allows him to properly and remotely control the execution of processes (`remoteProccessControl`). Since in the second rule a proxy is being used, there is no need to identify with which permissions the user is logged in the storage server because this information is borrowed from the user credentials already found in the cluster access rule.

```
if (user == "neisse" and startTime >= "11/25/2003 00:00:00" and
    endTime <= "11/25/2003 23:59:59"
) {
    if (resource == "LabTec Cluster") {
        allowAccess = true;
        login = gridUser;
        maxProcessing = 50%;
        networkQoS = remoteProccessControl;
    }
    if (proxy == cluster(1) and resource == storageServer(2)) {
        allowAccess = true;
        maxAllowedStorage = 40GB;
        networkQoS = highThroughputDataIntensive;
    }
}
```

Listing 1. Nested grid policies with domains

The grid policy language used supports rule nesting (i.e. one inner rule can be defined in the context of another outer rule) and domains [7], important when defining policy rules whose users, proxies, and resources can not be precisely defined, but only their classes. The grid policy presented state the required network QoS through the `networkQoS` clause and an associated class of service identification (e.g. `remoteProccessControl` and `highThroughputDataIntensive`). Behind these identifications, a set of QoS-related parameters is found. We suppose that the following parameters are available in defining new classes of services: minimum bandwidth, required bandwidth, minimum loss, maximum loss, priority, and a sharing flag that indicates if the bandwidth used by the class of services will be shared among the users. The

classes of services are supposed to be defined by the grid administrator and stored in a library of classes of services to be further used when new grid policies are defined.

Before advancing in this discussion, first we briefly observe how network policies, in terms of QoS, are defined. Listing 2 presents an example of a network policy. This policy states that the traffic generated by host 143.54.47.242 sent to host 143.54.47.17, using any source port (*), addressed to the HTTP port (port 80 over TCP), and with any value as DSCP (*) will have 10Mbps of bandwidth, will be marked with value 1 in the DS field [3], and will gain priority 4. The problem we have here is how to generate such a network policy given: a grid policy, a network QoS, and the network resources sharing issue.

```
if (srcAddress == "143.54.47.242" and srcPort == "*" and
    dstAddress == "143.54.47.17" and dstPort == "80" and
    DSCP == "*" and proto == "TCP" and
    startTime >= "11/25/2003 00:00:00" and
    endTime <= "11/25/2003 23:59:59")
{
    bandwidth = 10Mbps;
    DSCP = 1;
    priority = 4;
}
```

Listing 2. Network policy example

2.2 Mapping Architecture and Mapping Rules

The architecture for mapping grid policies to network policies is presented in Figure 1. The steps in a grid policy translation, identified with the numbers from 1 until 9, are: (1) the grid administrator defines grid policies and network classes of services and stores them in a global repository; (2) the network administrator of each administrative domain defines a set of mapping rules and store it in a local rule repository; (3) once the grid administrator wants to deploy a policy, the mapping engine retrieves such policy from the global repository; (4) the mapping engine retrieves the set of mapping rules from the local rule repository; (5) the mapping engine translates the grid policies based on the mapping rules and consults the toolkit to discover network addresses and protocols information; (6) once the mapping engine builds up new network policies related to the local domain, these policies are stored back in a local network policy repository; (7) the mapping engine signals a set of PDPs in the local domain in order to deploy the just created network policies in a set of PEPs; (8) the signalled PDPs retrieve the network policies from the local repository; (9) the PDPs translate the network policies to configuration actions in order to deploy such policies in the local domain PEPs.

New mapping rules are defined dealing with policy objects that addresses both original grid policies and network policies to be created. Four global objects are implicitly instantiated before a mapping rule evaluation: `schedule`, `srcResource`, `dstResource`, and `requiredQoS`. These objects identify a grid communication pair and hold,

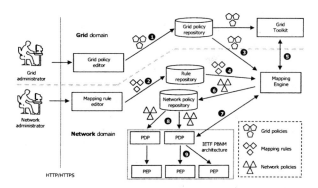

Figure 1. Policy Mapping Architecture

respectively, the period in which the communication has to be considered, the source grid resource, the destination grid resource, and the QoS required from the underlying network. If a proxy is defined, the `srcResouce` will address the proxy IP address and port instead of the user host.

To create new network policies, a mapping rule must first instantiate a `NetworkPolicy` object, and proceed manipulating its content in order to define the network policy conditions and actions. The `addCondition` and `addActions` methods help building up the new policy. Once created, the network policy (through its `NetworkPolicy` object) is stored in the policy repository of the local administrative domain. Listing 3 presents an example of a mapping rule that creates two new network policies from a single grid policy.

```
if (srcResource.address/24 == 143.54.47.0/24 and
    dstResource.address/24 != 143.54.47.0/24 and
    dstResource.port == 80 and dstResource.protocol == TCP)
{
    p1 = new NetworkPolicy();
    p1.addCondition(startTime,">=",schedule.startTime);
    p1.addCondition(endTime,"<=",schedule.endTime);
    p1.addCondition(srcAddress,"==",srcResource.address);
    p1.addCondition(dstAddress,"==",dstResource.address);
    p1.addCondition(dstPort,"==",dstResource.port);
    p1.addCondition(dstProtocol,"==","tcp");
    p1.addAction(DSCP,2);
    inPEPs = select pep
        .within[srcResource.address, 143.54.47.1]
        .direction["in"]
    from
        device.type["DiffServDevice"];
    inPEPs[0].deployPolicy(p1);

    p2 = new NetworkPolicy();
    p2.addCondition(startTime,">=",schedule.startTime);
    p2.addCondition(endTime,"<=",schedule.endTime);
    p2.addCondition(DSCP,2);
    p2.addAction(bandwith,requiredQoS.requiredBandwidth);
    outPEPs = select pep
        .within[srcResource.address, 143.54.47.1]
        .direction["out"]
    from
        device.type["DiffServDevice"];
    outPEPs.deployPolicy(p2);
}
```

Listing 3. Mapping rule example

This mapping rule defines the network policies `p1` and `p2` to mark packets and allocate bandwidth in the underlying network, typically operating with the IETF

DiffServ architecture [3]. However, `p1` and `p2` are only created if the original grid policy states that the source resource is located in the local network (143.54.47.0/24) and the destination resource belongs to another network, different than the local one. The network policy `p1` verifies the local and remote addresses, the remote port (80), and the transport protocol (TCP) of the network packets in order to mark the DS field with the DSCP 2. The policy `p2`, on its turn, only verifies the DSCP to guarantee the required bandwidth determined in the original grid policy.

We provide a mechanism to support the selection of the target network devices (PEPs) in the mapping rule using dynamic domains [4]. Such domains are defined through selection expressions introduced in the mapping rules. In the example from Listing 3, the previous policy `p1` is deployed in the ingress interface of the first router, while policy `p2` is deployed in the egress interface of all routers in the path (including the first router).

3 System Prototype

We have implemented a Web-based prototype of the proposed architecture using the PHP language. Through the prototype, a grid administrator can specify the grid policies and the network administrator, in each administrative domain, can specify the corresponding mapping rules. The prototype is part of the QAME (QoS-Aware Management Environment), a Web-based network management system (NMS) developed at the Federal University of Rio Grande do Sul (UFRGS) [5].

Figure 2. Grid Mapping Rule Editor

The user is allowed to create mapping rules using a list of commands presented to the user in the user interface. The mapping rule editor is presented in Figure 2 and allows the user (network administrator) to write a mapping rule without previous knowledge of the syntax of the language. The mapping rules are scripts defined through a subset of the PHP language.

Figure 3 presents a whole view of the prototype operation and the technologies used in the implementation. The grid policies, required to the mapping process, are retrieved by the mapping engines from a centralized repository, previously configured, and the extra information required by the mapping engine to create the communication pair objects, for instance, resources address and protocols, are queried in the Monitoring and Discovery Service (MDS) of a Globus toolkit copy. The network administrator in each domain creates the mapping rules considering the particular QoS architecture and network topology found in the domain. We tested the mapping engine in a network domain with PDPs implemented in Java to configure QoS in FreeBSD routers with AltQ.

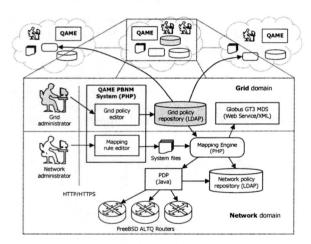

Figure 3. Prototype implementation

4 Conclusions and Future Work

This paper presented an architecture for mapping grid policies to network policies that uses mapping rules to control a mapping engine element. We proposed a set of elements to allow a richer specification of grid policies. These elements allow to express more adequate rules compared to the grid policies found in literature (more expression power). The grid policies can only be translated to network policies if the mapping engine is present. This engine depends on the toolkit used in the grid installation,

and also depends on the PBNMS used by the network administrators.

A Web-based prototype was presented as well. In the current implementation, the mapping rules are defined through a subset of the PHP scripting language. Although the mapping rules are very flexible, this flexibility forces the network administrators to learn a new language to define more adequate mappings. We believe that visual wizards would ease the definition of mapping rules. Currently, such wizards are under investigation through the introduction of more elaborated user interfaces.

The performance evaluation of the proposed architecture needs to be verified. Although we believe that the bandwidth consumption to transfer the policies from one element to other will be reduced, an observation of the impact of such transfer in the underlying network is about to be executed. More important, however, is the performance evaluation of the mapping engine, mainly related to the number of grid rules, level of rules nesting, and number of current mapping rules defined by the network administrator.

References

[1] The access grid (ag) user documentation, 2003. http://www-fp.mcs.anl.gov/fl/accessgrid.

[2] The globus project, 2003. http://www.globus.org.

[3] S. Blake, D. Black, M. Carlson, E. Davies, Z. Wang, et al. An architecture for differentiated services. Request for Comments: 2475, Dec. 1998. IETF.

[4] M. B. Ceccon, L. Z. Granville, M. J. B. Almeida, and L. M. R. Tarouco. Definition and visualization of dynamic domains in network management environments. In *International Conference on Information Networking 2003*, volume 2662 of LNCS, pages 828–838, 2003.

[5] L. Granville, M. Ceccon, L. Tarouco, M. Almeida, and A. Carissimi. An approach for integrated management of networks with quality of service support using qame. *IEEE/IFIP DSOM*, 2001.

[6] V. Sander, W. Adamson, I. Foster, and R. Alain. End-to-end provision of policy information for network qos. *10th IEEE International Symposium on High Performance Distributed Computing*, 2001.

[7] M. Sloman and J. Moffett. Domain management for distributed systems. In *Integrated Network Management I*, pages 505–516, 1989.

[8] B. Sundaram and B. M. Chapman. Policy engine: A policy-based framework for authorization and accounting in computational grids. In *2nd International workshop on Grid Computing*. Springer-Verlag lecture notes in Computer Science, Nov. 2001.

[9] B. Sundaram, C. Nebergall, and S. Tuecke. Policy specification and restricted delegation in globus proxies. In *SuperComputing 2000*, 2000.

[10] A. Westerinen, J. Schnizlein, J. Strassner, M. Scherling, B. Quinn, S. Herzog, A. Huynh, M. Carlson, J. Perry, and S. Waldbusser. Terminology for policy-based management. Request for Comments: 3198, Nov. 2001. IETF.

Automated Generation of Resource Configurations through Policies

Akhil Sahai, Sharad Singhal, Vijay Machiraju
HP Laboratories
1501 PageMill Road, Palo-Alto, CA 94304, USA
Rajeev Joshi[1],
Jet Propulsion Laboratories, Pasadena, CA
{asahai, sharad, vijaym}@hpl.hp.com, rjoshi@jpl.nasa.gov

Abstract

Resource Management systems have been attempting to undertake automated configuration management. Automated configuration management involves considering user requirements, operator constraints and technical constraints of the system to create a suitable configuration, and to create a workflow to deploy it. In this article we propose a policy-based model that we have used for automating these configuration management aspects.

1. Introduction

Resource management systems have been trying to create systems that provide automated provisioning, configuration, and lifecycle management of a wide variety of resources. The current trend in utility computing is a step towards creating such automated resource management systems. HP's Utility Data Center product [1], IBM's "on-demand" computing initiative [2], Sun's N1 vision and Microsoft's DSI initiative, Grid initiative are examples of this trend. However, the resources that are available to these resource managements systems are "raw" computing resources (e.g., servers, storage, network capacity) or simple clusters of machines. The user has to still manually install and configure applications, or rely upon a managed services provider to obtain pre-configured systems from service providers.

Because every user's needs are different, it is usually not possible to create custom environments for every user—managed service providers rely on a small set of pre-built (and tested) application environments to meet each user's needs. However, this limits the ability of users to ask for applications and resources that have been specially configured to meet their needs. In our research, we are focusing on how complex application environments (e.g., an e-commerce site, oracle clusters) can be automatically "built-to-order" for users. In order to create a custom solution that satisfies user requirements many different considerations have to be taken into account. Typically, the underlying resources have technical constraints that need to be met in order for valid operations, e.g., not all operating systems will run on all processors, and not all application servers will work with all databases. In addition, system operators may impose constraints on how they desire such compositions to be created. For example, when resources are limited, only certain users may be able to request them. Finally, the users themselves have requirements on how they want the system to behave. Thus, automating the design, deployment and configuration of such complex environments is a hard problem.

In this paper we describe a model for generating specifications for such environments based on policies. Policies have been traditionally described as rules that change the behavior of a system [3] and policy based management has been viewed as an administrative approach to simplify management by associating certain conditions with actions.

In our model for resource composition [4], the complex environments themselves are treated as higher-level resources that are composed from other resources. Policy is embedded in the various resource types, specified by the operators of the resource pool, or by users as part of the requests for resources, and restricts the composition choices used when composing higher-level resources from the component resources. Unlike traditional policy systems, our policy model does not couple actions to constraints, and actions (workflows) needed for realizing the specification of the higher-level resource are automatically generated. By guiding the composition using policy, our model offers the following advantages over other methods of resource composition:

Component specification is easier than traditional approaches. Policy can be specified in a distributed and hierarchical manner by specifying the behavior of individual entities in the system. The designer only needs to specify constraints (as policy) that relate locally to the component(s) of interest, without worrying about global conflicts during composition. All policies that are

---

[1] Work performed while author was at HP Laboratories.

107

relevant are automatically combined to ensure that the system conforms to the relevant constraints.

The system designer no longer has to be concerned with *how* a given composition can be realized. Because configuration workflows are also generated as part of the specification, the designer only needs to specify the configuration actions available on individual entities in the system.

Updating components becomes easy. If a particular constraint on a component is modified, a new set of attribute values are computed by the policy system that would satisfy all policy constraints in the system, as well as the new configuration workflow that is needed to realize the system.

Adding or updating new entities or components is simplified. Since policy may be attached to any entity, new (or updated) entity instances and entity types can be introduced freely with their associated policies. These new policy instances are automatically considered in the policy management system when the new or updated entities are used.

In the next section of the paper we describe the policy-based model, which is followed by a section on application of the policy model for automating workflow creation.

2. Policy-based Resource Composition

When resources are combined to form other higher-level resources, a variety of rules need to be followed. For example, when operating systems are loaded on a host, it is necessary to validate that the processor architecture assumed in the operating system is indeed the architecture on the host. To ensure correct behavior of a reasonably complex application, several thousand such rules may be necessary if the construction of such applications is to be automated. This is further complicated by the fact that a large fraction of these rules are not inherent to the resources, but depend on preferences (policies) provided by the system operator or indeed, by the customer as part of the request itself.

In this section, we propose a policy-based model for combining resources which allows specification of such rules in a distributed manner. By capturing the construction rules as part of the specification of resource types, and by formalizing how these rules are combined when resources are composed from other resources, we provide a very flexible policy-based model for generating configuration specifications for complex resources.

In our model, we visualize policy as the entire set of strict (enforced) constraints that restrict allowable configurations of some target entity to those that satisfy some goal. Policies are therefore formulated as constraints on system composition (as opposed to conditions that arise as a result of system operation). In our model, resources and configuration activities are considered as the target entities. Each entity is characterized by a set of attributes and values taken by those attributes. For resource entities, the attributes represent configuration or other parameters of the resource that are meaningful for resource composition. For configuration activities, attributes represent if a particular activity needs to be triggered by the deployment system, and if so, parameters that are required for that activity.

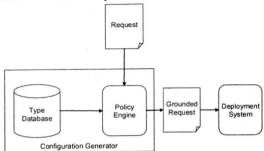

Figure 1: Resource construction process

Figure 1 shows the high level structure of the policy based configuration generator. The user creates a request (which may be minimally specific) for a composed resource. The configuration generator uses a type database and depending on the policies specified in the resource request and those associated with the resource types, generates a "grounded" request specification (i.e., a specification that is provably compliant with policy). The grounded request contains enough detail to allow a deployment system to instantiate the request. The policy engine treats the user's request and the corresponding policy constraints as a goal to be achieved. It uses a constraint satisfaction engine to select resource types and configuration activities, and assigns attribute values such that all of the policy constraints are satisfied.

Figure 2 shows the meta-model for construction policy. Construction policy is associated with both resources and activities that perform configuration operations on those resources. As part of creating the configuration specification, instances of resource types and activities are selected by the configuration generator such that the resulting model conforms to policy. The deployment system then uses that specification to initiate the appropriate activities to configure the resources to that specification.

Construction policy instances contain constraints that are defined using the attributes present in the associated resource type and activity type definitions. When a resource request is grounded, the configuration generator ensures that all policy constraints specified for that resource are satisfied. Because resource types can be derived from other resource types, this implies that all constraints for all composing resources are also satisfied. Activity models contain attributes that describe if a particular activity needs to be triggered during deployment. They may also refer to attributes of the associated resources or other associated activities. By capturing dependencies between the activities in the policy specification, workflows or methods may be modeled as composite activities. Since the configuration generator creates the union of all (relevant) constraints when creating the resource specification, it can also accommodate a variety of operator and user level policies during grounding.

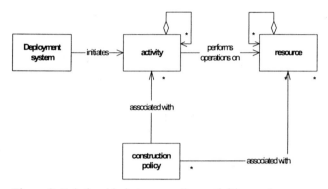

Figure 2: Relationship between policy, activities, and resources

The language that we use for describing policies is derived from the SmartFrog language [5]. Constraints contain first order predicates, arithmetic and logical operators, and other structural constructs.

5. Creating workflows for automated deployment

The deployment system has to execute a number of configuration activities to instantiate the composed resource. However, these activities cannot be executed in any arbitrary order. Just as the resources cannot be pre-composed (the composition depends on user requirements), the configuration parameters and the order of configuration cannot be pre-determined and provided to the deployment system. Depending on the exact composition, components may need to be configured differently and may need different work flows for configuration. Thus, for example, the configuration activities associated with an application server may change if the selected database server is different. Furthermore, depending on the composition, activities may need to be performed in different order. Some

activities could be executed in parallel while others may need to wait for others to complete before proceeding.

Our Activity model is loosely based on the notion of task-graphs as implemented in Microsoft® Project. In our Activity model, configuration activities are modeled similar to resources, and are associated with the resources in the composition hierarchy. As the policy engine selects resources appropriate for a given request, it also selects the corresponding configuration activities. The Activity model is shown in Figure 3. An activity has set of attributes that determine when the activity will be performed. It has a duration, a startdate, enddate, and a mechanism to specify whether there is a deadline associated with the activity. It has a constraintDate and a constraintType that determines when the activity has to be executed. The constraintType could be either, As early As Possible (ASAP), As Late As Possible (ALAP), Finish No Earlier Than (FNET), Finish No Later Than (FNLT), Must Finish On (MFO), Must Start On (MSO), Start No Earlier Than (SNET), Start No Later Than (SNLT).

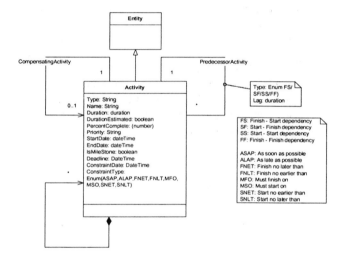

Figure 3: Activity Model

An Activity is made up of other activities. An activity may have a compensating activity and every activity may have a set of predecessor activities. Policies are associated with Activities and so the *pre-conditions* and *post-conditions* of an activity may be specified as policies. In our model, these pre-conditions and post-conditions may also be used to create a sequence of activities in a workflow. We have formalized the precedence through the type attribute defined in the association between an activity and its predecessor activities, which determines the order in which the activities are executed. These temporal planning based constructs enable creation of workflows.

- FS type means the predecessor activity is finished before the successor activity is started (sequence).
- SF means that the predecessor activity is started before the successor activity is finished
- SS means both the activities are started at the same time (parallel). Lag if present determines how much time after the predecessor activity is the successor activity started
- FF means both the activities must finish together (synchronize).

Policy constraints associated with each resource specify the associations between activities and predecessor activities of itself and its components. These predecessor activities have to follow the precedence relationships mentioned above with the successor activities. As a result of the constraint satisfaction a set of components are chosen along with a set of activities. These associations between the so chosen activities automatically establish ordering between the selected activities. A post-processor looks through all the enabled activities and using precedence relationships between the activities, creates a workflow. Figure 3 shows a part of a resource model for an e-commerce site with the associated activities. Note that where refinements exist (e.g.Oracle9i, IBMDB2 for a database) for resources, separate configuration activities may be associated with the refinements. The complete directed acyclic graph establishes the relationships between activities and their immediate predecessors.

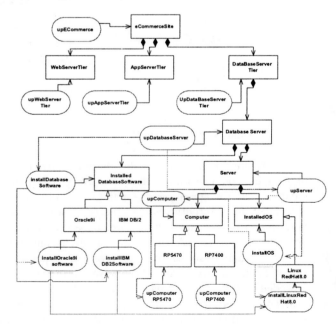

Figure 3: A resource model with associated activities

Figure 4 shows a part of the workflow generated when the model was used to instantiate an instance of an eCommerceSite. Note that the workflow contains both sequential and parallel activities as well as points where different activities need to be joined. Also note that it is not always possible to infer the sequence of activities from the composition hierarchy alone (e.g., the composition hierarchy does not show that the server has to be up before database software can be installed on it in order to instantiate the database server. Such sequences are determined from the dependencies specified as part of the activity model.

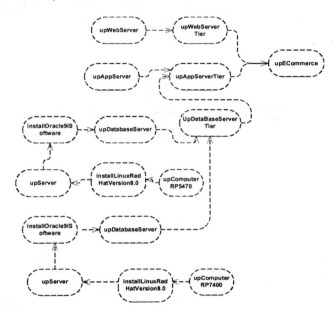

Figure 4: Part of the workflow generated when the e-commerce site is composed

Conclusion

In this article we have discussed how automated resource configuration may be undertaken using constraint satisfaction approach. The first-order logic and linear arithmetic based policy expressions are used to create system and workflow specifications of a system to be deployed.

References

[1] HP Utility Data Center (UDC) http://www.hp.com/enterprise
[2] IBM Autonomic Computing http://www.ibm.com/autonomic
[3] Nicodemos Damianou, Narankar Dulay, Emil Lupu, Morris Sloman: The Ponder Policy Specification Language. POLICY 2001: 18-38
[4] Sahai A, Singhal S, Joshi R, Machiraju V. Automated Policy-Based Resource Construction in Utility Computing Environments. In the proceedings of IEEE/IFIP NOMS 2004.
[5] SmartFrog http://www.smartfrog.org

People and Policies: Transforming the Human-Computer Partnership

Rob Barrett

IBM Almaden Research Center
650 Harry Rd, San Jose, CA 95120
barrett@almaden.ibm.com

Abstract

Policy-driven systems represent a significant change in the human-computer partnership as substantial responsibility is shifted from people to systems. In fact, the shift to policy-driven systems may be understood as a set of specific, distinctive changes in this partnership. This paper describes six such distinctive features of mature policy-driven systems from the human viewpoint and discusses the implications of these for the development of policies and the operation of policy-driven systems.

1. Introduction

This position paper describes a vision for the human side of running advanced policy-based systems. IBM's autonomic computing initiative [3][4] envisions a world of information technology (IT) that is governed by high-level policies rather than by low-level configuration settings. Such policy-based systems aim to reduce the cost, complexity, and frailty of current system management practices, while also enhancing system behavior with qualities such as self-configuration, self-healing, self-optimization, and self-protection. Shifting to such a model will require not only technical innovation, but also substantial changes in the partnership between computers and people. This paper describes the opportunity presented by policy-based systems, not necessarily the state of current systems.

In this paper, we explore some of the theoretical implications of this new sort of human-computer partnership as well as some practical implications of it for the human practice of working with policy-based IT systems. Specifically, we discuss policy-driven computing from the human perspective (as opposed to the technical and system perspective), the realities of the human policy development process, and the human implications of operating policy-based systems.

2. Distinctive Features of the Policy Model

What are policies? Why should IT organizations move from familiar configuration-based systems toward policy-based systems? Defining policy is a continual problem, as discussed by Westerinen [7]. As she explains, Webster's dictionary and the IETF agree on the core concept: policies provide guidance for decision making by providing goals, plans and methods. However, this is not a complete enough definition for differentiating between configuration-based and policy-based systems. For example, configuring a web server to listen on port 80 would fit the definition of a policy because it specifies a goal for the web server and thereby guides the decision making of the web server software when selecting a port. Even further specifying that policies are "high level" is not enough because in our example many "low level" details have indeed been left out, such as specifying that this goal can be accomplished by a plan that involves opening a socket and accepting connections on it, or that the low level plan involves using the open() and accept() methods on a Socket object.

We think it is helpful to define policy-based systems in terms of their appearance to their human operators in addition to their technological underpinnings. In this regard, we focus on six aspects of policy-based systems that present an opportunity for transforming the partnership between computers and their human operators: (1) vocabulary, (2) expertise embodiment, (3) span of control, (4) generality and specificity, (5) separation of goals and methods, and (6) progressive grounding.

Policy-based systems can shift the *vocabulary* of interaction between human and computer toward the domain of interest of the people. Instead of specifying port number 80, a policy-based system could allow the operator to specify that the web server should use its well known port number. Shifting from the computer-centric "80" to the human-centric "well-known" is an example of the sort of vocabulary change that can go along with policy-based systems. As another example, a storage policy might specify that "music files" receive "bronze-class" service, which are more human-centric terms than "files matching the regular expression '(.)+\.(mp3|wav)' are stored on devices with data rates of >1Mbps and access times of <5 seconds".

Policy-based systems *embody expertise* within them, decreasing the expertise required of operators. For example, a policy-based system might allow the operator to specify that all system operations comply with Security Directive 123 from SecurityExperts.com without requiring the operator to understand the directive's details or translate them into operational configurations and processes. Of course, this policy would resolve into many sub-policies. Westerinen describes this aspect of policy as "enabl[ing] reuse and duplication of an expert's knowledge and processes" [7].

Policy-based systems enlarge the *span of control* of the human operator from single components toward end-to-end systems, business processes, and even complete businesses. In the previous security example, a single policy governs all system operations rather than separate expressions covering each system. From the operator's point-of-view, this not only reduces effort but also reduces errors of omission and covers future systems. Policies naturally transcend the computer-centric component view of IT operations.

The move to policy-based systems can also provide the ability for operators to specify general guidelines that may be adjusted in particular cases. For example, a general policy may be that unused files will persist for at least one year from their last use. More specific policies may stipulate that certain files persist for longer while others have shorter lifetimes. This *generality and specificity* again moves the specification to more natural human terms.

Well-written policies *separate goals and methods*. Dijker's helpful manual on writing human-readable policy documents points out that policies should not contain processes for implementing the policies, but should reference other documentation [2]. This separation preserves the policy specification even as processes change. Ross points out that the adaptability of business rules directly results from this separation, which allows business processes to be replaced when adapting a system within stated constraints [5]. Tying policies too closely to implementation makes policies inscrutable, inflexible, and brittle. For example, a policy may specify the goal of maintaining backups that are less than a week old without specifying when and how backups are actually run.

Finally, policies should be described in a progressive fashion, moving fluidly between generalities and specifics, goals and methods, components and systems, levels of expertise, and domains of vocabulary. The result for human operators is that computers begin to act more as partners than tools. Human partnership requires *progressive grounding* where conversation between the partners is used to form common understanding that develops over time [1]. Just as a newly hired secretary may require extensive detailed guidance when making travel reservations for the boss, new systems will require extensive interaction to build common ground with its operators. Later interactions will require less detailed exchanges, but changing circumstances and needs will mean that new instructions, clarification on meanings, disambiguating earlier assumptions, questioning plans, and so on must occur continually. Computer partners will show similar interaction patterns.

These six features help to define what it means for a system to interact with its human operators by means of policies. Note that none of these—vocabulary, expertise embodiment, span of control, generality and specificity, separation of goals and methods, and progressive grounding—are either true or false for a given system but are more or less present in one system compared with another. By this description, from the human perspective there is a continuum of maturity for policy-driven systems.

3. Developing Policies

As systems become more policy-driven, there will be significant changes in the human organizations that manage systems. In this section, we discuss policy development and some of the human and organizational implications of moving to policy-based computing.

In describing IBM's autonomic computing vision, Kephart and Chess point out that "the enormous leverage of autonomic systems will greatly reduce human errors, but it will also greatly magnify the consequences of any error humans do make in specifying goals" [4]. This is also true for policies. For this reason alone, it is clear that the development of policies for policy-driven systems will be a complex social process. In the context of writing IT policies for people, Dijker insists that policies should be authored by teams: "There are too many potential consequences of establishing a policy to leave its development to a single individual" [2]. Therefore, policy-based systems must provide for different roles and responsibilities across a number of individuals when policies are being authored. For example, Dijker recommends that a policy authoring team include at least a senior system administrator, a high-level manager, a lawyer, a writer, and a user. This list reveals some of the important roles in policy development. The system administrator and lawyer represent *domain experts* who are necessary for determining the fitness of proposed policies. The administrator contributes technical expertise, and the lawyer, legal expertise. They can answer questions about the technical and legal implications of the policies. There might be many other experts whose domain knowledge is needed for developing good policies, such as human resource experts who understand what is important for employee morale, industry experts who know what policies competitors use, customer experts who understand the impact of policy decisions on customers, and so on.

Dijker's user is a *stakeholder*, a representative of the group that will be affected by the policies. The various stakeholders in the policy decisions must have a voice in specifying the policies so that the best tradeoffs can be made by the whole team. The high-level manager represents the *responsible agent* who authorizes the final policy decisions, is willing to defend and enforce their implementation, and is the appellate judge for future arguments for policy changes. Finally, the *writer* is the one who is responsible for encoding the team's policy decisions into the appropriate final form. In Dijker's case this is a conventional writer but policy-based systems will require one skilled in writing machine-readable policies that represent the team's decision. Policies of any realistic complexity will require special skills to encode them. These four roles classes of domain expert, stakeholder, responsible agent and writer should collaboratively interact with any policy development tools that are used in complex real-world systems.

Dijker also points out that good human-readable policies contain persuasive language for why these policies have been enacted and what the risks of alternative policies would be [2]. Computer-readable policies do not have the same problem of convincing their readers to comply; however, specifications for policy-based systems will still need to be read by people at various points in their lifecycle: initial implementation, verification, operation and revision. Therefore including complete documentation of when the policy applies, why it exists, how it can be implemented, and the risks of alternatives will be helpful when specifying policies. Otherwise later readers of the policy will have the doubly difficult task of determining what the policy actually accomplishes, and its original intent. It should not be assumed that the machine-readable form of the policy will naturally include this sort of critical information.

Policy development is not a one-time process, so policy writing tools must support continual development of improved policies. This is related to the need for progressive grounding in policy-based system interaction. Changes in policy will include such things as new exceptions to general policies, adjustment of details of policies, and changes to the implementations of the policies, as well as large-scale changes to the overall policy structure. Just as programmers have learned to separate algorithms from parameters and to internationalize text messages, policy writers will learn to specify varying details of policies separately from the policy itself. For example, gold customers may receive a 10% discount today and a 15% discount tomorrow. Reports might go to Joe today and Jane tomorrow, when she takes his job. Policy systems need to enable writers to manage relatively fixed and varying parts of the policy without modifying the entire policy.

Likewise, policies and implementations should be kept separate. Procedural detail not only obscures the actual goal of the policy, but is also likely to change more quickly than the governing policy. Procedures and policies should be cross-referenced so that their relationship is understood, but they should not be confused. In fact, the roles of policy development and procedure development may be very different.

Finally, Dijker points out that policy writing teams will need to make many policy decisions "on the fly" [2]. As policies are being defined, gaps in the current understanding will appear and need to be filled. For example, there might be a policy that all corporate communications must be archived, but it might not be clear whether dynamically generated fact sheets are a valid exception. The team must have rapid means for answering such questions as well as the power to make its own decisions as the policies are being authored. As noted previously, the power of policy-based management means that the authority of the policy writers must be carefully managed.

4. Operating with Policies

We have discussed features of policy-based systems from a human viewpoint and the process of developing policies for such a system. We now explore the operational flavor of a policy-based system. What are the implications for the system operator? In some scenarios, the system operator disappears, having become as obsolete as telephone operators. In others, the operator becomes a de-skilled babysitter who watches for alarms. In others, the operator moves up the value chain, integrating business and IT savvy into corporate impact. Regardless of the scenario, policy-based systems have different operational requirements than conventional systems, likely leading to different individual and organizational behavior.

First, operators must trust these systems or else they will either be left undeployed or subverted. Because the vocabulary of interaction will shift toward the human domain, the system will need to demonstrate that it has understood the human goals. There will be varying levels of automation that require varying degrees of trust. IBM's autonomic roadmap lists five: Basic, Managed, Predictive, Adaptive, Autonomic [3]; Sheridan lists ten [6]. At the lowest level is manual control; in the middle levels the system offers possible actions; at the highest levels the system takes actions automatically. These are fine taxonomies, but in real deployments, all levels will operate simultaneously in different parts of the system (*e.g.*, virtual memory allocation will remain fully automatic; purchase of new hardware will probably remain manual). Operators will need tools to manage the levels of automation as the system matures and becomes more trustworthy.

Second, policy-driven systems will become more highly coupled than conventional systems, requiring operators to maintain situation awareness over much larger domains. For example, changing a web server policy may affect network usage, which might change a database backup plan that shares the same network. Policy-driven systems will need to provide views and controls that operate at the proper level of abstraction (providing the right information, neither too much nor too little) for a given situation in order for the resulting complex to be controllable.

Third, policy-driven systems have the potential to be less predictable than their predecessors. For example, operators may be used to system backups running every Saturday evening. But a policy-driven system may decide to shift the backup to a maintenance window on Sunday in order to do a necessary data reorganization on Saturday. When the operators notice this change in behavior, an explanation must be forthcoming to calm fears that the backup has been "forgotten." These systems will also be unpredictable because constraint-oriented policy engines famously find unexpected solutions to problems. For example, an email application might discover that it can achieve throughput goals by deleting all attachments if it did not understand this to be an unacceptable solution. Highly-dynamic systems are also fundamentally less predictable because they change their configuration more quickly than their operators adjust their mental

models. In operational environments, policy-driven systems must be able to explain and justify their behavior, to disclose planned behavior, to have their plans adjusted on-the-fly, and to interact with operators to incrementally improve their common understanding of the goals. All of this communication should be done in a way that corresponds with the distinctive features of mature policy-driven systems, *e.g.*, in human vocabulary terms of general and specific policies, separating goals and methods.

In conclusion, the move toward policy-driven systems must be understood from the point of view of changes to the human-computer partnership—as well as from the point of view of technology. As more responsibility is shifted toward the computer, complex technological change will be required to handle the responsibility. But significant changes will also be required in human organizations and individuals to develop and operate these policy-driven systems, as well as in interface technologies that connect people and systems to work smoothly together in partnership.

5. References

[1] Clark, H. H. *Using Language*. Cambridge University Press, 1996.

[2] Dijker, B. L., "A Guide to Developing Computing Policy Documents," SAGE, http://sageweb.sage.org/resources/publications/policies/.

[3] IBM, "Autonomic Computing Concepts," http://www.ibm.com/autonomic/pdfs/AC_Concepts.pdf.

[4] Kephart, J.O. and D.M. Chess, "The Vision of Autonomic Computing," IEEE Computer, Jan 2003, http://www.research.ibm.com/autonomic/research/papers/AC_Vision_Computer_Jan_2003.pdf.

[5] Ross, R.G., "The Business Rules Approach," Policy 2003, IEEE 4th Intl Workshop on Policies for Distributed Systems and Networks, Lake Como, Italy, June 4-6, 2003, http://www.policy-workshop.org/2003/web/policy2003/common/RonaldPresentation.pdf.

[6] Sheridan, T. B., *Telerobotics, Automation, and Human Supervisory Control*. MIT Press, 1992.

[7] Westerinen, A., "What Is Policy? And, What Can It Be?", Policy 2003, IEEE 4th Intl Workshop on Policies for Distributed Systems and Networks, Lake Como, Italy, June 4-6, 2003, http://www.policy-workshop.org/2003/web/policy2003/common/AndreaPresentation.pdf.

6. Acknowledgments

We thankfully acknowledge helpful insights provided by Paul Maglio and Eser Kandogan.

Session 5:
Security Policy
in Large Scale Systems

A Framework for Contractual Resource Sharing in Coalitions

Babak Sadighi Firozabadi*

Policy Based Reasoning Group
Swedish Institute of Computer Science (SICS)
Box 1263, SE-16429 Kista, Sweden
babak@sics.se

Marek Sergot

Department of Computing
Imperial College London
180 Queen's Gate, London SW7 2BZ, UK
mjs@doc.ic.ac.uk

Anna Squicciarini†   Elisa Bertino

Dipartimento di Informatica e Comunicazione
Università degli Studi di Milano
Via Comelico 39/41, 20135 Milano, Italy
{squicciarini,bertino}@dico.unimi.it

Abstract

We develop a framework for specifying and reasoning about policies for sharing resources in coalitions, focussing here on a particular, common type of contract in which coalition members agree to make available some total amount of specified resource over a given time period. The main part of the framework is a policy language with two basic elements: 'obligations' (of a member enterprise to provide a total amount of resource over a given time period) express the coalition policy, and 'entitlements' (granted by an enterprise to other coalition members) express the local policies of the coalition members. We discuss the conditions under which a local policy can be said to be in compliance with, or meet, the obligations of a coalition policy, and the conditions under which an obligation, and by extension a contract, can be said to be violated or fulfilled.

1 Introduction

There is a growing interest in facilitating collaboration between independent and heterogeneous enterprises, in the form of coalitions. One of the reasons behind creating such coalitions is to share different types of resources that are owned and independently managed by the coalition members. The set of resources are made available by participating enterprises which agree on sharing them according to a *coalition policy* expressed in terms of a *contract* between the coalition members. The coalition policy defines the agreed rights of the coalition members to use others' resources and their obligations to provide their own resources to other coalition members.

The aim of the paper is to develop a framework for specifying and reasoning about policies for sharing resources in coalitions. We focus on a particular, common type of contract in which coalition members agree to make available some total amount of specified resource over a given time period. The main part of the framework is a policy language with two basic elements: 'obligations' (of a member enterprise to provide a total amount of resource over a given time period) express the coalition policy, and 'entitlements' (granted by an enterprise to other coalition members) express the local policies of the coalition members. We discuss the conditions under which a local policy can be said to be in compliance with, or meet, the obligations of a coalition policy, and the conditions under which an obligation, and by extension a contract, can be said to be violated or fulfilled.

2 Overview

In this section we give an overview of a framework for contractual sharing of computational resources in a coalition. The idea is that coalition members, which in our case are enterprises, can share resources among each other according to a coalition policy which can be seen as a contract between the coalition members. We see one member's

---

*The work by Sadighi Firozabadi was partly supported by the Policy Based Management project funded by the Swedish Agency for Innovation Systems.

†The work by Squicciarini was performed during her stay at the Swedish Institute of Computer Science (SICS).

obligation to provide a resource to another as the second member's right to access/use that resource. As a coalition member an enterprise will gain access to the resources of others and at the same time will have to release its own resources for use by the other members, according to the *rules of sharing* stated in the contract.

Resources in a coalition are shared but are still managed independently by their owners. Each member of a coalition has its own *local policy* which specifies how it intends to grant access to its resources. An enterprise may change the terms of use of its resources, in its local policy, to optimize the resource usage as time passes.

Each enterprise as a member of a coalition must publish a local policy that complies with the contract of the coalition. This local policy must be available for other coalition members to examine, in order that they may be able to plan how to make use of the shared resources available. It is a separate question whether an enterprise will in fact comply with its own local policies. An enterprise might promise to provide a total amount of resource that exceeds what it can actually deliver. An enterprise may also be a member of several coalitions, and it might produce several local policies for its resources, each compliant with the contract of one of the coalitions to which it belongs, but without being able to comply with all the coalition policies at the same time. This is similar to the way flight companies sell tickets to more people than they have available seats.

Although a member publishes a local policy specifying how it will make its resources available, it is still possible in practice that it will deny access to its resource upon a request. If a request to access a resource is not granted, although specified as available in the local policy, then the enterprise violates the corresponding obligation in the coalition policy. As a consequence of the violation, the enterprise must usually accept another obligation to be fulfilled, or in the absence of such an obligation, it will violate the entire contract. The assumption is that members always have an incentive to continue being members of coalitions, and hence they will avoid, as far as they are able, any breach of contract. In the case that a contract is violated, one can expect that some kind of punitive actions may take place, for instance, expulsion of the defaulter from the coalition. These further considerations however will be outside the framework presented in this paper.

It is important to note that all the member interactions are carried out without centralized control. Thus, a key issue of the proposed framework concerns monitoring systems. The framework provides both monitoring systems and enforcement mechanisms at different stages of the coalition life. First, a mechanism for verifying that local policies satisfy coalition policies is devised. Then, a level of monitoring is performed for controlling the actual granting of access requests. It is reasonable to assume that if a request is granted

then the resource is actually allocated for the requester to use. To make this explicit, the granting of a request can be in the form of a signed certificate stating that the requesting agent is entitled to access/use the resource, which in our case is the same as allocating the resource for use by the agent. In this way, we factor out of consideration the possibility that a request is granted but the resource or the promised level of quality is subsequently not provided. A system to enforce this would be one which has a central reference monitor controlling access to the coalition resources, even though these are owned by different coalition members. Note that the resources are released by the reference monitor, only if the user can show a valid certificate issued by the resource owner stating its right to use the resource. It is up to the resource owner to keep track of the use of its resource and it cannot grant access to a resource that is already in use. We do not consider the issue of blocking granted requests in this paper, but of course one can think of a system supporting this as a way of releasing resources that are in use in order to fulfill certain obligations as a cost of violating others.

As a running example, we consider an academic alliance ($\mathcal{AA}$, in what follows) involving a number of different systems cooperating on a common research project. The entities involved are, let us say, three universities ($Milano, Imperial, KTH$), two research centres ($SICS, CNR$), and two business companies ($ABCent, Micro$) sharing resources and services. We will use this scenario throughout the paper to show how the framework can be applied.

3   Formal Framework

In this section we formalize the ideas described informally in the previous section. We start by defining what a coalition consists of and its basic elements. We develop a policy language for describing local and coalition policies. We also define how a local policy conforms to an obligation and how it conforms to a coalition policy.

Definition 3.1 (Coalition Elements) The basic elements of a coalition are:

1. $\mathcal{R}$ denotes the set of resources shared among the coalition.

2. *Users* denotes the set of users of the resources pooled in the coalition. We assume only that each user is somehow uniquely identified, for example by its public key.

3. $\mathcal{E} = \{E_1, \ldots, E_n\}$ denotes a finite set of enterprises, the members of the coalition. Each enterprise has associated with it a (possibly empty) set of users, as given by the function $users \colon \mathcal{E} \to \wp(Users)$. $users(E)$ is the set of users who belong to enterprise E. The same user can belong to several different enterprises.

4. *Pol* denotes the set of policies regulating the sharing of the resources available in the coalition. *Pol* conveys the coalition policy *Contract* as well as the local policy $\mathbf{LP}_E^t$ of each member enterprise $E \in \mathcal{E}$ at each time point t. For simplicity, in this paper we assume that the coalition policy *Contract* does not vary over time.

5. Each member enterprise maintains an accounting/monitoring system which keeps track of all usage of its resources and all requests for access submitted to it by other coalition members. We assume that the coalition also has access to this accounting information, either by obtaining it from member enterprises, or by maintaining its own independent monitoring and accounting system where member enterprises cannot be trusted to supply the information reliably. The minimum requirements for the accounting system are described in section 3.3.

Resources are provided to users as member of enterprises. Here, we do not assume anything about the internal structure and behaviour of the users in a given enterprise, and consider them only as agents executing actions.

3.1 Resources

A key element in characterizing a coalition is the set of resources to be shared by coalition members. To be correctly enforced, policies must be specified according to the specific features of the resources to which they refer. Resource descriptions therefore must be expressed in terms of measurable parameters. For example, the resource type *bandwidth* can be specified by the parameters *amount, duration-time, latency*. We use a generic scalar metric to specify parameters and allow them to be composed to model resource features. Resource requirements can be expressed either by exactly specifying resource capacity or by constraining the ranges of capacity. Resources may be specified by the following type of metrics, similar to those used in [4]:

— **Time Metrics** where time points are expressed as a combination of date and clock time, e.g. $(22\text{-}09\text{-}2003, 13{:}54{:}23)$. For the examples in this paper, time points will be measured to the second, though of course this is very easily changed to the needs of an actual application.

— **Scalar Metrics** given as some suitable numerical value depending on the type of resource, such as integers for the amount of disc-space (50Gb).

— **Max limit–Min limit** specifying an exclusive or inclusive upper/lower limit on the given metric.

We assume that each resource is specified by means of a set of characterizing attributes, each expressed using one of the above metrics. This way of specifying resources defines an ontology for formally checking whether a resource is properly released, meeting the parameters describing the resource itself.

Definition 3.2 (Resource comparison) Let *ResType* be a resource type, measured according to some suitable metric m. Let R' and R'' be two instances of resource type *ResType*. $R' \sqsubseteq_m R''$ denotes that the two instances R' and R'' of resource type *ResType* are comparable and that R' is less than or equal to R'', according to metric m.

In what follows the subscript m is often omitted where context allows.

For instance, where bandwidth resource is characterized by the attributes {*amount, duration-time, latency*} we can write, e.g., $\{10Gb, 10h, 1.5ms\} \sqsubseteq_{bw} \{12Gb, 18h, 1.5ms\}$. Some amounts are not comparable. $\{10Gb, 10h, 1.5ms\}$ is not comparable with, e.g. $\{8Gb, 18h, 1.5ms\}$.

3.2 Obligations and Entitlements

The two basic elements of our policy language are *obligation* and *entitlement*. Here, we give formal definitions of these two notions. In the next section we will define how obligations can be fulfilled and violated.

Definition 3.3 (Obligation) An obligation for an enterprise P to provide a total amount R of a certain resource over the time interval I to each of a set S of enterprises is denoted as $Obl(P, S, R, I)$ where:

— $P \in \mathcal{E}$ denotes the *bearer* of the obligation, also referred to as the 'providing enterprise' or simply 'the provider';

— $S \subseteq \mathcal{E}$ is the set of enterprises to whom the obligation is owed;

— R is a specified amount of a resource in $\mathcal{R}$;

— I denotes the time period of the obligation, expressed as a time interval $I = [t_{start}, t_{end}]$.

The idea is that there is a total amount R of resource available over the time interval I. There is no restriction on how R will be claimed: it can be claimed all at once, or piecemeal. The policy language could be extended to specify also minimum and maximum amounts of R that can be claimed at any one time but we shall not do so here.

The intended reading is that obligation $Obl(P, \{E_1, \ldots, E_k\}, R, I)$ is equivalent to a collection of separate obligations $Obl(P, \{E_1\}, R, I)$, $\ldots$, $Obl(P, \{E_k\}, R, I)$. It is also possible to extend the policy language by introducing another form of obligation $CollObl(P, S, R, I)$ to represent an obligation owed by P to the set of enterprises S collectively, that is to say, to represent that enterprises S *share* access to P's resource R over interval I. The details for the *CollObl* form of obligation are not difficult but are sufficiently complicated that we omit them here for brevity. (There is in any case no loss of expressivity, since if necessary we can introduce another 'artificial' enterprise E_S such that $users(E_S) = \bigcup_{E \in S} users(E)$.)

Example 1

$Obl(SICS, \{Milano, KTH\}, \{10Gb, 600h, 1.5ms\},$
$\qquad [(12\text{-}07\text{-}2003, 10:10:50), (02\text{-}12\text{-}2003, 10:23:30)]\,)$
is an example of an obligation, stating that SICS is obliged to provide at least 10Gb of network bandwidth for a total of 600 hours over the specified time period to each one of Milano and KTH universities.

Definition 3.4 (Entitlements) Entitlements are expressions of the form $Ent_P(E, R, I)$ where:

— $P \in \mathcal{E}$ is the granter of the entitlement;

— $E \in \mathcal{E}$ is the enterprise to which the entitlement is granted;

— R is a specified amount of a resource in $\mathcal{R}$;

— I denotes the time period of the entitlement, expressed as a time interval $I = [t_{start}, t_{end}]$.

An entitlement can be regarded as a promise by an enterprise to grant access to its resource. By publishing the entitlement $Ent_P(E, R, I)$ in its local policy, the enterprise P promises that over the time interval I a total amount R of the resource will be released on request to any user belonging to the entitled enterprise E.

As in the case of obligations, it is possible to introduce another form of entitlement $SharedEnt_P(S, R, I)$ to represent that the set of enterprises S together *share* an entitlement to P's resource R throughout interval I. Again, we omit the details for brevity.

The first step for an enterprise to fulfill an obligation is to specify a local policy that is in compliance with the obligation, or, as we shall also say, one that *meets* the obligation. This step is a necessary but not sufficient condition for fulfillment of the obligation: it does not mean that the resource is actually allocated, but merely that the provider has published a plan specifying how it intends to fulfill its obligation. This plan may change as time goes on.

We now define the conditions under which a set of entitlements is *in compliance with*, or meets, an obligation. The key point is that $Obl(P, \{E_i\}, R, I)$ allows users in E_i to take up to the full amount R of the resource from P over the time period I, with no restriction on how much of the resource is requested at any time, up to the limits of the obligation. Users in E_i can take R at any time over I—all at the same time, spread evenly across the interval, or in whatever portions they choose. So in order to meet its obligation, P must publish entitlements in its local policy in such a way

that all of E_i's possible uses are accommodated. Clearly, an entitlement $Ent_P(E_i, R', I')$ meets this requirement when $I' = I$ and $R \sqsubseteq R'$. But suppose that I' is a (proper) sub-interval of I. Then $Ent_P(E_i, R', I')$ would not, by itself, meet the obligation since it restricts an entitled user to access R only during the sub-interval I'. A set of entitlements could meet the obligation, however, if together they cover the entire obligation interval I.

What if the entitlement interval I' extends beyond the obligation interval I? In this case, an entitled user is able to access the full amount R of obligated resource over the interval I, as long as I' does not start earlier than I (because in that case, some of the entitled resource may have been used up already before the obligation interval I commences).

Finally, we do not want to allow separate entitlements to be accumulated over the interval I in order to meet an obligation. For example, if there is an obligation to provide 100Gb of disk storage over the interval $[1, 10]$ (here and later we sometimes use integers for time points to reduce clutter), two separate entitlements of 50Gb each over $[1, 5]$ and $[6, 10]$ would not meet the obligation. Even though the sum total of entitled resource over the interval $[1, 10]$ meets the required 100Gb, two separate entitlements impose restrictions on how the entitled 100Gb can be accessed and thus do not meet the obligation. The only way that two separate entitlements over the intervals $[1, 5]$ and $[6, 10]$ could meet the obligation is if both granted at least 100Gb of disk storage each. Anything less would impose a restriction on how the 100Gb resource is accessed over $[1, 10]$.

This may seem like a very strict requirement, but the point is that if two separate entitlements of 50Gb each over time intervals $[1, 5]$ and $[6, 10]$ are to be regarded as meeting the agreed obligation, the provision that should have been specified in the contract is an obligation to provide 50Gb over time interval $[1, 5]$ and an obligation to provide 50Gb over time interval $[6, 10]$, not one single obligation for 100Gb over $[1, 10]$.

A case could be made for allowing entitlements for the same resource type which span the obligation interval to be summed up: one could say that an entitlement of, e.g., 70Gb over $[1, 10]$ combined with another entitlement of, e.g., 30Gb over $[1, 10]$ together would meet an obligation to provide 100Gb over $[1, 10]$. However, this possibility raises a number of further potential difficulties which still remain to be resolved and we therefore do not support it in this version of the framework.

The definition we use is as follows.

Definition 3.5 (l-cover) Let $I = [t_s, t_e]$ and $I_1, \ldots I_k$ ($k \geq 1$) be (closed) time intervals. $\{I_1, \ldots I_k\}$ is a *l-cover* for the interval I iff

i) $t_s \leq t'_s \leq t_e$ for every interval $[t'_s, t'_e]$ in $\{I_1, \ldots I_k\}$;

ii) for every time point $t \in I$ there is an interval I_i in $\{I_1, \ldots I_k\}$ such that $t \in I_i$.

Condition (ii) requires that the collection of intervals $\{I_1, \ldots I_k\}$ together cover the entire interval I. Condition (i) requires that none of the intervals in $\{I_1, \ldots I_k\}$ start earlier than the interval I.

Definition 3.6 (Obligation compliance) Let $\mathbf{E}_P$ be a set of entitlements granted by enterprise P. Let $S \subseteq \mathcal{E}$ be a set of enterprises. The set of entitlements $\mathbf{E}_P$ is in compliance with an obligation $Obl(P, S, R, I)$, denoted by

$$\mathbf{E}_P \text{ meets } Obl(P, S, R, I)$$

iff, for every enterprise $E \in S$, there exists a set of entitlements $\{Ent_P(E, R_1, I_1), \ldots, Ent_P(E, R_k, I_k)\} \subseteq \mathbf{E}_P$ such that $\{I_1, \ldots, I_k\}$ is a 1-cover for I and $R \sqsubseteq R_i$ for every $i \in 1..k$.

Example 2
Consider the following set of entitlements granted by research centre SICS:

1. $Ent_{SICS}(Milano, \{18Gb, 610h, 1.5ms\},$
   $[(12\text{-}07\text{-}03, 10:10:50), (20\text{-}10\text{-}2003, 08:43:30)])$
2. $Ent_{SICS}(Milano, \{12Gb, 650h, 1.5ms\},$
   $[(20\text{-}10\text{-}03, 08:43:31), (02\text{-}12\text{-}2003, 10:23:30)])$
3. $Ent_{SICS}(KTH, \{10Gb, 600h, 1.5ms\},$
   $[(12\text{-}07\text{-}03, 10:10:50), (02\text{-}12\text{-}2003, 10:23:30)])$

This set of entitlements is in compliance with the obligation of Example 1. Entitlements 1 and 2 together cover the obligation interval and each provides (more than) enough resources to meet the specified requirements for Milano. Entitlement 3 covers the obligation interval and meets the specified requirements for KTH.

The following restatement of Definition 3.6 is useful.

Proposition 1 *Let $\mathbf{E}_P$ be a set of entitlements granted by enterprise P. Let $Obl(P, S, R, I)$ be an obligation. Suppose $I = [t_s, t_e]$. Then $\mathbf{E}_P$ meets $Obl(P, S, R, I)$ iff, for every enterprise $E \in S$ and every $t \in I$, there exists an entitlement $Ent_P(E, R', [t'_s, t'_e]) \in \mathbf{E}_P$ such that $t_s \leq t'_s \leq t \leq t'_e$ and $R \sqsubseteq R'$.* $\square$

3.3 Local policies and obligation fulfillment

Definition 3.7 (Local Policy) For every enterprise $P \in \mathcal{E}$ and every time point t, the set of policies Pol conveys the local policy $\mathbf{LP}_P^t$ of P at time t.

The local policy $\mathbf{LP}_P^t$ is a (finite) set of entitlements $\{Ent_P(E_1, R_1, I_1), \ldots, Ent_P(E_n, R_n, I_n)\}$.

Note that we do not insist that the time point t must be within the validity interval of each entitlement in $\mathbf{LP}_P^t$. A local policy can thus specify future as well as past entitlements. Note also that since $\mathbf{LP}_P^t$ is a set of entitlements, the expression $\mathbf{LP}_P^t$ meets $Obl(P, S, R, I)$ is well defined. We can thus speak of a local policy at time t being in compliance with, or meeting, an obligation.

We assume that there is an accounting system at each enterprise P that keeps track, for each resource owned by P, the amount of that resource granted by P to each enterprise E of the coalition over any given time interval. We will also assume that the coalition itself has access to this information, either by trusting P to supply this information or by maintaining its own independent monitoring and accounting system.

Definition 3.8 (Accounting function) Let P and E be enterprises in $\mathcal{E}$, R a specified amount of a resource in $\mathcal{R}$, and t_s and t time points. *Consumed* and *Rest* are the accounting functions for resource usage: $Consumed(P, E, R, t_s, t)$ gives the amount of resource R that has been granted by P to E from time t_s up to but not including time t. $Rest(P, E, R, I, t)$ is the amount of P's resource R that was available at time t_s and remains available for the use of E at time t.

$$Rest(P, E, R, t_s, t) = R - Consumed(P, E, R, t_s, t-1)$$

In what follows the key role is that of the accounting function *Rest*. We will assume it has the following properties.

$$Rest(P, E, R, t_s, t) = \begin{cases} 0, & \text{if } t < t_s \\ R, & \text{if } t = t_s \end{cases}$$

$$0 \sqsubseteq Rest(P, E, R, t_s, t) \sqsubseteq R$$

$$Rest(P, E, R, t_s, t) \sqsubseteq Rest(P, E, R, t'_s, t) \text{ if } t_s \leq t'_s$$

$$Rest(P, E, R, t_s, t') \sqsubseteq Rest(P, E, R, t_s, t) \text{ if } t \leq t'$$

$$Rest(P, E, R_1, t_s, t) \sqsubseteq Rest(P, E, R_2, t_s, t) \text{ if } R_1 \sqsubseteq R_2$$

Having the accounting function, we are now able to define the conditions for a request to be supported by the coalition policy and the local policy of a resource provider, as follows.

Definition 3.9 (Supported request) Let $Req(u, P, R, t)$ represent a request submitted at time t from user $u \in Users$ to enterprise $P \in \mathcal{E}$ for access to an amount R of a resource owned by P.

$Req(u, P, R, t)$ is *supported* by an obligation $Obl(P, S, R', I)$ if $t \in I$, $u \in users(E)$ for some $E \in S$, and $R \sqsubseteq Rest(P, E, R', t_s, t)$ where $I = [t_s, t_e]$.

$Req(u, P, R, t)$ is a *locally supported* request if there is an entitlement $Ent_P(E, R', I)$ in the local policy $\mathbf{LP}_P^t$ of P such that $t \in I$, $u \in users(E)$, and $R \sqsubseteq Rest(P, E, R', t_s, t)$ where $I = [t_s, t_e]$.

A request $Req(u, P, R, t)$ is *trivial* if $R = 0$.

The following result gives further support for the choice of definitions above.

Proposition 2 *Let* $\mathbf{LP}_P^t$ *be the local policy of an enterprise* P *at* t. *Let* $Obl(P, S, R, I)$ *be an obligation. Let* $I = [t_s, t_e]$ *and* R *be a resource of type* $ResType$. $\mathbf{LP}_P^t$ *meets* $Obl(P, S, R, I)$ *iff, whatever requests are granted by* P *for resource of type* $ResType$, *every nontrivial request supported by* $Obl(P, S, R, I)$ *is locally supported by* $\mathbf{LP}_P^t$.

Proof. Left-to-right: suppose $Req(u, P, R_x, t_x)$ is supported by $Obl(P, S, R, I)$. Then for some $E \in S$, we have $u \in users(E)$, $t_s \leq t_x \leq t_e$, and $R_x \sqsubseteq Rest(P, E, R, t_s, t_x)$. Since $\mathbf{LP}_P^t$ meets $Obl(P, S, R, I)$ there is an entitlement $Ent_P(E, R', [t_s', t_e'])$ in $\mathbf{LP}_P^t$ such that $R \sqsubseteq R'$ and $t_s \leq t_s' \leq t_x \leq t_e'$.
We need to show $R_x \sqsubseteq Rest(P, E, R', t_s', t_x)$. We have $R_x \sqsubseteq Rest(P, E, R, t_s, t_x) \sqsubseteq Rest(P, E, R, t_s', t_x)$ because $t_s \leq t_s'$, and $Rest(P, E, R, t_s', t_x) \sqsubseteq Rest(P, E, R', t_s', t_x)$ because $R \sqsubseteq R'$.

For the converse: suppose $t_s \leq t_x \leq t_e$, $E \in S$, and $u \in users(E)$. Suppose further that the nontrivial request $Req(u, P, R, t_x)$ is the only request for resource of type $ResType$ granted by P during the interval I. Then $Rest(P, E, R, t_s, t_x) = R$ and $Req(u, P, R, t_x)$ is supported by $Obl(P, S, R, I)$. This request must also be locally supported, so there is an entitlement $Ent_P(E, R', [t_s', t_e'])$ in $\mathbf{LP}_P^t$ such that $t_s' \leq t_x \leq t_e'$ and $R \sqsubseteq Rest(P, E, R', t_s', t_x)$.

By Proposition 1, it just remains to show that $t_s \leq t_s'$. Suppose not: suppose $t_s' < t_s$. Suppose then that there is a granted request $Req(u, P, R', t_s - 1)$. This is outside the interval I and so does not contradict the assumption earlier. $Rest(P, E, R', t_s', t_s) = 0$, and hence also $Rest(P, E, R', t_s', t_x) = 0$ (because $t_s \leq t_x$). So $R \sqsubseteq 0$, and $Req(u, P, R, t_x)$ is a trivial request, which contradicts the assumption. $\square$

¿From the above one can see why condition (i) is essential in Definition 3.5.

As informally introduced, publishing a local policy in compliance with an obligation does not imply the actual fulfillment of the obligation. *Violation* of an obligation occurs whenever a *supported* request is not granted.

Definition 3.10 (Obligation violation) An obligation $Obl(P, S, R, I)$ is violated at any time $t' \geq t$ where:

— $t \in I$ and it is not the case that the local policy $\mathbf{LP}_P^t$ meets $Obl(P, S, R, I)$; or

— a request $Req(u, P, R_x, t)$ supported by $Obl(P, S, R, I)$ is not granted by P before time $t + \delta$, where δ is some suitably chosen (application specific) value to allow for the time delay between the submission of a request to P and the time at which the request can be acted upon by P.

Once an obligation is violated it remains violated at all future times. Notice that an obligation $Obl(P, S, R, I)$ cannot be violated before the start of time interval I, and that we have chosen to say it becomes violated at any time during I at which the local policy fails to meet the obligation.

An obligation $Obl(P, S, R, I)$ is *fulfilled* if the local policy meets $Obl(P, S, R, I)$ at each time point in the interval I and all supported requests during I are granted. We will say that the obligation becomes fulfilled at the time the interval I ends.

Definition 3.11 (Obligation fulfillment) An obligation $Obl(P, S, R, I)$ is fulfilled at any time $t' \geq t_e$ iff $I = [t_s, t_e]$ and:

— the local policy $\mathbf{LP}_P^t$ meets $Obl(P, S, R, I)$ for all $t \in I$; and

— every request $Req(u, P, R_x, t)$ supported by $Obl(P, S, R, I)$ (and hence during I) is granted by P within time $t + \delta$, where δ is the (application specific) time delay between the submission of a request to P and the time at which the request can be acted upon by P.

Once an obligation is fulfilled it remains fulfilled for all future times. Notice that before the time interval I, an obligation $Obl(P, S, R, I)$ is neither violated nor fulfilled, and after time interval I it is either violated or fulfilled (but not both).

We have chosen to say that an obligation $Obl(P, S, R, I)$ becomes fulfilled at the moment the time interval I ends. We could have chosen to say that an obligation could be fulfilled earlier than that, in the case where the resource R is completely used up before I expires. This complicates the presentation unduly however so we will not bother with it here.

Notice that an obligation $Obl(P, S, R, I)$ is fulfilled if no supported request is submitted to P during the time interval I, *as long as* local policy $\mathbf{LP}_P^t$ meets $Obl(P, S, R, I)$ for all times $t \in I$.

Of some special interest is the case where a resource providing enterprise P can be assumed to comply with its own published local policy, in the sense that a request submitted to P is granted by P if and only if that request is locally supported by P's local policy. For that special case we have the following.

Proposition 3 *Let* P *be an enterprise in* $\mathcal{E}$. *Suppose* P *grants any (non-trivial) request submitted to it at time* t *by time* $t + \delta$ *iff that request is locally supported by* P's *local policy* $\mathbf{LP}_P^t$.

Then an obligation $Obl(P, S, R, I)$ is fulfilled iff $\mathbf{LP}_P^t$ *meets* $Obl(P, S, R, I)$ *for every time* $t \in I$.

Proof. This follows immediately from Definition 3.11 and Proposition 1. $\square$

Notice that a provider P can over-comply with an obligation in the sense that P grants in its local policy an entitlement that exceeds what it is required to provide by the coalition policy. In that case, there can be locally supported requests that are not supported by any obligation: P might then fail to grant a locally supported request without violating any of its obligations under the coalition policy.

3.4 Contracts

Now we consider a special type of *contract*, which will convey the coalition policy. We call it a contract because it is a policy that all members of a coalition have to agree on. A contract specifies the members' obligations towards one another. Contracts are constructed from two basic building blocks: the *obligation sequence* and the *contract block*.

Definition 3.12 (Obligation sequence) An *obligation sequence* $Obl(P, S, R_1, I_1; \ldots; R_k, I_k)$ $(k \geq 1)$ is a set of obligations $Obl(P, S, R_1, I_1), \ldots, Obl(P, S, R_k, I_k)$ such that $R_1, \ldots, R_k$ are all instances of the same resource type and $I_1, \ldots, I_k$ is an ordered sequence of contiguous time intervals.

We will also write obligation sequences in the form $Obl(P, S; Seq)$ where Seq stands for the sequence of resource-interval pairs $R_1, I_1; \ldots; R_k, I_k$.

$Obl(P, S, R_1, I_1; \ldots; R_k, I_k)$ is *violated* at time t if any of its constituent obligations $Obl(P, S, R_i, I_i)$ is violated at time t.

$Obl(P, S, R_1, I_1; \ldots; R_k, I_k)$ is *fulfilled* at time t if all its constituent obligations $Obl(P, S, R_i, I_i)$ are fulfilled at time t. Clearly an obligation sequence $Obl(P, S, R_1, I_1; \ldots; R_k, I_k)$ is fulfilled when its last constituent obligation $Obl(P, S, R_k, I_k)$ is fulfilled.

A request $Req(u, P, R_x, t)$ is *supported* by $Obl(P, S, R_1, I_1; \ldots; R_k, I_k)$ if it is supported by any of the constituent obligations $Obl(P, S, R_i, I_i)$.

We do not define the 'meets' relation between arbitrary sets of entitlements and an obligation sequence, but we do want to define when the local policy $\mathbf{LP}_P^t$ of enterprise P meets (is in compliance with) an obligation sequence. Informally, $\mathbf{LP}_P^t$ meets $Obl(P, S, R_1, I_1; \ldots; R_k, I_k)$ if the obligation sequence is not violated before t and $\mathbf{LP}_P^t$ meets any constituent obligation $Obl(P, S, R_i, I_i)$ whose time interval I_i has not yet expired at time t. The following is an equivalent and more concise formulation.

Definition 3.13 (Obligation sequence compliance) A local policy $\mathbf{LP}_P^t$ is in compliance with ('meets') an obligation sequence $Obl(P, S, R_1, I_1; \ldots; R_k, I_k)$, denoted

$$\mathbf{LP}_P^t \text{ meets } Obl(P, S, R_1, I_1; \ldots; R_k, I_k)$$

if every constituent obligation $Obl(P, S, R_i, I_i)$ is either fulfilled at t or $\mathbf{LP}_P^t$ meets $Obl(P, S, R_i, I_i)$.

This means that obligations fulfilled in the past can be ignored by the local policy, which is clearly desirable. It also means that once a constituent obligation is violated the local policy can no longer be modified to meet the obligation sequence. In particular, if the local policy fails to meet an obligation sequence that has started, the local policy can never be modified later to meet the obligation sequence retrospectively.

The following property confirms that the definitions of obligation sequence compliance mirror the corresponding definitions for obligation compliance.

Proposition 4 *Let* $Obl(P, S; Seq)$ *be an obligation sequence with* $Seq = R_1, I_1; \ldots; R_k, I_k$. *Let* $I_k = [t_s, t_e]$. *Let* $\mathbf{LP}_P^t$ *be the local policy of enterprise* P *at time* t.

$Obl(P, S; Seq)$ *is violated at any time* $t' \geq t$ *iff:*

— $t \in I_1 \cup \cdots \cup I_k$ *and it not the case that* $\mathbf{LP}_P^t$ *meets* $Obl(P, S; Seq)$*; or*

— *a request* $Req(u, P, R_x, t)$ *supported by* $Obl(P, S; Seq)$ *is not granted by* P *before time* $t + \delta$, *where* δ *is the (application specific) time delay to allow a submitted request to be acted upon by* P.

$Obl(P, S; Seq)$ *is fulfilled at any time* $t' \geq t_e$ *iff:*

— $\mathbf{LP}_P^t$ *meets* $Obl(P, S; Seq)$ *for all* $t \in I_1 \cup \cdots \cup I_k$; *and*

— *every request* $Req(u, P, R_x, t)$ *supported by* $Obl(P, S; Seq)$ *is granted by* P *within* $t + \delta$. $\square$

The second building block for contracts is the *contract block*.

Definition 3.14 (Contract Block) A contract block CB_P of a coalition policy is an expression of the form:

$$Obl(P, S_1; Seq_1) \parallel \cdots \parallel Obl(P, S_k; Seq_k)$$

where each component $Obl(P, S_i; Seq_i)$ $(i \in 1..k)$ is an obligation sequence. P is the *bearer* of CB_P.

The contract block CB_P is *fulfilled* at time t if any of CB_P's components $Obl(P, S_i; Seq_i)$ is fulfilled at time t.

The contract block CB_P is *violated* at time t if all of CB_P's components $Obl(P, S_i; Seq_i)$ are violated at time t.

A request $Req(u, P, R_x, t)$ is *supported* by the contract block CB_P if it is supported by any of CB_P's components $Obl(P, S_i; Seq_i)$.

A local policy $\mathbf{LP}_P^t$ is in compliance with ('meets') the contract block CB_P, denoted $\mathbf{LP}_P^t$ meets CB_P, if $\mathbf{LP}_P^t$ meets $Obl(P, S_i; Seq_i)$ for any component $Obl(P, S_i; Seq_i)$ of CB_P.

The effect of the contract block is to give the bearer P a complete *free choice* about which of the component obligation sequences it wishes to fulfill. Although in principle these obligation sequences may differ in terms of the amount of a resource, the type of the resource, the set of enterprises to whom the resource is to be granted, and/or the time intervals over which the obligations hold, in practice only certain special forms are useful.

In particular, the contract block can be used to capture the common pattern of contractual obligations in which violation of one obligation can result in new obligations that then must be fulfilled. Often these new obligations will impose more stringent requirements, providing both an incentive to fulfil the original, easier obligation and a means of compensating for any violations that occur. By arranging the components of a contract block appropriately, violation of one component leaves only the choice of more stringent obligations if the contract block is to be fulfilled.

Example 3

Suppose SICS agrees to provide KTH with 100Gb of disk storage over the time interval $[1, 10]$ with 50Gb to be provided over the interval $[1, 5]$ and a further 50Gb to be provided over $[6, 10]$. (Here we employ integers for time points rather than the day-time notation simply to reduce clutter.) If, however, SICS fails (for whatever reason) to provide KTH with 50Gb over the interval $[1, 5]$, but manages to provide at least 30Gb over that period, then it must provide KTH with 90Gb over the interval $[6, 10]$ to compensate.

This coalition policy can be represented by a contract block with the following two components:

1. $Obl(SICS, \{KTH\}; 50Gb, [1, 5]; 50Gb, [6, 10])$
2. $Obl(SICS, \{KTH\}; 30Gb, [1, 5]; 90Gb, [6, 10])$

Suppose first that SICS violates its obligation to provide at least 30Gb of storage at some time t during $[1, 5]$, either by failing to include an appropriate entitlement in its local policy at time t or by denying a supported request at time t from a user at KTH. In that case, the obligations in component 1 are also violated at time t, and the whole contract block is violated.

Suppose that SICS fulfills its obligation to provide 50Gb of storage over $[1, 5]$. It therefore also fulfills its obligations for $[1, 5]$ in component 2. It can fulfill the contract block as a whole by providing 50Gb over $[6, 10]$. It can also fulfill it by providing more than 50Gb over $[6, 10]$ but that would be surplus to requirements.

Suppose now that SICS violates its obligation to provide at least 50Gb of storage (component 1) at some time t during $[1, 5]$ though it does not violate the obligation to provide

30Gb (component 2), for example, by including an entitlement for KTH to 40Gb in its local policy at time t. Since the first obligation of component 1 is now violated, the only way that SICS can fulfill the contract block as a whole is by fulfilling component 2. Effectively SICS now has an obligation to provide 90Gb of storage over $[6, 10]$, since that is the only available means of fulfilling the contract block. Notice that once component 1 is violated it remains violated. Having violated component 1 with its local policy at time t, SICS cannot undo the violation, for example, by altering its local policy later.

It should be clear that the example can be extended with further layers in similar fashion. Suppose that if SICS fails to provide 30Gb over the period $[1, 5]$ but manages to provide 10Gb, then it must provide 100Gb over the interval $[6, 10]$. This is represented by adding a third component to the contract block:

3. $Obl(SICS, \{KTH\}; 10Gb, [1, 5]; 100Gb, [6, 10])$

The reader may care to check how new obligations are effectively triggered by various kinds of violations in this extended example.

It is worth observing that the obligations in a contract block such as the one in the previous example are similar but not exactly the same as obligations of the 'contrary to duty' type [9]. In a 'contrary to duty' structure there is a primary obligation, and a secondary obligation which comes into force if the primary obligation is violated. To that extent the contract block is similar. The difference is that in a contract block there is no 'primary' obligation that gets special status: as long as at least one of the components of the contract block is fulfilled, there is no violation of the contract block as a whole.

We are now ready to define a contract. A contract is simply a set of contract blocks, with one important additional proviso. With the definitions constructed above, we must ensure that there are never two (or more) separate and independent obligations requiring one enterprise P to provide several instances of the same resource to the same enterprise E at the same time. In such circumstances (to be stated more precisely below), P can fulfill several obligations at once with just one single entitlement. Suppose, for example, there are two separate obligations $Obl(P, \{E\}, R_1, I)$ and $Obl(P, \{E\}, R_2, I)$. One might assume that E is thereby granted a total allowance of $R_1 + R_2$ over interval I. The treatment of obligation compliance developed above, however, gives a different effect: that of a single obligation $Obl(P, \{E\}, R, I)$ where R is the larger of R_1 and R_2. When formulating contracts care must be taken to ensure that this is the intended effect. The alternative would be to *name* all obligations and associate entitlements explicitly with named obligations. Fortunately, the

conditions under which problems can arise, and which need to be eliminated, are comparatively obscure.

Definition 3.15 (Contract) A contract is a (finite) set of contract blocks $\{CB_1, \ldots, CB_n\}$ ($n \geq 1$) such that, for any pair of obligations $Obl(P, S, R, [t_s, t_e])$ and $Obl(P, S', R', [t'_s, t'_e])$ in different contract blocks with R and R' both instances of the same resource type and $S \cap S' \neq \emptyset$, we have $t_s \neq t'_s$.

Given any set of contract blocks, the required conditions for a contract are easily and mechanically checked.

Definition 3.16 (Contract compliance) A contract *Contract* is violated at time t if any contract block in *Contract* is violated at time t.

Contract is fulfilled at time t if every contract block in *Contract* is fulfilled at time t.

A local policy $\mathbf{LP}^t_P$ complies with *Contract* iff $\mathbf{LP}^t_P$ meets CB for every contract block CB in *Contract* for which P is the bearer of CB.

4 Future work

The work presented in this paper is ongoing research, originally started with [5, 2], for designing and implementing a formal and sound framework for contractually regulated coalitions.

We are currently working on integrating the idea of *witness* and associated protocols, introduced in [2], as a trusted third party for monitoring the resource sharing between coalition members. We are also extending the framework with the delegation mechanism and the privilege calculus, given in [6], for decentralised management of privileges in coalitions. We will extend the privilege calculus for support of entitlements and obligations as presented in this paper.

For future work we are following three complementary directions. The first direction is to extend the policy language. The combination of obligation sequence and contract block presented here is still rather restrictive; we have not yet explored how restrictive it will prove to be in practice. We also plan to provide means of specifying polices about policies, that is to say, policies specifying what other (coalition) policies can be created and under what circumstances. In this paper, we have allowed local policies to vary over time but the coalition policy *Contract* is fixed. Finally, the focus in this paper is on obligations and entitlements to a specified amount of consumable resource over a specified period of time. We also need to speak of obligations and entitlements to non-consumable resources where there is no sense of measure, such as access to a file, which is either granted or not. There is no difficulty in extending the definitions to support non-consumable resources as well; indeed, the corresponding definitions are very much simpler than

those for consumable resources. We have concentrated on consumable resources in this paper precisely because they are more involved.

The second direction is to investigate the relationships between our framework and various methods for optimization and dynamic scheduling of resource allocations. We believe that there are interdependencies between coalition and local policies and the way planning of resource usage can be done. This is of course related to the idea that an enterprise can be a member of several coalitions offering the same resources. Hence, we need mechanisms for deciding which obligations to fulfill in order to minimize sanctions resulting from non-compliance whilst at the same time optimizing resource usage.

Thirdly, we plan to develop mechanisms and architecture to monitor contractual performance and enforce contractual agreements, enabling secure detection of contractual violations and triggering recovery mechanisms that apply to those violations.

5 Related work

Bettini and colleagues [3] formalize a rule-based policy framework that includes 'provisions' and 'obligations', and investigates a reasoning mechanism within this framework. They distinguish between actions (*provisions*) that have to be performed before a decision is taken and actions (*obligations*) that will be taken after the decision. These actions are represented as two disjoint sets of predicates. The system implementing the policy rules must deduce what actions (if any) may be performed to gain access, and what promises (if any) must be made after gaining the access. The system also monitors the progress of obligation fulfillment and, in case of failure, takes compensatory actions. Provisions are structured and have an associated weight, allowing the selection of the weakest obligation thus considering semantic relations between them. The main distinction between this work and ours is that Bettini's focuses on enhancement of policy rules with provisions and obligations to be accounted by systems implementing these rules, whereas we mainly focus on modeling policies for distributed communities sharing resources. Furthermore, Bettini's system is not integrated with any temporal reasoning technique, though the authors have indicated that this is a topic to be explored.

Xuhui Ao and Naftaly Minsky [1] have developed a fully implemented regulatory mechanism for coalitions, based on a very general view of the governance of coalitions. Similarly to our work, the coalition is governed by a global policy P_C, and each coalition member E_i is governed by a local policy, which must conform to P_c. Their definition of both coalition and local policy is provided using the LGI language [8], a general message-exchange mechanism that allows an open group of distributed agents to engage in a

mode of interaction governed by a policy. Our concept of coalition policy is different. We see it as a contract, and provide formal definitions of coalition and local policy and relationships between them. Furthermore in [1] local policies are obtained using a top-down approach, as refinements of coalition policies, whereas we consider local policy as a plan for enterprises to allocate resources under their own control while complying with coalition policy as expressed in the contract. Moreover in [1] no punitive mechanism is considered, since in that framework every obligation is necessarily fulfilled unless it is repealed.

In [7] there is proposed a contract monitoring system intended to provide automated checking of business to business contracts. It introduces a novel modelling approach to obligations, unifying the treatment of both permissions and obligations by reifying both and describing permit and burden passing in a way analogous to the established treatment of capabilities.

[4] deals with the problem of negotiating access to resources that exist within different administrative domains, presenting protocols for managing the process of negotiating access to resources in a distributed system. The approach taken is to define a general resource management model within which reservation, acquisition, task submission, and binding of tasks to resources can be expressed in a uniform fashion.

6 Conclusion

We have presented a framework for specifying and reasoning about policies for sharing resources in coalitions, focussing on the common case where coalition members agree to make available some total amount of consumable resource over a specified period of time. The simpler case of access to non-consumable resources, which can either be granted or not, can be treated in similar (simpler) fashion.

The framework provides a policy language with two basic elements: 'obligations', which are used to express the coalition policy (contract), and 'entitlements' which are used to express the local policies of the coalition members. Local policies may vary from time to time; for simplicity in this paper we have assumed that the coalition policy is fixed.

Each member of a coalition must publish its local policy so that other members can plan how to make use of the resources provided. A local policy must comply with, or 'meet', the obligations specified by the coalition policy. A member enterprise violates an obligation either by failing to publish a local policy that meets the obligation or by denying the resource in contravention of its own local policy. An accounting mechanism keeps track of which resources are granted over time. We have investigated the conditions under which violation of an obligation in the coalition policy

(contract) coincides with contravention of a local policy.

We have presented two basic building blocks for constructing coalition policies (contracts) from 'obligations'. An 'obligation sequence' collects a set of related obligations over an ordered sequence of contiguous time intervals. A 'contract block' specifies a set of alternative obligations with a free choice about which of them must be fulfilled. By combining these structures in various ways, one can represent common patterns of contractual provisions, such as the common case where violation of one obligation results in new, usually more stringent, obligations intended to compensate for the violation.

Our current work includes development of the mechanisms and infrastructure required to monitor contractual performance and enforce contractual performance.

References

[1] X. Ao and N. H. Minsky. Flexible regulations of distributed coalitions. In *Proceedings of the 8th European Symposium on Research in Computer Security (ESORICS)*, volume 2808 of *LNCS*, Gjøvik, Norway, October 2003. Springer Verlag.

[2] E. Bertino, E. Ferrari, and A. Squicciarini. A decentralized framework for controlled sharing of resources in virtual communities. In *Proceedings of the 17th IFIP Conference On Database and Applications Security, Estes Park, CO*, August 2003.

[3] C. Bettini, S.Jajodia, X. S. Wang, and D. Wijesekera. Provisions and obligations in policy management and security applications. In *Proceedings of the 28th International Conference on Very Large Data Bases (VLDB)*, Hong Kong, China, August 2002.

[4] K. Czajkowski, I. Foster, C. Kesselman, V. Sander, and S. Tuecke. Snap: A protocol for negotiating service level agreements and coordinating resource management in distribuited systems. In *Proceedings of the 8th Workshop on Job Scheduling Strategies for Parallel Processing*, volume 2537 of *LNCS*, pages 153–183, Edinburgh, Scotland, July 2002.

[5] B. S. Firozabadi and M. J. Sergot. Contractual access control. In *Proceedings of Security Protocols, the 10th International Workshop*, volume 2845 of *LNCS*, pages 96–102, Cambridge,UK, April 2002. Springer Verlag.

[6] B. S. Firozabadi, M. J. Sergot, and O. Bandmann. Using Authority Certificates to Create Management Structures. In *Proceeding of Security Protocols, the 9th International Workshop*, volume 2467 of *LNCS*, pages 134–145, Cambridge, UK, April 2001. Springer Verlag.

[7] P. Linington and S. Neal. Using policies in the checking of business to business contracts. In *Proceedings of the 4th IEEE Workshop on Policies for Distributed Systems and Networks*, pages 207–218, Como, Italy, June 2003.

[8] N. H. Minsky and V. Ungureanu. Law-governed interaction: a coordination and control mechanism for heterogeneous distributed systems. *ACM Transactions on Software Engineering and Methodology (TOSEM)*, 9(3):273–305, july 2002.

[9] H. Prakken and M. Sergot. Contrary-to-duty obligations. *Studia Logica*, 57(1):91–115, 1996.

A Formal Model for Hierarchical Policy Contexts

András Belokosztolszki, Ken Moody, David M. Eyers
University of Cambridge Computer Laboratory
JJ Thomson Avenue, Cambridge, United Kingdom
{firstname.lastname}@cl.cam.ac.uk

Abstract

Role-based access control (RBAC) models specify a policy interface for security administration, but do not provide guidelines for how large organisations should manage their roles. Parameterised RBAC systems are even more expressive; however, this adds to the risk of dangerous mistakes during policy specification. In this paper we define a formal model for hierarchical policy contexts: an RBAC metapolicy approach for subdividing the administration of large-scale security environments and for enforcing information flow restrictions over policies.

1. Introduction

Role-based access control organises and groups the users and privileges of organisations. This simplifies access control policies, since through roles policies can refer to aggregated component sets, as opposed to individual users and privileges. However in large organisations, where the number of users is measured in hundreds of thousands, the number of such aggregating roles can itself be very large.

Case studies like the one described in [16], which examine large commercial organisations, estimate the number of roles required to express the organisational policy to be well over one thousand. Even in the case of simpler policies, like the one described in [12], the number of roles is several hundred. All of these roles are mapped to users, privileges, or maybe other roles, and this mapping, usually in the forms of rules, also forms a part of the RBAC policy. In addition, roles and rules rely on policy components such as data types, environmental predicates, variables, and so forth, thus further adding to the total number of components in a policy. In this paper we provide means to structure policy components and to enforce restrictions, such as information flow, on policies. Contexts also facilitate scalable policy management through the differentiation of administrative tasks.

This paper is an extension of the work originally published in [6], and is based on [4]. Contexts were proposed for two main reasons; to group components for administrative purposes, and to impose restrictions on rules. We are at present examining the use of contexts to group dynamic credentials for the support of active security (e.g. work-flow management and dynamic separation of duties).

In §2 of this paper we first define contexts and context elements, the constituents of contexts. In §3 we consider information flow between contexts. Then, in §4, we describe the assignment of contexts to OASIS policy components. In §5 and §6 we look at the two primary functions of contexts: component grouping and information flow restrictions. We show further uses for contexts in §7, then we review related work and the applicability of contexts to other RBAC models (§8). We conclude in §9.

2. Context elements

In [6] we defined a non-hierarchical *context* as a finite set of labels. These labels, which are referred to as *context elements*, can be used to annotate policy components, such as roles and rules. In order to enforce information flow between policy components, we specified a flow relation ($\hookrightarrow$) for context elements. In this way we can control the prerequisites to roles, we can enforce information flow restrictions on role parameters, and so forth.

To support policy evolution our specification allowed wild-cards, so that we could express information flow to components that might appear in later policy versions. There was no scoping for such wild-cards, and, since context elements allow us to classify policy components according to a variety of aspects, we need a way of separating context elements that belong to different classifications.

2.1. Parallel context flow structures

In the following example, illustrated in Figure 1, we describe a scenario where our previous non-hierarchical context element specification proves insufficient.

Assume there are two context element groups that can describe two different information flows. One group has a web $\hookrightarrow$ secureWeb information flow restriction. This context element group takes care of information flow from

the web security aspect. The second group, consisting of the `CompLab`, `OPERA`, and `Security` context elements, describes information flow from an organisational perspective. The two context element groups thus describe two separate, orthogonal information flows.

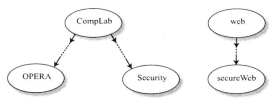

Figure 1. Parallel information flow example.

In our non-hierarchical model there is no way to support fine-grained wild-cards for specifying context elements, thus we cannot specify arbitrary information flow between context elements according to the organisational classification.

2.2. Motivation

We next present an extension to our previous context element specification, in which we add hierarchical information for context elements. The idea was first mentioned in our paper [6], but here we elaborate, and provide a more comprehensive formal description.

As context elements that are found on directed cycles (see Section 2.7) behave in the same way from an information flow perspective, it is vital to avoid creating such cycles accidentally. Unfortunately, it is easy to introduce cycles! A particular risk arises when specifying context elements that accept information from every other context element, or else potentially permit information flow to every other.

It would also be nice to group relevant context elements together. In our parallel information flow example we talk about two groups of context elements. The first group restricts information flow from the `CompLab` context element to the `OPERA` and `Security` context elements. The other group, which is independent of the first, contains two context elements, `web` and `secureWeb`, and permits information flow from the `web` to the `secureWeb`. These context element groups were separated in Figure 1, but in their specification, which puts all the context elements into a set, they would not be distinguished.

In the same example, the specification of wild-cards is also problematic, as it can introduce undesired information flow that could break the parallel context flow specification by joining the context component groups. With the hierarchies introduced in this section it is possible to specify free information flow within a group, i.e. we can specify that from the `CompLab` context element information may flow freely into any other context element in that group, which in our case is {`CompLab`, `OPERA`, `Security`}. This context element group can be extended later without the need

to modify the information flow restriction for the parent – `CompLab` – context element.

A further problem, which we shall address with hierarchical context elements, is the distributed administration of contexts. In the above example the Computer Laboratory must take care of its `CompLab` context element, but its subgroups are responsible for their own context elements. If additional context elements are introduced at subgroup level this must not affect the higher level context elements and information flow indirectly.

Using hierarchical contexts, participating context elements can be grouped together into a new context element, and can be referred to collectively via this new context element. For example, all the Computer Laboratory context elements can be grouped together under the `CompLab` context element. At university level this `CompLab` context element can be used to specify information flow to the Computer Laboratory, while within the Computer Laboratory the information flow can be further refined.

Context element hierarchies therefore introduce a layering in context specification. This is visualised in Figure 2.

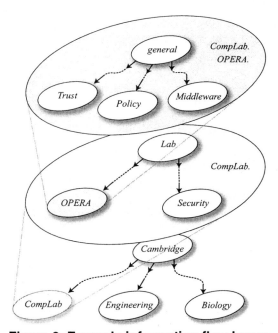

Figure 2. Example information flow layers.

2.3. Definition of context elements

We next present hierarchical context elements, to which we shall refer as C. C is a set, on which the following functions and relations must be defined. For consistent notation we shall use capital letters, e.g. A, B, or X, Y for variables that range over C.

Definition 2.1 (Hierarchy relation of context elements). *The hierarchy of the context elements is specified by the*

$Cparent \subset C \times C$ relation. This relation pairs together parent and child context elements.

In order to support hierarchical context administration, we do not allow multiple parents in our context element hierarchy, therefore the Cparent relation must satisfy the following restriction:

$$\forall X, P_1, P_2 \in C :$$
$$(P_1, X) \in Cparent \land (P_2, X) \in Cparent \Rightarrow P_1 = P_2$$

This restriction says that a context element may have at most one parent.

Context elements cannot be their own parents: ($Cparent = Cparent \setminus \triangle_C$). Furthermore, we require the reflexive-transitive closure of Cparent, for which we shall use the $\leq$ symbol, to be antisymmetric (no proper cycles).

$\leq$ is a partial order – reflexivity and transitivity are consequences of the closure, while anti-symmetry was required by the definition of *Cparent*. Thus the context elements, together with the *Cparent* hierarchy relation, form a forest of rooted trees ($C, Cparent$).

We also introduce the predicate *Croot* to denote root context elements, i.e. ones that have no parents: $Croot : C \rightarrow bool$

$$\forall A \in C : Croot(A) \equiv (\neg \exists B \in C : (B, A) \in Cparent)$$

Context elements that satisfy this predicate are the minimal context elements.

2.4. Labels

We decouple context element labels from context elements, thus we specify a function (*Clabel*), that returns the label associated with such a hierarchical context element. The range of *Clabel* is strings of English characters.

Just as in the case of non-hierarchical context elements, for which we required labels to be unique, we require that labels assigned to root nodes are unique. Similarly, siblings must use different labels:

$$\forall A, B \in C : \quad A \neq B \land ((Croot(A) \land Croot(B)) \lor$$
$$(\exists P \in C : Cparent(P, A) \land Cparent(P, B)))$$
$$\Downarrow$$
$$Clabel(A) \neq Clabel(B)$$

In the examples it is easier to refer to context elements if we use a path expression. To support this we introduce the *path* function, which returns a string consisting of the labels (separated by '.') on a path from the root of a context element to the context element. Using $+$ as concatenation the definition is as follows:

$$Cpath(X) = \begin{cases} Cpath(Y) + `.' + Clabel(X) \\ \qquad \text{if } \exists Y \in C : Cparent(Y, X) \\ Clabel(X) \quad \text{if } Croot(X) \end{cases}$$

Note that since the path from a context element's root to a context element is unambiguous, and because of our labelling restrictions, there is a bijection between path strings and context elements (C). Consequently, the *path* function is invertible on valid path expressions, with inverse $path^{-1}$.

This bijection enables policy administrators to refer more easily to hierarchical context elements using path expressions. In our examples we shall use labels (if this does not lead to ambiguity) and path expressions.

2.5. Wild-cards

In hierarchical context elements the meaning of the phrase *'information is allowed from everywhere'* can be interpreted at each context element. Therefore we shall introduce wild-cards for each context element. These wild-card symbols will have the form of $subtree(X)$, denoting the information source or target for the X context element and its entire subtree. We refer to the set of these parameterised symbols as $C_\star$.

To get the corresponding context element subtree from a wild-card symbol, we introduce the following function: $expand : C_\star \rightarrow \mathcal{P}(C)$.

$$expand(`subtree(X)') = \{Y | Y \leq X\}$$

We keep the $\star$ symbol from our non-hierarchical model [6] to refer to all existing context elements.

2.6. Information flow between context elements

For information flow restrictions we must store additional information with the context elements. This describes the direction in which information is permitted to flow. There are many ways to specify such a relationship between context elements. To make it easy to express information flow restrictions during access control (see [4]) we specify for each context element the set of context elements that it accepts information from, and the set of context elements it is willing to provide information to. Formally this can be expressed with the following two functions:

$$context\_in \quad : \quad C \rightarrow \mathcal{P}(C \cup C_\star \cup \{\star, \varepsilon\})$$
$$context\_out \quad : \quad C \rightarrow \mathcal{P}(C \cup C_\star \cup \{\star\})$$

For each context element the function *context_in* specifies the set of context elements that it accepts information flow from, and function *context_out* specifies the set of context elements that it allows information to flow to.

The range of both functions is extended by an additional element ($\star$) to support top-level wild-cards, i.e. to specify that information from or to any context element is allowed. The ranges also contain finer-grained wild-cards through subtree expressions ($C_\star$).

The range of *context_in* is further extended by a special value ε. The value ε indicates that a context element serves as an initial context element, thus no information flow check

129

is required for it. We shall use such initial elements in our context information flow definition.

As loop information flow from context elements to themselves will be ensured by our information flow definition (Definition 2.2), the information flow specification through *context_in* and *context_out* does not need to ensure reflexivity explicitly.

An explicit edge between two context elements in the information flow graph will exist if the set of context elements to which the source node permits information flow includes the target node, and the set of context elements from which the target node accepts information flow includes the source node. An extended, formal definition is provided below.

In order to evaluate the *context_in* and *context_out* sets for a given context element we must expand wild-card expressions. The *Ceval* function converts sets of context elements, wild-card expressions, and ε to a set of context elements. First specify *Ceval* for elements of the above set:

$$Ceval : C \cup C_\star \cup \{\star, \varepsilon\} \to \mathcal{P}(C)$$

$$Ceval(\omega) = \begin{cases} \omega & \text{if } \omega \in C \\ expand(\omega) & \text{if } \omega \in C_\star \\ C & \text{if } \omega = \star \\ \emptyset & \text{if } \omega = \varepsilon \end{cases}$$

Extending the *Ceval* function to sets of context elements, wild-card expressions, and ε:

$$Ceval : \mathcal{P}(C \cup C_\star \cup \{\star, \varepsilon\}) \to \mathcal{P}(C)$$

$$Ceval(\psi) = \bigcup_{\omega \in \psi} Ceval(\omega)$$

The following example shows how the *Ceval* function expands wild cards (for this we use the informal context specification in Figure 2) :

$$Ceval \left(\left\{ \begin{matrix} \texttt{CompLab.Security,} \\ \texttt{subtree(CompLab.OPERA)} \end{matrix} \right\} \right) =$$

$$\left\{ \begin{matrix} \texttt{CompLab.Security, CompLab.OPERA,} \\ \texttt{CompLab.OPERA.general,} \\ \texttt{CompLab.OPERA.Trust,} \\ \texttt{CompLab.OPERA.Policy,} \\ \texttt{CompLab.OPERA.Middleware} \end{matrix} \right\}$$

The information flow between hierarchical context elements is specified by the $\hookrightarrow$ relation.

Definition 2.2 (Direct information flow between hierarchical context elements). $\hookrightarrow \subseteq C \times C$

$$A \hookrightarrow B \quad \Leftrightarrow \quad (A = B) \vee \Big(\big(B \in Ceval(context\_out(A)) \big) \wedge$$
$$\big(A \in Ceval(context\_in(B)) \big) \Big)$$

According to the first part of this definition, information flow from a context element to itself is permitted. Also, information is permitted to flow from context element A to

context element B if B is included in A's expanded *context_out* set (i.e. wild-card expressions are evaluated and replaced by context elements of a subtree), and A is included in B's expanded *context_in* set.

It is worth considering direct information flow between parent and child context elements as a special case. In order for flow to be possible down an edge of the hierarchy, we require that the expanded *context_in* set of the child includes the parent, and also that the expanded *context_out* set of the parent includes the child. If the latter arises because of wild-card expansion, then the entire subtree of the child is contained in the expanded *context_out* set. However, direct information flow will be permitted only to those descendants whose *context_in* set includes the parent. Similar considerations hold for direct information flow up the hierarchy.

The final information flow graph is the transitive closure of the directed graph specified by the $\hookrightarrow$ relation. We shall use the symbol $\hookrightarrow^*$ to denote the relation that represents possible information flow between context elements.

One advantage of structuring context information as a hierarchy, as opposed to simply storing the edges of the information flow graph, is that the administration of context elements is more flexible. Context elements that use wild-cards may not need to be updated when new context elements are added or removed, in which case no access to those elements will be necessary. Hierarchic context elements also enable the principals responsible for particular context elements to specify information flow independently of the specification for other context elements, thus supporting distributed and multi-level administration.

2.7. Cycles in the information flow graph

Context elements on a directed cycle are equivalent in terms of information flow, but they may still differ from the perspective of policy structure. For example, access control privileges to a stored policy may depend on the specific context elements that annotate policy components [4]. Since policies evolve, the information flow graph will change through time, and currently equivalent context elements may become significantly different in the future.

3. Information flow relation between contexts

Policy components can be associated with contexts, i.e. with more than just a single context element. The assignment of a set of labels is similar to the assignment of a single label. Indeed, a possible formalisation would be to allow a single context element per policy component only, but to let the values be chosen from the powerset of the context labels. We have not followed this approach, since we think it is natural to specify the information flow relation in terms of flow between labels, and to extend this relation to define information flow between *sets* of labels.

The advantage of having a *set of labels* assigned to a component is that it allows policy components to be classified along multiple dimensions. For example, one dimension may identify components as relating to either procurement or marketing, and another may give a security classification such as 'web' or 'secure web'.

Based on information flow restrictions between context elements we can specify information flow between contexts.

If α and β are two contexts, then information flow between them is permitted only if: (1) for every context element in α there is a context element in the target context β into which information may flow, and (2) for every non-initial context element in β there is a context element a in the source context (α) from which information flow is permitted to the target context element. Formally this is defined by the following relation:

Definition 3.1 (Information flow between hierarchical contexts). $\hookrightarrow \subseteq \mathcal{P}(C) \times \mathcal{P}(C)$

$$\alpha \hookrightarrow \beta \iff (\forall A \in \alpha : \exists B \in \beta : A \hookrightarrow^* B) \land$$
$$(\forall B \in \beta : (\exists A \in \alpha : A \hookrightarrow^* B) \lor$$
$$(\varepsilon \in \text{context\_in}(B)))$$

Note that this definition allows information flow between two empty contexts.

The above definition has two consequences that are identified in the following two lemmas:

Lemma 3.1. *If α and β are two contexts between which information flow is permitted ($\alpha \hookrightarrow \beta$), and α has a context element ($a : a \in \alpha$) from which information may not flow anywhere else ($\text{context\_out}(a) = \{\}$), then this context element must be in β.*

Lemma 3.2. *If α and β are two contexts between which information flow is permitted ($\alpha \hookrightarrow \beta$), and β has a context element ($b : b \in \beta$) into which information may not flow from anywhere and which is not initial ($\text{context\_in}(b) = \{\}$), then this context element must be in α.*

3.1. Example

We next present an example that offers an alternative to part of our previous example in Section 2.1, this time using hierarchical contexts.

Instead of having two top-level context elements web and secureWeb we only have one context element, WSec. This has two child context elements with normal and secure labels. The information flow between these is shown in Figure 3. WSec groups together the two context elements that we use to annotate policy components that have something to do with web security. The two child context elements (normal and secure) represent the different classifications of policy components from the web security perspective.

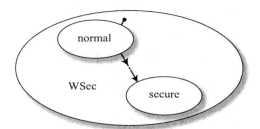

Figure 3. Example hierarchical inf. flow.

The same information flow of our old example is described next using the *context_in* and *context_out* functions:

$$\begin{aligned}
\text{context\_in}(\texttt{WSec}) &= \{\} \\
\text{context\_out}(\texttt{WSec}) &= \{\} \\
\text{context\_in}(\texttt{WSec.normal}) &= \{\varepsilon\} \\
\text{context\_out}(\texttt{WSec.normal}) &= \{\texttt{WSec.secure}\} \\
\text{context\_in}(\texttt{WSec.secure}) &= \{\texttt{WSec.normal}\} \\
\text{context\_out}(\texttt{WSec.secure}) &= \{\}
\end{aligned}$$

This example shows one advantage of hierarchical context specifications, since unlike the example in Section 2.1, we keep the web security related context elements together, and separate from other context elements.

Note the symbol **.** in the figure, which indicates that the WSec.normal context element is initial.

The parent component does not specify any permitted information flow in or out and it is not even initial! This makes this context element very limited, as information may only flow to itself, i.e. from WSec to WSec. If a role is marked with this context it must be initial, or in activation rules all its prerequisites must have WSec in their context.

But, as WSec.normal is an initial context it can be included in any target role's context. Every target role that uses this role as a prerequisite will have to have in its context the WSec.normal context component, or a context element to which information may flow from WSec.normal, which in our case is only WSec.secure.

We introduce an additional context element OPERA that is defined as follows:

$$\text{context\_in}(\texttt{OPERA}) = \{\varepsilon\}; \quad \text{context\_out}(\texttt{OPERA}) = \{\}$$

With this context element we can express the following context information flows:

$$\begin{aligned}
[\texttt{WSec.normal}] &\hookrightarrow [\texttt{WSec.normal}] \\
[\texttt{WSec.normal}] &\hookrightarrow [\texttt{WSec.normal},\texttt{WSec.secure}] \\
[\texttt{OPERA},\texttt{WSec.normal}] &\hookrightarrow [\texttt{OPERA},\texttt{WSec.secure}]
\end{aligned}$$

Note that since initial contexts are considered only in the information flow for contexts, as opposed to the information flow for context elements, the transitive closure of the information flow graph does not take account of them. As a consequence, information flow from [OPERA] to [OPERA, WSec.secure] is not permitted.

This example illustrates the expressive power of both normal and hierarchical context elements and contexts.

4. Context assignments

We have introduced contexts as an annotation for policy components. In this section we examine at syntactic level the OASIS [1] policy components that can have associated contexts. We consider other policy languages in Section 8.

The main constituents of OASIS policies, and indeed of many other RBAC policy languages, are role and prerequisite specifications, and the rules that govern role or privilege acquisition. Rules take two forms, authorisation and activation rules. These are used to assign a privilege to a role, and to prescribe prerequisites for role entry respectively. They follow these templates:

$$r, e_1, ..., e_{n_e} \vdash p$$
$$r_1, ..., r_{n_r}, ac_1, ..., ac_{n_{ac}}, e_1, ..., e_{n_e} \vdash r$$

where r and r_i are roles, p is a privilege, ac_j are appointment certificates[1], and e_k are environmental predicates. All of these rule components can be parameterised.

We allow context annotation of all rule components (prerequisites, target roles and privileges), their parameters, and the rules themselves. Consequently, it will often be the case that context-classified policy components have contexts associated with many of their constituent parts as well.

Allowing context specification for rule component parameters enables parameters within prerequisites to be differentiated. For example, in the case of the privilege *read_record(patient_id, record)*, information flow for the two parameters can be handled differently. Assuming that the *patient_id* parameter, which identifies a patient uniquely, is more sensitive than the *record* parameter, which specifies the record type and takes values such as 'haematology', contexts should be assigned in order to control the propagation of *patient_id* more strictly.

To show what context a policy component belongs to we use a superscript notation within square brackets. For example, to indicate that *RoleA* has the context elements web and secureWeb assigned to it, we write $RoleA^{[web, secureWeb]}$. Thus an activation rule can have the following form:

$$name^{[rulec]} : r_1^{[rc_1]}, ..., r_{n_r}^{[rc_{n_r}]}, ac_1^{[acc_1]}, .., ac_{n_{ac}}^{[acc_{n_{ac}}]},$$
$$e_1^{[ec_1]}, .., e_{n_e}^{[ec_{n_e}]} \vdash r^{[rc]}$$

where *name* is the name of the rule, r_i, ac_j and e_k are the n_r prerequisite roles, n_{ac} appointments, and n_e environmental certificates respectively, and r is the target role. The contexts are in superscript in square brackets; rulec is the rule context, while rc_i, acc_j, ec_k are the prerequisite contexts;

---

[1] these prerequisites are syntactically similar to roles

finally, *rc* is the target role context. The parameters of each rule component can also be assigned a context; thus any of the above rule components can look like:

$$rule\_comp^{[comp\_context]}(param_1^{[context_1]}, ..., param_n^{[context_n]})$$

Note that while we shall use the above form of a rule in our examples, it is not intended for policy administrators. Note also that rules are only associated with rule contexts. Rule component contexts and parameter contexts in the above forms of rules are specified with the rule component specifications, i.e. they can only be accessed when the appropriate component of a rule has been selected.

As the activation and authorisation rules illustrate, rules as well as other policy components can have many of their parts associated with contexts. Which of these contexts must be considered when a decision is made, or whether the union of the contexts must be considered, depends on the purpose for which the contexts are used. The possible purposes, as well as the use of contexts to support them, will be explained in the following sections.

5. Component grouping

By annotating policy components with contexts we form policy component groups. These groups provide a *view to the policy*, which can be used for several purposes; for example, structural component grouping can be used both to define coherent portions of a policy and for access control.

5.1. Structural groups

First of all, structuring introduced by contexts allows administrators to work with a smaller number of policy components. For example, policy components that are used for roles of one department of a hospital, say roles for haematology, can be grouped with the help of a context element called 'haematology'. Policy components that are annotated with this context element, i.e. whose contexts include the context element 'haematology', will belong to one group.

This can be used to structure a policy for the purposes of readability, and such groups or policy views can be visualised by appropriate graphical user interfaces.

For policy components that are built up from other components (e.g. roles encapsulate their parameters), we impose a restriction on the context specifications, and *require that subcomponents of a policy component belong to the context of their parent*. For example, the context of a role parameter must be a subset of the parent role's context. Note that data types are not considered to be child components of policy components, thus the above requirement does not apply to them.

132

6. Information flow restrictions

With the help of contexts and the information flow relation between context elements, we can express policy specification time restrictions, and decouple such restrictions from the policy itself. In this way we can control which policy components – belonging to a specific context – can be used as prerequisites to policy components of another group.

We discuss restrictions at four granularity levels: rule components, their parameters, rules, and data types.

6.1. Context specification for rule elements

Rule elements – roles, appointments, environmental predicates and privileges – can be assigned contexts. Information flow restrictions among these contexts control what can be used as a prerequisite for the target role or privilege in a rule.

The information flow requirement is that in both activation and authorisation rules, a rule component can be used as a prerequisite to the target component only if information flow is permitted from the prerequisite's context to the context of the target component.

The next example shows how to create two or more contexts that cannot be used as prerequisites of each other. We assume the context elements are encapsulated within a single hierarchical context element, thus we omit prefixes.

The context elements are CompLab, OPERA, and Security. Roles are *local_user(uid)*, *OPERA_webadmin(uid)*, *OPERA_meetingadmin(uid)*, and *Security_webadmin(uid)*. The CompLab is used to mark policy components that are under the direct control of the Computer Laboratory. OPERA and Security are used to mark components that are managed by the two research groups, the OPERA and the Security group. There is also an environmental predicate (*group_member*) that checks whether a particular user is in a specific research group.

The information flow restriction among the context elements is given next and visualised in Figure 4.

$$context\_in(\texttt{CompLab}) = \{\}$$
$$context\_out(\texttt{CompLab}) = \star$$
$$context\_in(\texttt{OPERA}) = \{\texttt{CompLab}\}$$
$$context\_out(\texttt{OPERA}) = \{\}$$
$$context\_in(\texttt{Security}) = \{\texttt{CompLab}\}$$
$$context\_out(\texttt{Security}) = \{\}$$

In this example, information may flow from the CompLab context element to any other – here the OPERA and Security context elements; no other information flow is

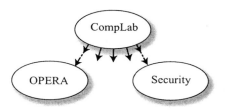

Figure 4. Information flow example for rule components.

permitted. The assignment of contexts to roles is:

$$local\_user^{[\texttt{CompLab}]}(uid)$$
$$OPERA\_webadmin^{[\texttt{CompLab,OPERA}]}(uid)$$
$$OPERA\_meetingadmin^{[\texttt{OPERA}]}(uid)$$
$$Security\_webadmin^{[\texttt{Security}]}(uid)$$
$$group\_member^{[\texttt{CompLab}]}(uid, group)$$

The information flow graph restricts the use of roles in the OPERA context so that these roles can be used as prerequisites only to roles in the OPERA context. Thus the rule

$$OPERA\_webadmin^{[\texttt{CompLab,OPERA}]} \vdash$$
$$OPERA\_meetingadmin^{[\texttt{OPERA}]}(uid)$$

is permitted, but the rule

$$OPERA\_meetingadmin^{[\texttt{OPERA}]}(uid) \vdash$$
$$Security\_webadmin^{[\texttt{Security}]}(uid)$$

cannot be part of the policy specification, because information is not allowed to flow from the OPERA context element to the Security context element. In other words, the roles of the OPERA group cannot be used as prerequisites to roles of the Security group. Note however, that a role from the OPERA research group can still be used for shared roles, i.e. for roles that are marked at specification time as belonging both to OPERA and Security contexts.

6.2. Context specification for parameters

Different parameters of the same rule component can themselves have different levels of sensitivity. In particular, they may be associated with contexts that their parent components do not share. Information from parameters with additional context elements may propagate only into parameters whose context includes context elements into which such information may flow.

In the next example there are three context elements involved: personal, hospital, and HIV_test. Components marked with personal indicate that these components handle or contain information that is personal to a patient. The hospital context element is used to mark hospital specific policy components. The HIV_test context is used to mark policy components that are used for HIV screening. To ensure anonymity it is expected that components marked with `HIV_test` contain no personal information.

Information is permitted to flow from `hospital` to `personal` and `HIV_test`, and from `HIV_test` to `personal`. This is visualised in Figure 5.

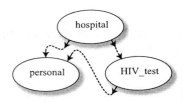

Figure 5. Example information flow for parameters.

The specification of the role involved is:

$$patient^{[\text{hospital}]}(patient\_id^{[\text{hospital,personal}]},$$
$$ward\_name^{[\text{hospital}]})$$

This role has the `hospital` context element associated with it, but one of its parameters (*patient_id*) is – in addition to the role context – also associated with the `personal` context element to indicate that it represents personal information.

There is also a privilege in this example:

$$HIV\_testable^{[\text{hospital,HIV\_test}]}(a\_parameter^{[\text{hospital,HIV\_test}]})$$

This privilege can be used to issue a magnetic card to a patient so that he may prove that he may be tested for HIV free of charge. The privilege has two context elements (`hospital`, `HIV_test`) in its context. Its parameter, which for the sake of this example is just called '*a_parameter*', has the same contexts as its parent component, the privilege.

The following authorisation rule (with contexts indicated) satisfies the context information flow restrictions:

$$patient^{[\text{hospital}]}(x^{[\text{hospital,personal}]}, y^{[\text{hospital}]}) \vdash$$
$$HIV\_testable^{[\text{hospital,HIV\_test}]}(y^{[\text{hospital,HIV\_test}]})$$

However, the following rule is an example in which the parameter level information flow restriction is not satisfied.

$$patient^{[\text{hospital}]}(x^{[\text{hospital,personal}]}, y^{[\text{hospital}]}) \vdash$$
$$HIV\_testable^{[\text{hospital,HIV\_test}]}(x^{[\text{hospital,HIV\_test}]})$$

This rule is not accepted, since according to the rule the value of the first parameter (x) of the prerequisite role propagates to the first parameter of the target privilege, but the information flow between the relevant contexts – [`hospital,personal`] to [`hospital,HIV_test`] – is not permitted (information may not flow from the `personal`

context element to either `HIV_test` or `hospital`). This result is to be expected, as there is no information flow from the `personal` context element, and according to Lemma 3.1, it is required that this context element is present in the target component's context.

6.2.1. Taxonomy of environmental predicates

Environmental predicates, a type of prerequisite within OASIS policies (similar environmental interaction mechanisms are found in many other policy languages), constitute a connection to services outside the policy enforcement environment. Their parameters can be either *in* or *out*, the latter of which are set after the evaluation of the predicate. Since such evaluations may propagate information from *in* parameters to either *out* parameters or outside the policy enforcement environment, it is prudent to provide a means to specify their information flow characteristics.

The next example shows the dangers of such undesired information flow. The environmental predicate $eq(a, b?)$ sets the value of b to be equal to the value of a. This information flow must be considered when a rule is checked. For example, the rule that was rejected earlier:

$$patient^{[\text{hospital}]}(x^{[\text{hospital,personal}]}, y^{[\text{hospital}]}) \vdash$$
$$HIV\_testable^{[\text{hospital,HIV\_test}]}(x^{[\text{hospital,HIV\_test}]})$$

could be extended as follows:

$$patient^{[\text{hospital}]}(x^{[\text{hospital,personal}]}, y^{[\text{hospital}]}), eq(x, z?)$$
$$\vdash HIV\_testable^{[\text{hospital,HIV\_test}]}(z^{[\text{hospital,HIV\_test}]})$$

Without the consideration of information flow within environmental predicates the above rule would be accepted.

In [6] we showed two approaches to handling information flow in such predicates.

6.3. Context specification for rules

Based on contexts, policy rules can be organised into groups. Administrators with different levels of trust and jurisdiction, and thus different privileges, can create rules that belong to specific contexts. Similarly to the context restriction for rule components, it is required that all the child components of such rules belong to the contexts of the rule. That is, the rule context is a subset of each child component's context.

This constraint can be used to restrict the policy components that are allowed in a rule. Consider for example the context elements specified in Figure 4. If a rule is marked with the `OPERA` context element, it will not be able to use components that are tagged with a context that does not contain a context into which information may flow from `OPERA`. For example, this rule may not contain a component tagged with the [`Security`] context.

This is useful for restricting the domain within which a policy administrator may work, as we can grant privileges to add and modify rules that have a specific context associated with them. In this way we can limit the rule components that the policy administrator may use for a given rule. For example, we can require that an internal policy administrator for the OASIS research group use only group specific roles and privileges in the group's policy.

6.4. Context-based restrictions for data types

In the same manner as for other policy components we have permitted context assignment to data types in order to restrict their use. But, unlike these other policy components, we do not consider data types to be child components within policy components, thus we define here separately the parent-child context relation for data types:

If a data type has no context associated with it we handle it as a general data type, and allow its use in any component specification. On the other hand, if a data type is assigned a context, then we require that it is used in components that have contexts associated with them into which information may flow from the context of the data type.

7. Further uses for contexts

Until now we discussed two main uses for contexts: grouping policy components for administrative and access control reasons, and to restrict information flow in rules. Next we consider other uses for contexts.

7.1. Organisational vs. functional roles

Roles are often classified as organisational or functional roles. For such roles it is expected that users first enter organisational roles, and then, according to the task they are performing, they enter functional roles. The restriction on such role entry order can easily be specified with the help of contexts. For this, two context labels are required (e.g. org and func). These labels shall be used to differentiate organisational and functional roles. By specifying information flow only from the org context element to func, we allow rules that use organisational roles as prerequisites to functional or organisational roles, and we disallow rules that would use functional roles as prerequisites to organisational roles.

7.2. Auditing

Proper auditing is crucial in systems that support access control. Since our contexts refer to aggregated policy components, they can be used to introduce an indirection in the specification of logging requirements. Thus logging requirements (the amount of information that needs to be logged) can be associated with contexts. Furthermore, log entries can contain the context information of the actions that they log, thus facilitating differentiated access control to the log itself.

7.3. Failure behaviour

In distributed environments where access control is managed by a service that is itself distributed over the network, mechanisms must be in place to handle network failure. In [5] we proposed extensions to OASIS policies to control heartbeat loss.

We propose to associate revocation behaviour with the context of roles. This has the advantage that revocation behaviour can be changed without policy modification, and it can also depend on external conditions, such as the organisational security level (like red and yellow alerts).

8. Discussion

We implemented contexts for OASIS as part of the policy management framework, Desert [4]. It was also a simple matter to extend the XML representation of OASIS policy to include context labelling. However, contexts are general enough to be used with other RBAC models and policy specification languages.

To extend the models of Sandhu and NIST [15] is relatively simple, since these models are very similar to OASIS. As in the case of other models that have no support for parameters (e.g. [13] and [11]) information flow restrictions can be used primarily for limiting prerequisites, i.e. what roles can be used as preconditions to other roles, and what roles can be assigned to what privileges.

Unlike OASIS, which expresses inheritance via its rules, many systems support role hierarchies. Contexts and information flow between them can limit this inheritance relation by restricting for a role the set of roles it may inherit from. This is achieved by analysing the inheritance graph, and ensuring that information is permitted to flow from less powerful roles to more powerful ones. Such restriction on role hierarchies is very useful, as it can restrict the use of a powerful privilege to a specific class of roles.

Ponder [9] can use contexts to mark both authorisation and obligation rules, libraries and objects. Contexts can restrict the use of certain libraries, for example ones that provide time information, or rule constraints. Thus we can restrict the use of temporal constraints for a certain category of rules. Contexts can also be assigned to different directories in Ponder's directory service, and in this way we can control the targets that can be used together with certain subjects.

Ponder supports component grouping with the help of hierarchical management domains. Contexts can express these domains, but they also extend management domains with information flow restrictions.

Contexts can also be applied to models that use certificates for roles [8]. We can associate certificate validity times with particular context elements. Thus it could be required that certificates for roles that are marked with a specific context element are issued for at most two hours.

8.1. Related work

Information flow control is a well researched area. Denning provides a unifying view of all systems that restrict information flow [10]. While in our work we consider only explicit and static information flow, she considers both static and dynamic information flow as well as implicit information flow.

Information flow restrictions can be found in many access controls, e.g. MAC [3]. In fact, the security labels in MAC inspired much of our work on contexts.

Bidan and Issarny model information flow as an extension to access control [7]. In their access control model, policies specify what a subject is authorised ($s \sim> o$) or prohibited to access ($s \not\sim> o$). This can also be interpreted as allowing information to flow from the subject to the object. Following this reasoning the authors extended their model with inverse information flow ($s <\sim o$). These information flow directions correspond to the *in* and *out* information flows of our context elements.

There has not been much work in the area of information flow analysis of RBAC access control policies. In [14], Osborn analyses her role graph model from an information flow perspective. Osborn's work is basically the reverse of ours, as it produces information flow graphs from role graphs. Such an approach is infeasible in the case of parameterised policies that may contain constraints.

The PCASSO (Patient Centered Access to Secure Systems Online) project aims to enable health care providers and patients to retrieve health information over the Internet [2]. To make this information access secure they use security classifications of objects together with RBAC in an access control system for health care. Their information flow restrictions can be simply expressed with the help of our contexts. In addition, through contexts, information flow restrictions can be extracted from policies. This helps to apply information flow restriction in environments that have existing, legacy policies.

9. Conclusion

In this paper we have specified a type of RBAC metapolicy; contexts. We extended our previous basic context model to support hierarchical relations between context elements, and provided formalism for both. Later we showed how these contexts can be used to group policy components and also to specify restrictions on RBAC policies. We used a relation on contexts, called the information flow relation, which can check information flow between parameter values within a rule, and between policy enforcement and the external world. With this relation we can also express constraints over policies, and thus assist policy evolution.

References

[1] J. Bacon, K. Moody, and W. Yao. A model of OASIS role-based access control and its support for active security. *ACM Transactions on Information and System Security (TISSEC)*, 5(4):492–540, Nov. 2002.

[2] D. B. Baker. PCASSO: A model for safe use of the internet in healthcare. *Journal of American Health Information Management Association (AHIMA)*, 71(3):33–38, Mar. 2000.

[3] D. E. Bell and L. J. LaPadula. Secure computer systems: Unified exposition and Multics interpretation. Technical Report MTR-2997, The MITRE Corporation, July 1975.

[4] A. Belokosztolszki. *Role-Based Access Control Policy Administration*. PhD thesis, University of Cambridge, Nov. 2003.

[5] A. Belokosztolszki and D. Eyers. Shielding RBAC infrastructures from cyberterrorism. In *Data and Applications Security*, volume 256 of *IFIP Information Processing*, pages 3–14. Kluwer Academic Publishers, 2003.

[6] A. Belokosztolszki, D. Eyers, and K. Moody. Policy contexts: Controlling information flow in parameterised RBAC. In *Policy 2003: IEEE Fourth Int. Workshop on Policies for Distributed Systems and Networks*, pages 99–110, 2003.

[7] C. Bidan and V. Issarny. Dealing with multi-policy security in large open distributed systems. In *Computer Security - ESORICS'98*, volume 1485 of *Lecture Notes in Computer Science*, pages 51–66. Springer, 1998.

[8] D. W. Chadwick and A. Otenko. The PERMIS X.509 role based privilege management infrastructure. In *Seventh ACM Symposium on Access Control Models and Technologies (SACMAT'02)*, pages 135–140. ACM Press, 2002.

[9] N. Damianou, N. Dulay, E. Lupu, and M. Sloman. The Ponder policy specification language. In *Policies for Distributed Systems and Networks, International Workshop (POLICY'01), Bristol, UK*, pages 18–38, 2001.

[10] D. E. Denning. A lattice model of secure information flow. *Communications of the ACM*, 19(5):236–243, 1976.

[11] L. Giuri and P. Iglio. A formal model for role-based access control with constraints. In *Proc. of the Ninth IEEE Computer Security Foundations Workshop*, pages 136–145, 1996.

[12] A. Kern, M. Kuhlmann, A. Schaad, and J. Moffett. Observations on the role life-cycle in the context of enterprise securi ty management. In *Seventh ACM Symposium on Access Control Models and Technologies (S ACMAT'02)*, pages 43–51. ACM Press, 2002.

[13] M. Nyanchama and S. Osborn. The role graph model and conflict of interest. *ACM Transactions on Information and System Security (TISSEC)*, 2(1):3–33, 1999.

[14] S. L. Osborn. Information flow analysis of an rbac system. In *Seventh ACM Symposium on Access Control Models and Technologies (SACMAT'02)*, pages 163–168, 2002.

[15] R. Sandhu, D. Ferraiolo, and R. Kuhn. The NIST model for role-based access control: towards a unified standard. In *Proc. of the Fifth ACM Workshop on Role-Based Access Control (RBAC'00)*, pages 47–63, 2000.

[16] A. Schaad, J. Moffett, and J. Jacob. The role-based access control system of a European bank: a case st udy and discussion. In *Sixth ACM Symposium on Access Control Models and Tec hnologies (SACMAT'01)*, pages 3–9, 2001.

Security Policy Reconciliation in
Distributed Computing Environments

Hao Wang,* Somesh Jha[†] , Miron Livny*
Computer Sciences Department
University of Wisconsin
Madison, WI 53706

{hbwang,jha,miron}@cs.wisc.edu

Patrick D. McDaniel
AT&T Labs-Research
Shannon Laboratory
180 Park Ave., Rm. A203
Florham Park, NJ 07932

pdmcdan@research.att.com

Abstract

A major hurdle in sharing resources between organizations is heterogeneity. Therefore, in order for two organizations to collaborate their policies have to be resolved. The process of resolving different policies is known as policy reconciliation, which in general is an intractable problem. This paper addresses policy reconciliation in the context of security. We present a formal framework and hierarchical representation for security policies. Our hierarchical representation exposes the structure of the policies and leads to an efficient reconciliation algorithm. We also demonstrate that agent preferences for security mechanisms can be readily incorporated into our framework. We have implemented our reconciliation algorithm in a library called the Policy Reconciliation Engine or PRE. In order to test the implementation and measure the overhead of our reconciliation algorithm, we have integrated PRE into a distributed high-throughput system called Condor.

1. Introduction

Security policy bridges the gap between static implementations and the broad and diverse security requirements of user communities. Security policy becomes more complicated in heterogeneous environments. When two or more

---

*Hao Wang and Miron Livny were supported by DOE under contract DE-FC02-01ER25464 and NSF/NASA under contract 795NAS1115A.

[†] Somesh Jha was supported by Office of Naval Research under contracts N00014-01-1-0796 and N00014-01-1-0708.

The U.S. Government is authorized to reproduce and distribute reprints for Governmental purposes, notwithstanding any copyright notices affixed thereon. The views and conclusions contained herein are those of the authors, and should not be interpreted as necessarily representing the official policies or endorsements, either expressed or implied, of the above government agencies or the U.S. Government.

entities share a security association, they must reach agreement on a governing policy (e.g., two end-points in an IPsec session). These entities express their requirements for the association through a security policy (called a domain policy). A *reconciliation algorithm* finds a policy that is consistent with all domain policies. Where a consistent policy can be found, the association is free to proceed. Where one cannot be found, the participants must alter their requirements or abstain from participating.

In the general case, policy reconciliation is intractable [15, 23]. As a result, past investigations have largely achieved tractability by limiting the policy representation or by using heuristic algorithms [11, 24, 26, 33]. Such approaches achieve the stated goals, but fail to efficiently capture dependencies between different aspects of a policy. Moreover, these systems do not consider *preferential policy* i.e., it is advantageous (and often necessary) for policy not only to specify what is legal and illegal, but to state what is desirable.

This work addresses the limitations of past work by developing a policy framework based on graphical policy representations. We exploit the graph representation to efficiently encode the complex dependencies inherent to contemporary policy. We formally define the representation and specify an efficient preference and dependency-respecting reconciliation algorithm. Before introducing our formalism, we present an overview of security provisioning policy and the intuition behind our framework in the following section.

1.1. Security Policy

The term *security policy* has come to mean different things to different communities. For example, access control policy defines who has access to what and under what circumstances [4, 29, 30]. Other forms of security policy specify under what conditions credentials are accepted [6],

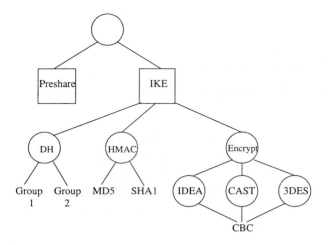

Figure 1. A graphical IPsec key management policy

or how a firewall is configured [3]. In its broadest definition, security policy is the specification of security relevant system behavior. This paper addresses session-specific configuration of security services. More commonly known as *security provisioning policy*, these configurations define the guarantees afforded the governed environment by explicitly identifying the algorithms, parameters, and protocols used to implement security.

To illustrate the importance and ubiquity of security provisioning policy, consider an email client (e.g., Netscape Communicator, MS Outlook). A user specifies a provisioning policy every time she adds an account. For example, the connection method (e.g., IMAP over SSL) dictates exactly the set of guarantees you will receive in obtaining and viewing your mail. Note that the decision to not use any security service is still a specification of policy. The policies defined for the applications and services used in an environment prescribe the security afforded its users.

In practice, provisioning policy is more complicated than our email example would suggest. It is often important that particular organization-wide goals are realized in the many policies implemented by the environment. Lower level policies must be constructed such that they are *compliant* with organizational goals [23]. Moreover, where an operation spans organizations, the policies of each organization must be *reconciled* to form a coherent and reasonable policy.

We now introduce our graphical provisioning policy representation. A graphical policy is a series of policy operations represented by cascading circular or square nodes in a singularly rooted directed acyclic graph (DAG) (formally this structure is an and-or graph). Policy is read from the root node. Each node may be a decision (circle) or a collection (square). A decision node requires that exactly one of the sub-graphs emanating from the node be resolved, and a collection node requires all sub-graphs be resolved. All leaf nodes are added to the policy. Any configuration derived from a policy respects these two simple rules.

Figure 1 shows a graphical provisioning policy for key management used in an IPsec VPN. This policy would be specified by a user or network administrator as part of, for example, VPN setup. One reads the example policy's root (decision node) as:

(configure) *Preshare (preshareed keys)* **or** *IKE*

The right-hand side of the graph (IKE, from the root) depicts a complex series of configurations used to specify the behavior of the Internet Key Exchange (IKE) protocol [16]. The IKE sub-policy consists of three independent configurations. We read the top IKE (collection node) as:

(configure) *DH group* **and** *HMAC* **and** *Encrypt*ion

The remainder of the policy is read as a selection of a single DH group, a hashing algorithm, and an encryption algorithm. Independent of the encryption algorithm, a mode (e.g., CBC) must be selected. Moreover, this policy mandates the use of CBC mode.

The example policy is used at the point at which an endpoint (host) is connected to the VPN. The policy is *evaluated* by identifying a subset of nodes and leaves in graph as defined by the structure of the collection and decision nodes. The IPsec implementation uses the resulting concrete specification, called an *evaluated policy* or *instance*, to implement the IPsec session. For example, one possible evaluated policy contains: *IKE, DH-Group 2, HMAC-MD5, IDEA-CBC*.

Two important factors are highlighted by this example. First, this is one of many possible policies for IPsec key management. Depending on the goals of the specified policy, the specifier may structure the policy in a number of different ways. For example, inasmuch as it is consistent with the IPsec implementation, the policy can allow other encryption modes (e.g., ECB) by adding an additional decision node.

The second factor of note is that unlike our email policy, this policy specifies a *range of behaviors*. That is, the policy states that there are a set of configurations that are equally acceptable. The structure of the graph directly mandates which sets of configurations should be considered acceptable. Having non-prescriptive policies allow the environment to make performance and security trade-offs at run time, and is essential to reconciling policies from different domains.

Now consider the case where there is not a single source of policy: for example, where the end-points of the VPN lie in different administrative domains. Each domain wishes to exert control over the session as specified through a *domain policy* (e.g., similar to Figure 1). Hence, the two parties must find an evaluated policy that is consistent with the domain policies supplied by both. This is performed by *reconciling* the domain policies. The session can continue only where a single governing policy can be found. If not, the domain policies are incompatible and the end-points must alter their policies or refrain from participating in the session.

The study of provisioning policy is unlike other policy efforts in several ways. First and most obviously, provisioning policy is a planning process. Traditional authorization policy systems determine whether a particular access is legal with respect to some larger governing policy. Conversely, provisioning policy attempts to find some configuration that is consistent with a governing provisioning policy.

Provisioning policy also embodies complex dependencies. That is, decisions about particular aspects of the policy affect subsequent options. Figure 1 illustrates a very simple dependency: the decision to use IKE over pre-shared keys has enormous impact on the further development of policy. The selection of IKE leads to decisions concerning the kinds of Diffie-Hellman groups to use, what encryption algorithms are necessary, etc. However, if pre-shared keys were selected, other configuration values (e.g., Diffie-Hellman group) should and would not be considered.

Provisioning is also subject to preferential behavior. That is, there is a often a set of configurations that is most desired among several choices. Again consider Figure 1. According to the policy, either group 1 or group 2 is acceptable. In practice, we have found the vast majority of IPsec configurations use group 2. As such, we (rightly or wrongly) may decide that group 2 is best for our environment, and is thus preferred. However, for compatibility reasons, we do not wish to preclude the use of group 1. Note that preferential configurations are more than simple default values, but a partial ordering of the available options. The existence of preferences is largely ignored by previous work in this area.

As we demonstrate in the following sections, reconciliation is made more complex by the introduction/appreciation of these deeper aspects of policy. While this work aspires to provide intuitive policy representations, it must do so within the constraints of these new complex semantics. Hence, our contribution lies not only in the representation or added semantics, but in the successful marriage of the two.

1.2. Contributions

This paper addresses the aforementioned deficiencies of existing systems by modeling dependencies and preferences in a graphical policy framework. The main contributions of this paper are:

●**Graph-based provisioning policy (exposes dependencies):** We present a model that represents policies as directed acyclic graphs (DAG). This model captures dependencies between policy components within a schema.

Hence, because policies adhere to the schema, it is impossible to define a correctly formed policy that is not consistent with the dependencies.

●**Efficient reconciliation:** In general, policy reconciliation is NP-complete [23]. However, a graphical representation of policies expose their structure and present a basis for an efficient reconciliation algorithm. We provide an efficient reconciliation algorithm for our graphical model. Our reconciliation algorithm is linear in the size of the policies.

●**Preferential policy:** Participant preferences, such as a server's preferences for authentication mechanisms, can be incorporated into our model. An important problem that arises in this context, is that of resolving multiple partial orders on the same set (intuitively, these partial orders represent preferences of different participants). We provide an efficient algorithm to resolve multiple partial orders and extend the reconciliation algorithm to handle preferences.

●**Implementation and deployment:** Based on our hierarchical framework, we have implemented a reconciliation module called the *Policy Reconciliation Engine* or *PRE*, which is available for download. We have integrated PRE with Condor [21], a high-throughput scheduling system used to manage resources in a complex distributed environment. We show experimentally that the cost of reconciliation is negligible.

2. Related Work

Other policy systems. Historically, policy systems have not addressed reconciliation. For example, trust management systems, such as KeyNote [5], SPKI/SDSI [12, 13], Binder [10], and SD3 [18] are concerned with compliance checking rather than reconciliation. In trust management systems, policies, called credentials, are simply cryptographic proofs that express authorization delegation. The compliance checker algorithm searches the available credentials for an accepting delegation chain that satisfies a specific request. Credentials can state a set of provisioning requirements. An action is only allowed where the provisioning of the environment matches the credential. Such approaches are useful for managing policy in a widely deployed or loosely organized environments [7]. However, because credentials mandate provisioning, there is no opportunity to perform reconciliation. Other systems simply assume a singular entity manually performs reconciliation when issuing policy for a domain [3].

Hardness of reconciliation. While reconciliation has only recently begun to be explored, the policy community has already developed a broad characterization of the problem. Gong and Qian discovered that reconciliation of authorization policy (in their work, called policy composition) is

NP-complete [15]. Similarly, the authors of Ismene found that reconciliation of general purpose provisioning policy is also NP-complete [23]. Such results do not mean that progress cannot be made, but suggests a required shift in the goals of investigation. Much of the ongoing work in reconciliation has centered on techniques that alter the environment or restrict policy to obtain efficient reconciliation. However, our paper demonstrates that by using a representation that exposes structure of the policies, the reconciliation problem becomes tractable for a larger class of policies.

Other reconciliation approaches. One way to address the inherent complexity of reconciliation is by essentially "flattening" the policy representation, i.e., explicitly enumerating the various choices. For example, the IPsec Security Policy System (SPS) [33] guarantees efficient two-party reconciliation by intersecting fixed and independent sets of policy values. The DCCM system extends this approach to the multi-party environments by providing a *Chinese menu* reconciliation algorithm [1, 2, 11]. Each participant chooses values from a fixed set of policy dimensions (e.g., one from column A, two from column, B, etc ...). The policy is reconcilable where an intersection of proposals is found for each dimension. Conflicts (where no such intersection is found) are resolved by an unspecified algorithm.

A limitation of both SPS and DCCM is that they assume that there are no dependencies between policy values. For example, in an IPsec policy, an encryption algorithm is needed when the ESP transform is selected. Therefore, to ensure that the resulting policy is enforceable, one must disallow any policy that defines the ESP transform but no encryption algorithm. In practice, these systems define policy as an enumeration of legal policy combinations, such as ESP-3DES-HMAC-SHA. Since only legal enumerations are available, no dependency can be violated. However, the number of enumeration values grows exponentially in the size of the domains, and therefore the "enumeration approach" is inherently not scalable.

Ismene policies are defined as expressions of provisioning variables [23]. The reconciliation algorithm tries to find a satisfying truth assignment for the universe of provisioning variables. Reconciliation is cast as an instance of satisfaction (over the conjunction of policy proposals). Efficiency is guaranteed by using a pair-wise satisfaction algorithm on restricted policy expressions. The iterative Ismene n-policy reconciliation algorithm is sound but not complete, i.e., some collections of reconcilable policies may be rejected. Furthermore, like SPS, the Ismene reconciliation algorithm does not consider dependencies. Dependencies are addressed in Ismene by evaluating the reconciliation result with respect to a set of "correctness rules" using an *analysis algorithm*. This approach is limited in that it occurs after the policy has been identified. Hence, reconciliation must be re-performed after each policy is rejected by analysis.

BANDS [32] addresses multi-domain policy reconciliation in the context of IPsec by describing the security requirements of each domain in a policy language [14]. The provisioning policy between two nodes (source and destination) is proposed by the source node through a gathering phase where security requirements from all domains along the path are gathered. From the gathered requirements, a policy is then proposed and passed along the path to the destination node. Each domain along the path must verify the policy against its own security requirements or return an error to the source node. If the proposed policy reaches the destination node without an error, it becomes the provisioning policy for the session.

A central limitation of the approaches defined above is that they are not sensitive to the structure of policy. Dependencies between different aspects of policy are either inefficiently encoded or externally evaluated. This is a prime motivation of the current work. Dependencies are captured through the graphical structure of the policy schema, and hence any policy resulting from reconciliation is guaranteed to be consistent with these dependencies. Previous reconciliation algorithms also make no distinction between reconciliation results. Since no distinction is made, every possible result is equally desirable. However, environments often desire to specify default behavior and allow others where the defaults are inefficient or infeasible. This work allows such desires to be expressed through preferences.

Other work on representation and analysis of security policies. Cholvy and Cuppens consider the complexities of detecting and managing inconsistencies introduced by access control policy specifications [8]. Our approach differs not only in problem domain (i.e., provisioning), but in that we avoid consistency evaluation by encoding dependencies within the policy structure. Hence, collections of individual policies cannot be inconsistent. Cholvy and Cuppens further considered preference in the context of the ordered application of access control regulations, but focused on access control applications.

While it has not been explored for other forms of policy, graphical representations are well suited to access control policy [20, 25]. For example, the LaSCO language specifies access control policy using graphical idioms [17]. The developers of LaSCO assert that the representation allows not only specification a more intuitive operation, but permits the use of well known graph algorithms for subsequent enforcement. We embrace a similar approach by using structural representation to enforce dependencies.

3. A Formalization of Policy Reconciliation

In this section we provide a precise semantics of policy reconciliation where the policies are represented hierarchically. Moreover, we describe how preferences can be incor-

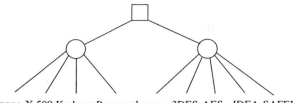

none X.509 KerberosPassword none   3DES AES   IDEA SAFER

Figure 2. Schemata S

porated into our framework. Finally, we present an efficient reconciliation algorithm.

Definition 3.1 A *schemata* is a directed acyclic graph or DAG $S = (N, E, root)$, where N is a set of nodes, $E \subseteq N \times N$ is a set of edges, and $root \in N$ is a distinguished node. We assume that $root$ has no incoming edge. Each node n has the following attributes associated with it:

- Each node is a $\wedge$ or $\vee$ node.

- A tuple of variables (denoted by $Var_T(n)$) $\langle V_1 : \tau_1, \cdots, V_k : \tau_k \rangle$ (where τ_i is the type of variable V_i). Currently, we only allow types string, int, real, and enum. For an enum type τ_i we assume that a set of values is given, e.g., $\tau_i = \{\text{DES}, \text{3DES}, \text{AES}\}$.

The set of successors of a node n in a schemata S is denoted by $succ_S(n)$. However, when the schemata S is clear from the context we simply write $succ(n)$ instead of $succ_S(n)$.

A schemata is shown in Figure 2. The root node is a $\wedge$-node and represented as a square. The left and right child of the root are $\vee$-nodes and represent various authentication and encryption mechanisms respectively. The leaf nodes, such as the ones labeled with none and 3DES, are $\vee$-nodes with no successors. The special keyword none signifies the fact that an authentication or encryption scheme is not required. Moreover, there are no variables associated with the $\vee$-nodes. However, if desired, associated attributes, such as key size for encryption schemes, can be associated with the $\vee$-nodes.

Definition 3.2 An *instance* I of a schemata $S = (N, V, root)$ is a subgraph $(N', V', root)$, where $N' \subseteq N$ and $V' \subseteq V$. Additionally, following conditions need to be satisfied:

- For a $\wedge$-node $n \in N'$, $succ(n) \subseteq N'$. In other words, all successors of a $\wedge$-node are in the instance I.

- For a $\vee$-node $n \in N'$, if $succ(n)$ is non-empty, then $|succ(n) \cap N'| = 1$. In other words, for a $\vee$-node with a non-empty set of successors, exactly one successor is in an instance.

- Consider a node $n \in N'$ such that $Var_T(n) = \langle V_1 : \tau_1, \cdots, V_k : \tau_k \rangle$. In this case, I assigns values v_i of type τ_i to each variable V_i in $Var_T(n)$. The tuple of values assigned by I to the node n is denoted by $Val_I(n)$.

Definition 3.3 A *policy* P for a schemata $S = (N, V, root)$ is a 2-tuple (S, C), where $S : N \rightarrow 2^N$ and C maps nodes to a tuple of conditions. For each $\vee$-node $n \in N$, $S(n) \subseteq succ(n)$, and $C(n)$ is a k-tuple of conditions $\langle c_1, \cdots, c_k \rangle$ where $Var(n) = \langle V_1 : \tau_1, \cdots, V_k : \tau_k \rangle$. Moreover, we assume that the condition c_i applies to values of type τ_i. Given a value v_i of type τ_i, we use $v_i \models c_i$ to denote that v_i satisfies c_i.

Two policies P_1 and P_2 are shown in figures 3 and 4 respectively. Consider the left child of the root. Policy P_1 specifies that only X509, Kerberos, and Password are allowed successors for the left node. Other edges and nodes can be interpreted in a similar manner.

Given an instance $I = (N', V', root)$ and a policy $P = (S, C)$, we say that I *satisfies* P (denoted by $I \models P$) iff the following two conditions are satisfied:

- For all $\vee$-nodes $n \in N'$, $(succ(n) \cap N') \subseteq S(n)$. In other words, instance I can only choose successors of a $\vee$-node from the subset $S(n)$ provided by the policy P.

- Let $Val_I(n) = \langle v_1, \cdots, v_k \rangle$ be the values assigned to the node n in I, and $C(n) = \langle c_1, \cdots, c_k \rangle$ be the conditions assigned to node n by the policy P. In this case, for $1 \leq i \leq k$, $v_i \models c_i$, or each value assigned in the instance I should satisfy the corresponding condition specified by the policy P.

Policy P for a schemata S is called *satisfiable* iff there exists I such that $I \models P$.

Next, we define conjunction of two policies. The conjunction of two policies $P_1 = (S_1, C_1)$ and $P_2 = (S_2, C_2)$ (denoted by $P_1 \wedge P_2$) is a policy (S', C'), where

- For each $\vee$-node $n \in N$, $S'(n) = S_1(n) \cap S_2(n)$ and $C'(n) = \langle c_1^1 \wedge c_1^2, \cdots, c_k^1 \wedge c_k^2 \rangle$, where $C_1(n) = \langle c_1^1, \cdots, c_k^1 \rangle$ and $C_2(n) = \langle c_1^2, \cdots, c_k^2 \rangle$.

Conjunction of the two example policies P_1 and P_2 is depicted in Figure 5.

Definition 3.4 A set of n policies $P_1, \cdots, P_n$ is *reconcilable* iff there exists an instance I such that $I \models (\bigwedge_{i=1}^{n} P_i)$ or in other words $\bigwedge_{i=1}^{n} P_i$ is satisfiable.

Remark: We have described the semantics of reconcilable policies using the satisfaction relation $\models$. One can give an alternative definition in terms of languages. A schemata S

141

defines a language of instances $L(S)$, i.e., $L(S)$ contains all instances I of the schemata I. A policy P for the schemata S also defines a language of instances $L(P) \subseteq L(S)$, i.e., $L(P)$ contains all instances I such that $I \models P$. In this context, policies $P_i, \cdots, P_n$ are reconcilable iff $\bigcap_{i=1}^{n} L(P_i)$ is non-empty.

3.1. Resolving multiple partial orders

Later in this section we discuss policy reconciliation in presence of preferences. In preparation for that, we need to develop some theory about resolving multiple partial orders. Assume that we are given a finite set S. Suppose n agents give their preferences on the set S, i.e., agent i specifies a partial order $\preceq_i$ on the set S. Intuitively, an agent i is an organization or process with a policy, and $\preceq_i$ specifies the preference of the organization or process. The question is how does one construct a *single partial order* on the set S (denoted by $\preceq_{1,\cdots,n}$) from the n partial orders $\preceq_1, \cdots, \preceq_n$?. Precise definition for combining partial orders is given in [31]. We also provide a a linear time algorithm to compute the combined partial order. For example, consider two partial orders shown in Figure 6 on the set { Kerberos, X509, Password }. Assuming that the agent giving the partial order (a) has higher preference than the agent with the partial order (b), the combined partial order is (b). Assuming no order between the agents the combined partial order is (a).

3.2. Reconciliation with preferences

This section describes reconciliation when policies are allowed to specify preferences. First, we define the concept of policy with preferences.

Definition 3.5 A *policy* P for a schemata $S = (N, V, root)$ is now a 3-tuple $(S, C, pref)$, where $S : N \rightarrow 2^N$, C maps nodes to a tuple of conditions, and $pref$ provides preferences. For each $\vee$-node $n \in N$, $S(n) \subseteq succ(n)$, $pref(n)$ is a partial order on $S(n)$, and $C(n)$ is a k-tuple of conditions $\langle c_1, \cdots, c_k \rangle$ where $Var(n) = \langle V_1 : \tau_1, \cdots, V_k : \tau_k \rangle$. Moreover, we assume that the condition c_i applies to values of type τ_i. Given a value v_i of type τ_i, we assume that $v_i \models c_i$.

A policy P induces a partial order $\preceq_P$ on the instances satisfying P. Given an instance I, the DAG rooted at a node n of I is called a *sub-instance*, i.e., a sub-instance consists of the node n and all of its descendants. The depth of a sub-instance is the length of the longest path from the root to one of its leaves. The partial order $\preceq_P$ is defined on sub-instances. Given two sub-instances $SI_1 = (N_1, V_1, root_1)$ and $SI_2 = (N_2, V_2, root_2)$, we say that $SI_1 \preceq_P SI_2$ iff the following conditions are satisfied:

- The roots are the same, i.e., $root_1 = root_2$.

- $root_1$ *is a* $\wedge$-*node.*
  Let the set of successors of $root_1$ be $\{n_1, \cdots, n_k\}$. Let I_i^1 and I_i^2 (for $1 \leq i \leq k$) be the sub-instances in SI_1 and SI_2 that are rooted at n_i. In this case the condition is that for all $1 \leq i \leq k$, $I_i^1 \preceq_P I_i^2$.

- $root_1$ *is a* $\vee$-*node.*
  Let the successors of $root_1$ and $root_2$ in SI_1 and SI_2 be n_1 and n_2 respectively, and I_{n_1} and I_{n_2} be the sub-instances rooted at n_1 and n_2 respectively. In this case, the condition is the following:

  If $n_1 = n_2$, then $I_{n_1} \preceq_P I_{n_2}$; otherwise, $n_1 \preceq n_2$ in the partial order $pref(root_1)$ given by the policy P.

Notice that $\preceq_P$ is inductively defined using the depth of the sub-instances. Intuitively, the partial order $\preceq_P$ extends the partial order $pref$ over nodes given by the policy P to sub-instances.

Next, we extend the definition of conjunction of two policies to incorporate preferences. The conjunction of two policies $P_1 = (S_1, C_1, pref_1)$ and $P_2 = (S_2, C_2, pref_2)$ (denoted by $P_1 \wedge P_2$) is a policy $(S', C', pref')$, where

For each $\vee$-node $n \in N$, $S'(n) = S_1(n) \cap S_2(n)$, $pref'(n)$ is equal to $\preceq_{1,2}$, and $C'(n) = \langle c_1^1 \wedge c_1^2, \cdots, c_k^1 \wedge c_k^2 \rangle$, where $C_1(n) = \langle c_1^1, \cdots, c_k^1 \rangle$ and $C_2(n) = \langle c_1^2, \cdots, c_k^2 \rangle$.

Given n reconcilable policies $P_1, \cdots, P_n$, an instance I is called a *most preferred instance* or *MPI* if $I \models (\bigwedge_{i=1}^{n} P_i)$ and I is a maximal element in the partial order induced by the combined policy $\bigwedge_{i=1}^{n} P_i$.

3.3. The Reconciliation Algorithm

Given n policies $P_1, P_2, \cdots, P_n$, the reconciliation algorithm proceeds as follows:

First, we compute the combined policy $P = \bigwedge_{i=1}^{n} P_i$.
Next, starting from the root the combined policy P is traversed recursively to find the most preferred instance according to partial order $\preceq_P$ induced by the combined policy.

The complexity of reconciliation algorithm is $O(n(|N| + |E|)$, where N and E are the nodes and edges in P. Details of the reconciliation algorithm can be found in [31]. Assume that we are given two policies P_1 and P_2 shown in Figures 3 and 4. The combined policy $P_1 \wedge P_2$ is shown in Figure 5. Suppose that the partial order on authentication mechanisms corresponding to policies P_1 and P_2 is as shown in Figure 6, and the partial order on the encryption schemes corresponding to the policies P_1 and P_2 is as shown in Figure 7. The partial orders are resolved so that policy P_1 has precedence over policy P_2. In this case, the partial orders on the authentication and encryption schemes in the combined policy $P_1 \land P_2$ is the one corresponding to policy P_2, i.e., the partial order labeled (b) in the two figures. The MPI computed by our algorithm is shown in Figure 8.

4. Applications of the policy reconciliation framework

This section illustrates the use of graphical policy in real application environments. To this end, we show how our policy reconciliation framework can augment IPsec's existing policy negotiation and support the Condor distributed computing system.

4.1. Graphical Policy in IPsec

The IPsec [19] suite of protocols provides *source authentication*, *data integrity* and *data confidentiality* at the IP layer. These services are implemented by the Authentication Header (AH) and Encapsulating Security Payload (ESP) transforms. Although not a security service, PCP implements data compression. Each IPsec node (host or security gateway) maintains a security and compression policy defined in terms of these transforms. Communicating peers establish one or more pairs of policy instances (an instance is represented as a *security association*, or SA) by reconciling configured local policies (called proposals). The Internet Key Exchange protocol (IKE) [16] is used to, among other things, negotiate this governing policy.

IKE policy can be modeled using our graphical approach. To illustrate, suppose that a host desires the following policy:

- All outgoing data must be protected by *ESP* and *AH* protocols, and must be compressed using the *PCP* protocol.
- *ESP* can use *3DES, 3IDEA* or *DES* encryption algorithms, and either *HMAC-MD5* or *HMAC-SHA* integrity/authentication algorithms.
- *AH* can use either *HMAC-MD5* or *HMAC-SHA*.
- *PCP* can use either *LZS* or *Deflate*.

An IPsec proposal and graphical representation for the example policy is depicted in Figure 9. The hierarchical DAG structure is clearly more expressive and efficient, i.e., one only needs to understand the difference between $\land$ (square) and $\lor$ (circle) nodes to interpret policy. Conversely, one needs a great deal of domain knowledge to in-

terpret the proposal/transform structure of IPsec. Such intuitive representation simplifies specification, and ultimately reduces policy errors.

Consider an extension to the above policy that states that the use of 3IDEA must use either 128-bit or 256-bit keys. In IPsec, attributes such as key length can be specified only once with each transform. Hence, a separate transform is required for each key length. More generally, the number of transforms grows exponentially in the number of independent attributes. Conversely, the graphical representation only needs to introduce a single subgraph that is shared by the relevant nodes.

4.2. Hierarchically Policy in the Condor system

The second example of the policy reconciliation framework is used in the context of Condor [9], a high-throughput distributed system designed to efficiently schedule the usage of distributed and heterogeneous resources such as idle CPU cycles and unused memory. Condor allows resources owners to place various policy requirements on the use of their resources. Our hierarchical DAG structure can succinctly encode Condor security policies. The design of the policy infrastructure and its integration with Condor are detailed in the following section.

5. Implementation

We have implemented our hierarchical reconciliation algorithm in the *Policy Reconciliation Engine (PRE)*. PRE reconciles (only) pairs of XML-encoded policies. The restriction of PRE to two-policy reconciliation is not a limitation of our approach, but rather an artifact of the initial target systems' point-to-point communication models (IPSec and Condor). We will extend the implementation to allow multi-party policy reconciliation (e.g., Ismene [23], DCCM [11]) as future needs dictate.

PRE implements an asymmetric requester/responder model. In this model, the requester supplies the relevant policy to the responder. The responder reconciles the received policy with local policies as needed, and the *reconciled policy* is returned to the requester. Both parties subsequently use the reconciled policy to control the session. We chose a requester/responder model because it most faithfully represents contemporary use of policy (e.g., IKE policy negotiation [16]). This model is similar to client/server communication models. Responders, acting as servers, govern access to the communication resources and requesters, acting as clients, submit requests for those resources. In PRE, the responders assert authority over the resources by placing a higher preference on their own (local) policy. Note that the requester may (and often should) validate that the received reconciled policy is consistent with the origi-

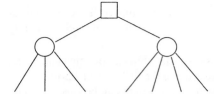

Figure 3. Example policy P_1

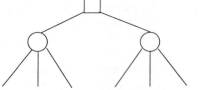

Figure 4. Example policy P_2

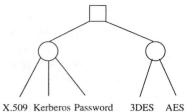

Figure 5. Combined policy $P_1 \wedge P_2$

Kerberos   X509   Kerberos

                X509

Password

        (a)   (b)

Figure 6. Two partial orders on authentication schemes.

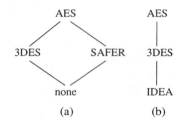

        (a)   (b)

Figure 7. Two partial orders on encryption schemes.

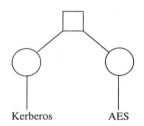

Figure 8. The most preferred instance.

nally proposed policy. Policy validation interfaces are provided by PRE.

PRE is both a library and a command line tool. Hence, it can be directly integrated into an application, or used as an external policy processor. Reconciliation is a three-step process in PRE. First, each security policy is parsed into internal data structures. Then each pair of policies is reconciled using the algorithms defined in section 3.3. Finally, the *verification engine* ascertains the correctness of the *reconciled policy* with respect to the local security policy (i.e., implements the consistency test described above).

The current implementation of PRE contains about 1000 lines of C/C++ code. Source code and documentation for PRE are available for download.

5.1. Integrating PRE with Condor

Much of our work in policy has been motivated by the requirements of the Condor system. As described in Section 4.2, Condor schedules resources based on the client requests and other environmental factors. Every Condor peer has a local security policy that governs the services providing the authenticity, confidentiality, and integrity of the session it supports. We have modified the Condor system to use PRE-based reconciliation to construct the security policy used by each session. Past versions of Condor defined security policy using flat structures called *ClassAds* [28]. ClassAds flexibly communicate resource advertisements and client requests. However, we found the

structure of ClassAds inherently limiting, i.e., we could not represent the appropriate range of acceptable or preferential policies because of their flat structure. Such statements of policy are, as previously argued, hierarchical in nature. This need for hierarchical policy drove our efforts, and ultimately lead to the development of PRE. For details on the implementation, we refer readers to [31].

Currently, Condor does not authenticate the policies or policy exchanges beyond that supported by the underlying transport layer. In general, how and by whom policies are issued and authenticated is an environmental and systems design issue. Environments often require external services for storing and validation of issued policies (e.g., LDAP collections of signed policies). These issues are defined by the larger policy architecture, and is beyond the scope of the current work. Interested readers are referred to [22] for a taxonomy of policy architectures addressing these issues.

5.2. Performance

Because of the relatively small policy size and the restriction to pairwise reconciliation, we did not anticipate the introduction of PRE into Condor would significantly impact performance. We sought to measure these costs through several controlled experiments. These experiments measured the total execution time of the policy negotiation protocol defined in the preceding section. All experiments were executed in an environment consisting of a single Central Manager *server* (333 Mhz duo-processor/Linux RedHat

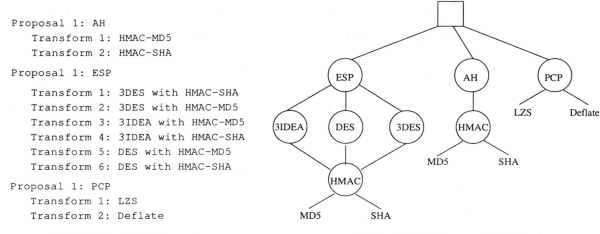

```
Proposal 1: AH
    Transform 1: HMAC-MD5
    Transform 2: HMAC-SHA

Proposal 1: ESP
    Transform 1: 3DES with HMAC-SHA
    Transform 2: 3DES with HMAC-MD5
    Transform 3: 3IDEA with HMAC-MD5
    Transform 4: 3IDEA with HMAC-SHA
    Transform 5: DES with HMAC-MD5
    Transform 6: DES with HMAC-SHA

Proposal 1: PCP
    Transform 1: LZS
    Transform 2: Deflate
```

a.) Original IPsec Policy Proposal   **b.) IPsec Policy Schemata in DAG Format**

Figure 9. IPsec Policy Example

7.2) and eight *clients* (three Ultra 10 Sparc Sun/Solaris 2.8 and five 750 MHz Pentium III/Linux Redhat 7.2).

The experimental results confirmed our intuition: the average protocol execution (without I/O), for a policy consisting of *authentication*, *integrity* and *secrecy*, only uses about 5.2% of the total execution time. When including I/O overhead, the cost is still small–at about 10% of the overall execution time. Startup cost (i.e. program initialization) is the most dominant factor of the overall execution time, followed closely by overhead incurred from Condor's internal data structures.

5.3. Future work

While the theoretical framework and implementation of our hierarchical policy model have reached maturity, we see further exploration of its application to a wide range of problem domains as essential. Initially, we will seek to integrate PRE with widely used policy systems. This will enable us to explore the ways of exploiting the PRE services in specific and policy reconciliation in general. One such work will realize our IPsec policy in software. Integration with tools such as FreeSwan [27] will provide important data-points in the use of extended policy services, and serve to further demonstrate the power of our approach.

We also seek to apply our work to domains which have immediate, but as yet unaddressed, requirements for policy. For example, reconciliation may play an important role in defining security for peer-to-peer (P2P) systems. Currently, there are few coherent security models for P2P. The egalitarian nature of P2P systems mandate autonomy. Each end-point must be able to assert and realize a set of security requirements deemed important. However, autonomy must be counter-balanced with interoperability. The collection of participants must be able to negotiate a shared view of security. This is precisely the definition of reconciliation. Hence, we claim that the fluid and heterogeneous security models of P2P systems would be well served by our work. Moreover, the clarity and succinctness of hierarchical models may enable more free and open use of security policies in these large communities.

This paper has discussed reconciliation only in the context of security policy. However, hierarchical policy models are applicable to other problem domains. To illustrate, GRID systems share the resources in heterogeneous environments. Participants in the GRID have diverse policies that govern the resource usage. Agreement is often achieved statically in current GRID systems by mandating the adoption of a single universal policy. This mandate is in direct conflict with the needs of dynamic environments whose resource constraints and requirements frequently change. Hence, policy reconciliation systems such as PRE can help to bridge such a gap between dynamicity and the needs for agreement. Furthermore, there is often a direct dependence between resource requirements and security settings and dynamic policy reconciliation can act as the agent between the two. For example, a system that handles sensitive data on remote hosts will require some minimum security policy be enforced.

6. Conclusion

Security policy reconciliation is the process of resolving different security policies. In this paper, we presented a formal framework for policy reconciliation. We also presented an efficient algorithm for reconciling different policies. Two distinguishing features of our work are hierarchical representation and preferences. We also implemented a simplified version of our algorithm in a software module called PRE and incorporated it in Condor. Experimental results in the context of Condor clearly demonstrate that for each session the reconciliation overhead is negligible.

References

[1] D. Balenson, D. Branstad, P. Dinsmore, M. Heyman, and C. Scace. Cryptographic Context Negotiation Protocol. Technical report, Network Associates, Inc., 1999.

[2] D. Balenson, D. Branstad, D. McGrew, J. Turner, and M. Heyman. Cryptographic Context Negotiation Template. Technical report, Network Associates, Inc., 1999.

[3] Y. Bartal, A. J. Mayer, K. Nissim, and A. Wool. Firmato: A novel firewall management toolkit. In *IEEE Symposium on Security and Privacy*, pages 17–31, 1999.

[4] D. Bell and L. LaPadula. Secure Computer Systems: Mathematical Foundations and Model. Technical Report M74-244, MITRE Corporation, Bedford, MA, 1973.

[5] M. Blaze, J. Feigenbaum, and A. Keromytis. KeyNote: Trust management for public-key infrastructures. *Lec. Notes in Comp. Sci.*, 1550:59–63, 1999.

[6] M. Blaze, J. Feigenbaum, and J. Lacy. Decentralized Trust Management. In *Proceedings of the 1996 IEEE Symposium on Security and Privacy*, pages 164–173, November 1996. Los Alamitos.

[7] M. Blaze, J. Ioannidis, and A. D. Keromytis. Trust management for IPsec. *Information and System Security*, 5(2):95–118, 2002.

[8] L. Cholvy and F. Cuppens. Analyzing Consistency of Security Policies. In *1997 IEEE Symposium on Security and Privacy*, pages 103–112. IEEE, May 1997. Oakland, CA.

[9] Condor. *http://www.cs.wisc.edu/condor/*.

[10] J. DeTreville. Binder, a logic-based security language. In *Symp. on Res. in Sec. and Privacy*, Oakland, CA, May 2002. IEEE Computer Society Press.

[11] P. Dinsmore, D. Balenson, M. Heyman, P. Kruus, C. Scace, and A. Sherman. Policy-Based Security Management for Large Dynamic Groups: An Overview of the DCCM Project. In *DARPA Information Survivability Conference and Exposition*, pages 64–73, 2000.

[12] C. Ellison. SPKI requirements. RFC 2692, Sept. 1999.

[13] C. Ellison, B. Frantz, B. Lampson, R. L. Rivest, B. Thomas, and T. Ylonen. SPKI certificate theory. RFC 2693, Sept. 1999.

[14] Z. Fu and S. F. Wu. Automatic Generation of IPSec/VPN Security Policies In an Intra-Domain Environment. In *Proceedings of the 12th International Workshop on Distributed System Operation & Management (DSOM 2001)*, pages 279–290, October 2001.

[15] L. Gong and X. Qian. The Complexity and Composability of Secure Interoperation. In *Proceedings of the IEEE Symposium on Research in Security and Privacy*, pages 190–200, Oakland, California, May 1994. IEEE.

[16] D. Harkins and D. Carrel. The Internet Key Exchange (IKE). *http://www.ietf.org/rfc/rfc2409.txt*, 1998.

[17] J. Hoagland, R. Pandey, and K. Levitt. Security Policy Specification Using a Graphical Approach. Technical Report CSE-98-3, The University of California, Davis Department of Computer Science, June 1998.

[18] T. Jim. SD3: A trust management system with certified evaluation. In *Proceedings of the 2001 IEEE Symposium on Security and Privacy*, May 2001.

[19] S. Kent and R. Atkinson. Security Architecture for the Internet Protocol. *http://www.ietf.org/rfc/rfc2401.txt*, 1998.

[20] M. Koch, L. V. Mancini, and F. Parisi-Presicce. A Graph-Based Formalism for RBAC. *Transactions on Information and System Security (TISSEC)*, 5(3):332 – 365, 2002.

[21] M. Litzkow, M. Livny, and M. Mutka. Condor - A Hunter of Idle Workstations. In *Proceedings of the 8th International Conference of Distributed Computing Systems (ICDCS)*, pages 104–111, 1988.

[22] P. McDaniel. *Policy Management in Secure Group Communication*. PhD thesis, University of Michigan, Ann Arbor, MI, August 2001.

[23] P. McDaniel and A. Prakash. Methods and limitations of security policy reconciliation. In *2002 IEEE Symposium on Security and Privacy*, pages 73–87, May 2002.

[24] P. McDaniel, A. Prakash, and P. Honeyman. Antigone: A Flexible Framework for Secure Group Communication. In *Proceedings of the 8th USENIX Security Symposium*, pages 99–114, August 1999.

[25] M. Nyanchama and S. Osborn. The Role Graph Model and Conflict of Interest. *Transactions on Information and System Security (TISSEC)*, 2(1):3 – 33, 1999.

[26] L. Pearlman, V. Welch, I. Foster, C. Kesselman, and S. Tuecke. A Community Authorization Service for Group Collaboration. In *Proceedings of the IEEE 3rd International Workshop on Policies for Distributed Systems and Networks*, 2001.

[27] T. F. Project. Linux FreeS/WAN. *http://www.freeswan.org/*.

[28] R. Raman, M. Livny, and M. Solomon. Matchmaking: Distributed Resource Management for High Throughput Computing. In *Proceedings of the Seventh IEEE International Symposium on High Performance Distributed Computing (HPDC)*, 1998.

[29] R. S. Sandhu, E. J. Coyne, H. L. Feinstein, and C. E. Youman. Role-Based Access Control Models. *IEEE Computer*, 29(2):38–47, 1996.

[30] R. S. Sandhu and P. Samarati. Access Control: Principles and Practice. *IEEE Communications Magazine*, 32(9):40–48, 1994.

[31] H. Wang, S. Jha, P. McDaniel, and M. Livny. Security Policy Reconciliation in Deistributed Computing Environments. Technical Report 1499, University of Wisconsin-Madison, March 2004.

[32] Y. Yang, Z. Fu, and S. F. Wu. BANDS: An Inter-domain Internet Security Policy Management System for IPSec/VPN. In *Integrated Network Management*, volume 246 of *IFIP Conference Proceedings*, pages 231–244. Kluwer, 2003.

[33] J. Zao, L. Sanchez, M. Condell, C. Lynn, M. Fredette, P. Helinek, P. Krishnan, A. Jackson, D. Mankins, M. Shepard, and S. Kent. Domain Based Internet Security Policy Management. In *DARPA Information Survivability Conference and Exposition*, pages 41–53, 2000.

Session 6:
Trust and Filtering

Responding to Policies at Runtime in TrustBuilder

Bryan Smith, Kent E. Seamons, Michael D. Jones

Computer Science Department
Brigham Young University
Provo, Utah 84602
E-mail: {bjcmit,seamons,jones}@cs.byu.edu

Abstract

Automated trust negotiation is the process of establishing trust between entities with no prior relationship through the iterative disclosure of digital credentials. One approach to negotiating trust is for the participants to exchange access control policies to inform each other of the requirements for establishing trust. When a policy is received at runtime, a compliance checker determines which credentials satisfy the policy so they can be disclosed. In situations where several sets of credentials satisfy a policy and some of the credentials are sensitive, a compliance checker that generates all the sets is necessary to insure that the negotiation succeeds whenever possible. Compliance checkers designed for trust management do not usually generate all the satisfying sets. In this paper, we present two practical algorithms for generating all satisfying sets given a compliance checker that generates only one set. The ability to generate all of the combinations provides greater flexibility in how the system or user establishes trust. For example, the least sensitive credential combination could be disclosed first. These ideas have been implemented in TrustBuilder, our prototype system for trust negotiation.

1 Introduction

In the physical world, individuals may establish trust by presenting paper credentials, such as a driver's license, passport, employee ID, credit card, etc., to demonstrate properties about themselves that prove their trustworthiness. These credentials serve as letters of introduction between parties with no pre-existing relationship.

In our research, we explore ways to facilitate similar kinds of interactions in the digital world. Traditional approaches to establishing trust on-line were designed for closed systems, where the participants know each other in advance. They frequently rely on identity-based approaches such as a username and password. In open systems like the Internet, these traditional approaches fail because the participants in a transaction are often strangers and are not in the same security domain.

Trust negotiation [15, 16, 17] is a new approach to establishing trust between strangers through the disclosure of digital credentials containing properties of the participants. Digital credentials are signed statements by trusted third parties that assert properties of the credential owner. Credentials are disclosed during trust negotiation to demonstrate trustworthiness. One approach to implementing digital credentials is to use X.509v3 attribute certificates.

A naïve approach to trust negotiation would be for Alice to disclose all her credentials to an unfamiliar server, Bob, whenever Alice makes a request. In the event the service is protected by an access control policy, Bob can check whether or not Alice possesses the requisite credentials. This simple approach is akin to a first-time customer plopping down their wallet or purse on the counter, and inviting the merchant to rifle through its contents to determine whether or not to trust the customer. Obviously, this is an unacceptable solution to the problem of trust establishment because it completely ignores credential sensitivity.

A more reasonable approach, which considers credential sensitivity, is to first associate an access control policy with each sensitive credential that specifies the credentials that must be received from the other party before the sensitive credential can be disclosed. A trust negotiation begins when one party discloses all non-sensitive credentials. Then the two parties take turns disclosing all the credentials whose access control policies have been satisfied by the other party's disclosed credentials. Eventually, the negotiation either succeeds when trust is established, or fails when one party has nothing further to disclose. A disadvantage to this approach is that credentials may be unnecessarily disclosed.

A third approach is for each party to disclose access control policies to each other that are relevant to the negotiation. Subsequent credential disclosures are then based on a need to know. This paper focuses on this third approach to trust negotiation.

When Bob receives a policy from Alice during a trust negotiation, he uses a compliance checker to determine two things: 1) whether or not his local credentials satisfy the policy, and 2) which credentials satisfy the policy. Bob needs to know which credentials satisfy the policy so that he knows what he must disclose in order to advance the negotiation. Compliance checkers designed for trust management [4] are usually not designed to provide this second capability.

Even if a compliance checker identifies the credentials that satisfy a policy, this is not enough for trust negotiation to succeed whenever possible. In this paper, we explain why a compliance checker must be able to generate all the ways that a policy can be satisfied. Some existing compliance checkers determine only one way that a set of credentials satisfies a policy. We present two practical ways to adapt such a compliance checker so that it is able to generate all the ways that a policy is satisfied. One approach requires rewriting the policy every time the compliance checker is invoked so that prior solutions are excluded in order to force additional solutions to be generated. Another approach involves modifying the set of input credentials each time the compliance checker is invoked in order to obtain all minimal satisfying sets.

Definition 1.1. A *minimal satisfying set* is a set of credentials that satisfies a policy such that no proper subset also satisfies the policy.

Throughout the remainder of this paper, all references to a satisfying set imply a minimal satisfying set.

Definition 1.2. A *compliance checker* is a function f : $\{C, P\} \Rightarrow S$, where C is a set of credentials, P is a policy, and S is a subset of C that $\models$ (minimally satisfies) P. If C is empty or contains no satisfying sets, then S is empty.

Once a compliance checker is able to produce all the satisfying sets, there are several ways to use this feature during trust negotiation. Generating some or all of the satisfying sets at once allows the negotiation agent to select the order that alternative ways of establishing trust are considered. We introduce several alternatives and discuss the merits of each approach.

The remainder of this paper is organized as follows. Section 2 presents an overview of trust negotiations involving policy exchanges and discusses the requirements this approach imposes on compliance checkers. Section 3 presents two approaches for generating all the minimal sets that satisfy an access control policy received during a trust negotiation. In Section 4, the three methods to generating satisfying sets and choosing which negotiation path to explore are presented. Section 5 contains related work and Section 6 contains conclusions and future work.

2 Policy Exchange during Trust Negotiation

The following hypothetical example of a trust negotiation illustrates how the participants can learn about each other's requirements for establishing trust by exchanging access control policies. This allows the participants to determine in private whether or not they satisfy the policy, and whether they are willing to disclose credentials that satisfy the policy.

Suppose Alice is registering online for community college. The server, Bob, requires some form of ID from Alice. Bob's access control policy specifies that several forms of ID are acceptable, including a driver's license, employee ID, and a military ID. Alice is employed by a major retailer and is a member of the Army reserve, so she has all three kinds of ID. Her employer requires that her employee ID only be used for business purposes, and Alice only discloses her military ID to authorized government servers.

Using semi-automated trust negotiation, Alice and Bob (or more precisely, their trust negotiation agents) could interact as follows. Alice requests to enroll in community college. Bob responds with an access control policy that requests that Alice submit a digital ID. Alice evaluates the policy and determines that she can satisfy Bob's policy in three different ways. Up to this point, Alice's trust negotiation agent completed these steps automatically on her behalf. At this point, the agent notifies Alice interactively that she must submit one of her three forms of ID, and Alice manually selects the form of ID that she is most willing to disclose.

With automated trust negotiation, Alice's trust negotiation agent relieves her of the need to manually select which credentials to disclose. Instead, credential disclosure is controlled by access control policies that specify the credentials the other party must first disclose in order to receive a sensitive credential. The following is one way the negotiation between Alice and Bob might proceed, and assumes a compliance checker that generates solutions to a policy in random order. Alice requests to enroll in community college. Bob responds with an access control policy that requests that Alice submit some form of ID. Alice evaluates the policy and determines that she can satisfy the policy using her military ID. Since it is sensitive, Alice discloses the access control policy to request that Bob demonstrate that he is an authorized military server. Bob notifies Alice that he cannot satisfy her policy. Alice then determines that her employee ID satisfies the policy. Since it is also sensitive, Alice requests that Bob demonstrate he is an authorized server representing Alice's employer, or someone that her employer trusts. Bob notifies Alice that he cannot satisfy this policy. Finally, Alice determines that her driver's license satisfies the policy, and she discloses her credential to Bob, allowing her to complete the enrollment process. Note in this exam-

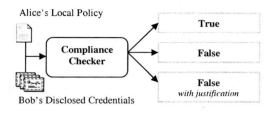

Figure 1. Compliance checker in a traditional mode of operation

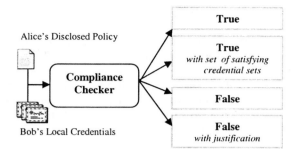

Figure 2. Compliance checker that is able to incrementally determine all minimal sets of credentials that satisfy a remote policy

ple that the negotiation could have been greatly simplified if Alice had considered her driver's license before the other more sensitive credentials. We will return to this point in Section 4.

There are two distinct modes of operation required by a compliance checker during trust negotiation. The first mode is the traditional way a compliance checker functions in a trust management environment, as shown in Figure 1. Alice's negotiation agent invokes the compliance checker to determine whether to grant Bob access to a sensitive resource. Alice's negotiation agent provides the compliance checker with Alice's access control policy for the resource, the credentials Bob has disclosed, and possibly other information that Alice has made available locally (e.g., time of day, proof of her age, the results of Alice's checks for revocation of the credentials Bob has submitted, etc.). The compliance checker produces a Boolean result indicating whether or not the credentials satisfy the policy. Policy-Maker has a compliance checker that returns a justification when access is denied [5]. KeyNote supports the specification of a user-defined justification whenever the result is false [3]. During trust negotiation, the compliance checker adopts this first mode of operation to determine whether to grant access to a sensitive service or to disclose a sensitive credential or policy.

The second mode of operation required of a compliance checker during trust negotiation is not usually necessary in traditional trust management environments, but is required if policies are disclosed during negotiation. Suppose Bob requests a sensitive resource and does not supply the necessary credentials. Rather than simply deny the request, Alice can disclose the access control policy governing the sensitive resource in order to guide the negotiation to a successful conclusion. Upon receipt of Alice's access control policy, Bob can make use of his compliance checker according to the diagram in Figure 2. Bob's negotiation agent invokes the compliance checker to determine whether Bob has credentials cached locally that satisfy Alice's disclosed policy. The compliance checker accepts Alice's disclosed policy and

Bob's local credentials as input, and possibly other information from Bobs environment (time of day, etc.). The compliance checker returns a Boolean result indicating whether Bob has credentials that satisfy Alice's policy. In addition, Bob's negotiation agent needs the compliance checker to return a set of local credentials that satisfies Alice's policy so that those credentials may be disclosed during the negotiation. In some cases, Bob may have more than one set of credentials that satisfies Alice's policy. However, some of Bob's credentials in a satisfying set may be sensitive, and Alice may not be able to qualify for access to them. Thus, Bob's compliance checker must be able to determine all minimal combinations of credentials that satisfy Alice's policy in order to exhaust all possibilities for establishing trust. REFEREE is an example of an early trust management system that returns a justification when a policy is satisfied [7].

Compliance checkers can be categorized according to the modes of operation supported. A type-1 compliance checker is the traditional type of compliance checker used in trust management systems, which determines whether to grant access to a protected resource. This type lacks support for the second mode of operation described previously. A type-2 compliance checker returns only a single set of credentials that satisfy the policy. The runtime engine for the IBM Trust Establishment (TE) system [9] is an example of this type of compliance checker. A type-3 compliance checker returns all the sets of credentials that satisfy the policy and is required by trust negotiation when exchanging policies [12].

A trust negotiation is said to be complete if it succeeds whenever possible. In order for the trust negotiation to be complete, Alice's compliance checker must be capable of determining all the ways that her credentials satisfy Bob's policy. If her compliance checker does not generate all minimal satisfying credential sets, then trust negotiation may be incomplete. This situation can occur when the following two conditions are met. First, the set of satisfying credentials returned by Alice's compliance checker contains credentials that are governed by policies that Bob cannot satisfy. Second, there is another set of satisfying credentials that Alice's compliance checker is unable to identify that are governed by policies that Bob can satisfy. When both of these conditions occur, Alice and Bob will not be able to establish trust even though it is theoretically possible for trust to be established.

3 Satisfying Set Generation

Most compliance checker implementations are either type-1 or type-2. They are not designed to satisfy the needs of policy exchange during trust negotiation, and so they do not generate all the sets that satisfy a policy.

TrustBuilder is our prototype trust negotiation system under development at BYU. The initial implementation of TrustBuilder leveraged the IBM TE system to provide a policy language for expressing the credential combinations necessary to establish trust and a compliance checker for making trust decisions. The TE system is freely available on IBM AlphaWorks, but the source code is proprietary.

Our experience using TE for trust negotiation was the impetus for the research presented in this paper. TE has a type-2 compliance checker. In order for trust negotiation to be complete when policies are exchanged, the compliance checker must generate all the minimal sets that satisfy a policy. One way to generate these sets using the TE compliance checker is a brute force approach. Given a policy P and a set of local credentials L, the compliance checker is invoked $2^{|L|} - 1$ times for each set from the power set of L. The disadvantage of this approach is that the cost grows exponentially with the number of local credentials.

In the remainder of this section, we discuss and analyze two approaches for generating all the sets that satisfy a policy, given a type-2 compliance checker. These approaches, known as policy modification and credential set modification, are more efficient than the brute force approach.

3.1 Policy Modification

The first approach to generating all of the sets that satisfy a policy is to repeatedly invoke the compliance checker with the same set of local credentials, but modify the policy to exclude all the satisfying sets that have already been generated. The process begins with no known satisfying sets. The compliance checker is invoked with the set of local credentials L and the policy P. If a set of credentials S_1 is returned by the compliance checker, then P is modified at runtime to exclude S_1 as follows: P AND NOT (P_1) where P_1 is a conjunction of all the credentials in S_1. Note that the set S_1 is excluded, but the individual credentials that

comprise S_1 can still be members of other minimal sets that satisfy P. The compliance checker is invoked a second time with the set of local credentials and the modified policy. After each invocation of the compliance checker, the policy is further modified according to the form P AND NOT $(P_1$ OR ... OR $P_n)$ where n is the number of satisfying sets generated thus far. The process of policy modification and compliance checker invocation continues until the compliance checker returns an empty set, which indicates that all satisfying sets have been generated. Using this approach, all of the satisfying sets will be generated after $N + 1$ invocations of the compliance checker where N is the number of satisfying sets.

The following illustrates how TrustBuilder adopts this approach using the XML-based Trust Policy Language (TPL) supported by the IBM TE system [9]. The TE system maps a subject to a role based on the subject's credentials, a role-assignment policy established by the owner of the resource, and the roles of the issuers of the credentials. The role assignment policy is a set of TPL role definitions. TPL role definitions contain a collection of ⟨GROUP⟩ tags. Inside the ⟨GROUP⟩ tag, ⟨RULE⟩ tags are used to state the requirements for role membership. If any of the rules are satisfied, then the supplicant is a member of the group. A RULE entity contains a series of INCLUSION tags and FUNCTION tags. An INCLUSION entity specifies constraints on credentials, such as type and issuer. Further constraints on credentials can be specified within a FUNCTION entity.

In the community college enrollment scenario discussed previously in Section 2, Alice has three identification credentials: an employee ID, a military ID, and a driver's license. Using TPL, the college server (Bob) requires that a person be a member of the $ValidIDHolder$ group to register. An example of a TPL policy for this scenario is shown in Figure 3.

The TE compliance checker is designed to return a single set that satisfies the policy. Suppose Alice invokes the compliance checker with the policy contained in Figure 3 and her three identification credentials as input. Assume the compliance checker first returns a set containing Alice's employee ID. In order for Alice to determine if there are additional satisfying sets using policy modification, the TPL policy is modified to exclude the set containing Alice's employee ID. Figure 4 illustrates how the $ValidIDHolder$ group can be modified to eliminate Alice's employee ID as a satisfying set, and force the compliance checker to return another satisfying set, if one exists.

Assume the modified policy in Figure 4 is fed to the compliance checker along with Alice's credentials, and her military ID is returned as another satisfying set. The policy can be further modified to also exclude Alice's military ID as a solution. The next invocation returns the set containing Al-

```
<GROUP NAME= "self" ></GROUP>

<GROUP NAME="Company ">
    <RULE>
        <INCLUSION ID="compcert" TYPE="TrustedCompany"
            FROM="self"/>
    </RULE>
</GROUP>

<GROUP NAME= "USArmedForces" >
    <RULE>
        <INCLUSION ID="usAFcert" TYPE="USArmedForces" FROM="self"/>
    </RULE>
</GROUP>

<GROUP NAME= "State" >
    <RULE>
        <INCLUSION ID="statecert" TYPE="State" FROM="self"/>
    </RULE>
</GROUP>

<GROUP NAME="ValidIDHolder">
    <RULE>
        <INCLUSION ID="empIDcert" TYPE="EmployeeID"
            FROM="Company"/>
    </RULE>
    <RULE>
        <INCLUSION ID="mIDcert" TYPE="MilitaryID"
            FROM="USArmedForces"/>
    </RULE>
    <RULE>
        <INCLUSION ID="dlcert" TYPE="DriversLicense" FROM="State"/>
    </RULE>
</GROUP>
```

Figure 3. Example TPL policy for community college enrollment scenario

```
<GROUP NAME="ValidIDHolder">
    <RULE>
        <INCLUSION ID="empIDcert" TYPE="EmployeeID" FROM="Company"/>
        <FUNCTION>
          <AND>
            <NE>
              <FIELD ID="empIDcert" NAME="issuerName"/>
              <CONST>CompanyX</CONST>
            </NE>
            <NE>
              <FIELD ID="empIDcert" NAME="X509serialNo"/>
              <CONST>2345</CONST>
            </NE>
          </AND>
        </FUNCTION>
    </RULE>
    <RULE>
        <INCLUSION ID="mIDcert" TYPE="MilitaryID"
            FROM="USArmedForces"/>
    </RULE>
    <RULE>
        <INCLUSION ID="dlcert" TYPE="DriversLicense" FROM="State"/>
    </RULE>
</GROUP>
```

Figure 4. Modified $ValidIDHolder$ role definition after a satisfying set containing an employee ID has been obtained

3.2 Credential Set Modification

The second approach to generating all of the sets that satisfy a policy is to repeatedly invoke the compliance checker with the same policy, but modify the input set of local credentials based on the satisfying sets that have already been generated. In this section, we present the Satisfying Set Generation (SSgen) algorithm, which accepts a policy and a set of credentials and returns all the credential sets that minimally satisfy the policy.

The SSgen algorithm assumes a restricted form of policies according to the following definition.

Definition 3.1. A *policy P* is a disjunction of rules, where rules are conjunctions of credentials. A rule specifies a minimal satisfying set.

By definition, a policy cannot be $(A$ AND $B)$ OR A because $A \subset \{A, B\}$.

A lattice can be formed from the subsets of the set of local credentials L according to the following rule: $Y \rightarrow^* X$, iff $Y \subseteq X$. Figure 5 illustrates a lattice formed from the set $\{A, B, C\}$. The SSgen algorithm uses the lattice to determine the sequence of sets with which to invoke the compliance checker.

A naïve implementation of the brute force approach to generating all the satisfying sets is to conduct a breadth-first traversal of the lattice, invoking the compliance checker for each non-empty set in the lattice. This results in $2^{|L|} - 1$ invocations of the compliance checker. This is impractical when $|L|$ is large.

The following properties provide insights into ways to improve on the naïve brute force algorithm. We will refer to sets in the lattice in Figure 5 for illustrative purposes.

ice's driver's license. Finally, the policy is modified to also exclude her driver's license, and the next invocation of the compliance checker returns the empty set because there are no more satisfying sets.

The policy modification approach results in fewer calls to the compliance checker compared to the brute force approach, especially when there is a large number of local credentials and only a few sets that satisfy a policy. As the number of satisfying sets grows, the complexity of the modified policy increases, requiring additional processing each time the compliance checker is invoked. Experiments using the TrustBuilder implementation of policy modification indicate that the added overhead for generating and evaluating modified policies using the TE system is negligible for typical problem sizes. For example, we developed two test scenarios involving 50 local credentials, policies with 4 or 5 satisfying sets each, and each satisfying set consisting of 2 to 3 credentials. The cost of each policy modification was approximately .02 seconds, with no noticeable increase in policy evaluation time. The experiments were run on a 1.4 GHz Pentium 4 processor with 512 MB of RAM.

In order to adopt the policy modification approach, the policy language must support the proper semantics for the AND and NOT operators. The recipient of the original policy is not able to treat the policy as a black box, but must be capable of rewriting the policy according to the satisfying sets that are generated.

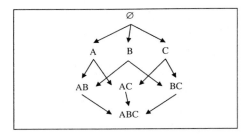

Figure 5. Lattice containing the subsets of $\{A, B, C\}$

Property 1. A search for a satisfying set can begin at the bottom of the lattice, and invoke the compliance checker with the set of all local credentials $\{A, B, C\}$. This is especially significant when there are no satisfying sets because the first call to the compliance checker will fail and the search is finished. If there are any satisfying sets, the first call to the compliance checker will find one.

Property 2. When the compliance checker returns a satisfying set, by definition, no proper subset of that set can also be a satisfying set. These proper subsets can be eliminated from the search space. For example, suppose the first call to the compliance checker returns the set $\{A,B\}$. The sets $\emptyset$, $\{A\}$, and $\{B\}$ can be eliminated.

Property 3. When the compliance checker returns a satisfying set, by definition, no proper supersets of that set can also be a satisfying set. These proper supersets can be eliminated from the search space. For example, suppose the first call to the compliance checker returns the set $\{A\}$. The sets $\{A, B\}$, $\{A, C\}$, and $\{A, B, C\}$ can be eliminated.

Property 4. When the compliance checker returns an empty set, by definition, no proper subset of the input set can be a satisfying set. These proper subsets can also be eliminated from the search space. For example, suppose the compliance checker is called with the set $\{A, C\}$ as input. If no satisfying set is returned, the sets $\{A\}$ and $\{C\}$ can be eliminated.

Property 5. Suppose the compliance checker returns a satisfying set S containing m members. To find additional satisfying sets, each proper subset of S can be combined with all the local credentials not in S and then passed to the compliance checker. If there are any more satisfying sets besides S, this approach will find one in at most $2^m - 1$ calls to the compliance checker. If no other satisfying set is found, then all other sets in the lattice will be eliminated during the process.

Property 6. In a lattice fashioned after the one shown in Figure 5, all nodes that are a distance i from the empty set comprise all of the i-subsets (i.e., subsets containing i members) in the lattice. For example, the nodes in Figure 5 that are a distance of 2 from the empty set form all the 2-subsets $\{A, B\}$, $\{A, C\}$, and $\{B, C\}$. For a lattice and a given i, suppose all of the i-subsets are input to the compliance checker and fail to return a satisfying set, or are proper subsets of failed input sets. According to Property 4, no other subset in the lattice with less than i members is a satisfying set. The remaining subsets are eliminated from consideration.

Property 7. Suppose the compliance checker returns a satisfying set S containing m members. If S is the only satisfying set in the lattice, this can be determined in $m + 1$ calls to the compliance checker based on Properties 1, 5, and 6. The first call to the compliance checker returns set S (Property 1). The next m calls to the compliance checker involve sets containing the $(m - 1)$-subsets of S (Property 5). If the m calls to the compliance checker fail to produce another satisfying set, all other subsets in the lattice are eliminated (Property 6).

The SSgen algorithm (see Figure 6) is based on the properties listed above. The following theorem states that the SSgen algorithm finds all the satisfying sets for a given policy.

Theorem 3.1. $R \subseteq L$ and $R \models P$ if and only if $R \in B$, where B is the set of sets returned by the SSgen algorithm, L is the set of local credentials, P is a policy, and R is an arbitrary set of credentials.

Proof. First, let $R \in B$. In the SSgen algorithm, the code to add R to B can only be reached by sets containing subsets of U unioned with $L \setminus U$ that satisfy P. The compliance checker on Lines 1 and 11 returns J such that $J \models P$ or J is empty. Lines 3 and 17 add J to B only if J is not empty nor already in B. Thus, if $R \in B$ then $R \subseteq L$ and $R \models P$.

Conversely, let $R \subseteq L$ and $R \models P$. Suppose to the contrary that $R \notin B$. In the SSgen algorithm, there are eight ways for R to not be in B. Lines 1 and 4-9 only consider sets containing subsets of U unioned with $L \setminus U$ for addition to B. Therefore, the first two cases that will cause R to not be in B are (1) R contains a non-empty proper subset of $L \setminus U$ and (2) $R \subset U$. Line 10 checks for sets that are not a superset nor a subset of a set in B and not a subset of a set in E. As a result, there are five more cases: (3) $R \subset$ a set in B, (4) $R \in B$, (5) $R \supset$ a set in B, (6) $R \subset$ a set in E, and (7) $R \in E$. Lines 1 and 11 invoke the compliance checker with a set and P and places the return value in J. Thus, another case is (8) R does not satisfy P. Lines 3 and 17 add sets that are not empty nor in B to B. However, the cases that R is empty and $R \in B$ are already covered. Line 18 causes sets to not be considered if all the n-subsets contain no subsets that satisfy P. Nonetheless, the case that $R \subset$

```
L is the set of local credentials
P is a policy
B is the set of known minimal satisfying sets, which can be empty
E is the set of sets known to contain no subsets that satisfy P, which can be empty
U is union of all sets in B
An n-subset is a subset that contains n members.
𝒫(U) returns the power set of U

1    J = complianceChecker(L, P)
2    if (J is not empty)
3        B = B ∪ {J}
4        Let S = 𝒫(U)
5        Let n = |U|
6        while (n > 0)
7            Let T be all the (n-1)-subsets ∈ S
8            For each set, D ∈ T
9                A = D ∪ (L \ U)
10               if (A is not a superset or a subset of a set ∈ B and is not a subset of a set ∈ E)
11                   J = complianceChecker(A, P)
12                   if (J is empty)
13                       E = E ∪ {A}
14                   else
15                       if (J \ U !-= φ )
16                           goto line 3 because |U| will increase
17                       B = B ∪ {J}
18           if ( ∀ t ∈ T (t ∪ (L \ U) ⊆ E))
19               n = 0
20           else
21               n = n-1
22       end-while
23   end-if
```

Figure 6. Pseudo-code for the SSgen algorithm

a set in E is covered. The following considers these eight cases and demonstrates that each ends in a contradiction.

Case 1: R contains a non-empty proper subset of $L \setminus U$. All minimal satisfying sets in R such that $R \cap (L \setminus U)$ is not empty and not equal to $L \setminus U$ are also in sets included in S. Therefore, any R that minimally satisfies P will be in B, which contradicts $R \notin B$.

Case 2: $R \subset U$. If R is a proper subset of U, then either $R \in B$, $R \supset$ a set in B, $R \subset$ a set in B, R is the empty set, or R is a mixture of credentials from different sets in B such that R is neither a superset nor subset of a set in B. $R \in B$ contradicts $R \notin B$. $R \supset$ a set in B contradicts $R \models P$. $R \subset$ a set in B contradicts $R \models P$. R is the empty set contradicts $R \models P$. All minimal satisfying sets in R such that R is a mixture of credentials from different sets in B such that R is neither a superset nor subset of a set in B are also in sets included in S. Therefore, any R that minimally satisfies P will be in B, which contradicts $R \notin B$.

Case 3: $R \subset F$, where F is a set in B. If a superset of R minimally satisfies P, then, by definition, R cannot satisfy P, which contradicts $R \models P$.

Case 4: $R \in B$ contradicts $R \notin B$.

Case 5: $R \supset D$, where D is a set in B. By the definition of a policy, if a subset of R minimally satisfies P then R cannot minimally satisfy P. This contradicts the fact that $R \models P$.

Case 6: $R \subset$ a set in E. If R is a proper subset of a set in E then R also does not satisfy P because otherwise the set would not be in E. But this contradicts the fact that $R \models P$.

Case 7: $R \in E$ contradicts $R \models P$.

Case 8: R does not satisfy P contradicts $R \models P$. □

The complexity of the SSgen algorithm is $O(2^{|U|})$ where U is the union of the satisfying sets. Although this worst case performance is exponential in the size of U, the algorithm is practical when $|U|$ is small and the number of satisfying sets is modest.

Figure 7 shows performance characteristics of an implementation of SSgen in TrustBuilder. All experiments were run on a 1.4 GHz Pentium 4 processor with 512 MB of RAM. Each test case consisted of a set of local credentials L where $|L| = 50$. The size of U varies from 1 to 24 credentials.

For a single satisfying set, the algorithm determines that there is only one satisfying set in well under one second in all cases. In this case, note that the complexity of the SSgen algorithm is $O(|U|)$.

The maximum number of satisfying sets for a given U is $\frac{n!}{r!(n-r)!}$, where $n = |U|$ and $r = |U|/2$. This case results in the most invocations to the compliance checker. The ex-

155

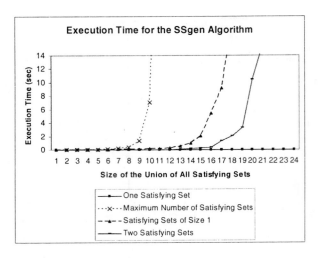

Figure 7. Execution time for the SSgen algorithm according to the size of the union of all satisfying sets and the number of satisfying sets.

periments show that SSgen starts to become impractical at approximately 10 credentials. However, since for 10 credentials there will be 252 satisfying sets, it is unlikely that an access control policy will ever reach that level of complexity in practice.

Another significant data point is the case where there are $|U|$ satisfying sets of one member each. This results in an exhaustive search of each lattice of size 1 to $|U|$. A single invocation of the compliance checker occurs for each lattice. The graph shows that the running time is below $\frac{1}{10}$ of a second as $|U|$ grows to 9 credentials, increases to 2 seconds as $|U|$ grows to 15 credentials, and then becomes impractical as $|U|$ grows beyond 15 credentials.

The graph also shows the performance when there are two satisfying sets. Each set is approximately three-fourths the size of U. The running time is below one second as $|U|$ grows to 16 credentials, increases to 3 seconds as $|U|$ grows to 19 credentials, and then becomes impractical as $|U|$ grows beyond 19 credentials.

4 Exploring Alternative Ways for Establishing Trust

This section presents three ways to utilize a type-3 compliance checker so that alternative ways to establish trust can be explored during a trust negotiation.

First, when a policy is received during a negotiation, the compliance checker can immediately generate all the minimal satisfying sets. This allows the trust negotiation agent the flexibility to determine the order in which each set will

be utilized to attempt to establish trust. The set ordering can be determined using heuristics, such as streamlining the negotiation or limiting the amount of sensitive information that is disclosed. For instance, the sets could be ordered by the number of sensitive credentials each set contains so that freely available sets will be considered first, possibly causing the negotiation to immediately succeed instead of pursuing additional rounds of negotiation to unlock sensitive credentials in another satisfying set. Another option is to prompt the user to provide guidance interactively regarding the order to explore satisfying sets based on the user's privacy preferences. Also, instead of considering each satisfying set individually, all the satisfying sets can be merged into a single set. This approach places a premium on reducing the number of rounds during a negotiation and is focused less on limiting the amount of information disclosed.

Second, the compliance checker may generate some of the sets that satisfy the policy, and then processes those sets using the same approaches that were discussed in the previous paragraph (e.g., order the sets according to sensitivity, prompt the user for guidance, and merge the sets). The reason for only generating some of the sets is to place limits on the amount of effort expended to generate the sets when there are many solutions. This can reduce the overall cost of the negotiation in case a successful negotiation can be reached without having to incur the cost to generate all of the sets. The amount of effort can be controlled by a threshold set on the amount of computation time expanded on set generation. Another method is to generate sets until the first set of non-sensitive credentials is returned, which could immediately lead to a successful negotiation without generating additional satisfying sets. If none of the sets leads to a successful negotiation, then the compliance checker must continue to generate additional satisfying sets in order for the trust negotiation to be complete.

Third, the compliance checker may generate one satisfying set at a time through an iterator-style interface. This approach avoids unnecessary generation of satisfying sets. However, the compliance checker dictates the order that satisfying sets are explored to establish trust. When a satisfying set leads to an unsuccessful negotiation, backtracking is employed to return to the previous point in the negotiation where the unsuccessful set was generated so that another attempt to generate a new satisfying set can be made.

5 Related Work

There are only a small number of compliance checkers that meet the requirement of returning the set of credentials that satisfy the policy passed to the compliance checker. The compliance checkers that are able to meet this requirement are: Rule-controlled Environment For Evaluation of Rules, and Everything Else (REFEREE) [7], Portfolio and

Service Protection Language (PSPL) [6], Trust Establishment (TE) [9], Role-based Trust management (RT) [11] and χ-TNL [2].

Chu et al. [7] present a general purpose execution environment for Web applications that require trust called REFEREE. Policies are treated as programs, which can be invoked and return an answer with justification. The justification is a statement or list of statements. A statement consists of two elements; the context or source of the statement and the content of the statement. A statement can be viewed as an attribute credential with the context being the issuer if the content contains some form of subject identification and states at least one attribute about the subject. It is unclear whether REFEREE returns all the sets of credentials that satisfy the policy. It also has a prototype implementation.

Bonatti and Samarati [6] present a uniform formal framework for specifying service access and information disclosure control. This framework was developed with trust negotiation in mind, so it meets the majority of the requirements of trust negotiation including a compliance checker that returns all the satisfying sets of credentials. Currently, no prototype implementation is available.

Herzberg et al. [9] present the Trust Policy Language, an XML-based language used primarily to map users to roles. The language is supported in the Trust Establishment (TE) system, which can determine a user's role based on certificates and TPL policies. TE is an example of a compliance checker that returns only one satisfying set. We incorporated TE in our TrustBuilder prototype because it supported many features needed in trust negotiation. The algorithms presented in this paper effectively transform the TE compliance checker into a type-3 compliance checker.

Li et al. [11] introduce RT, a family of Role-based Trust management languages for representing credential and policies in distributed authorization. An initial prototype implementation of trust negotiation based on the first RT language provides completeness during trust negotiation for unstructured credentials [14] and is an example of a type-3 compliance checker. The runtime engine is still under development to support the remaining languages in the RT family. We plan to explore the suitability of RT as a decision engine for TrustBuilder.

Bertino et al. [2] present χ-TNL, an XML-based language for conducting trust negotiation. χ-TNL provides a medium to transport information about the negotiating parties called a certificate. A certificate can be either a credential or a declaration. A credential is list of properties of a negotiating party certified by a Certificate Authority. A declaration contains helpful information (e.g., policies) for the negotiation process. χ-TNL is part of a more extensive project called Trust-χ, which extended from χ-Sec [1]. χ-Sec had no need to generate all satisfying credential sets, but the development of χ-TNL introduces this need.

6   Conclusion and Future Work

Access control policies can be exchanged between the participants in an on-line trust negotiation to inform each other of the requirements for establishing trust. A compliance checker is a runtime engine that answers the question of whether or not a set of credentials satisfies an access control policy. When a policy is received at runtime, a compliance checker determines which credentials satisfy the policy so they can be disclosed. In situations where several combinations of credentials satisfy a policy and some of the credentials are sensitive, a compliance checker that generates all the combinations is necessary to insure that the negotiation is complete (i.e., succeeds whenever possible). Compliance checkers designed for trust management do not usually generate all the ways a policy is satisfied.

In this paper, we presented two practical algorithms for generating all credential combinations that satisfy a policy given a compliance checker that generates only one combination. The policy modification approach requires rewriting the policy every time the compliance checker is invoked so that prior solutions are excluded in order to force additional solutions to be generated. The credential set modification approach involves modifying the set of input credentials each time the compliance checker is invoked in order to obtain all minimal satisfying sets.

The policy modification approach requires that an implementation be able to interpret and manipulate policies according to the semantics of the policy language. The credential set modification approach is policy language independent, although it requires policies to be expressed in minimal disjunctive normal form.

We incorporated these approaches in TrustBuilder, our prototype system for trust negotiation. TrustBuilder uses the compliance checker provided by the IBM Trust Establishment system that was designed for trust management. The extensions to TrustBuilder demonstrate one way to adapt existing compliance checkers to meet the needs of trust negotiation. The reason all satisfying sets need to be generated is because some of the sets may not lead to a successful negotiation. One reason failure can occur is that one or more of the credentials in a set is sensitive, and the other party is not authorized to receive them. If the sensitive credentials belong to another satisfying set, another failure will occur. Thus, one optimization in the search for additional satisfying sets is to remove from consideration the sensitive credentials that the other party is not authorized to receive. This will cut the search space in half for each sensitive credential.

Once a compliance checker is able to produce all the minimal satisfying sets, there are several ways to use that feature during trust negotiation. Generating some or all of the satisfying sets at once allows the negotiation agent to select the order that alternative ways of establishing trust are considered. We introduced several alternatives and discussed the merits of each approach. These ideas have also been implemented in TrustBuilder. Implementation details can be found in [13]. To our knowledge, this is the first example of a trust negotiation system that generates potential solutions to establishing trust and prioritizes them according to specific criteria. These ideas can be incorporated directly into the type-3 compliance checkers that are being implemented to support trust negotiation.

Disclosing access control policies during trust negotiation raises privacy issues, because policies themselves can contain sensitive information. Hidden credentials [10] address this problem by encrypting a policy so that it can only be understood if it is fulfilled. We are currently exploring ways to efficiently process these encrypted policies.

We plan to experiment with emerging compliance checker implementations designed for trust negotiation, including the RT runtime system [11] and the PeerTrust system [8] designed for trust negotiation in the Semantic Web.

7 Acknowledgments

The authors thank Marianne Winslett, Robert Bradshaw, Phillip Hellewell, Jim Henshaw, Tim van der Horst, and the anonymous reviewers for helpful comments that improved the quality of the paper. This research was supported by funding from DARPA through AFRL contract number F33615-01-C-0336 and SSC-SD grant number N66001-01-1-8908, the National Science Foundation under Grant No. CCR-0325951 and prime cooperative agreement no. IIS-0331707, and The Regents of the University of California.

References

[1] E. Bertino, S. Castano, and E. Ferrari. On specifying security policies for web documents with an XML-based language. In *Proceedings of the Sixth ACM Symposium on Access Control Models and Technologies*, pages 57–65, Chantilly, VA, May 2001. ACM Press.

[2] E. Bertino, E. Ferrari, and A. Squicciarini. χ-TNL: An XML-based language for trust negotiation. In *Fourth IEEE International Workshop on Policies for Distributed Systems and Networks*, pages 81–84, Como, Italy, June 2003. IEEE Computer Society Press.

[3] M. Blaze, J. Feigenbaum, J. Ioannidis, and A. Keromytis. The KeyNote Trust Management System Version 2. In *Internet Draft RFC 2704*, 1999.

[4] M. Blaze, J. Feigenbaum, and J. Lacy. Decentralized trust management. In *Proceedings of the 1996 IEEE Symposium on Security and Privacy*, pages 164–173, Oakland, CA, May 1996. IEEE Computer Society Press.

[5] M. Blaze, J. Feigenbaum, and M. Strauss. Compliance-checking in the PolicyMaker trust management system. In *Proceedings of Second International Conference on Financial Cryptography (FC'98)*, volume 1465 of *Lecture Notes in Computer Science*, pages 254–274. Springer-Verlag, 1998.

[6] P. Bonatti and P. Samarati. Regulating service access and information release on the web. In *Proceedings of the 7th ACM Conference on Computer and Communications Security (CCS-7)*, pages 134–143. ACM Press, Nov. 2000.

[7] Y.-H. Chu, J. Feigenbaum, B. LaMacchia, P. Resnick, and M. Strauss. REFEREE: Trust management for Web applications. *Computer Networks and ISDN Systems*, 29(8–13):953–964, 1997.

[8] R. Gavriloaie, W. Nejdl, D. Olmedilla, K. E. Seamons, and M. Winslett. No registration needed: How to use declarative policies and negotiation to access sensitive resources on the Semantic Web. In *1st European Semantic Web Symposium*, Heraklion, Greece, May 2004.

[9] A. Herzberg, Y. Mass, J. Mihaeli, D. Naor, and Y. Ravid. Access control meets public key infrastructure, or: Assigning roles to strangers. In *Proceedings of the 2000 IEEE Symposium on Security and Privacy*, pages 2–14. IEEE Computer Society Press, May 2000.

[10] J. Holt, R. Bradshaw, K. E. Seamons, and H. Orman. Hidden credentials. In *2nd ACM Workshop on Privacy and Electronic Society*, pages 1–8, Washington, DC, Oct. 2003. ACM Press.

[11] N. Li, J. C. Mitchell, and W. H. Winsborough. Design of a role-based trust management framework. In *Proceedings of the 2002 IEEE Symposium on Security and Privacy*, pages 114–130. IEEE Computer Society Press, May 2002.

[12] K. E. Seamons, M. Winslett, T. Yu, B. Smith, E. Child, J. Jacobsen, H. Mills, and L. Yu. Requirements for policy languages for trust negotiation. In *Proceedings of the Third International Workshop on Policies for Distributed Systems and Networks (Policy 2002)*, pages 68–79. IEEE Computer Society Press, June 2002.

[13] B. Smith. Responding to policies at runtime in TrustBuilder. Master's thesis, Computer Science Department, Brigham Young University, March 2004.

[14] W. H. Winsborough and N. Li. Towards practical automated trust negotiation. In *Proceedings of the Third International Workshop on Policies for Distributed Systems and Networks (Policy 2002)*, pages 92–103, Monterey, California, June 2002. IEEE Computer Society Press.

[15] W. H. Winsborough, K. E. Seamons, and V. E. Jones. Automated trust negotiation. In *DARPA Information Survivability Conference and Exposition*, volume I, pages 88–102, Hilton Head, SC, Jan. 2000. IEEE Press.

[16] M. Winslett, T. Yu, K. Seamons, A. Hess, J. Jarvis, B. Smith, and L. Yu. Negotiating Trust on the Web. *IEEE Internet Computing Special Issue on Trust Management*, 6(6):30–37, November/December 2002.

[17] T. Yu, M. Winslett, and K. Seamons. Supporting structured credentials and sensitive policies through interoperable strategies in automated trust negotiation. *ACM Transactions on Information and System Security*, 6(1):1–42, Feb. 2003.

Cassandra: Distributed Access Control Policies with Tunable Expressiveness

Moritz Y. Becker   Peter Sewell

Computer Laboratory, University of Cambridge
JJ Thomson Avenue, Cambridge, United Kingdom
{moritz.becker, peter.sewell}@cl.cam.ac.uk

Abstract

We study the specification of access control policy in large-scale distributed systems. Our work on real-world policies has shown that standard policy idioms such as role hierarchy or role delegation occur in practice in many subtle variants. A policy specification language should therefore be able to express this variety of features smoothly, rather than add them as specific features in an ad hoc way, as is the case in many existing languages.

We present Cassandra, *a role-based trust management system with an elegant and readable policy specification language based on Datalog with constraints. The expressiveness (and computational complexity) of the language can be adjusted by choosing an appropriate constraint domain. With just five special predicates, we can easily express a wide range of policies including role hierarchy, role delegation, separation of duties, cascading revocation, automatic credential discovery and trust negotiation.* Cassandra *has a formal semantics for query evaluation and for the access control enforcement engine. We use a goal-oriented distributed policy evaluation algorithm that is efficient and guarantees termination. Initial performance results for our prototype implementation have been promising.*

1. Introduction

The emergence of wide-area network-based services poses new and challenging problems to security management. The networks in question are generally heterogeneous, decentralised and large-scale, with possibly millions of autonomous entities (which may be individuals, agents, organisations or other administrative domains) that wish to share their resources in a secure and controlled fashion. Collaborating entities may be mutual strangers at first, thus access control cannot be based on identity, as it is the case in traditional approaches.

In the *trust management* approach [5], authorisation is based on credentials, digitally signed certificates asserting attributes about entities holding them. In systems supporting *trust negotiation* [19], peers establish trust between each other by exchanging sets of suitable credentials. A *policy specification language* is used to define a system's security policy, a set of rules specifying the security goals in a high-level language. This approach separates policy from implementation, simplifies security administration and facilitates policy evolution.

The diversity of emerging applications with widely differing security requirements has led to the development of a variety of increasingly expressive policy specification languages (e.g. [5, 6, 9, 11, 14, 13, 12, 7]). Existing ones are extended to accommodate more complex policies. For example, the role-based trust management language RT_0 [14] was extended to RT_1 to handle parameterised roles, and to RT^T to express separation of duties [13]. Another extension of RT, RT_1^C [12], provides constructs for limiting the range of role parameters using constraints. However, adding constructs to a language in an ad hoc fashion to increase its expressiveness has several disadvantages. Firstly, it is unlikely that the extension will cover all policies of interest; secondly, the semantics and implementations of the language have to be changed; thirdly, languages with many constructs are harder to understand and to reason about; and lastly, policy evaluation usually becomes computationally more expensive with increasing expressiveness (in some cases, the language is even Turing-complete).

We have designed a trust management system, Cassandra, in which the expressiveness of the policy specification language can be adjusted by selecting an appropriate *constraint domain*. The advantage of this approach is that the expressiveness (and hence the computational complexity) can be chosen depending on the requirements of the application, and can easily be changed without having to change the language semantics. In our prototype implementation of Cassandra, a constraint domain is a separate module that can be plugged into the policy evaluation engine. We have identified a condition on constraint domains, *constraint compactness*, which ensures that policy evaluation is decidable and guaranteed to terminate.

By factoring out the constraint domain, the language

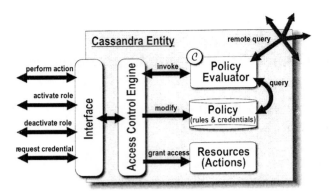

Figure 1. Cassandra components.

syntax and semantics are kept small and simple. In particular, Cassandra has no explicit provisions for standard policy idioms such as role hierarchy, separation of duties or delegation; instead, it is truly policy-neutral in that it can encode such idioms (and many variants). Its expressiveness suffices for policies found in highly complex real-world applications; this has been shown by our work on a large-scale security policy for a national electronic health record system [3].

In §2 we give an informal overview of Cassandra's policy specification language. Unlike most other systems, Cassandra not only formally specifies the policy language but also the access control semantics governing the dynamic behaviour of an entire Cassandra network. This operational semantics is described in §3. §4 shows how examples of standard policies, including role validity periods, role hierarchy, separation of duties, role delegation and trust negotiation policies, can be expressed in Cassandra. The policy specification language and semantics are formally defined and an algorithm for policy evaluation is given in §5. §6 briefly discusses our case study on security policies for a national electronic health record system. We also discuss our prototype implementation and preliminary experimental results. Finally we discuss related work and conclude.

2. Policy specification overview

Cassandra is a trust management system allowing a potentially large network of entities to share their resources under well-defined restrictions, specified by local access control policies, even if they are mutual strangers. Every entity runs its own copy of a Cassandra service, which acts as a protective layer around the resources. Figure 1 shows the internal components of a Cassandra service. Interaction with other entities is done via the interface that defines requests for performing an action (i.e. accessing a resource), activating and deactivating a role, and requesting a credential that can be used to support another request somewhere else. The *access control engine* handles the request by invoking the *policy evaluation engine*, which in turn queries the local Cassandra policy. The expressiveness of the policy specification language depends on the globally chosen constraint domain, $\mathcal{C}$, an independent module that is plugged into the policy evaluation engine. As policies can refer to policies of other entities, policy evaluation may trigger queries of remote policies (possibly the requester's) over the network. The answer of the policy evaluation engine is used by the access control engine to decide whether the request is to be granted. As a result of a request, the local policy may be modified. For example, if a role is activated, this new fact is put into the policy; similarly, deactivation of roles causes facts to be removed from the policy.

Cassandra's policy specification language is based on Datalog$_{\mathcal{C}}$, a generic extension of negation-free Datalog (Prolog without function symbols) where the expressiveness can be tuned by varying the constraint domain parameter $\mathcal{C}$ [10]. A Datalog$_{\mathcal{C}}$ rule is of the form

$$p_0(\vec{e}_0) \leftarrow p_1(\vec{e}_1), .., p_n(\vec{e}_n), c$$

where the p_i are predicate names and the $\vec{e}_i$ are (possibly empty) expression tuples (that may contain variables) matching the parameter types of the predicate. $p_0(\vec{e}_0)$ is the *head* of the rule, and the sequence of predicates on the right hand side of the arrow is the *body* of the rule; c is a *constraint* on the parameters occuring in the rest of the rule. Intuitively, to deduce the head of a rule, all body predicates must be deducable in such a way that the constraint is also satisfied. A set of Datalog$_{\mathcal{C}}$ rules can then be interpreted as the deductive closure of the set.

The constraint of a rule, c, is a formula from some fixed *constraint domain* $\mathcal{C}$, a language of first order formulae containing at least true, false and the identity predicate "=" between $\mathcal{C}$-expressions (variables, entities and possibly other constructs). It must be closed under variable renaming, conjunction ($\wedge$) and disjunction ($\vee$). Furthermore, it must be equipped with an interpretation that defines when formulae are satisfied.

The expressiveness of Datalog$_{\mathcal{C}}$ depends on the chosen constraint domain $\mathcal{C}$. For example, the least expressive constraint domain is the one where the only atomic constraints are equalities between variables and constants. Choosing this trivial constraint domain reduces the expressiveness of the language to standard Datalog or Horn clauses without function symbols. More powerful constraint domains often include boolean, arithmetic and set constraints, and make use of more complex expressions such as tuples, set expressions and (side-effect free) function applications (e.g. to access the current time). The computational complexity of evaluating Datalog$_{\mathcal{C}}$ programs increases with expressiveness: with set constraints it is already possible to encode the Hamiltonian cycle problem, and thus all NP-complete problems. Care must be taken not to choose a constraint domain that is too expressive as this can result in programs in which queries are undecidable. We will later introduce the notion of *constraint compactness* to restrict constraint domains to those that guarantee termination of queries.

In Cassandra, access control is role-based, and roles, as well as actions, are parameterised. Role-based access control (RBAC) [17, 8] was initially introduced to simplify security administration of large enterprises. In the context of distributed trust management, roles can more generally be used as a representation of authenticated subject attributes in decentralised access control [13]. Formally, a *role* is a typed role name applied to an expression (that may contain variables) of a matching type, e.g. Manager(Sales-dept). Similarly, an *action* is an action name applied to an expression, e.g. Read-file(*file*). For the remainder of the paper, variables will be written in small letters and italics (e.g. *file*), generic constants in italics but capitalised (e.g. some entity E), and concrete constants in typewriter font (e.g. Sales-dept).

Policies are specified by rules defining predicates that govern access control decisions: permits defines who can perform which action; canActivate specifies who can activate which roles (and thus implicitly defines the role membership relation); hasActivated specifies who is currently active in which role; canDeactivate specifies who can revoke which role; isDeactivated is used to define automatically triggered role revocation; and finally, canReqCred rules specify the conditions to be satisfied before the service is willing to issue and disclose a credential. User-defined auxiliary predicates are also allowed.

In the trust management approach, access control decisions are based on credentials asserting properties about the holders. In Cassandra, the properties asserted by credentials are (constrained) predicates. Therefore, in order to satisfy a predicate in a rule body, either the predicate can be deduced from the local policy or it is asserted by a foreign credential issued and signed by some other entity. Such credentials are either already stored locally, or are submitted to the service, or automatically fetched by the service from some other entity. To put constraints on the issuer and the storage location of credentials, each Cassandra predicate has an *issuer* and a *location* (constant or variable) parameter, and is written $loc@iss.p(\vec{e})$. For example, Alice@UCam.canActivate(Alice, Student(Maths)) is a predicate asserting that Alice is a Maths student. If this predicate is part of a rule body, Cassandra can contact Alice over the network (unless this is Alice's local policy) and request the corresponding credential issued by the University of Cambridge.

We will often write $iss.p(\vec{e})$ as shorthand for $E@iss.p(\vec{e})$ and $p(\vec{e})$ for $E@E.p(\vec{e})$, if E is clear from the context. Intuitively, if a predicate $loc@iss.p(\vec{e})$ appears in the body of a rule in E's policy, and loc is equal to E, it is deduced locally from E's policy (if iss is not equal to E, this must be a foreign credential). If, however, loc is not equal to E, this means that the authority over the predicate is delegated to the remote entity loc, so E requests a credential $iss.p(\vec{e})$ from loc over the network. loc will allow this only if her local policy lets her deduce both canReqCred($E, iss.p(\vec{e})$) and $iss.p(\vec{e})$. If these conditions are met, a credential containing $iss.p(\vec{e})$ (issued and signed by iss) is sent back to E. A more formal treatment of the language semantics is given in §5.1.

3. Access Control Semantics

Cassandra acts as a protective layer around the shared resources, allowing network access only through an interface. This interface defines requests for performing an action, activating a role, deactivating a role, and for requesting a credential. Incoming requests are checked by the access control engine against the local policy (Figure 1). Entities can support their requests by submitting credentials to the service; the service will then use the assertions in the credentials along with its own local policy to evaluate the query. Granting a request can have side-effects on policies, e.g. when a role is activated, a corresponding hasActivated credential rule is added to the policy.

We have formally specified the operational semantics of the access control engine by a labelled transition system where the labels are the requests and the transitions are between sets of policies of all entities. Due to lack of space, we will only give a brief overview of the request definitions.

Performing an action. Suppose the requester E attempts to perform the (parameterised) action A on S's Cassandra service. E's request is granted if permits(E, A) is deducible from S's policy (and submitted credentials).

Role activation. Suppose E attempts to activate the (parameterised) role R on S's Cassandra service. The request is granted if the role has not already been activated and if canActivate(E, R) can be deduced from S's policy (and submitted credentials). As a result of this transition, the corresponding hasActivated credential rule is added to S's policy.

Role deactivation. Suppose E requests to deactivate V's role R on S's Cassandra service. The request is granted if V is really currently active in the role R and if canDeactivate(E, V, R) is deducible from S's policy (and submitted credentials). Depending on the local policy rules, this deactivation may also trigger the deactivation of other role activations in S's policy (local cascading deactivation). For this purpose, we need to compute the set of all hasActivated credential rules in S's policy for which a corresponding isDeactivated credential can be derived under the assumption isDeactivated(V, R). The role activations in this set are then removed from S's policy.

Requesting Credentials. Suppose E requests the credential $I.p(\vec{x}) \leftarrow c$ (a digital certificate asserting $p(\vec{x}) \leftarrow c$, issued and signed by I) from S. S's service first computes the answer to the query canReqCred$(E, I.p(\vec{x})) \leftarrow c$. The answer is a constraint c_0 restricting the values that $\vec{x}$ can take.

If I and S are identical, the answer c_1 of the query $p(\vec{x}) \leftarrow c_0$ is computed, and, if c_1 is satisfiable, the new credential $S.p(\vec{x}) \leftarrow c_1$ is issued and sent to E. If I and S are different, this means that the requested credential is a foreign credential held by S, so it cannot be freshly issued and signed. In this case, S sends E all her credentials of the form $I.p(\vec{x}) \leftarrow c_2$ such that c_2 is at least as restrictive as c_0.

4. Standard policies

Unlike other policy specification languages, Cassandra does not have special constructs for expressing standard policies such as role hierarchies, separation of duties or delegation. Indeed, we can show that Cassandra, equipped with a sufficiently powerful constraint domain, can express these policies in a concise and readable way. Having no constructs in the language for specific policy idioms not only keeps the language and its semantics small and simple; it also avoids the necessity of having to constantly extend the language. Furthermore, our work on policies for a national electronic health record infrastructure has shown that, in large-scale real-world applications, these "standard" policies occur in many variants and combinations with subtle but significant semantic differences [3]. Cassandra was designed in such a way that the whole range of policy variants can be expressed without additional features. It should be noted that Cassandra was designed specifically for authorisation policies; in particular, we do not deal with obligation policies specifying the automatic triggering of actions (as in [7]).

In the following, we show how standard policies can be written in Cassandra.

Role validity periods. In the following rule, a certified doctor (with certification issued at time t) is also member of the role Doc() if t is at most one year ago. This is an example where the freshness requirement of a certification is set by the acceptor, not by the certificate issuer (as recommended in [16]). The chosen constraint domain must contain a (side-effect free) built-in function that returns the current time, and integer order constraints.

canActivate$(x, \text{Doc}()) \leftarrow$
    canActivate$(x, \text{CertDoc}(t)),$
    CurTime$() - \text{Years}(1) \leq t \leq \text{CurTime}()$

Auxiliary roles. Sometimes a role is used solely to express some property about its members and can be used without prior activation. In this rule, a logged-in user can read a file provided that the system can deduce she is the owner of that file. Ownership is here expressed with the auxiliary Owner role that need not be activated.

permits$(x, \text{Read}(file)) \leftarrow$
    hasActivated$(x, \text{Login}()),$
    canActivate$(x, \text{Owner}(file))$

Role hierarchy. In this variant of parameterised role hierarchy, members of a superior role (Engineer working in some department) are automatically also members of a more basic role (Employee working in the same department).

canActivate$(x, \text{Employee}(dep)) \leftarrow$
    canActivate$(x, \text{Engineer}(dep))$

Separation of duties. In this common example for separation of duties, a payment transaction requires two phases, initiation and authorisation, which have to be executed by two different people. The rule implements the dynamic and parameterised variant of separation of duties: an Authoriser of a payment must not have activated the Init role for the same payment. This restriction is implemented by the user-defined countInitiators predicate. Its definition is given by the second rule, an example of an *aggregate* rule. The count$\langle z \rangle$ aggregate operator counts how many different values of z satisfy the body. Therefore, the parameter n is 0 only if x has not activated the Init role for the same payment.

canActivate$(x, \text{Authoriser}(payment)) \leftarrow$
    countInitiators$(n, x, payment), n = 0$
countInitiators$(\text{count}\langle z \rangle, x, payment) \leftarrow$
    hasActivated$(z, \text{Init}(payment)), z = x$

Role delegation. Here, an administrator can delegate her role to somebody else by activating the DelegateAdm role for the delegatee. The delegatee can then subsequently activate the administrator role. The first parameter of the administrator role specifies who the delegator was. The second parameter n is an integer for restricting the length of the delegation chain: the delegatee can activate the administrator role only with a "rank" n' that is strictly less than the delegator's rank n but must be at least 0. Setting the parameter to 1 for non-delegated administrators (i.e. those at the top of a delegation chain) amounts to non-transitive delegation. Removing the constraint on n in the second rule results in unbounded delegation chains.

canActivate$(x, \text{DelegateAdm}(y, n)) \leftarrow$
    hasActivated$(x, \text{Adm}(z, n))$
canActivate$(y, \text{Adm}(x, n')) \leftarrow$
    hasActivated$(x, \text{DelegateAdm}(y, n)), 0 \leq n' < n$

With the following rule, the delegated role is automatically revoked if the delegation role of the delegator is deactivated.

$$\text{isDeactivated}(y, \text{Adm}(x, n')) \leftarrow$$
$$\text{isDeactivated}(x, \text{DelegateAdm}(y, n))$$

However, we need to specify who is allowed to deactivate a delegation role. In grant-dependent revocation (first rule below), only the delegator herself has this power. In grant-independent revocation (second rule below), every administrator (who has at least as high a rank as the delegator) can deactivate the delegation.

$$\text{canDeactivate}(x, z, \text{DelegateAdm}(y, n)) \leftarrow x = z$$
$$\text{canDeactivate}(x, z, \text{DelegateAdm}(y, n)) \leftarrow$$
$$\text{hasActivated}(x, \text{Adm}(w, n')), \ n \le n'$$

A rather paranoid policy may specify cascading revocation: if a delegated administrator is revoked from her role, all her delegation must also be revoked recursively.

$$\text{isDeactivated}(x, \text{DelegateAdm}(y, n)) \leftarrow$$
$$\text{isDeactivated}(z, \text{DelegateAdm}(x, n'))$$

The trust management system Oasis [21] has a language construct for role appointment, a generalisation of role delegation. Our work on real-world policies suggests that variants of general appointment are indeed far more frequent than role delegation [3]. Appointment and other stateful policies can be expressed in Cassandra in a very similar way as shown above for delegation.

Automatic trust negotiation & credential discovery. Suppose the following rule is part of the policy of a server holding the electronic health records (EHR) for some part of the UK's population. To activate the doctor role, x must be a certified doctor in some health organisation org, and furthermore the organisation must be a certified health organisation. Both requirements must be satisfied in the form of credentials signed by some entity $auth$ belonging to a locally defined set of registration authorities.

$$\text{canActivate}(x, \text{Doc}(org)) \leftarrow$$
$$auth.\text{canActivate}(x, \text{CertDoc}(org)),$$
$$org@auth.\text{canActivate}(org, \text{CertHealthOrg}()),$$
$$auth \in \text{RegAuthorities}()$$

In the rule above, there is no location prefix in front of the first body predicate, so the doctor certification credential is required to already be in the local policy or have been submitted by x together with the role activation request. No automatic credential requests are issued the credential is not found. On the other hand, there is a location prefix org in front of the second body predicate: the health organisation credential is automatically requested from org, or, more precisely, the entity the variable org stands for during actual evaluation. However, the health organisation (say, Addenbrooke's Hospital) will allow this retrieval request only if its canReqCred policy allows it. With the following rule, Addenbrooke's specifies that it is willing to reveal

its CertHealthOrg credential, signed by the registration authority of East England, to certified EHR servers.

$$\text{canReqCred}(x, y.\text{canActivate}(z, \text{CertHealthOrg}()) \leftarrow$$
$$x@auth.\text{canActivate}(x, \text{CertEHRServ}()),$$
$$y = \text{RegAuthEastEngland} \land z = \text{Addenbrookes},$$
$$auth \in \text{RegAuthorities}()$$

The $x@auth$ prefix specifies that the required credential must be signed by some registration authority and that it is to be retrieved automatically from x; in this case, x will have been instantiated to be the EHR server. The EHR server will in turn have canReqCred policy rules specifying to whom its CertEHRServ credential may be disclosed. As this example shows, a simple request can trigger multiple phases of credential exchanges between two or more entities over the network until a sufficient level of mutual trust has been established.

5. Language semantics and evaluation

This section defines the syntax and semantics of Cassandra's policy specification language. We also describe a goal-oriented algorithm for evaluating policy queries that is sound and complete with respect to the language, and discuss a condition for guaranteed termination of query evaluation.

5.1. Language Semantics

Each entity E_{loc} on the network protects its resources with a (possibly empty) Cassandra *policy*, a finite set of Cassandra *policy rules* of the form

$$E_{loc}@E_{iss}.p_0(\vec{e}_0) \leftarrow$$
$$loc_1@iss_1.p_1(\vec{e}_1), .., loc_n@iss_n.p_n(\vec{e}_n), c.$$

The *location* and the *issuer* of the rule, E_{loc} and E_{iss}, are entity constants, and the loc_i and iss_i are entities or entity typed variables. The $p_i(\vec{e}_i)$ are well-typed predicates, and c is a constraint from the globally chosen constraint domain $\mathcal{C}$.

A rule with empty body of the form

$$E_{loc}@E_{iss}.p_0(\vec{e}_0) \leftarrow c$$

is called a *credential rule* or just a *credential*. (These correspond to *facts* in Logic Programming.) If it is sent over the network, it can be thought of as a certificate asserting $p_0(\vec{e}_0)$, signed and issued by E_{iss}, and belonging to and stored at E_{loc}. The location and the issuer of a rule are usually identical; only in the case of a credential rule can they be different, as E_{loc} may hold a *foreign* credential signed by a different entity E_{iss}.

We will omit the prefix E_{loc} from a rule if it is clear from the context, and also E_{iss}, loc_i and iss_i if they are equal to E_{loc}.

Access control decisions are based on policy *queries* which have the same form as credentials: $E_{loc}@E_{iss}.p_0(\vec{e}_0) \leftarrow c$. The answer to a query is a set of constraints c_i such that $E_{iss}.p_0(\vec{e}_0) \leftarrow c \wedge c_i$ can be deduced from E_{loc}'s policy. For example, the query

$$\text{UCam@UCam.canActivate}(x, \text{Student}(subj)) \leftarrow$$
$$subj = \text{Maths}$$

may return the constraints $\{x = \text{Alice}, x = \text{Bob}\}$, and the query

$$\text{UCam@UCam.canActivate}(x, \text{Student}(subj)) \leftarrow$$
$$x = \text{Alice} \wedge subj = \text{Maths}$$

would simply return $\{\text{true}\}$.

The semantics of a policy is defined by the set of all credentials that can be deduced from it. To formally define the notion of deduction, we extend the notion of *consequence operator* known from constraint logic programming [18]. We construct a consequence operator $T_{\mathcal{P}}$, where $\mathcal{P}$ is the finite union of the policies of all entities. Given a set of credentials $\mathcal{I}$ (which we distinguish only up to variable renaming), $T_{\mathcal{P}}(\mathcal{I})$ returns the set of all credentials that can be deduced from $\mathcal{I}$ and the policies in $\mathcal{P}$ in one step.

The definition of $T_{\mathcal{P}}$ assumes the existence of two computable operations on $\mathcal{C}$-constraints, $\exists^{\mathcal{C}}$ and $\Rightarrow^{\mathcal{C}}$. $\exists^{\mathcal{C}} x.(c)$ computes the existential quantifier elimination of x and returns the set of conjuncts in the disjunctive normal form (DNF) of the result. If V is a set of variables, we also write $\exists^{\mathcal{C}}_{-V}(c)$ for the set of conjuncts in the DNF of c, with all free variables apart from the ones in V existentially eliminated. (This is in effect a projection of c onto the variables V.)

$\Rightarrow^{\mathcal{C}}$ is a computable subsumption relation on $\mathcal{C}$-constraints: if $c_1 \Rightarrow^{\mathcal{C}} c_2$ returns true then c_1 is *subsumed* by c_2, i.e. all substitutions that satisfy c_1 also satisfy c_2.

Then the consequence operator $T_{\mathcal{P}}(\mathcal{I})$ is defined to contain all credentials of the form $E_{loc}@E_{iss}.p(\vec{x}) \leftarrow c_0$ (for some entities E_{loc}, E_{iss}) if $\mathcal{I}$ contains no other credential that already subsumes it: if $E_{loc}@E_{iss}.p(\vec{x}) \leftarrow c_0' \in \mathcal{I}$ and $c_0 \Rightarrow^{\mathcal{C}} c_0'$ then $c_0 = c_0'$; and furthermore, if there is some matching rule

$$E_{loc}@E_{iss}.p(\vec{x}) \leftarrow P_1, .., P_n, c$$

in $\mathcal{P}$ (i.e. in the policy of E_{loc}) such that there is a constraint c_0 with the following property:

$c_0 \in \exists^{\mathcal{C}}_{-\vec{x}}(c_1 \wedge .. \wedge c_n)$, and c_0 is satisfiable, for some constraints $c_1, .., c_n$, such that each c_i is a contribution from P_i. We say c_i is a *contribution* from $P_i \equiv y_{loc}@y_{iss}.q(\vec{y})$ if one of the following two cases hold.

Either y_{loc} is taken to be local, so P_i has to be deduced from E_{loc}'s own local policy. This means that c_i must be

equal to some

$$(c_i' \wedge y_{loc} = E_{loc} \wedge y_{iss} = E_{iss}')$$

such that $E_{loc}@E_{iss}'.q(\vec{y}) \leftarrow c_i'$ is already in $\mathcal{I}$.

Alternatively, y_{loc} may refer to some remote entity $E_{loc}' \neq E_{loc}$, so P_i has to be deduced from E_{loc}''s policy. As this amounts to a credential request and E_{loc}''s credentials are protected by canReqCred rules, the corresponding canReqCred predicate must also be satisfied, as well as P_i itself. In this case, c_i is some constraint in

$$\exists^{\mathcal{C}} x_e.(c_i' \wedge c_i'' \wedge y_{loc} = E_{loc}' \wedge$$
$$y_{iss} = E_{iss}' \wedge x_e = E_{loc})$$

such that both credentials

$E_{loc}'@E_{loc}'.\text{canReqCred}(x_e, y_{iss}.q(\vec{y})) \leftarrow c_i'$ and $E_{loc}'@E_{iss}'.q(\vec{y}) \leftarrow c_i''$ are already in $\mathcal{I}$.

The consequence operator $T_{\mathcal{P}}(\mathcal{I})$ is continuous on the powerset of credentials and thus has a unique least fixed-point $\bigcup_{n \geq 0} T_{\mathcal{P}}^n(\emptyset)$ which we call the fixed-point semantics of $\mathcal{P}$. It coincides with our intuitive notion of deductive closure of the policy rules.

Sometimes we need to know not only whether a predicate can be satisfied but also how often. For example, it is often necessary to know that nobody has activated a certain role, i.e. the corresponding hasActivated predicate can be satisfied 0 times. For these purposes, we define rules with *aggregation operators* [15]. (These require the constraint domain $\mathcal{C}$ to contain equalities over set and integer constants and variables.) A Cassandra *aggregation rule* is of the form

$$E_{loc}@E_{loc}.p(\text{aggop}\langle x \rangle, \vec{y}) \leftarrow E_{loc}@iss.q(\vec{x}), c$$

where the aggregation operator aggop is either group or count. The predicate $q(\vec{x})$ is required to be one that can be satisfied with only finitely many different parameters on E_{loc}, and $\vec{x}$ must contain x. If the operator is group, the first argument of p stands for the finite set of all different values of x such that the rule body can be satisfied. If the operator is count, it stands for the cardinality of that set. For example,

$$\text{getSetOfActiveDoctors}(\text{group}\langle x \rangle, spcty) \leftarrow$$
$$\text{hasActivated}(x, \text{Doctor}(spcty))$$

finds the set of all active doctors with specialty *spcty*.

5.2. Evaluation

Recall that the access control engine makes access control decisions by invoking the policy evaluation engine, which queries the local policy. We now describe the algorithms used in the policy evaluation engine.

In deductive databases, queries are usually evaluated against a model that is pre-computed with a bottom-up algorithm that, starting from basic facts, iteratively adds derived facts until the fixed-point semantics is reached.

This would not be an acceptable evaluation strategy for Cassandra: firstly, the constraints may contain (side-effect free) function calls that depend on the environment, for example for getting the current time, and therefore cannot be pre-computed; secondly, the fact that rule bodies can refer to remote predicates would require a distributed form of bottom-up evaluation which would be highly impractical; and thirdly, the model would have to be re-computed after every activation or deactivation of roles as role activation and deactivation modify policies.

The standard SLD top-down resolution algorithm known from Logic Programming (e.g. Prolog) is not suitable either as it may run into infinite loops even when the fixed-point semantics is finite. Instead, Cassandra uses a modified version of Toman's memoing algorithm for evaluating constraint extensions of Datalog [18]. Based on SLG resolution, it combines advantages of both the top-down and the bottom-up approaches: it is goal-oriented and yet preserves the termination properties of the bottom-up algorithms by memoing (tabling) already seen subgoals and their answers. To solve a subgoal for which a table entry already exists, the algorithm uses the tabled answers as solutions; whenever new answers are added for the entry, they are automatically propagated to other waiting evaluation branches. If no relevant entry exists for the subgoal, a new table entry is created and populated. We have extended the algorithm in [18] to deal with goals referring to remote entities.

Suppose the query $E_{loc}@E_{iss}.p_0(\vec{x}_0) \leftarrow c_0$ is to be evaluated by the Cassandra service of E_{loc}. Evaluation is started by calling the Clause Resolution procedure on the query.

Clause Resolution. Find all policy rules with a matching head, i.e. of the form

$$E_{loc}@E_{iss}.p_0(\vec{x}_0) \leftarrow P_1, .., P_n, c_1.$$

For all such c_1, compute $c_2 \equiv c_0 \wedge c_1$ if the result is satisfiable. If the rule body is non-empty ($n \geq 1$), call the Query Projection procedure on the list $P_1, .., P_n, c_2$. Otherwise call the Answer Projection procedure on the combined constraint c_2.

Query Projection. This procedure operates on a list of predicates $P_1, .., P_n$ and a constraint c. Using the $\exists^{\mathcal{C}}$ operation, project the constraint onto the free variables of the first predicate P_1 in the list and compute the DNF constraint set. For all c_i from this set, call the Answer Propagation procedure on $P_1 \leftarrow c_i$, and the (possibly empty) list of remaining predicates, $P_2, .., P_n$.

Answer Propagation. This procedure operates on a subgoal $P \leftarrow c$, and a list of remaining predicates $P_2, .., P_n$. Check whether we have already encountered a query $P \leftarrow c'$ such that $c \Rightarrow^{\mathcal{C}} c'$, in which case the current goal can be solved using answers from that query. For each already

existing answer d, combine it with the current constraint and call the Clause Resolution procedure on the remaining predicates in the list, or the Answer Projection procedure, if the remaining list is empty. We also need to store the information that this query waits for answers from the proof of $P \leftarrow c'$.

If, however, no such $P \leftarrow c'$ exists yet, we need to spawn a new query for $P \leftarrow c$ and wait for its answers. If the location of P is remote, a credential request is sent to the remote entity. The remote entity will then call its Query Projection procedure on the list containing $\mathsf{canReqCred}(E_{loc}, P)$ and P with the constraint c.

Answer Projection. This procedure is called when the list of body predicates is empty. The remaining constraint is then projected onto the free variables of the query predicate. The resulting constraints are stored in the answers table and propagated to all queries currently waiting for such answers, and execution is resumed there. If the waiting party is a remote entity, the answers are sent to it over the network in the form of credentials. The remote entity will then invoke its Answer Projection procedure on these answers.

On exit, the table entry for the original query will be populated with all its answers. The algorithm is sound and complete with respect to the language semantics.

As in other database applications, we require query evaluation to always terminate. Clearly, if the chosen constraint domain $\mathcal{C}$ is too expressive, it is possible to write policies and queries that are uncomputable. Often, the features that make it too expressive seem rather innocuous at first glance. For example, constraint domains with untyped tuple constructors or with negative gap-order constraints of the form $x - c < y$ (where c is a positive integer constant) enable the construction of undecidable policies.

Constraint compactness [18] is a sufficient condition on constraint domains to guarantee a finite and hence computable fixed-point semantics for any finite global policy set $\mathcal{P}$. A constraint domain $\mathcal{C}$ is said to be constraint compact if any infinite set of $\mathcal{C}$-constraints in which only finitely many variables and constants occur has a finite subset subsuming the entire set, that is, for every constraint c in the infinite set there is a constraint c' in the finite set such that $c \Rightarrow^{\mathcal{C}} c'$.

Unfortunately, constraint compactness severely restricts the expressiveness of the constraint language and is also often hard to prove. We use *static groundness analysis* [1] to restrict policies in such a way that variables occuring in specific constructs will always have been grounded (so a unique value can be deduced for each) by the time existential quantifier elimination is performed on them, given the query patterns from §3 (e.g. canActivate queries are always fully grounded), so these constructs can be ignored.

We also use static groundness analysis to ensure that the location prefix of body predicates becomes ground by the time we evaluate it: otherwise the evaluator would have to query many different entities (all, in the worst case), which is clearly unpractical.

6. Discussion

EHR case study. Cassandra's design process was partially guided by our case study [3] on an access control policy for a national electronic health record (EHR) system. The background of the case study is the British National Health Service's current plan to develop an electronic data spine that will contain "cradle-to-grave" medical data for all patients in England. The project is highly risky and challenging for several reasons: it is extremely large-scale with 100 million records and billions of accesses per year; the requirements are likely to change frequently, in particular those concerning access control; and it is inherently distributed with interacting health organisations, registration authorities and the data-spine. These challenges can best be met by a distributed trust management system that allows policies to be specified in a sufficiently expressive high-level language.

In our case study, we propose a distributed three-level infrastructure to cope with the large scale. Based on official specification documents, we have developed Cassandra policies for the entire infrastructure. Our proposed policies contain a total of 310 rules, define 58 parameterised roles and implement all the required access control rules.

The requirements are not only highly complex but also contain principles unseen in traditional access control models. For example, the policies need to handle explicit patient consent, third-party disclosure consent, individualised access decisions (e.g. a patient could prohibit access to record items concerning a certain medical subject to a specific doctor), appointment of agents acting on a patient's behalf and workgroup-based access control (e.g. based on ward or consultant team membership).

One of the main lessons learnt from the case study is that standard policy idioms such as role appointment occur in many different variants. We thus had to design Cassandra in such a way that it could express all of these elegantly. Our approach was to identify the small number of underlying primitives concerning role membership, activation and deactivation, and to base the language solely on those. The distributed nature of the EHR policies also necessitated features for automatic credential discovery and credential protection (automatic trust negotiation).

For the case study, we devised a sufficiently expressive constraint domain containing tuple expressions and projections, disequalities, integer order inequalities, built-in functions to access state-dependent data and set inclusion constraints[3]. It is constraint-compact and thus guarantees query termination, but its relatively high expressiveness still makes it possible in principle to write policies that are prohibitively expensive to evaluate. However, such policies do not seem to occur in practice, as the recursion depth is usually small and variables are instantiated to ground values early on.

Implementation and performance. A prototype of Cassandra has been implemented in OCaml. The code is factored into independent modules as depicted in Figure 1. In particular, constraint domain implementations can be plugged into the policy evaluation engine as separate modules, as long as they provide fundamental operations of projection, satisfiability and subsumption checking. We have implemented the constraint domain used for the EHR case study, including a type inference mechanism that allows us to omit explicit variable typing.

At the time of writing, role deactivation and credential requests and the static groundness analyser are still in the process of being implemented. Furthermore, the current prototype only simulates the distributed system, and issued credentials are implemented without encryption and public key signatures.

The prototype was tested with the policies from the EHR case study. The system behaved as expected and handled all requests, including the most complex ones, within fractions of a second. The preliminary results suggest that Cassandra is indeed suitable for large-scale real-world application. Of course, authoritative results can only be produced after completion of a more complete and optimised implementation and under more realistic settings; we have for example so far only tested the system with up to 10,000 patients [3].

Our experiments have highlighted another requirement for policy-based trust management systems that neither our nor existing systems currently fulfil: human users expect textual justifications of access control decisions, especially if their request is denied; they feel rather frustrated and helpless if the answer is simply "request denied", especially if the policy is complex or unknown to the user. Such explanations could be collected from annotations of policy rules used during deduction. The problem is non-trivial as deduction proofs can be long and access denials can have many and far-reaching reasons. More worryingly, the textual justification may reveal more (and perhaps, sensitive) information than could have been deduced from the fact of request denial alone: consider, for example, a response such as "access denied because your daughter has prohibited you from accessing all her records with the subject 'abortion' ".

Related work. A large amount of work has been done on security policy specification in a non-trust-management context. For instance, Barker [2] uses constraint logic programming to encode RBAC policies in a non-distributed environment; as such, his approach does not deal with credentials, trust management and trust negotiation. Policy-Maker [5] introduced the trust management paradigm, and its successor, KeyNote [4] defined the first policy specification language. Since then, many other trust management systems have been proposed for policy specification and distributed access control (e.g. SPKI/SDSI [6], QCM [9], SD3 [11], RT [13], Oasis [21], Ponder[7]).

The Cassandra policy specification language was inspired by Oasis, a role-based trust management system in which Datalog-based rules specify which credentials are prerequisite for role activation and deactivation [21]. Oasis has a special construct for role appointment, which was introduced as a useful generalisation of the delegation mechanisms found in many other languages. Our case study supports the claim that role appointment (and its variants) is a very useful policy idiom. Oasis is the only other system we are aware of that supports cascading role revocation. Its revocation mechanism works even across the network between collaborating entities. This is implemented using a distributed event infrastructure. Another difference is that in Oasis, revocation is triggered whenever a specified subset of the role activation prerequisites ceases to hold. In contrast, role deactivations in Cassandra are allowed to be triggered by conditions that have nothing to do with the role activation prerequisites. Oasis does not deal with automatic credential discovery and trust negotiation. It also does not possess a full formal semantics and does not guarantee termination of queries.

The RT family of role-based trust management languages [13] bears some similarities to our system. In RT, the Datalog-based rules, or credentials, as they are called, specify only the role membership relation: either directly, by role hierarchy, by (direct or attribute-based) delegation of authority, or any combination of these. The subjects of the rule head and the body conditions are implicitly the same, which is sufficient to express delegation but not convenient for appointment policies. In RT's youngest offspring, RT_1^C [12], rules are translated into $Datalog_C$. Constraints are used only to define a range on each role parameter; constraints between two parameters are not permitted in order to keep policies more comprehensible and to guarantee tractability. We find that a more liberal use of constraints is useful and necessary, as our EHR policy shows, and can still be efficient in practice. RT roles are prefixed with the issuing entity, just like Cassandra's predicates are, but do not specify the location where a matching credential may be found. RT solves this by statically specifying for each role name whether credentials defining such roles are stored with the issuer or the subject. Our EHR policy has rules in which predicates have locations different from both issuer and the subject entity. A distinctive feature of the RT framework is that RT credentials contain a link to a so-called Application Domain Specification Document (ADSD) that defines a common vocabulary (types of role parameters, natural language descriptions of role names etc.) for collaborating entities.

SD3 is another Datalog-based trust management system [11]. Similar to Cassandra, SD3 predicates can be prefixed with an issuer (a public key), thereby delegating authority of predicate definition to that key. A predicate can further be tagged with an IP address which is used to refer to a remote policy. SD3 is a very general system that does not specify any access control meaning for any predicates and can be viewed as Cassandra without constraints, roles and access control semantics. SD3 passes the proof tree from its highly optimised policy evaluation engine through a simple and small proof checker to reduce the size of its trusted computing base. This would be a technique that could also be applied to Cassandra.

The problem of trust negotiation has been addressed in [19], where various different negotiation strategies (which, when and in which order credentials are disclosed) are discussed. Their Credential Access Policy (CAP) corresponds to Cassandra's canReqCred rules specifying the prerequisites for credential disclosure. Cassandra's uniform treatment of rules during evaluation gives us trust negotiation almost "for free", with a negotiation strategy similar to their "Parsimonious Strategy". It has been pointed out that this strategy can leak information about possession of credentials without actually disclosing them. The "Eager Strategy" does not have this problem but is less efficient. [20] prevents the problem by adding another policy protection layer. [22] argue that entities should be given the freedom to choose their own negotiation policy. They identify a large family of strategies that are mutually compatible.

Conclusions and future work. We have developed a trust management system, Cassandra, with a role-based policy specification language in which the expressiveness can be tuned according to need by choosing an appropriate constraint domain. Apart from management of role permissions, activations and (cascading) deactivations, the system also uniformly provides flexible automatic credential retrieval and automatic trust negotiation. With the constraint domain we devised for the EHR case study, Cassandra's expressiveness surpasses that of existing systems while preserving a strong termination property. The policy language is small, simple and devoid of any redundant constructs such as delegation or hierarchies and yet it can express a wide variety of policies. Cassandra, including the language, the access control engine and the goal-oriented distributed policy evaluation algorithm, is fully and formally specified and thus amenable to formal reasoning.

We plan to use Cassandra's formal framework to prove security properties about specific policies. Along the same lines, we wish to formalise a low-level model of Cassandra that specifies the underlying network protocols, the public key infrastructure and the design of certificates. We will also investigate possibilities for making answers to requests more descriptive and user-friendly without leaking sensitive information.

To gather more reliable test results, we need to build a complete prototype that is truly distributed and uses digital certificates for sending credentials over the network. We hope to improve efficiency by using a standard relational database for policy rule lookups. Such an implementation will enable us to test real-world policies in a more realistic setting, with millions of role activations and entities that interact via an unreliable network.

Acknowledgments We acknowledge support from a Gates Cambridge Scholarship (Becker), a Royal Society University Research Fellowship (Sewell), EPSRC grant GRN24872, and EC FET-GC project IST-2001-33234 PEPITO. The authors thank Arne Heizmann for corrections and comments. We also thank the reviewers for their valuable comments.

References

[1] N. Baker and H. Sondergaard. Definiteness analysis for CLP(R). In *Australian Computer Science Conference*, pages 321–332, 1993.

[2] S. Barker and P. J. Stuckey. Flexible access control policy specification with constraint logic programming. *ACM Transactions on Information and System Security*, 6(4):501–546, 2003.

[3] M. Y. Becker and P. Sewell. Cassandra: Flexible trust management, applied to electronic health records. In *Proceedings of the 17th IEEE Computer Security Foundations Workshop*, June 2004. To appear.

[4] M. Blaze, J. Feigenbaum, and A. D. Keromytis. KeyNote: Trust management for public-key infrastructures (position paper). *Lecture Notes in Computer Science*, 1550:59–63, 1999.

[5] M. Blaze, J. Feigenbaum, and J. Lacy. Decentralized trust management. In *IEEE Symposium on Security and Privacy*, pages 164–173, 1996.

[6] D. Clarke, J.-E. Elien, C. Ellison, M. Fredette, A. Morcos, and R. L. Rivest. Certificate chain discovery in SPKI/SDSI. *Journal of Computer Security*, 9(4):285–322, 2001.

[7] N. Damianou, N. Dulay, E. Lupu, and M. Sloman. The Ponder policy specification language. In *Policy Workshop*, 2001.

[8] D. F. Ferraiolo, R. Sandhu, S. Gavrila, D. R. Kuhn, and R. Chandramouli. Proposed NIST standard for role-based access control. *4*, (3):224–274, 2001.

[9] C. A. Gunter and T. Jim. Policy-directed certificate retrieval. *Software - Practice and Experience*, 30(15):1609–1640, 2000.

[10] J. Jaffar and M. J. Maher. Constraint logic programming: a survey. *Journal of Logic Programming*, 19/20:503–581, 1994.

[11] T. Jim. SD3: A trust management system with certified evaluation. In *Proceedings of the 2001 IEEE Symposium on Security and Privacy*, pages 106–115, 2001.

[12] N. Li and J. C. Mitchell. Datalog with constraints: A foundation for trust management languages. In *Proceedings of the 5th International Symposium on Practical Aspects of Declarative Languages*, pages 58–73, 2003 2003.

[13] N. Li, J. C. Mitchell, and W. H. Winsborough. Design of a role-based trust management framework. In *Proceedings of the 2002 IEEE Symposium on Security and Privacy*, pages 114–130, 2002.

[14] N. Li, W. H. Winsborough, and J. C. Mitchell. Distributed credential chain discovery in trust management: extended abstract. In *ACM Conference on Computer and Communications Security*, pages 156–165, 2001.

[15] P. Revesz. *Introduction to constraint databases*. Springer Verlag, 2002.

[16] R. L. Rivest. Can we eliminate certificate revocations lists? In *Financial Cryptography*, pages 178–183, 1998.

[17] R. Sandhu. Rationale for the RBAC96 family of access control models. In *Proceedings of the 1st ACM Workshop on Role-Based Access Control*, 1997.

[18] D. Toman. Memoing evaluation for constraint extensions of datalog. *Constraints*, 2(3/4):337–359, 1997.

[19] W. Winsborough, K. Seamons, and V. Jones. Automated trust negotiation. In *DARPA Information Survivability Conference and Exposition*, volume 1, pages 88–102, 2000.

[20] W. H. Winsborough and N. Li. Towards practical automated trust negotiation. In *Proceedings of the 3rd International Workshop on Policies for Distributed Systems and Networks*, pages 92–103, 2002.

[21] W. Yao, K. Moody, and J. Bacon. A model of OASIS role-based access control and its support of active security. *ACM Transactions on Information and System Security*, 5(4), 2002.

[22] T. Yu, M. Winslett, and K. E. Seamons. Supporting structured credentials and sensitive policies through interoperable strategies for automated trust negotiation. *ACM Transactions on Information and System Security*, 6(1):1–42, 2003.

A Policy Driven Approach to Email Services *

Saket Kaushik
ISE Department, MSN 4A4
George Mason University
Fairfax, VA 22030, U.S.A.
skaushik@gmu.edu

Paul Ammann
ISE Department, MSN 4A4
Center for Secure Inf. Sys.
George Mason University
Fairfax, VA 22030, U.S.A.
pammann@gmu.edu

Duminda Wijesekera
ISE Department, MSN 4A4
Center for Secure Inf. Sys.
George Mason University
Fairfax, VA 22030, U.S.A.
dwijesek@gmu.edu

William Winsborough
ISE Department, MSN 4A4
Center for Secure Inf. Sys.
George Mason University
Fairfax, VA 22030, U.S.A.
wwinsbor@gmu.edu

Ronald Ritchey
Booz Allen & Hamilton
Falls Church, VA, U.S.A.
ritchey_ronald@bah.com

Abstract

The primary original design goal for email was to provide best-effort message delivery. Unfortunately, as the ever increasing uproar over SPAM demonstrates, the existing email infrastructure is no longer well suited to the worldwide set of email users - particularly email receivers. Rather than propose yet another band-aid solution to SPAM, this paper rethinks email from the requirements perspective, albeit with the constraint of designing a system suitable for incremental adoption in the current environment. Our result to this exercise is a policy driven email service in which the interests of each principal can be articulated and accommodated. Our scheme rewards faithful senders with better quality of service and discourages misbehavior. Our scheme provides receivers with policy-driven control over whether and how a given message appears in the recipients mailbox.

1. Introduction

We replace the current notion that an arbitrary user has an implicit right to place a message in anyone's mailbox with a scalable, attribute-based access control policy in which a sender's access to a recipient's mailbox is controlled by the recipient. In this work we view a mailbox as a network resource of the recipient and email messages as access requests from senders, requesting write access to a mailbox. In addition to the sender and receiver, there are two other principals directly associated with the email pipe, namely the sender's and receiver's email service providers. Also, there are important third party participants in the scheme that provide reputation and adjudication services. We take the position that any solution that does not address the needs of all of the principals is unlikely to achieve its objectives. Our approach complements many existing proposals to improve email, such as the Project Lumos's initiative to control bulk email servers and Razor's reputation service for identifying SPAM.

The place to start with email service is sender authentication. Any approach to email that fails to incorporate some notion of sender authentication seems limited, at best. Somewhat surprisingly, sender authentication is widely believed to be a hard problem, usually due to an assumption that a widespread PKI infrastructure is necessary to support it. For example, Eric Allman's excellent overview of the SPAM problem [1], [2] takes exactly this position. However, as noted in the Project Lumos's white paper [6], most senders send email through an account with an Email Service Provider (ESP), and there is typically some sort of login required before mail can be sent. As for the ESP itself, there is already some infrastructure in place that allows mail servers to identify themselves when transmitting email. The fact that there are vastly fewer mail servers than there are email senders makes the task of securely authenticating ESPs (or, more specifically, an ESP's Mail Transfer Agent or MTA) far more manageable.

*This work supported in part by the National Science Foundation under grants: CCR-TC- 0208848, CCR-0113515 and CCR-0325951.

At the point at which a message originates, the sender's ESP typically can associate a password-authenticated account with the message, or, stated another way, the ESP knows which of the ESP's customers sent the mail. While this is not true for all email, it is true (or could be made to be true with relatively little effort) for most legitimate email. There are valid exceptions, such as deliberately anonymous email. While anonymous email is outside the scope of the current work, our policy-based approach certainly does not prohibit anonymous email. Rather, it is simply up to the recipient's policy whether and how to handle such email. In some cases, such as a corporate organization, the ESP knows quite a bit about the customer. Even in cases such as a HotMail message, the ESP is in a position to know, for example, how many email messages that customer has sent in the past hour. If the ESP passes this knowledge to the receiver, the receiver will be in a better position to decide how to handle the mail.

From our perspective, we view the level of sender authentication provided by email accounts at ESPs as relatively weak, but serviceable. The fact that the approach is essentially implemented and deployed makes it far more attractive than a full blown PKI approach. One of the interesting attributes of email account approach is that it gives the sender's ESP a central role in a policy based email approach. Specifically, an ESP is in a position to know what volume of email the sender has transmitted in the past, what complaints, if any, have been lodged against sender, and so forth. If information about how an ESP manages its customers is made public, which seems to be the direction in which the internet community is traveling, then ESPs that permit senders to misbehave will suffer a backlash from the outside world, which will, in turn, drive legitimate senders away from the ESP. Thus the sender and the sender's ESP each can have legitimate, but widely different, interests in the transmission of a given message. Sensible email policies need to accommodate both of these parties.

On the receiving end, users typically receive email through another ESP. In correspondence with the sender, both the receiver and the receiver's ESP have legitimate, but different, policy interests in how to process incoming email. The fact that there are also privacy interests involved complicates the issue. For example, a receiver may not wish to make public the fact that he or she rejects (or accepts) certain types of email.

Figure 1 illustrates the principals in a secure email pipe. In addition to the sender, the receiver, and the corresponding ESPs, the figure shows third party reputation and adjudication servers. These services provide evaluations of particular messages, senders, or ESPs. Recipients, or recipient ESPs provide the raw data that these servers use to make their evaluations. Adjudication services provide a third party mechanism for satisfying obligations that may

be incurred as the result of delivering a mail. For example, a sender or a sender's ESP may post a small bond as a guarantee to ensure recipient satisfaction.

The key contributions of this paper are the content of sections 3 and 4. Specifically, in section 3, the heart of the paper, we contribute 3 new types of policies. The first type of policy, a Service Level Agreement Policy (SLAP), addresses how a receiving ESP decides to interact with a given sending ESP that has announced that it has mail. The second type of policy, a Message Scheduling Policy (MSP), is the output of a SLAP evaluation, and specifies how each message at the sending ESP should be treated. The third type of policy, a Message Resource Allocation Policy (MRAP), encodes the specific requirements of an individual mail recipient, and is used to determine how (and whether) messages are presented to the actual human recipient. In section 4, we explain how the SMTP protocol can be extended to accommodate each of these three policies, thereby making an argument that the policies are plausible given the current protocol for sending email.

The paper is organized as follows. In the next section, we review the current mechanism for exchanging mail, the SMTP protocol, and enumerate its shortcomings. In sections 3 and 4, we present our main contributions in the form of 3 new types of policies and their relation to the existing SMTP protocol and introduce a candidate base set of predicates that principals in an email exchange could use to evaluate a given email message. Section 5 discusses related work, and section 6 concludes the paper.

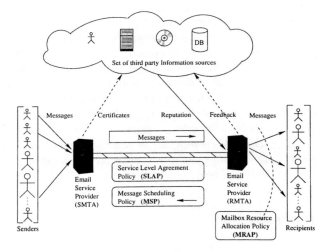

Figure 1. Principals in a Secure Email Pipe

2. Current SMTP Protocol

The current Internet mail system (or e-mail system) has three major components: *user agents, mail servers,* and the

Simple Mail Transfer Protocol (SMTP) [21]. A typical message starts its journey from the sender's user agent, travels to the sender's mail server, and then travels to the recipient's mail server, where it is deposited in the recipients' mail box [12]. SMTP, defined in RFC 2821 [21] transfers messages from the sender's mail server to the recipients' mail server. First, the SMTP client (running on the sending mail server host) has TCP establish a connection on port 25 to the SMTP server (running on the receiving mail server host). If the server is down, the client tries again later. Once this connection is established, the server and client perform some application-layer handshaking. During this handshaking phase, the SMTP client indicates the email address of the sender and the email address of the recipient. Next, the client sends the message. The client then repeats this process over the same TCP connection if it has other messages to send to the server, otherwise it instructs TCP to close the connection [12]. An simple explanation (not complete) of the protocol is provided in figure 2.

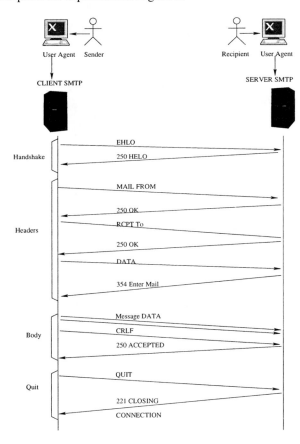

Figure 2. Current SMTP Protocol

Notation 1
Internet mail system entities discussed here are referred

to by their descriptions in [12]. For ease of understanding and brevity following notations are used interchangeably:

Symbol	Description
Sender, Recipient	Human users
MTA	Mail Transfer Agent [21]
ESP	Email Service Provider

Table 1. Industry Standard Symbols

Symbol	Description
SMTA, RMTA	Sending MTA, Recipient MTA
SESP, RESP	Sending ESP, Recipient ESP
SLAP	Service Level Agreement Policy
MSP	Message Scheduling Policy
MRAP	Mailbox Resource Allocation Policy

Table 2. Symbols introduced in the paper

Pseudo code in figure 13 in the Appendix provides a brief description of the algorithm that manages the state changes at the SMTA. A similar algorithm is presented in figure 12 in the Appendix which shows state changes for the RMTA.

2.1. Problems with the current protocol

The essence of the problem with original protocol is that the RMTA acts as a slave of the SMTA. The RMTA has no discretion regarding which and how many messages it receives, nor from whom. Numerous times in the past, this fact has been exploited by malicious entities to send unsolicited mail or spam [17], to the detriment of powerless recipient's. RFC 3207 [23] and RFC 2554 [22] add to SMTP support for authentication of SMTAs. They prevent impersonation of SMTAs, and so enable the RMTA to refuse service to specific SMTAs. This is an improvement, but does not provide a basis for accepting some messages (*e.g.*, a personal message) from a given SMTA, but not others (*e.g.*, bulk). It gives no basis for assessing whether a given, clearly identified SMTA is trustworthy. Moreover, it provides no control to the recipient, who is clearly an interested party. Factors other than the origin of a message could have an impact on its treatment, such as how the message is characterized by its sender (personal, bulk, ...), the current work-load level at the RMTA, or whether there are active virus alerts or the RMTA is under denial-of-service attack. In essence, what is absent in current email protocol is a framework for managing the allocation of mail-delivery resources based on the myriad of factors that could be of concern to the interested parties, *i.e.* the owners of those resources. In the next section we propose such a framework.

3. Policy driven email transfer

In this section we present a policy architecture for controlling the email pipeline. The goal of this architecture is to give the interested parties (*viz.*, the RESP and the recipient) control over the use of email-delivery resources (*viz.*, delivery service and mailbox access), thereby overcoming the shortcomings of the current SMTP protocol discussed above and enabling RESPs and recipients to prevent what they consider to be misuse of their resources.

The architecture consists of three forms of policy, introduced in each of the three subsections below. The first is associated with the RESP, and specifies what SESPs it will accept messages from, when, and under what terms; we call this *Service Level Agreement Policy* (SLAP). The second is optionally provided by the RESP(RMTA) to the SESP(SMTA) to specify which message should be sent when; we call this *Message Scheduling Policy* (MSP). The third is specified by the recipient, and is used to provide customization concerning whether email is accepted, and to which mailbox folder; we call it *Mailbox Resource Allocation Policy* (MRAP).

3.1. Service Level Agreement Policy (SLAP)

Connection-level actions of an RESP(RMTA) are governed by its *Service Level Agreement Policy (SLAP)*, which is pictured in figure 3.

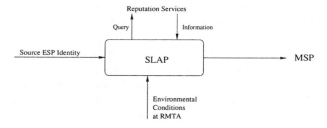

Figure 3. Service Level Agreement Policy (SLAP)

The inputs to SLAP include identity of the SESP, environmental conditions at the RESP, and the reputation of the SESP. This reputation is presumed to summarize past experiences in dealing with the SESP. These may be experiences that the RESP has had, or experiences had by third parties, which are then maintained and distributed by reputation services. The latter could take the form of white lists or black lists (such as provided by Open Relay Blacklists), or they could take some other, more dynamic form. The essential requirement is that the reputation service characterizes the past behavior of SESPs so that the SLAP can

give preferential treatment to SESPs with long records of favorable behavior. Relevant environmental conditions might include work load at the RMTA or Virus Alerts, etc. Together these inputs characterize the current SMTP session; based on them, the SLAP defines (*i.e.*, returns) a specification of what to do with messages waiting for transmission. Candidate specifications include: send them now ("as is"); send them later ("later"); do not accept messages from this SESP ("never"). In the most general case, however, this specification is itself a policy, called a *Message Scheduling Policy (MSP)*, that considers each message in turn, and determines whether and when it should be transmitted. MSP will be discussed further in the next section. SLAP's are not shared, so their format is organization-determined.

Example 1 *A certain ESP uses SESP identity and reputation to map each would-be sender to one of the following profiles: Business Partner, Trusted, Suspect, Black-listed, Unknown. Trusted SESPs are trusted by the ESP (RESP) to receive an MSP, and to apply it to waiting messages to determine whether and when to transmit them. The policy format used by the ESP is as follows:*

if(profile==Partner) return "as is"
if(profile==Black-listed) return "never"
if(load==heavy && profile==Trusted) return MSP_{heavy}
if(load==light && profile==Trusted) return MSP_{light}
if(Virus alert && profile==Suspect) return "later"
if(load==heavy && profile==Unknown) return "later"
$\vdots$

MSP_{heavy} *indicates that messages labeled "bulk" should be delayed, while MSP_{light} permits them to be transmitted.*

3.2. Message Scheduling Policy (MSP)

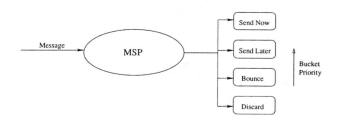

Figure 4. Message Scheduling Policy (MSP)

Message Scheduling Policy (MSP) is applied to each message awaiting transmission to determine whether and when it should be sent from the SMTA to the RMTA. The scheduling of a message will depend on characteristics of the message itself and of its sender, as well as the means of sender authentication. We model each of these characteristics as a predicate that takes a message and returns true if the message, its sender, or the SMTA involved has the characteristic in question; otherwise it returns false. The following is a (partial) list of such predicates:

Sender Attributes

1. Sender Auth: { Certificate | Password | None }
2. Reputation of sender provided by sending ESP: { Reputation Service specific }
3. Sender Activity in time $\mathcal{T}$: { No. of Messages in $\mathcal{T}$ }
4. Sender membership duration: { Duration of association with ESP }

Message Attributes

1. Bonded: { Guarantor, Bond }
2. Virus Scanned: { Scanner, version, patch-level }
3. Project Lumos attribute: { PLT-Personal | PLT-Service | PLT-First Class | PLT-Bulk }

MSPs are of two types: *portable* and *local*. The difference lies in where the policy is evaluated. A portable MSP is transmitted from the RMTA to the SMTA, which is trusted to apply the MSP to determine which messages to transmit. A local MSP can be used when the RMTA wishes to filter the messages transmitted, but does not wish to entrust the MSP and its application to the SMTA. When local MSP is used, the SMTA must transmit messages headers, which the RMTA then uses to evaluate the MSP on each waiting message. RMTA then provides the SMTA with instructions regarding if and when to transmit the waiting messages.

The format of local MSP is ESP-determined, but, because it is evaluated remotely, the format of portable MSP must be universal. In either case, the RMTA has the capability to check whether its MSP was adhered to by the SMTA, and contribute this information to build SESP reputation.

Example 2 *There are four messages $m_1 \cdots m_4$ in the transmit queue at the SMTA. These messages have following characteristics:*

$m_1 \rightarrow$ *sender auth:Password, Lumos-labeled Bulk*
$m_2 \rightarrow$ *No Sender authentication*
$m_3 \rightarrow$ *Bonded Mail, No sender authentication*
$m_4 \rightarrow$ *sender auth: Password, Lumos-labeled Personal*

Given its current load and environment, the MSP of the RMTA for the Sender in question is:
if(Password auth && Lumos-labeled Personal) send now
if(Bonded) send now
if(Lumos-labeled Bulk) delay
if(No sender authentication) discard

The application of this MSP to message (headers) in the Sender's transmit queue yields the following:
Send now $\rightarrow m_4, m_3$
Delay $\rightarrow m_1$
Discard $\rightarrow m_2$

3.3. Mailbox Resource Allocation Policy (MRAP)

Mailbox Resource Allocation Policy (MRAP) is specified by mail recipients and controls the utilization of their mailbox folders. User mail-reception preferences are captured and converted to MRAPs, which are evaluated at the user's ESP as part of the process of delivering a message to the user. MRAPs are pictured in figure 5. The input to MRAP includes: the *complete* message (including content); sender identity, characteristics, and reputation; SESP identities and reputations; message attributes; mailbox state. The result of MRAP evaluation is either to discard or bounce the message, in which cases the message is not delivered to the mailbox, or to assign a discrete category (*i.e.*, a mailbox folder) to route the message to.

Example 3 *The five messages shown in table 3 are sent. Evaluating the recipients' MRAPs on those messages has the following results:*

Alices evaluates m_1 by using reputation service $X \rightarrow$ discards.

Bob evaluates m_2 by using reputation service $X \rightarrow$ accepts — Bob's preferences lead him to a different action than Alice's, although he is sent the same message and gets the same information about it (from X).

Carol gets the same message as Alice and Bob, but does not consult a reputation service. Instead, she notes that the sender of m_3 has sender activity > 100 messages / hour $\rightarrow$ discards.

Bob evaluates m_4 with reputation service Y, which ranks it 'unobjectionable'; Bob then notes that his Advertisement folder is over 80% full $\rightarrow$ rejects.

Bob evaluates m_5 with reputation service Y, which ranks it 'interesting'; notwithstanding that his Advertisement folder is over 80% full $\rightarrow$ accepts.

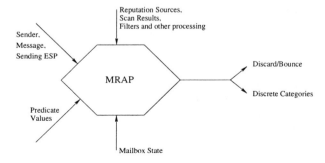

Figure 5. Mailbox Resource Allocation Policy (MRAP)

173

Message	From	To	Content
m_1	unknown	Alice	arbitrary string
m_2	unknown	Bob	same as m_1
m_3	unknown	Carol	same as m_1
m_4	commercial	Bob	advertisement
m_5	commercial	Bob	advertisement

Table 3. Messages with some characteristics

4. Proposed Extensions to SMTP

In this section we present how to modify the SMTP protocol to implement the decisions made by policy architecture introduced in section 3. The revised protocol is described in figure 6 and three additional message headers are described in figure 7.

To indicate policy based decision support, the EHLO [24] command is replaced by SHLO. SHLO should support all features of EHLO and in addition indicate extended handshake as shown in figure 6. SHLO implies authentication of MTA (as in [22],[23], [14] etc.), and in addition the SMTA would sign a hash of all the message headers and the hash of complete message and include it in the message as additional headers (see figure 7).

4.1. Extended Handshake

The first extended handshake *command* SHLO includes keywords for : server's identity, Message characterizations and other attributes like reputation references or certifications (keywords not defined) apart from the STARTTLS [23] or AUTH [22] and other usual EHLO parameters. The RMTA completes the negotiation by returning the keywords it supports. Figure 6 skips rest of the handshake commands and replies but details the identity and parameters transferred from SMTA to RMTA and the RMTA response. The SMTA reports the subset of the base predicates it supports described in section 3.2 (in the X-attribute header -figure 7) for the RMTA to define the MSP. Reputation references and certifications are included to get a higher priority SMTP session with the RMTA.

Reputation information is important for decision making at the RMTA. Source of reputations could be past behavior [8] with the same SMTA (maintained by RMTA) or a distributed information sharing mechanism like SpamNet [4] etc., open relay blacklists or provided by the SMTA (certifications on the lines of TRUSTe [26]). The onus to collect reputation lies on the RMTA (line 5 fig 8). RMTA evaluates these parameters based on its *Service Level Agreement Policy* and decides on the *Message Scheduling Policy* to apply to the Session. As will be discussed further in the next

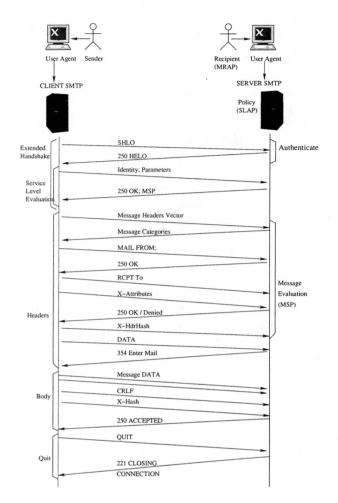

Figure 6. Proposed extensions to SMTP Protocol

Usual Headers [18]
- Mail From: Sender address

⋮

Additional Headers for policy support
- X-Attributes: Comma separated attribute list
- X-HdrHash: Signed hash of headers
- X-Hash: Signed hash of the complete message

Figure 7. Message Headers for Policy Support

```
1   if(state == connected)
2     then Wait for request;
3     if(request.hasParams)
4       then Parse params;
5     Reputation = getRep(params.ID);
6     MSP = SLAP(params, Reputation, Environ);
7     if (MSP.type==portable)
8       then Response = {Code, MSP};
9       state=portable;
10    else Response = {Code, send-Headers};
11      state=local;
12    Send Response;
```

Figure 8. Extended Handshake at RMTA

```
1   Send Command = {Identity, Params};
2   Wait for response;
3   if(response == 250 OK && response.hasParams)
4     then Parse Params;
5     MSP = response.Params;
6   if (MSP ≠ send-Headers )
7     then  state = schedule messages;
8   else state= send Vector;
```

Figure 9. Extended Handshake at SMTA

```
1   if(state == send Vector)
2     then (command = Header Vector(message queue))
3     Send command;
4     Wait for response;
5     if (response.hasParameters) then
6       MSP = response.Parameters;
7       state = schedule messages;
8     if(state == schedule messages)
9       Send now queue = response.SendNow;
10      Send later = response.SendLater;
11      Discard = response.Discard;
12      state = send sender; ;
```

Figure 10. MSP set up at SMTA

```
1   if(state==local) && request.hasParameters)
2     then (Header Vector = request.Parameters)
3     Send now queue = getNow(Header Vector);
4     Send later = getLater(Header Vector);
5     Discard = getDiscard(Header Vector);
6     response = Order(Send now queue, Send later, Dis-
      card);
7     Send response;
8     state = connected;
```

Figure 11. MSP set up at RMTA

section, message scheduling can be performed at either the SMTA or at the RMTA. In the latter case, the RMTA sends in the MSP parameter a keyword meaning "send all headers," which indicates to the SMTA that it should send a Vector of all transmit queue messages to the RMTA before any message is transferred. The pseudo code is described in lines 3 to 12 figure 8 (which replaces the steps between lines 5 and 6 in figure 12). Thus the handshake is completed.

4.2. Message Evaluation

At the SMTA, if the MSP parameter of the $250\ OK$ message is the keyword for "send all headers", then the next step for the SMTA is to provide a vector of all message headers in the transmit queue. It then waits for RMTA's response on the message scheduling of its messages (see lines 3 to 8 in figure 9). Otherwise, the SMTA proceeds to apply the received MSP to outbound queue and send messages in *send now* queue beginning with message headers (figure 10).

On receiving a message headers vector, the RMTA looks up its MSP to sort messages into different buckets of *send now, later, discard* etc It then sends the updated vector back to the SMTA (figure 11).

In the case that the MSP specified by the RMTA is portable, both parties proceed to the message-transfer stage.

On receipt of headers for a message, the RMTA can optionally verify that the MSP has been applied and, after the X-HdrHash header is transmitted, it can send back 250 OK response or a Denied response (see figure 11).

After a message arrives at the RMTA, the current SMTP session is not concerned with its further handling. Its disposition thereafter is controlled by MRAP, which reflects user preferences, and can depend on the complete body of the message. MRAP-determined bounce decisions are relayed as error messages out of band from the session in which the original message was transfered. The content of such feedback and whether any is provided depend on the level of trust that the RMTA places in the SMTA. This is a matter of policy for the RMTA, which can be controlled via an additional component of the SLAP policy.

5. Related Work

At the forefront of solutions against fraudulent email or spam are *laws and legislative provisions*. Laws are essential and helpful but certainly not the silver bullet we have been searching for, as summed up in [2]. They have limited jurisdiction and are ineffective against global spammers. Laws without technical support can be ill-directed. We aim to provide such a basis for laws to be effective.

Content based filtering solutions parse the content of a message (for keywords or phrases) to determine the probability of it being spam. Some of these approaches are showcased in ([9], [20], [28]). Naive Bayesian filters are considered most effective of all filtering solutions. Even though false positives might not be a big problem with them [11], the approach is reactive and does not discourage spammers from spamming. In fact, they work to defeat such filters and simply increase the number of messages sent. Our approach can take advantage of such pre-delivery processing of messages and add other essential mechanisms to be more proactive in reducing spam messages transmitted.

Project Lumos [6] includes the same notion of two-level sender authentication that we propose to use. The difference with the current work is that Lumos is set up, at heart, to serve the interests of the large commercial bulk mailers. The idea is to register bulk mailers, require them to respond to reports of abuse, and publish the corresponding reputations. If Lumos really does make headway in the marketplace, our scheme would be easier to implement, since we rely on the similar notions of sender authentication. Also, Lumos would be an excellent reputation service to include in an MSP or MRAP. Other examples of proposed or existing *reputation services* are Razor [19] and CloudMark [4], which aim to identify individual SPAM messages, and SmartScreen [16], which is a Microsoft effort with the same objective. Both Razor and SmartScreen would fit well with the approach that we propose. A weaker source authentication scheme proposed by Boykin and Roychowdhury [3] takes advantage of social networks to construct a list of trusted senders. The authors achieve limited success with this approach and note that the technique alone is insufficient to catch all spam in email. Spammer monitoring a network can get by such *whitelist* based solutions. Strong authentication based solutions [25] are clearly unscalable for email applications.

The third genre of email abuse solutions involve *economic solutions* like bonded mail [13], e-stamps [5], Penny Black [15] or computational or memory based costs [10]. These solutions would reduce spam drastically, but every one has to bear the cost and it is against the open internet flavor. In general, we would like the email service not to punish legitimate users for misbehavior of others. However, some organizations might have a realistic need for such a solution and we provide a model in which economic solutions can work on an incentive, rather than a punitive, basis. Specifically, it is straightforward to write an MSP or MRAP so that mail that otherwise might be reject is accepted if it is bonded. A sender who really wants to get through, and is prepared to pay a price set by the receiver, will get through. The important aspect we introduce is that the receiver, through an MRAP, has control over the ultimate de-cision of whether to accept a mail message with a specified set of attributes. Through appropriate additional attributes, buying interrupt rights ([7],[13]) is possible in our scheme.

Challenge/Response systems [27] hold promise by requiring the sender to pass challenge-response tests for human initiation; which would be a big improvement, although, overlaying SMTP with an interactive protocol signifies a substantial change in the way email is delivered and must be mandated by careful network traffic studies. Also, distinguishing a human from an automated program may not be enough for spam control, as recipients may need a finer grained control over the messages they accept or reject. In any case, our approach would only benefit from a challenge response mechanism as it can be included as another attribute to specify rules around.

Our approach provides an umbrella under which most realistic needs can be expressed as policies and negotiated during the SMTP connection set up. This involves extending the SMTP, but adoption is possible incrementally without breaking existing implementations.

6. Conclusion

In this paper, we have argued that email needs an end-to-end overhaul if it is to continue to serve as the valuable resource that it has been in the past. In particular, small, point patches cannot correct the fundamental design problem of the existing email system, namely, that by default arbitrary users have write access to arbitrary mailboxes and filtering solutions though effective are only a stop gap solution. As noted by author of `sendmail`, solutions which do not increase the cost of sending spam are insufficient as the spammer can get around such a solution. In essence, we need a feedback mechanism to allow recipients select the clients they communicate with and hence discourage the process of sending mails at will. We began our review by noting that a weak but serviceable notion of sender authentication for email is within reach of the existing internet infrastructure. Our main contributions are three types of policies:

- The first, Service Level Agreement Policy or SLAP, allows a RESP to determine the conditions under which it will communicate with a given SESP ((SLAP) in figure 1). Past experience with the sending ESP, third party evaluations of the SESP's reputation, the set of services supported by the SESP, and the RESP's load level all serve as inputs into a SLAP (figure 3).

- The result of evaluating SLAP is a Message Scheduling Policy or MSP, which is instructs the SESP on whether and when to send each particular message ((MSP) in figure 1). In contrast to the existing SMTP protocol, which sends every message as soon as possible in first come, first served order, an MSP evaluates the specific attributes of each email message and uses these attributes to assign the message a priority for transmission, a deferred transmission time, or a flat out rejection (figure 4).

- The last, Message Resource Allocation Policy or MRAP, allows an individual user to specify how incoming mail should be evaluated prior to appearing in the (human) user's mailbox. The attributes used by MSP are all available to the MRAP as well, and it is expected that the MRAP will use these attributes in a more restrictive manner than does the MSP ((MRAP) in figure 1). In addition, an MRAP may request third party reputation evaluation, and also base decisions on local state information, such as how full the user's mailbox is. The net result is to give each receiver fine-grained, attribute-based control over their mailbox.

We show how to integrate each of SLAP, MSP, and MRAP with the existing SMTP protocol, thereby completing our case that our proposal is reasonably compatible with existing email infrastructure. Twin issues of controllability achieved through these policies, and resolution of policy conflicts are not discussed in this work. Intuitively, the policies introduced allow a rich set of rules to be expressed (like selectiveness in SMTP communications based on SESP identity and prioritizing 'good quality' messages) and in future work we propose to investigate if these are enough to address the spam problem.

We envision an incremental adoption scheme in which SESPs that adopt the scheme are rewarded with better service for their customers. When adoption reaches a given point, those who lag behind in adoption will find themselves discriminated against by the SLAP policies of RESPs.

We deliberately do not attempt to detect misbehavior in our scheme. Instead, we expect that misbehavior will be noted externally - in part by end users who file complaints. Mechanisms to support this are already quite common on the Internet. The hashes on mail provided by the sending ESP help regulate complaints by ensuring that a actual email message can verifiably be associated with every complaint. Feedback about misbehaving ESPs or end users makes its way into the application of SLAP, MSP and MRAP policies to future mail.

References

[1] E. Allman. The economics of spam. http://www.acmqueue.com/modules.php?name=Content&pa=showpage&pid=108.

[2] E. Allman. Spam, spam, spam, spam, spam, the ftc and spam. http://www.acmqueue.com/modules.php?name=Content&pa=showpage&pid=66.

[3] P. O. Boykin and V. Roychowdhury. Personal Email Networks: An Effective Anti-Spam Tool, February 2004.

[4] CloudMark's SpamNet. http://www.cloudmark.com.

[5] E-Stamps. http://www.templetons.com/brad/spam/estamps.html.

[6] Email Service Provider Coalition. Project Lumos. http://www.networkadvertising.org/espc/lumos_white_paper.asp, Sept 2003.

[7] S. Fahlman. Selling interrupt rights: a way to control unwanted e-mail and telephone calls. *IBM Systems Journal*, 41(4):759–766, November 2002.

[8] E. Friedman and P. Resnick. The social cost of cheap psuedonyms. In *Journal of Economics and Management Strategy*, Aug 1999.

[9] P. Graham. A plan for spam. In *2003 Cambridge Spam Conference Proceedings*, 2003.

[10] Internet Mail 2000. http://cr.yp.to/im2000.html.

[11] Kristian Eide. Winning the War on spam: Comparison of Bayesian spam filters. http://home.dataparty.no/kristian/reviews/bayesian/.

[12] J. F. Kurose and K. W. Ross. *Computer Networking: A top down approach featuring the internet*. Addison Wesley, second edition, 2003.

[13] T. Loder, M. V. Alstyne, and R. Wash. Information asymmetry and thwarting spam. Technical report, University of Michigan, 2004.

[14] MicroSoft Corporation and Sendmail Corporation. Email Caller-ID in http://www.internet-magazine.com/news/view.asp?id=3930.

[15] Microsoft Corporation's Penny Black Project. http://research.microsoft.com/research/sv/PennyBlack/.

[16] Microsoft Corporation's SmartScreen Press Release. http://www.microsoft.com/presspass/press/2003/nov03/11-17ComdexAntiSpamPR.asp.

[17] S. Petry. Port 25: The gaping hole in the firewall. In *Proceedings of ACSAC'02 Annual Computer Security Applications Conference*, Dec 2002.

[18] M. Pop. Comparative study of electronic mail systems.

[19] V. V. Prakash. http://razor.sourceforge.net/, March 2000.

[20] M. Sahami, S. Dumais, D. Heckerman, and E. Horvitz. A bayesian approach to filtering junk E-mail. In *Learning for Text Categorization: Papers from the 1998 Workshop*, Madison, Wisconsin, 1998. AAAI Technical Report WS-98-05.

[21] Simple Mail Transfer Protocol. RFC 2821, Apr 2001.

[22] SMTP Service Extension for Authentication. RFC 2554, March 1999.

[23] SMTP Service Extension for Secure SMTP over Transport Layer Security. RFC 3207, Feb 2002.

[24] SMTP Service Extensions. RFC 1869, Nov 1995.

[25] T. Tomkins and D. Handley. Giving email back to the users: using digital signatures to solve the spam problem. In *First Monday 8, 9 in http://firstmonday.org/issues/issue8_9/tomkins/index.html*, September 2003.

[26] TRUSTe. http://www.truste.org.

[27] Visnetic MailPermit. http://www.deerfield.com/products/visnetic-mailpermit/requirements/.

[28] W. S. Yerazunis. Sparse binary polynomial hashing and the CRM114 discriminator. In *2003 Cambridge Spam Conference Proceedings*, 2003.

Appendix

```
1  state = not connected;
2  while (1) {
3    Wait for request from client; /* initiation */
4    if (request=HELO AND state == not connected)
5      then state =connected;
6      Send (250 OK) response;
7      Wait for request;
8      else state = not connected;
9    if (request=MAIL TO && state == connected))
10     then state = received sender;
11     Send (250 OK) response;
12     Wait for request;
13     if (request = RCPT TO && state == received
   sender)
14       then state =received rept;
15       Send (250 OK) response;
16       Wait for request;
17     if (request = DATA && state == received rept)
18       then state = receiving data;
19       Send (334 Enter Mail) response;
20       Wait for request;
21     if (request = CRLF && state == receiving data)
22       then state = received data;
23       Send (250 OK) response;
24       Wait for request;
25     if (request = QUIT && state == received data)
26       then state = not connected;
27       Send (221 Connection closing) response;
28   )endwhile
```

Figure 12. Parts of RMTA algorithm for communications with SMTA

```
1   while (1) {
2     Wait to receive message from clients; /* Message
   Queue initialization.  (Network service listening on
   port 25)*/
3     state = not connected;
4     if (message received) then append to message
   queue;
5     while (message queue not empty){
6       message = message queue.next();
7       if (state == not connected)
8         then state = connecting;
9         Send HELO / EHLO to SMTP server;
10        Wait for response;
11        if (response == (250 OK))
12          then state =send sender;
13          else break;
14      if (state == send sender)
15        then Send MAIL FROM: sender@domain.com;
16        Wait for response;
17      if (response = (250 OK))
18        then state = send recipient;
19        else remain in line 15;
20      if (state = send recipient)
21        then Send RCPT TO: recipient@recipient.com;
22        Wait for response;
23      if (response = (250 OK))
24        then Send DATA;
25        else remain in line 21;
26        Wait for response;
27      if (response = (354))
28        then input message body;
29        state = data;
30        else remain in line 25;
31      if (message body.end()) thenSend CRLF;
32      Wait for response;
33      if (response = (250 OK))
34        then go to line 5;
35        else append message in message queue;
36    )endwhile
37  )endwhile
```

Figure 13. Parts of SMTA algorithm for communications with RMTA

Session 7 (Short Papers): Security

A Decentralized Treatment of a Highly Distributed Chinese-Wall Policy

Naftaly H. Minsky*
Department of Computer Science
Rutgers University
New Brunswick, NJ, 08903 USA
Phone: (732) 445-2085
Fax: (732) 445-0537
Email: minsky@cs.rutgers.edu

Abstract

Access control (AC) technology has come a long way from its roots as the means for sharing resources between processes running on a single machine, to a mechanism for regulating the interaction among agents (software components, and people) distributed throughout the internet. But despite the distributed nature of the systems being regulated, the conventional enforcement mechanism for AC policies remains basically centralized, where a single (although possibly replicated) reference monitor (RM) is used to mediate the interaction between members of a given community of agents, according to a given policy. This papers demonstrates one of the main drawbacks of centralized AC mechanisms, when applied to distributed systems, and to shows the absence of this drawback under the inherently decentralized law-governed interaction (LGI) mechanism.

1 Introduction

Access control (AC) technology has come a long way from its roots as the means for sharing resources between processes running on a single machine, to a mechanism for regulating the interaction among agents (software components, and people) distributed throughout the internet. Distribution introduces several complicating factors to access control, such as insecure communication, heterogeneity, openness, and large scale. Some of the implications of these factors were addressed extensively,

and quite successfully, in recent years, by such techniques as: *encryption*, for securing communication; *public-key infrastructures* (PKIs), for scalable key distribution, and for authentication of the identity and roles of principals; *delegation certificates*, for distributed delegation of privileges; and *trust management*, for deciding which rights should be given to the holder of a given set of certificates.

But despite the distributed nature of the systems being regulated, the conventional enforcement mechanism for AC policies remains basically centralized, where a single (although possibly replicated) reference monitor (RM) is used to mediate the interaction between members of a given community of agents, according to a given policy. Although such centralized enforcement is often appropriate, it has some serious limitations, particularly when dealing with *communal policies*, which are not limited to the interaction of a single server with its clients, but govern the interactions among arbitrary members of a distributed community. Specifically, centralized enforcement does not scale well for *dynamic* (or "stateful") communal policies.

The purpose of this paper is to demonstrate this drawback of centralized AC mechanisms, when applied to distributed systems, and to show the absence of this drawback under the inherently decentralized *law-governed interaction* (LGI) mechanism *min00-6,min03-6*. This demonstration will be done via a highly distributed version of the Chinese Wall policy of Brewer and Nash [4], which is introduced in the following section; and by showing, in Section 3, how this policy is formulated and scalably enforced under LGI. Related attempts at distributed versions of the Chinese Wall policy are also discussed in Section 3.

---

*Work supported in part by NSF grants No. CCR-98-03698

2   The Distributed Chinese Wall Policy

Consider a distributed and heterogeneous collection of information systems, each serving some commercial company. And let these companies be grouped into a disjoint collection of "conflict sets," where each set contains companies that compete with each other in the market place—such as the set of banks, or the set of car dealers. Consider also a distributed collection of financial analysts whose business it is to consult for commercial companies. Now, suppose that the access of these analysts to the companies (i.e., to the information systems serving these companies) is subject to the following policy, to be called CW, for short:

(a) For an analyst to operate under this policy it[1] must authenticate its name, and its status as an analyst, via a certificate signed by a designated certification authority (CA); a company must similarly authenticate its name and the conflict set to which it belongs.

(b) A priori, each analyst can get information from *any* company. But once an analyst gets information from some company c, it is not allowed to get information from any other company in the conflict set of c.

(c) Copies of messages sent by companies to analysts must be sent to a designated *auditor*.

This is an inherently *communal policy*, which governs a whole community of companies, or company-servers, and their clients. If this policy is to be enforced via the traditional reference monitor, this monitor would have to be replicated for scalability. But replication is very problematic in this dynamic situation, because every state change sensed by one replica needs to be propagated, synchronously, to all other replicas of the reference monitor. specifically, all replicas would have to be informed synchronously about every access of each analyst to every company, lest an analyst sends requests to several companies in the same conflict set, but through different replicas. Such synchronous update of all replica is, of course, possible. But it could be very expensive.

We maintain that this policy calls for a more decentralized approach for the enforcement of distributed AC policies. In the following section we show how this can be done, in a scalable manner, under LGI.

---

[1]We are using "it" for an analyst, referring to the software component that might be operating on behalf of the human analyst.

3   A Decentralized Treatment of the Chinese Wall Policy

To show how all this works, we introduce here a formalization of our example policy CW, as a law CW under LGI. For simplicity, this law is left vulnerable to a significant kind of attack. The treatment of this vulnerability under the present LGI will be discussed briefly after the discussion of law CW itself. It should also be pointed out that policy CW itself is oversimplified, in that it ignores the fact that certificates generally have a limited lifetime. For a treatment of policies that specify what is to be done when a certificate expires or is revoked, and for the formalization of such policies under LGI, the reader is referred to [1].)

Law CW, displayed in Figures 1 and 2, has two parts: *preamble* and *body*. The preamble contains the following clauses: First there is the cAuthority(publicKey) clause that identify the public key of the certification authority to be used for the authentication of the controllers that are to mediate CW-messages. This authority is an important element of the trust between agents that exchange such messages—more about which in [2]. Second, there are two authority clauses, each of which identifies a certification authority acceptable to this community, one for certifying analysts, the other for certifying companies, identifying the name of each, and the conflict set to which it belongs. Each such CA is identified by its public-key, and is given a local name—"analystCA" and "companyCA" in this case—to be used within this law. Finally, the initialCS clause defines the initial control-state of all agents in this community—it is empty in this case.

The body of the law is a list of all its rules, each followed by a comment (in italic), which, together with the following discussion, should be understandable even for a reader not well versed in our language for writing laws.

By Rule $\mathcal{R}1$, one can claim the role of an analyst with a certified name n—recoding this information via the terms role(analyst) and name(n) in its control-state—by presenting an appropriate certificate issued by analystCA. Similarly, by Rule $\mathcal{R}2$, a server may authenticate itself as the server of some company c, belonging to a conflict set s—which would be recorded via the terms company(c) and set(s) in its control-state—by presenting an appropriate certificate issued by companyCA. Note that due to the rest of the law, one cannot function as an analyst or as a company without such terms.

An agent may claim the role of an analyst with name N, by presenting an appropriate certificate issued by analystCA).

```
R2. certified([issuer(companyCA),
        subject(X),
        attributes([C,S])]) :-
    do(+company(C)), do(+set(S)).
```

An agent may authenticate itself as the server of company C, belonging to set S by presenting an appropriate certificate issued by companyCA.

```
R3. sent(X,request(N,C,I),Y)
    :- role(analyst)@CS, name(N)@CS,
    do(forward).
```

A request message by an agent X will be forwarded only if X has the term role(analyst) in its control-state, and it must carry its authenticated name.

```
R4. arrived(X,request(N,C,I),Y)
    :- company(C)@CS, do(deliver),
    do(+requestedBy(X)).
```

A request for information about company C that arrives at an agent Y will be delivered to it only if Y has been certified as serving company C. Also, a term requestedBy(X) is added to the control state to record the fact that X requested information from this company.

Figure 1. Law $\mathcal{L}_{CW}$ for Chinese Wall Policy

```
R5. sent(Y,response(Data,C,S),U)
    :- company(C)@CS, set(S)@CS,
    requestedBy(X)@CS, do(forward).
```

A company-server Y which received a request from an analyst X can reply to him via a message response(D,C,S), where D is the information requested; and C and S are the certified name, and conflict set of the company served by Y, respectively.

```
R6. arrived(Y,response(Data,C,S),X)
    :- not blocked(S)@CS
    do(+blocked(S)),
    do(+permitted(C)), do(deliver),
    do(deliver(Y,[response(Data,C,S),
        X],auditor))
```

A message response(Data,C,S) arriving at an analyst X would be delivered if there is no blocked(S) term at the CS of X, and the term blocked(S) would be added to the CS of X, along with the term permitted(C).

```
R7. arrived(Y,response(Data,C,S),X)
    :- blocked(S)@CS, permitted(C),
    do(deliver).
```

A message response(Data,C,S) arriving at an analyst X would be delivered if there is blocked(S) term at the CS of X, but only if this CS also contains the term permitted(C).

Figure 2. Law $\mathcal{L}_{CW}$ continuation

By Rule $\mathcal{R}3$, a request message of the form request(N,C,I) will be forwarded only if the sender has been authenticated as an analyst (i.e., if it has the term role(analyst) in its control-state.) This message must contain the sender's authenticated name N, as well as the name C of the company for which information I is being sought. By Rule $\mathcal{R}4$, when this request arrives at its destination Y, it would be delivered *only* if Y has been certified as serving company C. Also, a term requestedBy(X) is added to the control state of Y, to record the fact that X requested information from it.

By Rule $\mathcal{R}5$ a company-server Y which received a request from an analyst X can reply to him via a message response(D,C,S), where D is the information requested; and C and S are the certified name and conflict set of the company served by Y, respectively.

Finally, the characteristic constraint of the Chinese Wall policy is carried out via the a pair of terms—blocked(S) and permitted(C)—that can be dynamically attached to a CS of an analyst by a response from a company server, and which determines the disposition of such a response. Specifically, by Rule $\mathcal{R}6$, a message response(Data,C,S) arriving at an analyst X would be delivered if there is no blocked(S) term at the CS of X, which, in effect means that X did not get any previous responses from a companies that belong to set S. Three additional operations are mandated by this rule: (a) the term blocked(S) would be added to the CS of X, blocking future responses from companies belonging to set S; (b) the term permitted(C) would also be added to the CS of X, permitting (by Rule $\mathcal{R}7$) the delivery of responses from servers of this company, even if the term blocked(S) is present; and (c) a copy of the response message is delivered to the distinguished agent auditor.

Note that this law does not prevent an analyst

from sending requests to several companies belonging to the same conflict set, nor does it prevent the companies from replying to these messages. But only the first such reply to arrive at the analyst would be delivered, all other replies will be blocked. Note also that such blocking is done strictly locally, and thus scalably.

A Limitation of Law CW, and its Resolution:
For simplicity we left an Achilles' heel in this particular law: a possible "double dipping" by an analyst. That is, a single analyst can operate via two (or more) agents under law CW—concurrently or at different times—using the same certificate to authenticate himself as an analyst. Law CW is not equipped to prevent two incarnations of a single analyst from getting information from different companies in the same conflict-set, which is, of course contrary to the CW policy.

This limitation can be fixed by regulating the membership of the group G of agents operating as analysts under law CW, ensuring the following two properties:

- Group G never includes more than one agent representing an analyst with a given name, as authenticated via a certificate issue by `analystCA`.

- If an analyst has been a member of G and left it, he (or she) will assume his latest control-state when rejoining the group.

The technique for controlling membership under LGI, which can be made to satisfy these properties, has been introduced in [7].

Related Work: There have been several recent attempts at the Chinese Wall policy in distributed context. Kajoth [5] described an implementation of this policy under the Tivoli system, but not in a scalable manner. Tivoli generally uses a replicated reference-monitor for enforcing its access control policies, this works well, and scalably, for regular, static policies, which is what Tivoli usually supports. In addition, Tivoli features what they call an *External Authorization Service*, which can support dynamic policies but is not replicated, and thus is not scalable. It is this centralized enforcer that they use for their implementation of the Chinese wall policy.

Atluri et al. [3] devised a Chinese-Wall-like security model to solve some difficulties with decentralized workflows. But they do not provide a solution to the full gladged distributed Chinese Wall problem itself, and their approach would not scale would they attempt to do that.

Finally, it should be pointed out that the author and his colleague published another solution to the Chinese Wall problem few years ago [6]. That solution was done under a more primitive version of LGI, which required a fairly complex process of initialization of the state of the various agents in a community, and required the law formulating this policy to specify the conflict set explicitly. The present solution is much simpler, and more powerful in some other respects, like the auditing part.

References

[1] X. Ao, N. Minsky, and V. Ungureanu. Formal treatment of certificate revocation under communal access control. In *Proc. of the 2001 IEEE Symposium on Security and Privacy, May 2001, Oakland California*, May 2001.

[2] X. Ao and N. H. Minsky. Flexible regulation of distributed coalitions. In *LNCS 2808: the Proc. of the European Symposium on Research in Computer Security (ESORICS) 2003*, October 2003.

[3] V. Atluri, S. A. Chun, and P. Mazzoleni. A chinese wall secuity model for decentralized workflow systems. In *Proceedings of the Eighth ACM Conference on Computer and Communications Security*, November 2001.

[4] D. Brewer and M. Nash. The Chinese Wall security policy. In *Proceedings of the IEEE Symposium in Security and Privacy*. IEEE Computer Society, 1989.

[5] G. Karjoth. The authorization service of tivoli policy director. In *Proc. of the 17th Annual Computer Security Applications Conference (ACSAC 2001)*, December 2001.

[6] N.H. Minsky and V. Ungureanu. Unified support for heterogeneous security policies in distributed systems. In *7th USENIX Security Symposium*, January 1998.

[7] C. Serban, X. Ao, and N.H. Minsky. Establishing enterprise communities. In *Proc. of the 5th IEEE International Enterprise Distributed Object Computing Conference (EDOC 2001), Seattle, Washington*, September 2001.

Unification in Privacy Policy Evaluation – Translating EPAL into Prolog*

Michael Backes
IBM Research, Switzerland
mbc@zurich.ibm.com

Markus Dürmuth[†]
University of Karlsruhe, Germany
markus.duermuth@web.de

Günter Karjoth
IBM Research, Switzerland
gka@zurich.ibm.com

Abstract

Privacy policy evaluation engines enable queries whether a specific user is allowed to access specific data for a specific purpose. While tools for authoring, maintaining, and auditing privacy policies already exist, no tool exists yet to deal with unification within such policies, e.g., to enable queries if data might *be modified by some* user, *or* how many *user entries satisfy a certain constraint. We show how this can can be achieved by embedding enterprise privacy policies into Prolog. We show this concretely for IBM's Enterprise Privacy Authorization Language (EPAL). Based on the unification mechanisms of Prolog, our work enables general queries for privacy policies as well as quantitative measurements.*

1. Introduction

An increasing number of enterprises make privacy promises to customers or, at least in the US and Canada, fall under new privacy regulations. To ensure adherence to these promises and regulations, enterprise privacy technologies are emerging [3]. An important tool for enterprise privacy enforcement is formalized enterprise privacy policies [4, 6]. Compared with the well-known language P3P [7] intended for privacy promises to customers, languages for the internal privacy practices of enterprises and for technical privacy enforcement must offer more possibilities for fine-grained distinction of data users, purposes, etc., as well as a clearer semantics.

Such languages define the purposes for which collected data can be used, model the consent that data subjects can give, and may impose obligations onto the enterprise. They can formalize privacy statements like "we use data of a minor for marketing purposes only if the parent has given consent" or "medical data can only be read by the patient's pri-

mary care physician". The evaluation mechanisms of enterprise privacy policies can then be used to decide if a specific user is allowed to access specific data for a specific purpose. However, the existing evaluation mechanism cannot be used to answer queries that involve unification, e.g., whether a user *exists* that can edit specific data, or, more generally, to give quantitative measurements like the number of user entries that satisfy a certain constraint. In practice however, such queries are highly attractive: Examples range from deciding if employees of the marketing department are allowed to access data that must not be used for marketing purposes, over identifying which data an application is allowed to access, to building up statistics over user entries without violating their individual privacy.

We show how such general queries can be handled by transforming enterprise privacy policies into Prolog. Since unification is a central construct in Prolog, and since Prolog offers very powerful decision procedures, our transformation allows for very general queries for privacy policies as well as quantitative measurements. We show the transformation concretely for IBM's Enterprise Privacy Authorization Language (EPAL) [1], which has recently become an accepted W3C member submission. The transformation has been implemented as an XSLT program.

2. EPAL

In this section we give a brief review of EPAL. Instead of the lengthy XML syntax, we use a corresponding abstract syntax [2] and omit all details that are not necessary for understanding. An EPAL privacy policy consists of a *vocabulary Voc*, a list of *authorization rules R*, a *global condition gc*, a *default ruling dr*, and a *default obligation $\bar{d}o$*.

The *vocabulary* defines the categories of users and data, the actions being performed on the data, the business purposes associated with the access requests, and obligations incurred on access. Note that purposes and obligations are not part of classical access control languages. Users, data, and purposes are captured in *hierarchies*. Formally, a hierarchy is pair $(H, >_H)$ of a finite set H and a transitive, non-reflexive relation $>_H \subseteq H \times H$, where every $h \in H$

---

*The long version of this paper has been published as IBM Research Report RZ 3541.

[†]This work was done when the author was on internship at the IBM Zurich Research Laboratory.

has at most one immediate predecessor (parent). We write $\geq_H$ for the reflexive closure of $>_H$. We write $h \gtreqless_H h'$ if $h \geq_H h'$ or $h' \geq_H h$ holds. Technically, a vocabulary is a tuple (UH, DH, PH, A, Var, O) where UH, DH, and PH are hierarchies called the *user*, *data*, and *purpose hierarchy*, respectively, and A is a set of *actions*. Var is a set of *variables* used to build conditions that determine when a rule of the policy is applicable, and O is a set of *obligations*.

The *authorization rules*, short *rule list*, is a list containing elements of the form $(u, d, p, a, r, c, \bar{o})$ called *rules*, where $(u, d, p, a) \in U \times D \times P \times A$,[1] c – the *condition* of the rule – is a well-typed formula of a subset of standard logic based on the set Var of variables, $r \in \{+, -\}$ is the *ruling* of the rule, and $\bar{o}$ is a set of obligations. Conditions are used to check context, consent, and other data subject properties. Formally, a rule list for a vocabulary Voc is a list containing elements of $U \times D \times P \times A \times \{+, -\} \times C(Var) \times \mathfrak{P}(O)$, where $C(Var)$ is the set of well-typed formulas of the underlying logic over Var, and $\mathfrak{P}(O)$ denotes the powerset of O. In EPAL, the precedences of the rules are contained implicitly by the textual order of the rules. The rulings $+$ and $-$ mean 'allow' and 'deny'. We say that a rule is *negative* if it has a 'deny' ruling, otherwise it is *positive*. For the ease of writing, we augment each rule $rule$ with a natural number $n(rule)$ called the rule's *precedence*, such that rules that come first in the rule list have higher precedence. Thus, we write $(u, d, p, a, r, c, \bar{o}, n(rule))$ instead of $(u, d, p, a, r, c, \bar{o})$.

Finally, the *global condition* gc, the *default ruling* dr, and the *default obligation* $\bar{do}$ are arbitrary elements from $C(Var)$, $\{+, \circ, -\}$, and $\mathfrak{P}(O)$, respectively, where $\circ$ corresponds to a 'don't care' decision.

A *query* to an EPAL policy is a tuple (u, d, p, a). Typically, queries belong to the set $U \times D \times P \times A$ for the given vocabulary; queries that do not fulfill this will yield a special *scope error*. EPAL queries are not restricted to "ground terms", i.e., minimal elements in the hierarchies, to handle policy extension, refinement, and composition [2].

Whether a rule with a satisfied condition matches a given query crucially depends on its ruling: First, every rule matches the query which it is defined for. Positive rules additionally match for all children of the defined query (component-wise in the hierarchies), i.e., positive rules are inherited downward the hierarchies. Negative rules are additionally inherited upwards the hierarchies, i.e., they apply also for parents of the defined query.

The semantics of an EPAL privacy policy is a function

eval that evaluates a query based on a given assignment χ of the variables in Var and returns as result a *decision* and a *set of associated obligations*. For a compact representation of the function eval, as depicted in Algorithm 1, we introduce the following parent-child notation on quadruples. Let $(u, d, p, a) \square (u', d', p', a')$ for $\square \in \{\geq, \gtreqless\}$ iff $u \square u' \wedge d \square d' \wedge p \square p' \wedge a = a'$.

```
if gc →χ false then return (dr, ∅)
if (u_R, d_R, p_R, a_R) ∉ U × D × P × A then return
  (scope_error, ∅)
foreach (u, d, p, a, r, c, ō) ∈ R (in the given order) do
    if c →χ true then
        if r = + ∧ (u, d, p, a) ≥ (u_R, d_R, p_R, a_R) then
        return (r, ō)
        if r = − ∧ (u, d, p, a) ⋛ (u_R, d_R, p_R, a_R) then
        return (r, ō)
return (dr, d̄o)
```

Algorithm 1: Query Evaluation

If the query is not contained in the considered vocabulary or the global condition is not satisfied under the given assignment then the result is $(\text{scope\_error}, \emptyset)$ respectively $(dr, \emptyset)$. Otherwise, the decision is determined by the first matching rule whose condition is satisfied. If no such rule exists, the decision equals the default ruling.

3. Translation

Our transformation imitates the inheritance mechanisms of EPAL in Prolog and transforms EPAL rules more or less one-to-one to Prolog rules. This approach is usually less efficient than a specialized translation, where the decisions of the policy are determined for all possible queries and assignments, allowing to implement query evaluation very efficiently by simple table look-up. However, it allows to answer more general queries.

3.1. A Brief Review of Prolog

In Prolog, a *clause* is an expression of the form $B :\text{-} A_1, \ldots, A_n. (n \geq 0)$ where B is a *goal* and $A_1, \ldots, A_n$ are *conditions* (or sub-goals) of the clause. In the above clause, the symbol :- reads *if* to indicate logical implication and the symbol ',' reads *and*:

B is true if (A_1 is true and ... and A_n is true).

If a clause does not have a condition, it is called a *fact*, and a *rule* otherwise. *Functors* are names that begin with a lower case letter or that are enclosed in single quotes, and numbers. *Variables* are names that either begin with an upper

---

[1] In the XML syntax of EPAL, rules may have subsets of each of these four sets instead of single elements which allow a more convenient way of specifying a policy. In the abstract syntax, rules are then flattened under adherence of the relative order, i.e., such a rule $(\bar{u}, \bar{d}, \bar{p}, \bar{a}, r, c, \bar{o})$ with $\bar{u} \subseteq U$, $\bar{d} \subseteq D$, $\bar{p} \subseteq P$, and $\bar{a} \subseteq A$ corresponds to the list of rules $((u, d, p, a, r, c, \bar{o}) \mid u \in \bar{u}, d \in \bar{d}, p \in \bar{p}, a \in \bar{a})$, where the order of the rules can be chosen arbitrarily.

case letter or an underscore. A *term* is either a functor or a variable. Any variable is implicitly considered to be universally quantified with the scope being the entire clause. A *predicate* is a collection of clauses whose goals have the same functor and arity.

If a predicate offers multiple clauses to solve a goal, they are tried one-by-one until one succeeds. In particular, Prolog's backtracking mechanism for non-determinism can return more than one answer. Unification is used to assign values to variables.

3.2. Transformation and Semantical Encoding

Hierarchies. The hierarchies of an EPAL privacy policy are mapped directly to Prolog by one fact for each edge of the hierarchy. We show this exemplarily for the user hierarchy. A user relation $userA \geq_U userB$ is transformed to the Prolog fact `uh(userA, userB)`, where `uh` abbreviates "user hierarchy". The transitive closure `deruh` of the rules `uh(·,·)` is defined by

```
deruh(X,X).
deruh(X,Y)  :- uh(X,Y).
deruh(X,Y)  :- uh(X,Z), deruh(Z,Y),
```

which we call the *derived user hierarchy*. By definition, we have $u_1 \geq_U u_2$ if and only if $\mathtt{deruh}(u_1, u_2)$ for all users u_1, u_2. The corresponding derived hierarchies *derdh* and *derph* for data and purposes are defined similarly.

Conditions. EPAL provides a set of predefined functions and predicates to build conditions. Most Prolog systems also have a rich set of built-in predicates, which can be used to implement EPAL conditions. Note that EPAL predicates and their corresponding Prolog predicate might differ slightly. We identify different degrees of converting conditions into Prolog. In the basic version, we assume that conditions are coded as Prolog facts. A more elaborated version deals with the individual attributes (variables) of the conditions. According to their type, we assign values as above, stating them as facts, and then evaluate the condition expressions accordingly.

Rules. Prolog clause `rule(u,d,p,a,r,o,n) :- c.` captures rule (u, d, p, a, r, c, o, n) from the rule list R, where rulings are defined as `allow` for + and `deny` for −. For a rule list R, we refer to the set $P(R)$ of these clauses as the *Prolog rules*.

To capture the semantics of EPAL within Prolog, i.e., the evaluation of queries based on the function eval, we first define that an EPAL rule is applicable for a given query $q = (u', d', p', a')$ if and only if there is a rule (u, d, p, a, r, c, o, n) such that $a = a'$ and $x \geq x' \vee (x' \geq x \wedge r = -)$ for every $x \in \{u, d, p\}$. Next, we define Prolog clauses as

```
ask(U,D,P,A,R,O,N)
   :- deruh(U,U1),ask1(U1,D,P,A,R,O,N).
ask(U,D,P,A,R,O,N)
   :- deruh(U1,U),ask1(U1,D,P,A,deny,O,N).
ask1(U,D,P,A,R,O,N)
   :- derdh(D,D1),ask2(U,D1,P,A,R,O,N).
ask1(U,D,P,A,R,O,N)
   :- derdh(D1,D),ask2(U,D1,P,A,deny,O,N).
ask2(U,D,P,A,R,O,N)
   :- derph(P,P1),rule(U,D,P1,A,R,O,N).
ask2(U,D,P,A,R,O,N)
   :- derph(P1,P),rule(U,D,P1,A,deny,O,N).
```

and we show that the Prolog goal `ask` corresponds to the individual rules in a natural way. Therefore, we introduce the scope of a Prolog rule.

Definition 1 *The scope of a Prolog rule is defined as*

$$scope(\mathtt{rule(u,d,p,a,+,o,n)} : -c)$$
$$:= \{(u',d',p',a') \mid u' \leq u, d' \leq d, p' \leq p, a' = a\},$$
$$scope(rule(u,d,p,a,-,o,n) : -c)$$
$$:= \{(u',d',p',a') \mid u \gneq u', d \gneq d', p \gneq p', a' = a\}.$$

If a query q is in the scope of a Prolog rule, we say that this rule is applicable *for q.*

We can now state the following simple lemma.

Lemma 1 *Let an EPAL policy with rule list R be given and let* `rule(u,d,p,a,r,o,n) :- c` $\in P(R)$*. Then the Prolog goal* `ask(u',d',p',a,r,o,n)` *is derivable if and only if this rule is applicable for $q = (u', d', p', a)$ and the condition c evaluates to true under the considered assignment.*

Because `?- ask(u,d,p,a,_,_,_)` returns all applicable rules independent of their precedences, we sort them based on their precedences:

```
query(U,D,P,A,R,O,N)
   :- ask(U,D,P,A,R,O,N),
      not(ask(U,D,P,A,_,_,Y),N > Y).
```

The goal `query` searches for applicable rules and succeeds if there is no other applicable rule with lower precedence. It uses negation, i.e., if the goal `ask(U,D,P,A,_,_,Y)`, `N > Y` has a solution, it fails; otherwise it succeeds. This algorithm has the advantage that it also permits queries with free variables for users, data, purposes, and actions, which is not possible for other algorithms.

The following theorem finally captures that this Prolog goal corresponds to the EPAL semantics.

Theorem 1 *Let P be an EPAL policy, let $P(P)$ denote the corresponding Prolog program obtained by applying above transformations, and let χ be an arbitrary assignment for Var. Then the goal* `query(u,d,p,a,r,O,_)` *is derivable in $P(P)$ and the Prolog variable O is bound to obligation o if and only if $eval_{P,\chi}(u,d,p,a) = (r,o)$.*

4. Benefits of the Embedding

Our transformation shows that all the information contained in EPAL can easily be stored in a Prolog database and inheritance can be canonically expressed within Prolog. A formal mapping ensures that no errors are introduced in the translation. Thus, we can use Prolog to perform consistency checks for privacy policies and to evaluate access queries.

Unification. First, we want to stress that after transforming a privacy policy into Prolog, much more general queries are possible compared to plain EPAL. Our Prolog representation enables queries of the form "Who is allowed to read personal data of category credit card number" by

```
| ?- query(U,creditCardNumber,anyPurpose,
             read,allow,_,_).
```

```
U = marketingDep
```

One can also ask Prolog to return other successful unifications which forms the basis to obtain quantitative measurements for queries. As an example, consider a query "Are employees of the marketing department allowed to access data that must not be used for marketing purposes?", which can be represented by

```
| ?- query(_,D,marketing,deny,_,_),
       query(marketingDep,D,_,_,allow,_,_).
```

Moreover, such queries may support the development of new business processes, for example by determining what personal data is accessible by department `salesDep` under purpose `statistics`. The following query returns the accessible data categories in variable `L`:

```
| ?- setOf(D,query(salesDep,D,statistics,
             allow,_,_), L).
```

```
L = [age,gender,citizenship]
```

Building up statistics. In EPAL, consent choices of the data subject are "stored" in (auditable) attributes (i.e., whether a certain data subject opted-in or opted-out to third-party marketing may be determined by an attribute called `consentToMarketing`). Having such a consent repository, for example expressed as Prolog facts, one can ask how many percent of the customer population could be reached by a marketing campaign.

Conflicts between stated policy and actual practice. The Platform for Privacy Preferences (P3P) specification [7] enables Web sites to describe their data collection practices, which can then be read and displayed by P3P-enabled browser software or other user agents. However, whether or not the data inside the organization is used as promised depends on the enterprise's actual privacy practices as expressed by a fine-grained privacy policy like EPAL.

There are two ways to assure that the EPAL policy correctly implements the privacy "promises" of the P3P policy. To achieve correctness by construction, the P3P policy is translated into an equivalent EPAL policy or vice versa [5]. However, these transformations are not trivial and must be verified. To achieve correctness by validation, it is checked whether each query granted by the EPAL policy is also granted by the P3P policy. If there is a P3P into Prolog mapping as well, Prolog offers the capability to verify the above property.

Assuming that goal `queryP3P(u,d,p)` returns a positive answer if the P3P specification grants access for user u on data d for purpose p, the below clause checks for implementation errors:

```
conflict(U,D,P) :- query(U,D,P,_,allow,_,_),
                     not(queryP3P(U,D,P)).
```

If the evaluation of goal `conflict` fails then the EPAL policy correctly implements the P3P policy; otherwise it outputs a triple for which access is granted by the EPAL policy but not by the P3P policy.

References

[1] P. Ashley, S. Hada, G. Karjoth, C. Powers, and M. Schunter. Enterprise Privacy Authorization Language (EPAL 1.2), 10 Nov 2003. www.w3.org/Submission/SUBM-EPAL-20031110/.

[2] M. Backes, B. Pfitzmann, and M. Schunter. A toolkit for managing enterprise privacy policies. In *8th European Symposium on Research in Computer Security (ESORICS)*, Lecture Notes in Computer Science 2808, pages 162–180. Springer, 2003.

[3] A. Cavoukian and T. J. Hamilton. *The Privacy Payoff: How successful businesses build customer trust*. McGraw-Hill/Ryerson, 2002.

[4] S. Fischer-Hübner. *IT-security and privacy: Design and use of privacy-enhancing security mechanisms, Lecture Notes in Computer Science* 1958. Springer, 2002.

[5] G. Karjoth, M. Schunter, and E. Van Herreweghen. Translating privacy practices into privacy promises — how to promise what you can keep. In *IEEE 4th International Workshop on Policies for Distributed Systems and Networks (Policy'03)*, pages 135–146. IEEE Computer Society, 2003.

[6] G. Karjoth, M. Schunter, and M. Waidner. The platform for enterprise privacy practices – privacy-enabled management of customer data. In *Privacy Enhancing Technologies*, Lecture Notes in Computer Science 2482, pg. 69–84. Springer, 2002.

[7] Platform for Privacy Preferences (P3P). W3C Recommendation, Apr. 2002. http://www.w3.org/TR/2002/REC-P3P-20020416/.

An Introduction to the Web Services Policy Language (WSPL)

Anne H. Anderson
Sun Microsystems Laboratories
Anne.Anderson@sun.com

Abstract

The Web Services Policy Language (WSPL) is suitable for specifying a wide range of policies, including authorization, quality-of-service, quality-of-protection, reliable messaging, privacy, and application-specific service options. WSPL is of particular interest in several respects. It supports merging two policies, resulting in a single policy that satisfies the requirements of both, assuming such a policy exists. Policies can be based on comparisons other than equality, allowing policies to depend on fine-grained attributes such as time of day, cost, or network subnet address. By using standard data types and functions for expressing policy parameters, a standard policy engine can support any policy. The syntax is a strict subset of the OASIS eXtensible Access Control Markup Language (XACML) Standard. WSPL has been implemented, and is under consideration as a standard policy language for use with web services.

1. Introduction

A web service has various aspects and features that can be controlled or described using policy rules. Examples of such aspects or features include authentication, authorization, quality-of-service, quality-of-protection, reliable messaging, privacy, and application-specific service options. Interoperability, usability, and reliability of web services will benefit from use of a common policy language for expressing these types of policies. The Web Services Policy Language (WSPL) [1] is an excellent candidate for accomplishing this goal.

WSPL is of particular interest in several respects. First, it allows policy negotiation by supporting the merging of policies from two sources. The result is a single policy that represents the intersection of the two source policies, assuming such a policy exists. Second, policies can be based on policy parameter comparisons other than simple equality matching. This allows policies to depend on fine-grained parameters such as time of day, cost, or network subnet address. Third, by

using a set of standard data types and functions for expressing policy parameters, a standard implementation of the language can support any policy.

The syntax of WSPL is a strict subset of the OASIS eXtensible Access Control Markup Language (XACML) Standard [2]. WSPL has been implemented, and is under consideration as a standard policy language for web services.

WSPL was developed based on use cases and requirements [3] that were collected and reviewed in a public forum.

The examples in this paper are shown in a general form rather than in the XML [4] syntax actually used by WSPL. Logically, the examples are equivalent to the corresponding policy expressed in the exact XML syntax, but the general form should be much easier for the typical reader to understand.

2. WSPL overview

A WSPL policy is a sequence of one or more rules, where each rule represents an acceptable choice for satisfying the policy. Rules are listed in order of preference, with the most preferred choice listed first.

A WSPL rule is a sequence of predicates. Each predicate places a constraint on the value of an attribute. The constraint operators are: equals, greater than, greater than or equal to, less than, less than or equal to, set-equals, and subset. A predicate may specify a constraint based on a literal value, as in "A > 3", or it may place a constraint based on the value of another attribute, as in "A > B". All of the predicates in a rule must be satisfied in order for the rule to be satisfied.

Each policy also states the target aspect of the web service that is covered by that policy.

An example WSPL policy, expressed in a general form, is shown in Figure 1.

```
Policy (Aspect = "Quality of Protection") {
   Rule {
      Signature-Algorithm = "RSA-SHA1",
      Key-Length >= 2048 }
   Rule {
      Signature-Algorithm = "RSA-SHA1",
      Key-Length >= 1024,
      Source-Domain = "EXAMPLE.COM" }
   Rule {
      Source-Domain = "MY.EXAMPLE.COM" }
}
```

Figure 1. QoP policy example

The target aspect of this policy is the web service's quality of protection (QoP) requirements and offerings. There are three rules, indicating that there are three choices for satisfying the QoP requirements of this web service. The first rule, the most preferred choice, says that the Signature-Algorithm attribute must have the value "RSA-SHA1" and the Key-Length attribute value must be at least 2048 (bits). The second rule states that, if the Source-Domain attribute is "EXAM-PLE.COM" (presumably a somewhat trusted domain), then the Signature-Algorithm must still be "RSA-SHA1", but the Key-Length may be shorter, but at least 1024 (bits). The third rule states that, where the Source-Domain attribute is "MY.EXAMPLE.COM" (presumably the service's local domain), digital signatures are not required at all.

A policy may state offerings or options rather than requirements. An example is shown in Figure 2. This policy might be published by a service that is selling access to a database.

```
Policy (Aspect = "Service Levels") {
   Rule {
      Member-level = "Gold",
      Transaction-Fee = 5 }
   Rule {
      Member-level = "Gold",
      Time >= 9pm,
      Time <= 6am }
   Rule {
      Member-level = "Tin",
      Transaction-Fee = 25 }
}
```

Figure 2. Service options policy example

This policy specifies that a "Gold" level member pays a fee of 5 (cents) per transaction normally, but between the hours of 9pm and 6am, transactions are free. A "Tin" level member pays a fee of 25 (cents) per transaction.

The policies for all aspects of a web service are collected into a "PolicySet". A PolicySet, like a Policy, has a target, but in this case the target specifies the service identifier and the service port type. In the case where a service needs different policies for different operations or messages supported by the service, there may be a second level of PolicySets nested inside the top, service level, PolicySet. The target for each second level PolicySet specifies the operation, and optionally the message, to which the policies within the PolicySet apply.

The policy model for a web service policy is shown in Figure 3.

```
PolicySet (target=<port type>) {
   PolicySet (target=<operation/message>) {
      Policy (target=<aspect>) {
         Rule {
            <predicate>, ...
         } ...
      } ...
   } ...
   Policy (target=<aspect>) {
      Rule {
         <predicate>, ...
      } ...
   } ...
}
```

Figure 3: WSPL policy model

There may be any number of operation/message PolicySets, Policies, Rules, and predicates. The use of the operation/message PolicySet level is optional. Where they are used, the Policies within an operation/message PolicySet all apply to the operation and message specified in the target of that PolicySet.

3. Policy negotiation

One of WSPL's strengths as a web service policy language is its ability to support the negotiation of mutually acceptable policies between two services or between a service consumer and the service itself. For example, a user may wish to use a service. Both the user and the service may have policies for the Quality of Protection parameters they are able to support. In order for the user to interact successfully with the service, the user's application must determine whether it can satisfy the provider's requirements, and, if there are multiple acceptable choices, which one is preferred by the user. This negotiation is accomplished by having the user's application merge the user's policy with the policy of the service.

In order to merge two WSPL policies, several steps are performed. First, the targets of the two policies must match. If they do not match, then the two policies are not compatible. Second, rules from the two policies are paired in all possible combinations, sorted first by the preference order of the party doing the merging, and second by the preference order of the other party (other algorithms could be used). Third, each rule pairing is combined to produce a single new rule. If the two rules in the pairing can not be combined, then the pairing is eliminated. The resulting set of rules represents the combined policy. If this set is empty, then the two policies are not compatible.

The step of combining a rule pairing is done by combining the predicates in the two rules. Predicates that constrain the same attribute must be combined in such a way that the resulting predicate represents the intersection of the original predicates. As an example, a rule stating "A >= 200" would be combined with a rule stating "A >= 300" to produce a result of "A >= 300". If predicates that constrain the same attribute from the two rules in the pair can not be combined, then the rule pairing is incompatible and is eliminated. WSPL specifies in detail how to combine all standard predicate types.

Once two policies have been merged, service-defined descriptions of attributes are used to select one rule from the merged policy and to apply its attributes appropriately. For example, one rule might specify "time of day" attribute values that are not compatible with the time at which this particular service request is being made, so that rule would be eliminated from consideration. Another rule might specify a "role" attribute value that this particular requester is unable to supply, so that rule would also be eliminated. Once inapplicable rules have been eliminated, the first remaining rule is typically selected. This rule might specify a "hash algorithm" attribute value to be used as input to the digital signature operation applied to the service request message. A "member status" attribute value might be obtained from a trusted authority as an attribute certificate and supplied as part of the service request. The specification and application of such attribute descriptions is outside the scope of WSPL.

In cases where all policies in a service's PolicySet are to be negotiated, all policies must be merged. In this case, the merging algorithm will first attempt to pair up operator/message PolicySets and Policies by their targets. If both PolicySets do not contain operator/message PolicySets and Policies that have matching Target values, then the two PolicySets are not compatible. In other cases, such as where the user's application is already coordinated with some aspects of a service's policy, it will be necessary to merge only specific policies. The choice of which policies must be merged depends on the service definition.

Policy negotiation may be either static or dynamic. That is, it may be done once for two parties that have static policies, with the result re-used for each communication between them. Alternatively, it may be done at runtime, based on policies that may represent dynamic constraints relevant to a particular service request. Specification of when policy negotiation must occur is outside the scope of WSP, and would be defined by a particular web service.

4. WSPL policy attributes

Very simple policy languages may support only named attributes that are "true" if present, and "false" if missing. WSPL uses XACML attributes, which are always name-value pairs. This allows the use of fine-grained attributes such as cost or time-of-day, where it would not be feasible to specify a policy for each possible value of the attribute, but where it is quite feasible to specify that an attribute must be greater than or equal to a certain value. An attribute that merely needs to be present, but has no other value, is defined as a named attribute with a Boolean value "true".

The definition of the attributes used by a particular service is outside the scope of WSPL. The semantic description of the attribute, while important in creating services and applications, is irrelevant to the WSPL policy and its evaluation. WSPL also does not specify how a policy user obtains values for attributes.

Each attribute must have a name and a data type. The name must be chosen by the service designer in such a way that it will not conflict with names of other attributes that may have different semantics (URLs can be used as attribute names in order to achieve such uniqueness).

Attributes may also be specified by using XPath [5] expressions. In this case, the policy user would be expected to present an XML instance containing values for the attributes when interacting with the service.

WSPL supports the rich set of data types used in XACML: string, integer, floating point number (double), date, time, Boolean, URI, hexBinary, base64-Binary, dayTimeDuration, yearMonthDuration, x500-Name, and rfc822Name. These data types are all taken from the XML Schema, with the exception of the two duration types taken from XQuery Operators [6], and the two name types taken from XACML. Each data type has a corresponding set of supported functions: equal, greater-than, greater-than-or-equal, less-than, less-than-or-equal, set-equals, and subset. This set of data types and functions is powerful enough to allow the expression of rich policies, yet is constrained enough to allow a precise definition of the rules for merging predicates in policies.

5. Design decisions and conclusions

Any language design must make a number of decisions about the underlying data and use models and also about the level of complexity to be supported. This section discusses some of the particular choices that were made in designing WSPL.

First of all, the WSPL language was developed to satisfy a set of use cases and requirements that were collected, reviewed, and published in an open, public forum. The functionality of the language was tailored to satisfy actual use case requirements.

Rather than starting from scratch, the WSPL language was defined as a strict subset of the OASIS eXtensible Access Control Markup Language (XACML) Standard. XACML has been used in a number of projects to date, is available in an open source implementation, has undergone a formal semantic analysis, and is an open standard. By using XACML as the base, WSPL inherits the considerable design work, public scrutiny, and implementation experience that XACML has undergone. Most of the design decisions involved in WSPL were actually made as part of the development of XACML.

One major design decision inherited from XACML is the use of name-value pairs and standard primitive data types for attributes, rather than depending on XML schema extensions. Using attributes defined via XML schema extensions would make merging policies difficult or impossible except where the values of the attributes are exactly equal, since there can be no standard merge algorithms. Use of non-standard algorithms would mean that the policies could not be supported using a base standard policy engine. Note that XACML supports extensibility of data types and functions, although the rich built-in set minimizes the need for such extensions.

Logically, a WSPL Policy is an "or" of "and" predicates, so is in Disjunctive Normal Form. This form makes it feasible to support the policy negotiation feature of the WSPL language. XACML supports full trees of logical expressions, which allows more compact policies. The value of being able to merge policies outweighed the compactness factor, especially considering that most web services will probably use fairly simple policies in their service definitions. Services may use more complex policies internally, and here the full XACML syntax may be used.

The WSPL specification includes bindings to WSDL 1.1 [7], WSDL 1.2, and to SOAP 1.1 [8].

These bindings may need to change as other standards evolve. The core WSPL language would be valuable as part of a number of protocols and standards, and should be considered whenever a "policy" component is being defined.

6. Acknowledgments

Tim Moses (Entrust) conceived of WSPL as a subset of the XACML syntax, and has continued to be the driving force in producing the definition of WSPL. Danfeng Yao (Brown University) implemented WSPL and provided valuable feedback on the language. Seth Proctor (Sun Microsystems Laboratories) and other members of the OASIS XACML TC contributed to the definition of the syntax and semantics of the language.

7. References

[1] T. Moses, ed., "XACML profile for Web-services", http://www.oasis-open.org/committees/download.php/3661/draft-xacml-wspl-04.pdf, Working draft 04, 29 Sept 2003 (also known as "Web Services Policy Language (WSPL)").

[2] S. Godik, T. Moses, eds., "OASIS eXtensible Access Control Markup Language (XACML) Version 1.1", OASIS Committee Specification, http://www.oasis-open.org/committees/download.php/4103/cs-xacml-specification-1.1.doc, 24 July 2003.

[3] T. Moses, ed., "Web-services policy language use-cases and requirements", http://www.oasis-open.org/committees/download.php/1608/wd-xacml-wspl-use-cases-04.pdf

[4] "XML Schema Part 2: Datatypes", W3C Recommendation, http://www.w3.org/TR/xmlschema-2/, 2 May 2001.

[5] "XML Path Language (XPath), Version 1.0", W3C Recommendation, http://www.w3.org/TR/xpath, 16 November 1999.

[6] "XQuery 1.0 and XPath 2.0 Functions and Operators", W3C Working Draft 2002, http://www.w3.org/TR/2002/WD-xquery-operators-20020816, 16 August 2002.

[7] "WSDL Services Description Language (WSDL) 1.1", W3C Note, http://www.w3.org/TR/wsdl, 15 March 2001.

[8] "Simple Object Access Protocol (SOAP 1.1)", W3C Note, http://www.w3.org/TR/SOAP, 8 May 2000.

Analyzing Information Flow Control Policies in Requirements Engineering

Khaled Alghathbar
King Saud University
P. O. Box 85373, Riyadh 11691,
Saudi Arabia.
ksa@ieee.org

Duminda Wijesekera
CSIS & ISE, George Mason University,
Fairfax, VA 22030, USA.
dwijesek@gmu.edu

Abstract

Currently security features are implemented and validated during the last phases of the software development life cycle. This practice results in less secure software systems and higher cost of fixing defects software vulnerability. To achieve more secure systems, security features must be considered during the early phases of the software development process. This paper presents a high-level methodology that analyzes the information flow requirements and ensures the proper enforcement of information flow control policies. The methodology uses requirements specified in the Unified Modeling Language (UML) as its input and stratified logic programming language as the analysis language. The methodology improves security by detecting unsafe information flows before proceeding to latter stages of the life cycle.

1. Introduction

Today, most security requirements such as the information flow control policies are considered only after completing functional requirements. Consequently, less secure systems are developed because security aspects are not properly engineered through the software development life cycle. Considered a non-functional requirement (NFR) security related requirements are considered difficult to express, analyze and test [10, 6]. The consequences of ignoring NFR result in low quality and inconsistent software, unsatisfied stakeholder and more time and cost to re-engineer.

Consequently, the need to formally analyze and validate security requirements during earlier phases of the software life cycle have been proposed earlier [8, 4] to detect and remove design vulnerabilities before proceeding to other phases.

Information flow control policies restrict information flowing between objects. Thus, it prevents unauthorized flows. This paper proposes a high-level methodology to analyze proper enforcement of information flow control policies during the early phases of the software development life cycle so that flow violations can be detected before proceeding to later phases where the cost of fixing them are amplified. Our methodology uses the Unified Modeling Language (UML) [13] as the source of design specification and integration. Also, the methodology uses stratified logic programming language as the language of analysis because it facilitates automated reasoning. Proposed methodology is not restricted to a particular meta-policy, and is flexible to facilitate the enforcement of a particular policy to any subset of the specification.

The remainder of this paper is organized as follows. Section 2 shows information flow specifications embedded in UML's sequence diagrams. Section 3 describes the methodology. Section 4 describes the larger scope of the methodology. Section 5 describes related work and section 6 concludes the paper.

2. Specifying flow in the UML

The UML is the de-facto design language for large software projects. The UML uses multiple diagrams (views) to represent requirements and designs. In UML based software design methodologies, requirements are specified using *use cases* at the beginning of the life cycle. They are textual descriptions of usage scenarios between the system and its intended users [5].

Use cases are refined into interaction diagrams that specify greater detail, such as how objects in the use case interact with each other to achieve system objectives. Interaction diagrams are important for us because they present detailed flow information between different objects of the system. Consequently we take them to be the beginning point for information flow control policies.

Sequence diagrams are specific interaction diagrams that show such interactions as a sequence of messages exchanged between objects and ordered with respect to time. The sequence diagram shown in Figure 1 consists of four objects and two actors, where *Actor A* initiates the first flow as a request to read information from *Obj3* which then returns the requested information. Secondly, *Actor A* writes information to *Obj4* and forwards it to the *control* object. The *control* object triggers other flows to other objects. Therefore, information may flow directly from an actor to an object or indirectly flow from an actor to an object through other object(s).

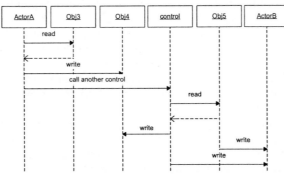

Figure 1: Sequence diagram

3. Methodology

Analyzing information flow control policies in the software systems requires two kinds of information:

1. Information flow requirements.

2. Information flow control policies.

Information flow requirements are embedded in general functional requirements. For example, in a functional requirement that allows a customer to place an order, there is an embedded information flow requirement from the customer to the billing department and another to the shipping department.

While information flow requirements are a kind of functional requirements, information flow control policies are not. The later are higher-level statements that must be enforced on functional specifications. Consequently, there can be one or more policies to be enforced on different parts of a design.

Therefore, identifying and separating each one of those information provides flexibility in analyzing the enforcement of the information flow control policies. We can now clearly know which policy to enforce on which information flow.

4. Steps of the proposed methodology

The methodology consists of four general steps, as shown in Figure 2. The first step starts by transforming information flows implied by each use case that is represented as a sequence diagram into predicates. Because sequence diagrams can be drawn in tools such as Rational Rose, this transformation can be automated. Because this step transforms direct flows, the second step enumerates all possible flows that traverse through several hops. For example, in Figure 1, if *Actor A* reads information from *obj3* then writes it to *obj4* then there will be a flow from *obj3* to *obj4*. Also, the second step enumerates all implicit flow that can be implied from the actor hierarchy. For example, if *Actor C* is a specialized actor of *Actor A*, then all flows that start or end from/in *Actor A* will be also start or end from/in *Actor C*. This step uses the predicates to specify information flows and it uses rules to derive transitive and implied information flows. The following predicates are examples of the predicates used in the first and second steps:

Flow(Initiator, Src_Obj, Dist_Obj,Value, Time)
for direct flow.

mayFlow(Initiator, Src_Obj, Dist_Obj,Value, Time)
for transitive flow.

Following is an example recursive rule that derives all possible transitive information flows.

$$mayFlow(X_a, X_{obj}, X'_{obj}, X_{att}, X_t) \leftarrow$$
$$Flow(X_a, X_{obj}, X'_{obj}, X_{att}, X_t)$$
$$mayFlow(X_a, X_{obj}, X'_{obj}, X_{att}, X_t) \leftarrow$$
$$Flow(X_a, X_{obj}, X_{BTWobj}, X_{att}, X_t)$$
$$mayFlow(X_a, X_{BTWobj}, X'_{obj}, X_{att}, X'_t),$$
$$X_t < X'_t$$

Previous steps specify information flow requirements. The 3rd step specifies information flow policies in the form of Horn clauses. Examples of policies are: (1) ensuring particular actor must not send information to another particular actor, (2) specific information must not flow from one entity to another. An example of policy written in rules is:

$$unsafeFlow(X_a, X_{obj1}, X_{obj2}, X_{att}) \leftarrow$$
$$Flow(X_a, X_{obj1}, X_{obj2}, X_{att}, X_t),$$
$$\neg dominates(X_{obj1}, X_{obj2})$$

The previous rule detects any information flowing between two objects where the recipient does not have higher or equal security label as sender.

After building the bases of requirements and policies, the last step is to analyze the information requirements and detects any violation of any specific policy. The process starts by taking the specified policies that are specified in rules and execute those rules on all existing information flow requirements that are specified in predicates. The outcome of this step is classifying each flow to either safe or unsafe flow.

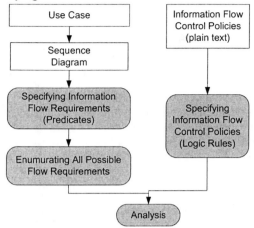

Figure 2: Steps of the Proposed Method

5. The larger scope

This section describes the larger scope and applicability of the methodology. As shown in Figure 3, the first step is to transform the geometric information in UML views to a set of basic predicates of information flow rules written as Horn clauses.

Beside the basic predicates used to capture the geometric information given in the UML sequence diagrams, other Horn clauses constitute the policies that are applicable at the early stages of the software design cycle. Thus, this division of predicate layers shows the clear separation of the basic geometry of the design from policy.

This separation of policy from the application has many consequences. The first is that it facilitates applying any policy to any design. As shown in Figure 3, policies B and C can be separately applied to the sequence diagram of use case A. Similarly, as shown, policies A and C can be separately applied to the sequence diagram of use case B. This shows that more than one policy applies to one design diagram and that one policy applies to more than one diagram.

Secondly, the same process can be used to check the consistency of two design diagrams with respect to a given security policy. That is, if two design diagrams are compliant with a given policy, then as far as that policy is concerned, they are indistinguishable. We propose to develop this concept further in designing *a notion of policy based equivalence* of design diagrams in UML. Thirdly, if UML policies can be separated from designs as shown here, then a policy composition framework for UML policy compositions along the lines of [14] can be developed. Lastly, by capturing more rules related to geometries of sequence diagrams, one may be able to capture deficiencies in the diagrams. If successful, this may lead to a rule based reverse engineering framework for UML diagrams.

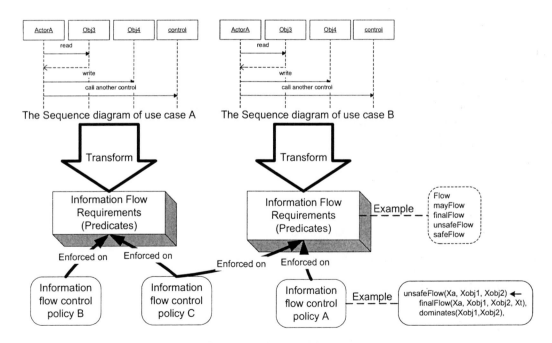

Figure 3 FlowUML's scope

6. Related work

Although information flow has a rich publication history, most papers concentrate on designing newer and richer flow control models such as [12, 3] that do not address flow policies and verifications techniques that go hand in glove with software design life cycle models.

At the other end, research such as Myers [9] focus on analyzing the information flow during the implementation phase while we propose is to be used during the requirements, design and analysis phases of the software development life cycle.

In the area of logic-based checking of policy violations during the requirement engineering, Alghathbar et al. [1] developed AuthUML, a logic program based framework for that analyzing access control requirements during the requirements engineering phase to ensure consistency, completeness and conflict-freedom. AuthUML approach is similar to this paper approach. However, AuthUML only focuses on the access control policies.

7. Conclusions

The main objective of this paper is to improve the security of software systems. We propose to do so by presenting a methodology to analyzes information flow requirements and ensures its compliance with specified information flow control polices. This analysis is to be applied at the early phases of the software development process.

Reference

[1] K. Alghathbar, D. Wijesekera. "authUML: A Three-phased framework to analyze access control specifications in Use Cases". In proc. of the Workshop on Formal Methods in Security Engineering, Washington, DC. Oct. 2003.

[2] D. Bell and L. LaPadula. "Secure computer system: United exposition and Multics interpretation". Technical Report, , MITRE Corp.. Bedford, MA, 1975.

[3] E. Bertino and V. Atluri. "The specification and enforcement of authorization constraints in workflow management". ACM transactions on Information Systems Security, February 1999.

[4] B. Boehm. *Software engineering economics*. Englewood Cliffs, NJ: Prentice-Hall. (1981)

[5] G. Booch, J. Rumbaugh, and I. Jacobson. *The Unified Modeling Language User Guide*. Addison-Wesley, MA, 99.

[6] L. Chung, B. Nixon, E. Yu, J. Mylopoulos. *Non-Functional Requirements in Software Engineering*. Kluwer Academic Publishers (2000).

[7] D. D. Clark, D. R. Wilson. "A Comparison of Commercial and Military Computer Security Policies". In the proc. IEEE Symposium on Security and Privacy. 1987.

[8] P. T. Devanbu and S. Stubblebine. "Software engineering for security:A roadmap". The Future of Software Engineering. ACM Press, 2000.

[9] A. Myers. "JFlow: Practical mostly-static information flow control". In Proc. 26th ACM Symp. on Principles of Programming Languages, San Antonio, TX, Jan. 1999.

[10] B. Nuseibeh and S. Easterbrook. "Requirements engineering: A roadmap". In A. Finkelstein, editor, The Future of Software Engineering. ACM Press, 2000.

[11] Rational Rose. http://www.rational.com.

[12] P. Samarati, E. Bertino, A. Ciampichetti, and S. Jajodia. "Information flow control in object-oriented systems. IEEE Transactions on Knowledge and Data Engineering", July-Aug. 1997.

[13] The Unified Modeling Language version 1.5. http://www.omg.org/uml/. Accessed in September 2003.

[14] D. Wijesekera, S. Jajodia, "Policy Algebras for Access Control - The predicate Case". In the Proc. 8th ACM Conference on Computer and Communications Security, Washington, DC, November 17-22, 2002.

[15] J. Rushby. "Security Requirements Specifications: How and What?" In the proc. of Symposium on Requirements Engineering for Information Security. Indianapolis, IN. March, 2001.

Towards a Multi-dimensional Characterization of Dissemination Control

Roshan K. Thomas
McAfee Research, Network Associates, Inc.
rthomas@nai.com

Ravi Sandhu
George Mason University and NSD Security
sandhu@gmu.edu

Abstract

Dissemination control (DCON) is emerging as one of the most important and challenging goals for information security. DCON is concerned with controlling information and digital objects even after they have been delivered to a legitimate recipient. The need for DCON arises in many different domains ranging from the dissemination of digital music and movies, eBooks, business proprietary and sensitive electronic documents as well as the propagation of mailing lists in relation to direct marketing. Our goal in this short paper is to present some of the multidimensional technical issues that need to be modeled and understood so as to provide a comprehensive set of DCON capabilities. It represents a first but necessary step in our ongoing work in formulating a family of DCON models.

1. Introduction

Dissemination control (DCON) is among the most challenging goals for information security. DCON seeks to control information and digital objects even after they have been delivered to a legitimate recipient. Control encompasses the usage of the digital object by the recipient (e.g., permission to view a document on a trusted viewer) as well as further dissemination (e.g., permission to distribute a limited number of copies of the document to colleagues but with no further dissemination allowed).

DCON arises in many different forms. A prominent example in recent years is the area of Digital Rights Management (DRM). DRM is concerned with distribution of copyrighted digital content for entertainment, such as music or movies, while ensuring that the revenue stream from this content remains protected. The high stakes in the DRM arena have led to a number of technology, legal and social initiatives that are transforming the entertainment industry. This is reflected in MIT's Technology Review rating of DRM as one of the top 10 emerging technologies that will change the world [4]. Requirements similar to DRM arise in other arenas such as distribution of scientific literature in digital libraries and distribution of high-cost analyst reports. Further, in business proprietary and national security arenas, DCON on sensitive information become

mission critical. Intellectual property has been an issue for software of all kinds, and so-called copy protection has been practiced for decades. Other instances of DCON include the need to preserve the privacy of medical information as it is disseminated as well as controls on the exchange of email lists to limit the proliferation of unsolicited email (spam).

The goal of dissemination control is inherently different from the classic security objectives of confidentiality, integrity and availability. Given the diverse contexts mentioned above it is not surprising that the treatment of dissemination control has been strongly driven by the specific context. Our goal in this short paper is to present some of the multidimensional technical issues that need to be modeled and understood so as to provide a comprehensive set of DCON capabilities. It represents a first but necessary step in our ongoing work in formulating a family of DCON models.

Dissemination control has been discussed in the formal literature under the term originator control [1, 3, 5]. However the focus has been rather narrow and the emphasis has been on mechanisms rather than policies. The literature on DRM is also focused on specific technical mechanisms such as watermarking. In our perspective DCON is a vast and policy-rich area. To develop appropriate models we need to understand the components of the dissemination problem and extract common elements and principles. Similar efforts have been successful in areas such as role-based access control [2, 8] and more recently in usage control [9]. Not surprisingly, the dissemination control arena turns out to be much richer than role-based access control.

2. High-level decomposition of DCON

Figure 1 shows a high-level decomposition of the DCON space. We distinguish the space along two axes. The vertical axis is related to the value of content being disseminated. This could be driven by the sensitivity and proprietary nature of the contents such as for intelligence reports, medical records, intellectual property etc. Content dissemination could also be driven by revenue generation policies such as in the case of digital entertainment objects like music and video files. There are some cases where the preservation of the sensitivity of contents as well as the driving of content-based revenue are both important.

Content type and value	Strength of Enforcement		
	Weak	Medium	Strong
Sensitive and proprietary	Password-protected documents	Software-based client controls for documents	Hardware based trusted viewers, displays and inputs
Revenue driven	IEEE, ACM digital libraries protected by server access controls	DRM-enabled media players such as for digital music and eBooks	Dongle-based copy protection, hardware based trusted viewers, displays and inputs
Sensitive and revenue	Analyst and business reports protected by server access controls	Software-based client controls for documents	Hardware based trusted viewers, displays and inputs

Figure 1. High-level decomposition of DCON

The other axis is characterized by strength of enforcement. For the purpose of this paper we consider three categories of strength – weak, medium and strong. Weak enforcement relies on server-side controls only (e.g., IEEE/ACM digital libraries) or weak document controls such as password-based protection of content. These schemes expose unprotected content on the client and the only real recourse in the presence of illegal dissemination is legal enforcement. Medium level enforcement includes DRM[1] schemes on current client-side platforms and digital players such as Windows Media Player and Apple's iPoD platforms. Strong enforcement utilizes trusted hardware to enforce DCON policies and is thus considerably more tamper-resistant and non-bypassable when compared to software based controls. Several trustworthy platform initiatives such as TCPA, NGSCB etc. are moving in this direction [10, 11]. Commercial products in this arena are still to emerge.

3. Technical dimensions to DCON

DCON applications demand a wide range of functionality which can be characterized along the multiple technical dimensions shown in Figure 2. The leftmost column shows various functional aspects and requirements that need to be considered when building DCON models (derived from analyzing multiple applications that use some form of DCON). For each functional area, the table indicates a range of simple to complex functionality, as well as strength of enforcement characterized as weak or strong.

Legally enforceable versus system enforced rights. One of the first dimensions that came to light in our analysis is the degree of reliance on legal versus system enforced rights. In some domains such as the ACM and

IEEE digital libraries, there is very little system enforcement of DCON using DRM and other security technologies. Thus in the presence of any abuse of the contents of these libraries, legal recourse is the only option available to the publishers. Now in the area of payment-based digital music, such as that provided by iTunes, some degree of system enforcement is present. An attempt to play a purchased song on a fourth machine would result in the user being asked to disable one of the three previously authorized machines (maximum number allowed is three).

Dissemination chains and flexibility. The simplest form of dissemination involves point-to-point single steps, i.e. the disseminator, such as a server A, disseminates an object to a recipient B, but B is not allowed to disseminate the object any further. A more flexible scheme would allow multi-step and multipoint disseminations. Peer-to-peer sharing (such as in the original Napster model for music dissemination) involved multi-step disseminations where an object released from a server would rapidly be re-disseminated by multiple peers. Incidentally, the rapid spread of spam (junk email) is now attributed to efficient peer-to-peer dissemination by exploited machines.

Object types supported. From the standpoint of object models, dissemination of objects such as music, involve read-only objects. However, in many domains, support is needed for modifiable, multi-version, and composite objects. For example, digital libraries (such as that of the ACM/IEEE) distinguish definitive versions from preprints. In the intelligence community, several versions of an intelligence report may be circulated with some versions having undergone sanitizations. Depending on the sensitivity of the contents, each version may be handled differently for the purpose of dissemination.

---

[1] We use DRM in the sense usually found in the trade press to mean the mechanisms that control entertainment content, and view it as a subset and enabling technology for the broader problem of DCON.

	Functionality		Strength of enforcement	
	Simple	**Complex**	**Weak/Medium**	**Strong**
Legally enforceable versus system enforced rights.			Reliance on legal enforcement; Limited system enforced controls.	Strong system-enforceable rights, revocable rights.
Dissemination chains and flexibility.	Limited to one-step disseminations.	Flexible, multi-step, and multi-point.	Mostly legal enforcement;	System enforceable controls.
Object types supported.	Simple, read-only and single-version objects.	Support for complex, multi-version objects. Support for object sensitivity/confidentiality.	Reliance on legally enforceable rights.	System supported and enforceable rights and sanitization on multiple versions.
Persistence and modifiability of rights and licenses.	Immutable, persistent and viral on all disseminated copies.	Not viral and modifiable by recipient.	Reliance on legally enforceable rights.	System enforceable.
Online versus offline access and persistent client-side copies	No offline access and no client-side copies.	Allows offline access to client-side copies.	Few unprotected copies are tolerated.	No unprotected copies are tolerated.
Usage controls	Control of basic dissemination.	Flexible, rule-based usage controls on instances.	Some usage abuse allowed.	No potential for usage abuse.
Preservation of attribution.	Recipient has legal obligation to give attribution to disseminator.	System-enabled preservation and trace-back of the attribution chain back to original disseminator.	Attribution can only be legally enforced.	Attribution is system enforced.
Revocation	Simple explicit revocations.	Complex policy-based revocation.	No timeliness guarantees.	Guaranteed to take immediate effect.
Support for derived and value-added objects.	Not supported.	Supported.	Reliance on legally enforceable rights.	System enforceable rights for derived and valued-added objects.
Integrity protection for disseminated objects.	Out of band or non-crypto based validation.	Cryptographic schemes for integrity validation.	Off-line validation.	High-assurance cryptographic validation.
Audit	Audit support for basic dissemination operations.	Additional support for the audit of instance usage.	Offline audit analysis.	Real-time audit analysis and alerts.
Payment	Simple payment schemes (if any).	Multiple pricing models and payment schemes including resale.	Tolerance of some revenue loss.	No revenue loss; Objective is to maximize revenue.

Figure 2. Characterizing the technical dimensions of DCON by functionality and strength of enforcement

Persistence and modifiability of rights. Rights may have to persist along the dissemination chain, as in some models of open software licensing, or they could be modified by the recipient.

Online versus offline access and persistent client-side copies. In certain applications, digital objects may be disseminated but clients may not be allowed to make client-side copies. For example, in satellite-based radio services, music is streamed and never stored. In many intelligence community systems, users are allowed to download and view documents but not allowed to save or print. The DCON problem is inherently more complex when client-side copies can be retained.

Usage controls. In the simplest case, usage controls prevent redissemination but do not limit the legitimate recipients in frequency or duration of usage. More complex usage controls can enforce such limits on a per instance and per recipient basis.

Preservation of attribution. In the simplest case, preservation of attribution (including copyright notices) during redissemination can only be done through procedural and legal controls. More complex functionality would involve system-enabled preservation and trace-back of the attribution chain back to the original disseminator. This is an important requirement in application domains such as that for the intelligence community.

Revocation. The ability to revoke rights on previously disseminated objects is an important one, but this is often difficult to enforce on client-side copies. The simplest case would be explicit revocations by the disseminator, but more complex rule-based schemes based on monitoring ongoing conditions are possible.

Support for derived and value-added objects. Objects may be derived from or bundled with disseminated objects. The simple cases of DCON would not support this functionality.

Other dimensions of DCON include integrity protection, audit and payment and these can be supported to varying degrees as indicated in the table. It is interesting to note that most revenue-driven services such as retailing of digital music support only a single pricing model. Also, the current pricing and DCON models for digital music don't support the resale of music.

4. Summary and conclusions

We have briefly presented a high level decomposition of the DCON space and presented some detailed technical dimensions that exhibit the diversity of requirements that need to be considered in the design of DCON models and schemes. The relevance, priority and level of sophistication of these dimensions vary considerably from one application area to another. Nevertheless, an elaboration and understanding of these individual dimensions and associated dependencies is important to having a unified approach to DCON.

The work presented here is an initial step towards the formulation of a family of DCON models. The richness of the DCON space and associated policies leads us to believe that this effort will inevitably be more complicated than past efforts at building families of models in areas such as role-based, discretionary and lattice-based access controls.

Acknowledgement
This work was supported by the Advanced Research and Development Activity (ARDA).

5. References
[1] Abrams, Marshall, et al., "Generalized Framework for Access Control: Towards Prototyping the ORGCON Policy." Proceedings of the 14th National Computer Security Conference, 1991, pages 257-266.

[2] David F. Ferraiolo, Ravi Sandhu, Serban Gavrila, D. Richard Kuhn and Ramaswamy Chandramouli. "Proposed NIST Standard for Role-Based Access Control." ACM Transactions on Information and System Security, Volume 4, Number 3, August 2001, pages 224-274.

[3] Graubart, Richard., "On the Need for a Third Form of Access Control." Proceedings of the 12th National Computing Security Conference, 1989 pages. 296-303.

[4] MIT Technology Review Editors. "Ten Emerging Technologies that will Change the World." MIT Technology Review, Jan/Feb 2001.

[5] McCollum, C.J., Messing, J.R. and Notargiacomo, L. "Beyond the pale of MAC and DAC-defining new forms of access control." Proceedings of IEEE Symposium on Security and Privacy, May 1990, pages 190-200.

[6] Jaehong Park, Ravi Sandhu and James Schifalacqua, "Security Architectures for Controlled Digital Information Dissemination." Proc. 16th Annual Computer Security Applications Conference, New Orleans, Louisiana, December 11-15, 2000, pages 224-233.

[7] Jaehong Park and Ravi Sandhu, "Originator Control in Usage Control." Proc. 3rd IEEE International Workshop on Policies for Distributed Systems and Networks, Monterey, California, June 5-7, 2002, pages 60-66.

[8] Ravi Sandhu, Edward Coyne, Hal Feinstein and Charles Youman, "Role-Based Access Control Models." IEEE Computer, Volume 29, Number 2, February 1996, pages 38-47.

[9] Ravi Sandhu and Jaehong Park, "Usage Control: A Vision for Next Generation Access Control." Proc. Mathematical Methods, Models and Architectures for Computer Networks Security, Saint Petersburg, Russia, September 21-23, 2003, Lecture Notes in Computer Science.

[10] The Next-Generation Secure Computing Base: An Overviewhttp://www.microsoft.com/resources/ngscb/ngscb_ove rview.mspx

[11] The Trusted Computing Group TPM Specification, https://www.trustedcomputinggroup.org/home

Protocol Decode Based Stateful Firewall Policy Definition Language

Pankaj N. Parmar   Priya Rajagopal   Ravi Sahita

Intel Corporation

Abstract

The policies for thwarting attacks on systems vary greatly in complexity, ranging from simple static firewall rules to complex stateful protocol state machine analysis. As intrusion detection systems are getting integrated into firewall solutions, there is a need for a language that can define both firewall policies and system intrusion behavior and exhibit inter-operable traits. This paper presents an XML based, self-documenting State-Aware Firewall Language (SAFire) that is designed to express the various kinds of firewall and intrusion behavior.

1. Introduction

The simplest type of firewalls includes simple stateless packet-based filters wherein a set of static rules is applied to every packet in isolation. The second type includes simple stateful firewalls that perform simple protocol decode analysis wherein they detect violations of network and transport layer protocol behavior. The third category of firewalls includes Application Level Gateways and proxies that analyze the more complex application-level protocol behavior. To reduce the processing overhead, these firewalls may be optimized to do selective and intelligent processing based on flow state information and control payload. Increasingly, Intrusion Detection Systems (IDS) are becoming an integral supplement to firewalls by providing comprehensive attack coverage. Hence, the firewall rule definition language must be capable of expressing the varying complexity associated with rules as well as system intrusion.

2. Existing Languages

In this section, we briefly discuss existing policy languages and how SAFire differs from them. One such language defined in academia is Ponder [8]. Ponder supports access control policies with meta constructs like roles and relationships. Ponder allows assigning policies to organization roles and their relationships. Via this abstraction, Ponder policies can map onto access control mechanisms for firewalls, software and other infrastructure elements. Compared to SAFire, Ponder is at a higher abstraction level for security policies. SAFire is the abstraction of firewall/IDS policies within a system, whereas Ponder is used for security policies across an organization. Another security policy language is the Security Policy Specification Language (SPSL) [9]. SPSL was designed to express policies for packet filters, security domains, and the entities that manage policies with focus on IP Security (IPSec). SAFire supports SPSL style filtering rules and extends it for autonomic configuration features. Autonomic configuration means the system itself creates dynamic filters when it notices configured events occurring. There are commercial firewall/IDS languages like Checkpoint's INSPECT* [5], Cisco PIX* configuration [4] and NFR's N-CODE* [7] that are used for defining firewall policies. One major drawback of these languages is that they use proprietary formats for expressing security rules, thereby making integration into other firewall implementations tedious. SAFire's XML based specification facilitates interoperability with other firewall vendors, for example, by the use of open standards like the Extensible Stylesheet Language Transformations (XSLT). XML based specification also allows administrators/developers to leverage well tested authoring, validation [12] and translation tools/APIs that make automation to express firewall policies across devices promising. An enterprise network may have firewalls with varying capabilities. In order to express the policies for these different firewalls using SAFire, the firewall vendors will have to indicate the SAFire features that map to their capabilities.

3. Overview

SAFire is a text-based, scriptable, self-documenting language designed to express protocol decode rules for firewalls. The language is specified as XML schema to define the inter-dependent set of filters and actions for protocol decode analysis. SAFire scripts or derivatives can be used to configure a firewall via a local or remote secure interface. The scripts can then be interpreted by a configuration component, which sets up the low-level sub-components of the firewall. One of SAFire's unique capabilities is that it supports autonomic configuration based on packet events. SAFire employs extensive use of string manipulation functions for application layer protocol processing and uses an abstract interface for calling user-defined functions. By design, SAFire allows for algorithmic translation to other firewall languages. SAFire retains features from existing languages such as minimal support for loops, implicit memory allocation, macros and functions with no recursion. Standard XML APIs allows integration of SAFire into a security framework like Checkpoint's OPSEC [11] via the Suspicious Activity Monitoring (SAM) or Content Vectoring Protocol (CVP) APIs. The goal of this language is to be able to express protocol decode rules to control overall protocol behavior. Section 3.1 enumerates the requirements of the language to achieve this goal.

3.1. SAFire requirements

The grammar has the following requirements:
R.1. Packet data extraction and filtering
R.2. Packet data, variables, constants declaration
R.3. Context-aware flow state table management
R.4. Multiple non-conflicting actions lists
R.5. Outsourcing policy decisions for specific flows
R.6. Express application layer information within rules
R.7. Definition of templates/macros for reuse
R.8. Math, binary, relational and logical operations
R.9. Packet variables like direction, interface, and host
R.10. String data manipulation
R.11. Dynamic rule creation /enabling /disabling
R.12. Implicit memory management
R.13. Support for integer data types of widths 8-64 bits

4. SAFire language details

This section describes SAFire capabilities and cross-references these with the requirements. It describes the functionality of the language elements.

4.1. SAFire functional elements

SAFire rules are built using XML schema elements that fall into the following functional categories:

4.1.1. Data extraction capability. Allows extraction of fixed or variable sized data from packet header or payload that can be saved for later use. The extracted data can be masked before extraction. Fulfills R.1.

4.1.2. String manipulation capability. Provides a rich set of string operation functions with the ability to store extracted strings for later use. Fulfills R.10.

4.1.3. Math operations. Allows basic math functions on integers of sizes 8-64 bits. The results can be stored in symbols for later use. Fulfill R.8.

4.1.4. Filter management. Allows dynamic creation, removal and modification of n-tuple bi-directional filters. Fulfills R.11.

4.1.5. State table management. Here, we introduce our concept of a General Protocol State Machine or GPSM. A PSM is a Deterministic Finite Automaton (DFA), which has a start state, multiple intermediate states, and one or more terminating states. The following seven states have been defined in SAFire to capture protocol state transitions: Suinit (Un-initialized), Sinit (Initialized), Scest (Connection Established), Sde (Data Exchange), Sctd (Connection Termination), Sterm (Termination), and Sabort (Abort). Protocol conditions or events cause the PSM to transition from one state to another. This capability in SAFire exposes the functionality to compute unique flow identifiers and based on these identifiers, the ability to create, delete, get or set state and context associated with a flow. Fulfills R.3 and R.12.

4.1.6. Pattern table management. Exposes intrinsics to create and populate a pattern table, and then search for these patterns in a given packet. Fulfills R.6.

4.1.7. Packet-related utilities. Exposes actions to be performed on packets such as allow, deny, copy, redirect or mark. Fulfills R.4 and R.5.

SAFire supports other actions like user-defined functions, generation of alerts, outsourcing or hold/resume of a flow, updating flow context, installation/removal of filters based on past events. The functional elements described above are arranged under *policyrule* and *policyaction* complex types. Autonomic configuration is achieved by recursively including the *policyrule* complex type as one of the attributes of *policyaction*. Such rules can be used for hierarchical protocol decode scripts. Requirements R.2, R.7, R.9 and R.13 are addressed with support for a declaration section for constants, variables and macros.

4.2 Creating SAFire scripts

This section describes the procedure to create SAFire scripts for analyzing protocol behavior. Firstly, the protocol is expressed in terms of a Deterministic Finite Automata (DFA) that is then appropriately mapped to the seven states described in section 4.1.5. An example of a protocol state machine for tracking active FTP sessions is shown in Figure 4.2.1 below.

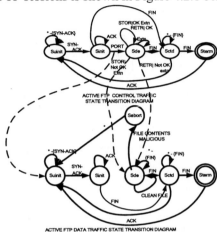

Figure 4.2.1. AFTP State Transition Diagram

Although the entire AFTP state machine as described in RFC 959 [2] can be described in SAFire, we present here only the subset of the state machine that pertains to file transfer tracking. Once that is done, all the transitions from the normalized DFA are extracted, noting the source state, destination state, the event that caused the transition, and any events caused due to the transition. Transition rules are logically grouped and are mapped to SAFire as follows - The transition causing events map to SAFire rules with a check for the source state and the events caused due to the transition map to SAFire action elements, with the state set to the destination state in the action. The resultant set of SAFire rules are then translated (using XSLT) to the firewall specific format.

For example, from Figure 4.2.1, consider the state transition that takes the control flow from Suinit to Sinit upon detection of a TCP packet with SYN - ACK flags set. The start state corresponding to the transition is Suinit, the event causing transition is the detection of SYN-ACK flags set in the TCP packet header and the destination state is Sinit. The corresponding SAFire rule creates a unique flow identifier (hash) in the setup portion of the rule. To compute this identifier, pattern

extraction templates are used to extract the 5-tuple data from all TCP packets. The rule's condition elements are then executed. These use other TCP pattern templates (or operations) to check if the TCP ACK and SYN flags are set. If they are, the state associated with the flow in the TCP flow table is updated to Sinit state (by default, all flows are in Suinit state). Section 4.3 gives a more detailed example.

4.3. SAFire examples

SAFire can be used to define a reusable set of scripts for common protocol definitions like TCP/IP. Each script has a name and a count of the rules described in the script. Typically, a script begins with the definitions of constants such as standard protocol values, for example, TCP 6, FTP port 21 and so on. This section of the script also defines pattern templates to be used in the script, for example pattern extraction template for IPv4 source and destination addresses etc. This is followed by the definition of the variables used in the script, for example, for the dynamic FTP port opened, a 16 bit unsigned integer variable is declared. Also associated with the variable is the format of the type as seen in the packet, namely, binary, ASCII, etc., and whether the data is expected in network byte order. The core part of the script is the set of SAFire statements explained in more detail below.

This sample SAFire FTP script:
- Captures outgoing AFTP PORT command packets
- Extracts the data port from the PORT command
- Creates a transient filter using the data port

To start with, the pattern extraction templates are used to extract the 5-tuple data from a flow and the flow identifier is computed. This part of the script is executed for all packets. The script then checks if the packet is an outgoing FTP control packet (i.e. is the destination port 21) with the ASCII data "PORT" at the expected offset, and if it is, it checks if the flow in the Sinit and Sde states. If the conditions are satisfied, the action section of the script defines the treatment to be given to the flow. The base action is to allow this packet, but other associated actions are to extract the port from the ASCII PORT command using the tokenizer action. ASCII data extracted also has to be operated upon using shift operations to store the port value in a variable. Based on the extracted and computed data, new flow states are created for the *expected* data flow and reverse traffic flow. This is also used to create a dynamic filter for these flows. When data traffic starts, the dynamic rules installed will be matched.

Further analysis can be performed on the data traffic as required. The script can finally be programmed to intercept the teardown of the control session and remove the dynamic rules installed for the data session.

5. Prototype Protocol Analysis Engine

This section provides implementation details of our prototype Protocol Analysis Engine (PAE) that executed SAFire firewall scripts. The PAE was implemented on Windows* XP as a Network Driver Interface Specification (NDIS) [14] intermediate driver. The SAFire script was compiled using Apache Xerces-C++ SAX libraries [10] [13] that generated the binary output that was interpreted and executed by the PAE. The PAE works on the principle of following the Protocol State Machine (PSM) of any protocol (FTP, HTTP, etc.), detecting flows that deviate from the defined protocol behavior and taking appropriate actions. Using SAFire, the PSM was expressed as a collection of rules that dictated state transitions and defined corresponding actions. The SAFire parser parsed the SAFire rules and passed it to the PAE via *ioctl()* calls. The PAE was comprised of a packet header based classifier and the filter database. The filter database stored static and transient filters. Static filters were applied to aggregate flows and remained in the filter database until explicitly removed. Transient filters were added and deleted by the PAE core to track per-flow state changes. A flow state table kept track of state changes and was PAE managed.

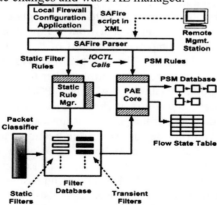

Figure 5.1. PAE architecture

6. Conclusion

With the heterogeneity in firewall capabilities and intrusion detection systems being increasingly integrated into firewall solutions, there is undoubtedly a need for a translatable, powerful language that can effectively express complex firewall behavior. In this paper we have identified the requirements of such a language and proposed a policy definition language, SAFire based on the requirements. The language is XML based, which enables the use of existing authoring and validation tools to write policies and to deploy them using web-based interfaces. A Birds-of-a-feather session was held at the 55th IETF meeting to discuss standards for distributed end-point firewall control. We feel SAFire is a good starting point for this effort.

7. References

[1] William R. Cheswick, Steven Bellovin, and Aviel Rubin, *Firewalls and Internet Security: Repelling the Wily Hacker,* Addison-Wesley, Second Edition.

[2] J.K.Reynolds, J.Postel, "File Transfer Protocol", RFC 959, STD 9, Internet Engineering Task Force, Nov 1998.

[3] "The Science of Intrusion Detection Systems Attack Identification, whitepaper", Cisco Sys, Inc.

[4] *Cisco Secure PIX* Firewall Command References,* Cisco Systems.

[5] *Check Point Reference Manual,* Check Point Software Technologies Ltd.

[6] *PAX Pattern Description Language Reference Manual,* Integrated Device Technology Inc.

[7] *NFR Network Intrusion Detection System* N-Code Guide,* NFR Security Inc.

[8] N. Damianou, N. Dulay, E. Lupu, M Sloman, "The Ponder Specification Language", Workshop on Policies for Distributed Systems and Networks, Policy2001.

[9] M. Condell, C. Lynn, J. Zao , "Security Policy Specification Language", Internet Engineering Task Force, October1998.

[10] *Xerces C++ Version 2.2.0,* The Apache XML Project.

[11] *Open Platform for Security (OPSEC)*, Checkpoint Software Technologies Ltd.

[12] *XmlSpy - XML Development Environment,* Altova Inc.

[13] *Simple API for XML,* Sourceforge Project SAX.

[14] *Network Driver Interface Specification*, Microsoft Windows XP* Driver Development Kit.

Session 8 (Short Papers):
Quality of Service

Implementation of the CIM Policy Model Using PONDER

Andrea Westerinen and Julie Schott
Cisco Systems
andreaw@cisco.com, jschott@cisco.com

Abstract

New work on the Distributed Management Task Force's CIM Policy Model emphasizes the definition of general event-condition-action semantics. These semantics are conveyed in an abstracted fashion, independent of any policy language or implementation. This approach allows vendor flexibility in designing policy writing tools and in choosing policy languages and implementations. Also, it allows products to communicate their policy rules in an interoperable and semantically rich manner. This short paper overviews the CIM Policy Model's approach and how it maps, via an example, onto the PONDER policy language, developed at Imperial College, London.

1. Introduction

The Common Information Model from the Distributed Management Task Force [1] is a structural model and semi-formal ontology describing the management of computing and networking environments, including policy. New work on the CIM Policy Model emphasizes the definition of general event-condition-action semantics. These semantics are conveyed using an object-oriented class hierarchy, as is the entire CIM Schema.

The CIM Policy Model is designed to be declarative, and independent of any policy language or implementation. Over the last several years, there has been much debate in the DMTF Policy Working Group over standardizing on a policy language. A vendor-independent solution was found by using CIM's query language as the mechanism for expressing the variables in a policy rule. This approach allows vendor flexibility in implementations by not choosing a policy language outright, and maps easily onto the CIM eventing and notification infrastructure which employs the query language to specify notification "filters".

This short paper overviews the CIM Policy Model, and compares and contrasts it to a particular policy language, PONDER developed at Imperial College, London [2]. The paper is divided into six sections. Sections 2 and 3 overview the CIM Policy Model and the PONDER language, respectively. Section 4 outlines an example that is used to compare the two approaches, while Section 5 is that comparison. Lastly, Section 6 presents conclusions.

2. Overview of the CIM Policy Model

In the CIM V2.8 release [3], policy is defined by instances (and groupings of instances) of the PolicyRule class. Each PolicyRule aggregates PolicyConditions and PolicyActions. This can be seen in Figure 1.

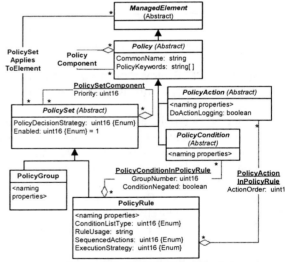

Figure 1. CIM Policy Model

Conditions are grouped into conjunctive or disjunctive sets for evaluation. The PolicyRule's ConditionListType property defines the grouping, while the GroupNumber property on the aggregation of a PolicyCondition into a rule specifies the particular group to which the condition belongs. Note that there is a similar property on the aggregation of PolicyActions into a PolicyRule. Actions can be sequenced, using the ActionOrder property on the aggregation.

Extensions to the model in CIM V2.9 define generic event/condition and method/action classes, subclassing from the existing object hierarchy [4]. Before CIM V2.9, all condition/action subclasses were domain-specific – for example, defining subclasses for IPsec Policy. Although domain-specific subclassing will continue, the goal of this new work is to limit the need for it, and to allow flexibility in the policy rules that can be defined.

The new classes in CIM V2.9 are QueryCondition and MethodAction, and are shown in Figure 2. They are very similar in that they both employ CIM queries to define the variables of the policy. (For specific examples, refer to Section 5.1.) Additionally, the model allows a policy system to distinguish "rule triggering" events from other conditions that should be evaluated in order to determine if a policy's action(s) should fire. "Rule triggering" events are denoted by setting a QueryCondition's Trigger property to TRUE.

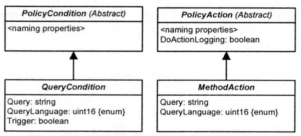

Figure 2. CIM Policy Model Addressing General Events, Conditions and Actions

Since policy conditions supply necessary contextual information, the results of specific QueryConditions and MethodActions may be used by other conditions and actions of a rule. The mechanism whereby query results are referenced is via transient (non-persisted) instances of the class, QueryResult. Instances of QueryResult are produced by the execution of a particular query. They are transient since they only exist within a CIM notification (an instance of CIM_Indication) or within the context of the execution of a PolicyRule. The properties of an instance of QueryResult are those attributes or other information (such as COUNT data) that are returned in the SELECT clause of a query.

Specific policy-related subclasses of QueryResult have been defined – QueryConditionResult and

MethodActionResult. In addition to the attributes and information requested by a SELECT clause, these subclasses also carry the naming information of the respective QueryCondition or MethodAction instance, whose execution resulted in the generation of the QueryResult.

Support for domain-specific rules, conditions and actions, as well as general policy definitions, permits great flexibility. Policies written against the general CIM Schema are comprehensible without additional model definition, but the flexibility to support domain-specific policy subclasses still exists.

3. Overview of PONDER

PONDER separates policy rules into three basic categories – authorization, delegation and obligation rules, both positive and negative. (Note that the negative aspect of obligation rules is defined as "refrain.") The basic rule structure is shown in the upper section of Figure 3. Below that is a specific rule taken from the PONDER overview document [5].

```
inst oblig <rule name> {
on <event identifier> ;
subject   <subject  name>   =   <domain  name  or
expression> ;
target <target name> = <domain name or expression> ;
do <one or more actions> ;
}


inst oblig loginFailure {
on 3*loginfail(userid) ;
subject s = /NRegion/SecAdmin ;
target <userT> t = /NRegion/users ^ {userid} ;
do t.disable() -> s.log(userid) ;
}
```

Figure 3. PONDER Policy Rule Structure

The event-condition-action semantics of PONDER are easily observed in the structure of the rules.

4. Mapping of the CIM Policy Model to PONDER

The CIM Policy Model makes similar distinctions as PONDER between authorization, delegation and obligation policies. There is great similarity between the CIM and PONDER concepts for obligation/refrain rules. This is established by use of an example, and is presented in Section 5.

As regards authorization and delegation, current thinking in the DMTF Policy Working Group is that these semantics will be modeled taking a domain-specific approach. This approach can already be seen in CIM V2.8's authentication policy modeling [3].

Given that the authorization and delegation work is still in development, and is not the focus of this paper, it will not be addressed further in this paper.

5. Example Mapping – Policy and Pigs

Demonstrating the mapping of CIM to PONDER highlights some of the issues that arise in any mapping from general semantics to a particular language or implementation. The example chosen here is based on a scenario first documented in the DMTF CIM Policy Working Group by Bob Moore of IBM. It is titled, "Policy, Pigs and PONDER" [6]. The goal of the example is to define a difficult policy problem, involving multiple domains and contexts, and utilizing a previously established model of the actors, their data and operations. (It is acknowledged that this is not a real-world example, and is used solely to demonstrate the complexity of policy.)

The following sections overview the example and its rendering in CIM and PONDER. Lastly, the correspondences and differences between the declarations are analyzed.

5.1. Policy Scenario – Farmers Feeding Pigs

The Farmer-Pig policy scenario is based on a farmer keeping animals, and determining when an animal is to be fed. The policy is stated as "If at least two of a farmer's pigs are squealing, then he/she must feed one of the pigs that is not squealing."

A few simplifying assumptions are made:

- Although multiple employees may work on a farm, only one is assumed on each farm. This simplifies the selection of the farmer who is requested to feed the pig.
- A notification mechanism is assumed to be in place, and provides an initiating event that carries sufficient information to define the subject and/or target environments.

Figure 4 illustrates the classes in the Farmer-Pig information model.

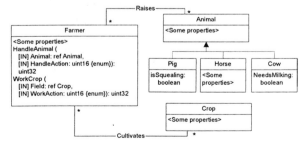

Figure 4. Farmer-Pig Information Model

5.2. Expressing the Farmer-Pig Policy in CIM

In order to express the Farmer-Pig policy ("if at least 2 pigs are squealing, feed a third pig"), the CIM instances shown in Figure 5 are defined. The CIM Query Language (CQL) [7] is used to express these instances. Note that the CIM Query Specification is still a work-in-progress of the DMTF, and changes are likely to occur in its definition in 2004.

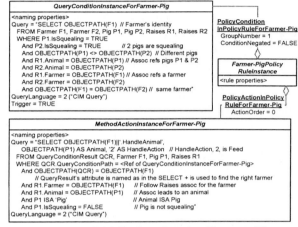

Figure 5. CIM Policy for the Farmer-Pig Scenario

CIM's query language is a variant of standard database query languages, but addresses the specific requirements of the CIM Schema. The general format of the CIM queries that are shown in Figure 5 is:

    SELECT <properties or other information>
    FROM <classes in a particular namespace,
    with optional aliases>
    WHERE <one or more expressions resulting in
    Boolean terms, combined via ANDs and ORs>
There are three items to note in this example:

- The SELECT clause of the MethodAction instance has an explicit format. According to the DMTF MethodAction class definition [4], the Query statement must define the object instance and method to be called (as the first attribute), and the method's input parameters.
- The triggering event is as precise as possible. If a simple SquealingPig event could trigger the policy, then the same pig could squeal multiple times and potentially result in a false activation of the policy action. A slightly complex query expression is needed to define "at least two different pigs squealing for the same farmer".

- As noted in Section 2, the result of the execution of a query can be referenced in other QueryConditions or MethodActions. This is seen in the Query statement in MethodActionInstanceForFarmer-Pig, where the policy rule's QueryCondition is referenced.

5.3. PONDER Expression of the Farmer-Pig Policy

Rendering the policy in PONDER can be accomplished by the rule shown in Figure 6. In this example, a notification (similar to the query shown in QueryCondition in Figure 5) triggers the rule. The notification is used to pass a reference to a farmer whose pigs are squealing. (The farmer can then be referenced as "self" in the remainder of the rule.) The "do" clause indicates that the Raises association is followed from a farmer to an animal, and any one that IsSquealing (=TRUE) is rejected. A resulting animal (labeled as t) is returned. All of this information is then used in the method invocation, HandleAnimal.

```
oblig feedNotSquealingPig {
    on CIM_AtLeastTwoSquealingPigs ;
        // 2 or more squealing pigs
    subject /farmers ;       // i.e., all farmers
    do (t = self.Raises->reject(isSquealing))
        -> self.HandleAnimal(t, 2) ;
}       // where 2='feed'
```

Figure 6. PONDER Policy for the Farmer-Pig Scenario

It is valuable to note the similarity in the rule rendering. The complexity of CIM's triggering event (defined in QueryConditionInstanceForFarmer-Pig) is identical to what would be required to generate the CIM_AtLeastTwoSquealingPigs notification. The domain of "/farmers" is specified in the FROM clause of the CIM Query statement and the "subject" statement in PONDER. However, in the CIM rendering, there is no need to explicitly distinguish subjects and targets. The queries simply specify the classes and instances of interest. Lastly, the necessity of traversing the Raises association to find a non-squealing pig is the same for both CIM and PONDER.

6. Conclusions

Similarity in rules between CIM and PONDER is reasonable since the focus of both is on declarative policy, and both utilize the semantics of a backing model or schema. The value of the PONDER rendering is its concise and explicit notation. The

value of the CIM rendering is that it does not dictate a specific language or implementation for a product, and utilizes existing query processing present in the CIM management infrastructure.

However, issues in rendering the CIM Policy classes exist, and are related to expression of the rules as queries. This is not a "natural" expression of policy, appears to add complexity to the problem space, and is not a language in which instrumentation/management software developers are versed. These issues must be taken into consideration in evaluating the CIM Policy Model, before finalizing it.

Clearly, further research and implementation experience are needed to evaluate the CIM Policy Model. Initial results indicate that rules ranging from the simple to the complex can be rendered and shared between different CIM-based implementations. This has been shown in the work of the Storage Networking Industry Association's Storage Management Initiative (SMI) [8].

7. References

[1] Distributed Management Task Force, http://www.dmtf.org.

[2] PONDER: A Policy Language for Distributed Systems Management, http://www-dse.doc.ic.ac.uk/Research/policies/ponder.shtml.

[3] DMTF Common Information Model V2.8 Schema, http://www.dmtf.org/standards/cim/cim_schema_v28

[4] PolicyCR00001 (Policy Model Change Request), submitted to the DMTF Policy Working Group, December 2003.

[5] The PONDER Policy Based Management Toolkit, http://www-dse.doc.ic.ac.uk/Research/policies/ponder/PonderSummary.pdf

[6] Email sent by R. Moore to the DMTF CIM Policy Working Group, "Policy, Pigs and Ponder", September 2002.

[7] DMTF CIM Query Language, DSP0202. http://www.dmtf.org/standards/published_documents.

[8] Storage Networking Industry Association Storage Management Initiative, http://www.snia.org/smi/home

Integrating Policy-based Access Management and Adaptive Traffic Engineering for QoS Deployment

Steven Van den Berghe, Filip De Turck, Piet Demeester
Department of Information Technology
Ghent University – IMEC
B-9000 Ghent Belgium
Email: {steven.vandenberghe, filip.deturck, piet.demeester}@intec.ugent.be

Abstract

In this paper, we describe our experiences of designing a platform that integrates distributed policy-based access control and trust management technologies with a developed QoS-aware network management platform. The main goal of this study is to demonstrate how the application of policy-based decision processes can help to deploy the platform in a scalable way offering adaptive services with enriching features such as flexible rule-based service definitions and roaming.

1 Introduction

The deployment of QoS in real-life networks has been an issue which has interested the network research community for quite some time now. Although the basic network components (Service Differentiation, routing optimisation, admission control schemes, etc.)[9] have been widely studied, the glue that is needed to tie them together is often neglected.

In order to design a flexible multiservice network architecture, three aspects need to be considered carefully: (i) performance differentiation, (ii) resilience differentiation, (iii) admission differentiation. It goes without saying that these should be addressed in both a scalable and practical (i.e. deployable and cost-effective) way. The requirements (i) and (ii) can be met by applying two networking technologies. The Differentiated Services architecture provides per hop differentiated forwarding behaviour. Additionally, a multi-path adaptive traffic engineering approach, combined with a fast rerouting mechanism allowed to build a flexible self-organising network layer, including robustness in a service-aware way. However, these requirements must also be fulfilled at the service management layer. This means that the service and traffic admission need to be operating in a highly distributed fashion. Dynamic distributed policy-based admission control, together with the application of concepts from trust management, is a (or even the most) suitable approach for implementing this. The added value of this aspect lies not only in the ability to extend the adaptive behaviour of Traffic Engineering (TE) towards the actual service offering (e.g. to avoid setting up a phone call if the network faces congestion). More importantly it allows to react more dynamically to the actual demand matrix and network state and adds opportunities for more flexible services (and a more flexible revenue stream, dynamic pricing, etc.). In summary, the quality of a service concept in this research is not only described by a discrete set of *classes of services* (CoS) which determines the behaviour in the network (both under normal and under degraded network circumstances), but also by a *Service Activation Policy* (SAP) which determines according to which policy users and their traffic are given access to the network.

This paper is a description of the integration of several existing components, rather than inventing new ones, it builds on related work that emerged from several areas. At the network-level, the basis is the IETF work on policy based admission control [8] together with recent advances in policy-based access and service management [7][4]. In the last few years, several projects (see [6][3] and their references) successfully looked at moving towards a closer integration between adaptive service and network management. In our research we focus on further weakening the requirement for centralised components and increasing the adaptiveness at the network level. In order to show the deployability the same adaptiveness must be made available in the service management. To achieve this, concepts from trust management [1] [2] and automated processing (e.g. XSL-T, XACML, etc.) were utilised.

Fig. 1 shows the most important aspects of the in-house developed adaptive TE platform (called SONAR, Service-Oriented Networking using Adaptive Resource manage-

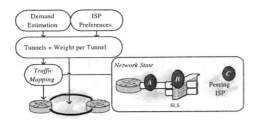

Figure 1. Basic SONAR operation

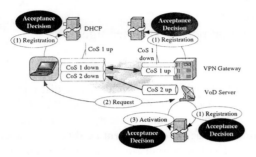

Figure 2. Example Exchange

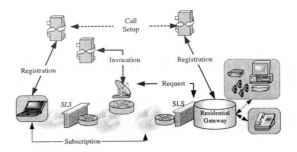

Figure 3. Typical Service Signalling

ment). The two main components are an off line centralised computation engine that is manually invoked by an operator to re-optimize the network configuration (so there is no real operational dependability on this centralised component). Based on an estimated demand matrix, it determines a set of paths through the network. This is then complemented with an on line distributed heuristic that, based on a weight per path outputted by the centralised computations and the current networks state, determines how these paths are used.

A critical requirement for this traffic mapping algorithm is that it can make its decisions purely based on information available in the network ingress. The remainder of this paper will describe the policy-based management mechanisms used to achieve that goal.

2 Service Signalling

Fig. 2 shows a user activating two types of services (one VPN-connection and a streaming request towards a Video on Demand, VoD, server). The first interaction that all "endpoints" in this system perform, is the registration with their local admission server. For the actual protocol to be used, a variety of mechanisms exist. In the example a DHCP server is shown, which is contacted when the user accesses the network. On this contact, the server checks if the user is actually allowed to access the network and which services he is subscribed to and delivers the corresponding connectivity information. In this example, 2 CoSs are available

(2 downstream, 1 upstream). Observe that another natural choice for this protocol is the Session Initialisation Protocol (SIP[5]) thanks to its extensibility, application-level transport, ease of implementation and support for both registration and session control. In a similar way, the VPN and VoD server endpoints register with their local access server.

The two services not only differ in the network CoS they will be using, they also differ in the way they are accessed. The VPN service typically requires a very flexible access method: we do not want to create a call every time we want to get something from a database server. Hence a host-based marking mechanism is used and both sides are given a certain ID which can be used to identify packets belonging to this service. In our case the IP DiffServ CodePoint (DSCP) field will identify the service (observe that in general this will not be corresponding with the actual CoS1 DSCP).

Opposed to this implicit service invocation method, the VoD server will typically be continuously and unidirectionally accessed for a specific duration. In this case an explicit service request can be performed. The client requests out-of-band (e.g. through a webpage) to receive a certain stream. Based on this request the server will send an activation request to its access server. If the admission process grants access to the network, again the packets belonging to this flow can marked at the source or alternatively the network ingress will configure the correct flow-to-CoS mapping. Observe that SIP would again be a natural choice to create and tear down these "QoS-sessions".

Fig. 3 shows the typical operations in the service management layer that can be identified in the scenario above: *(i) Subscription:* although we don not care how the actual subscription is done (e.g. : by buying a smartcard, signing a contract or accessing a web interface), we assume the client receives a document describing the service from the network provider to whom he subscribes. The content of this document is further discussed in the next section. *(ii) Registration:* given this document the user can gain access to a network by registering. This registration step (which is similar to a presence service) is introduced in order to support features such as "always-on" services and roaming.

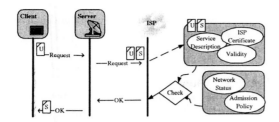

Figure 4. Sequential Message Exchange View

(iii) Call Setup or Service Request: both signals are a user-to-user communication to request a service, setup a phone call, etc. Although this is an out-of-band communication as far as the service management platform is concerned, it should allow for the service descriptions to be exchanged. *(iv) Service Invocation:* one or both sides (in case of respectively unidirectional and bidirectional services) communicate with the local network edge to actually activate the service.

The CoS and activation method are the first two "attributes" that define a certain service. We will now extend this into more generic service descriptions.

3 Service Profiles

For the registration process, we already mentioned that a service was described by a document. These are mostly referred to as Service Level Specifications. However in our case we would have two kinds of SLSs: one defining the aggregate pipes a user has to and from the local network, and one depicting the different services that use these pipes (i.e. subsets taken from the aggregate), together with additional information (like holding time etc.). To be able to differentiate between these two distinctive entities we will refer to the latter as service profiles.

Fig. 4 gives a more detailed view on how these profiles are used to activate the video streaming service. The user sends his profile (i.e. what he is capable of receiving) to the server in the request. This request is then combined with the server-side service profile. These two profiles are then combined with environmental aspects like the network status and the current time, and checked with the admission control policy for that service. Parts of this service profile are invariant (e.g. the fact whether a user has access to the network), while others might change dynamically (e.g. the time interval in which the service is accessible or the network circumstances).

Other attributes can limit the scope of services (e.g. only to certain servers), the type of user (e.g. residential or business), etc. This gives a second level of service differentiation that rises above the plain network level differentiation.

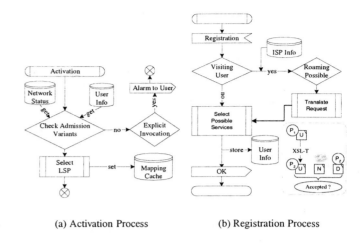

(a) Activation Process   (b) Registration Process

Figure 5. Decision Processes

A sample service policy for residential streaming can be: accept requests for this service if it is in the evening, and if none of the paths serving the corresponding traffic has received an alarm. It is interesting to note that all components required to deploy such a system are available today and in open standards (e.g. by carrying XACML requests over SIP) which can be a catalyst in the development of end-system support. A specific attribute that is worth looking at is the bandwidth indication. Instead of a complex negotiation, the endpoints indicate what can be sent/received in their respective profile. This means that each endpoint needs to manage the way his SLS is spread over the profiles himself. In a home environment this could for instance be done by a residential gateway (as shown in fig. 3).

The following section revisits the network-level QoS support and details how the SONAR approach interacts with the described service management.

As a result, the time spend in the activation process should be limited, so the policy decision process should make use of result caching mechanisms as much as possible. This requires the ability to make a distinction between static and dynamic attributes in the service profile, so that consecutive execution of the activation process (fig. 5(a)) can be based on just the dynamic attributes of the service profile). Another essential requirement for the service profiles is the ability to translate or map one profile into another while maintaining its semantics.

4 Profile Translation

The service profiles are derived from the SLS the user has with his network. As such, they have a meaning local to that network. In the case where both endpoints are located in different networks there must be a mean to translate the remote profile to a local service profile. One approach is trying to introduce a global meaning for the attributes. Also devising a corresponding trust management and accounting isn't that straightforward. A different approach is to make a translation mechanism part of the roaming agreement between a set of participating networks. The registration mechanism shown in fig. 5(b) demonstrates how this translation process integrates with the service management. To allow this, the service profile contains four parts:

(i) a certificate identifying the user's home (subscription) network provider, *(ii)* a user certificate identifying the user and signed by the network provider using a public key infrastructure (PKI) mechanism, *(iii)* the service attributes signed by the network provider using a PKI mechanism, *(iv)* a semantic subset of these attributes selected by the user (e.g. a reduced bandwidth indication),

By providing a key exchange as part of the roaming agreement (i.e. building a web of trust amongst the network providers participating in the roaming), this is sufficient to check whether a visiting user has roaming rights to the network, and the access he is requesting complies with his subscription. Another part of the roaming agreement, a translation mechanism between the visiting profile attributes and the local profile attributes is executed such that the user profile is understandable to the local access policy decision system. This translation can be more complex than just a rewrite: it can map one service into another (e.g. from a 5 Mbps video service offered by ISP1 to the 10 Mbps video service offered by ISP2). Since the service profiles are well-known between both network providers when the roaming agreement is established, we avoid complex real-time service translations. Limiting the service controlling communication to the local edge, and relying on trunking for the inter-domain part, enhances the scalability and deployability of this scheme. The diagram in the lower right hand corner of fig. 5(b) shows an example where a user profile (U) gets translated and is given, together with the current network status (N) and service description (D) to determine if a registration can be accepted.

5 Conclusion and Discussion Points

In this design study we investigated how a combination of adaptive traffic engineering and flexible, distributed, policy-based access decision processes can bring the deployment of QoS one step closer to reality. Although this initial work shows that existing components should be sufficient, further research must be done to check if other advanced features (like dynamic pricing) can fit in this picture. We experienced that the standardisation of service specifications with a global meaning might be less important. Rather, we would benefit more from a closer integration of existing rule-based decision mechanisms, easy trans-

lation technologies and trust delegation and management. However, we did notice the requirement for policy-based mechanisms to be able to make a difference between static and dynamic parts of the decision process which is correlated with the requirement for a distributed and "close-to-the-wire" operation (rather than outsourcing them). The basic ease of interpretation of XML and extensible (preferably application level) transport protocols such as SIP and HTTP (e.g. compared to using RSVP signalling) seem to complement this, allowing for a real-life deployment of multiservice networks. This deployment oppertunity is also be improved by offering roaming and user-based access to adaptive services in a scalable way.

Future work will focus on the exact implementation of this design and study what alternatives (such as the use of recent developments in the area of webservices) can complement or improve it.

Acknowledgment

Part of this work was supported through an IWT scholarship and the Fund for Scientific Research Flanders (FWO-V).

References

[1] M. Blaze, J. Feigenbaum, J. Ioannidis, and A. Keromytis. Rfc 2704, the keynote trust-management system version 2. Technical report, IETF, 1999.

[2] E. Freudenthal, T. Pesin, L. Port, E. Keenan, and V. Karamcheti. drbac: Distributed role-based access control for dynamic coalition environments. International Conference on Distributed Computing Systems, 2002.

[3] S. Giordano, S. Salsano, S. V. den Berghe, and G. Ventre. Qos advances in ip networks: architectures, protocols, and mechanisms. *IEEE Communications Magazine*, 41(1), 2003.

[4] A. Polyrakis and R. Boutaba. The meta-policy information base. *IEEE Network*, 16(2), 2002.

[5] H. Sinnreich and A. B. Johnston. *Internet Communications Using SIP*. John Wiley and Sons, 2001.

[6] P. Trimintzios, G. Pavou, P. Flegkas, P. Georgatsos, A. Asgari, and E. Mykoniati. Service-driven traffic engineering for intradomain quality of service. *IEEE Network*, 17(3), 2003.

[7] D. C. Verma. *Policy-Based Networking*. New Riders Publishing, 2001.

[8] J. Vollbrecht, P. Calhoun, S. Farrell, L. Gommans, G. Gross, B. de Bruijn, C. de Laat, M. Holdrege, and D. Spence. Rfc 2904, aaa authorization framework. Technical report, IETF, 2000.

[9] X. Xiao and L. M. Ni. Internet qos: A big picture. *IEEE Network*, 13(2), 1999.

Policy-based Congestion Management for an SMS Gateway

Alberto Gonzalez Prieto
KTH, Royal Institute of Technology
Stockholm, Sweden
gonzalez@imit.kth.se

Roberto Cosenza
Infoflex
Stockholm, Sweden
roberto.cosenza@infoflex.se

Rolf Stadler
KTH, Royal Institute of Technology
Stockholm, Sweden
stadler@imit.kth.se

Abstract

We present a policy-based approach to managing congestions in Short Message Service (SMS) systems. Congestion situations typically occur on SMS Gateways (SMSGs), which route SMS messages between different networks and domains. In our architecture, an SMS operator can dynamically define the maximum acceptable loss of messages of a non-guaranteed SMS service class, thereby controlling the trade-off between minimal message loss and maximum throughput in an SMS system. We present the functional architecture of a manageable SMSG and discuss the realization of the Policy Decision Point (PDP), which applies the congestion policy on the SMSG. An implementation of our architecture on a commercial SMSG, the EMG, is underway.

1. Introduction

The Short Message Service (SMS) is based on out-of-band message delivery, which permits users to send and receive text messages to/from their mobile phones.

SMS was introduced in 1992 and, since then, has experienced a remarkable success: by the end of 2002, 30 billion messages have been exchanged monthly, and the growth rate has been 0.5 billions per month. This makes SMS to represent about 10% of the revenue of mobile operators [1].

We consider two classes of SMS service. The first is the *guaranteed service*. It guarantees delivery, offering zero losses. The second, currently considered by service providers, is the *non-guaranteed service*. The rationale for offering two service classes is the existence of two different uses of SMS: person-to-person messaging, and bulk messaging. While the loss of person-to-person messages in not acceptable, bulk messages, such as promotional messages and messages from information services, can tolerate occasional losses.

Figure 1 presents the network architecture for SMS deployment in the GSM context. The key element is the SMSC, which acts as a store-and-forward system for short messages. Upon receiving an SMS, the SMSC queries the HLR database to get the location of the addressee of the message. With this information, the SMSC determines the servicing MSC for the addressee. Finally, the appropriate MSC delivers the message to the terminal of the receiver. This includes finding the appropriate base station to reach her.

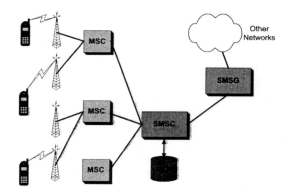

Fig 1: Architecture for SMS Deployment

The SMSC receives messages from two different parties. First, from mobile terminals. This is the case when a user sends a message from her mobile terminal. The second source of messages is SMS gateways. SMSGs interconnect the wireless network to others, like other mobile operator's network or TCP/IP networks. When the interconnected networks do not speak the same protocols, the gateway must perform protocol translations.

In this work, we will focus on the Enterprise Messaging Gateway (EMG), a commercial UNIX-based SMSG [2]. We use the model of the EMG shown in figure 2. On the left, we have the incoming ports, which receive the messages the EMG has to deliver. On reception, the message is routed to the appropriate outgoing port. After that, the message may need to be converted to a protocol understood by the receiving network. This conversion phase is irrelevant for this work.

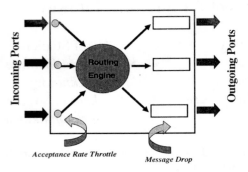

Fig 2: EMG Model

Each outgoing port of the EMG has an associated queue. This permits the EMG to cope with brief periods of congestion. Assuming the EMG is well-provisioned, longer periods of congestion can be caused by a persistent performance degradation of an outgoing port. In the rest of the paper, we will refer to such a port as a *"congested port"*.

If congestion is not addressed, the queue associated to the congested port will, eventually, get full. At that point, the EMG is designed to completely stop accepting incoming messages. Otherwise, all accepted messages routed through the congested port would be dropped. Such a situation is not acceptable.

The focus of this work is to provide the EMG with congestion management capabilities that permits us to address long periods of congestion.

In this paper, we propose a policy-based approach to congestion management for the EMG. We have chosen this approach for three main reasons. The first is that the use of policies permits us to raise the level of abstraction of the interaction with the EMG [3]. This permits the operator to focus on the management goals, the EMG's internal operation. A high level of abstraction is especially relevant for commercial SMSGs, like the EMG, due to the lack of specialists in such a specialized software.

The second reason is that a policy-based framework permits to modify the behavior of the system without having to re-implement it [4]. In our case, we can dynamically adapt the behavior of the queuing system without having to recode it. This feature gives more flexibility to the EMG operator.

The third reason is that task automation can be specified –in a relatively intuitive way—using event-condition-action policies. In this work, we aim to automate the reaction to congestion.

Congestion management in routing engines has been extensively studied in the context of IP routers. Our work differs from that field in both the problem space and the solution space. First, congestion management for IP routers considers physical networks. In contrast, an SMSG is a node in an *overlay network*, where the service rate of outgoing ports can vary, depending on the state of neighboring SMSGs. Second, the approaches to congestion management in IP networks often focus on flows. In contrast, flow-based mechanisms are not relevant in the SMS context, since an SMS message fits into a single packet.

2. Congestion Management in the EMG

In this section, we present the two strategies we can use to address congestion in the EMG.

The first strategy consists in reducing the load on the congested outgoing port by reducing the *acceptance rate* at the incoming ports (see figure 2). The acceptance rate at an incoming port controls the admission of messages from that port into the EMG. It indicates the number of messages per second an incoming port accepts. In the EMG, we can set the acceptance rate of incoming ports individually, with a granularity of 1 message per second (m/s).

By reducing the acceptance rate, we avoid the queue associated with the congested outgoing port from growing. However, this reduction affects the loads on all outgoing ports. Therefore the overall throughput of the EMG is compromised.

The second strategy consists in reducing the load on the congested port by dropping some of the non-guaranteed messages that are routed to its associated queue.

Both strategies –reducing the acceptance rate and dropping non-guaranteed messages— present a trade-off. If we want to maximize the overall throughput, we must avoid reducing the acceptance rate. But then, we are forced to drop messages to avoid the outgoing queue from overflow.

In contrast, if we want to minimize losses, we must avoid dropping messages. Then, we need to reduce the acceptance rate.

Therefore the EMG manager has to choose between giving priority to (i) having low losses or (ii) having high throughput.

3. The Congestion Control Policy and its Realization

This section describes our approach to congestion management in the EMG. We present how the EMG configures itself after the operator chooses an acceptable loss rate for the non-guaranteed service class. The configuration achieves an optimal throughput for the EMG and dynamically adapts to changes in the load pattern. Figure 3 shows the functional architecture of our approach.

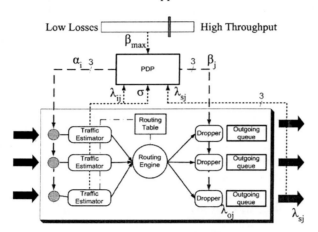

Fig 3: Functional Architecture for Realizing Congestion Control Policies on an EMG

3.1. Policy Specification

First of all, the operator specifies how he wants the system to behave during congestion. He chooses between giving priority to high throughput or to low losses.

As we have presented before, these two strategies present a trade-off: we achieve one at the cost of the other. Considering this, we propose to use a graphical interface where giving priority to one implies possibly penalizing the other: a sliding bar with one of the ends labeled "high throughput", and the other "low losses" (see figure 3).

The performance metric to favor is indicated by the position of the slider. The closer the slider is to the "high throughput" end, the more priority is given to throughput –at the cost of losses— and vice versa.

This qualitative priority is mapped to a quantitative parameter: the *maximum allowable dropping percentage* (β_{max}). It indicates the maximum percentage of non-guaranteed messages that can be dropped under congestion. β_{max} takes values from 0% (low losses) to 100% (high throughput), varying linearly with the position of the slider.

The *maximum allowable dropping policy* provides the maximum overall throughput under the constraint that, at most, β% of non-guaranteed messages is dropped.

3.2. Policy Refinement

The *maximum allowable dropping policy* is refined into two *second-level* policies: a policy for dropping messages and a policy for reducing the acceptance rate of incoming ports. These policies have the following forms:

TYPE 1.- ON congestion DO drop β % of non-guaranteed messages routed to the congested port

TYPE 2.- ON congestion DO reduce acceptance rate to α messages per second.

We have one policy of type 2 for each incoming port and one policy of type 1 for each outgoing port. That is, we have as many α_i as incoming ports and as many β_j as outgoing ports.

The PDP calculates the optimal values of α_i and β_j. They depend on the service rate (λ_{sj}), the EMG traffic matrix (λ_{ij}), the percentage of messages using the guaranteed service (σ), and β_{max}. This dependence is given by the vector equation:

$$(\lambda_{oj})_j = (\alpha_i)_i (\lambda_{ij})_{ij} [1-[1-\sigma](\beta_j)_j]$$

The calculated α_i and β are optimal in the sense that they maximize the overall throughput ($\sum \lambda_{oj}$) for the steady state, while $\beta_j \le \beta_{max}$ and $\lambda_{oj} \le \lambda_{sj} \forall j$

The traffic matrix and σ are estimated by the blocks labeled *traffic estimator*. They do so considering the incoming messages and the routing table of the EMG.

3.3. Policy Evaluation

In our context, congestion arises when $\lambda_{oj} > \lambda_{sj}$. During congestion, the PDP calculates the appropriate (α_1, α_2,..., α_i, ..., α_n) and (β_1, β_2,..., β_i, ..., β_m), and configures the incoming ports and the droppers (figure 3) accordingly.

This calculation is performed whenever any of the incoming parameters of the PDP (λ_{sj}, λ_{ij}, σ or β_{max}) changes significantly. If this re-calculation results in new values for α_i and β_j, the incoming ports and the droppers are re-configured.

3.4. Study Case

In this section, we illustrate the behavior of an EMG under congestion policies in a specific scenario. It consists of an EMG configured with three incoming ports (ip1, ip2 and ip3) and three outgoing ports (op1, op2, op3), like in figure 3. The port that will suffer the performance degradation is op3.

Each incoming port is configured to accept 6 m/s, which is also the offered load at those ports. The percentage of messages using the *non-guaranteed* service class is 90%.

The combined traffic of the three incoming ports (18 m/s) is evenly distributed among the outgoing ports: the load of each outgoing port is 6 m/s. Nevertheless, we assume that each incoming port contributes to the load of op3 differently. 70% of the traffic received in ip1 is routed through op3. For ip2 and ip3, the percentages are 20% and 10%, respectively.

Figure 4 shows the overall throughput of the EMG as a function of β for different service rates of the congested port (from 1 m/s to 5 m/s). The values in the figure correspond to the EMG in steady state.

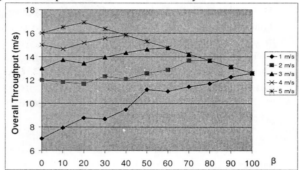

Fig 4: Overall Throughput of an EMG in function of β, the drop rate of messages of the non-guaranteed service class, for various rates of a congested output port

We make two observations to Figure 4. The first observation is characterized by the monotonic decrease of the throughput when β is increased. One example can be seen in figure 4, for a congested port performance of 5 m/s. In this case, from β=20% on, the overall throughput decreases monotonically.

The reason is that for β=20%, the percentage of dropped messages is high enough to permit setting the acceptance rate of all incoming ports to its initial value (6 m/s). Therefore, since we can not accept more messages, dropping a higher percentage only decreases the overall throughput.

The second observation is the occurrence of local minima. For instance, when the performance of the congested port is 2 m/s, the overall throughput is lower for β =20% than for β =0%. However, if we keep increasing β (to 30%), the throughput increases as well.

The reason is a constraint of the EMG: all α_i must be integers. This is imposed by the internals of the EMG implementation. Due to this, the λ_{oj} produced by the calculated (α_1, α_2,…,α_i, …, α_n) for β_{max} might be smaller than λ_{sj}. In such cases, the PDP calculates the smallest β (β < β_{max}) that keeps the load on the congested port smaller or equal to λ_{sj} for the calculated

(α_1, α_2,…,α_i, …, α_n). This permits non-guaranteed messages to utilize a capacity that would be unused otherwise.

The existence of these two situations implies that different *maximum allowable dropping* policies can result in the same configuration parameters (α_1, α_2,…,α_i, …, α_n), (β_1, β_2,…, β_i, …, β_m). For instance, for a congested port performance of 1 m/s, the configuration for both policies (i) β_{max} =50%, and (ii) β_{max} =60% is α_i= (0, 6, 6), β_j=(0, 0, 50).

Note that, for a given β_{max}, the PDP always chooses the operating point that maximizes the EMG throughput. As a consequence, the PDP chooses a value of β that is sometimes smaller than β_{max}. For example, in the scenario depicted in Figure 4, with a service rate of 1m/s, a policy with β_{max} =70% results in an operating point of the EMG with β=20%.

4. Current state and Future Work

In this paper, we presented our approach to congestion management in the EMG, a UNIX-based SMS gateway. Our architecture permits the EMG manager to control the tradeoff between high throughput of the EMG and low loss rate of the non-guaranteed service class. In situations of congestion and changes in load pattern, the system dynamically re-configures, following the manager's selected policy.

We are currently implementing our architecture on the EMG platform version 2.4 [2]. The prototype is programmed in C.

One of the issues we want to evaluate on the prototype is the behavior of different algorithms for the estimation of the parameters that influence the PDP.

Currently, messages receive different treatments based on their service class: guaranteed or non-guaranteed. We plan to study refined congestion policies, which are based on properties, such as the sender of a message, the message content or the source network.

References

[1] GSM Association, www.gsmworld.com
[2] Nordic Messaging, www.nordicmessaging.se
[3] M. J. Masullo, S. B. Calo, *"Policy management: an architecture and approach"*. Proc. of IEEE Workshop on Sys. Management, UCLA, Cal., April 1993
[4] M. Sloman, "Policy Driven Management for Distributed System", Journal of Networks and Systems Management, Vol.2, No.4, 1994

PROTON: A Policy-based Solution for Future 4G devices

Pablo Vidales*
Laboratory for Communication Engineering
University of Cambridge
pav25@cam.ac.uk

Rajiv Chakravorty, Calicrates Policroniades
Systems Research Group
University of Cambridge
{rc277,cbp25}@cam.ac.uk

Abstract

We present PROTON, a policy-based solution for 4G mobile devices – it allows users to seamlessly connect to highly integrated heterogeneous wireless networks. The key motivation behind PROTON stems from the statement that handover process complexity will increase in 4G systems, creating the need for augmented knowledge about context, as well as more flexibility. This paper demonstrates (1) how a flexible policy-based approach is suitable for 4G scenarios, and (2) how to incorporate richer context into policies and still maintain a light weight solution appropriate for mobile devices.

Table 1. Current and emerging radio access technologies will converge in a highly integrated and heterogeneous *ubiquitous* network (i.e. 4G system), in which handover process complexity will dramatically increase.

Network	Coverage	Data Rates	Mobility	Cost
Satellite (B-GAN)	World	Max. 144 kb/s	High	High
GSM/GPRS	Aprox. 35 Km	9.6 kb/s up to 144 kb/s	High	High
IEEE 802.16a	Aprox. 30 Km	Max. 70 Mb/s	Low/Medium	Medium
IEEE 802.20	Aprox. 20 Km	1-9 Mb/s	Very high	High
UMTS	20 Km	up to 2 Mb/s	High	High
HIPERLAN 2	70 up to 300 m	25 Mb/s	Medium/high	Low
IEEE 802.11a	50 up to 300 m	54 Mb/s	Medium/high	Low
IEEE 802.11b	50 up to 300 m	11 Mb/s	Medium/high	Low
Bluetooth	10 m	Max. 700 kb/s	Very low	Low

1 Introduction

An integrated network-of-networks (*i.e All-IP network*) is the vision for 4G mobile wireless systems architecture. This envisages that users can benefit in several ways from this unified access platform. The advantages, however, cannot be seized if we do not consider the dynamics and complexity in future environments. For instance, we believe that a model based on mobility hints, cross-layer activity information, and application-specific data can contribute to an effective network usage; what we need is a policy-based solution that can effectively expose context knowledge without a huge overhead.

The 4G architecture demands highly flexible and adaptive mobile clients that can cope with diverse, heterogeneous, and dynamic environments. More technologies, services, and devices join the fray every day, we can be sure that as the QoS gap offered by new access networks closes (see table 1), hard-coded handover algorithms will become obsolete and more flexible solutions will gain importance.

Diversity and heterogeneity in wireless systems' evolution have placed the integration of hybrid mobile data networks as an enormous barrier towards the success of seamless networking. This challenge outstrips embedded-system hard-coded policies (e.g. *handover to the strongest signal* or *always handover to the lowest available overlay*). We see in policy-based solutions the capacity to arise as a promising option for mobility management in future 4G systems.

Motivation – *Seamless roaming and connectivity to highly integrated and heterogeneous networks is the key idea that springs from the 4G vision. Dynamics, flexibility, and reactiveness to context, the main challenges that can be subdued by the deployment of policy-based solutions.*

Overview – The 4G vision poses the challenge of *seamless networking*, which involves (1) connection to many radio access networks (RANs) using a multimode device, (2) assistance for decision, execution, and adaption processes during vertical handovers, (3) minimisation of latency effects to support real-time services, and (4) related management issues such as access control, accounting, and security in the new consolidated platform [4].

Previous solutions [2, 5, 6, 9] have tackled particular aspects of seamless networking. In this paper, we present a policy-based solution, called PROTON, to support devices/users during vertical handovers in next generation mobile systems. This attempt differs from previous approaches in the following key aspects:

a) Application-specific policies: the policy model facilitates the cooperation between application and network layers in order to improve user experience.

b) Context-aware policy model: an important difference with all other previously proposed handover models is that policies here also imply *context* and reflect the relation between user/device and the mobility context.

c) Assistance during the entire handover process: cross-layer and context knowledge are used to support users in decision, execution, and adaptation processes triggered by vertical handovers.

d) Support for new services: 4G communication systems open new opportunities to mobile users. For example, access to multiple RANs poses the possibility for *integrated networks services*, not only high-speed connection with high usability, but users can use multiple services from different providers at the same time, and this results in novel services [4].

The rest of the paper is organised as follows: Section 2 describes the architecture of the Mobile IPv6 testbed used during experimental analysis. Section 3 explores in more detail the design rationale to build this solution and briefly describes PROTON components. In Section 4 we expose the core of the solution, the policy model. Finally, we contrast our work with previous approaches in Section 5, and conclude in Section 6.

2 PROTON MIPv6-based Testbed

To closely emulate the next generation (4G) integrated networking environment, our experimental testbed setup consists of a tightly-coupled, Mobile IPv6-based GPRS-WLAN-LAN testbed as shown in figure 1. The cellular GPRS network infrastructure currently in use is Vodafone UK's production GPRS network. The WLAN access points (APs) are IEEE 802.11b ones. Our testbed has been operational since March 2003, and results showing how we optimise vertical handovers are available [3].

In the testbed, the GPRS infrastructure comprises base stations (BSs) that are linked to the SGSN (Serving GPRS Support Node) which is then connected to a GGSN (Gateway GPRS Support node). In the current Vodafone configuration, both SGSN and GGSN node are co-located in a single CGSN (Combined GPRS Support Node). A well provisioned virtual private network (VPN) connects the Lab network to that of the Vodafone's backbone via an IPSec tunnel over the public Internet. A separate "operator-type" RADIUS server is provisioned to authenticate GPRS mobile users/terminals and also assign IP addresses.

For access to the wireless testbed, mobile nodes (e.g., laptops) connect to the local WLAN network and also simultaneously to GPRS via a Phone/PCCard modem. The

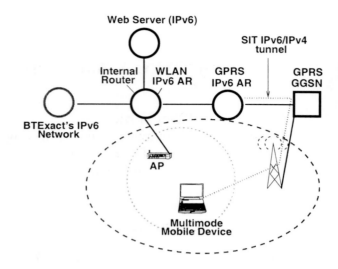

Figure 1. Experimental Testbed for PROTON.

mobile node's MIPv6 implementation is based on that developed by the MediaPoli project [1], chosen for its completeness and open source nature.

3 PROTON Solution

3.1 Design Rationale

PROTON's main objective is to tackle two obstacles in 4G systems: *heterogeneity* and *high dynamics*. To strike the first one, we propose to sense context and design the corresponding policy model to facilitate devices with the required flexibility and adaptiveness [8]. Moreover, to cope with dynamics, we propose a three-level context hierarchy according to sensed data and complexity in the rules applied.

3.2 Networking Context

Context is defined as any information sensed from the environment which may be used to define the behaviour of a system. This section outlines the concept of *Networking Context*, based on the introduction of the fragments in tables 2 and 3.

Networking context fragments are grouped into dynamic and static components. Moreover, these components are organised into a three-level hierarchy according to dynamics and complexity in the applied rules.

Upper level organises highly dynamic components on which simple local rules are applied.

Intermediate level arranges moderate fluctuation fragments that, together with data from the upper level, are used

Table 2. These components show the dynamics of heterogeneous 4G systems; a huge constraint in future policy-based solutions.

Sensed element	Context fragment	e.g. generated event
Presence	Device is attached to host	Interface [INSERT]
Status	Link-layer connectivity	Interface [UP/DOWN]
Connection	Network-layer connectivity	Incoming RAs at [eth0]
Signal Strength	SS received at the interface	[SS] below/above trigger
Handover Latency	Latency of vertical handover	[HL] from X to Y
Network	Profile of a specific network	Mobile host at home network
Congestion	Congestion in the network	Approximated [congestion]
Flows	Traffic classification	Traffic flow of [type] started
Velocity	Current speed of mobile host	Velocity [km/hr] above trigger
Position	Mobile host's position	Current [LAT,LON]
Direction	Moving direction of the MH	MH moving [NORTH]

to obtain aggregated contexts (host connectivity, activity, and location).

Lower level groups static components. We exploit collected data from all three levels to specify and evaluate the policy model.

Table 3. Dynamics in 4G systems demand intense context knowledge –expressed in a policy model– to cope with complexity. Static context components provide steady data which is essential to define and evaluate richer policies.

Component	Data elements	Capability
Network Profile	e.g., cost, bandwidth, RTT, packet loss, jitter, power consumption, and coverage	Information to exploit overlay model's diversity
Application Profile	QoS requirements such as packet loss, error rate, jitter, and latency.	Network aware applications that proactively adapt in 4G environments
User Profile	e.g., budget, security level, available power, priorities, and performance.	Consider user preferences as an input to the policy model
Infrastructure Profile	e.g., base stations and hotspots positions.	Increase proactiveness using network-provided static data

3.3 PROTON components

PROTON main components can be divided into three groups: *Context Management*, *Policy Management*, and *Enforcement groups* (see Figure 2).

Context Management group: *Sentinels* and *Retrievers* are the main components. These are responsible for gathering the Networking Context, applying local rules, and forming aggregated data.

Policy Management group: the *Policy Master* functions as the Policy Decision Point (PDP). Also, in this group we have the policy database, and two extra components: *Conflict Resolution module* and *Context-based profile selector*

dedicated to solve potential conflicts in the application of policies.

Enforcement group: *Executors* act as the Policy Enforcement Points (PEPs) –according to the IETF Policy Core Information Model (PCIM) [7]– for example, the *Handover Executor*.

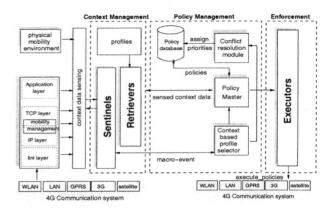

Figure 2. PROTON model stems from the vision of 4G systems.

4 Policy Model

4.1 IETF/PCIM and PROTON

PROTON follows the IETF/PCIM specification to define its policy model [7]. The main reasons for this are: (1) policies can be tagged with different roles, and this is useful to define subsets, (2) policies can be assigned a priority, useful for conflict resolution, and (3) IETF/PCIM can be translated to XML, this is useful for analysis and policy exchange.

4.2 Policy structure and classification

In PROTON's policy model, the condition expression can be simple or compound, and it is related to one or more Networking Context fragments, which belong to one of the following categories: *host connectivity*, *host location*, or *host activity*. Additionally, actions (i.e. operations) target one of the following processes: *handover decision*, *handover execution*, or *handover adaptation*.

4.3 Specification and evaluation

Within each context only a subset of the overall policies of the model needs to be specified, moreover, only a small subset of the specified policies needs to be evaluated under certain circumstances which in turn reduces the complexity dramatically. This argument follows the principle that

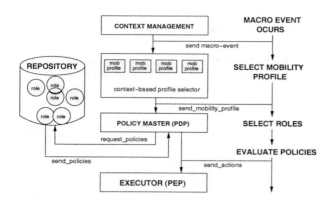

Figure 3. To minimise complexity, PROTON groups policies into roles that are then selected according to mobility profiles.

not all context fragments are important in every scenario. In praxis, policies are grouped in to *roles* such as "upward handover", and then associated to a *mobility-profile*, for example "in-building profile", which is selected due to the occurrence of a *macro-event* (e.g. velocity is 3mph). This process is shown in figure 3.

4.4 Scenario: 4G integrated services

Suppose a 4G system where a 4G mobile user, connects to different RANs. S(he) simultaneously accesses the following networks: *satellite GPS* (to track his location), *WLAN* (to receive video/audio from the closest restaurant), and *GSM* to reserve a table (using SMS) and ring some friends. In this scenario, PROTON-enabled device applies policies, according to current context and mobility profiles, to optimise network usage and maximise user experience.

5 Related Work

Helen J. Wang [9] first showed policy-enabled handovers. However, these policies focus exclusively in the decision making process. She argued that complete mobility assistance would be suboptimal and far too complex considering the environment dynamics. Nevertheless, we sustain that by using the correct data and policy model, we can provide support during the entire vertical handover process and still offer a light weight solution.

MosquitoNet [6] also addresses handover policy issues. This project was focused on choosing the most desirable packet delivery path based on the characteristics of the traffic flow. Instead, PROTON represents a complete support solution for 4G mobility management.

More recent work also considers policy-based handover decisions. POLIMAND [2] shows a policy model for Mo-

bile IP based handovers that uses link layer parameters to assist roaming hosts. However, this policy model is too simple. In contrast, PROTON explores the concept of incorporating Networking Context and building a richer policy model to deal with 4G complexities.

6 Conclusion and Ongoing Work

We presented PROTON, a policy-based solution for 4G mobile devices. This solution tackles three main challenges in future communication systems: decision, execution, and adaptation processes. PROTON stems from the fact that flexibility and adaptiveness will be demanded in future environments, and hard-coded handover algorithms will no longer be enough. Our ongoing work involves a full implementation of PROTON and its evaluation using our testbed.

Acknowledgements – The authors wish to thank Prof. Andy Hopper and Frank Stajano for providing the support and necessary advice for this project. Pablo Vidales and Calicrates Policroniades have scholarships from CONA-CyT.

References

[1] Mobile IP for Linux (MIPL) Implementation by HUT Telecommunications and Multimedia Lab, http://www.mipl.mediapoli.com.

[2] S. Aust, D. Proetel, N. A. Fikouras, C. Pampu, and C. Gorg. Policy based Mobile IP handoff decision (POLIMAND) using generic link layer information. In *5th IEEE International Conference on Mobile and Wireless Communication Networks (MWCN 2003)*, October 2003.

[3] R. Chackravorty, P. Vidales, I. Pratt, and J. Crowcroft. On tcp performance during vertical handovers: Experiences from gprs-wlan integration. In *Proceedings of The Second IEEE International Conference on Pervasive Computing and Communications (PerCom'04)*, March 2004.

[4] S. Hui and K. Yeung. Challenges in the migration to 4G Mobile Systems. IEEE Communications Magazine, December 2003.

[5] K. Jean, K. Yang, and A. Galis. A policy based context-aware service for next generation networks. IEE 8th London Communication Symposium, October 2003.

[6] K. Lai, M. Roussopoulos, D. Tang, X. Zhao, and M. Baker. Experiences with a mobile testbed. In *Proceedings of The Second International Conference on Worldwide Computing and its Applications (WWCA'98)*, March 1998.

[7] B. Moore, E. Ellesson, J. Strassner, and A. Westerinen. Policy Core Information Model. Internet RFC rfc3060.txt, , Work in Progress, February 2001.

[8] M. Sloman and E. Lupu. Security and management policy specification. In *IEEE Network*, volume 16, issue 2, pages 10–19, March/April 2002.

[9] H. J. Wang. Policy-enabled handoffs across heterogeneous wireless networks. Technical Report CSD-98-1027, 23, 1998.

Policy Control Model: a Key Factor for the Success of Policy in Telecom Applications

Fernando Cuervo, Michel Sim
Research and Innovation, Alcatel
600 March Rd, Ottawa, ON, K2K 2E6, Canada
{fernando.cuervo, michel.sim}@alcatel.com

Abstract

The application of policy in telecommunications networks is still in its initial stages. Since network elements lack native policy mechanisms, the impact of using policy, instead of SNMP or CLI based configuration, is not clearly understood. This paper presents a "Policy Control Model" and self-organising capabilities that network elements must exhibit to realise the policy potential for making service management simpler and more efficient. In this context, we discuss the importance of roles, propose a separation of functionality that makes policy solutions adaptable to diverse operational environments, and study the benefits of self-organising network elements obtaining their policy configurations through a stateless pull mechanism.

1. Introduction

It is expected that the application of policy-based management techniques in telecommunications will be instrumental in improving management of networks and services. While we believe that this expectation is not misplaced, there are a number of technical issues preventing the policy approach from realising its potential. Today there are many solutions in the market that are positioned as "policy-based". The truth is that they are focused on the configuration of network elements (NEs) via templates that help operators to express configuration data as "condition-action" pairs, but preserve the attributes of commonly used manager-agent models of management with no significant impact on the architecture of management systems or the fundamental way in which services are managed.

In this paper, we first identify shortcomings in the approach of current telecommunications network and service management. Then, we present a flexible Policy Control Model (i.e., how NEs obtain policy)

that is based on a "pull" style rather than the management layer pushing information into the NEs. Finally, we propose how to further exploit the relationship of service goals to roles to enable NEs to self-organise in order to configure policies in a dynamic and flexible manner, while reducing the complexity of top level management systems. The final sections offer potential areas of applications, along with future research topics.

2. Deficiencies in current approaches

Today, network and service management systems are designed to provide service intelligence to the networks they control. As such, policy-based solutions rely heavily on the top-down push model. In this model, once a configuration request is received, the policy server needs to identify the set of managed devices to configure, by consulting any number of databases, OSSs, pre-cooked lists, etc. This is a costly information process, where information is often affected by lack of completeness and inconsistencies. The complexity of this process is directly related to the number of devices that need configuration. These steps are further complicated by the need to handle pre-provisioning, using either traditional methods or policies, to prepare the managed devices to accept provisioning policies. Since a service order activation consists a set of configuration requirements that are often independently managed by several management systems, service activation is only realised once all configuration requests have been served by one or more telecom applications, and coordinated by a service activation environment (which is a workflow for service activations). This illustrates that, in a push-based environment, complexity is handled by adding complexity on top of complexity. Compounding the problem, each device also needs to be actively managed by the policy server in a stateful manner. The result is the massively complex management infrastructure currently used by service providers.

In our view, this complexity stems from the failure to provide more intelligence in the NEs and simplify management systems. The use of roles in current policy-based telecom applications is a prime example of this issue. Traditionally, roles have been viewed as selectors for policies to be implemented on NEs in the network [1]. In the process, we have lost sight of the semantics of roles, and how they can provide a useful level of abstraction to describe entities with similar behaviours that are required to implement network-services. Three categories of roles can be distinguished:

- *Network roles*, which are defined with respect to a set of capabilities that NEs offer.
- *Business roles*, which are labels that have significance in the context of the service provider's business, but are not related to capabilities [2].
- *Service-instance roles*, which identify a specific instance of a network-service implementation.

For each network-service, a set of network roles are defined in terms of the capabilities needed to perform these roles. These role definitions can then be deployed in the network, along with business roles defined by the operator, in order to provide Service Management and NEs with a higher level of abstraction for the services NEs can support. Subsequently, NEs can self-configure (i.e., tune its capabilities) to be ready to accept configurations in line with the assigned roles. NEs can then present their resources in terms of the roles they support within any given service, thus simplifying resource management at the service level. The introduction of true Policy Servers (PS) and Policy Enabled Devices (PED) in the network is required to exploit the power of the semantics of business and service-instance roles. We propose the use of self-organisation so PSs and PEDs can locate and arrange themselves such that the scalability and flexibility of the network is enhanced. We believe that a Policy Control Model that enables PEDs to locate and "pull" policy from available PSs, without requiring the PS to maintain state will be the foundation of the self-organisation mechanism.

3. Policy Control Model

The Policy Control Model includes the management entities and the protocols needed to instantiate, distribute and maintain the policy state of the network (Figure 1).

The **Role-Capability Manager (RCM)** is in charge of all aspects of roles. For instance, the RCM handles the creation of new roles when new network services are introduced. When a new service instance needs to be implemented in the network, the RCM can locate resources based on the required roles and capabilities. Those resources can then be assigned the appropriate roles, which triggers the pre-provisioning phase. Service-instance roles can also be used to ensure that resources are clearly identified as being used in the implementation of a service instance (e.g., for a specific end customer).

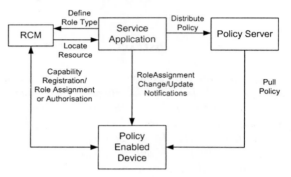

Figure 1: Policy Control Model

A **Policy Server (PS)** is in charge of handling policies. It is used by authorised NEs to retrieve policy or configuration information (for a state-of-the-art implementation of current practices, see [3]). A PS does not maintain management association with the PEDs nor synchronisation. The PED requests are served as long as the authentication of the PED to the PS succeeds. A PED uses a default PS as the source of all configurations unless a more specific server is specified in the role configuration request. A PS can also refer a PED to contact another PS. Notice that the approach suggested by COPS [5] does NOT implement the Policy Control Model suggested in this paper since policy associations in COPS are stateful.

The **Service Application (SA)** creates, configures and manages network services. It can be visualised as a "mini-workflow" that coordinates the definition of roles, the dissemination of configuration information and the inter-working with PEDs to indicate role assignments or configuration changes. It relies on service-instance roles to simply and effectively manage the identity and the configuration of each specific resource used for the implementation of service instances. The SA may also assume other functions, such as service verification and activation. This is however dependent on the capabilities of PEDs to support these operations.

A **Policy-Enabled Device (PED)** is a NE with native policy mechanisms. It can register its capabilities, potential and active roles to the RCM. It can also receive requests to configure/withdraw one of the registered roles, or receive notifications to update a role configuration. In order to implement services, a PED then retrieves policy or configurations from a PS, executes policy and maintains the integrity of policy specifications (i.e., enforce policy).

This functional separation adds flexibility, since the RCM, SA, and PS can be distributed to accommodate different deployments. It also makes SAs easier to create because inventories, reservation and allocation of resources are handled by the RCM and the PEDs themselves. Since the distribution and management of the configuration information is separated from the SA, each provider of service resources can create an infrastructure to distribute configurations that is transparent to the SA.

4. PED Self-organization for policy support

Self-organisation is a concept where PEDs can establish by themselves relationships to other PED or to the functional components of the Policy Control Model. While self-organisation may take different forms, we present a brief description of self-organisation into a tree-hierarchy, which occurs naturally in most complex management applications (telecom or otherwise).

PEDs organize themselves into "reliable-multicast" trees based on the roles that they perform. By reliable we mean that once a node has joined the multicast tree, its parent knows the state of each transmission, and the state of the node. Multicast addresses and credentials are provided by the RCM to each network component according to the "roles" it is intended to support. A PED should be configured to join any number of multicast trees that may be required for pull-configuring its functionality.

Filters can be used to restrict the scope to certain members of the destination set and can be applied by each node of the multicast tree. A filter could be as simple as a service instance role or an IP address prefix. *Directives* can also be used for a variety of functions: configure services, report on performance metrics, suppress alarms, bar traffic from entering the network, etc. They may be expressed in many different ways and do not have to directly point to a configuration (e.g., they may be evaluated by the NEs). Sophia [4] is an example of directives formally structured in a Prolog-like language. The protocol between SA and the devices to be configured ('the

destination set') must convey those filters and directives to the members of the destination set, along with references (e.g., a URL) to the PSs to be used for configuration by the members of the destination set.

For now, we will assume that the entire configuration for the destination set can be obtained from a single PS. A node in the tree can be notified by the PS when its children have pulled the needed configuration. The completion of the configuration request can thus be verified in a scalable, distributed manner. Figure 2 illustrates a possible sequence of the Pull steps after the PEDs have been assigned a role by the RCM and joined the multicast tree. The operations in this example revolve around one given destination D_i, but they are identical for any other members of the tree:

1. SA multicasts information such as filters, directives, or server references.
2. Each node below SA applies the filter before forwarding (in the example, D_v terminated the multicast on application of the filter, while D_i forwarded it to its children).
3. As D_i forwards the request and receives an acknowledgement (3a), it subscribes with the server to receive notifications (3b).
4. When D_j, D_k and D_m finish obtaining their configurations then D_i receives the notifications.
5. If D_i does not receive all notifications, then it can take actions to remedy the situation or to notify SA via a unicast message (not shown).

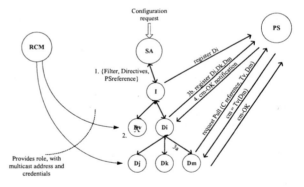

Figure 2: Pull Policy Control Model

This method can be easily extended to multiple configuration servers. Note also that Figure 2 shows a device in the multicast tree, labelled *I*, that is not necessarily part of the destination set but forms part of the hierarchy to process and ensure completion of the request. This type of device is introduced to account, for instance, for hierarchically organised element managers or dependencies in NEs between control and interface cards.

The advantages of a Policy Control Model based on the Pull method, and the multicast self-organisation mechanism can be summarised as follows: 1. configuration of the destination set is dynamic, cost efficient and highly scalable; 2. completion of the request is highly scalable; 3. distribution and configuration of the PS is flexible, allowing for ease of outsourcing. This capability enables enterprises or domains to supply their own configurations in a cross-domain manner; 4. The multicast method of communication is ideal to implement dynamic decisions where the limitation is to coordinate a large number of network resources to implement a configuration change.

5. Examples of Application

DSL access architectures because of their high fan out and their hierarchical organisation can be used to illustrate the advantages of the concepts presented above. DSL concentrators may support hundreds or thousands of access loops. Concentrators themselves may also be arranged in a hierarchical manner. DSL concentrators connect to an aggregation network that in turn connects to a service distribution network. As this hierarchy supports multiple services (voice, video, data) and multiple content providers, the large number of combinations is addressed by the operator through the use of service bundles. Service bundles may specify for instance "triple-play" or "video-sports". Policies that affect accounting, performance measurements, or package upgrades, can be efficiently distributed and applied through the mechanisms suggested in this paper. For instance, a change in the metering, monitoring policy or video channel availability for a given type of bundle subscribers can be easily issued by a service management application at the top of the hierarchy and enforced and verified in a distributed manner by many elements lower in the hierarchy. This provides operators with a very efficient model to tune and upgrade the operations of a large customer base.

Other policy applications such as IP routing policy also use hierarchies that involve several layers. BGP policy is captured at a higher level in Internet Route Repository Databases, which are in turn used for configuration of the routing layers which are themselves arranged in hierarchical ways (e.g., reflectors, route servers or confederations). We believe that automation of routing policy distribution

around the self-organisation concepts of the routing hierarchy can lead to more robust configuration of IP networks.

6. Conclusions and Future Work

The paper has proposed four main points: 1. the introduction of role semantics related to business and service instances that is managed by the PEDs in the network; 2. a functional architecture that decouples role management from configuration distribution and from service configuration management; 3. a Policy Control Model based on a stateless pull; 4. the introduction of self-organisation mechanisms to simplify the way in which the SA addresses large communities identified by roles.

We have shown that these concepts have the potential of simplifying the creation of SA applications and make management operations more efficient. Future research will fall into three topics: 1. the application of self-organising concepts at the PED level; 2. a trust-model between RCM, SAs and PSs that allows the application of the architecture in a cross-domain manner; 3. the introduction in PEDs of role management capabilities, notification, messaging and pull protocols.

7. References

[1] B. Moore, E. Ellesson, J. Strassner and A. Westerinen, "Policy Core Information Model -- Version 1 Specification", IETF, RFC 3060, February 2001.
[2] "Service Architecture version 5.0", Telecommunications Information Networking Architecture Consortium, June 1997
[3] R. Chadha et al. "PECAN: Policy-Enabled Configuration Across Networks", *Proc. 4th International Workshop on Policies for Distributed Systems and Networks (POLICY'03)*, Lake Como, Italy, June 2003.
[4] M. Wawrzoniak, L. Peterson and T. Roscoe, "Sophia: An information Plane for Networked Systems", Princeton U., Planetlab project, July 2003.
[5] D. Durham, J. Boyle, R. Cohen, S. Herzog, R. Rajan and A. Sastry, "The COPS (Common Open Policy Service) Protocol", IETF, RFC 2748, January 2000

Session 9:
Analysis and Refinement

A Goal-based Approach to Policy Refinement

Arosha K Bandara[1]   Emil C Lupu[1] Jonathan Moffett[2]   Alessandra Russo[1]

1: Department of Computing
Imperial College London,
180 Queen's Gate, London SW7 2AZ, UK
{bandara, e.c.lupu, ar3}@doc.ic.ac.uk

2: Department of Computer Science
University of York
Heslington, York YO10 5DD, UK
jdm@cs.york.ac.uk

Abstract

As the interest in using policy-based approaches for systems management grows, it is becoming increasingly important to develop methods for performing analysis and refinement of policy specifications. Although this is an area that researchers have devoted some attention to, none of the proposed solutions address the issue of deriving implementable policies from high-level goals. A key part of the solution to this problem is having the ability to identify the operations, available on the underlying system, which can achieve a given goal.

This paper presents an approach by which a formal representation of a system, based on the Event Calculus, can be used in conjunction with abductive reasoning techniques to derive the sequence of operations that will allow a given system to achieve a desired goal. Additionally it outlines how this technique might be used for providing tool support and partial automation for policy refinement. Building on previous work on using formal techniques for policy analysis, the approach presented here applies a transformation of both policy and system behaviour specifications into a formal notation that is based on Event Calculus. Finally, it shows how the overall process could be used in conjunction with UML modelling and illustrates this by means of an example.

1. Introduction

Policy based approaches to network and systems management are of particular importance because they allow the separation of the rules that govern the behaviour of a system from the functionality provided by that system. This means that it is possible to adapt the behaviour of a system without the need to recode functionality, and changes can be applied without stopping the system. Research into policy based systems management has focussed on languages for specifying policies and architectures for managing and deploying

policies in distributed environments. However, whilst there have been some promising developments in the area of policy analysis, policy refinement remains a much-neglected research problem.

Policy refinement is the process of transforming a high-level, abstract policy specification into a low-level, concrete one. Moffett and Sloman [1], identify the main objectives of a policy refinement process as:

- Determine the resources that are needed to satisfy the requirements of the policy.

- Translate high-level policies into operational policies that the system can enforce.

- Verify that the lower level policies actually meet the requirements specified by the high-level policy.

The first of these objectives involves mapping abstract entities defined as part of a high-level policy to concrete objects/devices that make up the underlying system. The second specifies the need to ensure that any policies derived by the refinement process be in terms of operations that are supported by the underlying system. The final objective requires that there be a process for incrementally decomposing abstract requirements into successively more concrete ones, ensuring that at each stage the decomposition is correct and consistent.

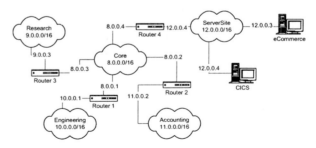

Figure 1: Example enterprise network

Figure 1 presents an example scenario, originally developed by Verma [2], where policy refinement might be applied. Here, an enterprise network must implement a Service Level Agreement (SLA) where one of the clauses specifies that "WebServices Applications on the eCommerce Server must receive Gold Quality of Service (QoS)". This requirement may be articulated as a policy which states that "On demand, the network should be configured to provide Gold QoS to WebServices applications on the eCommerce Server". Based on the objectives mentioned above, the policy refinement process should transform this high-level policy into lower-level policies that take into account:

1. The specific routers that need to be configured to handle the traffic for "WebServices applications on the eCommerce Server".

2. The set of operations, supported by these routers that will meet the objective of "Gold QoS for WebServices Applications on the eCommerce Server".

And the overall process should meet the third objective of ensuring that there is a means to verify that low-level policies actually meet the requirement defined by the high-level one. This example illustrates that the policy refinement problem is actually composed of two parts:

1. Refinement of abstract entities into concrete objects/devices.

2. Refinement of high-level goals into operations, supported by the concrete objects/devices, that when performed will achieve the high-level goal.

In order to solve these problems we need a formal representation for objects, their behaviour and organisation; a technique for refining high-level goals into more concrete ones; and finally a means of inferring the combination of operations that will achieve these concrete goals. To this end we use the formalism presented in [3] to model the behaviour and organisation of the objects, together with the goal elaboration technique developed by Darimont et al. [4], to refine high-level goals into concrete ones. However, the refined goals cannot be directly used in policies without first identifying the operations that will achieve them. To support this identification process, we introduce the concept of a *strategy*, which is the mechanism by which a given system can achieve a particular goal, i.e., a strategy is the relationship between the system description and the goal. By having a formal specification of the latter two types of information we can use abductive reasoning to infer the strategy.

In keeping with our previous work [3], we propose that the entire formalism be implemented in Event Calculus [5] since this is a particularly suitable notation for modelling the event-driven nature of the systems we are interested in; and also because this allows us to make use of the mapping from the Ponder policy notation to Event Calculus and the conflict detection techniques that we have already developed. We use the goal elaboration

technique presented in [4] because it provides the concept of domain-specific and domain-independent refinement patterns, logically proven goal refinement templates that can be easily reused. We can use such patterns to capture the refinement of goals that are commonly encountered in policy-based management, thus simplifying the refinement process for the user.

The paper is organised as follows. Section 2 presents background information on the techniques we are building on to develop our policy refinement solution. Section 3 presents the policy refinement approach together with the details for the formal notation being used; and Section 4 illustrates how the refinement technique might be applied to the example described above. In Section 5 we discuss the solution, its strengths and weaknesses; and in Section 6 we compare this work with existing research in the field. Finally Section 7 presents some conclusions together with directions for future work.

2. Background

2.1 Goal Elaboration

The first component of the policy refinement process to be considered is a technique for refining high-level goals, defined during the requirements gathering process, into concrete low-level policies. Figure 2 shows how the requirements of a system might be refined from high-level goals into implementable classes/modules. The decomposition of a goal can be either conjunctive (i.e. only by achieving all the sub-goals can we consider that the higher-level goal is achieved) or disjunctive (i.e. by achieving any one of the sub-goals we can consider the higher-level goal is achieved).

Note the two distinct phases of the refinement process. The first phase is one of goal refinement where the focus is on translating abstract goals into operationalised goals. An operationalised goal is one that has been assigned to specific agent whose capabilities enable the system to satisfy that goal. These goals are often referred to as the System Requirements. Taking the example presented previously, this process would transform the SLA requirement of providing gold QoS for a particular class of traffic into a set of goals that define the configuration changes that must be applied to the routers in the network. The second phase of the refinement process takes these system requirements and maps them to specific modules/operations that can be implemented within the context of the system architecture. This phase could be considered to be architectural or system design. In our example, this would involve identifying the operations to be invoked on the routers to achieve the desired goal.

In the above scheme, each high-level goal is refined into sub-goals, forming a goal refinement hierarchy where the dependencies between the goals at the different levels of refinement are based on the form of goal decomposition used (AND/OR). Additionally there can be dependencies between goals in different hierarchies. The process of refinement will involve following a particular path down the hierarchy, at each stage verifying the feasibility of achieving the higher-level goal in terms of the lower-level ones. If it is discovered that the goal cannot be achieved, it is necessary to elaborate the information at the higher-level such that suitable lower-level goals can be derived.

Work done by Darimont et al. [4], proposes a formal technique for elaborating goals grounded in Temporal Logic. Called KAOS, this approach represents each goal as a Temporal Logic rule and then makes use of refinement patterns to decompose these goals into a set of sub-goals that logically entail the original goal. Additionally, this technique makes use of obstacles (negated goals) which are then elaborated and resolved to provide new goals. This process results in a set of refined goals, and the identification of objects and operations that might operationalise them. The final stage of the procedure is to assign each of the refined goals to a specific object/operation such that the final system will meet the original requirements. Whilst the KAOS approach does not provide any automated support for the goal refinement process, it does define a library of domain-specific and domain-independent refinement patterns that have been logically proved.

A domain-independent goal refinement patterns uses properties of temporal logic operators to provide a proven relationship between a high level goal and a set of sub-goals. For example, the transitivity property of the ◊ R (R will eventually be true) operator provides the following simple domain-independent goal refinement pattern:

$$(P \Rightarrow \diamond R, R \Rightarrow \diamond Q) \vdash P \Rightarrow \diamond Q$$

```
If P is true then eventually R is true, AND
If R is true then eventually Q is true, THEN
If P is true then eventually Q is true.
```

In our example scenario, a domain-specific pattern might be one that describes the sub-goals required to guarantee QoS for a class of application traffic. The user could then refine the goal instance "provide Gold QoS to WebServices applications on the eCommerce Server", by instantiating this pattern with the Gold class of service and the appropriate application type. Once the user has specified appropriate sub-goals based on the particular pattern, the specification is checked for inconsistencies.

Policy-based systems use rules to govern their behavioural choices whilst satisfying the goals of the system. Therefore a policy refinement technique must provide a link between each goal and the underlying system behaviour in order to derive the different ways in which the system can satisfy the goal. This information can then be encoded into policies that control the behaviour of the system as needed. Whilst we can use the KAOS approach to refine abstract goals into lower-level ones, it does not provide a mechanism to connect the goals with the behaviour description of the system. Therefore, in this paper we show how the notation used by KAOS can be combined with state charts, Event Calculus and abductive reasoning to provide a practical refinement technique.

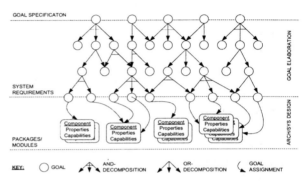

Figure 2: Goal refinement hierarchy

2.2 Event Calculus

We propose to use Event Calculus (EC) as the underlying formalism since it has well understood semantics; supports all modes of logical reasoning, including abduction; and the information we are interested in modelling involves events and temporal relationships. Event Calculus is a formal language for representing and reasoning about dynamic systems. Because the language supports a representation of time that is independent of any events that might occur in the system, it is a particularly useful way to specify a variety of event-driven systems. Since its initial presentation [4], a number of variations of the Event Calculus have been presented in the literature [6]. In this work we use the form presented in [7], consisting of (i) a set of time points (that can be mapped to the non-negative integers); (ii) a set of properties that can vary over the lifetime of the system, called *fluents*; and (iii) a set of event types. In addition the language includes a number of base predicates, initiates, terminates, holdsAt, happens, which are used to define some auxiliary predicates; and domain independent axioms. These are summarised in Figure 3.

This is the classical form of the Event Calculus where theories are written using Horn clauses. The frame problem is solved by circumscription, which allows the completion of the predicates initiates, terminates and happens, leaving open the predicates holdsAt, initiallyTrue and initiallyFalse. This approach allows the representation of partial domain knowledge (e.g. the initial state of the system). Formulae derived by the Event Calculus are in effect classically derived from the circumscription of the EC representation. To provide an implementation of such a calculus in Prolog, we use pos and neg functors. The semantics of the Prolog implementation assumes the Close World Assumption (CWA) and models are essentially Herbrand models where predicates are appropriately completed. The use of pos and neg functions on the fluents allows us to keep open the interpretation of fluents being true/false, in the same way as circumscription does in the classical representation. In this way we can guarantee that the implementation of our EC is sound and complete with respect to the classical EC formalisation. The correspondence between the classical EC with circumscription and the logic program implementation can be found in [6].

Base predicates:

initiates(A,B,T) event A initiates fluent B for all time > T.
terminates(A,B,T)   event A terminates fluent B for all time > T.
happens(A,T)   event A happens at time point T
holdsAt(B,T)   fluent B holds at time point T.
                    This predicate is useful when defining static
                    rules (e.g. state constraints)
initiallyTrue(B)   fluent B is initially true.
initiallyFalse(B)   fluent B is initially false.

Figure 3: Event Calculus predicates and axioms

The Event Calculus supports deductive, inductive and abductive reasoning. Deduction uses the description of the system behaviour together with the history of events occurring in the system to derive the fluents that will hold at a particular point in time. Induction aims to derive the descriptions of the system behaviour from a given event history and information about the fluents that hold at different points of time. However, the reasoning technique that is of particular interest to our work is abduction. Given the descriptions of the behaviour of the system, abduction can be used to determine the sequence of events that need to occur such that a given set of fluents will hold at a specified point in time.

3. Policy Refinement Approach

As mentioned previously, the KAOS approach provides a technique for refining abstract goals into lower-level ones. However these low-level goals cannot be directly used in refined policies. To do this, it is necessary to have a method for inferring the mechanism by which the system can achieve a goal at a given abstraction level.

At a given level of abstraction there will be some description of the system (SD) and the goals (G) to be achieved by the system. The relationship between the system description and the goals is the Strategy (S), i.e. the Strategy describes the mechanism by which the system represented by SD achieves the goals denoted by G. Formally this would be stated as:

(1) - $SD_x, S_x \vdash G_x$

x is a label denoting the abstraction level.

So, in our approach, it is expected that the user would provide a representation of the system description, in terms of the properties and behaviour of the components, together with a definition of the goals that the system must satisfy. The behaviour of the system is defined in terms of the pre- and post-conditions of the operations supported by the components, which the user can specify using a high-level notation such as state charts. Since the goals to be satisfied can be defined in terms of desired system states, they can be specified in a notation similar to that used to specify the post-conditions of the operations.

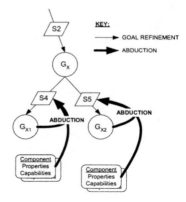

Figure 4: Deriving strategies from goals and system description

Once the user has provided this information, it is first necessary to transform it into a formal representation that supports automated analysis. Given the relationship between the system description, strategy and goal defined in (1) above we then use abduction to programmatically infer the strategies that will achieve a particular goal (Figure 4). Additionally, we can use the properties of the goal decomposition approach described previously to decompose the system description and strategies as follows:

$$(2) \quad - \quad G_{X1}, G_{X2}, \dots, G_{XN} \vdash G_X \quad \textit{Goal Decomposition}$$

$$(3) \quad - \quad SD_{X1}, S_{X1} \vdash G_{X1}$$
$$SD_{X2}, S_{X2} \vdash G_{X2} \quad \dots$$
$$SD_{XN}, S_{XN} \vdash G_{XN} \quad \textit{(from 1)}$$

This shows that if there is some combination of lower level goals from which we can infer the original goal, then for each of these sub-goals there must be a corresponding strategy and system description combination which will achieve it. Therefore, provided the goal decomposition is correct, intuitively the combination of the lower level system descriptions should allow inference of the abstract system description and similarly the combination of the lower level strategies should allow inference of the abstract strategy.

As mentioned previously, the other component of the refinement process is to refine abstract entities into concrete objects/devices in the system. For example, in the system illustrated in Figure 1, there might be an abstract entity called "Network" that logically consists of the "Engineering Network", "Core Network" etc., where each of these in turn consist of the routers and servers within them. We propose that a domain hierarchy be used to represent the relationships between the various abstract entities and the low-level concrete objects [8].

Domains provide a means of grouping objects to which policies apply and can be used to partition the objects in large systems according to geographical boundaries, object type, responsibility and authority. Membership of a domain is explicit and not defined in terms of a predicate on object attributes. An advantage of specifying policy scope in terms of domains is that objects can be added and removed from the domains to which policies apply without having to change the policies. The formal representation of the domain structure is as shown in [3].

In order to implement the approach outlined above, it is necessary to have a formal representation of the system description; and the strategies and goals. However, for the implementation to be usable, it would be ideal to be able to model the systems in a high-level notation and translate this into Event Calculus for analysis purposes. UML would be well suited for this purpose since it is widely used and is supported by many commercial tools.

This rest of this section outlines how UML would represent each of the types of information that need to be modelled together and describes how they can be translated into Event Calculus. The formal language being used is based on that described in [3], where in addition to the base predicates and axioms of Event Calculus we make use of the function symbols shown in Table 1.

3.1 System Description

The system description models the objects in the system in terms of their behaviour. The notation used to formally model the behaviour of objects is identical to that described in [3]. Using this notation, and building on the example used previously, it is possible to illustrate the use of these rules for modelling system behaviour. So, let us say there is an object of type DiffServRouter in the example system. This type has attributes to hold the IP interfaces and actions to configure various parameters of the router, which might be represented in UML as a class diagram. The actions for the DiffServRouter type can be specified in a UML state chart representation as shown in Figure 5.

It is possible to transform this state chart into the Event Calculus notation presented previously where the input shown on each transition arrow is the action being performed. For transition between different states, the current state values become the PostFalse fluents; any actions associated with the transition and next state values become the PostTrue fluents; and the current state values become the PreConditions. Self-transitions should not specify the current state as PostFalse fluents. So following this scheme, the transition labelled (**) in Figure 5 would be represented in the Event Calculus as follows:

Table 1: Function symbols.

Symbol	Description
state(Obj, V₀, Value)	Represents the value of a variable of an object in the system. It can be used in an initiallyTrue predicate to specify the initial state of the system and also as part of rules that define the effect of actions.
op(Obj, Action(V_P))	Used to denote the operations specified in an action event (see below)
systemEvent(Event)	Represents any event that is generated by the system at runtime. The Event argument specified in this term can be any application specific predicate or function symbol.
doAction(ObjSubj, op(ObjTarg, Action(V_P)))	Represents the event of the action specified in the operation term being performed by the subject, ObjSubj, on the target object, ObjTarg.

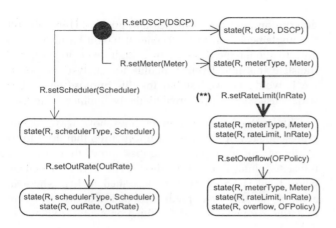

Figure 5: UML state chart for DiffServRouter type

```
initiates(
  doAction(_, op(diffServRouter,
                        setRateLimit(inRate))),
  state(diffServRouter,rateLimit, inRate), T) ←
  holdsAt(pos(state(diffServRouter,
                        meterType, Meter)), T).
```

The above rule also shows how we make use of the pos() function as described in Section 2.2. Note that, whilst we have shown the details of the Event Calculus representation of the system organisation and behaviour models, it is not necessary for the user to directly specify anything in the formal notation. Instead they would use UML class diagrams, state charts together with a domain model chart and the system will generate the Event Calculus code required for the refinement procedure.

3.2 Goals

A UML profile for modelling goals and goal refinement patterns described in the KAOS approach has already been developed and is presented in [9]. Figure 6 shows how an AND-decomposition of a goal would be represented in this notation. The profile defines a number of attributes for the <<goal>> stereotype, including one to hold the temporal logic representation of the goal. However, in order to support the formal analysis required for validating the goal refinements, it is still necessary to map the temporal logic formalism of KAOS into Event Calculus and describe a mechanism for verifying the correctness of a goal refinement.

The goal refinement patterns provided by KAOS make use of some of the temporal logic operators described in [10]:

X	X holds in the current state
◇ X,	X will eventually hold
◆ X,	X held at some time in the past
Y W X,	Y holds *unless* X holds

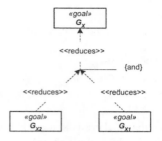

Figure 6: UML representation of the AND-decomposition of a goal

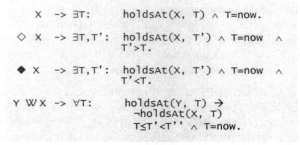

Figure 7: Event Calculus representation of temporal logic operators

The Event Calculus representation for each of these temporal operators is shown in Figure 7.

The UML profile in [9] also describes a high-level notation for representing these patterns, each of which can be mapped into a set of temporal logic formulas. These can be used by our system to guide the user in defining the sub-goals for a given goal and also to validate the correctness of the sub-goals. For example, applying the (P => ◇ R, R => ◇ Q) ⊢ P => ◇ Q pattern would present the user with a template of the following form:

```
If P is true then eventually R is true, AND
If R is true then eventually Q is true.
```

It would be up to the user to insert the appropriate value for the missing goal, R. The formal version of the goals would then be mapped into Event Calculus and the system would assert each of the sub-goals into the overall formal specification and attempt to prove the following properties of the refinement:

1. G1, G2, .. Gn ⊢ G *(entailment)*: validated by trying prove G after asserting all the sub-goals

2. ∀i: ∧ji Gj ⊬ G *(minimality)*: validated by checking the entailment property for each subset of the sub-goals.

3. G1, G2, ..., Gn ⊬ false *(consistency)*: validated by making sure that asserting the sub-goals does not nullify the entailment properties of any existing goal refinements.

If it is not possible to show the entailment property for the goal refinement, this indicates that either there is a missing sub-goal or the wrong goal refinement pattern has been applied.

3.3 Strategies

So far we have discussed the types of information that must be specified by the user for the refinement procedure to work. However, strategies do not fall into this category since they will be actually be derived by the abductive analysis procedure used in the refinement approach. Therefore, it is expected that the formal representation of a strategy is actually determined by the representation of the system behaviour and goals defined above.

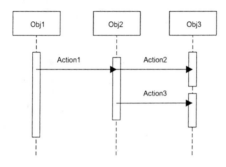

Figure 8: UML sequence chart for a strategy

As mentioned previously, a strategy describes the mechanism by which the system can achieve a given goal and is therefore defined by a set of operations to be performed sequentially or in parallel. Specifically, the strategy is defined using a conjunction of happens(doAction(...), T) predicates having a relationship between the time values that corresponds to the order in which the actions should be performed. For example, a strategy that defines Obj1 performs Obj2.Action1 and Obj2 perfoms Obj3.Action2 in parallel, followed by Obj2 performing Obj3.Action3 would be represented in our formalism as:

```
happens(doAction(Obj1, op(Obj2, Action1)), T0),
happens(doAction(Obj1, op(Obj3, Action2)), T0),
happens(doAction(Obj2, op(Obj3, Action3)), T1),
T0<T1.
```

In the interests of usability, it would be better if strategies are presented to the user in a high-level form. So, given that strategies define a method invocation trace for achieving a given goal, we can represent them in

UML using a message sequence chart. The UML model for the example above is shown in Figure 8.

A strategy is considered to be abstract if any of the actions defined in it is a method defined as part of an abstract entity. High-level, abstract policies can be defined using such strategies in the action clause. If the strategy is not abstract, it can be used in a concrete, implementable policy.

4. Policy Refinement: An Example

In this section we describe how the formal representation and approach presented in this paper can be used to refine Service Level Agreement policies for the example system shown in Figure 1. Figure 9a shows the UML model for the objects in this system, including the abstract entities, Network and Router. The behavioural model is as shown in Figure 5. The high level policy we wish to refine is stated as follows:

On demand the network should provide Gold quality of service to web services application traffic on the eCommerce server.

The goal we are interested in achieving is to provide gold QoS for network traffic to a particular application on the eCommerce server. The goal hierarchy for reducing this goal is shown in Figure 9b and the temporal logic representation for some of these sub-goals is presented below (tfc1 denotes the Traffic Class relevant to the goal):

G_1 - send(pkt, tfc1) ⇒ ◇qos(pkt,gold).

G_{11} - send(pkt, tfc1) ⇒
◇routed(pkt, R, tfc1).

G_{12} - routed(pkt, R, tfc1) ⇒
◇detected(pkt, R, tfc1).

G_{13} - detected(pkt, R, tfc1) ⇒
◇configured(R, tfc1, gold).

G_{14} - configured(R, tfc1, gold) ⇒
◇qos(pkt, gold).

G_{131} - detected(pkt, R, tfc1) ⇒
◇routerParmsKnown(R, gold, parms).

G_{132} - routerParmsKnown(R, gold, parms) ⇒
◇ parmsSet(R, gold, parms).

G_{133} - parmsSet(R, gold, parms) ⇒
◇ configured(R, tfc1, gold).

At each level of goal reduction, we use abduction to determine the strategy that will achieve the sub-goals. The absence of a strategy indicates that there is some information missing in the system description at one of

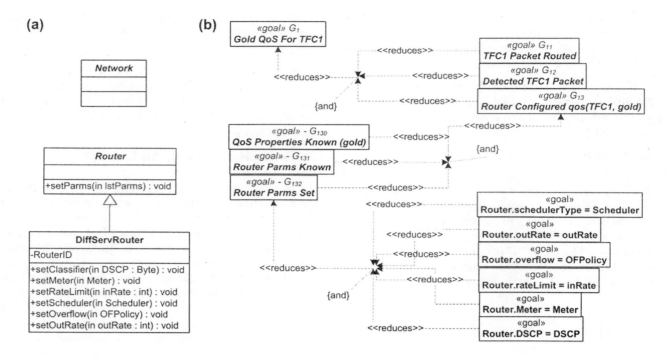

(a)

Network

Router

+setParms(in lstParms) : void

DiffServRouter
-RouterID
+setClassifier(in DSCP : Byte) : void
+setMeter(in Meter) : void
+setRateLimit(in inRate : int) : void
+setScheduler(in Scheduler) : void
+setOverflow(in OFPolicy) : void
+setOutRate(in outRate : int) : void

(b)

«goal» G₁
Gold QoS For TFC1

«goal» G₁₁
TFC1 Packet Routed

«goal» G₁₂
Detected TFC1 Packet

«goal» G₁₃
Router Configured qos(TFC1, gold)

«goal» - G₁₃₀
QoS Properties Known (gold)

«goal» - G₁₃₁
Router Parms Known

«goal» - G₁₃₂
Router Parms Set

«goal»
Router.schedulerType = Scheduler

«goal»
Router.outRate = outRate

«goal»
Router.overflow = OFPolicy

«goal»
Router.rateLimit = inRate

«goal»
Router.Meter = Meter

«goal»
Router.DSCP = DSCP

Figure 9: (a) UML representation of enterprise network example; (b) UML representation of goal hierarchy

the levels of abstraction. For example, at the top level of this example, there is no abducible strategy for the goal "G₁₃ - Router Configured for Gold Qos". This can be addressed by extending the abstract Router object with a method configureQos(gold). Similarly, the strategy for the lower level goal, "G₁₃₂ - Set the router parameters" can be achieved by defining the behaviour of the setParms(…) method of the Router object appropriately. Once these modifications have been made, the abduction process will yield abstract strategies (since the operations derived belong to abstract entities) for achieving each of the goals. In order to realise a concrete strategy, it is necessary to refine the goals further, into the lowest level ones shown in Figure 9b.

Now, attempting to abduce the lowest level goals yields a set of concrete operations that configure the DiffServRouter object in the appropriate way:

```
?- showStrategy([
    state(diffServRouter, dscp, Var_DSCP),
    state(diffServRouter, meter, Var_Meter), ..
    state(diffServRouter, ofp, Var_OFP]).

1 - happens(doAction(_, diffServRouter,
                     setDSCP(Var_DSCP), 0),
2 - happens(doAction(_, diffServRouter,
                     setMeter(Var_Meter), 0),
    ...
6 - happens(doAction(_, diffServRouter,
                     setOverflow(Var_OFP), 2).
```

Having identified the actions required in the lower level policy, all that remains is to refine the subject and target entities. In the original high-level policy we can identify the target entity as "the network". For the policy we are refining, we are only concerned with objects that are of type DiffServRouter (since this is the only object type in the policy's action clause). Therefore the refined target objects can be determined by traversing the domain hierarchy and selecting the objects of type DiffServRouter.

For ease of future specification, we can create a new domain DiffServRouters, and assign each of these target objects as members. Given there is no information about the subject entity in the top-level policy, it requires the user to apply some application specific knowledge to identify the correct subject for the low-level policy as DiffServConfigMgr. The event mentioned in the high-level policy is "on Demand" and given that there is no information in the system description about how this might be refined; it is up to the user to specify the lower level event to be used by the policy as adminRequest(Parms). This yields the final low-level policy as:

```
oblig /SLA/ConfigGoldQoS {
  on       adminRequest(Parms);
  subject  s = /PMA/DiffServeConfigMgr;
  target   t = /DiffDServRouters/;
  do       (t.setDSCP(Parms.DSCP) &&
            t.setMeter(Parms.Meter)) ->
            ...
            t.setOverflow(Parms.OFP);
}
```

5. Discussion

The approach described above provides a means of determining the strategy for achieving a particular goal, and identifying the specific objects in the system that are required to execute the strategy. However, there is no mention of how to decide whether a particular strategy should be specified as a policy, as opposed to directly implementing as system functionality. Using a policy specification differs from a direct implementation in that a policy controls the required functionality rather than implementing it directly. Therefore policies provide a great deal of flexibility in situations where there a several alternative strategies for achieving a goal, and it would be useful to dynamically switch between these strategies depending on the run-time state of the system. For instance, in the example scenario outlined above, the Gold QoS requirement might be met by either configuring the DiffServRouters in the manner described, or by dropping packets belonging to other applications. In this situation, two alternative low-level policies could be defined such that the strategy most appropriate for a given situation is used.

The exact circumstance in which a strategy should be encoded as a policy, rather than system functionality, will depend on the particular application domain. So, whilst there is no obvious way to automate this decision, we propose the following guidelines to determine the situations in which a policy-based implementation would be appropriate:

1. If the goal refinement process results in a disjunction of sub-goals (i.e. the high-level goal can be achieved by one of an OR-decomposed set of sub-goals), the strategies derived for each of the sub-goals could be encoded as policies.

2. If the system supports multiple strategies for achieving a given goal, each of these strategies could be encoded in a separate policy.

3. If a strategy has parameter values that the user is interested in changing at a future point in time, implementing such a strategy in a policy will provide the necessary flexibility to do this.

These guidelines should apply to all types of application. Additionally there may be application-specific guidelines that further guide the user in their decision to apply policies.

The policy refinement process described in this paper is built on a systematic, formal approach to refining goals thus ensuring that the strategies derived actually meet the requirements of the high-level policy. Also, the derivation of these strategies makes use of a description of the system, which means the policies derived are enforceable by the system. Using domain hierarchies to model the relationships between abstract entities and concrete objects, together with type information, allows the system to identify the objects that may be required to execute the strategies. These features illustrate how this solution satisfies the principal objectives of a policy refinement process identified in [1]. Additionally, by implementing the process using a formal representation it is possible to automate parts of the refinement process.

Automation of the technique presented here requires a tool that allows the user to specify the system behaviour and goal information in UML and then translates this representation into Event Calculus for analysis. Also, the results of the analysis should be presented in an easy to understand form. To achieve this, we envisage the final tool solution will integrate a UML editor, such as ArgoUML, with a Prolog system implementing an abductive reasoning engine. For the latter part of the solution, we will use the A-System with SICStus Prolog [11]. This latter part of the architecture has already been used to develop the policy analysis approach presented previously [5]. It is expected that this refinement and analysis tool will be integrated with a policy management system such as the Ponder Toolkit [8]. Development of an integrated refinement and analysis toolkit will form the core of our future work.

An important consideration when developing any formal technique is to ensure that the implementation is decidable and computationally feasible. In the Prolog implementation of the example, we have been able to ensure this by limiting ourselves to stratified logic programs. This permits a constrained use of recursion and negation while disallowing those combinations that lead to undecidable programs [12]. It is anticipated that we can remain within the realms of stratified logic programs for most applications of our technique. This would be advantageous since there are numerous studies that identify stratified logic as a class of first order logic that supports logic programs that are decidable [13, 14]. Moreover, such programs are decidable in polynomial time [14, 15]. A more detailed analysis of the computational complexity and expressive power of stratified logic can be found in [14].

One limitation of the work presented is that it does not provide a means of deriving the parameter values required by the operations to achieve a particular goal. Such a capability would be particularly useful when refining network management policies, where for example there might be a requirement that the network configure itself to provide optimal bandwidth utilisation by calculating the appropriate values for parameters like the input rate of the DiffServ meters. As part of our ongoing research, we plan to investigate the possibility of integrating constraint logic programming techniques to provide such capabilities. Another limitation is that at present we treat all the goals together, only accounting for whether their decomposition is based on the AND/OR connective. However, there may be situations where it is necessary to account for an explicit temporal ordering of the goals when performing refinement. Whilst this may be easily handled by making use of the time information provided by the Event Calculus representation, the implications must be fully considered and this requires further investigation.

6. Related Work

Work by Kelly [17], introduces the idea of annotating a goal refinement hierarchy with strategies for representing safety cases. However, in the context of safety case representation the strategies document the justification for the lower-level goals achieving the high-level goal. In contrast, the goal refinement approach used in this paper uses logical proofs to justify the validity of the goal decomposition and strategies are used to represent the mechanism by which the system can achieve a given goal. Therefore strategies provide the relationship between the system architecture and the goals.

In the wider software engineering context, there is a body of work on the synthesis of reactive systems [18], which aims to derive the system behaviour description based on temporal formulae that describe the output of the system. This is quite different from the approach presented in this paper, since our objective is to simply identify the sequences of actions, from the given system description, that will achieve a particular goal.

There are few examples of practical approaches for policy refinement. One such example is described in work done at Hewlett-Packard Laboratories, which outlines a policy-authoring environment that provides a policy wizard tool, called POWER, for refining policies [19]. Here, a domain expert first develops a set of policy templates, expressed as Prolog programs, and the policy authoring tools have an integrated inference engine that interprets these programs to guide the user through the refinement process. A major limitation of this approach is the absence of any analysis capabilities to evaluate the consistency of the refined policies. Also, the POWER approach depends on the domain expert having a detailed understanding of the entire system to develop a usable policy template. The refinement approach outlined in this paper avoids these problems by not only incorporating a complete analysis technique but also supporting abductive reasoning for deriving the action sequences required to achieve a goal.

7. Conclusions

In this paper we have presented an approach to policy refinement that allows the inference of the low-level actions that satisfy a high-level goal by making use of existing techniques in goal-based requirements elaboration and the Event Calculus. We have ensured the usability of the approach by showing how the user can specify the system using UML and how this specification can be translated into the formal representation for analysis. We have shown how the approach provides automation support for the refinement process when given a specification of the system behaviour and the goals to be satisfied. In order to relate the system behaviour specification with the goals, we introduce the concept of strategies and show how these can be used in the specification of policies.

There is ongoing work to investigate how the presented formalism can be extended to support the identification of the events and constraints to be included in the low-level policies. However, the immediate focus of our future work is to develop adequate tool support that uses the technique described here together with the analysis approach presented previously [3] to provide a comprehensive environment for policy specification. Additionally we will be investigating the use of the technique described here for refining and analysing traffic management policies for network QoS management. The areas of further investigation identified in the discussion will also be addressed as part of this work.

Acknowledgements

We acknowledge financial support for this work from the EPSRC (Grant Nos: GR/R31409/01 and GR/S79985/01) and CISCO Systems Inc. Additionally, we would like to thank Morris Sloman and Naranker Dulay for their valuable feedback during the preparation of this paper.

References

[1] J. Moffett and M. S. Sloman, "Policy Hierarchies for Distributed Systems Management," *IEEE JSAC*, vol. 11, pp. 1404-14, 1993.
[2] D. C. Verma, *Policy-Based Networking: Architecture and Algorithms*: New Riders Publishing, 2001.
[3] A. K. Bandara, E. C. Lupu, and A. Russo, "Using Event Calculus to Formalise Policy Specification and Analysis," presented at 4th IEEE Workshop on Policies for Networks and Distributed Systems (Policy 2003), Lake Como, Italy, 2003.
[4] R. Darimont and A. van Lamsweerde, "Formal Refinement Patterns for Goal-Driven Requirements Elaboration," *4th ACM Symposium on the Foundations of Software Engineering (FSE4)*, pp. 179-190, 1996.
[5] R. A. Kowalski and M. J. Sergot, "A logic-based calculus of events," *New Generation Computing*, vol. 4, pp. 67-95, 1986.

[6] R. Miller and M. Shanahan, "The Event Calculus in Classical Logic Alternative Axiomatisations," in *Computational Logic: Logic Programming and Beyond, Essays in Honour of Robert A. Kowalski, Part II.*, vol. 2048, *Lecture Notes in Computer Science*, A. Kakas and F. Sadri, Eds.: Springer, 1999, pp. 452-490.

[7] A. Russo, R. Miller, B. Nuseibeh, and J. Kramer, "An Abductive Approach for Analysing Event-Based Requirements Specifications," presented at 18th Int. Conf. on Logic Programming (ICLP), Copenhagen, Denmark, 2002.

[8] N. Damianou, T. Tonouchi, N. Dulay, E. Lupu, and M. Sloman, "Tools for Domain-based Policy Management of Distributed Systems," presented at Network Operations and Management Symposium (NOMS 2002), Frorence, Italy, 2002a.

[9] W. J. Heaven and A. Finkelstein, "A UML Profile to Support Requirements Engineering with KAOS," *IEE Proceedings - Software*, 2003.

[10] Z. Manna and A. Pnueli, *The Temporal Logic of Reactive and Concurrent Systems*: Springer-Verlag, 1992.

[11] B. van Nuffelen and A. Kakas, "A-System : Programming with abduction," presented at Logic Programming and Nonmonotonic Reasoning (LPNMR 2001), 2001.

[12] K. R. Apt, H. A. Blair, and A. Walker, "Towards a Theory of Declarative Knowledge," in *Foundations of Deductive Databases*, J. Minker, Ed. San Mateo, CA: Morgan Kaufmann, 1988, pp. 89-148.

[13] G. Jager and R. F. Stark, "The Defining Power of Stratified and Hierarchical Logic Programs," *Journal of Logic Programming*, vol. 15, pp. 55-77, 1993.

[14] E. Dantsin, T. Eiter, G. Gottlob, and A. Voronkov, "Complexity and Expressive Power of Logic Programming," presented at 12th Annual IEEE Conf. on Computational Complexity (CCC'97), Ulm, Germany, 1997.

[15] S. Jajodia, P. Samarati, and V. S. Subrahmanian, "A Logical Language for Expressing Authorisations," presented at IEEE Symposium on Security and Privacy, Oakland, USA, 1997a.

[16] E. Giunchiglia, J. Lee, V. Lifschitz, N. McCain, and H. Turner, "Nonmonotonic causal theories," *Artificial Intelligence*, vol. To appear, 2003.

[17] T. Kelly, "Arguing Safety – A Systematic Approach to Managing Safety Cases," in *Department of Computer Science*. York: University of York, 1998, pp. 341.

[18] A. Pneuli and R. Rosner, "On the Synthesis of a Reactive Module," presented at ACM Symposium on the Principles of Programming Languages (POPL'89), pp. 179-190, 1989.

[19] M. Casassa Mont, A. Baldwin, and C. Goh, "POWER Prototype: Towards Integrated Policy-Based Management," HP Laboratories Bristol, Bristol, UK October 1999.

Incremental Validation of Policy-Based Systems

A. Graham +
angus@angusgraham.ca

T. Radhakrishnan +
krishnan@cs.concordia.ca

C. Grossner *
cliff.grossner@newstepnetworks.com

+ Dept. of Computer Science, Concordia University, Montreal, Canada
* NewStep Networks, Ottawa, Canada

Abstract

Management and control of systems are becoming more and more automated and based on policies that are expressed in a suitable policy specification language. Such policies need to be validated to ensure correct operation of the managed or controlled systems. The set of policies in a system is dynamic and is constantly changing. When this set is very large, incremental policy validation is a topic worth exploring. In this paper, such a notion of incremental policy-validation is introduced. The well-known decision tables, a systems analysis tool, are adapted for representing policies. Based on such adaptations, two algorithms are developed for incremental validation and they are compared, with respect to the number of computations they require.

1. Introduction

Policy based systems offer the capabilities to dynamically change the behavior of software. Such systems are gaining wide popularity in the industry today. Applications for these systems range from event notification software [1],[2],[3] to network management [4],[5],[6],[7] to electronic commerce [8],[9].

Policies can be used in a system to control the behavior of the system, to control who is permitted to perform particular actions, and who is not. The system can either have all end-users enter their own policies, or have one or more policy administrators to be in charge of policy specification. Policies can be entered before the execution of the system begins, but many systems allow the entry of policies to occur during system execution as well. The form in which the policies are entered varies from system to system. Some systems require that policies be entered in a strict code-like format, whereas others allow natural language input.

When policies are entered into the system, they must be validated. When a new policy is entered into the system, it is not necessarily consistent with the rest of the system. A policy could lead to a combination of actions that are illegal in the application, or actions that conflict with actions specified by another policy. To detect any such anomalies, a validation process is needed. Validation can be performed at specification time, when a policy is entered into the system, or at runtime, catching conflicts as they are triggered but before they are executed. Detecting conflicts between policies is an important concern, and solutions have been provided to tackle the problems of both specification time and runtime policy validation. In this paper we are concerned with the former.

As policy based systems get larger, the problem of policy validation becomes more complex. Systems may have a very large number of policies, which would mean the validation process would take a long time if all policies were considered. However, if a small change is made, the number of policies affected by this change could be relatively small. If the entire set of policies is validated every time a small change is made, then the system would spend a great deal of time performing validation which may not be practical, or necessary. In some cases, the system may have to be brought offline in order to perform the validation. If the policy set were changed often, this would pose a serious problem when providing users with continuous service. Clearly this delay makes it unacceptable to revalidate the entire set of policies every time a change is made if the set of policies is large.

In this paper, we suggest "incremental policy validation" as a new approach. More specifically, we will examine how to determine if a set of policies is consistent after a small change to the set has been made. Finding only those policies which are affected by the change, and then validating that small subset will do this. This method will be analyzed and compared to a non-incremental validation solution.

We introduce the notion of storing policies in "decision tables format" and show how this format can help to check a set of policies for completeness. Also we indicate that the method used for checking decision tables for consistency could possibly be used in future to detect conflicts in policies. In order to accommodate all of the policy information, the decision table format is modified.

The concept of trigger chaining has been introduced in this paper in order to see which policies will trigger other policies upon firing. This concept introduces a new kind of conflict, in that a policy firing immediately after another may undo the actions of the first. This new type of conflict is explained and a method of incremental validation is developed in order to detect these conflicts. The method is analyzed and compared to performing an exhaustive revalidation of the entire system. The concept of trigger chaining also introduces the notion of cyclic conflicts, which is introduced but not discussed in detail in this paper.

2. Policy Based Systems

In recent years the software industry has been moving towards building software that can be customized by the user so it can meet the individual's needs. Policies are one way in which this customizability can be delivered. Policies also separate the behavior aspect of the software from the main functions. This allows either the main functionality of the software or the user's custom behavior to be changed without affecting the other [4]. Users can enter policies directly using some formal policy definition language, or can enter them at a higher level and have them translated to the definition language automatically. A policy can be analyzed for correctness and consistency before it is translated to the final code to be executed [6].

Because there are multiple policies in a given system, it is important to examine how one policy will affect another. If there are two policies which are triggered to fire at the same time, and they contradict one another, these policies are said to **conflict**. The process of checking policies to see if they conflict is called **policy validation**. Often conflicts can be detected when the policies are entered into the system (specification time) [10]. Although it is often advantageous to detect potential conflicts at specification time, this may not always be possible. Some conditions are based on states of the system, which are not known at the time of policy specification [10],[11]. In this case, the only way to detect the conflict is while the system is executing (runtime) [4]. Although the notion of runtime policy validation is important, this paper will focus on the problem of specification time policy validation.

Lupu and Sloman define two types of conflicts that can occur between policies in their model: **modality conflicts** and **application specific conflicts**. In their work, policies are associated with a mode. According to their definition, a modality conflict arises when two policies with opposite modality refer to the same subject, actions, and targets. This can happen in three ways:

- The subjects are both obligated-to and obligated-not-to perform actions on the targets.
- The subjects are both authorized and forbidden to perform actions on the targets.
- The subjects are obligated but forbidden to perform actions on the targets [11].

Application specific conflicts occur when two rules contradict each other due to the context of the application. Examples of this are: conflict of priorities for resources, conflict of duties, conflict of interest, actions that perform opposing tasks. Two rules may or may not conflict depending on the application and the "common sense" rules associated with that application. Therefore, in order to detect these kinds of conflicts, the system must have some sort of extra application specific knowledge. This extra knowledge is entered in the form of meta-policies. The meta-policies describe assumptions the system must make and explains how the system's "world" works. A set of policies may be consistent in one application and inconsistent in another due to the difference in the applications' meta-policy [11].

Lupu and Sloman provide a method of checking policies as they are specified for conflicts. Their method of policy validation involves examining the entire set of policies, or at very least all the policies found in one domain. They do not provide any method of incrementally checking a very small number of policies when a new policy is added or modified, to determine if the new set of policies is consistent. Although Lupu and Sloman acknowledge the need for run-time conflict checking, they do not discuss any methods to perform this type of checking [11].

Fraser and Badger [12] propose a way to detect conflicts for new rules that are introduced at run-time. Their approach first examines the new rules to see if the new policy is well formed. If so the next test is to see if it conflicts with the rest of the rule base, and if so, the new rule is rejected. The technique they propose, however, is for use with the Domain and Type Enforcement (DTE) prototype kernel, and so is specific to DTE.

Chomicki, Lobo, and Naqvi [8] propose a way to resolve conflicts. Instead of detecting conflicts at specification time, they perform detection and resolution at run time. There are monitors in the system, which detect actions that cannot occur together, and then decide whether to delete one of them, or delete one of them plus the other actions that were meant to execute along with it. They suggest obtaining priorities for each policy from the user in order to decide which actions should be canceled when conflicts arise. Since the detection and resolution is performed at run time, predicting which rules will conflict is not a problem. However, there may be some rules, which by examining them at specification time, we know will always conflict. If these conflicts were detected at specification time, the policy administrator could modify the rules so that this conflict would be avoided at run time. Their approach offers no specification time conflict detection, which could eliminate some of the automatic conflict resolution needed.

Out of all the specification languages we examined, Lupu and Sloman's language appears to be the most flexible. It offers both positive and negative modifications of authorization and obligation policies, and allows policies to have priority values. For these reasons we have chosen to use their policy specification language (PSL) for our policy model. Although we do not focus on policy entry in this paper, we assume that all policies entered into the system are done so in the form of Lupu and Sloman's policy specification language.

Our model will store policies in an internal policy format in order to perform conflict checking and other analysis on the policies. In order to execute the policies, they must be transformed from this internal representation into a form that can be executed. Although we are not concerned with how this is done, for the purposes of this article we assume that after conflict checking and analysis, the policies are transformed into rules that can be entered in a rule engine such as an expert system.

3. Representing Policies as Decision Tables

Decision tables are a formal way to specify the behavior of a software system. It groups conditions with actions that will be performed upon the conditions being met. These groups of conditions and actions are called rules and stored as columns in the table. Decision tables offer an easy way to analyze whether a set of rules is complete and consistent. This will benefit us by allowing policy rules to be checked for completeness, as shown further on.

A decision table is made up of four parts. The top left quadrant of a decision table is called the condition stub. The condition stub lists all the possible conditions that can occur in the system. The bottom left quadrant is called the action stub. The action stub lists all the possible actions that can be performed by the system [13]. The top right quadrant of a decision table is made up of condition entries. The condition entries hold the answers to the questions asked in the condition stub. The bottom right quadrant is made up of action entries. The action entries hold the answers to the questions asked in the action stub. Each column of answers in the table is called a rule [14]. Each rule indicates which conditions must be met in order for its actions to be performed [13]. When the events and states in the system match the conditions specified in a rule, the actions in that rule are executed [14].

As mentioned earlier, policy is concerned with two overall types of inconsistency: modality conflicts and application specific conflicts. In classic decision table theory, the concern is with two other types of conflicts: inter-column inconsistency and intra-column inconsistency. Inter-column inconsistency occurs when two rules in the decision table have overlapping conditions. When the conditions for the two rules are matched at run time, the system does not know which rule it should act upon [13]. This is also referred to as having an ambiguous table. When the two rules with overlapping conditions have the same actions, the ambiguity is said to be apparent. If the rules specify different actions to be performed, the ambiguity is said to be real [15]. In decision table terminology, having a real ambiguity means the table is inconsistent [16].

It has been said that ambiguities must be detected and removed from decision tables [17]. However, King and Johnson have argued that this is an unnecessary restriction to those applications which require only one action for a set of conditions. They argue that some applications may require that two or more actions be performed when one set of conditions is matched, and that this is perfectly acceptable [15]. Lew also used these kinds of rules by providing a vector action set as opposed to a single action for each rule [16]. For our purposes, it is perfectly acceptable to have more than one action executed upon a set of conditions being matched. Therefore, detecting the presence or lack of ambiguities in our table will not lead to concluding whether or not our set of policies is consistent, since our notion of consistency is different from that associated with single-action-rule decision tables.

Intra-column inconsistency refers to a rule having conflict within itself [13]. For example, say one rule includes two conditions $x = 6$ and $x + y < 3$. If x and y must be positive integers, this rule's conditions are inconsistent. The inconsistency notion can be extended to cover an action combination that does not make sense according to the "world" the system operates in. Intra-column inconsistency checking, therefore, seems to map quite well to the notion of application specific conflicts in policy. Using existing intra-column consistency checking algorithms to solve the problem of policy consistency checking is not discussed in this paper and is left for future work.

In what follows, we describe how to transform policies into a decision table representation. Firstly, for the purpose of storing policies as rules in decision tables, we will consider an event to be a specialized form of "condition" in a decision table. In this way, we will not need to modify our decision tables to be able to specify which events will trigger particular rules. We can simply make a condition indicating that "event E has occured". This solves the problem of representing both events and conditions in the table, which was originally meant only to represent conditions. For the remainder of this paper the word condition in a decision table will refer to our expanded notion of condition, which is either a condition from the rule or an event from the rule.

Decision tables lack two important attributes that are represented in the PSL we are using, however: the notion of modality, and rule priority. In Sloman's PSL, each rule has a single modality value. Therefore, we extend the decision table structure such that each rule has a value representing the modality. We add a new section to the decision table format (see Figure 1), called *Modality*, which will consist of exactly one row representing the modality values for all the rules.

	Rule1	Rule2	Rule3	Rule4	Rule5
Modality	A+	A+	A+	A+	A-
Priority	MED.	MED.	MED.	HIGH	MED.
All Reports Submitted	YES	NO	YES	NO	NO
Room Booked	YES	NO	NO	YES	
Chair Appointed	YES	NO	YES		
Book a Room		3	2	1	
Announce Exam	√	1		2	
Appoint Chair		4			
Find Examiners		2	1	3	
Defend					√

Figure 1. An example of our modified decision table format

If two rules are triggered at the same time, we may wish there to be priority values associated with each rule as suggested by Sloman, in order to determine which rule should be fired first. Therefore, we need to add a *Priority* section to the decision table in order to indicate this priority value. The entries in *Priority* can be varied depending on the sort of priority used in the policy specification language. It could be numeric values, strings such as HIGH, MEDIUM, LOW, or some other form of priority indicator.

The order of appearance of actions in a classic decision table rule does not affect the order of execution of these actions. If it did, then a particular action X would always be performed before another action Y because actions in the same table always appear in the same order. This may be contrary to what is desired. Therefore, we modify the decision table such that it gives us a way to represent the desired sequence of execution of the actions. There are two ways this can be done: absolute ordering and relative ordering. Using absolute ordering we can specify that a particular action will be the first to execute, another action will be the second, etc. Using relative ordering, we can specify relative execution priorities for each action. That way, some actions could have the same priority, when it is not important which is executed first. An example of our modified decision table format is shown in , with the new and modified areas shaded.

Our next concern is how the policies should be grouped. A policy rule is stored in a decision table as a rule in the table. How to store entire policies or policy sets is not as obvious a choice. A single decision table could be used to store the rules of one single policy, all the policies in a particular policy set, or all the policies in the entire system. There is really no restriction in this respect. However, large decision tables could become

unwieldy in terms of memory usage, thereby increasing the time needed to update the table or analyze it for consistency [18]. Therefore, it may be beneficial to store each policy as a separate decision table. This is also advantageous because in order to check for local consistency, often only one policy will need to be compared with itself. On the other hand, storing entire sets of policies in a single decision table can help to organize policies by keeping related policies together. Thus, there exists a trade-off in representing the policies of an organization in the form of a set of decision tables.

In the case where multiple policies are being checked for consistency, two or more tables can be temporarily merged into one larger table for the purpose of analysis. Research has been done on how to best merge decision tables into larger tables in order to optimize performance [18]. In our case, merging the tables would be a similar process, but for a different reason.

Then, the decision tables must be transformed into some form that can be executed. There have been several algorithms devised on how to translate the information given in decision tables into an executable code form [16],[19],[20],[21]. Generally these algorithms translate the contents of the decision table into a flowchart or execution tree. However, with declarative languages such as CLIPS [22], JESS [23], and PROLOG [24], we could simply form rules in the desired language directly from the rules in the decision table. Rule engines have been developed over many years with algorithms designed for the execution of declarative rules. In that case, all we need is a translation from the policy terms in our decision table rules to actual executable terms in the declarative language. Vanthienen and Wets [25] have discussed how easy it is to convert decision tables into rules that are executable by an expert system shell.

4. Incremental Policy Validation

Clearly stated, the problem of incremental policy validation is this: Let there be a pool of rules R. Assume that these rules have been validated somehow to check for conflicts, and R has been determined to be consistent. Suppose a change ΔR is made to R, such that the number of rules that have changes is much smaller than the total number of rules in R. We want to see if the set of rules R is still consistent without having to revalidate the entire set. We are aiming to revalidate R with significantly less effort than is needed to revalidate the entire set of rules. In particular we will show that this can be done in linear time.

First, let us make the restriction on our rule-based system that events cannot happen concurrently. One event must occur before or after another, even if they are separated by only an extremely small time interval. Based on this assumption, two rules can be triggered at the same time if and only if they contain the same triggering event in their conditional statements.

For our discussion, let us assume the change ΔR made to R, is in the form of adding a new rule R_N. If the change is in fact a modification to a rule, instead of a new rule, we can treat the modified rule as if the old rule was removed from R and the new rule containing the modifications was added.

Proposition 1: Two rules can be triggered at the same time if and only if the condition entries for both rules contain at least one common condition.

Corollary 1: Out of all the conditions in the condition entries for both rules, one of the common conditions must occur last, in order for both rules to be triggered at the same time.

Definition 4.1: If a set of rules S is the union of two sets of rules S_1 and S_2, where S_1 is consistent, and S_2 is inconsistent, then S will be inconsistent.

Definition 4.2: Any set of rules containing a rule which is inconsistent with itself, is an inconsistent set. Example: if rule R_1 states that it should lock door A and open door A, this is inconsistent. Therefore the entire set of rules S in which R_1 is contained is inconsistent.

Proposition 2: If the set of rules S is the union of the sets of rules S_1 and S_2, where S_1 is consistent, and S_2 is also consistent, then S cannot be guaranteed to be consistent. Example: Say S_1 contains one rule R_1: on event X open window A. Say S_2 contains one rule R_2: on event X close window A. It is obvious that S_1 is consistent, since there are no other rules in S_1 and R_1 does not conflict with itself. The same can be said of S_2. Now if we take $S = S_1 \cup S_2$, we can see that R_1 and R_2 will be triggered at the same time, and that they have conflicting actions. This means that if event X occurs, then a conflict will occur between R_1 and R_2. Therefore S is non-consistent.

Definition 4.2 and Proposition 2 lead us to two important observations. From Definition 4.2 we can see that if we find a rule which is inconsistent with itself, then we can stop the validation process and declare that the set of rules is inconsistent. From Proposition 2 we can determine that if we add a new rule to a set of rules previously said to be consistent, we cannot say that the new set is consistent without re-validating the set, even if the rule is consistent with itself. There are two cases in which a rule can be inconsistent with itself: if it contains mutually exclusive conditions, or if it contains opposing actions. These cases are explained below:

Case-1: If a rule depends on two conditions that can never occur together, then the rule is said to be inconsistent. For example: a rule with the condition "(x = 6) ^ (x = 9)". These two statements can of course never be true at the same time, so we know that the rule will never be triggered. Although this will not result in a runtime conflict, it means that the rule is useless as it will never be fired, so the policy administrator should be warned. We consider such a rule to be inconsistent.

Case-2: If a rule contains two actions that oppose each other, then the rule is said to be inconsistent. For example: a rule with an action "Close Door A" and another action "Open Door A". The end result of these actions is completely dependent on the order that these two actions are performed. Therefore, we consider this rule to be inconsistent.

Our incremental policy validation algorithm should check the new rule R_N that is incrementally added to the decision table, to make sure it is not inconsistent with any other rules. We know that in order for two rules to conflict with each other, they must be triggered at the same time. From Proposition 1 we know that in order for two rules to be triggered at the same time they must contain at least one common condition. Therefore if two rules do not have any conditions in common, we know they can never conflict. We also know that each rule must contain an opposing action with the same modality, or the same action with opposing modality. Therefore we are only interested in the following two subsets of rules:

(a) those rules which have a condition found in the new rule, an action opposite to one in the new rule and the same modality as the new rule.

(b) those rules which have a common condition with the new rule, an action found in the new rule but has the opposite modality as the new rule.

Any rule, which is in either of these subsets, does not even need to be compared with the new rule, since it automatically meets the definition of potentially conflicting with the new rule. Therefore, it is enough to know which rules fall in either of these subsets – these are the rules that potentially conflict with R_N.

Algorithm V₁(Input: R_N,D):

R_N: the new rule added

D: the input decision table

Step 1. Make sure R_N is consistent with itself. If it isn't, we know the set of rules is inconsistent, and we halt the validation process.

Step 2. Create a duplicate of the policy decision table D. Call this table D'.

Step 3. Eliminate from D' any conditions not found in R_N. We know that in order for a rule to conflict with R_N it must contain at least one common condition with R_N. Therefore we can eliminate all conditions from the table that R_N does not have.

Step 4. Eliminate from D' any rules whose condition entries are all empty.

Step 5. Partition D' into three sub tables T_M, T_A, and T_g such that T_M contains all rules with the opposite modality to R_N, T_A contains all rules with the same modality as R_N, and T_g contains the remaining rules. We know that for two rules to have a modality conflict they must have opposite modality values (T_M). In order for two rules to have an action conflict they must have the same modality values (T_A). Therefore, we must examine T_A, and T_M and ignore T_g.

Step 6. In T_A, eliminate any actions that are not opposing actions in R_N. In T_M, eliminate any actions that are not found in R_N. In T_M, we are looking for modality conflicts. In order for two rules to have a modality conflict, they must contain at least one common action. Therefore we eliminate all actions in T_M that are not found in R_N. Similarly in T_A, we are looking for action conflicts. In order for two rules to have an action conflict, one rule must contain an opposing action to an action in the second rule. Therefore we eliminate all actions in T_A that are not opposing actions to actions found in R_N.

Step 7. In T_A and T_M, eliminate any rules whose action entries are all empty.

Step 8. Eliminate R_N from T_A and T_M.

Step 9. The rules that remain potentially conflict with R_N, and the non-empty entries correspond to the conditions and actions that overlap with R_N. Table T_A contains rules that have action conflicts with R_N. Table T_M contains rules that have modality conflicts with R_N.

We know that any rule found in T_A has at least one condition in common with R_N. In fact, we know that the conditions it has in common are the conditions that are indicated in T_A after performing the steps above. We also know that any rule in T_A has at least one action, which is an opposing action to one found in R_N and they are the ones indicated in T_A. Finally we know, of course, that any rule in the table has the same modality value as R_N. These rules then meet all the requirements necessary to have an action conflict with R_N, therefore we know that all these rules have a <u>potential</u> action conflict with R_N. All the actions and conditions that would be responsible for each rule's conflict are the non-empty entry values in each rule in T_A.

Similarly, in T_M, we know that all rules have at least one condition in common with R_N. As with T_A, the common conditions are indicated in the table. We also know that any rule in T_M has at least one action in common with R_N, and again, these actions are indicated for each rule in the table. Finally, we know that each rule in T_M has the modality value opposite to R_N. These rules meet all the necessary requirements to have a modality conflict with R_N, therefore we can say that these rules have a potential modality conflict with R_N.

4.1. Analysis of V_1

Let C = number of conditions in the table
     A = number of actions
     n = number of rules

Our approach in V_1 starts by examining each condition once and eliminating it if necessary. This takes C operations. Next each rule is examined to see if its condition entries are all empty, and the rule is removed if so. This takes n operations. Let us assume as the worst case that no rules were removed in this step, leaving us with n rules. The table is then split into two smaller tables, by examining each rule and putting all rules of opposite modality into one table and all rules of the same modality into another table. Let us assume the <u>worst case</u>, that all rules in the original table had a modality value either the same as or opposite to R_N's modality value. Then this takes n operations and all the rules are still present. Say that the first new table contains n_1 rules and the second contains n_2 rules. Next each action is examined to see if it is a possible conflicting action. This is done for each action in each of the two tables so this takes *2 * A* operations. Finally each rule is examined in each of the tables, to check if all its action entries are empty, and the rule is removed if so. This takes n_1 operations for the first table and n_2 operations for the second table. Note that in the worst case $n_1 + n_2 = n$, therefore this step takes at most n operations. Then we can say that our entire process takes $C + n + n + 2 * A + n = C + 2A + 3n$ operations <u>in the worst case.</u>

5. Trigger Chaining and Indirect Conflicts

In what follows we introduce the notion trigger chaining, how this leads to indirect conflicts, and present an algorithm to detect these conflicts.

Definition 5.1: A rule R_1 that upon firing produces (or 'throws') k events $E_1, E_2, \ldots E_k$, is said to trigger R_2 if and only if R_2's conditions are a subset of all the events thrown by R_1, and no others. Since R_2's conditions are a subset of all the events thrown by R_1, we know that all R_2's conditions will be met when R_1 fires. Therefore R_1's firing will certainly cause R_2 to be triggered.

Definition 5.2: A rule R_1 that upon firing throws k events $E_1, E_2, \ldots E_k$, is said to <u>potentially trigger</u> R_2, if and only if R_2's conditions contain at least one of the events thrown by R_1.

Having rules that potentially trigger other rules, or **'trigger chaining'** as we call it, means the notion of conflict introduced earlier needs to be refined further.

Let us say a new rule R_N has an action opposite to one in R_2 but the two rules do not share any of the same triggering conditions. Let us also say that R_N has a triggering condition in common with R_1, which upon execution causes event E to occur, a triggering event for R_2. It is possible that R_N and R_1 could be triggered at the same time, and that the execution of R_1 will trigger R_2. The actions performed in R_N and R_2 will conflict. This conflict does not meet the strict definition of conflict we mentioned earlier. In this case we consider it a conflict because the action in R_2 could possibly undo an action performed in R_N, therefore the action in R_N has no lasting effect. A method to detect these conflicts is needed in addition to conflicts that meet our earlier definition.

Definition 5.3: Suppose a directed graph G is drawn where each vertex represents a rule in a system, and an edge from vertex P to another vertex Q represents that the rule P potentially triggers the rule Q. If there is a path from one vertex R_1 to another vertex R_2 of length n, then we say that R_1 <u>potentially triggers R_2 by degree n</u>.

We can now say that if R_1 potentially triggers R_2 by some degree n, and R_2 has an opposing action to an action in R_1, that R_1 and R_2 have a potential for a conflict. Let us call such a conflict an 'indirect conflict', and a potential conflict of degree 1 a 'direct conflict'.

Note that earlier, we restricted the system such that only one event could occur at the same time. With indirect conflicts, although the chain of events caused by a rule firing do not occur simultaneously, we can treat them virtually as if they do, since we know the events will be thrown one immediately after another. The actions caused by these events could neutralize each other's effects, or cause unknown results, since the effects could depend on which events are processed first. For this reason, we find it necessary to take note of these situations and consider them conflicts. Conversely, although any two events in the system could theoretically occur at almost the same time, we note these chain reactions because they indicate a likeliness of two or more events occurring at almost the same time, rather than just a random occurrence.

5.1. Development of Algorithm V_2

To detect indirect conflicts, first we start by adding R_N to the graph G of the system. Let us assume for now that no rule can potentially trigger itself (i.e., there are no cycles in G). We draw a directed edge from R_N to any rule (node) that contains an event in its condition that is found in R_N's action entry. This connects R_N to the nodes in G that R_N potentially triggers. Let us use C_N to refer to the connected component of the graph that contains R_N, and T_N to refer to a spanning tree of C_N. If there is more than one possible spanning tree for C_N, it is not important which one is used. We use U_N to refer to the subtree of T_N that has root R_N (see Figure 2).

Suppose we have R_A, which has opposite modality to R_N and some actions in common with R_N. Let us say that R_N gets triggered upon event E_1 occurring, and R_A gets triggered upon event E_2 occurring. Looking at these two rules alone, they will not be triggered at the same time, and therefore do not potentially conflict. Let us say, though, that there is a rule R_B that causes two events E_1 and E_2 to occur. When R_B fires, R_A and R_N will be triggered and could have a conflict. Thus, it is not only

important to look at U_N <u>from R_N down</u>, but to examine all of T_N.

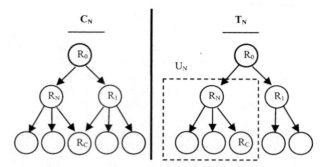

Figure 2. An illustration of our terminology

One way to do this is to keep a list of all rules that cause each event to occur, sorted by event. Then when we add R_N to the graph, we see what events cause it to fire. In this case event E_1. We look up event E_1 in our list and see that rule R_B causes event E_1 to occur. Then we draw arrows from R_B to R_N. We must keep track of the roots of the spanning trees we have just connected R_N to (in this case T_B). These trees will be used to find any conflicts. A motivation for using spanning trees is to avoid checking rules that have multiple trigger paths more than once (R_C in Figure 2).

Suppose that we have previously validated these rules and so no rule in our graph potentially conflicts with any other rule in our graph. This is a consistent set of rules. There are now three cases that could occur upon adding a new rule R_N.

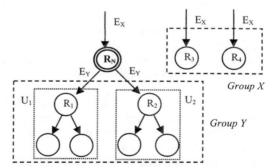

Figure 3. Case 1: R_N throws one event, no rules trigger R_N

Case 1: a new rule R_N, which throws one event, is added to graph G, such R_N is the root of T_N. Let us say event E_X causes R_N to fire, and R_N throws event E_Y that triggers R_1 and R_2. All the rules in U_N are triggered when R_N is triggered, in this case: U_1 and U_2. This means there is the possibility of R_N conflicting with any of the rules in these two sub trees. Therefore we must compare R_N with every rule in U_N to see if there is a conflict. Not only this, but say event E_X also causes R_3 to fire. Since none of the rules in U_N were previously triggered upon event E_X occurring, all these rules must be checked to see if they conflict with any of the rules U_3. Since R_1 and R_2 are both triggered by the same event E_Y, they would have been triggered at the same time before we added R_N. We know that the system of rules was consistent before R_N was added, therefore no conflicts will arise between rules in U_1 and U_2.

This gives us two groups of rules that need to be checked: those in subtrees triggered by E_X, and those in subtrees triggered by E_Y. Let us call these groups group X and group Y respectively. In order to validate the system after R_N has been added, we need to compare R_N with all the rules in group X and group Y, and all the rules in group X need to be compared with all the rules in group Y (see Figure 3).

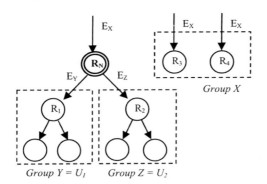

Figure 4. Case 2: R_N throws multiple events, no rules trigger R_N

Case 2: a new rule R_N, which throws more than one event, is added to graph G, such that R_N is the root of T_N. Let us say event E_X triggers R_N, and R_N throws events E_Y and E_Z, which trigger rules R_1, and R_2 respectively (see Figure 4). As in the previous case, the rules in U_1 and the rules in U_2 must be checked to see if they conflict with the new rule R_N. This time, however, R_1 and R_2 are not triggered by the same event. Although the system was consistent before R_N was added, that conclusion was based on R_1 and R_2 being triggered by different events, and therefore they could never be fired at the same time. Now R_N firing could cause both R_1 and R_2 to fire at the same time. This means that the rules in U_1 could possibly conflict with the rules in U_2. We can once again group the subtrees by the events that trigger their root node. This time R_N will have to be compared against all the rules in group X, group Y, and group Z, and all the rules in those groups will have to be compared with the rules in each other group.

Case 3: a new rule R_N, is added such that it is not the root of T_N, linking two or more connected components of graph G (see Figure 5). Say that R_N is triggered by event

E_X, which is thrown by groups V and W. R_N throws one or more events, which trigger R_2 and R3. As in case 1 and 2, we must check to see if R_N will conflict with any of the rules in its spanning tree. This time, since R_N is not the root of T_N, it is not just R_N's children we must check against R_N. In this case when the rules in groups V and W fire, the rules in U_N are also triggered, which was not the case before R_N was added. Therefore we must check the rules in the predecessor groups V and W to see if they conflict with any rules in U_N. However, the rules in V need not be checked with those of W as they still remain independent of each other.

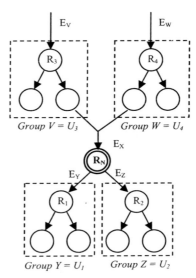

Figure 5. Case 3: R_N throws multiple events, one or more rules trigger R_N

There are three things we can conclude from all this:
➤ First, we know that no matter where R_N is added, R_N must be checked to see if it potentially conflicts with any of the rules in its sub spanning tree.
➤ Second, if the connected component containing R_N is triggered by events $X:\{X_1, \ldots X_n\}$, then all the rules in U_N must be compared with all the rules in any connected component triggered by one or more events $X_k \in X$.
➤ Third, if multiple connected components $C:\{C_1, C_2, \ldots, C_M\}$ are merged into one connected component, then the rules of each $C_i \in C \mid C_i$ is a successor to R_N must be compared with the rules of each $C_j \in C \mid C_j$ is a predecessor of R_N.

With this information we can build an algorithm to check for the consistency of the rules using minimum number of comparisons.

In order to find all conflicts, we must perform three steps in the **Algorithm V_2**:

Step P1: Find any conflict between a rule in R_N's predecessors ($T_N - U_N$), and R_N's new sub tree U_N.

Step P2: Find any conflict between rules in U_N and rules in U_A where R_A is triggered by an event that also triggers the root of T_N.

Step P3: Determine if any of the rules in one of R_N's child groups conflict with another rule in a different child groups of R_N.

A detailed discussion of the algorithm V_2 and its complexity analysis can be found in the thesis [26] and they are not given here for want of space.

Both algorithms V_1 and V_2 could in theory be used to create a consistent set of rules by starting with an empty set, and adding rules one by one. However, although this is theoretically interesting, it has not been examined in depth because we believe a system will be designed with a number of rules. At that time it would have been validated and converted to our format so that it can be maintained in an incremental fashion.

5.2. Complexity of V_2.

Let us use the following notations:
R_O = the root of the tree T_N.
k = the number of trees R_{Ti} that each have at least one triggering condition in common with R_O.
t = the average number of rules in each R_{Ti}.
n = the number of rules in U_N.
m = the number of rules in U_O.
N = the total number of rules in the system.

It can be shown that the entire process of Algorithm V_2 in the worst case takes $20 + 4C + 8A + 3kt + 3m + 9n$ operations [26]. Assuming m, n, and t are proportional to N, our algorithm is $O(N)$ in the worst case.

In the best case, Step P1 and P2 are completed without detecting a conflict. In this case, the entire process takes $20 + kt + m$ operations. If once again we assume that m and t are proportional to N, our algorithm is $O(N)$ in the best case.

5.3. Cyclic-Conflict Detection

Another possibility for a conflict is if a rule R_I triggers a rule R_J that triggers a rule R_K etc., until finally a rule R_T is triggered which triggers R_I again. This causes a cycle of triggers. This means that rules are constantly being triggered, and may never stop executing. This behavior needs to be detected in the rules and reported. Let us make a graph showing each rule as a vertex in this graph. Now let us connect the vertices using directed edges, each edge drawn from one vertex to another representing that the first rule triggers the second. Now if we examine the graph and detect a cycle, we know that one rule may, after a trigger chain reaction, effectively trigger itself. This needs to be researched further.

6. Future Work

One restriction of our algorithms is that in order for two rules to conflict, they must be fired at the same time. This does not take into account rules that may be triggered at different times but have overlapping execution times. Whether we can extend our algorithm to handle such cases is left for future work.

Another restriction made is that events cannot occur concurrently. If we consider a world where events can occur simultaneously, our problem becomes more complex. If any two events can occur at the same time, then any two rules could potentially fire at the same time, and we must examine the entire set of rules to determine if two rules conflict. This is not very helpful nor very likely. Instead we would require more information about the world in which the events are thrown, such as which events can occur at the same time, and which events are likely to occur at the same time. With this added event information, we could then make reasonable decisions about which subsets of rules need to be compared to look for conflicts. Exactly what additional information is needed, and how it should be stored is left for future exploration.

7. Summary and Conclusion

The main contribution of our work was exploring the problem of incremental policy validation, and providing a method of solving this problem. Incremental policy validation is an area in which no prior work has been done so far. With the increase in number of systems that use policies, and the large size of policy systems, incremental policy validation will become an important problem. By validating only those rules which have a chance of conflicting, we can substantially reduce the execution time of the validation process of policy systems.

As a way of solving this problem, we have developed an algorithm in a step-by-step manner. Then, we analyzed the algorithm for its performance and compared it to the complete revalidation approach of revalidating all policies in the system. This analysis showed that incremental policy validation offers a significant advantage over complete revalidation, as the number of rules in the system becomes large.

The concept of trigger chaining was introduced in this paper. Trigger chaining consists of looking at policies to see which chain of policies they trigger. This lead to the problem of indirect conflicts, and so an incremental validation algorithm was suggested to find these conflicts. This algorithm was analyzed and compared to a complete revalidation method. Our incremental validation method was shown to operate in linear time, as opposed to the complete revalidation method, which is quadratic in complexity.

Trigger chaining also introduced a second new type of conflict. Cyclic conflicts were introduced as a policy, which triggers a chain of policies to fire, results eventually in its own execution. This new type of conflict needs further research.

We have also introduced the idea of representing policies in the form of well-known decision tables. Decision tables have given us a benefit in the form of conceptual simplicity. With this simple representation, we found it easy to see the differences between policies, what happens when new policies are added or old policies are removed, etc. This view makes it simpler to develop algorithms related to policies. In fact, this representation helped in the task of developing an incremental validation algorithm, by providing a simple way to eliminate conditions, actions, and entire rules from the search space. We presented policies in the form of decision tables and then showed the limitations of this format. We then extended the decision table format to meet the requirements of representing policies. There has been much work done related to decision table completeness and consistency, which can benefit the policy domain.

Acknowledgements

We acknowledge the funding provided by Nortel Networks. We thank the anonymous reviewers for their careful reading and helpful comments.

References

[1] Gruber, R. E., Krishnamurthy, B., Panagos, E., "High-Level Constructs in the READY Event Notification System", *Eighth ACM SIGOPS European Workshop*, Sinatra, Portugal, Sep. 1998.

[2] Krishnamurthy, B., Rosenblum, D. S., "Yeast: A General Purpose Event-Action System", *IEEE Transactions on Software Engineering*, vol. 21, no. 10, Oct. 1995.

[3] Rosenblum, D. S., Wolf, A. L., "A Design Framework for Internet-Scale Event Observation and Notification", *Proceedings of the 6th European conference held jointly with the 5th ACM SIGSOFT symposium on Software engineering*, Sep. 22 - 25, 1997, Zurich Switzerland, pp. 344-360

[4] Lupu, E., Sloman, E., "Conflicts in Policy-Based Distributed Systems Management", *IEEE Transactions on Software Engineering* vol. 25, no.6. Nov./Dec. 1999.

[5] Omari, S., Boutaba, R., "Policy-Based Control Agents for Boundary Routers in Differentiated Services IP", *First International Workshop on Mobile Agents for Telecommunications Applications*, pp.477-490, Oct. 1999.

[6] Koch, T., Krell, C., Krämer, B., "Policy Definition Language for Automated Management of Distributed Systems", *Proceedings of the Second IEEE International Workshop on Systems Management*, pp. 55-64, 1996.

[7] Howard, S., Lutfiyya, H., Katchabaw, M., Bauer, M., "Supporting Dynamic Policy Change Using CORBA System Management Facilities", *Proceedings of the 5th IFIP/IEEE International Symposium on Integrated Network Management (IM '97)*, pp. 527-538, 1997.

[8] Chomicki, J., Lobo, J., Naqvi, S., "Conflict Resolution in Policy Management", www.cs.buffalo.edu/~chomicki/papers-tkde01.ps, Submitted Jun. 12, 2000.

[9] Grosof, B. N., Labrou, Y., Chan, H. Y., "A Declarative Approach to Business Rules in Contracts: Courteous Logic Programs in XML.", *Proceedings of the First ACM Conference on Electronic Commerce*, Nov. 1999.

[10] Michael, J., Sibley, E., Littman, D., "Integration of Formal and Heuristic Reasoning as a Basis for Testing and Debugging Computer Security Policy", *Proceedings of the New Security Paradigms Workshop*, Los Alamitos, California, pp. 69-75, 1993.

[11] Lupu, E., Sloman, E., "Conflict Analysis for Management Policies", *Proceedings of the 5th International Symposium on Integrated Network Management IM'97*, 1997.

[12] Fraser, T., Badger, L., "Ensuring Continuity During Dynamic Security Policy Reconfiguration in DTE", *Proceedings of the 1998 IEEE Symposium on Security and Privacy*, 1998.

[13] Montalbano, M., Decision Tables, Science Research Associates, USA, 1974.

[14] Welland, R., Decision Tables and Computer Programming, Hyden & Son, Great Britain, 1981.

[15] King, P. J. H., Johnson, R. G., "Some Comments on the Use of Ambiguous Decision Tables and Their Conversion to Computer Programs", Comm. of the ACM, vol. 16, no. 5, pp. 287-290, May 1973.

[16] Lew, A., "Optimal Conversion of Extended-Entry Decision Tables with General Cost Criteria", Comm. of the ACM, vol. 21, no. 4, pp. 269-279, Apr. 1978.

[17] Ibramsha, M., Rajaraman, V., "Detection of Logical Errors in Decision Table Programs", Comm. of the ACM, vol. 21, no. 12, pp. 1016-1025, Dec. 1978.

[18] Shwayder, K., "Combining Decision Rules in a Decision Table", Comm. of the ACM, vol. 18, no. 8, pp. 476-480, Aug. 1975.

[19] Muthukrishnan, C. R., Rajaraman, V., "On the Conversion of Decision Tables to Computer Programs", Comm. of the ACM, vol. 13, no. 6, pp. 347-351, Jun. 1970.

[20] Shumacher, H., Sevcik, K.C., "The Synthetic Approach to Decision Table Conversion", Comm. of the ACM, vol. 19, no. 6, pp. 343-351, Jun. 1976.

[21] Dathe, G., "Conversion of Decision Tables by Rule Mask Method Without Rule Mask", Comm. of the ACM, vol. 15, no. 10, pp. 906-909, Oct. 1972.

[22] Giarratano, J., Riley, G., Expert Systems Principles and Programming, PWS Publishing, USA, 1998.

[23] Jess the Java Expert System Shell, http://herzberg.ca.sandia.gov/jess; accessed Mar. 12, 2001.

[24] Rowe, N. C., Artificial Intelligence Through Prolog, Prentice Hall, USA, 1998.

[25] Vanthienen, J., Wets, G., "From Decision Tables to Expert System Shells", Data & Knowledge Engineering 13(3), pp. 265-282, Oct. 1994.

[26] Graham, A. "Incremental Validation of Policy-Based Systems", M. Comp. Sci. Thesis, Concordia University, May 2001

Finite State Transducers for Policy Evaluation and Conflict Resolution

Javier Baliosian and Joan Serrat
Universitat Politècnica de Catalunya,
Network Management Group
{jbaliosian,serrat}@tsc.upc.es

Abstract

This paper presents a formal framework for a policy representation model based on Finite State Transducers (FSTs). The main motivation for this approach is to produce the formalities to represent the body of policies in an unambiguous way.

Using well-known entities such as finite state machines, we propose interpretations and adaptations to the basic theory to fit in the domain of policy based management. Policies are modeled as finite state transducers that consume events, and a function we call a tautness function *is defined to be on the transitions.*

The operations of finite state transducers are revised accordingly. In particular, we present determinization and intersection operations for FSTs that will mimic the modality conflict resolution process between policies. We also demonstrate how the composition of transducers could be used to express constraints or meta-policies. In our approach, all the tasks associated with the conflict resolution process can be done "a priori," and the computing of a policy-evaluation is linear in the number of events, and independent of the number of policies.

1. Introduction

As defined in [14], policies are rules governing the behavior of a system. They are often used as a means of implementing flexible and adaptive systems for the management of Internet services, distributed systems, and security systems. As in all rule-based systems, one of the major issues of Policy-Based Management (PBM) is the detection and resolution of the conflicts between rules. Some partial approaches to this problem have been undertaken. Representative examples are the static resolution of conflicts between obligation and/or authorization policies in [11] and a logic programming approach, with attention on the dynamic conflicts in an *event-condition-action* paradigm [4]. Others such as [5] have made an intensive study of formal and practical aspects of conflict detection but not conflict resolution. This field is still open, with some major issues to be addressed, among them the issue of efficiency.

In this paper we propose an approach consisting of an adapted subset of finite state automata concepts with the aim of detecting and solving conflicting rules.

Finite state automata are classical computational devices used in a variety of large-scale applications. Finite State Transducers (FST), in particular, are automata whose transitions are labeled with both an input and an output label. They have been useful in a wide range of fields, but particularly in Natural Language Processing. This discipline makes intensive use of grammatical rules, which are ambiguous by nature, and require quick decisions based on those rules, in particular in fields as speech recognition, with major needs on performance.

While our approach has several points of contact with the approaches that use symbolic logic, the morphology of transducers, with an underlying *if-condition-then-action* structure, allows us to use the analytic and computational advantages of restricting rules to fit them.

In the following section, we introduce transducers in a general way as a necessary background for interpreting the paper's main idea, and we define the concept of tautness function as an abstraction of condition specificity. In that section we also show how these functions are placed into classical transducers to give them the expressiveness we seek. Section 3 summarizes operations that apply to our transducers, and section 4 explains the semantics of those operations for PBM. Other related work is presented in section 5 and several future trends are suggested in section 6. These trends, including far more technology-dependent work, are the main motivation of this basic work.

2. Finite State Transducers

2.1. Recognizers

Finite State Recognizers (FSR) can be seen as a class of graphs and also as defining languages [13]. In the context of this paper, the word "language" should be understood as a set of ordered sets of events.

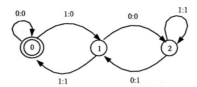

Figure 1. Transducer representing division by 3 of binaries numbers

Graphically a recognizer is an oriented graph with a set of start states (nodes), a set of final states and labeled transitions (arcs) between nodes. A string is consumed symbol by symbol, and in each state, the process follows the transitions labeled with a matching symbol. The common terminology of automata theory uses the word "symbol" to refer to what automata consume, but in our field the word "event" it is more accurate. In this paper we will use both words as synonyms. Common conventions when describing an FSR graphically are as follows: final states are depicted by two concentric circles; ϵ represents the empty string; and, unless otherwise specified, the initial state (usually labeled 0) is the leftmost state appearing in the figure.

In-depth information about finite state machines can be found in [8, 13].

2.2. Transducers

Finite State Transducers (FSTs) can be interpreted as a class of graphs or a class of relations on strings. Under the first interpretation, an FST can be seen as an oriented graph with a pair of symbols in each arc, for example in Figure 1 we can see a transducer that performs a division by 3 of binaries numbers.

Deterministic transducers are a category of transducers that present no ambiguities. This means that at any state of such transducers, at most one outgoing arc has a label with a given element of the alphabet. Output labels might be strings, including the empty string ϵ. However, the empty string is not allowed in input labels.

Deterministic transducers are computationally very interesting, because their computation load does not depend on the size of the transducer but rather only on the length of the input since that computation consists of following the only possible path corresponding to the input string and in writing consecutive output labels along this path. More information on transducers can be found in [13].

2.3. Our Extension for FSTs

Some of the main strategies used for solving what are known as "modality conflicts" [11] are:

· priority is always given to negative policies;

· the policy with highest priority is the one that is at the shortest distance from the managed object;

· the more specific a policy's domain is, the more priority the policy has;

· explicit priorities are directly assigned.

Our current work covers the first, second and third strategy; the fourth will be addressed in future work.

The idea of calculating distance between a rule or policy, and the objects on which it is being applied, has already been used in the network management context and object oriented databases. In the latter, priority is given to the policy applying to the closer class in the inheritance hierarchy when evaluating access to an object referenced in a query.

One particular case of distance to the rule is the specificity related to *domain nesting* (or in a more general way to *condition nesting*) as explained in [11]. A sub-domain of objects is created for a specific management purpose to specify a policy that differs from those applying to the objects in the parent domain. We are making use of this idea, generalizing it to any condition as follows:

A policy has a condition delimiting a region where a given event can or cannot lay in. When such an event is inside two or more overlapping regions, a modality conflict may arise. We are concerned about how tautly a condition fits on an event instead of how far from the border it is. Then, our preferred condition will be that which is the most "taut" around the event under consideration.

In order to quantitatively represent the aforementioned "tautness," we will define a metric called *tautness function* (TF), so that the more taut a condition is, the closer its TF is to 0.

To provide an intuitive example of TF, let us assume that one policy specifies *users* and another policy specifies *administrators*, that are a special kind of users. For an action attempted by an administrator, the second policy should define a TF that is closer to 0 than the first policy. However, as with the distance-to-a-policy concept, much more complicated expressions could be computed, for example using the last modification date of a policy or the person responsible for it. TFs represent an issue in themselves, and their implementation shall be part of future work.

Definition 1 *A tautness function associated with a condition c, denoted τ_c, establishes a mapping from $E \times C$ to the real interval $[-1, 1]$ where:*

· *E is the set of possible network events or attempted actions,*

· *C is the set of policy conditions,*

251

$\cdot$ $\tau_c(e) \in [-1, 0) \Leftrightarrow e\ not\ satisfies\ c$,

$\cdot$ $\tau_c(e) \in [0, 1] \Leftrightarrow e\ satisfies\ c$,

$\cdot$ $\tau_c(e) = 1 \Leftrightarrow \forall f \in E, f\ satisfies\ c$,

$\cdot$ $\tau_c(e) = 0 \Leftrightarrow \{e\}$ is the set of events that satisfies c.

Considering, inside the condition c, the subject, target or any other condition such as temporal constraints.

This follows the *event-condition-action* (ECA) paradigm used, for example, in [4].

Notice that in the TF definition we are stating only the general rules that a TF should comply with. How it will be implemented or how it maps events and conditions to real numbers should be decided in the context of a specific PBM system. Thus a TF is a sort of abstraction layer of technology dependent issues that allow us to work in a more generic way.

2.4. An Algebra for Tautness Functions

The logic we use for tautness functions is inspired by the algebra used with **fuzzy sets**. Nevertheless it does not mean that we adopt any kind of fuzzy logic to solve a policy conflict. But we realized that the same logic behind fuzzy sets can be useful to decide how taut the condition of a certain combination of policies is for an event.

Definition 2 *Disjunction. The TF of the* disjunction *of two policy conditions A and B with TFs τ_A and τ_B respectively is defined as the maximum of the two individual TFs: $\tau_{A \vee B} = max(\tau_A, \tau_B)$. This operation is the equivalent of the OR operation in boolean algebra.*

Definition 3 *Conjunction. The TF of the* conjunction *of two policy conditions A and B with TFs τ_A and τ_B respectively is defined as the minimum of the two individual TFs: $\tau_{A \wedge B} = min(\tau_A, \tau_B)$. This operation is the equivalent of the AND operation in boolean algebra. Please note that with this definition, when the event is inside the intersection of both conditions, its TF has the value of the tautest, and if the event is outside the intersection, we can say that the event is just as far outside as the one that is furthest outside.*

Definition 4 *Negation. The TF of the* negation *of a policy condition A with TFs τ_A, is defined changing the sign of the specified TF: $\tau_{\neg A} = -\tau_A$. This operation is the equivalent of the NOT operation in boolean algebra.*

Definition 5 *Tauter-than. The* tauter-than *operation ($\rightarrow_\tau$) is an ad hoc operation created to simplify the notation*

involved in the determinization process which will be explained in 3.6. The TF of the tauter-than of two policy conditions A and B with TFs τ_A and τ_B respectively is defined as:

$$\tau_{A \rightarrow_\tau B} = \begin{cases} \tau_A, & if\ \tau_A < \tau_B \\ -1, & else \end{cases}$$

This operation is intended especially for the distance concept behind our TFs. It tell us when A fits more tautly around an event than B.

Definition 6 *As-taut-as. The* as-taut-as *operation ($\rightleftarrows_\tau$), like* tauter-than, *was created to simplify the notation involved in the determinization process. The TF of the* as-taut-as *of two policy conditions A and B with TFs τ_A and τ_B respectively is defined as:*

$$\tau_{A \rightleftarrows_\tau B} = \begin{cases} \tau_A, & if\ \tau_A = \tau_B \\ -1, & else \end{cases}$$

2.5. Transducers with Tautness Functions and Identities

Let us start defining *finite state recognizers with TFs* (TFFSR) because they are the starting point for presenting the corresponding transducers and because, in some cases, transducers should be "reduced" to recognizers in order to compute some operations.

The main idea is to replace classic symbol labels on FSTs for TF labels. Thus, instead of trying to match an incoming symbol with a label on a transition, a recognizer with TFs will evaluate the TF on a transition for the incoming event.

Therefore, the mechanics of processing an incoming stream of events with a TFFSR is as follows: starting at an initial state, **an event is consumed if there is a transition with a positive (or zero) tautness function value evaluated for that event**[1]. The new current state will be the one at the end of the chosen transition. Then the process is repeated. We can see a TFFSR as a set of rules that accept a certain pattern of events.

The following two definitions (TFFSR and TFFST) are extensions of the definitions for predicate-augmented finite state recognizers (PFSR) and predicate-augmented finite state transducers (PFST) introduced in [15].

Definition 7 *A finite state recognizer with tautness functions (TFFSR) M is a tuple (Q, E, T, Π, S, F) where:*

$\cdot$ *Q is a finite set of states,*

$\cdot$ *E is a set of events,*

---

[1] Although one possibility could be to choose the one with the lowest positive TF value, this would interfere with our intentions of adding weights to these automata in future work.

· T is a set of tautness functions over E.

· Π is a finite set of transitions $Q \times T \cup \{\epsilon\} \times Q$.

· $S \subseteq Q$ is a set of start states,

· $F \subseteq Q$ is a set of final states.

The relation $\widehat{\Pi} \subseteq Q \times E^* \times Q$ is defined inductively:

· for all $q \in Q$, $(q, \epsilon, q) \in \widehat{\Pi}$.

· for all $(p, \epsilon, q) \in \Pi$, $(p, \epsilon, q) \in \widehat{\Pi}$.

· for all $(q_0, \tau, q) \in \Pi$ and for all $e \in E$, if $\tau(e) \geq 0$ then $(q_0, e, q) \in \widehat{\Pi}$.

· if $(q_0, x_1, q_1) \in \widehat{\Pi}$ and $(q_1, x_2, q) \in \widehat{\Pi}$ then $(q_0, x_1 x_2, q) \in \widehat{\Pi}$.

The "language" of events $L(M)$ accepted by M is defined to be $\{w \in E^* \mid q_s \in S, q_f \in F, (q_s, w, q_f) \in \widehat{\Pi}\}$

An extension could be defined to allow the recognizer to deal with strings of events in each transition, in order to make some operations easier and produce more compact transducers.

A TFFSR is called ϵ-free if there are no $(p, \epsilon, q) \in \Pi$. For any given TFFSR there is an equivalent ϵ-free TFFSR. It is straightforward to extend the corresponding algorithm for classical automata to TFFSRs. We will assume this equivalence afterward for the sake of simplicity.

Analogous substitution between symbol-labels and TF-labels is performed on finite state transducers. Thus, the FSTs outgoing label is also substituted by a TF. This means that, following a transition produces an event with a positive (or zero) value for the TF in the outgoing label of the transition.

Definition 8 *A finite state transducer with tautness functions and identities (TFFST) M is a tuple (Q, E, T, Π, S, F) where:*

· Q is a finite set of states,

· E is a set of symbols,

· T is a set of tautness functions over E.

· Π is a finite set of transitions $Q \times (T \cup \{\epsilon\}) \times (T \cup \{\epsilon\}) \times Q \times \{-1, 0, 1\}$. The final component of a transition is a sort of "identity flag" used to indicate when an incoming event must be replicated in the output[2].

· $S \subseteq Q$ is a set of start states.

---

[2]The negative identity value is to express the obligatory difference between input and output, this is needed to compute the complement of a TFFST.

· $F \subseteq Q$ is a set of final states.

· For all transitions $(p, d, r, q, 1)$ it must be the case that $d = r \neq \epsilon$.

Note that we are assuming that the input and output sets of tautness functions are the same, and the same for input and output set of events. This could be refined but does not diminish the generality of this paper.

We define the function str from $T \cup \{\epsilon\}$ to 2^{E^*}.
$$str(x) = \begin{cases} \{\epsilon\} & if \ x = \epsilon \\ \{s \mid s \in E, x(s) \geq 0\} & if \ x \in T \end{cases}$$

If $\tau \in T$ and $str(x)$ is a singleton set, then the transitions (p, τ, τ, q, i) where $i \in \{-1, 0, 1\}$ are equivalent.
The relation $\widehat{\Pi} \subseteq Q \times E^* \times E^* \times Q$ is defined inductively:

· for all p, $(p, \epsilon, \epsilon, p) \in \widehat{\Pi}$.

· for all $(p, d, r, q, 0)$, $x \in str(d), y \in str(r)$, $(p, x, y, q) \in \widehat{\Pi}$.

· for all $(p, d, r, q, -1)$, $x \in str(d), y \in str(r)$, $x \neq y$, $(p, x, y, q) \in \widehat{\Pi}$.

· for all $(p, \tau, \tau, q, 1)$ and $x \in str(\tau)$, $(p, x, x, q) \in \widehat{\Pi}$.

· if $(q_0, x_1, y_1, q_1) \in \widehat{\Pi}$ and $(q_1, x_2, y_2, q) \in \widehat{\Pi}$ then $(q_0, x_1 x_2, y_1 y_2, q) \in \widehat{\Pi}$.

The relation $R(M)$ accepted by a TFFST M is defined to be $\{(w_d, w_r) \mid q_s \in S, q_f \in F, (q_s, w_d, w_r, q_f) \in \widehat{\Pi}\}$.

An extension could be defined to let the transducer deal with strings of events in each transition.

TFFSTs will be the base model for a policy rule. In the ECA paradigm the incoming label will model the condition part of a policy, and the outgoing label will model the triggered action.

3. Operations on TFFST

In several cases the operations on TFFSTs could be easily generalized from FSTs or from PFSTs. In this section, we present the main operations and their new algorithms on TFFSTs, with special emphasis on the determinization algorithm.

3.1. Identity

The identity relation for a given language of events L is $id(L) = \{(w, w) \mid w \in L\}$. Further on, we will see that a *right* will be a identity relation applied to the incoming authorized event. For a given TFFSR $M = (Q, E, T, \Pi, S, F)$, the identity relation is given by the TFFST $M' = (Q, E, T, \Pi', S, F)$ where $\Pi' = $

$\{(p, \tau, \tau, q, 1) \mid (p, \tau, q) \in \Pi\}$. Note that several events could be positive under τ so the "identity flag" is set to 1 in order to force the event produced to be the same that the one that entered. A more in-depth explanation of this can be found in [15] but one difference from the identity defined for PFSTs, is that we are defining a -1 value for the identity flag.

Symbols "<" and ">" around TFs in the labels express identity between the input and the output, and symbols "[" and "]" express difference.

3.2. Union

The union of two transducers results in a transducer that defines the relation which is the union of the relations defined by each of the two original transducers. This means that the new transducer Hill recognize the union of sets of "words" of events recognized for both original transducers and produce the same events that the original ones would produce. The union algorithm for TFFSTs is simple and analogous to the one for classical transducers. No ϵ labels should remain in the input part of transitions, thus an algorithm such as the one in [12] should be used to avoid those labels. That algorithm does not ensure that the final transducer will be deterministic. Later we will see how to solve this using determinization algorithm. Typically, adding a new policy will mean computing the union of the TFFST modeling the new policy.

3.3. Intersection

The intersection of two transducers results in a transducer that defines the relation resulting from the intersection of the relations of the two original transducers. It is one of the most important and powerful operations on automata. As TFFSTs are not always closed under intersection, it is necessary to start thinking about recognizers instead of transducers.

In the classical case, the intersection of two given automata M_1 and M_2 is constructed by considering the cross product of states of M_1 and M_2. A transition $((p_1, p_2), \sigma, (q_1, q_2))$ exists in the intersection iff the corresponding transition (p_1, σ, q_1) exists in M_1 and (p_2, σ, q_2) exists in M_2. In the case of TFFSR, instead of requiring that the symbol σ occur in the corresponding transitions of M_1 and M_2, the resulting tautness function must be the conjunction of the corresponding tautness functions in M_1 and M_2.

Given two ϵ-free TFFSRs $M_1 = (Q_1, E, T, \Pi_1, S_1 F_1)$ and $M_2 = (Q_2, E, T, \Pi_2, S_2 F_2)$, the intersection $L(M_1) \cap L(M_2)$ is the language accepted by $M = (Q_1 \times Q_2, E, T, \Pi, S_1 \times S_2, F_1 \times F_2)$ and $\Pi = \{((p_1, q_1), \tau_1 \wedge \tau_2, (p, q)) \mid (p_1, \tau_1, p) \in \Pi_1, (q_1, \tau_2, q) \in \Pi_2\}$.

The transducers used in our model will always be analogous to the letter transducers presented in [13]. Then we will be able to use this intersection definition on the underlying TFFSRs, which we will define below, to calculate the intersection of the transducers themselves.

Definition 9 *Underlying TFFSR. If* $M = (Q, E, T, \Pi, S, F)$ *is an TFFST, its underlying TFFSR is* $M' = (Q, E, T, \Pi', S, F)$ *where:*

$$\Pi' = \{(p, (x, y), q) \mid (p, x, y, p, i) \in \Pi\}$$

All properties of finite state automata apply to the underlying automaton of a transducer. For example, the intersection algorithm could be applied to the underlying TFFSR and in our conditions, properly interpreted as the intersection of two TFFSTs.

3.4. Complement

This is the *complement* of the relation defined by a transducer. This operation will be useful to compute a subtraction between relations or sets of rules. As in basic sets theory, $A - B$ will be expressed as $A \cap \overline{B}$.

In Figure 2.a you can see a simple TFFST with identities expressing a *right*. When an action is attempted and is positive under the tautness function a, then the transducer replicates the same action in the output. Remember that the symbols "<" and ">" express identity between the input and the output. We can say that this machine transduces a certain set of actions A into themselves, and rejects its complement $\overline{A}$. *Complement* operation creates the transducer that expresses the opposite relation. In other words, it transduces $\overline{A}$ into itself and rejects A. This transducer can be seen in Figure 2.b.

Although it is true that transducers are not closed under *complementation* in all conditions, our "axiomatic" transducers will never accept ϵ as a valid input string nor ϵ symbols in the input part of loops. Therefore we can compute the complement of a policy/transducer considering the transducer as a recognizer that consumes pairs x:y in the set $E \times E$ and computing the complementation algorithm on it as seen in [15]. To make this possible we needed to include a "non-equal" flag into TFFST definition, although it makes no direct sense in expressing a policy.

3.5. Composition

The meaning of composition here is the same as for any other binary relations: $R_1 \circ R_2 = \{(x, z) \mid (x, y) \in R_1, (y, z) \in R_2\}$. This can be seen as a chain of events processing: the events outgoing from the first transducer are take as input of the second one. Later we will see how this is useful to represent constraints or meta-policies.

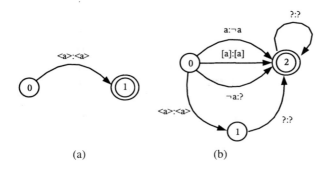

(a)   (b)

Figure 2. The *complement* (b) of a *right* (a)

In the classical case, the composition of two transducers M_1 and M_2 is built considering the cross product between the states of M_1 and M_2. A transition $((p_1, p_2, \sigma_i, \sigma_o, (q_1, q_2))$ exists iff there is some σ such that $(p_1, \sigma_i, \sigma, q_1)$ exists in M_1 and $(p_2, \sigma, \sigma_o, q_2)$ exists in M_2. The case of TFFSTs is equal to that of PFSTs plus an extra condition for non-identity. We will require that the conjunction of both TFs be positive. Identity is required in the new transition only when it is required in both, and the same with the non-identity mark; it will remain in the new transition only if it existed in both original ones. Transitions with ϵ in the input or output should be handled specially.

Given two TFFST $M_1 = (Q_1, E, T, \Pi_1, S_1, F_1)$ and $M_2 = (Q_2, E, T, \Pi_2, S_2, F_2)$, the relation $R_1 \circ R_2$ is defined by $M = (Q_1 \times Q_2, E, T, \Pi, S_1 \times S_2, F_1 \times F_2)$ where:

$$\Pi = \{((p_1, p_2), d, r, (q_1, q_2), i) \mid \\
(p_1, d, \tau_1, q_1, i_1) \in \Pi_1, \\
(p_2, \tau_2, r, q_2, i_2) \in \Pi_2, \\
\tau_1 \wedge \tau_2, \\
i = 0 \; if \; i_1 = 0 \; or \; i_2 = 0 \; or \; i_1 \neq i_2, \\
i = 1 \; if \; i_1 = 1 \; and \; i_2 = 1, \\
i = -1 \; if \; i_1 = -1 \; and \; i_2 = -1\} \\
\cup \{((p_1, p_2), \epsilon, d, (q_1, q_2), 0) \mid \\
(p_1, \epsilon, d', q_1, i_1) \in \Pi_1, (p_2, d', d, q_2, i_2) \in \Pi_2\} \\
\cup \{((p_1, p_2), r, \epsilon, (q_1, q_2), 0) \mid \\
(p_1, r, d', q_1, i_1) \in \Pi_1, (p_2, d', \epsilon, q_2, i_2) \in \Pi_2\}$$

3.6. Determinization

This is the most important operation for our objectives, but also the one that exhibits the highest computational cost. To solve the conflicts between a set of rules, we must determinize the transducer representing that set in order to eliminate ambiguities.

We will say that a TFFST M is *deterministic* if M has a single start state, if there are no states $p, q \in Q$ such that $(p, \epsilon, x, q, i) \in \Pi$, and if for all states p and events e there is at most one transition (p, τ_d, x, q, i) such that $\tau_d(e)$ is positive. If a TFFST M is deterministic then the process of

computing the output events for a given stream of events ω as defined by M, can be implemented efficiently. This process is linear in ω, and independent of the size of M.

In order to extend the determinization algorithm of PFST [15] to TFFST, we must take into account the case where, although an event satisfies two conditions, one of these conditions fits more tautly than the other. We must also take into account the case where both conditions have the same specificity. In this way, all possible combinations between TFs are computed as with PFSTs, but instead of using conjunctions only, we use *conjunction, tauter-than* and *as-taut-as* operations defined in subsection 2.4.

For now, we will assume that the output part of a transition contains a sequence of TFs; this implies an extension to the above-defined TFFSTs, which will not be described in this paper. We will also assume that there are no ϵ input functions, because an equivalent transducer without ϵ input functions could be computed for a transducer which has these functions [13].

In this algorithm, outputs are delayed as much as possible. This is because a local ambiguity may not be such if we look at the whole transducer and realize that only one path would be possible until the final state. This is the case of the ambiguity shown in state 0 in Figure 3.

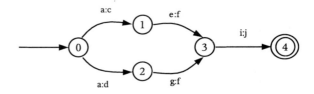

Figure 3. Before determinization

The algorithm maintains sets of pairs $Q \times T^*$. Each of these sets corresponds to a state in the determinized transducer. In the example of Figure 3, once an event that satisfies condition a is read, we can be at states 1 and 2, with pending outputs c and d, then $P = \{(1, c), (2, d)\}$. In order to compute the transitions leaving such a set of pairs P, we compute (as in PFSTs) $Trans^P(\tau_d) = \{(q, xy) \mid (p, x) \in P, (p, \tau_d : y, q) \in \Pi\}$. In the example, $Trans^P(e) = \{(3, cf)\}$ and $Trans^P(g) = \{(3, df)\}$. Let T' be the TFs in the domain of $Trans^P$. For each split of T' into $\tau_1 ... \tau_i$ and $\neg\tau_{i+1} ... \neg\tau_n$, and each possible order of $\tau_1 ... \tau_i$ we have a proto-transition with the operator $\rightarrow_\tau$ and another with the operator $\rightleftarrows_\tau$ between two consecutive TFs τ_j, τ_{j+1}:

$$(P, \tau_1 ... \tau_j \rightarrow_\tau \tau_{j+1} ... \tau_i \wedge \neg\tau_{i+1} \wedge ... \neg\tau_n, A) \\
(P, \tau_1 ... \tau_j \rightleftarrows_\tau \tau_{j+1} ... \tau_i \wedge \neg\tau_{i+1} \wedge ... \neg\tau_n, A)$$

where A is $[Trans^P(\tau_1), ..., Trans^P(\tau_i)]$. In the example we have proto-transitions:

$$(P, e \wedge \neg g, [(3, cf)])$$
$$(P, g \wedge \neg e, [(3, df)])$$
$$(P, e \rightarrow_\tau g, [(3, cf), (3, df)])$$
$$(P, g \rightarrow_\tau e, [(3, df), (3, cf)])$$
$$(P, e \leftrightarrows_\tau g, [(3, cf), (3, df)])$$
$$(P, g \leftrightarrows_\tau e, [(3, cf), (3, df)])$$

The last two proto-transitions are equivalent and one should be erased.

A transition is created from proto-transitions putting in its output the longest common prefix of TFs in the target pairs (ϵ in the example). Before removing the longest common prefix, the sequences of output TFs should be packed, putting together the sequences associated with the same target state. This is done using a combination of conjunction and disjunction in the case of a *tauter-than* relation or including an XOR with an ERROR event in the case of a *as-taut-as*. This means that, in the case that no decision can be made, an ERROR is marked[3]. Thus, two pairs of target states and TF sequences (p, s_1) and (p, s_2) can be combined into a single pair (p, s) iff (p, s_1) is in $A[j]$ and (p, s_1) is in $A[j + 1]$ and $s_1 = \tau_1...\tau_i...\tau_n$, $s_2 = \tau_1...\tau_i'...\tau_n$ and $s = \tau_1...(\tau_i \vee (\tau_i \wedge \tau_i'))...\tau_n$ if the operator between τ_j and τ_{j+1} is $(\rightarrow_\tau)$, or $s = \tau_1...(Error \oplus (\tau_i \wedge \tau_i'))...\tau_n$ if the operator between τ_j and τ_{j+1} is $(\leftrightarrows_\tau)$. In the example the third proto-transition is packed in

$$(P, e \rightarrow_\tau g, \{(3, (c \vee (c \wedge d))f)\})$$

and the fourth

$$(P, e \leftrightarrows_\tau g, \{(3, (Error \oplus (c \wedge d))f)\})$$

as can be seen in Figure 4.

Despite the fact that $a \vee (a \wedge b) \equiv a$, we have chosen to use the expression on the left because we are working with events that must sometimes be replicated in the output. This expression is closer to the behavior of the actual implementation when computing identities.

We realize that this version of the algorithm could be highly optimized, although it should be addressed in future work. For instance a lot of transitions could be eliminated by manipulating the queue of incoming events in a more complex way and ignoring the non-sense combinations of conditions.

3.7. Kleene Closure

Kleene closure (Kleene*) of a given "language" L, denoted for L^*, is the language that results from concatenating any number (including 0) of "words" of the language

---

[3]This would be useful to detect non resolvable conflicts and report them to an operator.

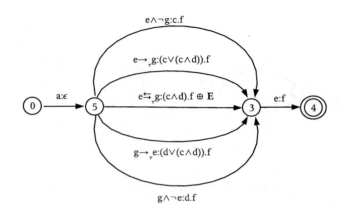

Figure 4. After determinization procedure

L. Thus $\epsilon \in L^*$always. Kleene+ or L^+requires at least one occurrence of words of L. Remember that we are using "word" as a synonym of finite ordered set of events and language as a set of words.

It is easy to demonstrate that TFFSTs are closed under Kleene* and Kleene+, and this will be useful to build a final TFFST that accepts a continuous stream of events.

4. TFFST Semantics in Policy-Based Management

In this section we will give meaning, in the context of PBM, to the operations presented in the last section.

The entities defined so far will be used to represent policies. Then policies will be represented as TFFSTs and as such, they will be combined using the above defined operations. In fact, the target is a system wide TFFST representing the system behavior free of conflicts. To this end, we propose the sequence of processes of Table 1 as the overall algorithm.

In terms of policy classification, and for reasons of clarity, we prefer the terminology used in Rei project [10] in which policy objects are *rights, prohibitions, obligations* and *dispensations*. These terms correspond, respectively to the conditions of positive and negative authorization, and positive and negative obligation. Due to space limitations only a couple of simple examples of policy rules are depicted. More detailed and representative examples shall be included in future work.

4.1. Rights

Since the underlying model consumes events, our approach is to think of a requested action as an event. Then, the *right* or *positive authorization* can be modeled as a transducer that replicates the incoming requested action in

256

Table 1. The overall process

1. Compute the union of all transducers representing *rights* and *obligations*
2. Subtract the transducers representing *prohibitions* and *dispensations*
3. Compose the resulting transducer with each constraint transducer
4. Determinize the resulting transducer to solve conflicts

the output. That is the Identity relation described in subsection 3.1.

Thus, a *right* expressed in terms of an TFFST is as depicted in Figure 5:

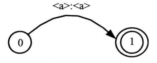

Figure 5. A right expressed with a transducer

4.2. Prohibitions

We express *prohibitions* as the subtraction of a *right*[4]. Therefore, if we have a prohibition expressed by policy P, it is possible to express it by the subtraction of the *right* R_P. If our policy model up to now is the transducer B, after inserting a *prohibition* it will be $B - R_P$. In other words: $B \cap \overline{R_P}$. This is because we are assuming conditions given in subsection 3.4. Also, and because of the restricted PBM environment in which we are working, we can use the algorithm in subsection 3.3 for the intersection. In Figure 6 we can see a *prohibition* obtained from the complement of a *right* (Figure 2.b) in a "permit all" environment.

4.3. Obligations

A rule expressing that when an event fulfills a certain condition, a given action shall be executed, is represented as a transducer with a main link with the event in the input and the action in the output.

Typically the incoming event will report the occurrence of a fact and the outgoing event will order the execution of

---

[4]We know this means making a decision in favor of negative policies. However, this will be revised in future work in light of transducers with weights.

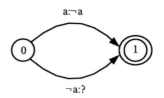

Figure 6. A prohibition modeled by a transducer

a given action. However, other combinations are possible as well, for instance to be *unobtrusive* (as defined by [4]), the incoming event could be replicated in the output.

To express an action as a consequence of a set of events, you can build a transducer like the one in Figure 7. This transducer models the rule:

Rule 1: if the user *dial-up* (d in the figure) and the system send the order of *charge* (c in the figure) then, the action *connect* (k in the figure) should be executed.

For the sake of simplicity, we disregard the fact that events can arrive without order, and we do not include other possible events before and after the sequence of interest in the model. The symbol "?" represents the TF associated to the "all events" condition.

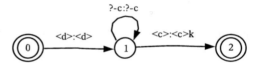

Figure 7. TFFST model for the obligation in Rule 1

4.4. Dispensations

As in the case of prohibitions, dispensations should be expressed as the intersection of the existent *policy body* with a transducer expressing the complement of an obligation. Note that this is because, in formal terms, a dispensation is equivalent to a prohibition; however, semantically it is not, as explained in [11].

4.5. Constraints

Constraints, or meta-policies, are expressed using the **composition** operation introduced in subsection 3.5. Once all rights, prohibitions, obligations and dispensations are represented in a single transducer, the transducer representing constraints should be composed after it.

To see how constraints work, let us re-assume the *dial-up-charge-connect* example in subsection 4.3. If we rely only on Rule 1, in the event of an error in the connection, the user will be charged anyway and this must not be allowed. One possible solution, among others, is to create the following constraint:

Rule 2: if an *error* (e in the figure) occurs *charge* action should not be triggered.

The transducer shown in Figure 8 represents this constraint.

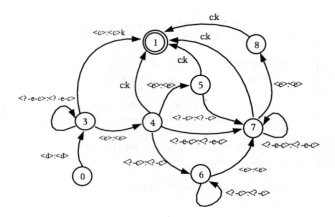

Figure 9. TFFST model for composition of rules 1 and 2

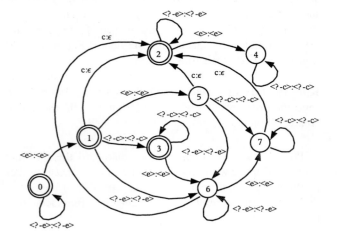

Figure 8. TFFST model for the constraint in Rule 2

Computing a *composition* of both transducers results in the transducer shown in Figure 9, where what is underlying is that all possible system responses are computed in advance when a dynamic conflict like this occurs.

5. Related Work

Important work emphasizing the static resolution of conflicts between obligation and/or authorization policies is found in [11], and was used in this paper as a main reference in the analysis of the problems arising in conflict resolution. As in that work, most of the proposals on policy-based management focus on practical issues.

The work presented in this paper relies on the ECA paradigm and is related to the formal work on event notification languages found in [16, 7]. These have the main goal of network monitoring, but without emphasis on the actions; thus, the conflict issue does not arise. In [2] we have a formal and complete approach to an event calculus based specification language. Our work does not directly overlap with those works, since our main goal is to produce

an internal model with intrinsic conflict resolution procedures, practically unrelated to the policy specification language. Although the work presented in [5] makes use of a database of conflicts, our work is akin to it in the way in which all possible conflicts are considered; however they limit the work to conflicts detection. Conflict resolution among *production rules* has been studied in *artificial intelligence* and databases, for example OPS5 [3]. Priorities are used in active database systems, to choose among conflicting rules [1].

The work in [9] deals with a model where the conflicts studied are between the rules, not actions, and the events are not taken into account. The *Action constraints* concept can be found in [4] and [6], and is the main inspiration for the solutions with composition of transducers presented in this paper. In [4] the *Epoch* concept is also introduced as a set of events assumed occurring simultaneously. This concept could be seen as analogous to the concept of "word" mentioned in this paper. Eiter et al. [6] introduce a modal policy specification language for software agents and conflict resolution is only one of the many issues addressed in that article.

In general, conflict resolution methods in current active rule literature are not *unobtrusive*. The solution with transducers is flexible enough to express unobtrusiveness or not.

6. Conclusions and Future Work

We have proposed a modeling approach for policies directly linked to the finite state automata theory. The purpose is the formalization of rules encountered in policy based management systems and hence to derive an algorithm for policy conflict resolution. One of the genuine advantages of this approach is that related implementations can exhibit good efficiency figures like their homologous transducer implementations found in applications to other fields. In fact, transducers can be well implemented with performance oriented languages and this would be a distinguishing characteristic compared with other approaches, especially dealing with implementations on network devices.

Another interesting aspect of our approach is that the computation of the model is done beforehand, prior to the use of the model itself and re-computations are only required when policies are added, modified or deleted. At runtime, the complexity of the conflict resolution algorithm is directly proportional to the amount of events in an epoch. This has a very positive impact on the scalability of systems based on such a model.

The *tautness function* defined in this paper could be seen as an abstraction layer inside which technology-dependent issues can be solved, leaving the conflict resolution process as general as possible.

Additionally, we should note that work is still in progress and therefore it must advance in several directions. Up to now we have only implemented the algorithms presented in this paper, but they require an intensive test process with representative policy scenarios. Another direction we plan to follow consists of the improvement of the modeling method. In this sense we plan to use weights in the TFFSTs to provide them the capacity to distinguish explicit priorities. Through the use of such weights the model will allow the resolution of conflicts that in the current model are only detectable.

Although our modeling approach seems to be relatively independent of the language used to express policies, the question has not been tackled up to now.

Finally, another open question concerns the distribution of the resulting implementation. From a straightforward application of the proposed model, a unique PDP would be used to drive the system. This has obvious problems and in some cases would be unfeasible. A possible distribution strategy would consist of associating finite state recognizers with PEPs representing the "language" of actions that a PEP is able to perform. Once these recognizers were obtained, they could be intersected with the second projection of the general transducer obtained from the execution of the above proposed algorithm. The results of such intersections would then be sent then to specific PDPs.

7. Acknowledgments

This work has been performed in the framework of the project IST CONTEXT (http://context.upc.es) co-founded by the European Union.

References

[1] R. Agrawal, R. J. Cochrane, and B. G. Lindsay. On maintaining priorities in a production rule system. In *Proceedings of the 17th Conference on Very Large Databases, Morgan Kaufman pubs. (Los Altos CA), Barcelona*, 1991.

[2] A. K. Bandara, E. C. Lupu, and A. Russo. Using event calculus to formalise policy specification and analysis. In *4th IEEE Workshop on Policies for Distributed Systems and Networks (Policy 2003)*, 2003.

[3] L. Browston, R. Farrell, E. Kant, L. Browston, and N. Martin. *Programming Expert Systems in OPS5: An Introduction to Rule-Based Programming*. Addison-Wesley Longman, Incorporated, 1985.

[4] J. Chomicki, J. Lobo, and S. Naqvi. Conflict resolution using logic programming. *IEEE Transactions on Knowledge and Data Engineering*, 15(1):245–250, Jan/Feb 2003.

[5] N. Dunlop, J. Indulska, and K. Raymond. Dynamic conflict detection in policy-based management systems. In *Enterprise Distributed Object Computing Conference, 2002. EDOC '02. Proceedings. Sixth International*, pages 15–26, 2002.

[6] T. Eiter, V. Subrahmanian, and G. Pick. Heterogeneous active agents i: Semantics, 1999.

[7] M. Z. Hasan. An active temporal model for network management databases. In *Integrated Network Management*, pages 524–535, 1995.

[8] J. E. Hopcroft and J. D. Ullman. *Introduction to Automata Theory, Languages and Computation*. Addison Wesley, 1979.

[9] H. V. Jagadish, A. O. Mendelzon, and I. S. Mumick. Managing conflicts between rules. *Journal of Computer and System Sciences*, 58(1):13–28, 1999.

[10] A. Joshi. A policy language for a pervasive computing environment. In *Policies for Distributed Systems and Networks, 2003. Proceedings. POLICY 2003. IEEE 4th International Workshop on on*, pages 63–74, 2003.

[11] E. Lupu and M. Sloman. Conflicts in policy-based distributed systems management. *IEEE Transactions on Software Engineering*, 25(6):852 –869, Nov/Dec 1999.

[12] M. Mohri. Finite-state transducers in language and speech processing. *Computational Linguistics*, 23(2):269–311, 1997.

[13] E. Roche and e. Yves Schabes. Finite-state language processing. Technical report, MIT Press, Cambridge, Massachusetts., 1997.

[14] M. Sloman. Policy driven management for distributed systems. *Journal of Network and Systems Management*, 2:333, 1994.

[15] G. van Noord and D. Gerdemann. Finite state transducers with predicates and identities. *Grammars*, 4(3):263–286, December 2001.

[16] O. Wolfson, S. Sengupta, and Y. Yemini. Managing communication networks by monitoring databases, 1991.

Notes

Author Index

Press Operating Committee

IEEE Computer Society Publications

The world-renowned IEEE Computer Society publishes, promotes, and distributes a wide variety of authoritative computer science and engineering texts. These books are available from most retail outlets. Visit the CS Store at *http://computer.org* for a list of products.

IEEE Computer Society Proceedings

The IEEE Computer Society also produces and actively promotes the proceedings of more than 160 acclaimed international conferences each year in multimedia formats that include hard and soft-cover books, CD-ROMs, videos, and on-line publications.

For information on the IEEE Computer Society proceedings, please e-mail to csbooks@computer.org or write to Proceedings, IEEE Computer Society, P.O. Box 3014, 10662 Los Vaqueros Circle, Los Alamitos, CA 90720-1314. Telephone +1-714-821-8380. Fax +1-714-761-1784.

Additional information regarding the Computer Society, conferences and proceedings, CD-ROMs, videos, and books can also be accessed from our web site at *http://computer.org/cspress*

Revised: 20 February 2004